Sexual Meanings

THE CULTURAL CONSTRUCTION OF GENDER AND SEXUALITY

Sexual Meanings
THE CULTURAL CONSTRUCTION
OF GENDER AND SEXUALITY

EDITED BY

Sherry B. Ortner and Harriet Whitehead

Cambridge University Press

CAMBRIDGE
LONDON   NEW YORK   NEW ROCHELLE
MELBOURNE   SYDNEY

Published by the Press Syndicate of the University of Cambridge
The Pitt Building, Trumpington Street, Cambridge CB2 1RP
32 East 57th Street, New York, NY 10022, USA
296 Beaconsfield Parade, Middle Park, Melbourne 3206, Australia

First published 1981

Printed in the United States of America
Typeset by Rainsford Type & Graphics, Ltd., Ridgefield, Connecticut
Printed and bound by the Murray Printing Co., Westford, Massachusetts

Library of Congress Cataloging in Publication Data
Main entry under title:

Sexual meanings, the cultural construction of gender
and sexuality.

1. Sex role – Addresses, essays, lectures.
2. Sex symbolism – Addresses, essays, lectures.
I. Ortner, Sherry B., 1941–   II. Whitehead, Harriet.
GN479.65.S49   305.3   80–26655
ISBN 0 521 23965 6 hard covers
ISBN 0 521 28375 2 paperback

Contents

Contributors

Stanley Brandes is in the Department of Anthropology at the University of California, Berkeley, where he received his doctorate in 1971. He has carried out extensive field research in rural Mexico and Spain. He is the author of *Migration, Kinship, and Community: Tradition and Transition in a Spanish Village; Metaphors of Masculinity: Sex and Status in Andalusian Folklore*; and, with Mary LeCron Foster, was editor of *Symbol as Sense: New Approaches to the Analysis of Meaning*. Correspondence may be addressed to him at the Department of Anthropology, University of California, Berkeley, CA 94720.

Jane F. Collier received her Ph.D. in Anthropology from Tulane University. She is interested in the relationship between political processes and systems of social inequality. She studied conflict management procedures among the Maya Indians of Zinacantan, Chiapas, Mexico, and has done limited field work in an Andalusian village in Spain and in a Kpelle community in Liberia. She is presently an assistant professor of Anthropology at Stanford University and can be reached at the Department of Anthropology, Stanford University, Stanford, CA 94305.

Salvatore Cucchiari is a doctoral student in Anthropology at the University of Michigan and is currently in the field investigating charismatic Protestantism in Western Sicily. Whether in the domain of gender or religion, his main theoretical interest is in the part played by the structure of belief and value in the historical process. Correspondence may be addressed to him in care of the Department of Anthropology, University of Michigan, Ann Arbor, MI 48109.

Melissa Llewelyn-Davies (BBC Bristol, UK) is currently working in television, coproducing a series of anthropological documentaries. She is a doctoral candidate at Harvard University and has made several films and written articles based on her research among the Maasai.

Leslee Nadelson is a doctoral student in the Department of Anthropology, the Graduate Center, City University of New York. She is completing her dissertation research on the nature of social and ritual sexual opposition in New Guinea. Her general interest is in the comparative study of social organization and religion. She has taught at Brooklyn College and Queens College. Correspondence may be addresed to her at 452 Bridlewood Circle, Decatur, GA 30030.

Sherry B. Ortner is an Associate Professor of Anthropology at the University of Michigan (Ann Arbor, MI 48104.) She is the author of *Sherpas through their Rituals* and was the consulting anthropologist for the film "Sherpas" (Granada Television, Manchester, England). She has written articles on Sherpa culture, symbolic anthropology, and gender. She is currently working on a social history of Sherpa religion.

Fitz John Porter Poole is Assistant Professor of Anthropology at the University of Rochester. He received his Ph.D. in Anthropology and in Social Psychology in 1976 from Cornell University. His dissertation research, conducted among the Bimin-Kuskusmin of Papua New Guinea, focused on social structure, political and ritual leadership, and ritual symbolism. He is the author of several articles on cultural, psychological, and social aspects of Bimin-Kuskusmin ritual, and is completing a monograph on *Rites of Childhood* among Bimin-Kuskusmin. He may be contacted in care of the Department of Anthropology, 334 Harkness Hall, University of Rochester, Rochester, NY 14627.

Michelle Rosaldo received her Ph.D. in anthropology from Harvard University in 1972. She has done extensive field work among the Ilongot of the Philippines and is the author of *Knowledge and Passion: Ilongot Notions of Self and Social Life*. She has a long-standing interest in symbolism and gender, has written numerous articles on these subjects, and is coeditor of *Woman, Culture and Society*. She is currently associate professor of anthropology at Stanford University. Correspondence may be addressed to her at the Department of Anthropology, Stanford University, Stanford, CA 94305.

Bradd Shore received his Ph.D. from the University of Chicago in 1977. He has done extensive field work in Western Samoa and has written numerous articles and a book based on his research on kinship, conflict resolution, and social control. Before taking up his current teaching position at Sarah Lawrence College, he taught at the University of California, Santa Cruz, where he had a joint appointment in Anthropology and at the Center for South Pacific Studies. Correspondence may be addressed to him at the Department of Anthropology, Sarah Lawrence College, Bronxville, NY 10708.

Marilyn Strathern is a Fellow of Girton College, Cambridge University, Cambridge CB3 0JG, England. She began work in Papua New Guinea in 1964 and continued intermittently till 1976. Her major publications include *Official and Unofficial Courts: Legal Assumptions and Expectations in a Highlands Community* (1972) and *No Money on Our Skins* (1975) (a study of migrants in Port Moresby). She has always sustained the interest in gender studies that led to her first book, *Women in Between* (1972), and has since written several articles in this area and recently coedited a collection of essays entitled *Nature, Culture and Gender* (1980).

Harriet Whitehead received her Ph.D. in Anthropology from the University of Chicago in 1975. She did her dissertation research on religious cult phenomena in the United States, and is currently completing a book on the role of symbolic form in religious conversion and psychotherapy. She is also interested in the cross-cultural study of gender systems. She has taught at Stanford University and Haverford College. Correspondence should be addressed to her at 905 S. 47th St., Philadelphia, PA 19143.

Preface

This is a book about the ways in which gender and sexuality are conceptualized in various cultures, and about the sources and consequences of such cultural conceptions. It is not primarily about what men and women normatively do ("sex roles") although the roles of men and women both shape and are shaped by cultural conceptions. Nor is the book primarily about gender asymmetry ("male dominance," "the status of women") although again this dimension of gender relations systematically influences and is influenced by cultural notions of gender and sexuality. The book, in short, is about what we have called "sexual meanings," taking "sex" in the double English sense – pertaining to gender, and pertaining to the erotic – and considering it as a symbol, or system of symbols, invested with culturally variable "meanings."

We consider the attempt to understand gender and sexuality in social and cultural context to be among the most important tasks of contemporary social science, and this book is first and foremost a contribution toward that understanding. In addition, however, we view the book as a contribution to the field that has come to be known as "symbolic" or "hermeneutic" anthropology, in two ways: First, the symbolic approach is shown to be particularly powerful in dealing with the tangled domain of gender problems; seeing sex and gender as symbols liberates this whole area of inquiry from constraining naturalistic assumptions and opens it to a range of analytic questions that would otherwise not be asked. Second, as we discuss more fully in the Introduction, the symbolic-analysis or hermeneutic approach is itself significantly expanded by its encounter with some of the problems peculiar to the domain of gender. Thus, for example, where symbolic anthropology often tends toward a somewhat uncritical cultural relativism, the systematic asymmetry of gender relations in all known cultures forces the analyst toward a more critical analytic stance. Similarly, although symbolic anthropology, like anthropology in general, tends to ignore the individual, the fact that gender symbols always pertain simultaneously to individual and social processes forces the analyst to maintain the vital analytic link between the individual and society, between "the personal and the political."

Originally, the impetus for doing the book came from knowing that there were a number of people independently working on issues of gender from a symbolic-analysis perspective. It seemed worthwhile simply to try to bring their work together in a volume, with an introductory essay explicating the value of such an approach to gender and related issues. This minimal objective, however, has been continually expanded in relation to the wealth of insights that emerged in the essays. We came to realize that the collection was more than simply a state-of-the-art compendium of symbolic approaches to gender; it also opens up a number of theoretical approaches that appear significant for future research in this important field of inquiry. Drawing on the essays, but going somewhat beyond any single one, we have tried in the Introduction to summarize and systematize these theoretical prospects.

We should probably say a few words about what is underrepresented, or not represented, in the collection.

First, complex societies are underrepresented. This was unintentional. We would have liked to have had more papers on European and Asian societies, but this simply did not work out. There is thus an unevenness of ''coverage'' in the collection, not only in terms of geographic ''spread'' (which we do not think is critical in itself), but more importantly in terms of certain theoretical issues. In particular, none of the essays directly address issues of interaction between gender and class. Many of the essays, however, do address the relationship between gender and other forms of social inequality, at least those forms to be found in non-class-based societies. In the Introduction we have tried to summarize some of the main points of these discussions, and to suggest their implications for the analysis of more complex systems.

Second, none of the essays in the collection systematically analyze gender culture from the ''female point of view,'' although many of them incorporate a discussion of women's viewpoint within an analysis of the hegemonic (male-biased) ideology. We consider this approach to be theoretically justified, in that some form of asymmetry favoring men is present in all cultures, and that women's perspectives are to a great extent constrained and conditioned by the dominant ideology. The analysis of the dominant ideology must thus precede, or at least encompass, the analysis of the perspective of women.

Most of the essays were submitted in first draft in 1978. The manuscript was subjected at various stages to a total of five readings by anonymous referees. Although it is often thought that collected volumes are subject to less, or less stringent, refereeing than journal articles, this has not been the case with this collection. We thank the Press readers for their careful and helpful comments and criticisms.

Ann Arbor, Michigan   S.B.O.
Haverford, Pennsylvania   H.W.
July 15, 1980

Introduction: ACCOUNTING FOR SEXUAL MEANINGS

Sherry B. Ortner & Harriet Whitehead

It has long been recognized that "sex roles" – the differential participation of men and women in social, economic, political, and religious institutions – vary from culture to culture.[1] It has also long been recognized that the degree and quality of social asymmetry between the sexes is also highly variable between cultures. What has not been generally recognized is the bias that often underlies studies of both sex roles and male dominance – an assumption that we know what "men" and "women" are, an assumption that male and female are predominantly natural objects rather than predominantly cultural constructions.

This book assumes a radically different premise: that natural features of gender, and natural processes of sex and reproduction, furnish only a suggestive and ambiguous backdrop to the cultural organization of gender and sexuality. What gender is, what men and women are, what sorts of relations do or should obtain between them – all of these notions do not simply reflect or elaborate upon biological "givens," but are largely products of social and cultural processes. The very emphasis on the biological factor *within* different cultural traditions is variable; some cultures claim that male–female differences are almost entirely biologically grounded, whereas others give biological differences, or supposed biological differences, very little emphasis.

Margaret Mead, of course, argued these points – one might even say "discovered" them – over forty years ago, and few anthropologists today work with an explicit theoretical model of biological determinism. Yet until recently, few have bothered to identify in any systematic way the cultural and social processes to which culturally variable sex and gender notions might be related. Either by referral of all such matters to biologically grounded psychological theory, or simply by neglect of the subject, anthropologists have allowed the naturalistic bias to dominate the field of sex and gender. This volume assumes the challenge of correcting this imbalance by focusing upon gender and sexuality as cultural (symbolic) constructs, and inquiring into the sources, processes, and consequences of their construction and organization.

Thus, all of the authors in the collection systematically begin by asking what male and female, sex and reproduction, *mean* in given social and cultural contexts, rather than assuming that we know what they mean in the first place. Gender, sexuality, and reproduction are treated as *symbols*, invested with meaning by the society in question, as all symbols are. The approach to the problem of sex and gender is thus a matter of symbolic analysis and interpretation, a matter of relating such symbols to other cultural symbols and meanings on the one hand, and to the forms of social life and social experience on the other. The shared view of gender and sexuality as meaningful symbolic forms that require interpretation before explanation unites the entire collection.

The results of applying such a perspective are, first, to bring to light previously unrecognized diversity in the meanings of the sexes and sexuality cross-culturally, while simultaneously making us more aware of those cross-cultural similarities that do exist. And second, the symbolic approach helps to draw our attention to those societal and cultural factors that impinge most immediately upon the culture of gender.

Before examining these results, however, it is important to make clear what is meant by a "symbolic approach" to sex-gender data, and to specify some of the methodological differences that exist among our contributors. In the present essay, we will first discuss methodologies, then survey the sorts of cross-cultural differences and similarities in gender ideas brought to light by the symbolic perspective, and finally consider the question of which areas of society and culture appear to be most influential in shaping cultural notions of gender and sexuality.

Aspects of method

The essays can be grouped broadly into two sets: one in which the methodological emphasis is upon working out the inner logic and structural relations *among* cultural symbols, and one in which the emphasis is on analyzing the relationships between symbols and meanings on the one hand, and aspects of social relations on the other. We may label the first set as more "culturalist" and the second as more "sociological," while stressing that even the more sociologically oriented studies are committed to a symbolic (or "cultural") view of gender, and that even the more culturally oriented papers have important sociological underpinnings.

The culturalist approach, first, stresses that no particular gender symbol can be well understood without an appreciation of its place in a larger system of symbols and meanings. In other words, it is not only that we must understand what "male," "female," "sex," and "reproduction" mean in any given culture, but that those meanings are best understood in terms of a larger context of interrelated meanings. The emphasis, then, is on "making sense" of sex and gender symbols in terms of other cultural beliefs, conceptions, classifications, and assumptions.

This approach is illustrated, with variations, by the essays in Part I of the collection: Whitehead on native North American gender crossing, Poole on the "androgynous" ritual leader among the Bimin-Kuskusmin of New Guinea, Strathern on the culturally perceived moral orientations of Hagener (New Guinea) men and women, Shore on the "algebra" of maleness and femaleness in Samoa, Brandes on male sexual ideology in Andalusia, and Nadelson on myths of the origin of women among the Mundurucú of Amazonia. Cucchiari's speculative essay on the origins of gender categories, although not purely a cultural analysis, also belongs in this methodological category because it too deals primarily with internal relations (in this case, contradictions) among elements of an ideological system. In all of these essays, the meanings of maleness, femaleness, sex, and reproduction emerge in large part from the systematic relations, both logical and associational, in which they are shown to participate with other symbols.

For example, it emerges from a contextual analysis of Andalusian gender symbolism, that popular symbols of the Devil (the goat, the serpent of Eden) are predominantly identified in this area with the female sex rather than the male, contrary to their masculine associations in other branches of Western tradition (Brandes). Another example: In three of the culture areas dealt with in the collection – New Guinea, native North America, and Polynesia – gender-anomalous persons are culturally recognized (even created), but as our authors make clear, Western categories of sex perversion and hermaphroditism are inappropriate to describe them. In each case, their special status is based upon a culturally specific, non-Western, configuration of gender traits (Poole, Whitehead, Shore). These findings, as well as Nadelson's revelation of the fantasy of male self-sufficiency underlying Mundurucu mythic ruminations about the origins of women, or Strathern's explication of why the Melpa women's point of view on gender parallels that of the men, arise from a careful unraveling of the premises behind particular usages, classifications, and associations.

Although these essays focus primarily on the cultural level, that is, on the *interrelations* among symbols and meanings, it should be noted that such an approach does not in itself preclude raising further questions concerning the social, political, and economic contexts of the symbolic constructs in question. Indeed we would argue that systematically executed symbolic analyses often evolve in such a way as to indicate which aspects of social (or economic or political) relations will prove most significant for further analysis. All of the more "culturalist" essays contain, implicitly or explicitly, such indications. The analyses of Whitehead, Strathern, and Brandes suggest that the social organization of prestige and status is critical for understanding gender conceptions in the cultures of their studies. On the other hand, the analyses of Poole, Shore, and Nadelson suggest that the social organization of kinship and marriage is central to the construction of gender in their cases. In fact we will argue later that aspects of *both* prestige *and* kinship-marriage organization systematically influence cultural conceptions of gender in specific ways, but for the moment we wish to continue the discussion of more strictly methodological issues.

We are arguing here that the culturalist approach, emphasizing the relations among cultural symbols, does not preclude asking more conventional sociological questions, questions concerning the effects of political, economic, and other social arrangements on cultural notions. We would go further and claim that a culturalist approach provides a less reductionistic basis for framing such questions in the first place. One of the persistent problems of social anthropology (mostly British) has been, that in the rush to connect "culture" to "society," analysts have often taken culture in bits ("female pollution," "virgin birth"), nailing each bit to some specific feature of social organization (marriage between enemy groups, matrilineal clan organization) without going through the crucial intervening phase of analyzing what that bit means. There is a failure in such accounts to understand that culture itself has the properties of a system, a system that mediates between any given symbol and its social grounding. The meaning of specific cultural features is as much a function of their fit within a wider symbolic context as it is of their relevance to (or reference to) a particular social institution, and serious interpretive distortions may arise when this wider cultural context is slighted in favor of a quick Durkheimian fix.

For instance, one could argue – with justice – that the "importance of patriliny" is being expressed in the Bimin-Kuskusmin's ritualized androgynous character, the *waneng aiyem ser*. But the very possibility of such a character is, as Poole demonstrates, contingent upon a cultural complex in which *both* kinship *and* gender identities are expressed, and interfused, in a code of bodily substances. The prior analysis of the systematics of cultural relations thus acts as a brake against oversimplifying sociological reductionism.

This brings us to the second broad approach represented in this collection – what we have called the more "sociological" approach. Whereas culturalist analysis works from the top down, as it were, the sociological approach works from the bottom up. Although both analytic modes as represented in this book share the same problematic – to elucidate the culture (symbols, meanings, ideologies) of gender – the more sociologically oriented essays approach this by considering how certain types of social orders tend to generate, through the logic of their workings, certain types of cultural perceptions of gender and sexuality. The approach is most directly represented by the essays in Part II: Collier and Rosaldo's analysis of gender in "brideservice" societies, Llewelyn-Davies's analysis of gender among the Maasai of East Africa, and Ortner's analysis of gender and sexuality in Polynesia. The nature of this approach, and particularly its distinctiveness from more traditional sociology-of-meaning approaches, is again best considered by comparing it with certain standard patterns of social anthropological analysis.

In the traditional social anthropological view, cultural features have been seen largely as "reflections" of primary jural structures (lineages, castes, classes), serving essentially to "reinforce" those structures. In the Marxist variant on this view, culture has been seen largely as "ideology," "justifying" the status quo and "mystifying" the sources of oppression and exploitation. The Marxist view has the distinct advantage of stressing that culture is rarely an accurate "reflection" of the whole, but rather a distortion of a systematic sort. All of the more sociologically oriented authors in this collection have been influenced, implicitly or explicitly, by the Marxist refinement, at least in part because the study of gender is inherently a study of relations of asymmetrical power and opportunity.

Yet traditional Marxism, like traditional Durkheimianism, suffers from an inadequate conception of culture as anything other than, or more than, a handmaiden of the social process. For sociological analysts with a strong background in symbolic anthropology, on the other hand, more sophisticated analytic tools are available. Of particular importance is the method of actor-centered, more precisely, actor-mediated, analysis, which has its roots in Weber and which carries through into modern symbolic anthropology by way of Parsons and Geertz. The concept of the "actor" is central to the sociology of symbols and meanings in a way that it is not central to more conventional social anthropology, partly for the simple reason that meaning does not inhere in symbols but must be invested in symbols and interpreted from symbols by acting social beings; thus social actors must be part of the analysis.

In actor-centered (or actor-mediated) analysis, the focus is not only on the formal characteristics of the structure, but on the ways in which, in operating within such structures, actors' perceptions of the world – of nature, of the self, and of social relations – are shaped in certain ways. Gender conceptions, and notions of sexuality and reproduction, are seen as emergent from varying forms of action, or practice, within varying forms of organization of social, economic, and political life. Thus Collier and Rosaldo show why, "in a world where a man needs a wife, and nothing else, to achieve the highest status available to him in his society, . . . sexual intercourse takes on the character of a truly 'political' act," and operates as a "dominant idiom for political relations." Llewelyn-Davies shows how among the Maasai the process of becoming an "autonomous" "elder" depends in part on obtaining "property" – wives and cattle; in this context the period of (male) transition from propertyless to propertied is ritualized and takes on great cultural "glamour." And it is in this period, Llewelyn-Davies argues, that "the [Maasai] *idea* of masculinity is constructed." Finally, Ortner shows how in Polynesia, where prestige is importantly maintained and augmented through enlargement of descent lines, kinswomen – sisters and daughters – appear as particularly valuable beings who have the capacity to attract men and to retain children for their lines, and who are thus treated with (rather contradictory forms of) respect.

In these examples, then, the method of analysis consists not of mapping certain symbols onto certain features of social structure as "reflections of" or "justifications for" institutional arrangements. Rather, it consists of showing how, for actors operating within certain kinds of institutional orders, and complying in effect with the rules of the game, the world tends to take on certain seemingly inevitable and "natural" appearances. The political nature of sexual intercourse in "simple" societies, the "glamour" of Maasai warriors, and the high cultural value of sisters and daughters in Polynesia – all of these become comprehensible as features of the "common sense" world *as it appears* to actors participating in social relations organized in particular ways. Obviously the process is circular. The structure of social relations itself is shaped and crystallized by the very cultural notions that social dynamics have acted to inspire.

For these more sociologically oriented analyses, certain questions emerge that had only been lurking in the background of the more culturalist essays, particularly the question of *which* aspects of social relations have greater influence upon the shape of gender ideology than others. We will take up this question in the section on the social contexts of gender culture. Here, however, we simply wish to reiterate that the two broad approaches just outlined must be seen not as opposed and mutually exclusive types, but as differing methodological emphases within the broader attempt to interpret and analyze gender as a cultural system. As noted previously, the contributors share a commitment to the proposition that male and female, sex and reproduction, are cultural or symbolic constructs, whatever may be the "natural" bases of gender differences and human reproduction. Each contributor thus begins by questioning the *meanings* of sex and gender as symbols in the societies with which he or she is concerned. Analysis then proceeds by seeking and showing the *contexts* within which such constructs "make sense," whether the context is a wider set of symbols and meanings, or whether it is some particular ordering of social relations.

Before considering the substantive issues, we should say a few words about the essay by Cucchiari on the origins of gender in cultural thought. This essay is essentially a thought experiment. Cucchiari asks the reader, by way of asking himself, to imagine a world without gender, and at the same time asks what other features of social organization and cultural thought would be absent, or present, in such a world. In the process, he discusses in greater detail than we do in this Introduction the sense in which gender *is* a cultural (and social and historical) construct. We have placed his essay after the Introduction both for its expanded discussion of the symbolically constructed nature of gender ideology, and for the general purpose of unhinging the reader's mind from standard modes of thinking about gender-related matters.

General features of gender ideologies

Although cultural gender ideologies vary greatly, certain general themes concerning the nature of men, women, sex and reproduction appear across a wide variety of cases. In this section we call attention to some of these themes, particularly those that emerge from the essays in this collection.

It must first be noted that the degree to which cultures have formal, highly elaborated notions of gender and sexuality is itself variable. One may think, for example, of the contrast between the Mediterranean and northern European cultures; the former have highly complex and explicit views on the nature of gender, views that, in turn, organize and define many other spheres of life – work, leisure, religious activity, and so forth. In northern Europe, on the other hand, notions of gender and sexuality appear to be less highly elaborated, and they do not seem to operate as master organizing principles for other domains of social life and activity.

Furthermore, not all cultures elaborate notions of maleness and femaleness in terms of symmetrical dualisms. Collier and Rosaldo point out, for example, that although notions of manhood are highly developed in "brideservice" societies, notions of womanhood are relatively unsystematized. Men are glorified as hunters and killers, but women are not by that fact glorified as mothers and "life givers." In these cases, cultural beliefs about the sexes do not form systems of logical oppositions or complementarities; the sexes appear more as gradations on a scale (see also Llewelyn-Davies).

In the majority of cultural cases, however, the differences between men and women are in fact conceptualized in terms of sets of metaphorically associated binary oppositions (and even a single scale, after all, has its top and bottom, its polar points). Moreover, there are certain oppositions that recur with some frequency in gender ideologies cross-culturally, and we wish to call attention to, and reflect upon, a number of them here.

First, some version of the "nature/culture" opposition makes an appearance in some of the studies in this book. In a 1972 article, Ortner argued that there is a universal tendency in cultural thought to align male with culture, and to see female as closer to nature (see also Ardener 1975; Barnes 1973; Mathieu 1973). In the present collection, Strathern, Shore, and Llewelyn-Davies find resonances of this tendency in their material. All of them, however, find reasons to modify the formulation in various ways. It seems worthwhile to review briefly these modifications and the theoretical status of universal oppositions between the sexes generally.

Of particular interest is the formulation that appears in Strathern's and Llewelyn-Davies's essays. Both contributors suggest that the dimension of opposition between the sexes most relevant for the peoples they studied (the New Guinea Mt. Hageners and the African Maasai, respectively) is the contrast between what Strathern calls "self-interest" and the "social good." Women are seen as tending toward more involvement with (often divisive) private and particularistic concerns, benefiting themselves, and perhaps their children, without regard for larger social consequences, whereas men are seen as having a more universalistic orientation, as being concerned with the welfare of the social whole. It appears likely that this association obtains in a large number of cultures throughout the world, and that it relates to a widespread sociological distinction between the sexes suggested by Rosaldo (1974): Nearly universally, men control the "public domain" where "universalistic" interests are expressed and managed, and, nearly universally, women are located in or confined to the "domestic domain," charged with the welfare of their own families.

This basic structural relation has been sensed and articulated, with varying emphases, by earlier theorists, notably Talcott Parsons and Claude Lévi-Strauss. In fact, it was Lévi-Strauss who, seeing the domestic domain primarily as a biological entity (the "biological family") and the public domain as that network of alliances brought into being by the first truly "cultural" act, the institution of the incest taboo, invoked the nature/culture opposition in reference to the domestic/public distinction. Ortner, following Lévi-Strauss's train of thought, closed the circle by suggesting that men will tend to be culturally aligned with "culture" and women with "nature," one reason (among others) being that men control the sphere of wider social coordinations, while women occupy the subunits being coordinated (Ortner 1972).

As we reflect upon these points, it seems clear to us that all of the suggested oppositions – nature/culture, domestic/public, self-interest/ social good – are derived from the same central sociological insight: that the sphere of social activity predominantly associated with males encompasses the sphere predominantly associated with females and is, for that reason, culturally accorded higher value. The different ways in which this insight has been formulated have to do with theoretical interests. Rosaldo, for instance, is concerned primarily with articulating male and female positions in parsimonious sociological terms, and maintains only that her formulation is consistent with the ways in which men and women are culturally perceived, not that her terms – domestic/public – replicate the native perspective. Ortner's nature/culture opposition, by contrast, was intended as a rather global approximation of the categorizing tendencies of many cultures. (The variations of its appearance at the level of *explicitly* articulated cultural ideology constitutes a separate analytic problem). The self-interest/social good contrast proposed by Strathern, finally, also captures a dimension of native viewpoint, and one that is perhaps closest to the central sociological insight itself: that men do indeed control the larger social operation (whether or not this invariably redounds to the good of everyone), while women's social horizons are narrowed to the small range of closely related kin and their immediate needs. The question of which of the cited male–female contrasts will show up in the idiom of a particular culture is, of course, empirical. But all could be present without inconsistency; all are in a sense transformations of one another.

A further permutation of the themes raised by the interrelation of men's and women's spheres of action may be seen in the general cultural tendency to define men in terms of status and role categories ("warrior," "hunter," "statesman," "elder," and the like) that have little to do with men's relations with women. Women, by contrast, tend to be defined almost entirely in relational terms – typically in terms pertaining to kin roles ("wife," "mother," "sister") – that, upon closer inspection, center around women's relationship to men. This contrast is not in most cases an explicit component of cultural thought. Nonetheless it constitutes a very general feature of the *way* in which the categories of male and female are differentially defined and organized cross-culturally.

The tendency for the image of women to be refracted through different modes of attachment to men is brought out especially clearly in Ortner's and Shore's analyses of Polynesian cultures, and in Poole's analysis of the ideas of the New Guinea Bimin-Kuskusmin. In the Polynesian case, both Shore and Ortner further note that the female relational categories, "wife" and "sister," which dominate the Polynesian concept of woman, embody among other things an important distinction between women who are, from any male ego's point of view, sexual and those who are not. The distinction between sexual women ("wives") and nonsexual women ("sisters"), and more importantly, the relatively greater cultural prominence of "sisters," has broad implications for the Polynesian cultural valuation of women and for patterns of cross-sex relations.

In what seems to be an extension of the androcentrism of defining women relationally, one finds a number of cultural cases in which there is an explicit conceptual split between a ''world of men'' and a ''world of heterosexual relations.'' Nadelson finds such a split in Mundurucu (South America) myths, and Collier and Rosaldo see it in the gender ideologies of ''brideservice'' societies generally. Associated with this pattern are themes of male unisexual reproduction (Nadelson) or at least male ritual control over female reproduction (see also Poole). Male–male sexual relations also tend to be a cultural issue, whether as positive ideal (see Kelly 1976 on New Guinea), or as a culturally exaggerated threat (see Brandes on Spain). Here we are in the realm of more specialized gender ideologies that are found only in certain types of society. But the pattern may also be seen as a particular transformation of the more general tendency to define women in terms of their relations with men (the ''world of heterosexual relations'') as opposed to defining men in terms of their occupation of certain exclusively male roles or statuses (the ''world of men'').

There is one additional widespread feature of the organization of gender ideas that must be noted here: the fact that very commonly the same axes that divide and distinguish male from female (and indeed rank male over female), also cross-cut the gender categories, producing internal distinctions and gradations within them. Both Strathern and Shore bring out this pattern clearly in their essays. Strathern lays out a set of oppositions that distinguish male and female among Hageners: not only the distinction between concern for the social good (male) and an orientation toward private self-interest (female), which we have already discussed, but also parallel distinctions between investors and consumers, prestigious and ''rubbish,'' and success and failure (the male term being first and best in each case). She goes on to show, however, that these same categories also order statuses *among* men (for example, especially ''big'' or prestigious men versus ''rubbish'' men) and, at least situationally, *among* women (for example, those who contribute to their husbands' investments versus those who simply consume the family resources). Similarly, Shore shows that the question of control over sexual behavior that divides Samoan men from women (women must be controlled, whereas, men need not, and indeed should not, be) also generates internal rankings of both males and females, although in inverse fashion for the two sexes. The highest female category, the ceremonial virgin princess, is the most sexually controlled, followed by the sister, the wife, and the ''wanton woman.'' For men, on the other hand, although the issue of sexual control does not actually generate *categories* of masculinity, there is nonetheless a correspondence between status and sexual activity that is the inverse of the female system – higher-ranking men are supposed to be more sexually active and expressive, lower-status men less so (see also Ortner).

In both cases, then, the axes of distinction between male and female also cross-cut each gender category. This suggests a point to which we will return in greater detail later: that many axes of gender distinctions are not in fact unique to the domain of gender, but are shared with (both derived from and exported to) other important domains of social life. It is to the question of what ''other domains of social life'' might be particularly relevant for the understanding of gender ideologies that we now turn.

The Social Contexts of Gender Culture

The field of gender studies has been plagued with the so-called "myth and reality" problem – the problem that cultural gender notions rarely accurately reflect male – female relations, men's and women's activities, and men's and women's contributions in any given society. Some argue that we must ignore the "myths," that is, the cultural representations, and focus on the realities; others argue the reverse. Neither approach is satisfactory. The problem is precisely one of understanding why certain "realities" emerge in cultural thought in distorted forms, forms that in turn feed back upon and shape those realities.

Thus our purpose in bringing together this collection is not simply to map a variety of cultural gender ideologies – although such an enterprise is in itself of fundamental importance – but to raise questions about the principles of their production and transformation. A consideration of the essays in this volume suggests a number of spheres of social life that seem particularly critical in shaping – and in turn being shaped by – cultural notions of gender and sexuality. In this section we wish to call attention to those "critical spheres," and to discuss why (in our view) they are significant.

We will begin with a consideration of the domain of kinship and marriage, commonly supposed to be one of the most important contexts within which gender ideology is produced and reproduced. We will then consider the sphere of prestige relations, and suggest that this sphere in fact mediates between the organization of kinship and marriage on the one hand, and the ideology of gender on the other, in any given society. Finally, we will suggest that certain very general features of prestige systems cross-culturally can account for some of the equally general features of gender ideologies discussed in the preceding section.

In considering critical spheres, it must be noted that we will be going beyond simply contextualizing and reviewing the contributions of the authors. We will be expressing our own theoretical hunches concerning what area of the social enterprise bears most immediately upon the cultural construction of sex and gender. The area we have chosen to emphasize, the organization of "prestige," is featured implicitly or semiexplicitly in several of the essays contained in this collection (and explicitly of course in our own essays); indeed certain of the essays have greatly strengthened our sense of the importance of prestige relations to sex and gender concepts. However, we must stress that we do not attempt to speak for our contributors on this matter. Any or all of them may prefer other interpretations of the data or other ways of stating our particular interpretations.

KINSHIP AND MARRIAGE

In even the most conventional ethnographies, one could always be sure to find women in the section on kinship and marriage, if nowhere else in the book. Because analysis of kinship and marriage relations always entails specifying whether the actors involved are male or female, studies of kinship and marriage systems have always been at least latently "genderized." The fact that such studies have long been central to anthropology may in part account for the fact that gender issues have consistently found more of a place in this field than in many of the other social sciences, even before the current wave of feminist-inspired work.

In contemporary feminist anthropology, in turn, kinship and marriage organization was the obvious place to start looking for important insights into the ways in which cultures construe gender, sexuality, and reproduction. Rubin (1975) specifically called attention to the fact that whatever else kinship and marriage are "about," they are always "about" gender, requiring two varieties of persons, "male" and "female," and reproducing persons in those two varieties (see also Rivière 1971, and Cucchiari). Rubin's article provides an analytic framework that is worth sketching briefly.

Using as a point of departure Lévi-Strauss's (1969) perception that the "exchange of women" in marriage transactions in some sense constitutes human society, Rubin explores both the social and psychological implications of the (universal) fact that "men have certain rights in their female kin, and that women do not have the same rights either to themselves or to their male kin. In this sense," she continues, the notion of "the exchange of women is a profound perception of a system in which women do not have full rights to themselves" (1975: 177). Rubin goes on to call for a "political economy of sex," an analysis of the ways in which marriage transactions are "tied into" economic and political arrangements (207), suggesting that such analysis will be key to understanding the varying ways in which "sex as we know it – gender identity, sexual desire and fantasy, concepts of childhood" – is socially produced and culturally organized (166).

In the present collection, Collier and Rosaldo most closely follow Rubin's lead, examining the ways in which marriage in "brideservice" societies reproduces certain hierarchical relations between a husband and his in-laws, and how the structure of these affinal relations in turn shapes cultural notions of men, women, and sexuality. Llewelyn-Davies similarly discusses the ways in which bridewealth arrangements articulate with male authority structures, and these in turn with gender conceptions among the African Maasai. Ortner discusses the ways in which Polynesian men enhance chances of status advancement by "holding" their daughters and sisters (and eventually the chidren of those women) after marriage, with systematic consequences for the views and treatment of women in this area. Aspects of kinship, marriage, descent, residence, and family also enter into the analyses of Cucchiari, Poole, Shore, Brandes, and Nadelson.

The sphere of kinship and marriage relations then is clearly consequential in various ways for cultural notions of gender and sexuality. Indeed, given the inherently genderized nature of kinship/marriage relations, one would hardly expect otherwise. Yet although we might suppose, in a common-sense way, that cultural notions of gender, sexuality, and reproduction would reflect directly the shape of kinship, marriage, and other structurally and affectively important cross-sex bonds, the ethnographic record has proven frustrating in this regard. The obvious (to us) connections are often missing. For example, the Trobriand Islands notwithstanding, "matrilineal" societies do not typically neglect the facts of physical paternity; nor do "patrilineal" systems (for example, the Nuer) necessarily emphasize these facts. So too, women's universal and highly visible kinship function, mothering, is surprisingly underrated, even ignored, in definitions of womanhood in a wide range of societies with differing kinship organizations (Collier and Rosaldo, this volume). Heavy symbolic stress on the brother–sister bond may show up equally well in the "matrilineal" Trobriands, the "patrilineal" South African Lovedu, and the "bilateral" Mediterranean peasantry. And so on. In other words, however important formal kinship organization may be for shaping concepts of gender and formulations of cross-sex relations, this organization has its impact only in an indirect and mediated way.

Rubin's article provides the lead to the relevant mediations. Rubin stresses the necessity of analyzing the ways in which marriage transactions tie into more encompassing political and economic arrangements, and Collier and Rosaldo carry Rubin's suggestions forward by systematically showing how a particular structure of links between marriage and political relations can account for a particular set of gender conceptions.

Both Rubin and Collier and Rosaldo describe the relevant encompassing structures as "political-economic" in character. We would like to pick up the gist of their argument, but reformulate it in a more particular way. We suggest that the structures of greatest import for the cultural construction of gender in any given society are the structures of prestige. Let us be careful about phraseology here, for this is partly a matter of phraseology. There is no disagreement with Rubin or Collier and Rosaldo in seeing political-economic organization as a dynamic interdependence between transactions of an economic-material nature and those of a more ideologically constituted – Collier and Rosaldo would say "political" – nature. There is no question, in other words, of opposing our viewpoint to that of mere "material reductionism." Rather, where Collier and Rosaldo have tended to highlight the political character of gender-relevant social relations, we prefer to speak of the prestige-oriented character of such relations, feeling that this emphasis brings into fuller articulation what it is about the political-economic organization of a society that most immediately and intelligibly affects that society's formal understanding of sex and gender.

We wrote earlier of the Weberian tradition of examining cultural constructs from the viewpoint of actors within the social system. Our principle interest in the organization of prestige derives from this perspective. It will be argued that many aspects of particular conceptions of the sexes, sexuality, and so on, make sense if interpreted as emanating from the perspective of actors operating within their society's rules and mechanisms governing status differentiation. More specifically, we find that the cultural construction of sex and gender tends everywhere to be stamped by the prestige considerations of socially dominant *male* actors. In effect, the way in which prestige is allocated, regulated, and expressed establishes a lens through which the sexes and their social relations are culturally viewed.

Obviously, this shift of emphasis involves some reorganization of what is considered to be a direct, and what a more mediated, influence on gender constructs. Kinship and marriage, the distribution of the means of violence, the relations of production – all are viewed here as of importance in the degree to which they enter into the structuring of prestige situations. We would thus interpose prestige structures as a screen between the various material, familial, and political structures that have been considered to impinge in varying and complex ways upon cultural conceptions of manhood, woman-hood, sex, and reproduction. The case for doing so is not altered by the fact that prestige systems can be viewed as part of the political-economic order. Our point is that it is this – the prestige – part (or dimension) that specifically has the clearest and most intelligible implications for gender ideas.

The importance of prestige systems for the understanding of particular sex-related beliefs has not gone altogether unrecognized in the anthropologi-cal literature. Certainly treatments of gender relations in the Mediterranean area and India have brought prestige considerations to the forefront (e.g., Pitt-Rivers 1966; Yalman 1963). But these studies seem to have accom-plished little more than the adding of yet another social determinant of gender ideas to a long list of suggested determinants, a list that includes the produc-tive system, the inheritance modality, the dominant social ideology, the higher cosmological system, the kinship organization, and the patterns of warfare. Our contention is that instead of being simply another item on the list, prestige systems provide us with the analytic catalyst that brings organ-ization into the remaining assortment of suggested possibilities.

In the following section, we will explain briefly what is meant by prestige structures, and examine the reasons why, and some of the ways in which, these are interwoven with cultural constructions of gender. We will then return to the question of the impact of kinship organization and marital practices upon sex-gender ideology, placing these factors into what we consider a more useful perspective.

PRESTIGE STRUCTURES

Prestige – or "social honor" or "social value" – assumes slightly different qualities and falls in different quantities on different persons and groups within any society. The sets of prestige positions or levels that result from a particular line of social evaluation, the mechanisms by which individuals and groups arrive at given levels or positions, and the overall conditions of reproduction of the system of statuses, we will designate as a "prestige structure."

Of course it is not particularly easy to arrive at a hard and fast definition of such structures. Although they are ordinarily *culturally* salient – that is, actors are well aware of them, and often invoke prestige motives in explaining their actions to each other and to outsiders – questions concerning the nature and workings of prestige systems have received surprisingly little systematic attention from social scientists (Dumont 1970, Goldman 1970, and Bloch 1977 are exceptions). Even Max Weber, who is noted for taking the position that prestige systems are structurally significant and historically dynamic (Weber 1958), nonetheless did not organize his observations on the subject very clearly. Anthony Giddens summarizes Weber's views on the subject as follows:

> The status situation of an individual refers to the evaluations which others make of him or his social position, thus attributing to him some form of (positive or negative) social prestige or esteem. A status group is a number of individuals who share the same status situation. Status groups, unlike classes, are almost always conscious of their common position . . .
>
> Status groups normally manifest their distinctiveness through following a particular life-style, and through placing restrictions upon the manner in which others may interact with them . . .
>
> Stratification by status is not, for Weber, simply a "complication" of class hierarchies: on the contrary, status groups, as differentiated from classes, are of vital significance in numerous phases of historical development . . . Both class and status group membership may be a basis of social power. [Giddens 1971: 166–7]

Weber's careful distinction between status groups and classes, that is groups defined by their relationship to production, should be borne in mind in our subsequent discussion. When we speak of gender ideas being motivated by prestige (status) concerns, we do not mean to suggest that such ideas are aimed, in the Marxist sense, at maintaining a situation of economic domination. Gender ideas may in some cases serve this function, but whether they do so or not would have to be determined in every specific case.

Considered abstractly, the sources of status or prestige, for individuals and groups alike, are relatively few and straightforward. Command of material resources (including human labor power), political might, personal skill, and/or connectedness through kinship or other reliable bonds to the wealthy, the mighty, and the skilled are, if conjoined with (a) effective use of these factors in dealing with others or the environment, and (b) a modicum of largesse and concern for the social good, all sources of prestige. This picture is complicated in an important way by the fact that historical reputations of efficacy, wealth, might, good connections, and social generosity compound, and to a degree stand in for, the "real" thing, and reputation thus serves to solidify and in some cases rigidify the social standings of groups or persons. This is one of the reasons why prestige systems are seldom simple and direct reflections of material power (see also Bloch 1977).

Insofar as the modes of prestige allocation have crystallized into formal, above-ground mechanisms, they are similarly few and simple in theory. There are the ascriptive channels, which assign people to status positions through kin affiliation and natural surface characteristics; there are the achievement channels, which assign prestige according to group or individual success in designated endeavors; and there are sundry hybrids of both modes.

Finally, prestige structures are always supported by, indeed they appear as direct expressions of, definite beliefs and symbolic associations that make sensible and compelling the ordering of human relations into patterns of deference and condescension, respect and disregard, and in many cases command and obedience. These beliefs and symbolic associations may be looked at as a legitimating ideology. A system of social value differentiation, founded on whatever material base, is fragile and incomplete without such an ideology.

When we turn to the examination of specific cases, the general sources of prestige, modes of allocation, and supporting ideologies translate into an incredible variety of highly distinctive structures and substructures. Some better-known examples of prestige structures are the Polynesian aristocratic ranking system, the Hindu caste system, the medieval European estates, the "honor" and "shame" complex of the Mediterranean (perhaps best described as a substructure), and the rather amorphous fusion of income, education, occupation, and lifestyle (what the sociologists call S.E.S. – socioeconomic status) that generates the culturally perceived "upper," "upper-middle," "middle," (and so on) "strata" of contemporary American society. Obviously, how prestige is culturally articulated and justified in any given case must be empirically determined: One must ask what ideas are invoked to transform "raw" social power into "cooked" esteem, and to establish the rules (often exquisitely nuanced) that govern how this esteem may be enhanced, diminished, adulterated, parlayed, or cashed in.

In every case too, it will remain to be determined how various sets of prestige structures (there is never only one such structure to a society) are harmonized with each other, and how they arise from and in turn play back upon deeper, more distant, or less obvious social arrangements such as the organization of production. Although we have tentatively included under the concept of "prestige structure" the conditions of that structure's reproduction, an inclusion that would in most cases enjoin delving into the social relations of production in the society in question, we think it important to recognize some theoretical distinction between these two analytic levels even while emphasizing their interdependence. In our view, prestige structures are "emergent," or partially autonomous structures, with properties not directly reducible to relations of production in the Marxist sense (thus "socioeconomic status" is distinguishable from Marxist-defined "class" position under capitalism) nor to material power in the more general ("vulgar Marxist") sense (see Parsons 1937; Bloch 1977). In part, this autonomy is a function of the importance of tradition in maintaining a state of affairs crystallized in the past, in part a function of the presence of a legitimating ideology that acts as a filter between social power and efficacy in its raw form and publically agreed upon status distinctions. The specifically cultural elements of the sociocultural phenomenon of prestige thus seem to give structures of status differentiation a certain life of their own.

Recognizing this partial autonomy, theorists have argued that a prestige system may feed back upon underlying relations and forces of production, sometimes dominating and conserving a certain pattern of economic relations, as Dumont believes has been true of the Hindu caste system (Dumont 1970); sometimes having a destabilizing and even developmental effect, as Goldman speculates was the case with the Polynesian system of rank (Goldman 1970); in yet other instances, interlocking with production so as to give rise to long cyclical patterns wherein both productive and prestige relations undergo systematic alternations, such as the *gumsa/gumlao* cycle of the Kachin of Burma (Leach 1954; Friedman 1972).

The relationship between a particular prestige system and its deeper social supports must thus be viewed as historically specific and complex. Nor can this relationship be ignored in favor of treating prestige systems in artificial isolation from their social roots. Certainly in studies of the impact of prestige concerns upon gender notions, one may find that tensions between a formally instituted prestige arrangement and those components of the productive system essential to its maintenance are the wellspring of a number of sex-related beliefs. For instance in a given society it may seem, and men may assert, that masculine prestige is purely a function of ritual knowledge, or bravery in warfare, or hunting prowess. But deeper investigation may uncover the importance to a man's position of wifely productive labor, or female kin links to trading partners, or property rights in women and children; and these factors in turn can be shown to motivate particular images of women, procreation, or sexual activity (see Collier and Rosaldo, Llewelyn-Davies, this volume; Kelly, n.d.).

At this point we may elaborate more fully upon our contention that the social organization of prestige is the domain of social structure that most directly affects cultural notions of gender and sexuality. This contention has several interrelated aspects that must be distinguished. We will first simply list these, then unravel them slowly, with illustration. (a) A gender system is first and foremost a prestige structure itself. This is the most central point. (b) Prestige structures in any society tend toward symbolic consistency with one another (on the order of what has been called "logico-meaningful integration"). (c) Gender constructs are partly functions of the ways in which male prestige-oriented action articulates (in structural-functional terms) with structures of cross-sex relations. Let us take each of these points in turn.

(a) The point that gender systems are themselves prestige structures, once stated, seems self-evident. Indeed the point has been articulated many times before, the feminist-inspired anthropological discussions of "women's status" being only the most recent of these articulations. In every known society, men and women compose two differentially valued terms of a value set, men being as *men*, higher (Rosaldo 1974; Ortner 1972). In the simplest societies, there are often only two principles of status differentiation: One that distinguishes between senior (or "elder" or "initiated") men and juniors, ranking the former over the latter; and one that distinguishes between male and female, ranking men over women. In such simple systems, needless to say, gender as a prestige system has enormous social salience, and is interwoven with the political-economic fabric of the society in direct and transparent ways. In more complex societies, in which larger systems of nongender-based ranking (ranked lineages, castes, classes) attain social structural prominence and historical dynamism, and in which gender recedes into the background as a formal social organizational principle, the genders remain nonetheless among the most psychologically salient of status groups.

Once the point that gender is a prestige structure is moved to the center of the analytic project, a number of features of gender ideologies cross-culturally begin to make sense. It will be immediately noted, for example, that the concepts used to differentiate men from women in terms of social worth are often identical to the concepts used to distinguish other differentially valued social types, and identical as well to the concepts used to grade individuals of the same gender. These concepts in fact simply denominate common axes of social valuation – the selfish versus the altruistic, the controlled versus the uncontrolled, the cultured versus the beastly, the strong versus the weak. In Strathern's essay this point is explicit: among New Guinea Hageners, male is to female *as* concern for the social good is to private, selfish concerns *as* prestigious is to "rubbish." Collier and Rosaldo also point out that selfless generosity and concern for the social whole is an attribute that distinguishes senior from junior men in brideservice societies, and not just men from women.

By the same token, it becomes intelligible why prestige positions outside the immediate gender realm are often rendered in gender terms. The Andalusian man who is humiliated by another is said to have "lowered his trousers" to the other (Brandes); the Piegan women whose age and accumulated wealth enable her to assume a position of general social dominance is spoken of as "manly hearted" (Whitehead). In Polynesia, sexuality is not merely an idiom of gender relations but of transgender rank relations as well: Chiefliness and aristocracy are associated with active sexuality and with the stimulation of the fertility of nature (Ortner). And of course in our own culture, the boy who does not care to participate in violent sports – a major source of prestige for young American males – is said to be like a girl. Again, Strathern articulates the process at work in such usages when she speaks of the relationship of mutual metaphorization that often obtains between gender categories and categories from the larger prestige system.

But the point that gender is a prestige structure has larger implications than those just noted. It raises analytic questions that in turn produce additional insights into the ways in which sexual meanings are organized cross-culturally. Specifically, it directs us to inquire into the relationship between gender and other prestige orders, from a number of analytic viewpoints. The two points that follow are addressed to two general dimensions of such relationships and the implications of these for gender ideas.

(*b*) Prestige structures tend toward symbolic consistency with one another. This means not only that certain general scales and polarities, such as culture/nature, and so on, will be commonly invoked in explaining any sort of social value differential; and not only that one prestige structure will be metaphorically invoked in regard to another and vice versa; but furthermore, that two or more dimensions of prestige may appear conceptually fused into a single system. Such fusings seem to run in either of two directions. On the one hand, it is possible to find social systems in which gender and some other dimension of prestige are simply not differentiated. In many New Guinea societies for instance, gender status is so well harmonized with age status through the symbolic emphasis upon reproductive substances, that the gender structure is simultaneously an age structure (Rubin, n.d.). This is apparent for the Bimin-Kuskusmin (Poole), and it emerges as well in Meigs's study of the Hua (Meigs 1976), Kelly's study of the Etoro (Kelly 1976) and others. In many of the societies of native North America, gender was partially fused with occupational specialization, the latter being an important arena of prestige (Whitehead).

On the other hand there are clearly systems in which a recognition of the different axes of prestige is evident, but in which a unity of sorts has nevertheless been imposed upon them by a deliberate rationalizing effort. This appears to be the case with gender and caste in India. The same pollution–purity ideology that divides the castes divides the sexes as well, but this does not mean that gender and caste are simply undifferentiated. At the same time, it is more than a matter of spontaneous mutual metaphorization. The similarities between gender distinctions and caste distinctions seem instead to be the result of the secondary application of a general philosophy of hierarchy to both gender and caste spheres. Gender and caste are seen as different manifestations of the same principles, but different nonetheless.

It should be pointed out that the gender hierarchy is not the only prestige hierarchy that forms amalgamations with other prestige structures. Political and ecclesiastical structures also seem to have a fatal attraction for one another in certain types of societies, and one finds as a result priest-kings, divine kings, and the like.

We note this widespread tendency of prestige structures to align with one another or to form amalgamations primarily in order to direct further inquiry. The reasons why gender should fuse with X in one society and with Y in another remain to be determined. When some highly explicit status stratification system has the effect of dominating the entire organization of society, as Hindu caste does, it seems unsurprising that it should cast its shadow upon sex ranking too; but one can hardly argue that in New Guinea for example, age-phase stratification dominates or is even particularly explicit. Rather, it seems almost to be "inveigled" into gender status via the cultural obsession with reproductive substances. Whitehead suggests that the identification of gender with occupational specialization in most of the relatively unstratified native North American societies may have arisen from that fact that, in the absence of strong systems of gender-linked surplus appropriation that tend to be associated with highly ritualized and symbolically "loaded" definitions of the sexes, and in the absence as well of transgender prestige hierarchies (caste, class, rank), occupation rose to the surface as simply the most salient (and prestige-relevant) sex marker. Needless to say, this is an area of "sexual meaning" that requires further analytic attention.

(c) Gender concepts are functions of the ways in which male prestige oriented action articulates with structures of cross-sex relations. In contrast to the preceding point, we are not concerned here with how gender as a cultural system is symbolically harmonized with other prestige orders as cultural systems; rather, we are concerned with how cross-sex social relations in all their manifestations – the sexual division of labor, marriage, consanguinity – ramify upon male prestige from the point of view of the male actor, and how these ramifications are interpreted.

We begin this discussion by noting that, with the possible exception of contemporary Western society, there are no larger-than-gender prestige structures that are not in fact partially "genderized." We relate this to the fact that the "public domain" or the "sphere of wider social coordinations" is, as we have argued, dominated by men, and that it is in this domain that larger prestige structures take their shape. Simply put, the other-than-gender prestige hierarchies of most societies are, by and large, male games.

In less complex societies, this is often clearly the case. Men compete for "big man" status, and are differentiated accordingly, whereas women remain a relatively homogeneous social mass – at least from the official cultural point of view. Even when birthright status groups have formed – ranks, castes, classes – the primarily male face of prestige concern is not entirely overcome. For even though both sexes participate in a designated social rank and follow behavioral codes appropriate to that rank, the feminine version of this code overwhelmingly emphasizes the woman's position as a ward of her menfolk. Hers is, in other words, a "dependent rank."

We noted earlier that men tend to be defined in terms of role categories such as warrior, statesman, Brahmin, or elder, whereas women are defined largely in terms of their cross-sex relations (as wives, mothers, and so on.) We tentatively related this pattern to the "public" orientation of men and the "domestic" orientation of women. This point can now be refined. We can see that the primary categories of maleness are not simply from the "public" domain in general, but specifically from the sphere of prestige relations. To be a warrior or an elder in societies in which these are primary categories of manhood is not simply to perform a certain role in the public domain, but to be located at a certain point in a hierarchical scheme of culturally ordered prestige.

The tendency to define women relationally, in turn, must be seen as a reflex of their exclusion from – yet crucial linkages with – the world of male prestige. If it were simply a matter of there being two parallel value-equivalent domains – domestic and public, female and male – then the categories of womanhood might appear as parallel to the categories of manhood. Women might be described, for example, primarily as "childtenders" or as "hostesses," categories derived from their primary activities or role performances in their (domestic) domain. In fact, however, the categories of femaleness are not generated in terms of some sort of abstract symmetry with masculinity, but in terms of women's relationships with men, and terms of the relevance of those relationships to male prestige.

The existence of larger prestige structures and their rootedness in the male-dominated public sphere of social activity has consequences for cultural notions of the sexes beyond merely this tendency to designate a man in terms of social position and a woman in terms of her menfolk. We are suggesting that cultural notions of the genders and sexuality will vary from culture to culture in accordance with the way in which women, the woman-dominated domestic sphere, and cross-sex relations in general are organized into the base that supports the larger (male) prestige system.

In saying this, we return to the point at which we digressed from Collier and Rosaldo. We said earlier, in agreement with them, that political-economic relations and marital-kinship relations (the two being, as they clearly demonstrate, often inseparably connected) have consequences for the cultural construction of gender and sexuality. Here we are interjecting our particular way of understanding how these consequences come about. Specifically, we are proposing that economic and kinship-marriage relations ramify upon sex-gender ideology as these relations are filtered through the perspective of the male ego situated within the prestige structure (or structures) of the society under consideration. Thus, analysis of the implications of kinship, marriage, and other important cross-sex relations for the cultural construction of gender must proceed by way of examining the consequences of these factors for (male) prestige relations.

In considering the ways in which cross-sex relations impinge upon male prestige-oriented action, probably the first question to ask in any given case is simply to what degree there is such impingement. For example, in an unpublished paper, Raymond Kelly analyzes beliefs about female pollution in different parts of New Guinea (n.d.). He notes that, in areas such as the Sepik, male prestige is generated through activites like hunting or warfare that are organized independently of women and of relations with women; in such areas there is relatively little elaboration of beliefs about female pollution. In the Highlands, on the other hand, male prestige depends heavily upon female productive labor: Women raise the pigs that men need for their prestige-generating exchange relations, and obviously have the capacity to undermine their husbands' ambitions. In this part of New Guinea beliefs about female pollution tend to flourish, as do male cults that both defend men against such pollution and ritually assert male self sufficiency.

From the point of view of this argument, the situation described by Brandes for Andalusian villagers parallels the Highlands (rather than the Sepik) New Guinea case. An Andalusian man's honor is bound up with the defense of his "domus" (to borrow the useful Occitan term [Ladurie 1978]) – defense of the house, land, and family that together constitute the base of his social standing in the community. Here it is not so much women's productive activities (or failures to produce) that threaten to undermine male prestige, but rather women's overall personal comportment, and an Andalusian man's concern for maintaining his honor takes the form of an almost paranoid obsession with the sexual conduct of his womenfolk. And, as in the New Guinea Highlands, Andalusian women are portrayed as highly threatening creatures who are capable of, indeed intent upon, destroying a man's social standing and even his health and survival. Even though the economic organization of Highlands New Guinea and Andalusia are obviously utterly different, because of certain similarities in the way prestige, for men, is organized, the two areas' notions of gender relations bear a striking similarity.

In contrast, we see two cases in this collection analogous to the more benign Sepik example: native North America, as discussed by Whitehead; and Polynesia, as discussed by Ortner and Shore. In neither area does male prestige depend heavily upon women's activities and/or men's relations with women, and in both areas notions of female pollution, disruptiveness, and threat are not developed. A corollary of Kelly's argument is that, in New Guinea, the disjunction between sources of male prestige on the one hand and male–female relations on the other, allows for the development of independent female social groupings and/or independent sources of female prestige. In the Sepik area of New Guinea, for instance, women have their own rituals, whereas Highlands women do not. Although one must be cautious in deriving any universal hypothesis from the New Guinea materials, it is interesting to note that Kelly's point seems to hold true for the analogous cases in this volume: Samoan women have organizations that perform valued communal tasks, and North American Indian women's craftwork and curing are significant sources of wealth and, with this, feminine prestige.

Most societies probably have some sources of male prestige that, as in these cases, are relatively disconnected from relations with women. But in perhaps the majority of cases, male prestige is deeply involved in cross-sex relations. Women may be cast as the prize for male prowess or success; having a wife may be the prerequisite to full adult male status; good or bad liaisons with women may raise or lower one's status; the status of one's mother may systematically affect one's status at birth; the sexual comportment of one's sisters and daughters may polish or dull one's honor; and so on. Although we would not expect such dependency of male honor upon female behavior to necessarily always be reflected in beliefs in female pollution, it is remarkable how widespread such beliefs are.

Once we start speaking of situations in which male prestige is closely involved with relations with women, it is clear that we are back once again on the subject of kinship and marriage. Now, however, we are in a position to observe that these structural bonds are themselves differently construed, and reverberate differently into the general area of sexual meanings, depending upon what these bonds accomplish for the actor in the larger prestige game, and in what way. At this point, then, we refocus on the subject of kinship and marriage relations from the vantage point of prestige.

KINSHIP AND MARRIAGE FROM THE POINT OF VIEW OF PRESTIGE

It is not our intention to catalog the myriad ways in which kinship and marriage relations may be implicated in the organization of prestige systems; quite the contrary. It is precisely our contention that one must focus on the *particularities* of the relationship between the two domains in any given case, in order to understand the sources of cultural gender notions in that case. In this section of the discussion, then, we will summarize and organize some of the patterns of relations between kinship/marriage, prestige, and gender ideologies that have emerged in the essays in this collection, as well as in a number of earlier studies.

We have already noted several times that distinctions among women as wives, mothers, or sisters are critical to cultural definitions of femininity in ways that analogous distinctions among men are not critical for masculinity. In order to see the interactions between prestige and kinship more clearly, we must now extend this point. It emerges from various essays in this collection (Poole, Shore, Brandes, Collier and Rosaldo, Ortner) that in different cultural systems, different female relational roles – mother *or* sister *or* wife – tend to dominate the category of "female" and to color the meanings of all the other female relational roles. In brideservice societies it seems to be "wife," (or perhaps more generally "affinal women"), in Polynesia "sister" (or perhaps more generally "kinswomen"), and in American society throughout much of the twentieth century (to use an example with which we are all familiar) it has been ''mother.'' The dominance of one or another of these types within the larger category of ''female'' is highly consequential for the ways in which *all* women are viewed in a particular culture. But this dominance in turn emerges precisely as a function of the ways in which male prestige does or does not hinge on marriage, or on sibling relations, or on filiation, or (in the American case) on something like ''early socialization.'' The prestige system, in other words, ''highlights'' certain cross-sex bonds within the total range available in the society, insofar as they are central to generating or maintaining status.

In perhaps the majority of societies, the cross-sex bond most critical to a man's social standing is marriage. The frequency with which marriage is in fact the most prestige-relevant cross-sex relationship, relates to the extraordinary versatility, both functional and symbolic, of this institution. In many societies, production for both use and exchange is based in the domestic unit. A wife is thus often a productive asset, and particularly a producer of goods utilized in male prestige-generating exchange activities, or in hospitality events that allow a husband to be seen as a big and generous man. Wives also bear children, who are themselves often productive assets (and sometimes exchange items as well), but who may also represent the continuity of a man's (or a group's) line or ''name.'' With the appearance of large scale, nongender-based, status groups (castes, estates), domestic production recedes in importance for at least some sectors of the society, but the issue of continuity of descent lines becomes even more prominent. Marriage then takes on new meanings and functions: preserving or enhancing the purity or pedigree of the group (see Yalman 1963). For these and many other reasons, the marriage system in most societies is the cross-sex relational system that has the greatest implications for male prestige, and ultimately for cultural notions of gender, sex and reproduction.

One result of a situation in which marriage is central (in whatever way) to status, is that notions of femininity tend to be dominated by *affinal* female roles (wife, mother-in-law, daughter-in-law), and even female kin tend to be seen largely in terms of (past or future) affinal status. In the brideservice societies discussed by Collier and Rosaldo, for example, a man needs a wife (or wives) for the domestic and sexual services that make him ''independent,'' and thus ''equal'' to other men. Marriage itself creates for a husband what amounts to the highest status available in these societies. In the context of such a pattern of relationship between marriage and prestige, womanhood is defined largely by wifehood, and the ''essence'' of womanhood is that which is of greatest value in a wife – sexuality and economic usefulness.

But in some cases the cross-sex bonds most significant for prestige may not be marital-sexual bonds at all; they may be bonds of consanguinity. In Polynesia, for example, within the system of hereditary ranking, relative position within a sibling set plays a great role in determining individual status. Siblingship in general is of great structural importance. In addition, from a man's point of view, sisters are of great potential value in building up descent lines for purposes of status advancement (as discussed by Ortner). Sisters then dominate the category of female, and all women, even wives and lovers, are seen to some extent as sisters (Ortner, Shore). This has both positive and negative consequences. On the one hand, because sisters are respected, all woman get the respect of being metaphoric sisters. On the other hand, the tendency to see all women as sisters may partly account for the high incidence of rape in Polynesia, insofar as there is difficulty in transforming the asexual sibling relationship into a sexualized one (Shore).

Other effects of defining women largely through kinship rather than affinal roles may be seen in systems in which the mother–son bond is of central importance for prestige, and in which "mother" dominates the category of female, as in most Catholic cultures (see, for example, Brandes) and in the twentieth-century United States. In these cases it may be proposed that wives are seen (and used) largely as mothers, but compared to mothers they are felt to be defective in various ways; such a view has implications for the meaning and quality of the sexual relationship between husband and wife, as well as for many other aspects of male–female relations in these cultures.

Although the complex of meanings surrounding any particular kin role will vary greatly from culture to culture, one can anticipate certain very general repercussions on the image of women depending upon which type of cross-sex bond – wife, mother, sister – is highlighted by prestige concerns. One may assume, for example, that because wives are normally sexual partners, and mothers and sisters normally are not, an emphasis on wives will tend to give more ideological prominence to the sexual aspects of women in general.

Ortner expands on this point and suggests that, where affinal role defini-tions, and emphasis on female sexuality, dominate a culture's notions of femininity, women in such cultures are generally viewed and treated with less respect than in those cultures in which women are construed largely as kin. She argues that women in roles with a major sexual component are more easily seen as different kinds of "natural" beings than men, whereas kins-women are more easily seen simply as different social actors. Thus cultures in which kinship (especially sibling) definitions of womanhood have hegemony over sexual and marital definitions appear to be both more sex-egalitarian and less sex-antagonistic (for example, not only Polynesia, but also much of South-east Asia), than cultures (such as India) in which the opposite is the case.

Beyond such general points, however, one must enter into the systematic analysis of particular cases. Different prestige systems will not only give central place to different cross-sex bonds, but, depending upon the system in question, the "same" bond (siblingship, marriage) may be endowed with different meanings. "Mother systems" are highly variable in terms of what mothers mean. Catholic cultures, for instance, emphasize mother's nurturance and merciful protection, whereas Protestant-dominated American culture tends to emphasize mother's controlling and manipulative nature. "Wife systems" are perhaps even more variable, for reasons discussed earlier. From the prestige point of view, marrying a woman effects very different things in different systems: It may be the sheer *fact* of being married that counts, or that marriage obligates a man to his in-laws in brideservice systems, or to his kinsmen in bridewealth systems; it may be that marriage above all brings property, or children, or the productive labor of a wife, or the assistance of a brother-in-law, and so on. And in each instance, the category "wife" will carry a distinct meaning. A consideration of which cross-sex relations are of greatest consequence for male prestige, and hence of which relational categories dominate the category of women, is thus only the beginning of the analysis. One must then proceed to consider the specific ways in which the marital, or sibling, or filiative, bond affects prestige, and hence why wives are seen as disruptive, sisters as sacred, mothers as merciful, or whatever it is the culture proposes.

Where's the Sex?

Perhaps the reader is beginning to wonder when this book is going to get down to the implied promise of its title: What about sex in all these cultures? Do the natives engage in foreplay (and what sort)? What does cliterodectomy do to a woman's sexual responsiveness? Is it true that the ancient Chinese were sexually excited by bound feet? At the very least one might expect to hear more bout what Samoan men fantasize about their women, or Maasai women about their men, or the American Indian berdache about his male lovers. After all, this is a large part of what sex means to *us* – erotic techniques, medical facts, Freud. Undoubtedly some disappointment will set in as, in essay after essay, the erotic dissolves in the face of the economic, questions of passion evaporate into questions of rank, and images of male and female bodies, sexual substances, and reproductive acts are peeled back to reveal an abiding concern for military honors, the pig herd, and the estate.

We might defend ourselves here by answering that the collection was not aimed primarily at the erotic dimension of sexual meanings but at the social and the latter is what our contributors have abundantly provided. But this would be an incomplete defense. The erotic and the social are too deeply mutually implicated to be passed off as entirely different dimensions. When two of our contributors, Nadelson and Brandes, treat gender lore and gender-related myth from the point of view of the underlying fantasy structures that these betray, they find not some garden of eroticism unconditioned by social concerns, but instead a world of status-anxious psyches, perseverating on the ways in which the erotic may threaten cherished social positions, and trying to imagine ways in which this might be forestalled. Furthermore, we need only observe Sudanese women readily enforcing the brutal Pharaonic circumcision upon their daughters and granddaughters *in the name of lineage honor* (Hayes 1975), or the fact that Imperial China seemed never to have lacked for recruits to the palace eunuch staff (eager young men from the provinces showed up to apply, carrying their genitals in a jar [Mitamura 1970]), to be reminded of the power of social considerations to override libidinal ones, both in fantasy and in practice.

At the same time, a brief checklist of the attributes of the person that various cultures have singled out as erotically stirring – the artificially pale complexion of the sheltered lady, the brutish musculature of the lower-status man, the elaborately scarified abdomen, the cinched waist, the subincised penis, and yes, the bound foot – is sufficient to jolt us into the realization that we are on social, and more precisely "status," territory once again. In other words, although the war between civilization and discontented eros is waged at the front, the two seem to have established a quite fruitful collaboration behind the lines.

The point is not just that sexuality is socially shaped and, in the course of this, inevitably curbed, but that the forms of society are themselves eroticized. It is worth investigating whether it is necessarily social inequality that receives the strongest erotic charge. The psychic energy that has been rallied and rerallied behind egalitarian social movements and utopian ideals suggests strong possibilities at the other end of the spectrum as well. It may be that these possibilities will not be fully realized until gender itself, the home ground of the erotic, ceases to be a status hierarchy. But equally, it may be that gender itself will not cease to be a status hierarchy until the wider system surrounding it has become more egalitarian.

Conclusion

When we initiated this collection, our idea was simply to bring together the latest and finest anthropological attempts to comprehend sex and gender as cultural constructs, shaped in various ways by the larger social and cultural matrixes in which they are embedded (and in turn shaping those matrixes). We felt it was time for some of the analytic sophistication applied in the last decade to unraveling women's status historically and cross-culturally, to carry over into the entire realm of gender and gender-related matters. This would amount in a way to a new assault upon the problem of the cultural variability of sex-gender concepts, a problem thrust into the foreground of anthropological attention by Margaret Mead in 1935, but subsequently buried (with Mead's assistance too) under a mountain of psychological and sexological (that is, eclectic biological-psychological) theories.

True to our expectations, we had no trouble finding excellent contributions that cast conceptions of woman and man, sex and reproduction, within sociological and cultural frameworks, and we have tried to break down the basic dimensions of their methodologies in the first section of this essay. We then turned to the content of the contributions, to the patterns discovered by our authors in the course of their analyses. We looked first at some common features of "gender systems," that is, cultural constructions of male and female, that emerge cross-culturally. We then raised the question of the most probable "roots" of such conceptions, as seen by our contributors. It was in the course of playing our own ideas off those developed in the essays, that we decided to confront more directly the central question that seems to lurk behind any study of this sort, namely, which areas of social life interact most critically with cultural constructions of sex and gender. Our answer – that the social-cultural formations most directly bound up with conceptions of gender (and gender-related matters) are prestige structures – was elaborated in the final sections of this essay.

We do not pretend that our suggestions regarding the importance of prestige systems amount to a comprehensive theory of the social and cultural forces affecting gender ideas. There are influences on sexual meanings not readily, nor entirely, subsumable under the prestige system. The highly rationalized "world" religions, which have, historically, been powerful sources of sexual doctrine, come to mind as examples. Although religion clearly qualifies as a cultural (as opposed to biological) shaper of male–female relations and perceptions thereof, we have not attempted to situate this influence within our suggested prestige model. And, of course, even within its proposed range of applicability, the prestige theory needs to be subjected to much further analytic and ethnographic scrutiny before it can be considered an established analytic tool. Yet we feel this is an area of investigation that holds great promise, and we hope the points made here, if far from definitive, are nevertheless sufficiently thought provoking to encourage future investigative effort.

Note

1 We wish to thank Raymond Kelly, Michelle Rosaldo, and Judith Shapiro for their helpful critical and editorial commentary on this essay.

References

Ardener, Edwin. 1975. "Belief and the problem of women." In *Perceiving women*, ed. S. Ardener, pp. 1–28. New York: Wiley.

Barnes, J. A. 1973. "Genetrix: genitor:: nature: culture?" In *The character of kinship*, ed. J. Goody, pp. 61–74. Cambridge: Cambridge University Press.

Bloch, Maurice. 1977. "The disconnection between power and rank as a process." *Archives Européennes de Sociologie* 18: 107–48.

Dumont, Louis. 1970. *Homo hierarchicus*. Chicago: University of Chicago Press.

Friedman, Jonathan. 1975. "Tribes, states, and transformations." In *Marxist approaches in social anthropology*, ed. M. Bloch, pp. 161–202. New York: Wiley.

Giddens, Anthony. 1971. *Capitalism and modern social theory*. Cambridge: Cambridge University Press.

Goldman, Irving. 1970. *Ancient Polynesian society*. Chicago: University of Chicago Press.

Hayes, R. O. 1975. "Female genital mutilations, fertility control, women's roles and the patrilineage in modern Sudan: a functional analysis." *American Ethnologist* 2: 617–33.

Kelly, Raymond. 1976. "Witchcraft and sexual relations: an exploration in the social and semantic implications of the structure of belief." In *Man and Woman in the New Guinea Highlands*, ed. P. Brown and G. Buchbinder, pp. 36–53. Washington, D.C.: American Anthropological Association.

    n.d. "Sanctions and symbolic domination: patterns of male–female relations in New Guinea." Unpublished manuscript.

Ladurie, Emmanuel LeRoy. 1978. *Montaillou: the promised land of error*. Translated by B. Bray. New York: George Braziller.

Leach, E. R. 1954. *Political systems of highland Burma: the study of Kachin social structure*. Boston: Beacon Press.

Lévi-Strauss, C. 1969. *The elementary structures of kinship*, trans. J. H. Bell, J. R. von Sturmer, and R. Needham. Boston: Beacon Press.

Mathieu, N.C. 1973. "Homme-culture, femme-nature?" *L'Homme* (July–Sept.): 101–13.

Mead, Margaret. 1935. *Sex and temperament in three primitive societies*. New York: New American Library.

Meigs, Anna S. 1976. "Male pregnancy and the reduction of sexual opposition in a New Guinea Highlands society." *Ethnology* 15: 393–408.

Mitamura, Taisuke. 1970. *Chinese eunuchs: the structure of intimate politics*. Rutland, Vt.: Charles Tuttle.

Ortner, Sherry B. 1972. "Is female to male as nature is to culture?" *Feminist Studies* 1:5–31. Reprinted in *Woman, culture and society*, ed. M. Z. Rosaldo and L. Lamphere, pp. 67–88. Stanford: Stanford University Press, 1974.

Parsons, Talcott. 1937. *The structure of social action*. New York: Free Press.

Pitt-Rivers, Julian. 1966. "Honor and social status." In *Honor and shame: the values of Mediterranean society*, ed. J. G. Peristiany, pp. 19–78. Chicago: University of Chicago Press.

Rivière, Peter. 1971. "Marriage: a reassessment." In *Rethinking kinship and marriage*, ed. R. Needham, pp. 57–74. London: Tavistock.

Rosaldo, Michelle Z. 1974. "Woman, culture and society: a theoretical overview." In *Woman, culture and society*, ed. M. Z. Rosaldo and L. Lamphere, pp. 17–42. Stanford: Stanford University Press.

Rubin, Gayle. 1975. "The traffic in women: notes toward a political economy of sex." In *Toward an anthropology of women*, ed. Rayna Reiter, pp. 157–210. New York: Monthly Review Press.

n.d. "Coconuts." Unpublished manuscript.

Weber, Max. 1958. "Class, status, party." In *From Max Weber*, ed. H. H. Gerth and C. Wright Mills, pp. 180–95. New York: Oxford University Press.

Yalman, Nur. 1963. "On the purity of women in the castes of Ceylon and Malabar." *Journal of the Royal Anthropological Institute* 93: 25–58.

PART I
The cultural organization of gender

1

The gender revolution and the transition from bisexual horde to patrilocal band: THE ORIGINS OF GENDER HIERARCHY

Salvatore Cucchiari

Introduction

This essay is about the origin of one of the most fundamental, and unquestionably universal, characteristics of human cultures – gender.[1] To some readers the origin of gender as a sociocultural system may appear to be a nonquestion. After all, aren't these categories given to us by nature and then modified by culture? This essay will take a totally different approach and assume the unthinkable – the possibility of human society without gender. Let us assume that the seemingly absurd is justified as long as it yields fresh views of objects so common that they resist our efforts to understand them. And what could be more common, "natural," or central to personal identity than our assigned gender category? Only the reader can finally judge if this thought experiment succeeds in elucidating the nature and origin of gender and gender hierarchy.

Despite its universality, gender as a principle of social organization is historically relative. Although the gender system has biological referents or markers, in no way is it determined or made inevitable by those sexual markers. Like other social organizing principles, such as class, gender made its appearance on the human stage at some point in the past, has since become elaborated in a number of different directions, and will most likely yield the stage to other actors in the future. Thus, whatever it is that defines our common humanity with thousands of generations past and future, it is *not* the idea of gender any more than it is the idea of class or hierarchy.

Let me stress again that genderless human organization cannot be observed in either present or historical ethnography. I am *postulating* the existence of a nongender stage in human cultural evolution because I found that until I did so I could not begin to explain another cultural universal – gender hierarchy or universal male dominance; and it is an explanation of gender hierarchy that constitutes the main problem of this essay.

The task of constructing a model that not only describes genderless society but accounts for its transformation to gender-stratified society becomes immensely complicated when we realize that such a model must also account for the origin of institutions and principles that depend for their existence on the concept of gender: kinship, marriage, the family, incest taboos, and exclusive heterosexuality. Indeed, an important part of the model will be to demonstrate how the advent of the gender system created conditions that ultimately brought forth these gender-dependent social forms, hence the "gender revolution.'' In the section on ''Conditions and constraints'' I will discuss in detail why the gender question logically implies these other issues.

For some, origin scenarios are useless endeavors – just-so stories for which there is little or no evidence and for which there can never be any definitive test. With this I both agree and disagree. Untestable? – in a strict sense quite true; useless? – definitely not. The objection to origin theorizing misses the all-important point: The answer to an origin question is not nearly as significant as the way the question is posed, how the question is linked to other questions, and the methodology with which the question is tackled. In fact, the answer as such may never be forthcoming, but through intelligent asking, our questions can become more sophisticated and profound. In this way creative and disciplined speculation on the big-why origin questions can be another route to sharpening our overall perspective on the more immediate and perhaps more testable aspects of culture theory. It is not stretching the point to say that the way problems, particularly universal ones, are reformulated is an important index of the maturity of anthropology.

The essay is in three parts. The section on ''Conditions and constraints'' defines our present state of knowledge with respect to gender issues, outlines and critiques some approaches to the origin question, and delineates the constraints and conditions to be satisfied by the model. The section on ''Pre-gender society'' presents a model that describes the principles around which a genderless, pre-kinship society might operate and how those principles, via a dialectic, transform to principles based on the gender idea. The section on ''Gender and the archaeological record'' applies the model to a segment of the archaeological record – Paleolithic Europe – and explores a tantalizing interpretation that suggests that the gender revolution may be more than mere theoretical possibility.

Conditions and constraints

THE GENDER SYSTEM: IDEOLOGY VERSUS BIOLOGY

Under the social and political impact of the feminist movement, recent anthropology has been forced to reexamine the question of gender. This challenge to generations of male bias in the theory and practice of the subject has been constructive, creative, and productive of exciting and useful ideas. [2] One result of these efforts is the important concept of the gender system.

A gender system is a symbolic or meaning system that consists of two complementary yet mutually exclusive categories into which all human beings are placed. Among the features that distinguish the gender system from other category systems is the fact that the genitals are the sole criterion for assigning individuals to a category at birth. Associated with each category is a wide range of activities, attitudes, values, objects, symbols, and expectations. Although the categories – man and woman – are universal, the content of the categories varies from culture to culture; and the variation is truly impressive. Thus, in some cultures men weave and women make pots, whereas in others these roles are reversed; in some places women are the major agricultural producers, and in others the fields are barred to them. Even those aspects of life we imagine are most tied to biology, such as childbirth, are subject to a gender reinterpretation. Through a complex of customs called the couvade, men in some cultures share in the pain, discomfort, and postpartum recuperation that are only assigned to women in our own (Wilson and Yengoyan 1976: passim; Oakley 1972: 134, 135). Also varying is the degree of polarity of the gender duality, that is, the extent of role overlap: from slight dichotomization in Southeast Asia to extreme polarity in the Mediterranean Basin.

Developing the notion of the gender system further, we note that it is not a balanced opposition. Everywhere, to the best of our knowledge, gender categories are hierarchically arranged with the masculine valued over the feminine. Although symbols of masculinity are always positive, feminine symbols are often negative or at least ambiguous. No matter how variable women's status and power, it is men who dominate the kinship system and political arena and have rights in and over women – everywhere woman is ''other.'' Again I want to stress the variability of male dominance, in both its ideological expression and actual exercise. For example, Ortner reports a male-biased gender ideology among the Sherpas but near equality in actual behavior (personal communication). The aspect of hierarchy in actual relations between men and women is a complex historical problem involving all the material and symbolic processes of social life; all of these are outside the scope of this essay. In the model presented here the crucial point to be accounted for is the universal and hierarchical nature of gender ideologies, and not their various and sundry empirical manifestations.

That human beings are thought to come in two distinct varieties is primarily a cultural fact; this system of meanings is related to other meanings in the realm of culture. This does not mean, however, that the gender system is unrelated to biology. But how is it related? One is tempted to see the obvious connection between the two gender categories, man/woman and the two biological categories, male/female. The obvious in this case, however, is misleading: Our notion of the biological or sexual dichotomy is more a product of our gender ideology than the reverse.

To avoid confusion let me state from the outset that biological science does indeed tell us that there are two developmental processes, male and female. These two developmental cycles are defined with respect to five physiological areas: genes or chromosomes, hormones, gonads, internal reproductive organs, and external genitals (Money 1965: 11). Hence, the scientific view of sexual classification is based on a complex developmental process that is not readily observable. In fact, the external characteristics of sexuality (genitalia and secondary features) are quite variable and from a purely morphological perspective do not lend themselves to easy dichotomization. More important, an estimated 2 to 3 percent of the world's people are born hermaphroditic – with ambigious genitalia (Edgerton 1964: 1289). Yet despite this continuum of outward sexual characteristics, the world's cultures insist on seeing only two biological sexes. There is one firm exception, the Navajo, who give special status to hermaphrodites. Martin and Voorhies devote a whole chapter in their book to the Navajo and other groups who, they claim, recognize not only more than two biological sexes but more than two genders as well (1975: 84–107). A brief examination of their argument will show that these apparent exceptions prove the rule that cultural systems universally operate on a two-gender model only.

The authors proceed from a position identical to the one taken here:

> The fact that more than two physical sexes can coexist has seldom been recognized by investigators concerned with the interrelationship between physical sex and culture. Social scientists usually assume that human sexual attributes are perceived by all societies as exclusively dichotomous. [Martin and Voorhies 1975: 85]

Their strongest case is the Navajo among whom a special category called *nadle* (''hermaphrodites'') is recognized, the authors maintain, as both a sexual class and gender category. However, when we examine the characteristics of the *nadle* we find few that distinguish it as an independent gender. Persons in the *nadle* category share characteristics of both genders and mediate disputes between men and women but have few if any features that establish them as a gender category. The role of the *nadle* as mediators in the power relations between the genders is reflected in myth, where a mythological hermaphrodite is said to have aided men in asserting dominance over women. Furthermore, one need not be a hermaphrodite to become *nadle*, which means this category is not ascriptive – uncharacteristic of gender. Perhaps most important is a fact ignored by Martin and Voorhies: *Nadle* is a sacred category, removed from the normal plane of social intercourse – which is where we must look for any gender system (Edgerton 1964: 1290). This may explain why the *nadle* have special property rights not shared by others. Thus we cannot conclude that the *nadle* are a separate gender category; to the extent that they function as a gender class in some contexts their identity is *derived* from the characteristics of the masculine and feminine genders.

The other ethnographic cases are even weaker examples of ''supernumerary'' (more than two) gender systems: the Mohave, the Canadian North Piegan, and the Siberian Chukchee. In all these cases there are named cross-gender categories, none of which are ascriptive. Thus men may live and behave as women and vice versa once they have achieved or chosen membership in a cross-gender category. The Chukchee, for example, have three categories for men seeking feminine status, each category differing from the others in its degree of feminization. Women have an analogous two-category system. Martin and Voorhies would count these five as separate gender categories, giving the Chukchee a total of seven. Although these examples are intriguing illustrations of the degree to which biology is genderized, they clearly are not examples of supernumerary gender societies. All of the cross-gender categories are derived categories that, far from undermining the two-gender model, underwrite it. They do so by institutionalizing behavior that falls between or outside of the two polar gender categories: In effect, uncharacteristic behavior is defined as a movement toward the opposite gender, thereby rendering the gender system immune to behavioral deviations.

Therefore, there are no convincing exceptions to the bi-polar gender model. This, of course, makes explanation even more difficult. If gender runs counter to biology – even molds it to its own image – what are the constraints on the gender system that produce its universally dual character? This is a key problem for our origin model.

GENDER AND KINSHIP

The argument between the extensionist and social-category exponents of kinship theory has a nearly institutional status in anthropology by now (Buchler and Selby 1968: 4–6, 33–46). Like Barnes and Pitt-Rivers I take a middle position between those who say kinship is genealogy reified and those who view kinship as a set of sociocultural categories that also have genealogical referents (Barnes 1973: 72; Pitt-Rivers 1973: passim). Pitt-Rivers articulates this middle position. Following Fortes, he views kinship as relations of "prescribed amity." Unlike friendship, a set of dyadic relationships, kinship is a *system* of relationships or categories over which rights, duties, statuses, and roles are *differentially* distributed and inherited. What distinguishes kinship, as a social system, from other systems is its underlying notion of shared substance: "consubstantiation." Pitt-Rivers underscores the word "notion" and it is essential that we do likewise here. The idea of shared substance is culture specific and may have little or nothing to do with the concepts of physical science. As we move from culture to culture the critical substance may be semen, menstrual blood, mother's milk, or even food. As can be seen from this list, consubstantiation encompasses the whole continuum of kinship systems, from those that emphasize procreation (child bearing) as defining characteristics of kin bonds (semen, blood) to those that stress nurturing or fostering criteria (milk, food). The utility of this broad concept of consubstantiation is its ability to handle both "real" and adoptive kinship as variants of one type of cultural system.[3]

Despite the fact that kinship systems can and do stress either a nurturing or procreative notion of consubstantiation, everywhere, kinship categories have procreative referents; indeed, kinship systems seem universally capable of being expressed in terms of some *cultural* model of procreation rather than nurturing. That is, even where parents are defined more as the people who protect, feed, and raise the child, the relationship is still expressed in genealogical idiom. Note, for example, that although the Navajo idea of motherhood can be *either* the woman who bore or the one who raised the child, a mother can only be a woman – a person at least theoretically capable of bearing the child (Witherspoon 1976). One would expect that a completely nurturing model of the mother–child relation would be capable of including both men and women.

In saying that even kinship systems that stress nurturing/fostering are expressed in a procreative idiom, we seem to be caught in a logical contradiction. Perhaps the issue can be clarified this way. All kinship systems partake of both procreative and nurturing notions of shared substance; some can be said to be procreative dominant whereas others are nurturing dominant. But, regardless of the stress, nurturing dominant systems rely – if only in latent form – on a procreative model in order to map the total kinship system. Procreative dominant systems, however, need never refer to the content of kinship relations, that is, nurturing behavior, in order to map the social universe. American kinship may be taken as an example. Although nurturing values are considered important elements of what kin relations should be, it is genealogical ("blood") relations that determine who one's kin are; surrogate and adoptive relations are sharply distinguished. The native view is sum-marized by the expression "you only have one mother and father."[4]

Shortly I will suggest reasons why the procreative model assumes the independence and importance it does. For now, however, let us note that in keeping with the cross-cultural significance of the procreative idiom at least two key distinctions are reflected in all kinship terminologies: sex and generation. If we recall that kinship systems are systems of statuses and roles, rights and duties that are differentially distributed, then the universal pres-ence of the sexual distinction takes on added meaning. For in essence we are saying that the gender distinction is embedded in every kinship system. This fact has been recognized by a number of theorists but assigned varying significance. For example, Fox explicitly builds it into the axiomatic structure of his universal kinship model, where it appears as the axiom of male dominance – unquestionably a gender concept (Fox 1967: 31). Turning the question around somewhat, Rivière says that no matter how the functions of marriage may vary from culture to culture marriage accomplishes one key structural task – it affirms, defines and reproduces the gender duality (Rivière 1971: passim). Perhaps most interesting is Needham's left-handed confirma-tion of this point. He maintains that kinship, as a bounded, coherent class of phenomena, does not exist. That is, there is no element or set of elements common to all kinship systems, *except* one – the gender distinction. But Needham does not find this "so remarkable as to deserve a special designa-tion to call for a distinct type of theory" (Needham 1971: 4).

So, the first main point I wish to make is this: Kinship – a sociocultural system of differentially distributed rights, duties, roles, and statuses, founded on an ideology of shared substances – is inextricably bound up with an embedded system of gender categories. Moreover, as Rivière reminds us, gender in turn is reproduced by the kinship system – particularly by its marriage structure. But I want to take this argument one step further. Gender and kinship are not merely two independent structures that happen to be functionally enmeshed in the ethnographic record. Rather, gender is inherent in the very nature of kinship, which could not exist without it – kinship's historical precondition, not temporary bedfellow. How can I justify this assertion?

We can approach the problem by exploring the viability of a hypothetical kinship system that totally lacks the gender distinction. We first note that the sexual distinction is also necessarily absent from such a system; for it is hard to imagine a sex-specific social system (that is, kinship) that does not use the sexual distinction in the way it differentially distributes statuses and roles – that is not also gender bound. But such a hypothetical kinship system, blind to the sexual distinction, would place severe constraints on its foundation concept of consubstantiation. Clearly, procreative substance would be ruled out, as would the genealogical model in general. This follows from the fact that inherent in procreative ideologies is the distinction between male and female substances and the roles they play in constituting the physical and social being of the child. Even those cultures that deny the importance of either male or female substance are implicitly making a sexual distinction. Therefore, our genderless kinship system must rest on some kind of nurturing ideology to the exclusion of the procreative. But even here, suckling and mother's milk must be ruled out as the symbolic foundation of the system because it too is sexually specific. This leaves us with some, more general notion of nurturing (feeding and caring for the child) upon which to construct our kinship model. I do not believe that a kinship system, built on so narrow a segment of the consubstantiation continuum, could unambiguously reproduce its relational categories from generation to generation or viably carry out important functions. Space will not allow a complete derivation of this position so I will state only the general conclusion here.

In primitive societies characterized by a pervasive general reciprocity, a kinship system based *exclusively* on the nurturing idea would fail clearly to mark off categories even within the nuclear unit – parents from older siblings, for example. If the defining characteristic of the category "parent" is the one who feeds and cares for the child, even the generational distinction would be weakened as parent and grandparent cooperated in child rearing. Indeed, all categories – parent, child, sibling, and spouse – would tend to be semantic domains with variable boundaries and include no fixed catalogue of relationships. It is for this reason that procreative models are essential to kinship systems in providing the discrete genealogical points that connect broad social categories – a kind of social map. There are other weaknesses in this system as well. Due to the blurring of generational distinctions, clear lines of descent would be difficult to lay out. Moreover, critical social functions such as procreation and the important alliance mechanism of child adoption lie completely outside the kinship system, raising questions about its viability. In short, a genderless kinship system does none of the things a kinship system should do. Indeed, it is not kinship at all.

The consequences of the preceding discussion burden the task at hand, for it is now apparent why a pre-gender society must also be a pre-kinship society. Hence, in accounting for the origin of the gender system we cannot appeal to kinship structures or kinship-related causes. Our model must then describe a viable and thoroughly human social system that operates on principles other than what we have come to think of as the very essence of being human – kinship.

GENDERIZED SEXUALITY: EXCLUSIVE HETEROSEXUALITY AND OTHER INCEST TABOOS

At the heart of any gender system are notions of what constitutes appropriate sexual expression. This includes not only the mechanics of sexuality and the gender of one's erotic fancy, but the whole complex of objects, symbols, and fantasies that constitute normative or permissible eroticism. (Of course eroticism goes beyond the normative, but that is not my concern here.) Not surprisingly, there is much cross-cultural variation in the erotic domain as in other aspects of the gender system (Pomeroy 1969: 4–6; Marshall and Suggs 1971: 206–17). The range goes from peoples like the Etoro of New Guinea who grudgingly engage in heterosexual sex (Kelly 1976) to the Judeo–Christian tradition, which phobically insists on it. The variation in the ethnographic record suggests that human sexuality is plastic, not subject to rigid genetic or hormonal patterning, but determined by the learning and symbolic areas of the brain. This has been repeatedly verified over the past 30 years by researchers in the field of psychosexual development (Beach 1947: 310; Money 1965: 3–23; Stoller 1974). Money's pioneering work on the sexual identity of hermaphrodites shows complete disjunction between the physiological sex of the hermaphrodite infant (defined by the five criteria outlined earlier) and the eventual erotic/sexual identity adopted by the child. The key to predicting the eventual sexual identity of the hermaphrodite infant, according to Money, is the expectations of its parents. Parents convinced that their child is male will raise an individual who in all respects thinks, feels, and acts male – regardless of its genetic or hormonal sex. What is crucial to the attitude of parents is "genital appearance," and for this reason Money recommends early cosmetic surgery (Money 1965: 10–12). The results of Stoller's work are identical to Money's on this score.

Summarizing the relationship between hormones and psychosexual development, Money is emphatic.

> The hormones that bring about sexual maturation do not according to all the evidence available, have any differential determining influences on the psychosexual, male–female direction and content of perceptual, memory, or dream imagery that may trigger or be associated with erotic arousal. On the contrary, there is strong chemical and presumptive evidence . . . that the libido hormone is the same for men and women and is androgen.
> Psychosexually, the androgenic function is limited to partial regulation of the intensity and frequency of sexual desire and arousal, but not the cognitional patterns of arousal. [Money 1965: 14]

The plasticity of human sexuality has been placed in an evolutionary schema by Saul Rosenzweig (Rosenzweig 1973). In his view, as one moves up the evolutionary ladder from lower mammals through primates and then to the hominids, there is a change from periodic to continuous sexual activity and from external/internal (hormonal) control over sexual behavior to autonomous (learned) control. Reproduction and sexuality become uncoupled in the human line; sex becomes a highly imaginative, culturally elaborated activity not confined to the genital areas as in lower animals but "extragenital" in every sense.

All this leads to the inescapable conclusion, long recognized by psychoanalysis and confirmed by modern researchers such as Money: Human beings come into this world as bisexual creatures (Freud 1923: 31; Stoller 1974; Money and Tucker 1975: 16). Exclusive heterosexuality, then, must be

viewed, in Gayle Rubin's words, as an "instituted process" (Rubin 1976:
180). If we define incest taboos broadly, as institutional or cultural restrictions on sexuality, then exclusive heterosexuality is an incest taboo – a structural feature of the social systems in which it is present.[5] In defining incest
restrictions in this way I sharply separate them from marriage rules (with
which they may or may not overlap) and from genealogical relatedness (with
which they may or may not positively correlate). Lumping these three classes
of phenomena together under the heading of incest has led to considerable
confusion on the subject.[6] The incest taboo is after all an analytic category –
our concept, not the native's – and for this reason we ought to be clear as to its
meaning. We know, for example, that clan mates may be perfectly legitimate
bed partners but totally off limits with regard to marriage; and that equally
close cross cousins may be viewed quite differently with respect to marriage
and sex. In all the discussion of brother–sister marriage among royal families
in Incan, Egyptian, and Hawaiian society, it is not clearly demonstrated to
what extent they are breaking intrafamilial incest taboos, that is, having sex.[7]
In other words, if sex does not imply marriage, marriage may not always
imply sex.[8] Given the highly political nature of this kind of marriage, it is not
out of the question that it may often be a ritual affair having little to do with
sex, and therefore with incest. Confusing incest rules with marriage rules
and/or genealogical relationships is one of many sins of sociobiology, which
would like to see sex rules and marriage rules as the same and to correlate both
kinds of behavior with genealogical distance.[9]

   In the last section I argued that we should keep kinship and gender
analytically distinct, no matter how finely enmeshed we find them. I would
make the same argument about incest restrictions on sexuality and sexual
restrictions related to kinship statuses or other kinds of structures (such as
adultery), even though in practice they obviously overlap and interpenetrate.
Indeed, Goody (1969) reminds us that if we regard restrictions on sexuality as
a large cultural domain, each culture partitions the domain differently.[10]
Nevertheless, for our own analytic purposes it is useful to regard all institutional restrictions on sexuality as falling within the locus of the gender
system, despite the fact that those restrictions may be expressed in a kinship,
religious, caste, or racial idiom and fulfill functions peculiar to these cultural
domains. I offer three points to justify this position.

   First, all sexual restrictions of a structural type make gender statements.
That is, no matter what the idiom or cultural domain, they structure, prescribe, or create attitudes and conduct with respect to intragender and intergender relations. Consider, for example, that a racial bar to sexual relations
not only says what is wrong with the men and women of another race but
conversely what is desirable and right about the men and women of one's own
race. An ostensibly racial prohibition is implicitly making normative statements about all men and women – about gender.

   Second, although all restrictions on sexuality make gender statements –
can be translated into the idiom of gender – the reverse is not always true. That
is, some institutional restrictions, although justified or validated by religious
or other cultural forms, originate and primarily function as part of the gender

system; these defy reduction. Exclusive heterosexuality and exclusive homo-sexuality are two such restrictions.

Third, by placing all sexual restrictions within the gender domain we are free to view at least some incest forms as independent of kinship, and like gender prior to it. This allows us to see incest as a causal force in the evolution of kinship rather than just its outcome. This is exactly the role exclusive hetero-sexuality will play in the arguments I will make concerning pre-gender society.

In summary, human sexuality is innately plastic – bisexual. Exclusive heterosexuality is therefore an institutional restriction on sexuality, an incest taboo that runs counter to our biology and part of the structure of the gender system. Another way of stating this is to say that sexuality becomes a social ordering principle only when limited and controlled – only when it is incor-porated into a gender ideology. Incest taboos in general and exclusive hetero-sexuality in particular, like kinship, are gender elaborated social forms. Thus, pre-gender society is necessary bisexual and totally lacking in con-straints on sexuality. The problem for our model is to explain how this can be a viable state of affairs and how sexuality ultimately becomes genderized.

GENDER HIERARCHY: THEORIES OF ORIGIN VERSUS THEORIES OF REPRODUCTION

In general, how and why a sociocultural form comes into the world may have little or nothing to do with the means by which it is reproduced from generation to generation and how it relates to other features of the social system. The first question is an evolutionary problem, the second a functional one. A complete explanation attempts to unite the evolutionary model and the functional model at some other theoretical level.

One of the problems with origin accounts in the gender literature is a failure to distinguish between these two kinds of endeavors: Their attempts at explaining gender hierarchy presuppose what they wish to explain – the gender system. In other words, they are really theories of reproduction. This is true of four papers that have greatly influenced my own thinking: Chodorow 1974; Rosaldo 1974; Ortner 1974; and Rubin 1975. Each, from its own perspective, makes an important contribution to a theory of reproduction of the gender system. Let me briefly characterize these positions.

Chodorow analyzes the structural dynamics of the socializing unit, the family, to account for the universal features of masculine and feminine personality, whereas Rosaldo, with a wider focus, points to the split of public domain (male) and domestic domain (female) as the social structural under-pinning of universal male dominance. Both of these views are consistent with and complementary to one another. From a different angle Ortner sees the structure of the meaning system itself – which projects that male equals culture and female equals nature – as having reproductive momentum of its own. Again, this is thoroughly complementary to the first two views in that actors in a social process must be able to lay hold of an available stock of gender symbols: A social process must be infused with meaning before it can reproduce meaning. Still another approach is shown in Rubin's paper on the role of kinship and marriage exchange in reproducing the gender hierarchy.

This brilliant attempt to synthesize Marx, Freud, and Lévi-Strauss places the major burden of the symbolic reproduction of gender hierarchy on the exchange of women in marriage systems. This exchange fixes and institutionalizes the idea of woman as "other," object and subordinate. Rubin argues, and I think rightly, that no matter how bound up the gender system is with other aspects of complex systems, such as class, it remains autonomous by virtue of its reproductive locus in the kinship system.

In the course of developing my model I shall invoke all of these ideas.

SUMMARY

Let me conclude this part of the essay with an inventory list of the conditions the model must satisfy and the constraints on its construction.

First, it must explain how gender as a system of meanings arose – why the system is universally bipolar and why the two categories are universally stratified.

Second, because kinship, marriage, and the family are all gender-related institutions, the model must account for the advent of the gender system without reference to any of these; indeed it is kinship that must be accounted for by the advent of gender. At the same time the model must describe a workable pre-gender society, organized around nonkinship principles and consistent with what we know about the technology and ecological constraints in foraging society.

Third, because exclusive heterosexuality and other forms of the incest taboo represent genderized restrictions on a plastic sexuality, they also can have no place in a pre-gender society. The model must explain how and why nonrestricted sexuality can be socially viable and how it ultimately gets incorporated in a gender system.

Fourth, this plastic, autonomous human sexuality implies a fully developed brain and fully developed symbolic and cultural capacity. That is, pre-gender society must be a human one – not primate or early hominid. This point will be elaborated in the section on "Gender and the archaelogical record," but it should be clear now that the model does not propose to account for the transition from hominid to human society but rather from one kind of human society (pre-gender) to another kind of human society (gender stratified).

Fifth, the model must attempt to integrate its evolutionary perspective with mechanisms of reproduction: It must explain both the genesis of gender forms and their persistence.

The model: pre-gender society and its transformation

ANATOMY OF THE BISEXUAL HORDE

Like contemporary hunter-gatherer society, pre-gender or pre-kinship society (these terms will be used interchangeably) is organized into small groups or hordes, each with primary use-rights to the resources of a definite territory. There are two main categories of persons in the pre-kin horde: those who forage (Foragers) and those who tend children (Child Tenders). The categories of Forager and Child Tender are more than functional groups, for they embody principles of social organization. That is, they are ideal social groups tied to one another by reciprocal obligations and expectations. To understand this we must note another social distinction made in pre-kin society: that between helpless children and self-sufficient, socially responsible adults. Children as a social category are the means or idiom through which the complementary relationship of Foragers and Child Tenders is articulated. Thus Child Tenders think of themselves as caring for the children of the Foragers and, similarly, Foragers view themselves as providing for the tenders of their children. This ideal relationship is celebrated in various horde rituals.

Before I discuss other features of the Forager–Child Tender system let me say a parenthetical word about terminology. "Proto-man" and "proto-woman" will be understood as anatomical designations only. It is important that we totally separate in our minds all the activities, values, and meanings associated with the concepts "man" and "woman" from these genderless anatomical designations.

The ideal or structural nature of the categories Foragers and Child Tenders should not be confused with their on-the-ground or empirical manifestation. As social groups their membership is neither fixed, permanent, nor prescribed. One is not born a Forager or Child Tender, nor is there any basis for claiming permanent membership in either group. In fact, the composition of these groups shifts considerably through time. Yet, at any one time, there are individuals who are primarily Foragers or Child Tenders.

Most important, the Forager–Child Tender division should not be confused with the sexual division of labor found in kinship societies. As Lévi-Strauss recognized long ago, the division of labor is in fact "artificial," that is, a cultural dichotomy – "a device to institute a reciprocal state of dependency between the sexes" (Lévi-Strauss 1971: 346). In other words, the sexual division of labor is in reality the *gender* division of labor. For this reason I avoid the terminology "hunting and gathering" because the delineation of a separate category called "hunting" seems to be a gender-valued distinction, rather than a designation of a particular kind of activity. For example, women do "hunt" small animals in the course of foraging, yet somehow this is seen as "collecting"; and men are always hunters, no matter what proportion of their subsistence activities is the pursuit of game. Thus, the existence of a separate activity category "hunting" seems predicated on the existence of the gender division of labor.

It is true that at any one moment one finds in pre-kin society a statistical preponderance of proto-men foraging and proto-women child tending; but these empirical characteristics are not the defining characteristics of these categories as seen by the actors themselves. It is also true that although proto-men participate as Child Tenders, only proto-women can bear and suckle children. This will indeed figure prominently in the evolution of gender; not as a biological fact, however, but as part of a social and ideological dialectic to be discussed shortly. For now, the important point is that at one time or another everyone can expect to play both roles.

There is another aspect to the Forager–Child Tender relationship that we need to understand: the spatial dimension. Foragers, operating out of a horde camp, generally go far afield in search of food, whereas Child Tenders stay close to camp. In addition to their main task, Child Tenders routinely exploit local resources, thereby adding to the total calorie pool of the horde. On many occasions their contribution even exceeds that of the Foragers; but by maintaining the convenient fiction that food collected by Child Tenders is not ''proper'' food, the social contract between Foragers and their complements is never violated. Similar fictions are maintained in contemporary hunting and gathering societies of the kinship type. Thus, Forager and Child Tender are not only ideal social categories, functional groups, and specific activities, but also activities set within certain spatial relations: Child Tender/camp and environs; Forager/the external world.

This spatial–social dichotomy is played out in other ways as well. Foragers are the traders and solely responsible for interhorde contact and relations, whereas Child Tenders are responsible for all the activities of the camp including the construction of shelters. Left solely to each group also is the ritual handling of relationships to the spiritual beings that inhabit their respective domains.

Therefore, we can say of the social structure of pre-kin society, that although structural principles divide activity and space, they do not divide people into exclusive groups. Roles and statuses are not prescriptive or permanent and tend to be shared by everyone.

This has consequences for the structure of ideology and cosmology. I take it as an article of faith that human beings tend to view the world they define as nonhuman, namely, nature, *through* the lens of their social relationships. Thus I see the worldview of pre-kin society as a unitary one, and one that deemphasizes *rigid* dualisms as an immanent quality of nature. This perceived unitary quality of nature then serves as a standard, even moral injunction on what the good and correct society should be. Pre-kin society is therefore fiercely democratic in its insistence that all its members share in one unitary life experience. I prefer to label this ideology unitarianism rather than egalitarianism, because the latter is characteristic of kinship society, which is gender stratified – hence its concern with equality. Pre-kin society, on the other hand, has no such contradiction to mediate, no categories to equate; rather, its preoccupation is with identity – universal identity. As will be shown, unitarianism is a double-edged sword with respect to the stability of pre-kin society.

Before moving on to the critical area of sexual relations, several issues remain to be addressed. If it is true that participation in the Forager–Child Tender social system is nonprescriptive and flexible, what ensures that necessary survival tasks will get done? First, we should note that there would tend to be a relatively stable core of people within each category, a core based on biological imperative (only proto-women can have and suckle children) and on personal talents and skills (for example, skilled hunters). Second, limits on the numerical division of the horde into both categories would be set by the labor requirements of child tending; excessive personnel would be morally compelled to put their energies to use in foraging. Third, it should also be noted that the division of labor itself is not airtight; that is, Child Tenders also forage. This provides a great deal of flexibility for individual participation.

This view of a flexible pre-gender division of labor runs counter to the hypothesis that the sexual division of labor (man equals hunter, woman equals gatherer) in foraging societies is the outcome of the interaction of demographic–ecological imperatives. Ernestine Friedl puts forward such a model in her book *Women and men: an anthropologist's view* (1975). This important position must be examined.

The author underscores the point, fully accepted here, that the physiological differences between men and women cannot account for the exclusion of women from hunting. About the advantages men have over women with regard to hunting, she says:

> But though such advantages undoubtedly make men in the top range of
> these physical characteristics the best potential hunters, it is hard to see
> why they should make the general run of men the only hunters. The overlap
> between the sexes in respect to the physical characteristics listed is con-
> siderable. [Friedl 1975: 18]

The problem then is "why cannot both men and women be responsible for both hunting and gathering?"

The answer, for Friedl, lies in the fact that women must bear children in the double sense: both giving birth to children and carrying them around. Furthermore, because women gatherers must carry their children around while foraging they must space them widely apart, to insure the survival of themselves and their infants. This imposes a demographic constraint on women's activities: For hunting-gathering society to reproduce itself women must be either pregnant or nursing continuously, leaving no opportunities to learn or participate in hunting.

The difficulty with this plausible-sounding argument is in its underlying assumptions. It assumes: that each woman is responsible for the caring and nursing of her own child, that is, that child care is not collective; that each woman must carry her own infant and in general only women transport children; that men will not participate in child care and women's activities. These assumptions faithfully describe conditions in contemporary foraging societies– the very conditions we need to explain, not take as givens.

If we proceed with a different set of assumptions, the logistics and demographic dynamics of hunting-gathering society begin to look quite different. For example, children could easily be tended at camp while some women went off hunting or gathering. Is this practical? Oakley reports several primitive societies in which women collectively breast feed (Oakley 1972: 133). Furthermore, if men lent a hand in child care and transport, as older children and older people of both sexes do, this would allow women the time and mobility to hunt. I know of no ecological, demographic, or adaptive reasons why men remain aloof from women's activities during the sometimes lengthy slack periods between hunts. This aspect of male behavior can only be understood as expressing a gender ideology that in no way can be reduced to ecological variables. Communal child care of *all* members of the foraging band would allow for a greater variability in women's fertility (some women having more children, others having fewer or none) and probably an overall higher birth rate. In short, different social and productive relationships yield different demographies.

Friedl takes the family/household mode of organizing work and reproduction as a given and then points to the demographic dynamics it creates as primary causes of the division of labor. This is circular on two counts. First, as I have argued, the family and household are themselves expressions of the division of labor based on the gender idea. Second, demography can never be given primary causal efficacy. As Godelier's work on Australian marriage systems demonstrates, demography is a summation or expression of social relations of production, not their cause (Godelier 1975). Thus, we can say that *given* the division of labor, *given* the family, and *given* the gender system, the ecological and demographic considerations cited by Friedl do have constraining or conservative effects in foraging society. But again this is properly a theory about social reproduction, not origins.

PRE-GENDER SEXUALITY: GENITOFUGAL AND SELF-SUBLIMATING

As indicated in the section on "Conditions and constraints," sexuality in pre-gender society is both bisexual and unrestrained. Thus far in our discussion these terms have meant little more than flexibility in choice of sexual object and promiscuity, respectively. In this section we will go beyond these superficial working definitions to uncover the deeper significance of these terms. We proceed from the negative to the positive: first, with four points on what pre-gender sexuality is not and then a positive examination of its possible structure.

1. Anatomical differences between proto-men and proto-women are not systematically cognized. For us who regard the world through the spectacles of gender this idea may seem ludicrous; but we must remember that perception is conditional. We perceive vaginas and penises not merely as biological features but apperceive them as meaningful signs representing gender categories – signs that are opposite but of the same fundamental type. Nothing about the morphology of genitalia necessitates this point of view. In a heterosexual culture where opposite genitalia are habitually contrasted and united, and where heterosexual sex and reproduction are firmly linked, it is then only "natural" that the anatomical differences between men and women should appear so all-consumingly obvious. Pre-gender society is bisexual, however, and heterosexual sex and pregnancy are not associated. It is well known that the degree to which the causal link between sex and reproduction is recognized in primitive, heterosexual societies is problematic (see Barnes 1973). In bisexual, pre-gender society the connection between a proto-women's pregnancy and her sexual encounters (with both sexes) would not be even remotely obvious. But there is a more compelling reason to suppose that sex and reproduction are not seen as connected in pre-gender society: People have no reason for wanting to know; such knowledge has no relevance to any aspect of social life. Filiation and descent are simply nonissues, because children belonging to the horde have full jural rights by virtue of being born to

any (proto-) woman of the group. We can make this point even stronger by saying that *not* knowing is consonant wih prevailing social relations, whereas knowing could be disruptive, that is, would violate the notion of *common* rights over children. Thus, the first characteristic of pre-gender sexuality is its cognitive separation from reproduction.

2. Sexuality is not an important part of self-identity. People may differ in their sexual capacity, ability, and need; but there is no way to link these differences to stable social groups, social categories, or symbols. This of course is closely related to the fact that sexuality is not a social ordering principle, that is, not genderized.

3. Sexuality is not an important aspect of interpersonal bonds. This follows directly from point two; for if persons do not define themselves sexually neither can relationships between persons be so defined.

4. For all these reasons, intense and unrestricted sexual expression within the horde is compatible with harmonious social relations. Another way of saying this is that sexuality is peripheral to group organization and self-identity and therefore poses no threat to interpersonal relations. This unrestricted sexuality, however, cannot be equated with the adjective "promiscuous," for this term implies the transgression of implicit or explicit sexual rules; there are none in pre-gender society. In this important respect (and others) the concept of the bisexual horde differs from the older anthropological notion of the "promiscuous horde."[11]

This discussion establishes that, in striking contrast to gender society, sex in pre-gender society is: not a social structural element; not significant in self-definition; and in general is a more limited category of thought. But all this does not mean that pre-gender sexuality plays no social role or, more important, that it lacks a characteristic organization on the individual level. Indeed, I will argue that psychosexual development in pre-gender society, as in gender society, lies well below conscious structures – roles, selfhood; and that its underlying psychic dimension is organized along qualitatively different lines than is characteristic of gender society. To justify advancing this hypothesis we must take a short excursion into Freudian sexual theory and come better to understand the term "bisexual."

In *Psychoanalysis and feminism*, Juliet Mitchell evaluates Freud's notion of bisexuality as his great initial "hunch" and at the same time the final, unsolved "crux" of the problematic of human sexuality – a problematic uniquely defined by the father of psychoanalysis (Mitchell 1974: 49). Breaking sharply with his predecessors and contemporaries, Freud views "normal" adult sexuality not as a unitary instinct, a preadaptive response activated in the organism at puberty, but rather as a composite of independent drives that, unmodified in the infant, seek expression over the entire surface of the body and through bodily functions (seeing, smelling, excreting). Ultimately, this anarchy of instincts becomes orchestrated and localized in certain erogenous zones – oral, anal, and so on. Localization is accompanied by dominance as a particular zone comes solely to assume the function of discharging sexual tension, while subdominant zones and instincts lose the means of their own satisfaction and function only as "fore pleasure" or as intensifiers of sexual tension.

Freud's model of psychosexual development, with its succession of dominating zones, specifies the dominance of the genitalia as the ultimate stage in the process. Along with genital primacy Freud sets out other normative conditions that ultimately take shape in the adult by means of this complex and tortuous development: object love versus infantile autoerotism; heterosexuality versus homosexuality; the division of the sexual universe into masculine and feminine types.[12] The motive force behind this evolution is repression, taking the forms of moral convention, shame, and loathing.[13]

Broadly speaking, then, the psychosexual process operates between two polar extremes. The polymorphous, perverse, and decentralized sexuality of the infant is channeled, molded through repression into its genital, localized, and centralized adult form. The pre-genital sexual organization of childhood, then, is one of the important senses in which Freud uses the term bisexual and the one most important to us here.[14]

It must be stressed that despite Freud's use of the language of instinct his is not a biological problem but a psychosocial one: Instincts are always *ideas* in Freud, only knowable through their psychic representations. As Ricoeur has forcefully argued, Freud's instincts are *meanings* wed to energy quanta or drives – desire vectors.[15] As such they are constructed and inherited, both in the socialization of individuals and in the cultural history of the entire species. But herein lies both the genius and weakness in Freud's sexual problematic; for although sexuality is presented as an elaborate organization of meanings, Freud does not posit a culture theory capable of generating and transmitting these meanings. On the contrary his cultural theories are essentially static and regressive – analogues of *individual* dream process and neurotic fixation that are extended to the status of identities.[16] Therefore, to account for the universal tendencies in psychosexual development – genital primacy or the Oedipus complex – Freud relies heavily on phylogenetic inheritance of memory traces of *past cultural* events. Meaning tends always to be generated in the past and implanted via racial memory in the here-and-now. Most important, this renders archaic events such as the primal scene as historical readbacks of clinically observed phenomena. Perhaps for this reason Freud's cultural ideas seem to go well beyond speculation and take on a timeless, mythic quality.[17]

The Freudian sexual problematic, then, requires a two-pronged explanation: of the universally observed tendencies in psychosexual development – tendencies that *appear* biologically given – and of the contingent, variable cultural/historical forces that give rise to these universals. This is, of course, the way I have defined the entire question of the origins of the gender system; and I believe there is more than mere analogy here. Genital primacy, as a highly structured and centralized form of sexuality may be historically contingent – a correlative of the gender system and another of its universal aspects. Thus, as human sexuality moved from the realm of nature to become a cultural ordering principle, as it began to acquire a highly structured social form, a parallel development took place on the psychic level. Despite Freud's fatalism and ahistoricism, his theory of sexuality invites the possibility that humanity (past and future) need not choose between the tyranny of genital primacy or the anarchy of infantile bisexuality. Indeed, an intermediate sexual form between these extremes is found theoretically possible within the Freudian problematic by Marcuse in his *Eros and civilization*.

Marcuse begins his reinterpretation by recognizing that "civilized" sexuality is the product of a repressive "reality principle." That is, culture is opposed to free libidinal development – sexual aims must be deflected or sublimated in order to effect wide social bonding and for society's work to proceed smoothly and dependably. But, asks Marcuse, is the reality principle an absolute and unchanging set of external conditions? What would be the characteristics of a nonrepressive society, sexuality, and sublimation?

As part of his program to purge Freud of his ahistoricism, Marcuse rejects the notion of *the* reality principle, noting that repression is a sociocultural phenomenon and thus is relative to a given historical situation – we can only speak of *a* reality principle. Extending this idea, he speculates that a nonrepressive sexuality is only possible in a nonalienated society, that is, where the contradiction between work and play, labor and leisure has not ripened – where social domination has not subordinated one part of the society as mere means to the other. This of course rules out both class and gender societies, and we must therefore look for nonrepressive sexuality either forward in a new liberated age or backward in pre-gender society.[18]

Continuing this line of thought,[19] Marcuse maintains that sexuality in the liberated or nonrepressive society must also be nonalienated – not subordinated to either the functions of *an* organ or to ends other than its own satisfaction, such as reproduction. Nonrepressive sexuality, therefore, is not genitally dominant but rather pre-genital in organization – diffuse, polymorphous, and flexible. Borrowing a term from Sandor Ferenczi, Marcuse dubs it "genitofugal" (away from the genitals – Ferenczi 1968). What are the implications of a psychosexual development that does not "desexualize" the organism or centralize erotic expression in the genitalia? Marcuse states:

> The process just outlined involves not simply a release but a *transformation* of the libido: from sexuality constrained under genital supremacy to erotization of the entire personality. It is a spread rather than explosion of libido – a spread over private and societal relations which bridges the gap maintained between them by a repressive reality principle. [201, 202, author's emphasis]

This extension of erotism means that all individual activities – even thinking – and collective activities, including work, become erotic expressions as well. The contradiction between culture and sexuality is transcended and libidinal strivings become culture binding rather than culture threatening. In this way genitofugal sexuality is what Marcuse calls "self-sublimating"; and a self-sublimating erotism need not always be satisfied through coitus. Marcuse says:

> With this restoration of the primary structure of sexuality, the primacy of the genital function is broken – as is the desexualization of the body which

has accompanied this primacy. The organism in its entirety becomes the substratum of sexuality, while at the same time the instinct's objective is no longer absorbed by a specialized function – namely, that of bringing ''one's own genitals into contact with those of someone of the opposite sex.'' [205]

We are now in a position to consider pre-gender ''bisexuality.'' In keeping with Freud's use of the term and Marcuse's interpretation of its possibilities, pre-gender sexuality is pre-genital in organization but at the same time not infantile or regressive in nature. As a mature, adult form it lies somewhere on the Freudian psychosexual continuum bounded by infantile polymorphism, on the one hand, and genital primacy on the other, that is, it is genitofugal. The self-sublimating character of this form of sexuality is consonant with the four other hypothesized properties of pre-gender eroticism. Thus, we would expect a culture that has not welded the genitalia into systematic cultural categories to also deemphasize the genitalia at the psychosexual level (point one). Similarly, a society in which sexuality is not structured into a system of cultural rules is also most likely a society in which sexuality at the individual level maintains a more fluid organization (point four). But what about points two and three? They maintain that the sexuality of pre-gender society is not a significant element of self-identity or of interpersonal relations, yet the concept of genitofugal psychosexuality includes a universal erotization of both the personality and social relationships. The contradiction is only apparent. Because erotic expression is a universal aspect of human thought and action it cannot function as a principle or category that separates, defines, or distinguishes one self from another or one kind of relationship (or aspect of a relationship) from another.

It is precisely this universal character of sexuality that is transformed by the transition to gender society: At the social level, rules come to separate time, space, and persons into sexual and nonsexual spheres and relations; at the individual level, mind and body become polarized along an erotic axis. The former (social level transformation) is embodied by gender relations, the latter by genital primacy. We will return to this set of transformations later; for now, having completed the anatomy of the bisexual horde, let us examine interhorde relations.

CHILD EXCHANGE AND ALLIANCE

Our description of pre-kinship society must be completed by sketching the mode of interhorde relationships. The first question to be answered is why hordes should want or need to form bonds with other hordes. After all, sexual relations are basically within the group, and the horde is both the production and reproduction unit. But it is the reproduction unit only in a narrow sense. Hordes must ensure their survival against erratic demographic and ecological conditions: People-to-resource ratios must be continually readjusted. In kinship societies this requires the establishment of affinal bonds under the cover of which people and resources are shuffled around. But genderless society has neither kinship nor marriage. By what means, then, are hordes brought into meaningful relationships with each other?

In and of itself, trade cannot provide this means because the exchange of goods must take place within a mutually predictable and previously existing relationship. Kinship society solves this problem by exploiting one of its chief characteristics: By the exchange of women, groups are immediately brought into a relationship that both parties understand. That is, the exchange itself implies an ordered set of mutual obligations and expectations. This relationship, then, provides the social cover for a whole host of useful material exchanges. Moreover, an important productive and reproductive resource has been transferred – namely, women. This whole system rests on the gender hierarchy: the notion that men have rights over women (Rubin 1975).

In genderless society, however, groups of adults do not have rights over other adults – but adults do have rights over children, who again form the glue in the social system. When Horde A bestows an infant on Horde B, both parties immediately understand the terms and implications of the exchange. Horde A is saying, ''You, Horde B, are Child Tenders to us, and we will be your Foragers.'' Horde B might reciprocate, bringing both groups into reciprocal relation as Child Tenders–Foragers. Or, hordes might exchange children in systems of generalized exchange. Whatever the arrangement, the same affective and moral bonds that unite Child Tenders and Foragers in mutual aid and cooperation within the horde would also unite several hordes. Whereas kinship society transfers the rights to future generations indirectly through the exchange of women, pre-kinship society does so directly through child exchange. Another point of consequence is that Foragers, as keepers of the external realm, are mainly responsible for carrying out these exchanges, although the choice of the exchanged child would most likely fall to the Child Tenders.

Child exchange is not restricted to pre-gender society. It has been and is a structural element in several societies. Oceanic societies are perhaps the most prominent examples, but it is reported as an important alliance technique among the Eskimos, West Indians, and African tribes. The point here is not that contemporary child adoption is some sort of ''survival'' but that it is a workable form of social exchange and alliance.[20]

THE GENDER REVOLUTION

The model of pre-kinship society I have constructed, although viable and stable, contains a dynamic or dialectic that leads to the creation of gender and ultimately to the dissolution of pre-kin social structure. Succinctly stated, it is the contradiction between unitarian ideology, with its insistence on sharing one life experience, and the biological asymmetry or exclusivity of proto-women's ability to have and suckle children. Once this exclusivity becomes a firm part of consciousness, the crisis in pre-kin society becomes acute and must be resolved.

Resolution here means attempting to contain the corrosive effects of this awareness. One way to do this is to sanctify proto-women and their special abilities, much as the Navajo sanctify the *nadle*. This lifts the problem out of the social realm: The special power of proto-women is now supernatural, no longer a challenge to the social system as it is constituted. But this proves to be only a temporary solution, with consequences more disruptive than the problem it seeks to solve.

Once elevated to the sacred, proto-women become separated as a category of thought and marked as a group by distinguishing anatomical character-istics. Those features closely associated with reproduction – genitalia, breasts – now become symbols of a new social category. At the same time, this process calls into being, through contrast and opposition, the category of persons lacking special power – proto-men. Thus, the masculine gender is formed negatively at first – by what it is not. Symbols of this category are not as well defined. As noted, there is nothing obviously complementary about male and female genitalia, particularly in a bisexual society: The vagina and breast become symbols of feminine gender because of their association with child bearing, *not* sex. We will return to the symbolic representation of gender in the section on "Gender and the archaeological record," where we will observe in the archaeological record an initially vague rendering of the phallus in contrast to elaborate feminine gender symbols.

The subversiveness of this new sacred category (women) becomes decisive when it is linked to the established category of Child Tender. This linking is predictable because of the infectious and dangerous nature of the sacred. That is, sacred things and people can make all they come in contact with sacred, but such power, beyond normal control, also has the potential for great destruction. Hence, much of primitive ritual is designed to seal off this polluting aspect of the sacred from nonsacred areas of life. The idea of identifying sacredness and pollution may seem strange to us, yet it is never-theless real in societies that do not rigidly cordon off separate realms of the universe labeled natural and supernatural.[21]

Because proto-women are themselves immune to the danger of their new sacred status, the problem of the polluting character of the sacred is resolved by proto-men abandoning the role of Child Tender and proto-women being excluded from external foraging.

The result is, of course, that the sacred, originally marshalled to contain a contradiction, only intensifies it. The final stages of this dialectic find the established categories of Child Tender and Forager mutually exclusive and dominated by newer but equally exclusive categories – men and women. Gender has taken definite shape, and exclusivity – once an exceptional source of contradiction – is now a main characteristic of social life. This accom-plished, unitarian ideology is unalterably transcended and the sacred charac-ter of proto-women ceases to exist; the sacred becomes profane once again, but not until pre-kinship society takes a fundamental step toward its own destruction.

Let me summarize this argument. Awareness develops of proto-women's exclusive power to bear and suckle children. To resolve the contradiction be-tween this exclusivity and unitarian ideology, proto-women are made a sacred category of person. This identifies and symbolizes a new social category by sexual characteristics – proto-women; and by contrasting opposition delineates the category of proto-men. Sacredness is contagious and the category Child Tender soon becomes dominated by proto-women. Similarly, Foragers become exclusively proto-men. Exclusivity is now a generalized condition and unitarian ideology ceases to be dominant. Therefore, sacredness of proto-women and child tending is no longer necessary, although many aspects of this new gender category remain tainted with notions of pollution.

This scenario raises a number of critical questions that need to be addressed before continuing. From its inception, wouldn't pre-gender society be conscious of the exclusive reproductive power of proto-women and of the incompatibility of that exclusiveness with the constituted social and ideological order? That is, wouldn't the gender revolution be contemporaneous with pre-gender society and not its outcome? Closely related to this question is the perceptual-cognitive one: Wouldn't the dramatic and patently significant fact of reproduction be an obvious element of human knowledge from the very beginnings of human history?

The viability of the entire enterprise here depends on how we answer these questions, affirmative or negative. An affirmative answer means that our model has no temporal dimension: Gender and the advent of human consciousness burst onto the stage together. At best it describes a cognitive process – how gender comes to be recognized. At worst, the model reduces to the absurdity of a pre-gender society that is also gender conscious. The negative answer, however, implies that the process is not perceptual-cognitive at heart but cultural and historical: The gender revolution is not the dawn of a new cognition as much as it is the creation of new *meaning*. And the genesis of meaning versus perception-cognition is the crux of the argument.

Pre-gender society was as cognizant as any society of the facts of reproduction: who gets pregnant, for how long, who suckles children, and so on. But the question is, what do these facts mean? Are they viewed as the characteristics of a category of person known as "women," embedded in a mesh of special roles, symbols, tasks, and values, and bearing a complementary relation to a category "men"? Or, are they viewed as aspects of the open, ascriptive category Child Tender related to an equally open category Forager? In short, are the facts of reproduction also gender facts? I have argued that biological facts do not speak for themselves. The biological asymmetry between proto-men and proto-women becomes the biological substratum of the gender system when these empirical data become anomalous – foreground in a contrasting symbolic background – threats to the constituted order of things. I have also posited the social system of pre-gender society and its unitarian view of human experience as that cultural matrix or background that renders reproductive facts anomalous and propels their revolutionary redefinition. Perhaps a more familiar example, racial systems, will clarify the distinction that I am drawing.

Racial categories are close analogues of gender categories. As with the gender system, people are assigned to them at birth (determined by parentage) and often tagged for life by certain phenotypic markers. Like the gender system too, racial categories seem to always be set within a hierarchical social system. The question that concerns us here is, do populational differences (skin color, eye shape, hair texture, and so on) yield these racial categories? That is, are our notions about races or a particular race simple reflections of "naturally" occurring units? I agree with those anthropologists who view the long-standing debate on what constitutes a biological race as fundamentally misguided.[22] Racial categories, whether of the "common sense" variety (street view) or "scientific" variety, are cultural constructs – elements of a particular discourse. This does not mean that population differences are figments of our imaginations; they are undoubtedly real, can be measured and quantified, but do not of themselves bring racial types or groups into being. The construction of racial categories entails: emphasizing certain physical differences between populations, simultaneously underplaying the similarities; and endowing the distinctive features of the racial type with certain meanings. In short, racial categories are constructed meanings and must be accounted for by some underlying sociocultural process that causes people to "see" quite selectively. Indeed, genetic variation between two contact populations can only be maintained by cultural rules that prohibit or discourage intermarrying. Otherwise, these differences would soon disappear under the random mixing of the gene pools. So we can say that, on balance, racial categories have more to do with the creation and maintenance of populational differences than the other way around.

We can highlight the cultural essence of racial status by demonstrating the way a population takes on and sheds racial identifications with no apparent change in its gene pool or phenotype, and conversely, how racial categories are often unaffected by considerable changes in a population. Consider, for example, the titanic upsurge of American "nativist" racism provoked by the new waves of post-Civil War immigration. Very different populations from eastern and southern Europe came to be lumped together and thought of by Americans as a vast racial underclass; and like Blacks and other dark-skinned races, the newcomers were considered inherently unassimilable. Besides being perceived as radicals and criminals, the "racial inferiors" flocking to American shores were considered a grave threat to the racial purity of native American stock, a degenerative influence on the physical and mental well-being of future generations (Curran 1975; Higham 1955; Weiss 1970: 121–43). The essential point is that American opposition to immigration, although having many causes and a long history, was deliberately fashioned into a racial opposition by elite propagandists and intellectuals within a relatively short period of time. These individuals literally created a race where none had existed. Higham summarizes the phenomenon.

> To the development of racial nativism, the thinkers have made a special contribution. Sharp physical differences between native Americans and European immigrants were not readily apparent; to a large extent they had to be manufactured. A rather elaborate, well entrenched set of racial ideas was essential before the newcomer from Europe could seem a fundamentally different order of men. [Higham 1955: 133][23]

Most contemporary Americans would find the idea of categorizing Hungarians, Poles, Jews, Italians, or Greeks along with Blacks as bizarre, because these groups have again been redefined as belonging to White America. The interesting thing about the American racial system is its amazing stability. Groups may undergo repeated redefinition, but the American two-race model remains unaltered. Even a considerable amount of gene flow through interracial unions has not changed the bipolar structure of the system. R. P. Stucket maintains that twenty-eight million Americans, the majority classed as White, in fact have African ancestry. Asserting the primacy of cultural forces in maintaining racial ideas, he says: "One conclusion stands out from the data. The belief in racial uniformity of an individual's ancestors may be the basic myth of the white man's past" (Stucket 1959: 563–4).

Examples could be multiplied of racial categories coming into and going out of existence, others fusing together or coming apart without any corresponding change in phenotype or gene frequency; or conversely of real physical changes occurring in population structure without any alteration of the structure of the racial system. But the point has been demonstrated: Physical or biological features, even the most prominent, are not inherently meaningful. To become the markers or referents of race or gender, these features must be welded in categories, given a broad range of meanings, and in the case of racial categories the very features themselves must be maintained by cultural sanctions.

So much for our distinction: The gender revolution is a revolution in meaning, not perception. But the original question still remains unanswered: If the ideology of pre-gender society forms the necessary condition for the genesis of this new meaning, what took the gender system so long to emerge?

The model of pre-gender society constructed in this essay was presented as a completed product, not as a work in progress. But if it is to resemble life we must recognize that this epoch too has a developmental history – imperceptible beginning, middle, and final periods. It is on this latter, mature stage that I have focused. When we view the social structure and ideology of pre-gender society from this developmental perspective, it becomes clearer why the gender revolution was the product of its mature stage and not its ever-present companion. It is precisely when unitarian ideology becomes a fixed, integrated formal aspect of mental life, when the Child Tender–Forager structure becomes most defined, elaborated, and firmly rooted in consciousness, that the hitherto *latent* empirical or perceptual category "women" becomes troublesome, anomalous, and plainly contradictory. We can say that this perceptual category emerges as a meaning or cultural category *by virtue* of its contrast and contradiction to the Child Tender–Forager structure and the unitarian ideal. Thus, the transition from latent perception to full-fledged cultural category depends on the evolution of the manifest structure of pre-gender society. Remember that the category "women" does not develop in relation to its sexual opposite, "men," but rather in contradistinction to its sociocultural milieu. Indeed, the category "men" emerges later as a latent category in opposition to the category "women."

This whole discussion, of course, pushes the explanation back in time and we are forced to ask about the nature of the *pre*-pre-gender period and its internal logic. Here I can say little. As I have maintained, pre-gender society is fully human; the prior period was a formative one stretching deep into our hominid past. This period is marked by a transition to fully human symbolic capacity and the uncoupling of instinctive drives from their behavioral consequences: Sexuality gains its characteristically human plasticity and the infant-mother bond dissolves as a biological imperative. Beyond this I have not speculated.

This limitation aside, there are still other issues to be tackled. Outside of internal forces driving the gender dialectic forward, what other conditions retard or hasten the crisis? The concept of a "latent" category implies an active process of nonrecognition. This idea has been developed in different ways: as repression (Freud) and false consciousness (Marx). Both of these are at work in pre-gender society. As the development of pre-gender society proceeded to greater consistency and sharper contours, thereby infusing the latent perceptual category of "women" with meaning, this dangerous awareness must have been actively repressed, that is, systematic and vital connections were not drawn. The contradiction between the category "women" and the category Child Tenders had to be blurred, forced away from conscious investigation. Evans-Pritchard's *The Nuer* comes readily to mind as an example. Although the Nuer think of their lineage system as agnatic, localized, and segmentary, it is in fact cognatic, dispersed, and flexibly aligned. The Nuer, who are perfectly aware of maternal links and of the ad hoc local lineage alliances, nevertheless speak in the idiom of agnation, segmentation, and localization; the contradiction is never raised to the conscious level (Evans-Pritchard 1970: 192–248).

If we consider the processes of "not knowing" as retarding the crisis in pre-gender society by delaying the transformation of perceptual into broad, meaningful cultural categories, how can we account for the ultimate breakdown of these stabilizing forces? The major part of the explanation lies in the dynamic of the contradiction itself: As the latent category becomes more defined, more contrasting and apparent, repression and false consciousness simply become more difficult to maintain. But there must surely have been external factors as well – ecological, for example – that contributed to pushing the contradiction to the point of no return. Again I cannot be more specific, not having extended the model in that direction. Perhaps I can evaluate the gender revolution account as an explanation by saying that whereas it specifies the *necessary* conditions for the emergence of gender (the internal dialectic) it is not complete because it fails to provide all the *sufficient* conditions: the developmental process that brings pre-gender forms into being from the formative period; the external conditions that propel the gender dialectic to the breaking point.

In summary, the main dynamic in pre-gender society turns on the incongruity between the biological asymmetry of reproduction and the social and ideological structure of pre-gender society – its ideal of unitary experience. Or more specifically, it turns on the incongruity between the latent category "women" and the manifest cultural category Child Tender. As pre-gender society develops from its formative hominid origins – as its structure and ideology surfaces into bolder, more consistent outlines – it gives meaning to the latent category by making it more anomalous. The phenomenon of "not knowing'' stabilizes the situation for a time but ultimately gives way to the burgeoning crisis. The disintegrating effect of the newly emerged category ''women'' is contained by its elevation to sacred status. But again this rear guard attempt fails and the crisis of exclusivity is generalized by the emergence of another latent and negatively defined category – ''men.'' In this way gender categories arise but not in the form we recognize today: They are still not hierarchically arranged nor are they yet indissolubly linked to new social forms of kinship. We now turn to these developments.

HETEROSEXUALITY AND GENDERIZED SEX

In this discussion of the development of exclusive heterosexuality, as throughout this section of the essay on the transformation of pre-kinship society, I will outline a number of different yet related causal processes. Despite their diversity they derive a unity by being set in motion by conditions brought forth by the new gender system. I want to stress the mutual causal nature of this process because the linear character of written language easily obscures the simultaneity and interconnectedness of the phenomena. For example, the trend toward exclusive heterosexuality results from three causal forces: intensification of *intra*-gender competition; gender-related repression inherent in the socialization process; and the symbolic need to mediate a severely dichotomized perception of the social and natural world. We could label these three as social, psychological, and symbolic, but that would tend to destroy the unity and interpenetrating nature of the process – exactly what I want to avoid.

In my description of pre-kin society I neglected to speak of the interpersonal struggle for prestige or individual honor. This is an important aspect of kinship societies but little developed in pre-kin society. The reason for this shift lies in the nature of social recognition, which is bound or set within social categories. Hence, the hunter's struggle for honors depends on a socially recognized category called ''hunter'' and a set of activities associated with that category. Individual struggle for prestige is constrained by the number and kind of outlets that the culture makes available. Other things being equal, the more rigidly defined the activity or role – the more limited the range of possible activities and roles available to individuals – the more intense the competition within them. We come upon the same phenomenon if we approach from a different direction, from the question of self-identity and worth, which is closely related to a culture's role structure. The more limited and constrained that structure, the greater the pressure on individuals to achieve recognition within a smaller cultural sphere.

This explains why pre-kinship society, with its flexible and nonascriptive categories of Child Tender and Forager, would tend to underplay the struggle for prestige within each of these categories. More specifically, intracategory competition is undercut because membership in the activity groups corresponding to these categories is constantly shifting. The advent of the gender system changes all this. Foraging and Child Tending are now prescriptive roles in life – ones in which competitive peers and competitive activities are fixed. Moreover, these gender-associated activities and roles, once they are acquired at birth, take on the aspect of being "natural" and thus begin to define a significant portion of self. These conditions are conducive to a much more intense intracategory competition – now intra*gender* competition.

The consequences for the character of sexuality and gender are significant. Competition within gender-related activities – and all activities are now circumscribed by the gender dichotomy – tends to reinforce and elaborate the very meanings of masculinity and femininity. For example, as men compete for honors as hunters the category "hunter" not only becomes more delineated but becomes more firmly associated with male gender. Thus, the identity male equals hunter encourages the idea that the better hunter is more the male. It is not a big step from competing as hunters to competing as *men*, yet this small step implies important consequences. One critical aspect of this new intragender competition – competing as men and as women – surely must be sexual attractiveness and conquest. This follows from the new emphasis and meaningfulness of the genitalia in defining gender membership. But sexual competition tends to skew sexual preference into one of two exclusive directions: intragender homosexuality or intergender heterosexuality. Why is this polarization of the previously bisexual framework a necessary result of sexual competition?

It must be emphasized that our problem here is one of sexuality not in a statistical but an ideological sense; which sexual patterns are viewed as superior or preferred? These are value judgments that emerge from a set of socially validated standards, and the standards in turn are intimately connected to the new competitive arena in which the sexuality of gender society finds itself. This common set of standards, by which men and women now evaluate themselves as sexual persons vis-à-vis each other, also specifies the characteristics of a desirable sexual choice, the criteria of winning and losing, and in general the rules of the new sexual game. It is precisely because sexual performance is evaluated competitively by a set of shared values that sexuality tends to become skewed in either of the two exclusive directions. That is, the standards of sexual performance themselves cannot escape the gender dichotomy; it was this very dichotomy that gave rise to sexual competition in the first place. Thus, the criteria of sexual desirability will tend to rank sexual objects along a continuum of desirability based, among other things, on the gender of the object. It would seem inevitable under these conditions for *either* intragender homosexuality or intergender heterosexuality to assume dominance as a preferred form. It is this polarization of bisexuality that constitutes what I call the genderization of sexuality.[24]

The preceding line of reasoning, which moves from intragender competition to sexual competition and then to genderized sexuality, is not meant to reduce intragender competition to sexual competition or reduce sexuality in general to its competitive dimension. Rather, I posit this as one causal trend among others – part of an explanation. It cannot, for example, account for the dominance of exclusive heterosexuality (as opposed to homosexuality), which I believe to be the *predominant* outcome at this historical juncture of the polarization of sexuality.[25] For this we turn to psychological and symbolic processes.

Within the individual the gender system generates psychic forces that promote heterosexual sex. We begin by noting the obvious but crucial fact that women dominate the socialization process after the gender revolution. Chodorow has incisively analyzed the dynamics of this situation in which little boys must fashion their identity in *opposition* to their most immediate gender model, mother; the socialization process for girls is more positive and smoother but nevertheless leaves its own brand of scars (1974). The aspect of this phenomenon I wish to emphasize is its inherent repression. In a world of different activities, personality types, and aspirations to which the human infant is exposed, he/she must reject some in favor of others with hardly the ability to know why. This must lead to a sense of loss. Thousands of years of androgynous myths and folk tales testify to the unconscious need to be reunited with a repressed part of ourselves (see Singer 1977). This is another powerful force behind heterosexuality. Repression not only leaves each of the genders with a sense of incompleteness, but tends to fetishize the opposite gender.

At the unconscious level also, we note the already well-entrenched tendency toward genital primacy. The genitalia have become charged with intense meaning and symbolism – a symbolism that once internalized comes to occupy the central regions of the self. In psychoanalytic terms the genitalia become psychic representatives of the ego. Hence, the continual contrast and unity of the genitalia in heterosexual sex serves as an unconscious metaphor of individual distinctiveness and integration in the cultural universe.

Compelling social-psychological forces still do not amount to norms or rules. The gender duality, however, creates conditions within the symbolic domain that would tend not merely to validate but to prescribe exclusive heterosexuality. Recall, the worldview of pre-kinship society was unitary. This changes drastically with the establishment of mutually exclusive gender categories. The world now appears divided into a whole series of dualities – all of which have a gender component or association. Would it not seem necessary for those who view the world thus to attempt to put it back together again, to mediate these divisions? In this way, heterosexual sex might be viewed as "natural" and necessary to maintain social and cosmic harmony.

Working in concert, these three forces or trends could extend the gender system to include exclusive heterosexuality. Soon I will discuss other developments that even more thoroughly institutionalize heterosexuality, but even at this point we can say the culture's first incest prohibition has taken shape.

THE HOUSEHOLD: CHANGING RELATIONS IN THE HORDE

The gender system, now heterosexual and genitally dominant, elevates sex simultaneously to a social ordering principle, an arena of competition, and a key element of self-identity. This makes sexuality a powerful social force and one that can bring disorder in exact proportion to its ability to order human relations. What was once a generalized aspect of human interaction is now a central focus and one that above all must be *controlled*.

The destructive aspect of the new sexuality manifests itself at the interpersonal level as sexual jealousy and possessiveness. So familiar and powerful are these ways of relating that we have come to think of them as innate to human nature. Yet I argue that this emotional complex is a consequence of the gender system – a historically relative phenomenon. Once "maleness" or "femaleness," attractiveness, sexuality, and mate getting become significant in the way men and women carve out their identities and in the way they compete among themselves, it is not difficult to understand why "cheating" or mate stealing can be threatening acts leading to severe emotional reactions. I do not want to overstate the case; we know that people overcome possessiveness, that there are institutions and social arrangements designed to transcend it. Nevertheless, it is an ever-present force or tendency to be overcome or transcended. It not only potentially but actively leads to violence and social schism.

Exclusive heterosexuality and sexual possessiveness tend to lead to a more defined method of mate selection and to further restraints on sexual relations in the horde – what is called "pair bonding" by the ethologists. Heterosexual pairing, however, creates a crisis in the mate-selection process – a subject I will return to soon. For now let us note other profound effects of pairing on the internal organization of the horde.

In pre-kinship society the complementing categories of Child Tenders and Foragers were made mutually exclusive gender categories by the gender revolution. Under the impact of pairing, all vestiges of the contractual and functional relationship between these categories of people disintegrate. A woman is now dependent on a particular man for meat ("hunted" food) and sex. But aside from sex, what ties a man to a particular woman?

It will be remembered that the gender revolution made the external domain exclusively male. This left the crucial area of interhorde relations and child exchange exclusively to men, who now must obtain children under very different conditions. In addition, a man's ability to forge external relations has also become an important part of the more intense struggle for prestige. Hence, men need the alliance of particular women to obtain children. In a parallel fashion, women, within their gender sphere of competition, now tend to view (their ability to bear) children as a resource – a means to attract men and perhaps to express or declare their own gender identity.

The overall movement or development is that the moral contract between Child Tender and Forager is replaced by subunits of the horde, composed of male–female pairs. Child tending, once an open communal responsibility, is now primarily considered the responsibility of the particular mother. The Forager's primary responsibility has also shifted from feeding the collective to feeding a particular woman and her children. The maternal bond has not appeared until now. As with other important elements of the model, I see the maternal bond as a cultural-historical gender phenomenon. This is not to deny that among primates and early hominids the mother–child bond is and was in some sense innately programmed. Tanner and Zihlman have persuasively argued for the importance of the mother–child unit in early hominid evolution (Tanner and Zihlman 1976). But to argue that this mechanism carried over into fully human cultural systems is another story. As I have maintained, and will maintain in more detail in the section on "Gender and the archaeological record," there is a basic discontinuity in human evolution. Just as human sexuality represents a break or freedom from rigid somatic controls, so too with other patterns including the mother-child bond. Thus, it is a mistake to argue for similar function, meaning, and origin of social forms, such as the family, that superficially look the same in human and prehuman social systems.

With pairing the household mode of organization (though not the family) takes definite shape. Along with its appearance and the dissolution of the older Child Tender–Forager system, however, new critical problems arise: How to find mates when the small horde size is frequently unbalanced sexually? And how to link these new moral–economic household units within the horde to achieve social cohesiveness? Concerning the last question, it should be remembered that households, although important productive and reproductive units, are by no means self-sufficient.

These new relations of production, once they become customary, take on powerful causal efficacy. That is, these new arrangements become necessary for economic survival and therefore compel the solution of contradictions they pose. Thus, the need to solve problems created by the existence of the household, such as suprahousehold organization and mate selection, will call new social principles and forms into being: the family, marriage, and horde exogamy.

THE FAMILY, MARRIAGE, AND HORDE EXOGAMY: MORE ON INCEST PROHIBITIONS

As I have indicated, the internal reorganization of the horde into household units should not be confused with the nuclear family. The former is a functional group that produces and reproduces. The family, however, is a set of ideal relationships and principles (incest prohibitions, marriage rules) that are imposed on the activities and internal dynamics of the nuclear household (Buchler and Selby 1968: 19–23). In another sense we can view the family as the resolution of contradictions posed by the household form of organization. Its evolution involves several interwoven causal strands in addition to the ones already discussed (exclusive heterosexuality, the household).

First, with pairing and the concomitant competition for mates within the group, a trend is begun: People are compelled to seek mates in other hordes. This follows from the crisis in mate selection and the potentially explosive nature of the new sexuality – both offspring of the gender revolution. The trend easily becomes a rule as soon as a regular means is established for providing interhorde mate exchange. Indeed, a mechanism already exists for this purpose – child exchange. It will be recalled that under the old system of pre-gender society, Foragers exchange children to cement and establish interhorde networks. Now they do so for an additional reason – to import mates.[26] Initially, this does not change the nature of interhorde dependence but just adds a new dimension to it. Within the horde, however, a new condition is created: Formerly children were adopted as full members of the horde but now, as incoming mates, it is their nonmembership (as potential mates) that must be maintained in accordance with the rule of horde exogamy. Thus, the relationship between parents and children must be marked, named, and remembered; and children must be able to distinguish their own siblings and horde mates from future spouses. To a certain extent this new emphasis on genealogical connection (the relation need not be actually genealogical, see the section on "Gender and kinship") had already begun with the advent of the household, but now it has become a structural feature – filiation and descent are now stable features of gender society. Therefore, horde exogamy and the idea of descent must be viewed as two sides of the same process, taking shape together in a complementary way.

Second, it must be stressed that it is men who are exchanging child spouses among themselves, and hence, most of the exchanged children are female. This is a consequence of the gender revolution and of the external domain having fallen to men. Male control of mate exchange cannot be overemphasized: Rosaldo's (1974) distinction between the masculine public domain versus the feminine domestic domain is firmly established by this time and shortly will be a decisive element of permanent male dominance. The reader should note, however, that male control of the external domain, as with other effects of the gender transformation of pre-kin society (such as the asymmetrical nature of socialization) are also causes – agencies of persistence that reproduce the very forces that give rise to them.

Third, intrahousehold incest prohibitions emerge. This appears anomalous, because with the exception of mother–son mating all possible nonparental sexual relationships within the household are already tabooed by existing restrictions on sexuality. For example, brother–sister and father–daughter sex are barred by the horde exogamy rule, while all homosexual relationships (mother–daughter, brother–brother, and so on) are forbidden by the rule of exclusive heterosexuality. It is true that household and horde solidarity requires further restriction be placed on father–son competition for mother, that is, prohibition on mother–son incest; but even so, why the emergence of the full set of intrahousehold incest prohibitions – why the redundancy?

Part of the answer lies in the fact that dyadic relationships within the household (mother–son, sister–brother, and so on) are themselves newly emerging at this point in our model. Under the impact of principles such as filiation and exogamy these relationships are being named and given social recognition for the first time. Thus, it can be expected that the extant incest restrictions would be reformulated to cover these new relationships. But there is a more fundamental reason: The incest taboos that hold between members of the household have their own causes peculiar to the internal dynamics of the primary unit of socialization itself. Thus, although intrafamilial incest taboos are isomorphic to other incest prohibitions, they cannot be reduced to them.

That family incest rules have their own foundation is evidenced by their universally tenacious nature: Other incest restrictions may come and go, but they remain. This independent foundation lies in the complex of child-to-parent psychosexual identification that Freud called the Oedipal complex (1923; 1925: 31–9). We can view it more broadly, however, as the asymmetrical process of gender socialization that takes place in the family, most decisively between mother and child. Inherent in this process are rejection and repression; and both contribute to the phobic sexual attitudes of children toward parents and toward each other. Needless to say, the Oedipal complex is not only an effect of a gender–related structure (the family) but, once established, a key force in the reproduction of the gender system.

Thus, with the establishment of horde exogamy, a well–defined marriage system (the exchange of child brides) and intrahousehold incest prohibitions, all the conditions for the existence of the family are met; and the problems posed by the advent of the household mode of organization are solved. As Lévi-Strauss has argued, these are also the same conditions necessary for kinship (Lévi-Strauss 1967: 43–50; 1971: passim). That is, exogamous family units are linked through both affinal and consanguineal ties; moreover, these relationships may be unambiguously represented and reproduced each generation, via a marriage system that continuously produces new family units.

Because the horde is now internally differentiated into family units enmeshed in a regionwide kinship network, we can drop the word horde and use the more familiar anthropological term ''band''; and because wives are imported into the band we can also designate it as patrilocal. However, the transformation of pre-kinship society is not yet complete.

GENDER HIERARCHY, AMBIGUOUS SYMBOLS, AND THE EXCHANGE OF WOMEN

It is a small step from the exchange of child brides to the exchange of adult women in daughter or sister exchange. With this step the transformation of pre-gender society is completed. The exchange of adult women by men represents the exercise of dominance by some adult members of the community over other adults, a principle totally antithetical to pre-gender society. As Rubin maintains, the marriage exchange of women institutionalizes male dominance, fixing the status of women as objects and ''other'' (Rubin 1975). Most important, it reifies gender hierarchy, which becomes encoded right into the heart of the kinship system – marriage. The symbolic expression of male dominance does not merely reflect the gender hierarchy, however; it also causes and actively maintains that hierarchy.

Recall that the need to mediate symbolically a severely dichotomized cosmos was one of the active principles invoked in the development of exclusive heterosexuality. At that time the female and male symbolic representations were not weighted one over the other. This symbolic coexistence is inherently unstable as the transformation to kinship society deepens. Ortner's work is particulary useful here. She notes that woman becomes an ambiguous symbol that is associated with nature and is contrasted negatively to the positive symbol of culture (human intervention, control) – man (1974). As the model here has developed, three of woman's roles have evolved, each reinforcing the association of woman equals nature and ambiguity. As child bearer she is nature; as socializer of men she is ambiguous, to be both embraced and rejected; as wife she is both outsider (again ambiguous) and passive object (nature). Once the transition from the pre-kinship horde to the patrilocal band is complete, the simple symbolic formula woman equals passive nature and man equals dominant culture becomes a well-defined code, a powerful mechanism for reproducing gender hierarchy.

Gender and the archaeological record

I would now like to turn to a practical application of our thought experiment exercise by testing its usefulness in interpreting archaeological data.

Fully erect, bipedal, tool-using hominids appear in the archaeological record at least three to three and a half million years ago. Throughout this period the assemblages of artifacts and skeletal remains show an increasing mastery over raw nature paralleled by an expanding cranial capacity. Because the model I have constructed of pre-kin society and its transformation is prior to anything we, or history, can observe directly, its plausibility as a model rests on the archaeological interpretation of those remains. I have neither the expertise nor the space to carry out such a grand project, so I will select a small slice of that long record – the European Upper Paleolithic – to see if the model of the gender revolution makes sense of the evidence. The enterprise is made more difficult both by the relative scantiness of the remains and the divergent opinions of experts on their meaning.

Despite these limitations, however, the material from the Upper Paleolithic (35,000 B.C. to 12,000 B.C.) suggests strongly, for Europe at least, a gender revolution in human history closely paralleling the one in our discussion. The pattern of symbolic expression of gender concepts during this epoch closely follows that in the model: an initial stage characterized by a well-defined, highly specified feminine concept and correspondingly weak masculine representation: a middle period of elaboration in which both gender signs are related to each other in different contexts and mapped onto other kinds of signs; and finally, toward the end of the Upper Paleolithic, a clear, graphic representation of the phallus but concomitant weak and abstract rendering of feminine signs. The whole sequence seems to confirm the negative definition of the masculine gender category I postulate as the logic of the evolution of gender. But to postulate a transition to gender society in Europe during the Upper Paleolithic implies a pre-gender period in the latter part of the Mousterian (the culture period preceding the Upper Paleolithic) to early Upper Paleolithic. I would like the reader to suspend this critical question until we have completed reviewing the evidence for the Upper Paleolithic. Through the work of Leroi-Gourhan we will see that the art and ritual of this epoch explodes with gender symbols.

THE UPPER PALEOLITHIC AND THE SYNTAX OF GENDER SIGNS

The Upper Paleolithic, spanning approximately 25,000 years, is subdivided into five major periods that are, from earliest to latest, Chatelperronian, Aurignacian, Gravettian, Solutrean, and Magdalenian. Except for the exclusively prefigurative art of the Chatelperronian, the subjects of Paleolithic art consist of a variety of animals, male and female figures, and a number of signs classified as "narrow" and "wide." These sundry subject elements appear on portable objects such as pendants, tools, weapons, and figures; and are engraved, sculpted, and painted on the walls of caves and rock shelters (Leroi-Gourhan 1968: 54–104).

Allowing for temporal and regional variation in style, the entire spectrum of Paleolithic art maintains a remarkable unity and constancy over an immense area (France to Russia). This unity consists in more than just the constancy of subject elements. Leroi-Gourhan argues that if we treat the animals, male and female figures, and the like, as signs in a meaningful symbolic system we note a syntax of signs that remains unvarying from the early Aurignacian to late Magdalenian. Hence, certain signs will occur together as regular motifs whereas others never occur together; some signs will appear on certain objects and in certain contexts and not others. This thematic regularity is not confined to durable objects; even on less durable objects the signs appear in a more abbreviated form. From this syntax of signs Leroi-Gourhan maintains:

The invariability of the subjects represented, which we find in every category of object or on the cave walls, presupposes deep-rooted oral traditions and testifies to a precisely codified body of beliefs. [Leroi-Gourhan 1968: 63]

The author characterizes this body of beliefs as a dualistic religious system that uses the idiom of sexual symbolism as a model of expression. He notes that all of the abstract signs, animals, and anthropomorphic figures are in fact masculine and feminine signs; and these are continually found juxtaposed to one another in a number of different contexts (1968: 144). So invariant is this syntax of pairing that Leroi-Gourhan has used the class of "wide signs" as a principal means of dating the difficult-to-date cave paintings (1968a: 63).

Cave painting represents the most mature and elaborate form of Paleolithic art. On the walls and ceilings of multichambered caves, in seemingly bewildering chaos, Paleolithic artists exquisitely and often breathtakingly rendered late Pleistocene fauna: bison, ibex, stag, mammoth, and horse. Their achievement is highlighted by the dark and perilous conditions in these decorated "sanctuaries," some of which descend a mile into the earth.

Leroi-Gourhan has made an exhaustive study of a large percentage of the known Spanish and French caves.[27] Prior to this work it was believed that the paintings were the piecemeal work of Paleolithic hunters practicing sympathetic magic. This is no longer a tenable interpretation. For one thing, only a small minority of the animals are depicted with "symbolic wounds" (1968: 34). Second, the cave animals are only a small portion of the species known to exist at that time, nor were the depicted animals necessarily the most important economically (1968: 111). Third, and most importantly, the pairing and spatial arrangement of the animals and other painted signs shows a definite and regular pattern, suggesting that the whole cave is a planned, meaningful organization of signs. Space does not permit a complete description of the complexities in Leroi-Gourhan's argument, so I must regrettably oversimplify.

When caves are broken down into three spatial components (central area, periphery, and entrance/rear) the author notes that large herbivores such as the ox, bison, horse, and mammoth are overwhelmingly found in the central areas; ibex and stag in the periphery; and the dangerous animals such as bear, lion, and rhinoceros at the cave entrances and rear. All of the central animals are associated, in other contexts, as feminine; the horse and other peripheral animals are similarly linked to the masculine. The horse, along with other peripheral animals, Leroi-Gourhan calls "framing" animals; indeed, the horse/ox and the horse/bison are two of the most prevalent themes in cave art. Thus, the general pattern in cave painting demonstrates the principle of complementary sexual pairing: center (female) with periphery (male); and within the center, ox, bison, mammoth (female) with horse (male). The pairing idea is carried through with masculine and feminine figures and abstract signs as well. Vulvas and wide signs are found in the central areas where they are paired to male figures and signs. In the periphery, particularly at entrances and in the rear chambers, only male signs are found, however (1968: 108–20).

Leroi-Gourhan is not attempting to establish the existence of a gender system in the Upper Paleolithic; he never uses the term. Yet, his interpretation solidly establishes the existence of a very well-developed system. Moreover, the system is unmistakably asymmetrical: paired feminine signs in the center and unpaired masculine signs in the periphery. The overall impression is one of containment, neutralization, or control of femininity. The author even suggests that the deep caves themselves are metaphors of the womb and supports older interpretations of the caves as initiation centers (Leroi-Gourhan 1968: 148, 174). One can very well imagine the caves being used to reveal the mysteries of gender to young initiates. The gender implications of cave art are seen even more clearly when it is placed in chronological perspective.

The deep caves (as opposed to the open rock shelters) are late developments in Leroi-Gourhan's chronology – Magdalenian III to Magdalenian V. They come at, or shortly before, a time when carved phalluses are graphically represented on artifacts and when feminine signs are weak and more abstract. In short, the late Upper Paleolithic represents the culmination or resolution of the gender revolution: The firm establishment of gender hierarchy. This period is in marked contrast to the early and middle Upper Paleolithic in which the really definitive gender signs are not masculine but feminine – vulvas, "wide" signs, and most importantly the venus figurines of the Gravettian.

These figures, found all over Europe, are highly conventionalized representations with exaggerated breasts, thighs, and vulva circumscribed within a circle; and correspondingly the head and limbs are almost nonexistent. Most interpretations have explained their use as fertility symbols, but Leroi-Gourhan and others have rightly questioned the validity of a fertility interpretation especially when applied to a nonagricultural people (Leroi-Gourhan 1968: 174; Mouvis 1961: 37). In my view, the early and middle Upper Paleolithic, with its strong feminine forms and weak masculine ones, reflects the beginnings of gender consciousness; the delineation of the feminine gender category; its elevation to sacred status; and the less pronounced, negatively formed male gender category.

The reversal in the emphasis and status of gender signs from the early to late Upper Paleolithic is exactly what our model of the evolution of the gender system would predict. Leroi-Gourhan notes this reversal:

A survey of human representations in the Upper Paleolithic seems to show, as we move from epoch to epoch, that the proportion of male to female figures is wholly reversed. In the earliest period, statuettes and low reliefs of women are fairly numerous, then they grow scarce, giving way to abbreviated figures or signs. On the other hand, complete representations of men are rare in the early periods, and much more frequent in the caves during the peak period of the interior sanctuaries . . . The earliest figures of men that we can place – though unfortunately not as accurately as we could wish – belong to the Gravettian and Solutrean and are far less characterized according to sexual typology, than the statuettes and low reliefs of women from the same period. [1968: 123]

This interpretation places consolidated gender hierarchy in the late Magdalenian. It is difficult to resist making the observation that with this phase of human evolution hardly completed, another leap into evolutionary history was about to take place – agriculture. What is the connection between the revolution in social relations and the subsequent revolution in technology? That is the subject of another paper.

If the symbolic material from the Upper Paleolithic reflects the evolution of the gender system, we must raise the question – actually two questions – patiently suspended by the reader: Was the preceding epoch a pre-gender one, and if so, how far back in time can we trace it?

Unfortunately, we cannot answer the first question directly; unlike the Upper Paleolithic, the Mousterian lacks a gender symbolism and to my knowledge there is no convincing evidence from the Neanderthal remains that gender-related forms such as kinship structures existed. Hence, the most we can say is that the known record does not preclude a pre-gender interpretation of Neanderthal culture. The second question raises a more fundamental issue regarding the applicability of the model. If we hypothesize that all or part of Mousterian society was pre-gender, we are at the same time maintaining, in accordance with the model, that it was also fully human in its ability to formulate and express concepts. The contrary position seriously vitiates the argument for a gender genesis in the Upper Paleolithic. For if the elaboration of gender and the advent of fully human culture are contemporaneous then we imply that a long-standing, *de facto* gender system was merely given symbolic expression in the Upper Paleolithic: that gender *is* human nature rather than *a* human nature. Thus, the important questions we turn to now are: Can the society preceding the Upper Paleolithic be characterized as human? If so, how far back in the hominid record does human culture go? What criteria can be used to decide these questions?

WHAT IS HUMAN?

Anthropologists have confirmed over and over again that humans, in whatever culture we find them and at whatever sociotechnical level, share a basic psychic unity – identical thought processes. This psychic unity is a fundamental operating principle of the discipline; it ties the human capacity for culture (symbolic expression) to a certain given development of the human brain. In an insightful essay, ''The Growth of Culture and the Evolution of the

Mind,'' Clifford Geertz shows how this operating assumption runs into serious trouble as soon as it is changed from a functional statement into a statement about human evolution, that is, when mental capacity and culture are seen as developing sequentially (Geertz 1973). This position is best expressed by those who see a critical point in the development of brain physiology spawning humanity's leap into culture: An independently developing brain provides the basis for a subsequent cultural florescence.

The contradiction in this argument is revealed quickly. The Australopithecines, with an average cranial capacity of 550 cc, made stone tools, foraged cooperatively, and built shelters – all the things we associate with cultural behavior. Yet, hominid cranial capacity did not stabilize to within a human size range till the late Pleistocene, millions of years later. Geertz summarizes the difficulty.

> In fact, as the *Homo sapiens* brain is about three times as large as that of the Australopithecines, the greater part of human cortical expansion has followed, not preceded, the ''beginning'' of culture, a rather inexplicable circumstance if the capacity for culture is considered to have been the unitary outcome of a quantitatively slight but qualitatively metastatic change of the freezing-of-water sort. [Geertz 1973: 64, 65]

How then do we save the valid proposition of the psychic unity of humankind and at the same time avoid the contradictions inherent in the critical point notion? Geertz suggests, I think correctly, that we view tool making and other cultural behavior evidenced in the hominid record as part of the selective environment operating on the evolution of the human brain. That is, culture and the human brain should be seen in a mutually causal relationship, each having given rise to the other in the course of a long evolutionary sequence. Australopithecus and Homo erectus undoubtedly had communicative and expressive forms more advanced than those of extant primate species but well below those of Homo sapiens. The all-important point, however, is that both the somatic and extrasomatic components of culture should be seen evolving in a mutually interactive unity.

This unity leads Geertz to suggest that we may be searching in vain for *purely* morphological differences in the brain to account for the vast gulf that separates the cultural capacity of primates and early hominids from Homo sapiens. The determining difference is not *in* the brain but in that mutually dependent unity of brain and culture: the human mind is extracerebral. The compelling conclusion of all this is that the human mind can neither survive, nor indeed function, without culture. Moreover, although the brain has the capacity for symbolic thought, that capacity is only actualized by the manipulation of cultural objects, principally language.

How far back in history can we trace the human condition? With what group of hominids do we share the same psychic unity that ties White Americans, Bushmen, and ancient Near Eastern agriculturalists into a common human experience? Geertz hedges somewhat about this in his argument, but the implication of his essay is clear: at the point when the physiological aspect of the brain-culture unity stabilizes its development, that is, when cranial capacity falls within the modern range. Hence, the psychic unity of contemporary humanity can be dated to a time when organic evolution "slowed to a walk" (Geertz 1973: 69).

In summary, Geertz's model provides us with two markers or criteria for the advent of fully human culture in the archaeological record. The first is the capacity for language, which is the highest expression of a two-sided process: the power of the human mind to construct models of the world and its dependence on cultural (public) objects with which to do it. The second is the leveling off of cerebral development, which can be roughly dated to the Neanderthal period (110,000 to 35,000 years ago; Kottak 1974: 117). If we view both criteria as expressions of the same event, however, we must give a very late date for the development of language, leaving millions of years of hominid evolution with prelinguistic forms of communication. This position runs counter to a great deal of anthropological thinking on the question, yet it was the predominant view of archaeologists and other experts at the 1976 New York Academy of Science's conference on the origins of human language.

THE MOUSTERIAN: A PRE-GENDER CULTURE?

One of the participants at the conference, Glynn Isaac, having devised his own index of complexity, gauges the relative cognitive ability reflected in stone tool assemblages (Isaac 1976). He surveys the entire hominid record and argues that tools attained a certain minimum adaptive efficiency very early; their increased differentiation and standardization beyond that minimum point reflects an increase in cortical development. When he combines the complexity of tool assemblages with the archaeological evidence for ritual, he concludes that the period dating from 200,000 to 40,000 years ago was "transitional between subhuman and fully human capabilities" (1976: 283).

Another discussant, Alexander Marshack, lays greater emphasis on symbolic material. He says of the Mousterian (Neanderthal culture dating from 110,000 to 35,000 years ago):

> Add to the above artifacts the evidence of ritual burial and the ceremonial arrangements of bones and skulls, and one has a picture of a symbolized cultural complexity that was fully *sapiens*.[Marshack 1976: 305]

The artifacts that Marshack refers to are objects incised with patterns that recur repeatedly. The incised pattern represents a mapping of one symbolic system onto the symbolic form of the object itself: a complex and sophisticated mental operation.

Marshack is convinced that the evidence for language is to be sought in these kinds of nonutilitarian artifacts and in evidence of ritual behavior such as burials, grave offerings, and cult complexes rather than tool making and subsistence activities. He argues that tool making is a visible activity that proceeds to verifiable ends and does not require the complex use of language. On the contrary, it is behavior that suggests the unseen, unknowable, and unverifiable that bespeaks of a complex symbolic process. Hence, Marshack's conclusion: Mousterian culture, with its consistent evidence of ritual and linguistic behavior, expresses the fully human nature of our Neanderthal ancestors.

The last participant I will discuss here is Julian Jaynes, who also argues for the beginnings of language in the late Pleistocene (after 70,000 B.C.). He maintains, even more forcefully than Marshack, that tool making and other subsistence skills do not require language for their transmission. He is worth quoting at length.

> At this point, some objections could possibly be raised. How was it possible for proto-man to function, to live in caves, to hunt, to use fire, to make pebble choppers or hand axes if he could not speak? The answer is that he communicated just like all the other primates, with an abundance of visual, vocal, and tactile signals very far removed from the syntactical language that we practice today. Nor is language necessary for the transmission of such rudimentary skills as simple tool using and making from one generation to another. Indeed language might even have hindered. It is almost impossible to describe the method for chipping flints to make simple choppers and hand axes with language. This art was transmitted solely by imitation in exactly the same way in which chimpanzees transmit the trick of inserting vine stems into ant hills to get ants or Japanese Macaques the method of using leaf-sponges and other nutrient-handling tasks that have then diffused without vocal language. In our own culture, it is doubtful if language is at all necessary in the transmission of such skills as swimming, riding, or other motor skills. [Jaynes 1976: 314]

In summary, given the evidence for language and the modern size of the brain, for all or part of the sixty to seventy thousand year period of the Mousterian, we can reasonably assume that we and the Neanderthals share a psychic unity. This becomes meaningful when considered together with the absence of gender symbolism throughout this period. As a minimum it indicates that the gender transformation of society is a possible interpretation. I want to stress that possible interpretations are just that: *possible* interpretations. Nothing like verification or proof is being suggested here. Anything approaching confirmation would entail a large-scale and detailed weighing of the mass of data from the Mousterian and Upper Paleolithic against the features of the model; I leave it to those more qualified than myself to determine whether a nonkinship, sociocultural model proves superior in being able to account for prehistoric materials. At the very least I would hope that this suggestive application of the model will convince some archaeologists that there may be a definable historical limit beyond which we can no longer read back the current realities of gender and kinship.

Conclusion

In seeking the origins of gender I have admittedly taken an extreme position. I began with a few ideas, gave them a logic and some room to develop, and then set them free only to find them far afield of intuition and common sense. A world without gender is, after all, unthinkable, and a self without gender self a seeming absurdity. But as Marx noted well over a hundred years ago, "The forming of the five senses is the labor of the entire history of the world down to the present" (Marx 1844: 108). Can any less be said of common sense or self sense than of the five senses?

A look to the future is the unspoken purpose of backward-looking origin investigations. This is not unreasonable; the past and future meet in the collective image of our humanity and that image is more faithfully projected there than in present realities. For this reason anthropology must always come back to ultimate questions: From where? To where? Asking these questions defines the humanity of the discipline. So, as I began this essay by comparing the historical relativity of gender and kinship with the historical relativity of class, let me now end it by projecting the gender-class relationship as a question about the future.

Many of us have come to see that human liberation is contingent on the eventual end of the state – the ultimate institution of hierarchy – and of the class system in which it is embedded. We naively assumed this would mean the end of sexism as well; however, Rubin, Ortner, and others have shown us that gender hierarchy has a life of its own. But can the gender system be *re-formed* any more than the class system can? Is sexual equality anything more than a way station on the road to total sexual liberation?; and does human liberation demand anything less than the end of the gender system itself? In Rubin's words, do we need "a revolution of kinship" as well as in polity?

Notes

1 This essay grew out of Sherry Ortner's gender course at the University of Michigan. I am indebted to her not only for creative inspiration and encouragement but for her critical reading and rereading of the text. Others have been equally essential in seeing this work to its final form. Bruce Knauft, Kathy Loring, and Harriet Whitehead have taken time out of very cramped schedules to read one or more drafts of the essay and to discuss with me their recommendations, approvals, and reservations. Although the responsibility for the content of this essay is solely mine, I have incorporated the suggestions of all these critics whenever possible.
2 See Naomi Quinn's thorough survey (Quinn 1977) for a useful guide to the gender literature.
3 Pitt-Rivers is explicit about the cultural nature of consubstantiality.
   He says:

   > The "substance" on which consubstantiality is founded is the *notion* of substance only, a notion as far divorced from the physical scientist's concept as that of Christian consubstantiality . . . Thus, blood, saliva, semen, milk, meat, fruit, vegetables or beer can make consubstantial those who are related through no womb, vagina or breast. [1973: 92, 93]

   This strikingly broad and flexible idea of consubstantiality can be achieved in an equally impressive number of ways. Two interesting cases cited by Pitt-Rivers are: Through an act of love a man and a woman "become one flesh" in Christian marriage; and brotherhood can be established among the Eskimos by virtue of being delivered by the same midwife.
      Although consubstantiation is a necessary element of kinship, the converse is not true. Many nonkinship bonds are established using the idea of shared substance,

for example, various kinds of ''blood'' brotherhood. Consider, also, the ritual of Holy Communion in which Christian community is confirmed by those who partake of the body and blood of Christ.

4 Harold Scheffler articulates this position in his critique of David Schneider's *American kinship: a cultural account* (Scheffler 1976). Scheffler argues that American kinship is defined by the notion of shared ''blood'' (the American procreative ideology); in-laws, ''step'' relatives, adopted relatives, and other classes of relatives are ''simple'' and metaphoric extensions of this distinctive feature of common blood. In contrast to Schneider he maintains that codes of behavior and legal and social rituals are nondistinctive features of the American notion of what constitutes a relative. Although nondistinctive, these features are, however, important to what kinship signifies: the meaning of kinship as opposed to the definition of a relative.

5 Rubin's paper (1975: 178–80) contains the first and only reference to this idea that I have come across.

6 The reader may wish to consult Aberle et al. 1971: 346–55; Ellis 1963: 123–32; and Fox 1967: 54–76 for capsule descriptions of the main approaches to the incest issue.

7 See, for example, Murdock's handling of this issue (Murdock 1949: 13, 266).

8 Despite Fox's generalization, ''No society (I believe) is bloody-minded enough to ban sex from marriage'' (1967: 54) there is at least one important exception. In thirty Southern Bantu societies the practice of women taking ''female husbands'' is legitimate and not uncommon. This formal marriage arrangement does not include homosexual sex; ''husbands'' allow their wives male lovers in order to produce heirs – an important function of this type of marriage. Interestingly, this form of ritual marriage is prevalent among royal or politically prominent women (O'Brien 1977: 107).

9 Such are the views of Norbert Bischof (1975), who maintains that the incest taboo is a cultural expression of a genetically based tendency to avoid inbreeding. He points to behavioral mechanisms in the animal world that prevent close matings and then argues that because this is adaptive it eventually becomes part of the genetic code; in this way homo sapiens have acquired an innate predisposition to avoid close matings. Citing Bischof's work specifically in a recent paper, Frank Livingstone vigorously argues against the weaknesses in this position (1978). He first disputes Bischof's assertion that close matings are rare in the wild with evidence to the contrary; and then notes that if there is selection against close matings it is not operating in many populations all over the world where we find very high inbreeding coefficients. For example, the Yanomamo have a coefficient of 0.5; pure brother–sister mating would yield a coefficient of only 0.25! Why, asks Livingstone, are only some kinds of close matings selected against and not others? Here, he zeros in on the confusion alluded to: Bischof wants to argue that just as there is a close fit between mating and genealogical distance among subhumans (debatable), so also with homo sapiens, but it is just not so.

10 In Chapter 2 of his book *Comparative studies in kinship*, Goody (1969) notes that it is not only the classificatory schemes that differ but the sanctions associated with the types of sexual offenses and the severity of the emotional reactions to those offenses. Hence, among the Ashanti, father–daughter incest, although punished as severely as mother–son incest, is classed with a different set of sexual prohibitions. And again, contrary to our cultural expectations, the patrilineal Tallensi consider brother–sister sex disreputable but less serious than the heinous crime of having sex with the wife of a clan brother. The matrilineal Ashanti, closer to our expectations,

reverse these moral judgments. Goody's point is that our culture-specific distinction between adultery and incest is based on our bilateral notion of kinship and may be inappropriate and misleading when applied to other cultures, particularly unilineal ones. He argues that the descent and/or alliance structure of a society orders the way the domain of sexual restrictions is cognized and how sanctions are applied. Goody suggests a critical analytic distinction for the cross-cultural study of sexual restrictions: intragroup prohibitions versus group-wife prohibitions.

This distinction is useful, particularly in societies characterized by unilineal corporate descent groups, but it is not sufficient in accounting for the general nature of sexual prohibitions. The attempt to reduce incest to social-structure determinants (descent/alliance) is doomed to severe limitation. The universality or near universality of intrafamilial prohibitions, prohibitions on homosexuality (or restrictions on heterosexuality), must be approached from the more basic principles that organize the structure of gender relations, and from an analysis of the way those principles in turn shape dynamics in the socializing unit, psychosexual development, and psychodynamic processes in general.

11 The idea of promiscuity, as used by the early evolutionists, denoted the contrast between the original, immoral condition of humanity and its ultimate stage of monogamous family life, i.e., the moral perfection of Western civilization. Through a series of stages or key developments humankind moved from licentiousness to chastity. Thus, certain forms of non-Western marriage – polygamy, polyandry – were viewed as moral improvements compared to the absolute promiscuity of the original state. The task of laying out the moral evolution of the species is typified in the works of C. S. Wake (1878), Westermarck (1922), and C. M. Williams (1893); but the idea of moral advancement is deeply ingrained even in the works of the more social-structural evolutionists – Morgan (1871), Bachofen (1861), McLennan (1886), and Lubbock (1871).

Needless to say, the idea of the bisexual horde and of pre-gender society has nothing in common with these moralizing outlooks. Furthermore it should be noted that, in contrast to the concept of a pre-gender society, the promiscuous horde is a formless condition on the boundary between nature and culture, no more than a staging area for a particular evolutionary schema. Pre-gender society, on the other hand, is a structured and fully human culture. As a final contrast, the early evolutionists implicitly assumed that primeval promiscuity was heterosexual promiscuity. Exclusive heterosexuality was taken as a given fact of nature and not, as I insist here, a structural element of a culture.

12 The following are some of Freud's important writings on the subject of psychosexual development: 1905; 1915; 1923a; 1923b; 1924; 1925; 1931.

13 The reader may wish to pursue the following references, which exemplify Freud's varying usage of the concept, including its "racial" or historical aspects: Fliess (1956: 41–2); Freud (1905: 572, 617, 627; 1923a: 36–9; 1930: 99, 100).

14 Both Mitchell (1974: 42–52) and Stoller (1943) recount the complex and by no means consistent way Freud uses the concept of bisexuality: biologically, as the inherent bipolar potentiality of living tissue; psychically, as both pre-genital sexuality and as the androgynous nature of psychic processes in general; and finally sociologically, in connection with conventionalized aspects of male–female sex roles. The idea of bisexuality is central to Freud's whole enterprise; it challenged and frustrated him throughout his career, during which it evolved away from the biological and toward the psychic. Yet at the end of Freud's life it still remained, in Mitchell's words, "the unsolved crux of the matter" (Mitchell 1974: 49).

15 See Ricoeur 1970: 65–7, 368, 369, 375; Mitchell 1974: 22.

16 The author of *Freud and philosophy* also sheds critical light on the nature of psychoanalytic culture theory. With dream work and symptom formation as the models of the cultural process, regression comes to the fore as the key concept in Freud's cultural analysis. Dreaming is a kind of temporary, nocturnal regression in which the unconscious expresses forbidden, repressed ideas by means of a *pre-existing* stock of cultural symbols. That is, the dream work is not a creative process but rather the rehash of an old problem with stereotypic cultural symbols. Similarly, neurotic symptoms are the return of past, repressed traumas in an altered form. Ricoeur identifies the central difficulty: Psychoanalysis has no way of dealing with the genesis of *new* meanings; hence it must look to past events for the birth of critical meanings (Ricoeur 1970: 512). This partly explains Freud's steadfast adherence to phylogenetic inheritance of ideas, in the face of considerable opposition within and without psychoanalytic circles (Paul 1976: 312–14). Thus, Ricoeur characterizes Freud's ideas on culture as an "archaeology" and "a revelation of the archaic, a manifestation of the ever prior" (Ricoeur 1970: 440).

This judgment must be altered somewhat by Freud's final typology of the instincts (Freud 1921; 1930) into Eros (life instincts) and Thanatos (death instincts). Here culture is the outcome of the cosmic struggle between Eros and Thanatos, assisted by Ananke (necessity). Although this new formulation moves decidedly away from reductionism it is doubtful that many cultural theorists have found it useful. Most, like Geza Roheim, have looked to Freud's earlier works. Roheim's work is typical of this approach, which views *whole* cultures as so many different manifestations of neurotic fixation, each stuck at some point along the psychosexual continuum (Roheim 1943: 81–2).

17 Ricoeur 1970: 207, 208.

18 Of course, Marcuse never refers to pre-gender society. In fact, his distinction of "civilization" versus primitive society is quite vague. His clear implication, however, is that nonrepressive sexuality may have been possible in a prior (primitive) nonstratified society and a definite possibility in the classless society of the future (see 1955: 215–17).

19 Marcuse develops most of this thinking in his Chapter 10, "The Transformation of Sexuality into Eros."

20 Oceania: Levy 1973 and Carroll 1970; Eskimos: Friedl 1975: 42; West Indies: Sanford 1974; African: Schildkrout 1973.

Adoption everywhere is a complex and multifunctional institution. The alliance aspect of adoption in the enumerated societies distinguishes it from: (a) adoption in contemporary Western societies where it functions primarily to rescue children from an inadequate domestic system; and (b) adoption in traditional Eurasion societies (Roman, Greek, Chinese, Hindu India) where it served as a method of obtaining heirs for childless family and lineage heads. In the former, the child has a problem and in the latter the parent has one. Goody (1969) discusses this and other contrasts.

The term alliance is used here in a broad sense to include both interkin group bonds and interpersonal networks. In Oceanic and West Indian societies adoption takes place mostly within the kin group but African adoption effects both types of alliance. To a large extent the kin/nonkin distinction is blurred by the interesting fact reported by Schildkrout that child fostering creates, maintains, and solidifies kinship bonds (1973: 59, 60). Thus, adoption is an important way that urban Ghanaians have of extending kinship across ethnic lines in communities where dozens of different ethnic groups have taken up common residence.

In all of the societies in question, parenthood, viewed as a bundle of rights and responsibilities, tends to be distributed over a wide segment of the kinship network.

Hence, parents' siblings and parents' parents often exercise these rights as a request for a child.

Adoption, then, seems to have alliance functions analogous to marriage, although there are no ethnographic cases, to my knowledge, where child exchange replaces marriage or is the main alliance mechanism. An interesting case in which the adoption system and the marriage system are articulated into one institution is the *pogsime* of the West African Mossi. Here, chiefs make adoption claims on their subjects' children; in return they give their adopted daughters back to their subjects as brides. (Male adoptees become palace servants and officials.) Schildkrout explains that this institution is not limited to the chieftainship. Mossi lineage heads also engage in this two-way exchange of adopted daughters, although on a less spectacular scale (1973: 51).

21 Mary Douglas has developed this idea extensively in her book, *Purity and danger* (See, for example, pp. 16–40).

22 Jean Hiernaux's (1964: 486–95) work is an eloquent example of this position. Echoing an earlier paper by Livingstone (1962), he argues that the whole attempt to apply a concept of race to human variation has been and is doomed to failure because human genetic variation is inherently unclassifiable. All attempts at racial classification that have divided the human species from three to a theoretical upper limit of a million races are arbitrary breakdowns based on some select group of characteristics; change the characters and the taxonomy is altered. The arbitrary character of classificatory schemes means that they can tell us little about human phylogeny and the evolutionary processes that have given rise to the bewildering array of human variation. Hiernaux then asks, why spend so much energy on an enterprise that is nonproductive and even misleading?

The construction of a racial taxonomy based on true classificatory principles would, in Hiernaux's judgment, involve: (a) grouping human populations by enough genetic criteria so that any addition of characteristics to the schema would not alter the taxonomy; and (b) classifying groups in such a way that the genetic variation between categories is greater than the range of variation within them. The feasibility of (a) is problematic but even if it were possible, argues Hiernaux, (b) has not been and probably never will be achievable. Based on his own work in Central Africa and the endeavors of others, Hiernaux shows that genetic variation just refuses to ''cluster.'' Invariably, the populations at the extreme ends of racial taxa have more in common with populations in adjacent taxa than they do with populations within their own class. The author concludes that human variation is essentially continuous and not susceptible to genuine classification.

23 My point is not that upper-crust ideologists such as Henry Cabot Lodge, Frances A. Walker, Charles B. Davenport, and Madison Grant singlehandedly created American racism. They did, however, shape American nativist sentiment along racial lines and furthermore, systematized and elaborated the already existing racial model by wedding it (albeit in a distorted way) to Mendelian genetics and Darwinian evolutionary theory. The result was a new ''scientific racism'' considerably more virulent than the racial ideologies of the early nineteenth century. Higham's chapter, ''Toward racism: the history of an idea'' is a particularly useful account of this process.

24 In passing it should be noted, the view that both homosexuality and heterosexuality are permutations or possible outcomes of the same underlying gender process runs parallel to the psychoanalytic account. In the more mature thought of Freud, the outcome of psychosexual development is decribed as a complex, four-way identification of the child – positive and negative for both the same-sex and the cross-sex parent (see Freud 1923: 31–4).

25 Again I stress that we are not discussing heterosexuality or homosexuality at the behavioral level but at the ideological. (The relationship between sexual ideology and sexual behavior in preliterate cultures may theoretically cover all the possibilities except two: A homosexual society that never violated its ideal would obviously not be in an ethnographic sample for very long, nor would an ideologically heterosexual society that always broke the rules.) "Dominance" here means the following: (a) the total exclusion of one or the other of the possible structural outcomes of the polarization of sexuality; (b) the restriction of homosexuality or hetereosexuality to some limited but legitimate domain; and (c) symbolic dominance of the kind outlined by Rabinow (1975). Proceeding in reverse order, examples of (c) can be found in societies in which actual homosexual relations are expressed at least partially in a heterosexual idiom or where the actors themselves see their relations as heterosexual. Same-sex marriages consequent to the ritual change of gender status (see the section on "Ideology versus biology") should be viewed in this way, as should certain forms of institutionalized homosexuality, as among the ancient Greeks, in which one of the partners was expected to conform to "feminine" ideals (Slater 1968: 61, 62). Dominance in the second sense is illustrated in the several societies that, although predominantly heterosexual, prescribe homosexual relations within certain well-defined situations, for example, between young initiates and unmarried men (Ford and Beach 1951: 132). Cases of simple exclusion are perhaps rarer (a) but it would appear that the heterosexual Sherpas come very close (Ortner, personal communication). What can be said, then, about the broad, cross-cultural outlines of the relationship between homosexual model and heterosexual model within the present framework?

In either the Rabinowian sense or in the sense of (b), I cannot think of any examples in which homosexuality is the dominant model. Certain New Guinea societies, however, in which institutional homosexuality is clearly preferred, would seem to be cases of dominance in the first sense, i.e., exclusion. That is, homosexuality is not only the preferred model but heterosexuality is looked on as dangerous and polluting. (The already cited Etoro are a good case in point. See Kelly 1976). In many New Guinea societies, the two models of sexual behavior are antagonistic and the overall tendency is toward the exclusion of heterosexuality. Indeed, in some of these societies there is evidence that the strain to bring behavior in line with ideology may be bringing them to the brink of extinction (Tom Ernst, personal communication).

Overall, it appears that we can find many primitive societies in which the heterosexual model is dominant in all three senses I have outlined, but few in which homosexuality molds ideological dominance and then only in an exclusive sense. In the text, in the section on "Heterosexuality and genderized sex," I set forth symbolic and psychological reasons why I think heterosexuality as a dominant ideology is the more common route. It in no way, however, explains why homosexuality is dominant in some societies, achieves subdominance, or is excluded in others. That is well outside the scope of this essay.

26 The reader should note that the regular practice of betrothing children is not uncommon in the ethnographic record (Lévi-Strauss 1971: 345).

27 Leroi-Gourhan is one of the leading analysts of Upper Paleolithic symbolic remains; his work is unquestionably the most systematic and extensive on the subject. Another key student of the period is Alexander Marshack, whose book, *The roots of civilization*, although significant in its own right, is important to us here because it claims to be a critique of Leroi-Gourhan's position. By way of introduction, it should be noted that Marshack's research is predominantly confined to small, moveable artifacts of the Upper Paleolithic and not the impressive

cave art. Therefore, although his analysis tends to be more intensive it lacks the extensiveness and completeness of Leroi-Gourhan's.

The emphasis of Marshack's critique is that some of the signs and figures that Leroi-Gourhan calls "sexual" are in fact elements of myth, folk tales, or notational devices and are not primarily sexual (1972: 148, 173, 196, 221–7, 296, 297, 305, 311–13, 318). A careful reading of Marshack's fascinating book will convince the reader that the author misreads Leroi-Gourhan and fails to appreciate the fact that the two interpretations are perfectly compatible with each other. Leroi-Gourhan's concern is with the broad outlines of a system of signs – the deep structure of Paleolithic symbolism. Marshack, on the other hand, deals with the content and function of certain sets of symbols. These are two different kinds of analysis and need not be – are not – contradictory.

Marshack reads Leroi-Gourhan's use of the word "sexual" much too narrowly. It is clear from Leroi-Gourhan's argument that he is really talking about a dualistic, gender worldview – a worldview more than capable of subsuming the multiplicity of ecological, folk and mythic meanings that Marshack says Paleolithic art embodies. In fact, on more than one occasion Marshack notes the multiplicity of meanings in Paleolithic symbolism (1972: 261–75) but cannot reconcile himself to the idea that Leroi-Gourhan's deep structural approach may encompass the polysemy.

References

Aberle, David F.; Miller, Daniel F.; Bronfenbrenner, U.; Schneider, David M.; Hess, E. H.; and Spuhler, J. N. 1963. "The incest taboo and the mating patterns of animals." Reprinted in *Readings in kinship and social structure*, ed. Nelson Graburn, pp. 346–55. New York: Harper and Row.

Bachofen, J. J. 1861. *Das Mutterecht*. Stuttgart: Krais and Hoffman.

Barnes, J. A. 1973. "Genetrix: genitor:: nature: culture?" In *The character of kinship*, ed. Jack Goody, pp. 61–73. Cambridge: Cambridge University Press.

Beach, Frank A. 1947. "Evolutionary changes in the physiological control of mating behavior in mammals. *The Psychological Review* 54: 297–313.

Bischof, Norbert. 1975. "Comparative ethology of incest avoidance." In *Biosocial anthropology*, ed. Robin Fox, pp. 37–67. New York: Wiley.

Buchler, I. R., and Selby, Henry A. 1968. *Kinship and social organization: an introduction to theory and method*. New York: Macmillan.

Carroll, Vern. 1970. *Adoption in Eastern Oceania*. Honolulu: University of Hawaii Press.

Chodorow, Nancy. 1974. "Family structure and feminine personality." In *Woman, culture and society*, eds. Michelle Zimbalist Rosaldo and Louise Lamphere, pp. 42–66. Stanford: Stanford University Press.

Curran, Thomas J. 1975. *Xenophobia and immigration, 1820–1930*. Boston: Twayne.

Douglas, Mary. 1966. *Purity and danger: an analysis of concepts of pollution and taboo*. London: Routledge and Kegan Paul.

Edgerton, Robert. 1964. "Pokot intersexuality: an East African example of the resolution of sexual incongruity." *American Anthropologist* 66: 1288–99.

Ellis, Albert. 1963. "The origins and the development of the incest taboo." In *Incest: the nature and origin of the taboo*, by Emile Durkheim, pp. 121–74. New York: Lyle Stuart.

Evans-Pritchard, E. E. 1970. *The Nuer: a description of the modes of livelihood and political institutions of a Nilotic people*. Oxford: Oxford University Press.

Ferenczi, Sandor. 1968. *Thalassa: a theory of genitality*. New York: Norton.

Fliess, Robert. 1956. *Erogeneity and libido*. New York: International Universities Press.

Ford, Clellan S. and Beach, Frank A. 1951. *Patterns of sexual behavior*. New York: Harper and Brothers.

Fox, Robin. 1967. *Kinship and marriage: an anthropological perspective*. Harmondsworth, Middlesex, England: Penguin Books.

Freud, Sigmund. 1915. "Instincts and their vicissitudes." In *The standard edition of the complete psychological works of Sigmund Freud*, ed. James Strachey. Vol. 14: 111–40. London: The Hogarth Press and The Institute of Psychoanalysis.

    1921. "Beyond the Pleasure Principle." In *Ibid.*, Vol. 18: 3–64.

    1923a. "The ego and the id." In *Ibid.* Vol. 19: 3–66.

    1923b. "The infantile genital organization: an interpolation into the theory of sexuality." In *Ibid.* Vol 19: 14–145.

    1924. "The dissolution of the Oedipus complex." In *Ibid.* Vol. 19: 172–9.

    1925. "Some psychical consequences of the anatomical distinction between the sexes." In *Ibid.* Vol. 19: 243–58.

    1930. "Civilization and its discontents." In *Ibid.* Vol. 21: 59–145.

    1931. "Female sexuality." In *Ibid.* Vol. 21: 223–43.

    1938. "Three contributions to the theory of sex." In *The basic writings of Sigmund Freud*, ed. A.A. Brill, pp. 553–629. New York: Random House.

Friedl, Ernestine. 1975. *Women and men: an anthropologist's view*. New York: Holt, Rinehart and Winston.

Geertz, Clifford. 1973. *The interpretation of cultures*. New York: Basic Books.

Godelier, Maurice. 1975. "Modes of production, kinship and demographic structures." In *Marxist analyses and social anthropology*, ed. Maurice Bloch, pp. 3–27. London: Malaby Press.

Goody, Jack. 1969. *Comparative studies in kinship*. Stanford: Stanford University Press.

    1969. "Adoption in cross-cultural perspective." *Comparative Studies in Society and History* 17: 55–78.

Hiernaux, Jean. 1964. "The concept of race and the taxonomy of mankind." Reprinted in *The origin and evolution of man: readings in physical anthropology*, ed. Ashley Montagu, pp. 486–95. New York: Thomas Y. Crowell.

Higham, John. 1955. *Strangers in the land: patterns of American nativism 1860–1925*. New Brunswick, N.J.: Rutgers University Press.

Isaac, Glynn L. 1976. "Stages of cultural elaboration in the Pleistocene: possible archaeological indicators of the development of language capabilities." In *Origins and evolution of language and speech*, ed. Stevan R. Harnad, Horst D. Steklis, and Jane Lancaster. Annals of the New York Academy of Sciences, 280: 275-88.

Jaynes, Julian. 1976. "The evolution of language in the Late Pleistocene." In *Origins and evolution of language and speech*, ed. Stevan R. Harnad, Horst D. Steklis, and Jane Lancaster. Annals of the New York Academy of Sciences, 280: 312–25.

Kelly, Raymond C. 1976. "Witchcraft and sexual relations." In *Man and woman in the New Guinea Highlands*, eds. P. Brown and G. Buchbinder. Washington, D.C.: American Anthropological Association.

Kottak, Conrad P. 1974. *Anthropology: the exploration of human diversity*. New York: Random House.

Leroi-Gourhan, André. 1968. *The art of prehistoric man in Europe*. London: Thames and Hudson.

    1968a. "The evolution of Paleolithic art." *Scientific American* 218: 59–66.

Lévi-Strauss, Claude. 1967. *Structural anthropology*. Garden City, N.Y.: Doubleday.
    1971. "The family." In *Man, culture and society*, ed. Harry L. Shapiro, pp. 333–57.
    London: Oxford University Press.
Levy, Robert I. 1973. *Tahitians: mind and experience in the Society Islands*. Chicago:
    University of Chicago Press.
Livingstone, Frank. 1962. "On the nonexistence of human races." *Current Anthro-
    pology* 3: 279–81.
    1978. *Biological and cultural determinants of human behavior*. Manuscript.
Lubbock, John. 1871. *The origin of civilization and the primitive condition of man*. New
    York: D. Appleton and Company.
Marcuse, Herbert. 1955. *Eros and civilization: a philosophical inquiry into Freud*.
    Boston: Beacon Press.
Marshack, Alexander. 1972. *The roots of civilization: the cognitive beginnings of
    man's first art, symbol and notation*. New York: McGraw-Hill.
    1976. "Some implications of the Paleolithic symbolic evidence for the origin of
    language." In *Origins and evolution of language and speech*, eds. Stevan R.
    Harnad, Horst D. Steklis, and Jane Lancaster. Annals of the New York Academy
    of Sciences, 280: 289–311.
Martin, M. K. and Voorhies, Barbara. 1975. *Female of the species*. New York:
    Columbia University Press.
Marx, Karl. 1961. *Economic and philosophic manuscripts of 1844*. Moscow: Foreign
    Languages Publishing House.
McLennan, John Ferguson. 1886. *Studies in ancient history*. London: Macmillan and Co.
Mitchell, Juliet. 1974. *Psychoanalysis and feminism*. New York: Pantheon Books.
Money, John. 1965. "Psychosexual differentiation." In *Sex research: new develop-
    ments*, ed. John Money, pp. 3–23. New York: Holt, Rinehart and Winston.
Money, John and Tucker, Patricia. 1975. *Sexual signatures: on being a man or a
    woman*. Boston: Little, Brown and Company.
Morgan, Lewis H. 1871. *Systems of consanguinity and affinity*. Smithsonian Contribu-
    tions to Knowledge. Vol. 17. Washington, D.C.: Smithsonian Institute.
Movius, Hallam L. 1961. "Aspects of Upper Paleolithic art." In *Three regions of
    primitive art*, eds. Hallam L. Movius, S. Kooijam, and George Kubler, pp.
    12–40. New York: University Publishers.
Murdock, George P. 1949. *Social structure*. New York: The Free Press.
Needham, Rodney. 1971. "Remarks on the analysis of kinship and marriage." In
    Rethinking kinship and marriage, ed. Rodney Needham, pp. 1–34. London:
    Tavistock Publications.
Oakley, Ann. 1972. *Sex, gender and society*. London: Temple Smith.
O'Brien, Denise. 1977. "Female husbands in Southern Bantu societies." In *Sexual
    stratification: a cross-cultural view*, ed. Alice Schlegel, pp. 109–26. New
    York: Columbia University Press.
Ortner, Sherry B. 1974. "Is female to male as nature is to culture?" In *Woman, culture
    and society*, eds. Michelle Zimbalist Rosaldo and Louise Lamphere, pp. 67–87.
    Stanford: Stanford University Press.
Paul, Robert A. 1976. "Did the primal crime take place?" *Ethos* 4: 311–52.
Pitt-Rivers, Julian. 1973. "The kith and the kin." In *The character of kinship*, ed.
    Jack Goody, pp. 89–105. Cambridge: Cambridge University Press.
Pomeroy, W. B. 1969. "Homosexuality." In *The same sex: an appraisal of homo-
    sexuality*, ed. Ralph W. Weltge, pp. 3–13. Philadelphia: Pilgrim Press.
Quinn, Naomi. 1977. "Anthropological studies on women's status." *Annual Review
    of Anthropology* 6: 181–225.

Rabinow, Paul. 1975. *Symbolic domination*. Chicago: University of Chicago Press.

Ricoeur, Paul. 1970. *Freud and philosophy: an essay on interpretation*. New Haven: Yale University Press.

Rivière, P. G. 1971. "Marriage: a reassessment." In *Rethinking kinship and marriage*, ed. Rodney Needham, pp. 57–74. London: Tavistock Publications.

Roheim, Géza. 1943. *The origin and function of culture*. New York: Nervous and Mental Disease Monographs.

Rosaldo, Michelle Z. 1974. "Woman, culture and society: a theoretical overview." In *Woman, culture and society*, eds. Michelle Zimbalist Rosaldo and Louise Lamphere, pp. 17–42. Stanford: Stanford University Press.

Rosenzweig, Saul. 1973. "Human sexual autonomy as an evolutionary attainment, anticipating proceptive sex choice and idiodynamic bisexuality." In *Contemporary sexual behavior: critical issues for the 70's*, eds. J. Zubin and John Money, pp. 189–229. Baltimore: Johns Hopkins University Press.

Rubin, Gayle. 1975. "The traffic in women: notes on the political economy of sex." In *Toward an anthropology of women*, ed. Rayna R. Reiter, pp. 157–210. New York: Monthly Review Press.

Sanford, Margaret. 1974. "A socialization in ambiguity: child lending in a British West Indian society." *Ethnology* 13: 393–400.

Scheffler, Harold W. 1976. "The meaning of kinship in American culture: another view." In *Meaning in anthropology*, eds. Keith H. Basso and Henry A. Selby, pp. 57–91. Albuquerque: University of New Mexico Press.

Schildkrout, Enid. 1973. "The fostering of children in urban Ghana: problems of ethnographic analysis in a multi-cultural context." *Urban Anthropology* 2: 48–73.

Schneider, David M. 1968. *American kinship: a cultural account*. Englewood Cliffs, N.J.: Pretice-Hall.

Singer, June. 1977. *Androgyny: toward a new theory of sexuality*. Garden City, N.Y.: Anchor Press/Doubleday.

Slater, Phillip. 1968. *The glory of Hera: Greek mythology and the Greek family*. Boston: Beacon Press.

Stoller, Robert J. 1974. "Facts and fancies: an examination of Freud's concep of bisexuality (1973)." In *Women and analysis: dialogues on psychoanalytic views of femininity*, pp. 343–64.

Stuckert, Robert P. 1959. "African ancestry of the white American population." Reprinted in *The origin and evolution of man: readings in physical anthropology*, ed. Ashley Montagu, pp. 558–64. New York: Thomas Y. Crowell.

Tanner, Nancy and Zihlman, Adrienne. 1976. "Women in evolution. Part I: Innovation and selection in human origins. *Signs* (Spring 1976): 585–608.

Wake, C. S. 1878. *The evolution of morality: being a history of the development of moral culture*. Vol. 1. London: Trubner and Co.

Weiss, Richard. 1970. "Racism in the era of industrialism." In *The great fear: race in the mind of America*, eds. Gary B. Nash and Richard Weiss, pp. 121–43. New York: Holt, Rinehart and Winston.

Westermarck, Edward. 1922. *The history of human marriage*. Vol. 1. New York: The Allerton Book Company.

Williams, C. M. 1893. *Evolutional ethics: a review of systems of ethics founded on the theory of evolution*. New York: Macmillan.

Wilson, H. C. and Yengoyan, Aram A. 1976. "Couvade: an example of adaptation by the formation of ritual groups." *Michigan Discussions in Anthropology*. Vol. 1: 111–33.

Witherspoon, Gary. 1976. "Kinship and human procreative process." *Michigan Discussions in Anthropology*. Vol. 2: 29–45.

2

The bow and the burden strap: A NEW LOOK AT INSTITUTIONALIZED HOMOSEXUALITY IN NATIVE NORTH AMERICA

Harriet Whitehead

Sexual exoticisms in exotic lands, when they are highlighted in the social science literature, typically appear not exotic at all but seem instead to be familiar items from our own sexual behavioral repertoire dressed up in foreign garb. The moral of the social scientist's discussion is often that a particular element of our sexual behavior appears in other cultures, but in other places meets a different cultural fate. Sexuality itself, that infinitely variable human capacity, paradoxically presents us with few surprises, but cultural responses to it are wildly unpredictable.

Nowhere does this construction of the data appear more commonly than in the case of what is called in the literature "institutionalized homosexuality." The homosexuality that other societies prescribe or condone is immediately taken to be something very much like one of the forms of homosexuality familiar to the modern West, and the explanation of the foreign culture's institutionalizing response, when offered, proceeds in accordance with the chosen meaning of the behavior in our own culture. Is homosexual behavior the result of an enduring erotic disposition to which a certain percentage of the population will inevitably fall prey? If so, it is noted that certain other cultures meet this universal problem by providing a specialized niche for such individuals (Kroeber 1940). Is homosexuality the result of irregularities in the early socialization process? In that case, those cultures in which it is widespread or institutionalized must have a correspondingly widespread or institutionalized kink in their early socialization processes (Slater 1968). Is homosexuality a practice to which people resort when heterosexual outlets are unavailable? Then look to the barriers that exist in some cultures against heterosexual expression (Bullough 1976). And so on. It is evident from the approaches cited that there is not much agreement as to what this phenomenon is that is supposedly the same wherever we find it. In fact, a good many of the cross-cultural investigations have been, explicitly or implicitly, aimed at mustering support for one or another interpretation of "our" homosexuality rather than at laying bare the meaning of "theirs."

A corollary of this ethnocentrism of interest is an anthropological solecism that often appears in studies of this sort, that of interpreting the styles of homosexuality that are fully institutionalized in the light of those that are not (again, "theirs" in the light of "ours"). Intriguing though the similarity of types often is, brief reflection should counsel us that cultural processes (and psychological ones as well) operate in a quite different fashion in behaviors that are formally instituted as opposed to those that are spontaneously expressed. Sexual behaviors that occur within the context of normative expectations tell us something about normative expectations but very little about human desire; and conversely, spontaneous (noninstituted) sexual expressions indicate the presence of characteristic desires without giving us any clear message about the operations of the formal cultural system. The cross-cultural data on spontaneous homosexuality around the world is too deficient to permit much clarification of its nature, but the rate of it in any particular area appears to vary independently of the official cultural "attitude" toward it. The rate may be high where it is condemned (twentieth-century America) or low (Trobriands); low where it is permitted (Nambikwara) or high (Desana). And it is not universal. Some groups genuinely have never heard of homosexuality in any form.[1] In other words, spontaneous expression is neither an automatic outcome of human psychological and social processes, nor is it an artifact of culture in any straightforward sense. (Heterosexual expression might appear equally elusive were it not, in some form, universally "institutionalized.") Whatever the forces are that generate homosexual desires in the population at large and bring these desires to expression, there is no evidence that these same forces, even when intensified, necessarily cause the expression to become formally instituted. Consider the relatively simple case of lack of heterosexual outlet as a motive for homosexual behavior. Among the Azande of Central Africa, young bachelors, deprived of women during their military service to the king, substituted "boy wives" in their place; the practice was explained in terms of substitution, and it was embedded in its own set of rules and standards of decorum (Evans-Pritchard 1970). Here we seem to have an "institution" of sorts flowing straight-forwardly from a structurally engendered need. But we cannot predict when such a principle will operate. Neither the heterosexual deprivation nor the emotional intensity of the sex-segregated upper-class boarding school environment in European societies has been, in the entire history of these establishments, sufficient to produce any comparable acceptance of the resulting homosexual relationships. In native America, as we shall see, spontaneous homosexual expressions appear in societies where a fully institutionalized form is available, but the former, rather than being channeled into the latter is dismissed as some type of possibly dangerous foolishness. If in such cases the natives see no meaningful connection between an instituted form and a spontaneous one, should the anthropologist?

In all fairness to the discipline of cultural anthropology, the theoretical weaknesses in the cross-cultural study of sexuality (not just homosexuality) of which I complain, are largely confined to the "Culture and Personality" school and to assorted theorists from other fields similarly dominated by biological or psychiatric models. More strictly cultural studies have much better fulfilled the anthropological mandate that one put a practice into its cultural context before attempting to generalize about its meaning. These studies have often helped considerably to illuminate the meaning of certain sexual exoticisms, even when not always directly addressing them. The recent studies of New Guinea belief systems and social organization are notable examples. These studies include Kelly (1976), Meigs (1976), Schieffelin (1976), Buchbinder and Rappaport (1976), and Poole (this volume). Because of the nature of New Guinea culture, these studies focus upon sex-roles and sex-related practices and ideas.

One of the customs clarified in this recent literature is that of prescribed man–boy homosexual relationships common throughout the south-central lowlands of New Guinea. These relationships, of limited duration, are similar in intention to ancient Greek pederasty. In both instances it is thought that the younger male generation is raised to full manhood through erotic connection to the older male generation, but the New Guineans, unlike the more abstract Greeks, consider this beneficial result to be a function of the fact that "manhood," in both its physical and cultural aspect, is embodied in semen, hence some regular mode of transmitting the stuff is in order (Kelly 1976: 450; Schieffelin 1976: 124; Van Baal 1966: 493–4). Comparably, full "womanhood," throughout New Guinea, is held to be embodied in menstrual and parturitional blood, and the males of pederastic tribes speculate that women too have some means of transmitting their substance to the next generation (Kelly 1976: 47).

What findings like this make clear is that a particular instituted sexual custom – in this case pederasty – is but one manifestation among many of a way of classifying and thinking about the sexes that, if traced in all its detail (a task I will not undertake here) is found to be rooted both in a wider set of cosmological premises and a characteristic pattern of social privilege and obligation that divides the sex and age categories. Furthermore, it is often the "offbeat" (to our eyes) sexual and sex-related practices such as pederasty (or ritual semen eating, or menstrual pollution taboos, or the use in headhunting of weapons that symbolize copulation, to mention only a few items from the Southern Lowland New Guinea repertoire) that help to bring the native theory most clearly to the fore, probably because being unclouded by obvious utilitarian aims their "symbolic" nature stands out more boldly.

The "peculiarity" reveals the underlying thought system and the underlying thought system explains the peculiarity. This is, of course, one of cultural anthropology's classic findings, now used as a starting premise in most cultural studies. This starting premise is gradually coming into more frequent and more rigorous use in studies of gender and sex-related beliefs and practices everywhere, including the West (see Barker-Benfield 1976; Smith-Rosenberg 1979). This trend has been greatly inspired by recent feminist rejection of the conservative natural-destiny idiom that prevailed in so much previous theory. As the cultural and ideological dimension of sex and gender is made clearer, it is to be hoped that this dimension will be more revealing of the social – as opposed to natural – processes at work in the shaping of sex roles, sexual identity, and even eroticism itself.

In the interests of furthering this enterprise and simultaneously introducing more clarity into the subject of institutionalized homosexuality, it is my intention here to examine the cultural and social underpinnings of another ethnographically well-known style of homosexuality, the transvestitic version that abounded among tribal peoples of northern Asia and North America.[2]

In contrast to New Guinea pederasty wherein a boy was considered to become fully a man through homosexual intercourse, in native North America, it was permissible for a man to become, in important social respects, a woman. Homosexual practice was one of the common accompaniments to this alteration in gender status. In some areas too, a female-to-male transition was possible. These two styles of institutionalized homosexuality, the New Guinea and the North American, (which are the two styles most often encountered in tribal societies), could not be further apart in their primary meaning, and indeed as far as I can determine, they never coexist. The meaning of each is also significantly different from the culturally "recognized" but not instituted homosexuality of the modern West. Yet there is a dimension of similarity (aside from the common element of homoerotic contact) that continues to prompt "theirs"-to-"ours" comparisons, especially in the North American case. The differences and similarities can be sorted out and understood, I will argue, if it is realized that each of the "homosexualities" rests upon a different cultural construction of gender – a different gender system, so to speak – while, at the same time, cultural constructions of gender, however dissimilar in content, all have certain points of structural similarity.

When I speak of cultural constructions of gender, I mean simply the ideas that give social meaning to physical differences between the sexes, rendering two biological classes, male and female, into two social classes, men and women, and making the social relationships in which men and women stand toward each other appear reasonable and appropriate. A social gender dichotomy is present in all known societies in the sense that everywhere anatomic sexual differences observable at birth are used to start tracking the newborn into one or the other of two social role complexes. This minimal pegging of social roles and relationships to observable anatomic sex differences is what creates what we call a "gender" dichtomy in the first place, but in no culture does it exhaust the ideas surrounding the two classes thus minimally constituted. Additional defining features of gender status, some related to further real or further supposed physiological differences between the sexes, and some related to a host of other dimensions, such as fate, temperament, spiritual power, ability, and mythical history, are brought into play as well, and it is these additional hypothesized attributes of the sexes that vary significantly from culture to culture. As we shall see in the case of native North America these additional defining features often form clusters, with one or another feature being, in a sense, the "core" of the cluster. Cultural variation in "gender systems" may then appear both in regard to the content of clusters and in regard to their core features. In addition, as long as gender is not fully defined by any one feature alone, there is always the possibility that for various reasons – and the reasons will vary depending on the gender system – a mixed gender or deficient gender status may arise for certain persons or categories of persons. In New Guinea, boys are "deficient" in manhood, for instance. Although homosexuality does not inevitably accompany such situations, they may provide occasions where it is deemed appropriate: In both New Guinea and native North America the institutionalization of homosexual relations is occasioned by peculiar gender statuses constituted on other grounds. In our own society, by contrast, it is spontaneous homosexual activity as such that occasions the cultural recognition – if not condonement – of a peculiar gender status, that of the ''homosexual.'' All of these points will be considered in further detail as I proceed with the analysis of the native North American gender system and the ''gender-crossers'' who proliferated in the context of it.

A word of caution is needed about the concept ''gender system.'' My ambitions for this term are modest. I am positing here only that there will be some degree of structure in any culture's notions of manhood and womanhood, sexual relations and reproduction. I am not implying that the content of this ''system'' is in any way self-contained. Rather, starting off in the selected area of sex and gender, the investigator will soon find him/herself handling meanings that seemingly take their shape from the ''kinship,'' ''religious,'' ''economic,'' and other systems of the culture in question, just as starting off in any of the latter areas one is apt to receive meanings from the ''gender system.'' Culture is like this: a hall of mirrors. My viewpoint on the culture of gender is close to David Schneider's views on the culture of kinship (Schneider 1968, 1972, 1973). I also take a page from Schneider's book by easing into the analysis of gender systems through a ''defining-features'' approach. I do not wish to imply, however, that such an approach exhausts the analysis.

North American Indian gender concepts and the berdache status

Gender-crossers of some variety have been reported in almost every culture area of native North America. A word is necessary about the objectivity of some of these reports. Very early accounts are typically of this sort:

> It must be confessed that effeminacy and lewdness were carried to the greatest excess in those parts; men were seen to wear the dress of women without a blush, and to debase themselves so as to perform those occupations which are peculiar to the sex, from whence followed a corruption of morals past all expression; it was pretended that this custom came from I know not what principle of religion. [Charlevoix in Katz 1976: 290 in reference to the Iroquois and Illinois]

> Among the women I saw some men dressed like women, with whom they go about regularly, never joining the men . . . From this I inferred they must be hermaphrodites, but from what I learned later I understood that they were sodomites, dedicated to nefarious practices. From all the foregoing I conclude that in this matter of incontinence there will be much to do when the Holy Faith and the Christian religion are established among them. [Font, in Katz 1976: 291 in reference to the Yuman]

Despite the obvious indifference of these early travelers to the niceties of native form and concept, later accounts lead us to believe that their judgments did not so seriously distort the facts as one might at first think. American Indian gender-crossing, which largely takes the form of anatomic males dressing as women and assuming the tasks of women, appears to have been a relatively visible phenomenon. Early travelers and missionaries remark upon the incongruity of these transvestite figures among the natives and we may assume that no extensive knowledge of the indigenous language or close rapport with members of the culture was required to uncover the practice. Even the frequent horrified assertions about sodomy did not necessarily represent a hasty conclusion on the part of these reporters (whose first impulse was to consider them hermaphrodites rather than homosexuals), and such assertions have not proved inconsistent with later, and better, documentation. It is, however, difficult to establish from such accounts the native attitude toward the gender-crosser. One wonders whether in those cases where the ordinary natives were said to share the visitor's disgust with the berdache, he was in fact despised, whereas in those cases where the "nation" as a whole was dismissed as depraved he was respected; but this is undoubtedly too crude a rule of thumb. What is not to be doubted is that some practice similar to the gender-crossing that later and more sophisticated ethnographers have detailed for us existed at one time over an extensive area of the continent. Kroeber was inclined to consider the trait present unless proven absent. Some geographical constriction of it, however, seems to have been afoot from the beginning of the historical period. The berdache role appears to have dwindled drastically or vanished altogether from much of the subarctic and northwest coastal areas by the late nineteenth century, and there is some question of how strong its foothold in these parts ever was (Bancroft 1875, v. 1: 58, 81–2, 92, 415, 515, 773–4; Hallowell 1955: 291–305; Landes 1938: 177, 180; Delaguna 1954: 178). There is no report of it among the Eskimo. Even moving southward, where one begins to encounter the custom extensively, there are occasional tribal groups that seem to have been abstainers: the Comanche of the Plains for instance, and the Maidu of California (Munroe et al. 1969; Dixon 1905: 241). One Plateau group, the Kaska, manifests the anomaly (perhaps an artifact of poor reporting) of having had only female-to-male crossers, not the more usual male-to-female (Honigmann in Katz 1976: 237). These occasional gaps and anomalies aside, however, the presence of the berdache and his less frequent female counterpart is traceable throughout the Plateau, Plains, Southwest, Prairie, and Southeastern regions of the continental United States and deep into Mesoamerica. (Data are missing for the Atlantic and Northeastern states regions. In the case of the Mesoamerican civilizations, early Spanish accounts provide little more than allusions to effeminate male prostitutes and to sanctions against homosexuality.)

Rather than search for a focal or "classic" version of the custom, an approach that tends to beg more questions than it resolves, I will begin with a few simple common denominators and statistical generalities. Minimally, gender-crossing in North America consisted of the permissibility of a person of one anatomic sex assuming part or most of the attire, occupation, and social – including marital – status, of the opposite sex for an indeterminate period. The most common route to the status was to manifest, in childhood or early adolescence, behavior characteristic of the opposite sex. These manifestations were greeted by family and community with a range of responses from mild discouragement to active encouragement according to prevailing tribal sentiment, but there was seldom any question as to the meaning of certain opposite-sex-tending behaviors: They were signals that the youth might be destined for the special career of the gender-crossed. Supplementing and sometimes substituting for youthful behavioral cues were messages that came to the future gender-crosser in dreams and visions. Less commonly, men acquired the gender-crossed status by being taken captive in war and integrated into the household of a captor in the status of ''wife.'' Although it was not inconsistent with North American notions of gender to assimilate anatomically intersexed (hermaphroditic) persons, or animals, to the gender-crossed category, there is little reason to believe that physical hermaphroditism occurred any more frequently among native Americans than among other populations or that the occasional appearance of such figures in any way inspired the gender-crossing custom. Despite the probings of Western observers predisposed toward physiological explanations, the number of cases of genuine hermaphrodites reported is negligible.

All evidence suggests that the gender-crossed status was more fully instituted for males than for females. The vast majority of reported cases are ones of anatomic males assuming aspects of the status of women. For these the term ''berdache'' (from the French word for male prostitute) has come down to us in the ethnographic literature. Female deviations into aspects of the male role were far from infrequent, but in most areas – with exceptions to be discussed – these excursions were not culturally organized into a named, stable status category comparable to that of ''berdache.'' The asymmetry in the ease with which passage was made into the status of the opposite sex is consistent with the status asymmetry of the sexes in North America. The man was everywhere considered superior in worth to the woman. As in most hierarchical systems, downward mobility was more easily achieved than upward mobility. In more particular terms, however, the asymmetry of gender-crossing must be seen as a function of the relative weight given the principal defining features of gender, which differed inversely for the two sexes.

The institution of gender-crossing can be used analytically as a means of discerning the principal defining dimensions of gender and the proportions in which these dimensions were weighted for each sex. My focus will be first upon the man, then the woman.

The defining features of gender in North America can be seen as falling into two broad clusters, the one having to do with anatomy and physiology, the other with behavior and social role. In regard to the first, the sexual anatomy visible at birth was, in North America (as in every other part of the world), the baseline for the social differentiation of the sexes. The kind of genitalia established a prima facie case for the individual's social destiny. According to this criterion, normally the child was routed to one or the other side of the division of productive labor, to one or the other set of marital, parental, and kinship responsibilities, and to either a partially restricted (for women) role or an unrestricted (for men) role in political affairs and communal ceremonies. Even in the case of the berdache, as we shall see, the sheer fact of anatomic masculinity was never culturally ''forgotten,'' however much it may have been counterbalanced by other principles. Yet beyond this basic anatomical marker, little attention devolved upon the details of male reproductive physiology. Unlike the New Guinea peoples mentioned earlier, American Indians were not given to using semen as a reification of manhood, vitality, and so forth, nor did they try, magically, to rid themselves of, or conversely acquire, the reproductive attributes of women. In a word, the physiological obsessions so common in Oceanic cultures do not appear in North America, at least not in regard to the male. [3]

THE MALE BERDACHE

Turning now to those aspects of social behavior most definitive of gender status in North America, the evidence from the material on male gender-crossing indicates overwhelmingly that pride of place was given to participation in productive labor. In instance after instance, he became "woman" who did woman's work, preferred the tools of the female trades, or had this work or those tools, through perverse fate, thrust upon him.

From the Yurok of northern California:

> The *wergen* usually manifested the first symptoms of his proclivities by beginning to weave baskets. Soon he donned women's clothing and pounded acorns. [Kroeber 1925: 46]

The Crow of the Plains:

> I was told that when very young, those persons manifested a decided preference for things pertaining to female duties . . . as soon as they passed out of the jurisdiction of their parents . . . they donned women's clothing. [Simms 1905: 581]

The prairie-dwelling Miami:

> There were men who are bred for this purpose from their childhood. When they are seen frequently picking up the spade, the spindle, the axe, but making no use of the bow and arrows, as all the other small boys are wont to do, they are girt with a piece of leather or cloth which envelops them from the belt to the knees, a thing all women wear . . . They omit nothing that can make them like the women. [Liette in Katz 1976: 288]

Similar accounts of the importance of cross-sex occupational preferences in childhood or adolescence can be found for the Southwest (Hill 1935: 274–5; Underhill 1939: 186; Devereux 1937: 501–3). When tests were used to confirm the nature of the opposite-sex-tending child, these took the form of a forced choice between characteristic male and female implements (Underhill 1939), and when it was a vision that commanded the change, the stereotypic elements of the vision again involved the posing of occupational alternatives:

> It is said that the moon would appear to a man having in one hand a burden strap, in the other a bow and arrows, and the man would be bidden to make a choice. When he reached for the bow, the moon would cross its hands and try to force the strap on the man. [Fletcher and LaFlesche 1972: 132]

That this strong association of manhood and womanhood with specific areas of productive activity was not confined to a narrow complex surrounding the berdache is shown by the fact that tests and visions to establish the sex of an unborn child follow the same pattern. Among the Omaha, a pregnant woman seeking to learn the sex of her future child presented the young child of a neighbor with a choice between bow and burden strap, in this case taking the child's choice to be conditioned by the influence of the fetus, not the inclinations of the chooser (Fletcher and LaFlesche: 1972: 329). The Mohave expectant mother paid attention to whether her dreams were primarily of male or female implements and clothing (Devereux 1937: 501). Given the gender-defining character of labor activities, there is no particular contradiction between the usual reports that the berdache was a self-recruited position and the reports that in certain Woodlands and Prairie tribes male war captives were incorporated into the capturing group as berdaches (Angelino and Shedd 1955: 122). Lurie points out that both routes to berdache-hood existed among the Winnebago, the self-initiated route being the honorable one, the enforced route dishonorable (Lurie 1953: 712). (The Plains and Western tribes did not as a rule take adult male captives.)

Clothing and mannerisms were also strongly defining of gender in North America. Spontaneous use of female speech patterns, a piping voice, or feminine ways of laughing and walking are sometimes mentioned as identifying the budding berdache (Fletcher and LaFlesche 1972: 132; Devereux 1937: 502; Lowie in Katz 1976: 319), and cross-dressing (or attempted cross-dressing) was an almost invariable concomitant of gender transformation. Typically this dimension of gender was in harmony with occupational choice, but it was possible in the twentieth century for persons to maintain the gender-crossed status by occupation alone while dressing, in response to white pressure, as befitted anatomic sex (Landes 1970: 201–2; Stevenson in Katz 1976: 314). It is not known whether a gender-crossed status could be maintained by cross-dressing alone, because examples of this are not reported. Probably the two "social" criteria, work and external appearance, were mutually reinforcing. Each in itself was suggestive of a gender-crossed destiny and conducive to reclassification, but it was expected that with the appearance of one cross-over trait, the other would and should follow. Of the two attributes, occupational preference and dress, it is the first that is most often mentioned and commented upon, inclining us to believe that it was the most central of the social attributes definitive of gender.

By anatomy the berdache was a man, by occupational pursuit and garb, a woman. In the eyes of the American Indians, he was therefore a mixed creature. The most frequent thumbnail description of the berdache given investigators is "man-woman," "part-man, part-woman," or, phrased in the negative, "not-man, not-woman" (McKenny in Katz 1976: 299–300; Holder in Katz 1976: 312; Simms in Katz 1976: 318, Munroe et al. 969: 90; Kroeber 1925: 180). Hermaphroditism was the analog to berdachehood in the animal kingdom when such an analogy was drawn (Lurie 1953: 709; Hill 1935: 273–4). Navajo, Cheyenne, and Mohave lore about the berdache's exceptional abilities as a matchmaker, love magician, or curer of venereal disease again expresses the logic that the berdache unites in himself both sexes, therefore he is in a position to facilitate the union of the sexes (Hill 1935: 275;

Hoebel 1960: 77; Devereux 1937: 506). Although he was not infrequently dubbed ''coward,'' that is, less than a full man, the male gender-crosser was at the same time viewed as more than a mere woman – for reasons I will discuss later (see Landes 1938: 136). It was not unheard of for the berdache, while taking on female tasks, to retain certain of the male ones as well, excluding those strongly stamped with the seal of masculinity such as warfare. The Navajo, for instance, prized the berdache precisely because he was thought capable of doing the productive work of both sexes. The Navajo *nadle* was often promoted to the head of his natal household, the family holding to the idea that his presence guaranteed them wealth (Hill 1935: 275). Because there is only the finest line between doing what both sexes do and doing what neither sex does (neither sex ordinarily does what both sexes do), we find in several instances specialized duties reserved only for the berdache. Among the Yokuts, the berdaches were corpse handlers (Kroeber 1940: 314), and this seems to have been the case as well in parts of Florida where, in addition, berdaches tended the ill and carried provisions for war parties (LeMoyne in Katz 1976: 286). Specialized ritual functions, such as the cutting of a particular ritual lodge pole (Crow), or officiating at scalp dances (Papago and Cheyenne) are also reported (Lowie 1956: 48; Hoebel 1960: 77; Underhill 1939: 186). Judging from the usual American Indian division of labor and ritual activity, these special berdache functions were probably appropriated from the women's sphere; but not all instances can be so neatly diagnosed. Among the Illinois for example, the berdache could go to war but bearing only a club, not, as in the case of ordinary men, the bow and arrow (Marquette in Katz 1976: 287).

In order for this peculiar mixed status to come into being, the two defining dimensions of gender – anatomical and social – had to be given equivalent weight, for then, when a nonconcordance arose, when occupational interest was one way and anatomy another, neither criterion was used as a final determinant of gender status. Instead, the individual became half the one thing, half the other. Attempts can be made to circumvent this logical outcome only by mystifying anatomy, as Westerners do when they say of an effeminate man or a masculine woman, ''his/her genes are mixed up.'' But this reasoning has the ultimate effect of making anatomy the final determinant. In most areas of North America, Indian informants seem to have quickly disabused investigators of the idea, which the investigators favored, that the berdache was anatomically intersexed. But mystifications of anatomy were not entirely absent from North America. They crop up primarily in the Southwest and there for two superficially contrary reasons – either to shore up the gender-crossed status by appeal to the inevitability of the anatomical, or conversely to undermine the status on the same grounds! In either case a certain insecurity concerning the gender-crossing practice is suggested. The Navajo, who respected the gender-crosser, furnish an example of the ''shoring-up'' strategy. Their term for gender-crosser, *nadle*, which is derived etymologically from the expression ''changing'' or ''being transformed,'' has come to mean ''hermaphrodite,'' and the Navajo will claim that the ''real'' *nadle* is physically intersexed. Gender-crossers not actually hermaphroditic are called "pretend" *nadle*. However, no distinction is made between "real" and "pretend" in degree of social worth; rather, the implicit idea seems to be that a status that is mixed because social appearance contradicts anatomy should really be thought of in terms of a mixed or "changing" anatomy. The ideal validates the imitation. (Hill 1935: 273. One of the Navajo *nadle* known to Hill may have been a genuine hermaphrodite.)

The Mohave present a contrasting situation. Here the gender-crossing custom was "humoristically viewed" according to Devereux, and ordinary Mohave seized upon every opportunity to bait the gender-crosser with the charge of anatomic fraudulence.[4] The gender-crossers in turn responded with apparently serious attempts at fakery to support their position. Several known *alyha* (berdaches) were said to have shammed a menstrual flow and even pregnancy (Devereux 1937: 511–12). In other words, baited with the "real" facts of anatomy, called in effect an imposter, the Mohave gender-crosser was thrown back upon the only defense he thought would be acceptable, namely, that in his case the "real" facts were otherwise.

With one or two possible exceptions (see note 5), this anatomical flummery seems to be confined to the Southwest. Throughout most of the continent, the "part-man, part-woman," was not thought to be, nor forced into the pretense of being, woman in the physiological "parts." It was sufficient that he do as women did in regard to occupation, dress, and demeanor. This established the female component of his identity as anatomy did the male and the mixture of the two dimensions gave rise to his special cross-sex status.

THE FEMALE BERDACHE

For someone whose anatomic starting point was female, the infusion of an official opposite-sex component into her identity was by no means so easily effected. Throughout most of North America, there was no recognized female counterpart to the male berdache. Yet women willing and able to traverse the sex boundary do not seem to have been in short supply. Wherever ethnographic attention has been turned to this subject, the impression is given that for every boy who dreamed of the burden strap, there was a woman who actually picked up the bow. Not uncommonly the examples are of married women, sometimes with children, whose excursions into the male domain were episodic. On occasion, economic necessity drove them to the hunt or other male tasks (Landes 1938: 163–6, 169); at other times, they, like men, took to the warpath in response to a sudden vision or the requirement to avenge a slain kinsman (Landes 1938: 152; 1968: 152–3, 166, 212; De Smet in Katz 1976: 303). Whereas in some cases it was the absence of a husband, or his ineptitude, that provided the occasion for a woman's masculine debut (Landes 1970: 36; 1938: 126–77), just as often we hear of a husband or father encouraging the women to learn male skills or to act in his place in male curing, cermonial, or even warlike duties (Landes 1970: 37; 1938: 124–77; Denig in Katz 1976: 309). With appropriate circumstances or encouragement, some women consistently cultivated male skills from an early age (Landes 1968: 49; Denig in Katz 1976: 308–11). All such transgressors, if successful in their actions, were honored by the community as a man would be.

Women of the preceding tales, receive the title and symbolic eagle feather of "brave," *ogitcida*, which is a male title ideally, and grammatically is not conjugated for female sex gender . . . The people are untroubled by the contradiction between a woman's carrying this title and the conventional belief that war is a male occupation. [Landes 1938: 144. The Ojibwa]

> A few individual women in each village did drive buffalo on horseback, and did stalk, scalp and mutilate the enemy; often they were young women, of childbearing age. Their deeds were accepted simply by the men, who not only failed to criticize them but even accorded them the honors of men. [Landes 1968: 49. The Sioux]

One captured Gros Ventre girl ultimately rose to the position of a chief among the Crow, having from girlhood practiced masculine arts and, as an adult, repeatedly distinguished herself in battle and in horse raiding. This woman, after apparently trying and failing to find a husband, converted her horse wealth into marriage payments and founded a household by taking wives (Denig in Katz 1976: 310). But was she reclassified as a man, or as "part-man, part-woman"? It seems not, for the Crow had no such slot for the anatomic female, nor did most of the other Plains, Prairie, and Woodland groups, many of which sported splendid examples of the male berdache.

What was the problem here? It might be thought significant that none of these women reportedly cross dressed (not even the Crow chief), but the importance of this feature is equivocal given that berdaches were not always consistently transvestites; and the absence of full-scale imitations of the opposite sex can be explained as proceeding from the absence of a cross-sex category as easily as the other way round. Landes has speculated that a crystallized masculine status for women was rendered unlikely by the casual and sporadic approach of most women to manly activities. This in contrast to the single-minded dedication of the male berdache to his feminine tasks, or, for that matter, of ordinary men to their careers. Men were, in her view, "careerist" in whatever they did; women, inconstant and undisciplined (Landes 1938: 136, 156). But again, the lack of a masculine "career" for women might be the explanation for casualness and inconstancy in male pursuits rather than the other way round. Besides, some women were reported to have been disciplined and steady in their orientation to male activities. The young male berdache's career was commonly launched on the basis of less evidence of cross-sex talent than that shown by a number of the reported female cases. In short, when women did the equivalent of what men did to become berdaches, nothing happened.

The reason for this, I would suggest, is that throughout the continent, the anatomic-physiological component of gender was more significant in the case of the female than in the case of the male, and was thus less easily counter-balanced by the occupational component. The greater significance of the anatomical for the female had to do with the reproductive capacities of the mature women. As in so many other parts of the world, in North America, menstrual and birth blood was the symbolic door at which women's social disadvantage in relation to the men was laid (Lowie 1924: 205–17; Landes

1938: 124; Underhill 1939: 163). This area-wide belief in the inimical effect of female blood upon male activities, upon sacred power, or simply upon men, was ostensibly used to justify the exclusion of women from the occupational and ceremonial domain of men. In fact, this belief served more as simply a rationalization of women's less frequent participation in the male world for everywhere it seems, people shrugged at female intrusions as long as the woman nominally observed the monthly restrictions. Nevertheless, female blood and its attendant associations seems to have anchored women more firmly in their womanly identity than male anatomy anchored the man in his masculinity.

Support for this interpretation can be derived from those North American groups in which there was a cross-sex identity for women. Significantly, almost all reported cases are found in the Southwest. A female-to-male type, sometimes called by the same term as the berdache, is reported for the Mohave, the Cocopa, the Zuni, the Apache, and the Navajo. In these tribes women, either through dream inspiration or cross-sex occupational preferences, or both, established themselves as destined for the cross-sex identity early in life and thereafter cross-worked, cross-dressed, and even cross-married (Hill 1935: 273; Devereux 1937: 501–2; Forde in Katz 1976: 324; Gifford in Katz 1976: 325). Although there do not seem to have been many takers for the position because parents and community more actively discouraged the female-to-male crosser than the male-to-female, nevertheless the position was available. Southwestern tribes placed symbolic emphasis upon women's menstrual and parturitional blood just as did the other North American groups, but it was in the Southwest that a mystique of anatomical change had crept into the gender-crossing custom. As male crossers were found claiming that they menstruated, so, conversely it was bruited that female crossers did not. Gifford noted female transvestites in the Cocopa:

> Female transvestites (war'hameh). Male proclivities indicated by desire to play with boys, make bows and arrows, hunt birds and rabbits. Young men might love such a girl, but she cared nothing for them; wished only to become a man. Hair dressed like a man's, nose pierced. Such females not menstruate or develop large breasts. Like men in muscular build, but external sexual organs of women. (Gifford in Katz 1976: 325)

Forde wrote on "female inverts" among the Yuman:

> Female inverts (kwe'rhame) are rare, but they too realize their character through a dream at puberty. The characteristic dream is of men's weapons. As a small child the kwe'rhame plays with boy's toys. Such women never menstruate; their secondary sexual characteristics are undeveloped or in some instances are male. [Forde in Katz 1976: 324]

Obviously it could not be clear during the supposedly tomboyish childhood of such a woman whether or not she would grow up to menstruate or develop her secondary sexual characteristics; therefore all that one can conclude from this sketchily recorded lore is that the postpubertal indicators of cross-sex identity were made to jibe with the prepubertal ones, or vice versa, in the minds of informants, and that the absence of the mature woman's reproductive process was one of the critical attributes of the gender-crossed. Only one case of a known Southwestern female "berdache" has ever been detailed – that of the nineteenth-century Mohave, Sahaykwisa, remembered by Devereux's informants. She claimed and others believed that she did not menstruate, but she was otherwise of fully developed female form.(Devereux 1937: 523).

Whether or not the claim of nonmenstruation in any particular case was true, the point remains: Inasmuch as the gender-crossing custom had become mixed up with redefinitions of physiology, females could, by accident or design, find themselves relieved of that physiological factor that made them so resolutely women. The occupational component of their identity could then hold effective sway. The vast majority of other North American groups lacked the physiological elaborations on gender-crossing known to the Southwest, and lacked as well the female berdache.[5]

A type of masculine status for women, that of the "manly-heart" as it was called, existed in one Plains-culture group, the Piegan (Canadian Blackfoot). It has been well documented for us by Oscar Lewis (Lewis 1941). Although the "manly-heart" was not the equivalent of the berdache, the category is significant for our understanding of gender-crossing and I will consider it again when I turn to the larger cultural and social context of the custom. For the moment let me note that this status, for various social reasons, grew upon a woman with advancing age, so that even though menopause was not mentioned as a prerequisite to the title, the overwhelming majority of known "manly-hearts" were postmenopausal.

To recapitulate: Two dimensions of personal identity stood out as central to North American Indian notions of gender. On the one hand, there was one's sexual anatomy and physiology, on the other, one's participation in the sexual division of labor and – somewhat less salient – one's public appearance (dress, demeanor). For those starting off as anatomically male, no further bodily processes came into play to reinforce the image of their masculinity – at least not in the official cultural mind of the American Indian. The masculine identity had thus to be reinforced, or conversely contradicted by a feminine identity, through the social medium of work and dress. When not reinforced by the quintessentially manly activities of hunting and warfare, and at the same time contradicted by stereotypically feminine tasks, the male identity that emerged was that of the "part-man, part-woman," the berdache. For the female, by contrast, the phenomena of adult reproductive processes added to and underscored an image of femininity that could weaken and be counterbalanced by masculine occupations only if the physiological processes themselves were held to be eliminable. Throughout most of North America, they were not so held, at least not for that period of a woman's life when she was realistically capable of taking up the hunter-warrior way of life. Becoming a member of the opposite sex was, therefore, predominantly a male game.

GAY AMERICANS?

The sexual life of the berdache has been the subject of endless curiosity on the part of Westerners, for reasons that are not hard to discern. American Indian berdaches, male and female, conformed for the most part to a social, rather than anatomic, heterosexuality. In our terms, then, their sexual activity was heavily "homosexual." Apparently under no necessity to marry, the male berdache rather resembled in status the woman who, after several marriages and sundry affairs, had attained a certain looseness of reputation (Catlin in Katz 1976: 301–2; Devereux 1937: 513). In the Plains and Prairie area, he might be treated as the village bawd or as everyman's "sister-in-law" or "cross-cousin," the kin categories with whom a man enjoyed, in Landes's words, "extensive and boorish flirting privileges" (Landes 1968: 98). Men might boast publicly of their exploits with the berdache (Catlin in Katz 1976: 301–2), or he of his exploits with them (Hill 1935: 278). Fragmentary evidence suggests that the same "secondary marriage market" of divorced and widowed women to which the male berdache was assimilated, provided the female gender-crosser with a source of (real female) lovers and mates (Devereux 1937: 515).

When marriages between gender-crossed and ordinary individuals took place, they seem to have been in the form of secondary marriages – the taking of an additional wife by a polygynist in the Plains area (Boscana in Katz 1976: 614; Tanner in Katz 1976: 301), the rematch of divorcees in the Southwest (Devereux 1937: 515). The data on these marriages are insufficient to permit much generalization. Economic motives were cited as the reason for an ordinary person marrying a gender-crosser, but this did not imply an asexual relationship (Devereux 1937: 513–14, 515, 521–6; Parsons 1916: 526).

Given these practices, berdaches appeared in the eyes of Western observers as dominated by a homoerotic drive. Because spontaneous erotic orientation in our culture is the basis for dividing people into socially significant categories and is strongly linked in our view with gender identity as a whole (the more so in the late nineteenth century when homosexuality was considered a sign of gender "inversion"), it is not surprising that attention has been riveted upon this feature in the literature and that it has been the starting point for some of the more influential theories of institutionalized gender-crossing. But the need to gratify a conviction of underlying identity between the American Indian berdache and the homosexual of Western society has threatened to obscure the meaning of the former in American Indian culture, as well as to obscure the nature of cultural processes. I will take up these difficulties *seriatim*.

Foremost among the explanations of the North American berdache is that given by Kroeber, who saw institutionalized gender-crossing as part of a larger pattern whereby American Indian society made accommodation for instances of individual abnormality. He explicitly assumes that a certain number of sex variants appear in any population and they must be dealt with somehow; a regularized status was the American Indian way of dealing with them. Implicitly Kroeber also assumes that cultural institutions may arise out of the need to accommodate individual deviance (Kroeber 1940).

Let me start with the first assumption. Although Kroeber himself was hesitant on this point, not a few writers have interpreted the recurrent "sex variant" in question to be the person of homosexual erotic orientation. In their *Patterns of sexual behavior*, Ford and Beach classified the native American custom as one of the forms of "institutionalized homosexuality" (Ford and Beach 1951). Jonathan Katz, on whose careful scholarship I have relied heavily in putting this essay together, felt no hesitation in subsuming native American gender-crossers under the rubric "gay Americans" for his *Gay American history*. The most insistent anthropological exponent of the homosexuality interpretation is George Devereux, whose essay, "Institutionalized homosexuality of the Mohave," is something of a classic in the literature on the subject. Devereux sums up his understanding as follows:

> Socially speaking Mohave civilization acted wisely in acknowledging the inevitable. The airing of the abnormal tendencies of certain individuals achieved several aims . . . In creating metaphorically speaking, "reserved quarters" for permanent homosexuals and for the passing whim of bisexually inclined active male homosexuals and passive female ones, they [the Mohave] gave the latter an opportunity to satisfy their passing longings, and left the door wide open for a return to normalcy. [Devereux 1937: 320]

In support of this paralleling of berdachehood with Western-style homosexuality (though not of Devereux's evaluative slant), there is not only the documented homosexual activity of gender-crossers, but also the strong element of self-selection to the role. The Mohave explain it – and their statements are echoed in other tribes:

> When there is a desire in a child's heart to become a transvestite, that child will act different. It will let people become aware of that desire. They may insist on giving the child the toys and garments of its true sex, but the child will throw them away and do this every time there is a big [social] gathering. [Mohave informant quoted by Devereux 1937: 503]

However, assessed against the data more closely and its logic scrutinized, the "niche-for-homosexuals" argument begins to unravel at the edges. First, there is no evidence that homosexual behavior as such was used as a reason for promoting reclassification of an individual to the gender-crossed status. In contradistinction to occupational and clothing choice, cross-sex erotic choice is never mentioned as one of the indicators of the budding berdache.[6] It was not as if homosexual behavior was unrecognized in North America. Homosexual acts between persons of ordinary gender status were known to occur or were recognized as a possibility among a number of tribes on which data are available. In some cases such behavior seems to have met with no objection (Forde in Katz 1976: 324; Honigmann in Katz 1976: 327; Holder in Katz 1976: 313); more often, it was negatively sanctioned as some sort of evil, inadequacy, or foolishness (Hill 1935: 276; Jones in Katz 1976: 317–18; Lowie in Katz 1976: 321–2; Landes 1938: 103). But homosexual acts were not in any way immediately suggestive of an enduring disposition such as that which characterized the gender-crosser (or the "homosexual" in our culture), and such acts were not confused with gender-crossing in the native mind. Forde's ethnography of the Yuman tribes (closely related to the Mohave) brings this point out clearly:

> Male and female inverts are recognized; the females are known as kwe'rhame, the males as elxa' . . . Casual secret homosexuality among both women and men is well known. The latter is probably more common. This is not considered objectionable but such persons would resent being called elxa' or kwe'rhame. [Forde in Katz 1976: 324]

As to the practice of (anatomic) homosexuality by recognized gender-crossers, the social expectation of it as well as its permissibility seems to have been the consequence of the crosser's social redefinition. The process did not work the other way round. Hill reports of the Navajo:

> The usual tabu placed on abnormal sex relations by normal individuals are lifted in the case of the nadle . . . Sodomy with a nadle is countenanced by the culture and the insanity believed to follow such an act with a normal person does not occur if the relation is with a nadle. [Hill 1935: 276]

One wonders of course why the process did not work the other way around, as one way seems to logically imply the other. If sexual object choice should conform to public gender, then why should not public gender conform to sexual object choice? The American Indians seem to have followed only one step of this logic, and even that not consistently. That is, berdaches seem to have lapsed into anatomic heterosexuality and on occasion even marriage without any loss of their cross-sex status (Liette in Katz 1976: 288; Devereux in Katz 1976: 305, 307; DuLac in Katz 1976: 612; Fletcher and LaFlesche 1972: 133; Stevenson in Katz 1976: 314). Hill records of the Navajo, "Transvestites are known to marry both people of the same and opposite sexes," and "Transvestites have sex relations both normally and unnaturally with both sexes" (Hill 1935: 276). One of Hill's *nadle* was known to have a *nadle* grandfather and a Zuni *la'mana* (male berdache) of Stevenson's acquaintance was credited with having fathered several children (Stevenson in Katz 1976: 314).

One way of construing this rather contradictory state of affairs is to say that sexual object choice was indeed gender-linked, along heterosexual lines (man to woman, woman to man), but that because the berdache had a foot in both camps, being by anatomy one thing, by occupation the other, he had a claim on the favors of either sex. His (or her) partners meanwhile retained their ordinary gender status because, whatever their gender, they could be interpreted as conforming to the heterosexual norm. (There is never a report of a berdache getting together with another berdache.) But this begs the question of why homosexual acts between ordinary individuals had no gender-transformative consequences. The only solution to this paradox is to conclude that sexuality, heterosexually typed though it may have been in the native mind, fell outside the realm of what was publicly and officially important about the roles of the two sexes. Sexual object choice was very much the trailing rather than the leading edge of gender definition. In itself, it did not set in motion the process of gender reclassification. And the inconsistency of some berdaches in regard to object choice was a function of the lesser relevance of this feature to the maintenance of their gender-crossed status.

Some may wish to carry Kroeber's "sex variant" argument onto deeper ground and rather than view the berdache as a homosexual, place him in the recently conceived Western category of "transsexual." As defined by Benjamin, transsexualism, the drive to assume the behavior and public identity of the opposite sex, is a psychological orientation in its own right, distinct from homosexuality. Anatomically homosexual behavior within the context of the transsexual orientation is merely the expression of a psychological hetero-sexuality; it follows from rather than leads to the transsexual orientation (Benjamin 1966: 27 ff.). Just so, in the American Indian mind, the salient fact about the gender-crosser was his/her preference for the external social iden-tity of the opposite sex. If all a person really wanted to do was engage in homosexual activity, there were opportunities for doing so without all the ballyhoo of a special identity. But proponents of the homosexuality view, moving onto deeper ground themselves, can counterargue, as Jonathan Katz is inclined to do, that "transsexualism," as a psychological stance, whether appearing in our own culture or any other, arises by default from the absence of cultural categories sophisticated enough to permit homosexuals to concep-tualize their nature. Having inadequate cultural tools for self-understanding, they tend to cast their desires into the socially dominant heterosexual frame-work (Katz 1976: 278).

Obviously, one can go round and round with this. Without attempting to resolve the debate as to the actual psychodynamics of the berdache, and leaving aside the strong political and social motivations that enter into this discussion, let me try to clarify what it is in the cultural logic of the West that strains theory toward positing an identity between berdache and Western homosexual. In the last couple of centuries, the homosexual has come to be the nearest thing to a cross-sex, or dual-gender, category in Western society. Although there have been and still are competing understandings of homo-sexuality, a recurrent one stresses the "intermediate" sexuality or androgy-nous character of the homosexual practitioner. Medical investigators keep returning to the possibility that opposite sex genetic or hormonal material lurks in the body of the homosexual (Ellis 1963), whereas social reformers have frequently adopted the "body of a man, mind of a woman" (conversely in the case of a lesbian) formula (DeBecker 1969: 153–88). The homosexual thus emerges as part the one thing, part the other. At this level of abstraction (and ignoring that the condition was anathematized in the West), the Western homosexual *is* the logical counterpart of the native American berdache. But when we move down to the level of which features are conceived to be the crux of this gender dualism, the two types, "homosexual" and "berdache," part company. I say the "crux," because in both American Indian and Western gender systems, the same three social attributes of gender appear: occupation, dress/demeanor, and sexual object choice. What differs is the center of gravity in the two gender systems. For the American Indians, occupational pursuits clearly occupy the spotlight, with dress/demeanor coming in a close second. Sexual object choice is part of the gender configura-tion, but its salience is low; so low that by itself it does not provoke the reclassification of the individual to a special status. In the Western system, the order of salience is virtually the reverse. A marked cross-sex occupation may engender "suspicions," to be sure (decreasingly so in modern times), but by itself it has never defined a unique sex-gender status. Homosexual activity, on the other hand, has been so strongly definitive of an enduring, gender-anomalous condition that it has long been impossible to engage in it casually. In both Western and native American gender systems, dress and demeanor function as strong but not essential supports for the dualistic status established through the core variable. Esther Newton's comments on the relationship in our culture between dress/demeanor ("sex-role presentation of self" in her words) and homosexuality deserve to be repeated here:

> Homosexuality consists of sex-role deviation made up of two related but distinct parts: "wrong" sexual objects and "wrong" sex-role presentation of self. The first deviation is shared by all homosexuals . . . The second deviation logically (in this culture) corresponds with the first, *which it symbolizes*. [my emphasis] It becomes clear that the core of the stigma is in "wrong" sexual object when it is considered that there is little stigma in simply being effeminate, or even in wearing feminine apparel in some contexts, as long as the male is known to be heterosexual, that is, known to sleep with women or, rather, not to sleep with men.

Newton makes note of the fact that there is class variation in this system: lower-class men consider a man "gay" only when he assumes the feminine role in the sex act with another man (Newton 1977: 341).

The new Western mixed type, the transsexual, who emerged with the dawn of the sex-change operation, is still persistently seen in terms of the dominant mixed type, the homosexual. That is, he/she, like the berdache, is thought to be a homosexual who misunderstands him/herself, or is misinterpreted by society. Yet, as one recent treatise argues, the rise of Western "transsexualism," with its formidable array of psychiatric, medical, and legal mediators, may in fact represent a movement within Western culture for the reestablishment of a strong connection between gender and dichotomized occupational spheres (see Raymond 1979). This reestablishment will not be easy for the trend of history is in the opposite direction, one probable reason why erotic object choice, not occupation, has been drawn into the foreground of Western gender identity.

To return to the North American berdache, and to give the arguments of Kroeber and others their due, the indifferent role of homosexuality in the establishment of berdache status does not in any way prove that homoerotic desires were absent from the psyche of the budding gender-crosser, or that such desires might not develop as a psychological offshoot of the young crosser's resocialization into the public status of the opposite sex. But it does make it hard to argue that the institution of gender-crossing was the way in which American Indian culture "dealt with" homosexuality.

There is another reason for demurring from this interpretation, one that applies with equal force to the now tempting proposal that institutionalized gender-crossing was the way in which American Indian culture "dealt with" sex-role deviance in the occupational realm. Hoebel has proposed this second explanation (Hoebel 1949: 459). The male berdache, according to his reasoning, is a fellow too timid to face the daunting warrior role of the adult Indian male, whereas the female-crosser is a girl too aggressive for feminine pursuits. Although accurate in terms of native American gender criteria, these suggestions, like those of Kroeber and Devereux, posit cultural forms as simple reactions to personality patterns, and minority patterns at that. If culture were by its nature so accommodating, one would expect deviants and role failures the world over to be provided with institutionalized "niches," "reserved quarters," and the like; this is far from being the case. Thus even if we were to clear up the mystery of the American Indian gender-crosser's inner psychic orientation, the cultural mystery would remain unsolved. We would still have to ask, if native American culture was permissive in regard to this particular "variation," why was it permissive?

The larger cultural and social context of gender-crossing

Any really thorough answer to the question just posed takes us so deeply into the warp and woof of native American society and culture as to exceed the scope of this essay. I will content myself here with merely making some headway on this issue. Two lines of speculation present themselves. One is that American Indian culture was, in some sense, very permissive, and that therefore all sorts of – to our mind – surprising things received a routine stamp of approval. The other is that there was something special about the sex-role organization of Indian society, something we have not fully uncovered yet, that made it permissible, or at the very least understandable, for an occasional individual to stray over the sexual line, the institutionalization of this straying constituting a statement that the culture was, for these as yet obscure reasons, not unhappy to make. Both lines of speculation carry us a certain distance. The first thought takes its inspiration again from Kroeber, who had a way of being close to if not always on the point. As explained earlier, he was of the opinion that the gender-crossing custom was part of a larger pattern whereby American Indian culture made accommodation for instances of individual abnormality. There is virtue to the idea of a larger pattern, but it is not well understood as one of providing niches for individual abnormality. Rather, it consisted of a principle of letting all individual careers, sex-related or otherwise, be shaped by an extrasocietal destiny.

It does not require social identities as dramatic as that of the berdache to illustrate the pattern in question. All over North America, as persons matured they were expected to show special luck or ability in certain areas more than in others, and the consequent social differentiation of individuals was rationalized in terms of a fate over which neither the individual nor the community had much control. In wide areas of the continent – the Plains, Plateau, Prairie, Woodland, and Subarctic areas in particular – men and occasionally women received their particular destiny through visions of supernatural helpers who bestowed upon them special powers and protections. Usually supernatural visions were deliberately solicited through fasting, solitude, and self-mortification. Landes's characterization of the Ojibwa philosophy surrounding visions is widely applicable:

> All those talents and traits of character which we think of as functions of a total personality are regarded by the Ojibwa as isolated, objective items which may be acquired in the course of life by individuals who are fortunate enough to coerce them from the supernaturals. In Ojibwa thought, there is no original and absolute "self" – a person freshly born is

"empty" of characteristics and identity. Consequently tremendous pressure is exerted upon a young person to pursue the supernaturals and move them to fill up his "emptiness." [Landes 1938: 124]

Appearing in the vision was the spiritual manifestation (often in human form) of some natural species or phenomenon – bear, crow, rabbit, morning star, thunder, and so forth – who taught the visionary songs and instructions that, if used properly, would insure success in some designated area. Treating the vision casually or ignoring the instructions (which often included taboos of one sort or another), occasioned not just the loss of the special powers bestowed by the guardian but often additional misfortune as well. Typically, men hoped for visions that would bring them success in the conventional male pursuits of warfare and hunting, although receiving a special curing or craft ability through vision was by no means despised. But fate could be cantankerous. A vision could deceive and the expected success fail to materialize. Some were blessed with abundant visions, whereas some received none at all; and not everyone received the powers he (or she) purported to want. Visions that instructed berdachehood, and those that involved the individual in the more rigorous forms of shamanism are often mentioned as unwanted destinies; but the individual ignored such a calling at his risk. Among many of the vision-questing tribes, it was possible to pass on vision-inspired luck to someone else by selling the collection of symbolic items – the "medicine bundle" – that the original visionary had constructed to embody and preserve his/her special fortune. Like the vision itself, bundle ownership inspired the possessor toward feats he or she might ordinarily fear to undertake and rallied community confidence behind the possessor's leadership of collective enterprises (or his/her curing activities). However, a bundle was not guaranteed to retain its powers any more than was a vision, and the new possessor might find himself out of luck.

In those areas where the vision ideology was highly developed, a complex casuistry of supernatural assistance, trickery, or neglect underlay the gradual differentiation of social identities that took place as each generation reached its social prime, and gender-crossing, along with many another distinctive idiosyncrasy, was readily encompassed by this ideology.

One might speak of the vision complex as simply a full articulation of attitudes that were generally present in American Indian society. Even in areas where vision was of minor significance, personal proclivity, talent, or peculiarity was handled with a vocabulary of preconceived stereotypes that excused both individual and community from worrying very deeply over why someone was the way he or she was or whether this should be changed. Among the Pima and the Papago for instance, some women eschewed the burdens of marriage, engaged in casual liaisons with men of their choice, and spent their time embellishing their appearance and going to dances. They were called "light women" or "playful women" and, as it was considered in their nature to be this way, their parents offered little protest against the behavior (Underhill 1939: 183–4). In parts of California, "bear men" – men born with the nature of the bear – were a culturally recognized category. A case is reported by Kroeber:

When [the] child was born, he had tufts of hair on each shoulder. He grew up apparently stupid and sluggish, not participating much in ordinary activities. Once, when he was being teased, he grew angry, growled, turned into a bear, scattered the coals of the fire, and began to cuff people around. After this incident, he was carefully let alone, except when his anger could be directed against the enemy Yuki. [Kroeber 1940: 315]

A young man behaved and appeared rather like a bear: Very well then, he was a ''bear-man.'' The same principle could be, and was, applied if he behaved rather like a woman; he became a ''woman-man.''

Although recognizing that the berdache fell under a broader rubric of culturally stereotyped individual careers, Kroeber interpreted this as ''culture'' putting the best face on a psychopathological condition of some sort. The ''bear man'' is an overgrown dullard, the shaman a stabilized psychotic, the berdache a sexual deviant. But the phenomenon of American Indian individualism extended well beyond the area of what, to our minds, is the ''problematic'' or the ''abnormal.'' The able hunter had his stereotypic destiny too, as did the woman with a knack for curing low back pains. Rather than being a special dispensation, the institutionalization of gender deviation was only one of the many examples of the use, in North America, of various forms of distinctiveness as a guideline for future conduct on the part of the individual, and as a signal to the community of how destiny had decided to carve up the human landscape.

Undoubtedly the notion of a whimsical personal destiny to some degree fostered a generalized acceptance of all varieties of nonnormative personal outcomes; but this may be of less relevance to the understanding of gender-crossing than the fact that the ethic of individual destiny was invoked primarily in regard to activity patterns that established a person's productiveness and prestige within the community. What the ethic ''said'' about these activity patterns, and thus about wealth and prestige as well, was that their social distribution was unpredictable and that they could not be anchored to any sure determinants. In this respect, religious individualism (or just plain individualism among groups such as the Southwestern Pueblo where the vision quest was undeveloped) accorded well with the status organization of the majority of American Indian societies. Prosperity, or at the very least a brief moment of glory, was available through a diversity of avenues, for American Indian society was profuse with semispecialized trades and part-time communal positions: the war leader, the hunt leader, the various prophets and diviners, the unscatheable warrior, the craft adepts, the many curers of such delimited ailments as snowblindness, bear-bite, or urinary disorder in horses. The relative absence of heritable forms of wealth and status made it possible for personal determination and talent, in combination with a number of unobvious processes such as the careful management of kin obligations and marriages, to result, each generation, in an unforeseen distribution of these leadership, ritual, curing, and craft functions that underlay social prominence (see Collier 1977). True, the odds were tipped in favor of the vigorous and well-connected for these were the persons best in a position to cultivate and capitalize upon semispecialized activities; but even within their ranks, a strong element of chance entered into social fortune. Doctrines of a capricious supernatural underlined this element of chance and pacified the unfortunate with the belief that their misery, if sufficiently extreme, might move the supernaturals to pity. Plains Indian legend, for example, abounds with "Horatio Alger" tales of downcast orphans who, having inspired the pity of the supernaturals, turn the tables on their persecutors, capture many horses, or win over the supercilious maiden (Lowie 1956: 237).

In such a context, in which prestige- and wealth-garnering skills and activities settled upon individuals in what seemed, and what many could only hope was, a rather haphazard manner, and in which, as we have seen, many of these activities and skills were gender-linked, it was not so unusual that there should be a certain haphazardness to gender as well, especially in the case of the male who was less firmly rooted in the physiological component of sex status. It was as if the various occupational complexes dragged with them, connotatively, the gender category with which they were most commonly associated, while being at the same time cut loose, on the ideal plane, from such automatic determinants. The potential "wandering" of sex-associated activity patterns and social attributes was all of a piece with the potential wandering of activity patterns and social attributes generally. If the attributes of a wealthy man could alight upon a poor orphan, why not those of a woman upon a man?[7] Another way of explaining this is that, as in all cultures, so in American Indian culture, gender was a "status," in the sense of a rank or standing. As such it was drawn into, in this case placed on a par with, all other available status positions and participated (to a degree) in their mode of allocation. In a vast number of American Indian societies, social distinction was linked to luck and ability in some established pursuit or set of pursuits, and so too was masculinity and femininity. Accordingly, just as a knack for these other pursuits was allocated by unobvious and officially unpredictable processes, so likewise – in its social as opposed to anatomic aspect – was gender.

Thus, it is apparent that the idea that North American Indian society was simply "permissive" in regard to individual variation must be significantly modified. Whether one calls the value complex of which the vision-quest ideology was the fullest expression, "permissiveness" in the sense of a passive acceptance of individual behavior, or "individualism" in the sense of an active encouragement of individual expression, the pattern in question was of a more specialized emphasis than noted by previous theorists. Rather than being simply supportive of individuality in all its personal ramifications, including the erotic, the American Indian ethic was really centered largely upon individual variation in prestige-relevant occupations. The reason this ideology bore upon gender-anomalous behavior at all is that gender itself was heavily defined in terms of prestige-relevant occupations.

It is this matter of the prestige potential of occupational specializations that leads us from the question of "permissiveness" to the other question raised earlier, that is, whether gender-crossing cannot be seen as tied in some more specific way to the sex-role organization of American Indian society. Obviously, it can, and the strong association of gender with occupational specialization leads us to look for the social sources of gender-crossing in the sexual division of labor.

It would be inadequate to argue that the way for gender-crossing was paved by the mere existence of a sexual division of labor. All known societies have some degree of division of labor by sex; thus, all known societies lay the groundwork for an association of manhood and womanhood with certain predetermined areas of work. I would venture that all known societies give some cultural expression to this association as well. Yet one need run only a quick survey of ethnographic cases to realize that not every cultural system brings occupation to the forefront of gender definition in the way that American Indian culture has done, nor does every system treat transgressions of the occupational boundary in the same accommodating manner as the American Indians. I am not arguing that American Indian society was unique in this respect; certainly there are other societies in other culture areas with similar types of organization (see Shore, this volume). But a sexual division of labor alone is insufficient to account for either a strong cultural association of gender with work specialty or for the toleration of gender ''individualism.'' In short, it is insufficient to account for the meaning complex we are examining here.

New Guinean systems, for instance, offer a striking contrast to native North America. In New Guinea, there is men's work and there is women's work, but New Guineans seldom seem to elaborate upon this particular dimension of masculinity and femininity: Rather, their focus is upon the reproductive substances associated with the sexually mature male and female. (American Indians, as we have seen, are not immune from this concern, but for the moment I am putting their relatively abbreviated use of this concept to one side.) And in paradoxical contrast to the gender-defining occupations that in North America are assigned by ''fate,'' the gender-defining substances of New Guinea are believed to be controlled by the collectivity (the male collectivity to be precise) so that any gender redefinition to be done must be engineered by collective ritual action (see Poole, this volume; Kelly 1976; Schieffelin 1976; Van Baal 1966). Finally, in New Guinea, the occupational boundary between the sexes, although culturally unstressed, is strongly defended in an indirect way through sanctions that warn the errant individual that his or her intrusions into the gardens, ritual lodges, or seating areas of the opposite sex (any of which might happen if cross-sex occupations were attempted) will result in mystical harm to self or opposite-sex kinfolk.

What is it then that the North American Indians (and others with similar cultural conventions) are doing differently? To begin with, it is important to reassert what numerous investigators into the status of women have already been at pains to make clear: The ''sexual division of labor'' is a term that tells us very little about the political and social significance of an organization of production. There is the ''work'' of simple production for instance, and there is the ''work'' of surplus appropriation, to name only the most crucial distinction that gets glossed over by bland ''division of labor'' concepts. Furthermore, even within the sphere of production, different labors are of different consequence for the eminence and social power of the "laboring" group. With these perspectives in mind, some observations can be made about the sex-divided organization of production in native North America that bear upon the cultural salience of occupation in the conceptualization of gender and upon the acceptability of gender-crossing. These observations illuminate as well the differences between the North American system and such culturally antithetical examples as the New Guinea one. Let me caution that my interpretation here will be sketchy and unrefined; I wish only to propose a line of thinking rather than to hone one to perfection.

First, almost everywhere in native North America, the woman's domain of economic activity included within it the production of significant durable goods: basketry in California; textiles, basketry, and pottery in the Southwest; in the buffalo-rich Plains and Prairie areas, a huge inventory of leather-goods including tipis, parfleches, garments, and the multipurpose robe, any of which might be decorated by painting, quillwork, or (in later periods) beadwork; in the Eastern Woodland areas, basketry, pottery, leather, and fur goods. These female products entered into intratribal gift exchange and intertribal trade, their circulation in both spheres accelerating with the arrival of the European trader. Many of the more difficult and time-consuming crafts – pottery in the Southwest, quilling, beadwork, tipi and earth-lodge construction in the Plains and Prairie areas – became the preserve of part-time female specialists who were remunerated both for supplying the craftwork and for passing on the skill. Various curing specializations tended to fall to women (different ones in different areas), and these were similarly a source of remuneration. Men of course had their own craftwork and curing specialties as well and were more apt than women to command and transmit expensive supernatural lore; but the point is that a woman's productive labor was not necessarily exhausted, any more than a man's, in the service of immediate consumption needs, and a woman's products circulated beyond the bounds of the domestic unit.

Second and more importantly, a good deal of a woman's wealth and talent redounded to her own credit officially, and not simply informally. Women's labor was not subject to total or even very extensive appropriation by men. Men, because of their position in warfare, intertribal contact, and the organization of often wide-scale cooperative hunting, held sway in communal decision making and were, as a class, accorded greater social esteem than women. But they were not privileged to appropriate the products of female labor into some higher distributive game from which women qua women were excluded. They were not organized in relation to women as "transactors" to "producers," to borrow the terms M. Strathern has applied to the New Guinea sex-role organization (Strathern 1972).

This is not to say that North American society lacked distributional structures whereby some parties could lay claim to the labor of others while simultaneously gaining rank through the economic generosity that these labor claims made possible. Such systems were present, but they did not sharply divide the sexes. To generalize from the better-analyzed Plains culture examples, it seems that insofar as the labor of some was appropriated to the prestige machinations of others, it was the well-positioned elder or household head of either sex who benefited from claims on the labor of his/her juniors. The mature householder with the right assortment of married or marriage-age children, junior in-laws, wives – or in the case of women, junior co-wives – and a credible record of personal achievement, was the individual in a position to begin sponsoring ceremonials, purchasing ritual memberships and renowned "bundles," obligating others through timely acts of generosity, and devoting him/herself more fully to lucrative craft specializations (Collier 1977; Lewis 1941). Wives and husbands often worked in concert to put together the admission feasts and gifts for, and were admitted jointly to, select religious societies; there were single-sex societies for women as well as for men in those areas where such "sodalities" were present (Fletcher and La Flesche 1972: 440–540; Lowie 1924: 206, 211; Driver 1969: 351–4). Wealth objects produced (or stolen in raids) by one sex could circulate to and through either sex, because it was generally the case that women had the right to dispose of property independently of their husbands (Fletcher and LaFlesche 1972: 363; Driver 1969: 284; Lowie 1956: 61; Lewis: 177–80). The ability to be an independent economic actor would, of course, buttress the position of the industrious female craft or curing specialist. It should be pointed out that this pattern of production and allocation did not favor *all* women, but it routinely favored a certain percentage of women in every generation. This female elite consisted heavily of first or favorite wives in polygynous house-holds (because divorce was not difficult an ambitious woman could some-times engineer a better marital "location" for herself) and only or favorite children of a prosperous parent (Lewis 1941: 178–9; Fletcher and LaFlesche 1972: 507–9).

The situation just outlined bore upon gender-crossing in a number of ways. Because prestigious goods and services (such as curing) were located within the realm of female, and not just male, production, and because women, and not just men, had the right to dispose of property and command the labor of others, the "meaning" of the gender distinction in native American society rested more heavily upon differences in productive specialization than upon position within a system of sexual-political interaction. Sexual identities were not overwhelmed by hierarchical relational attributes such as "overlord/ ward" or "exchanger/exchanged," but were pinned primarily to the tradi-tionally demarcated spheres of activity. This laid the groundwork for a cross-sex category based upon cross-sex occupation, and it suggests, in part, how "crossing" came to be acceptable. An occasional gender maverick did not threaten to prick the bubble of an elaborate domination mystique, because sexual domination in North America was not elaborate, therefore neither were its mystiques. Thus the boundary between the sexual spheres was not strongly defended. (Only in one respect was male hegemony encoded in "absolutist" terms: This was in the notion that women's menstrual and parturitional blood was antipathetic to male enterprise, hence to true pre-eminence. The woman's child-tending responsibility, to which the symbol-ism of blood metonymically alluded, was not seen as an occupation of the sort that any human – including a man – could take up; and not having the status of a fully social activity, which translated into American Indian terms meant a supernaturally bestowed activity (!), it was not subject to variable allocation. As a consequence an asymmetry in access to the cross-sex status did appear throughout most of North America.)

However, the relatively nonthreatening character of occupational boundary transgressions only accounts in a negative way for the permissibility of gender-crossing. There may have been more positive influences at work as well. The prestige available to women operating simply as women in many ways narrowed the social gap that the gender-crosser of either sex had to jump in taking up cross-sex status, and may indeed have increased the incentive for ''jumping,'' at least in the case of the male. Limited but striking evidence suggests that a woman's work and capacity to command resources (including kin obligations) could, when carried to its full potential, ''masculinize'' her status in and of itself. Witness the status of ''manly hearted woman'' among the North Piegan, a Canadian Plains-culture group. ''Manly heart'' was not a title bestowed upon a girl who manifested cross-sex inclinations in occupation and dress; indeed there is no evidence that a manly heart ever had to participate in the strongly male-connotive hunting-and-warfare activity patterns. Rather, manly heartedness was a position toward which all successful Piegan matrons gravitated with age, economic achievement, sponsorship of ceremonials, and the ability to dominate husbands and co-wives (Lewis 1941: 175–7). Wealth, if not sufficient, seems to have been the most ''necessary'' prerequisite for the status. (''Informants laughed at our question, Are manly hearted women poor? The answer invariably was that a poor woman would not have the nerve to do the things that are considered manly hearted. [Lewis 1941: 177]). Wealth could be accumulated through established female routes – the gifts of husbands and parents, the woman's own excellence in her crafts.

> It takes most women six days to tan a hide which a manly hearted woman can do in four or five days. A manly hearted woman can bead a dress or a man's suit in a week of hard work, while it takes most women a month. An average worker makes a pair of moccasins in a week, while a manly hearted woman can make it in little over a day. These excellent workers were able to produce over and above the personal needs of the household. A manly hearted woman was therefore an economic asset, which is the only justification the Piegan give for a woman dominating her husband. [Lewis 1941: 178]

Although we do not have any indication of the existence of this masculine label in other parts of the Plains, there is no reason to believe that the Piegan manly heart was anything more than the Plains matron at her epitome.[8] The fact that she was then called manly hearted reveals that, at the height of her powers, she came close to matching the successful male in prestige. She must certainly have surpassed the unsuccessful male.

If success in the female sphere could hold a reasonable candle to success in the male, if, at the very least, femininity represented a positive sort of power rather than being, as it is in many cultures, overwhelmingly connotive of powerlessness, then it is conceivable that the female sphere held an attraction for men over and above anything to do with the erotic. If manliness did not, for whatever reason, seem available to a boy, why not manly heartedness? The berdache, while quitting the battlefront (quite literally) of male prestige rivalry, found it possible to take up a respectable sort of lateral position – that of ultra-successful female. To be sure, such a status was not as high as the higher masculine statuses. The berdache had to renounce a higher status potential when turning into the female channel, and, in doing so, he took on, to a degree that varied by tribal area, the stigma of masculine failure. But, in compensation, he took on as well – again, to a degree that varied by tribal area – the charisma that tends to attach itself to those who voluntarily renounce social position. And he made available to himself the forms of material prosperity and cultural respect that accrued to the assiduous practitioner of female crafts.[9]

In the latter regard, we are reminded of the frequent assertions made to (or by) investigators about the berdache's excellence and prosperity in his chosen career. The two Zuni berdaches of Stevenson's acquaintance were ''the finest potters and weavers in the tribe,'' and one of them among the richest men in the village (Stevenson in Katz 1976: 314). Simms was told of Crow berdaches that they often had ''the largest and best appointed tipis'' (Simms 1903: 580). The Navajo berdaches who were mystically associated with wealth already seem typically to have laid an empirical foundation under their mystical reputations:

> They knit, tan hides, make moccasins, are said to be excellent sheep raisers, and excel as weavers, potters and basket makers. The last three pursuits contribute substantially to their wealth, as especially are basketry and pottery making restricted technics and they are able to trade these products extensively with their own and other people. [Hill 1935: 275]

Among the Yurok of California, women apparently had cornered the market on a particularly lucrative form of shamanism, and it was precisely this specialty into which the Yurok berdaches (*wergen*) moved. The Yurok themselves interpreted the berdaches' motives in this light:

> The Yurok explanation of the phenomenon is that such males are impelled by the desire to become shamans. This is certainly not true, since male shamans are not unknown. It is a fact, however, that all the *wergen* seem to have been shamans and esteemed as such. [Kroeber 1925: 46]

The merit of psychosexual explanations of gender-crossing notwithstanding, the Yurok explanation embodies an important point: In Yurok society (as I would argue in many American Indian societies), the ways of woman could lead to material prosperity and social distinction *and were so perceived*. In the long run, it does not matter whether such perceptions entered into the consciousness of gender-deviating pubescent boys, as long as the prevailing culture was content to view the matter in this light and in doing so extend its toleration. At the same time, it is simplistic to discount such motivations in the young berdache, or arbitrarily oppose them to psychosexual ones. Certainly at the level of individual consciousness, prestige and psychosexual concerns are often bound up in indissoluble combinations.

It must be added that the cultural perception of women's potential was a complicated one. Common explanations of the successful berdache, as of the successful woman, testify to this. In actuality, it does not appear that berdaches were inevitably successful in their feminine careers. Besides the esteemed berdaches, some rather buffoonlike characters are reported in the literature (Katz 1976: 292, 300–1). Nor is it clear that, when successful, their achievements were of a higher order than those of women who, through age and household dominance, also enjoyed freedom from child-rearing responsibilities.[10] Nonetheless, investigators were frequently told that the berdache performed the tasks of women better than actual women. After all, he was a man! (Landes 1938: 136; Underhill 1939: 186; Simms 1903: 580; Stevenson in Katz 1976: 314). Comparably, the Piegan case illustrates the (less pronounced) tendency of the culture to view successful women as "manly." Both reactions reveal an unwillingness or inability to distinguish the sources of prestige – wealth, skill, personal efficacy (among other things) – from masculinity. Rather there is the innuendo that if a person performing female tasks can attain excellence, prosperity, or social power, it must be because that person is, at some level, a man.

At the same time, the entire male berdache institution, the predominant form of gender-crossing in native North America, demonstrates a reverse lack of distinction between the sources of prestige in the female sphere and femininity in a larger sense. Thus if men were to aspire to the socially and economically significant achievements available to a person in the feminine role, they had to infiltrate the realm of woman in the guise of women. Again, sources of prestige were conflated with gender, only the other gender.

The point here is not to fault a cultural system for conflations and contradictions that show up only within an analytic framework that the culture has no particular access to nor reason to adopt. As the reflex of persons inhabiting a certain social order, and as their way of understanding it, the various gendercrossovers, recategorizations, and double-entendres of American Indian culture were an ingenious comprehension of a situation in which social and economic powers tended to assume more complex distributions than those that could be readily encompassed by a simple gender hierarchy and in which, at the same time, class or caste structures were not sufficiently consolidated so as to delineate a transgender system of rank. Stated broadly, the culturally dominant American Indian male was confronted with a substantial female elite not perceivable as simply dependents of powerful men. Within such a context, the response to feminine transgressions into the traditional male sphere (hunting, warfare) was amazingly dispassionate: A woman who could succeed at doing the things men did was honored as a man would be. Few, if any, tortured rationalizations were brought to bear upon her achievement. What seems to have been more disturbing to the culture – which means, for all intents and purposes, to the men – was the possibility that women, within their own department, might be onto a good thing. It was into this unsettling breach that the berdache institution was hurled. In their social aspect, women were complimented by the berdache's imitation. In their anatomic aspect, they were subtly insulted by his vaunted superiority. Through him, ordinary men might reckon that they still held the advantage that was anatomically given and inalterable.

Conclusion

The primary purpose of this essay has been to show what sorts of meanings emerge from the ethnographic data regarding sex and sexual practices when proper respect is accorded the native cultural system. In many respects, I have simply tried to perform upon an ethnographic example of "institutionalized homosexuality" the sorts of contextualizing operations anthropologists typically perform upon cultural items that they feel require explanation. As it happens, in the area of gender, sex, and sex-related matters, neither anthropologists nor anyone else have, until recently, cared to take these well-established analytic steps, a situation that can be attributed in part to neglect of the subject matter in general, and in part to the theoretical hegemony of biological-psychiatric models in this field over the past three decades.

It would be disingenuous to assert, however, that respect for the native categories is all that is involved in cultural interpretation. Anthropologists are certainly familiar with the more intuitive and solopsistic forms of culture-specific interpretation. These typically consist of endless circles of metaphors aimed at conjuring up in our minds what is presumed to be going on in the native's, but in terms of social and cultural theory they are often, in the end, quite sterile. If this style of interpretation is to be avoided, some deeper sociological theoretical grounding, and theoretical persuasion, must inform the analysis from the start.

In terms of the analytic method used here, I have absorbed, partly from Max Weber, partly from the Durkheim-inspired British social anthropology tradition, the conviction that sociocultural orders, however special each may be, are never so unique as to be incomparable. Indeed, it is only by relentless comparison that useful understanding of specific cases is achieved and the theoretical framework of social science expanded. The very switching of our perspective back and forth from one system to another helps to bring out the essential features of each, while simultaneously causing more abstract social or cultural principles to precipitate out in our thinking (or, alternately, confirming or disconfirming abstractions already present).

In the foregoing pages I have been always implicitly, and at points explicitly, comparing the gender meanings of native North America with both those of my own culture (an inevitable implicit comparison) and those of tribal New Guinea. Within this cross-cultural framework, I have performed a great many "internal" comparisons of details from one culture area, native North America, to try to bring into relief the defining features of North American Indian gender, and the relative weights of these features.

What emerges from this comparative analysis is first what one might call the basic "Margaret Mead" points. One is that the principle attributes of manhood and womanhood, outside of birth anatomy, are culturally variable. Closely linked to this point is a second: that particular sexual practices and beliefs must be understood within the context of the specific gender-meaning system of the culture in question. Although these ideas have been accepted in anthropology for years, there has been little systematic application and illustration of them. I hope this essay stirs interest in further attempts of this sort.

But my ambition has been to proceed beyond these basic and accepted ideas, especially beyond the position of unanchored cultural relativism in which they, by themselves, leave us. To say that gender definitions and concepts pertaining to sex and gender are culturally variable is not necessarily to say that they can vary infinitely or along any old axis. Look again, for instance, at the three "homosexualities" touched upon in this essay. In New Guinea, homosexual practice is part of a set of theoretically dictated ritual practices designed to grow boys into men. In native North America, homosexual practice was anomalous, faintly suspect, but largely meaningless behavior except when practiced by someone whose gender had been redefined to a mixed-gender type in accordance with this person's preference for opposite-sex occupation and clothing. It was acceptable in such cases for this person's sexual orientation, like his or her clothing, to imitate that of the opposite sex. Finally, in our own culture, homosexual behavior itself tends to redefine a person to the status of an intermediate (and, except in liberal circles, strongly disapproved) sex type.

Although it is true that the three homosexualities could hardly be more different from the point of view of actors living within any one of these systems, there is, at a higher level of abstraction, a limit to their difference. In the New Guinea case, homosexual practice is deemed appropriate because one of the two parties is held to be deficient in the traits normally associated with his anatomic sex; in native North America, homosexual practice was deemed appropriate because one of the two parties was held to be possessed of traits normally associated with the opposite anatomic sex; and in modern Western culture, homosexual practice, although not deemed appropriate, gives rise, when it occurs, to the idea that one or both of the parties involved is mixed and/or deficient in their expected gender attributes. In a word, in all three cases, we see some manifestation of the dominance of heterosexuality as the model for sexual exchange. Those familiar with Gayle Rubin's provocative essay, "The Traffic in Women," will recall that in surveying the varieties of culturally recognized homosexuality, she noted, "the rules of gender division and obligatory heterosexuality are present even in their transformations" (Rubin 1975: 182). The findings here reaffirm this observation.

But should we consider the dominance of the heterosexual paradigm a case of "nature" exercising a constraint upon cultural variation? Certainly nature constrains at some level; but the question is, which level? Rubin points out that the omnipresence of gender division and obligatory heterosexuality is in line with the presence everywhere of socially organized kinship systems and the marital alliances that reproduce these systems while reproducing human beings (Rubin 1975: 178–83). Thus one might just as well argue that what we are seeing in the common denominator of the styles of homosexuality discussed here is *society* exercising a constraint upon cultural variation, and upon the nature of the individual organism as well.

Outside of looking for biological irreducibles, which go only so far and then ambiguously, if we are to get to the bottom of both the "Meadian" cultural variation in sexual and gender conceptions and the limits of that variation, we must begin to work through the range of variation of social and cultural systems, placing gender relations within this context. This brings us to the next aspect of my theoretical emphasis.

One line of sociological inquiry that I have tried to suggest here is investigation of the relationship between gender constructs and the organization of prestige in a given society. The reasons and methods for such an investigation are discussed in the Introduction to this collection. Let me here summarize the nature of the interlock in the North American case.

In the sorts of North American societies in which the institution of gender-crossing was to be found, there was little development of general social stratification. Instead, as in many tribal societies, age and sex were the principle lines along which prestige hierarchy manifested itself. It is not uncommon in such societies to find further development of individual prestige-differentiating mechanisms operating among men as well, and this was so in native North America. The very military, hunting, ritual, and material craft skills that served ascriptively to establish men's higher standing vis-à-vis women continued on, so to speak, to create achieved status differences between men. However, at the same time, for reasons having to do with the sorts of productive activities charged to women and for reasons that I would speculate lay in the organization of kinship and marriage (a subject inadequately treated here), a distinctive arena of female prestige differentiation existed as well. Moreover, it was an arena of prestige that could not have remained trivial in men's eyes, for some women seemed regularly capable, through their own doings, of rivaling men in wealth and social influence.

Gender stratification, which was strongly linked to the occupational specializations of the two sexes, had, shall we say, begun to leak around the edges. The leak, or more precisely contradiction, did not exist because it was unclear which sex should be doing what, but because the doing of these clear things did not generate the consistent inequalities in power and influence associated with full prestige differentiation. Accordingly, gender differentiation, which is a prestige differentiation, manifested its contradiction as well – the mixed-gender figure. Inasmuch as women's activities generated wealth and influence comparable to that of men, men appeared who were willing to take up these activities. Inasmuch, however, as these activities were still marked as monopolies of the female sex, the men who took them up had to be those who were willing to assume the general guise – dress, demeanor, even sexual object – of women. In this analysis then, North American gender-crossing was a cultural compromise formation founded on an incipient, though never fully realized, collapse of the gender-stratification system.

Notes

1 Wyatt MacGaffey, personal communication in reference to the BaKongo (Africa); Michelle Rosaldo, personal communication in reference to the Ilongot (Philippines); Sherry Ortner, personal communication in reference to the Sherpa (Nepal).

2 I am indebted to Jane Collier, Lynn Eden, Sherry Ortner, Michelle Rosaldo, and Judith Shapiro for invaluable critical and editorial assistance in the preparation of this essay.

3 Jane Collier has pointed out to me that some ambiguity in regard to these generalizations exists in the case of the Cheyenne. Cheyenne had notions that a man's supernatural vitality was depleted by sexual intercourse – also by childrearing and by hunting. They did not, however manipulate sexual substances in rituals of manhood as New Guinea people do (personal communication).

4 From Devereux's account, the Mohave closely resemble unsophisticated ''Anglo-Americans in their attitude toward gender ambiguity. Because Devereux's study is one of the more recent ones, the influence of acculturation cannot be ruled out. On the other hand, another anthropologist has commented that attitudes toward the berdache are more ambivalent among the Southwestern tribes (Hill 1938: 339n).

5 The Kaska, a Plateau group, considered it acceptable for a girl to be raised as a boy if the family had no sons. In this case, she had to wear from early childhood a magical talisman, the dried ovaries of a bear, to prevent conception. No mention is made of her menstruation (Honigmann in Katz 1976: 327). Another Plateau group, the Kutenai, was the home tribe of a female ''berdache'' figure widely known among European traders in the early nineteenth century. This transvestite woman was definitely an idiosyncracy among the Kutenai who seem to have lacked even male berdaches, and it is likely that she adopted the idea of switching her sex from the example of male berdaches in neighboring groups (she was known among the Flathead). At any rate, returning home after a long sojourn with a Canadian husband, she perpetrated the hoax that her former husband had ''operated'' upon her and changed her into a man. Her brother, discovering that there was no anatomical foundation to the claim, exposed her to the community. She returned to wandering among tribal groups (Schaeffer in Katz 1976: 293–8).

6 Even Devereux's data let him down on this point. The homosexual play of Mohave adolescents was not considered ''homosexuality,'' he writes, meaning by this that it was not associated with their gender-crossing custom. Also, ''A subsidiary informant . . . claimed that if a man was found to have submitted to rectal intercourse he was compelled to undergo the initiation [to berdache status], but this statement has been unanimously discredited'' (Devereux 1937: 507–8).

7 Age status as well could be disassociated from chronological age because of the association of age with experience and knowledge. Thus among the Santee Sioux, persons experienced in an activity were always spoken of as ''old'' in comparison to novices, and shamans of whatever chronological age were referred to as ''old ones'' (Landes 1968: 46, 209).

8 The ''manly heart's'' public display of domination over her husband may, however, have been atypical of the Plains matron pattern. It should be added as well that not every Plains group had this ''wealthy matron'' syndrome. Jane Collier, from whose excellent study of Plains marriage and labor organization I have abstracted this dimension of the female role, points out that among the Comanche, senior wives chose to maximize leisure rather than generate wealth, and used their free time to accompany their husbands on raiding expeditions (Collier 1977: 10). The Comanche, however, are said to have no berdaches.

9 Examining geographically just the connection between surplus-based female craft specializations and the institution of male gender-crossing, we find that in the wealthy and socially stratified Northwest Coast societies, the greater number of prestigious crafts were in the hand of male specialists and there were few, if any, berdaches. In the stratified Mesoamerican area, the same situation obtained in

regard to craft specialization, but there is mention of male prostitutes; one might speculate that some wholly eroticized version of the berdache existed there but evidence is too skimpy to permit conclusions (see Guerra 1971). In much of the subarctic area, there were no berdaches, but there was also little surplus and craft specialization. Among the Eskimo, curing and artistic craftwork was entirely the domain of men as was much of the crucial foraging; high rates of female infanticide give one an idea of the position of women. There were no berdaches (see Driver 1969).

10 In some areas, the berdache was subject to a disadvantage not suffered by the dominant female householder – no household to dominate. The Potawatomi actually exiled the berdache from his natal village (Landes 1968: 31–2). Among Plains groups, a berdache, when married, seems to have been taken as a subsidiary wife, never the first, and this in all likelihood cut him off from household leadership (at least in his marital household). Only in the Southwest, among Zuni and Navajo, do we find definite reports of his being permitted a position of domestic headship, and here in his natal, not marital, household (Stevenson in Katz 1976: 314; Hill 1935: 275). Obviously, in other areas, some arrangements must have existed whereby the berdache was supplied with the raw materials needed to practice female crafts, but the ethnography on this point is silent.

References

Angelino, Henry, and Shedd, C. L. 1955. "A note on berdache." *American Anthropologist* 57: 121–6.

Barker-Benfield, G. J. 1976. *The horrors of the half-known life. Male attitudes toward women and sexuality in nineteenth-century America*. New York: Harper and Row.

Buchbinder, G. and Rappaport, R. 1976. "Fertility and death among the Maring." In *Man and woman in the New Guinea Highlands*, ed. P. Brown and G. Buchbinder. Special publication of the American Anthropological Association, no. 8, pp. 13–35.

Bullough, Vern. 1976. *Sexual variance in society and history*. New York: Wiley.

Collier, Jane F. 1977. "Women's work, marriage and stratification in three nineteenth-century Plains tribes." Unpublished manuscript.

De Becker, R. 1969. *The other face of love*. New York: Bell Publishing.

Devereux, G. 1937. "Institutionalized homosexuality of the Mohave Indians." *Human Biology* 9: 498–527.

Driver, H. E. 1969. *Indians of North America*. 2d ed. Chicago: University of Chicago Press.

Ellis, Albert. 1963. "Constitutional factors in homosexuality: a reexamination of the evidence." In *Advances in sex research*, ed. Hugo G. Beigel, pp. 161–86. New York: Harper & Row.

Evans-Pritchard, E. E. 1970. "Sexual inversion among the Azande." *American Anthropologist* 72: 1428–34.

Fletcher, Alice, and LaFlesche, Frances. 1972. *The Omaha tribe*. Lincoln: University of Nebraska Press.

Ford, C. S. and Beach, F. A. 1951. *Patterns of sexual behavior*. New York: Harper & Bros.

Guerra, Francisco. 1971. *The pre-Columbian mind: a study into the aberrant nature of sexual drives, drugs affecting behavior and the attitude towards life and death, with a survey of psychotherapy, in pre-Columbian America*. London: Seminar.

Hallowell, A. I. 1955. *Culture and experience*. Philadelphia: University of Pennsylvania Press.

Hill, W. W. 1935. "The status of the hermaphrodite and transvestite in Navaho culture." *American Anthropologist* 37: 273–9.

1938. "Note on the Pima berdache." *American Anthropologist* 40: 338–40.

Hoebel, A. E. 1949. *Man in the primitive world: an introduction to anthropology*. New York: McGraw-Hill.

1960. *The Cheyennes: Indians of the Great Plains*. New York: Holt, Rinehart & Winston.

Katz, Jonathan. 1976. *Gay American history: lesbians and gay men in the U.S.A*. New York: Crowell.

Kelly, Raymond. 1976. "Witchcraft and sexual relations: an exploration of the social and semantic implications of the structure of belief." In *Man and woman in the New Guinea Highlands*, ed. P. Brown and G. Buchbinder. Special publication of the American Anthropological Association, no. 8, pp. 36–53.

Kroeber, A. L. 1925. *Handbook of the Indians of California*. U.S. BAE Bulletin No.78. Washington, D.C.: U.S. GPO.

1940. "Psychosis or social sanction." In A. L. Kroeber, *The nature of culture*. Chicago: University of Chicago Press, 1952, pp 310–19.

Landes, Ruth. 1938. *The Ojibwa woman*. New York: Norton.

1968. *The Mystic Lake Sioux: sociology of the Mdewakantonwan Santee*. Madison: University of Wisconsin Press.

1970. *The Prairie Potawatomi*. Madison: University of Wisconsin Press.

Lewis, Oscar. 1941. "The manly-hearted woman among the North Piegan." *American Anthropologist* 43: 173–87.

Lowie, Robert. 1924. *Primitive religion*. New York: Liveright.

1956. *The Crow Indians*. New York: Rinehart.

Lurie, Nancy O. 1953. "Winnebago berdache." *American Anthropologist* 55: 708–12.

Meigs, Anna S. 1976. "Male pregnancy and the reduction of sexual opposition in a New Guinea Highlands society." *Ethnology* 14: 393–407.

Munroe, Robert; Whiting, John W. M.; and Hally, David J. 1969. "Institutionalized male transvestism and sex distinctions." *American Anthropologist* 71: 87–91.

Newton, Esther. 1977. "Role models," in *Symbolic anthropology: a reader in the study of symbols and meaning*, ed. J. Dolgin et al. New York: Columbia U. Press.

Parsons, E. C. 1916. "The Zuni La'Mana." *American Anthropologist* 18: 521–8.

Raymond, J. G. 1979. *The transsexual empire: the making of the she-male*. Boston: Beacon Press.

Rubin, Gayle. 1975. "The traffic in women: notes on the 'political economy' of sex." In *Toward an anthropology of women*, ed. R. Reiter, pp. 157–210. New York: Monthly Review Press.

Schieffelin, Edward. 1976. *The sorrow of the lonely and the burning of the dancers*. New York: St. Martin's Press.

Schneider, David. 1968. *American kinship: a cultural account*. Englewood Cliffs: Prentice-Hall.

1972. "What is kinship all about?" In *Kinship studies in the Morgan Centennial year*, ed. P. Reining, pp. 32–63. Washington D.C.: Washington Anthropological Society.

and R. T. Smith. 1973. *Class differences in American kinship*. Ann Arbor: University of Michigan Press.

Simms, S. C. 1903. "Crow Indian hermaphrodites." *American Anthropologist* 5: pp. 580–1.

Slater, Philip. 1968. *The glory of Hera: Greek mythology and the Greek family.* Boston: Beacon Press.

Smith-Rosenberg, Carroll. 1978. "Sex as symbol of Victorian purity." In *Turning points: historical and sociological essays on the family*, ed. John Demos and Sarane Spence Boocock. Chicago: University of Chicago Press.

Strathern, M. 1972. *Women in between*. London: Seminar (Academic) Press.

Underhill, Ruth M. 1939. *The social organization of the Papago Indians*. New York: Columbia University Press.

Van Baal, J. 1966. *Dema: description and analysis of Marind-Anim culture*. The Hague: Martinus Nijhoff.

3

Transforming "natural" woman: FEMALE RITUAL LEADERS AND GENDER IDEOLOGY AMONG BIMIN-KUSKUSMIN

Fitz John Porter Poole

Ortner (1974:69) maintains that a study of women's social power and position requires ''...first understanding the overarching ideology and deeper assumptions of the culture that render...'' them in a distinctive way. In general, this analysis will examine certain central aspects of the ideological construction of gender among the Bimin-Kuskusmin of the remote West Sepik interior of Papua New Guinea.[1] In particular, it will focus on the apparently anomalous, androgynous image of the *waneng aiyem ser* (paramount ''female ritual leader'' or ''sacred woman'') in order to illuminate some dimensions (and their structures) of femaleness and maleness that characterize, *mutatis mutandis*, all Bimin-Kuskusmin social persons, but that are ''embedded'' differently in persons of distinct (and also ambiguous) gender.[2] Through the lens of the *waneng aiyem ser*, I shall demonstrate that Bimin-Kuskusmin gender concepts, rather than being static, immutable images of male and female in simple contrast, involve a recognition of process, of flow, of transition, and of dynamic (and different) balances in relation to (different and similar) substances that are given form in their articulation.[3] A particular construction of gender may crystallize in a particular context or at a particular moment of the life cycle only to be disarticulated and transformed into a new synthesis of ''natural'' dimensions as the life cycle progresses or the context shifts. Gender among Bimin-Kuskusmin involves a consideration of attributes, capacities, and signs (corporeal and noncorporeal – ethnobiological, ethnopsychological, and social) that are associated with different aspects of personhood and kinship in different ways in different contexts, for kinship relationships are the relationships par excellence that are interwoven with gender differences. But the system of meanings that constitute gender is anchored in (cultural ''representations'' of) ''natural'' phenomena (substances), which, in themselves, are seen to form complex structures.

Every analytic perspective may require a metaphor to organize it. Here one is provided in the ethnography. A key focus in ''making sense'' of the Bimin-Kuskusmin symbolism of gender is the persona of the *waneng aiyem ser*. A significant aspect of ''her'' analytic value is that she is apparently paradoxical in gender and thus presents an ethnographic puzzle that I shall attempt to probe, disentangle, and even solve. Among Bimin-Kuskusmin, the *waneng aiyem ser* stands in rather stark contrast to other women. The adult, married woman largely ''appears'' to be disvalued in stereotype, disenfranchised in political and economic power, dissociated from religious matters, and relegated to the domestic domain of children, gardens, and pigs in a manner long enshrined in the Highland Papua New Guinea ethnography.[4] Yet, the *waneng aiyem ser* is respected, powerful, wealthy, and prominent in male ritual. Her unique initiation substantially removes her from the concerns and obligations of the domestic-familial domain to install her in some semblance of a ritual "office" (see Fortes 1962, 1968). Once initiated, she is significantly embedded in *both* male *and* female ritual domains as the female agnate (of her patriclan) par excellence. Until her death, she will dwell in relative isolation and be surrounded by ritual *sacrae* that are associated with her obligations in male and female initiation, rites of purification, curing, divination, and other ritual matters. Her remaining life will be almost entirely encompassed by her "sacred" (*aiyem*) identity.

The ambiguous gender of the *waneng aiyem ser* is immediately apparent. In male ritual, she participates centrally throughout the long initiation cycle in the guise of primordial, hermaphroditic ancestors, and her skull eventually will be placed among male *sacrae* in her clan *katiam* cult house. She alone is said to "own" both sweet potato (female) and taro (male) gardens, and her gardens are "sacred" and set apart. She will handle sexual substances in ritual contexts, for she alone cannot be polluted by them. Yet, she is highly sacred and in *this* capacity can be polluted by and polluting to all other persons, with the sole exceptions of other *waneng aiyem ser* and their male "counterparts" (*kunum aiyem ser*).[5] Hence, as *waneng kusem ser* (paramount "female curer–diviner"), she is focal in rites of purification from sexual contamination for *both* females *and* males, and in divinations concerning the dreaded, highly polluting "female witch" (*tamam*). In female ritual, she often appears to represent the interests of her (male) clan agnates. She presides over the single female initiation at first menses, acts as paramount ritual midwife at births, bestows "female names" (*waneng win*) upon the uninitiated, and participates in the initiation of neophyte *waneng aiyem ser* of her clan.

In her distinctive initiation rite, ritual adornment, "taboo" (*aiyem mesem*) restrictions, and social identity, the ambiguous *waneng aiyem ser* appears to be neither female nor male, but rather "betwixt and between." She is old, no longer married, asexual, and postmenopausal, yet she remains a bodily reservoir of female "fertile fluids" sealed in a more or less male vessel for purposes of male ritual. Her unique initiation seems to be focused on this peculiar transformation of her gender attributes through ritual "operations" on substance. As a participant in ritual, her regalia is constructed of elements that are drawn from distinct phases of male initiation, that are female, and that are unique. Similarly, her myriad taboos are partly female and partly male, forming a unique constellation. Her possession of and rights of disposal over male valuables seem bizarre, as does her right to speak formally in a distinctively male *genre* on certain public occasions. Indeed, she bears a "male name" (*kunum win*) and a "sacred name" (*aiyem win*),[6] and she may be called a "male mother" (*auk kunum imok*). In the social and "natural" (as culturally conceived) peculiarities of her person, the *waneng aiyem ser* is a complex assemblage of "man" (*kunum*) and "woman" (*waneng*), "female" (*yangus*) and "male" (*imok*).

The ideological construction of gender among Bimin-Kuskusmin, seen in terms of the separation and articulation of natural substances and the image of the *waneng aiyem ser*, is very complex (cf. Barth 1975:204, 228). Both men and women are fascinated by the subject, and exegesis is highly elaborated (cf. ibid., p. 226).[7] But generally, it is natural substance focused within and between human bodies that forms the foundation of discussions that deal with the particular social identities of men and women, girls and boys. And embodied substances (originating in procreative contributions) become a basis for not only gender constructs, but also social relationships that are related to a fundamental differentiation of male and female. Thus, the intent of analysis is twofold: (a) to reveal some central "meanings" of man and woman, male and female, masculine and feminine, in Bimin-Kuskusmin culture through the exploration of an anomalous gender image; and (b) to link these meanings, as they unfold, to those sociostructural dimensions that seem to be most central to Bimin-Kuskusmin concepts of gender and to the institution of the *waneng aiyem ser*. Indeed, the figure of the *waneng aiyem ser* provides a privileged instance in which the sociocultural dimensions of gender may be seen most clearly, and these dimensions (their nature and structure) may suggest, in turn, why there is a *waneng aiyem ser* among Bimin-Kuskusmin.

Both the mode and the subject of this analysis are somewhat unusual in trying to "make sense" of gender and sexuality in Highland Papua New Guinea. Most early investigations of the Highlands dealt primarily with man–woman relations and sociostructural variations that might account for gender difference, rather than the cultural construction of gender per se.[8] Only a few selected features or a global impression of gender were invoked before turning to a comparative search for sociostructural correlates or determinants. Only recently have anthropologists recognized that different social identities assume paramount metaphorical significance for gender in different societies.[9] Langness (1976: 97), however, remarks that "The issue involved respecting the relative position of the sexes is not merely of men versus women but, rather, one involving absolutely fundamental historical, philosophical, and religious convictions about the nature of the life process itself." Indeed, recent attention to the symbolism of gender has raised new analytic problems.[10] Thus, for the Hua, Meigs (1976: 406) notes that, "A person's gender does not lie locked in his or her genitals but can flow and change with contact as substances seep into and out of his or her body" (cf. Strathern 1978b). And these problems have become linked to renewed attention to ritual,[11] procreative process,[12] ideas of maturation,[13] and relations between patrilineal recruitment and matrilateral influences.[14] Thus, natural substances (embedded in persons by procreative process) may become a basis for reckoning not only gender, but also social relations that are related to gender differences.

Two modes of illuminating the image of the *waneng aiyem ser* are used throughout analysis. The first follows the progression of the female life cycle. The generic term *waneng aiyem* denotes three "graded" identities: *seib aiyem*; *waneng imok aiyem*; and *waneng aiyem ser*. All *waneng aiyem ser* are said to have been *waneng imok aiyem* and, before that, *seib aiyem*. The *seib aiyem* is a young, premenstruous, unmarried, virginal maiden. She and the *waneng imok aiyem* undergo no special initiation and are selected for superficial participation in particular male ritual performances. The *waneng imok aiyem*, who should have once been a *seib aiyem*, is a mature, menstruous, married, sexually active mother. The *waneng aiyem ser*, however, is an old, postmenopausal, no longer married, asexual androgyne. She undergoes special initiation and is selected for central and permanent participation in most male *and* female ritual performances. The second involves a developing contrast between the *waneng aiyem ser* and the "mother" (*auk*), on the one hand, and the "female witch" (*tamam*), on the other. The contrast focuses on the ends to which these three females devote fertile fluids, menstrual blood, and semen. All three are seen to represent different constructions of natural substance and of gender.

The data on which the analysis is based are very dense. Therefore, it seems useful to outline the structure of presentation. After a brief sketch of Bimin-Kuskusmin culture and society, I turn to the foundation of the gender system in "Procreation and substance." Here I demonstrate that natural substances are separated and articulated in structures that relate to the (cultural) constitution of persons in body, spirit, personality, and behavioral tendencies. I argue that the basic "nature" of *both* gender *and* genealogy is seen in terms of these substances. Thereafter, I explore the implications and symbolic (ritual) transformations of substance at strategic points of the female life cycle. In "Birth," where the *waneng aiyem ser* appears as ritual midwife, I demonstrate how ritual, taboo, and prestation are linked to a recognition of the flow and strength of natural substances. In "Female naming," where the *waneng aiyem ser* appears as ritual officiant, I show how a rite of passage involves a focus on natural substance and process in marking the early gender and social identity of the child. In "Female initiation," where the *waneng aiyem ser* appears as ritual leader, I argue that the genesis (female) and control (male) of menstrual blood is central to all (natural and social) reproduction and to marriage and motherhood. Here menstrual blood appears as the most ambiguous of all natural substances – essential to fertility and a polluting impediment to health, strength, and growth. In "Marriage and motherhood," where the *waneng aiyem ser* appears as former wife and mother, I note the significance of rights *in uxorem*, *in genetricem*, and *in rem* in relation to substance and the natural social identity of children. Finally, in "The *Waneng Aiyem Ser*" and the conclusion, drawing on the legacy of prior analysis, I demonstrate how natural and ritual transformations of substance and prior social identities (in relation to substance) make sense of the image of the *waneng aiyem ser* as a focal model of gender among Bimin-Kuskusmin.

There are three interlinked themes that form the background to this analysis: (a) a dialectic between perceptions of the human body (including gender attributes) and the "social body"(see Douglas 1970; cf. Ellen 1977: 369 and Firth 1973: 307); (b) a dialectic between gender concepts (including the male–female or masculine–feminine attributes they generate) and living persons (see Strathern 1976, 1978b) or other phenomenal referents (see Buchbinder and Rappaport 1976); and (c) a dialectic between ideological models grounded in "nature" and codes for social conduct (see Barnett 1976; Geertz 1973a, 1973b; Ortner 1973; and Schneider 1968). At the high level of generality at which they are phrased, all of these themes seem to be supported in the present case. Indeed, what is particularly interesting about Bimin-Kuskusmin gender is the way in which natural substances and processes (and ritual manipulations thereof) have been elaborated so that contours of the social body, attributes of the person, codes for conduct, and features of the cosmos seem almost encompassed by gender idioms drawn from these natural models. But it is important to note that this analysis is an exercise in illuminating the cultural logic and social basis of a *particular* ideology of gender. Cultural constructions of gender are founded upon different conceptual bases and, consequently, have different ramifications in different societies. In the Bimin-Kuskusmin case, the conceptual basis of gender ideology is bound up with ideas of procreation and natural substance, which serve to discriminate not only gender categories, but also age and descent categories. And, whatever else it may be "about" (in a metaphoric sense), Bimin-Kuskusmin gender ideology is an explicit indigenous "theory" about sex (as well as age and descent) distinctions. It will become apparent that these partially linked distinctions are of enormous importance to Bimin-Kuskusmin, but an explanation of this importance (and complexity) of gender ideology must deal with the contradictions and tensions of sociopolitical organization, warfare, ethnohistory, and socialization (see Poole, forthcoming "a") in another analysis. The present endeavor seeks only to unravel some key dimensions of the system of gender ideology.

Thus, my approach to female (and male) gender and the *waneng aiyem ser* will be founded on an examination of notions of procreation and substance among the Bimin-Kuskusmin. I shall also be concerned with women (in relation to both men and women) as wives and mothers, sisters and daughters, and so on. I shall be particularly interested in the sense in which a woman (in any of several social identities) can be considered an agnate (or non-agnate). My focal image ultimately will be that of the *waneng aiyem ser*. When I first encountered the Bimin-Kuskusmin, I was disconcerted to discover that fear of female pollution "seemed" more rampant, female–male conflict more ferocious, and sexual segregation more rigid and pervasive than in many Highland societies. To some extent, I was enmeshed in an illusion. Yet, my consternation increased upon discerning an anomaly in this apparent pattern. In putatively exclusive male realms, where men claimed that female intrusion would be punishable by severe maiming or even death,[15] there were powerful female elders present. They appeared prominently in male and female rituals, wore bizarre regalia, controlled male valuables, and spoke in public with manly force and authority. They were known by special names and endured special initiations. Their skulls appeared among male *sacrae* in clan cult houses after elaborate (male) funerals. Eventually, they became powerful, yet rather special agnatic ancestors.

Bimin-Kuskusmin men, perhaps in the manner of some Highlands anthropologists, tended to articulate rather nasty stereotypes of women in general that, in fact, referred largely to inmarried wives, particularly the childless and those from alien groups beyond Bimin-Kuskusmin territory. With respect to mothers and to sisters and daughters, however, the image shifted and often softened with restrained affection and pride. But on the subject of *waneng aiyem ser*, both gleeful distaste and friendly warmth vanished from the discussion; for they were sacred women, with admired ritual "hotness" and "strength," and worthy of the respect granted to the great ancestors Afek and Yomnok,[16] whom they represent. Therefore, I shall attempt to unravel some of the complexities of their social identity and gender. By way of introduction, I shall delineate some general features of Bimin-Kuskusmin society and culture in relation to males and females.

The Bimin-Kuskusmin

About one thousand Bimin-Kuskusmin occupy a rugged, ecologically diverse, mountainous area in the extreme southeast of the West Sepik Province. In a Mountain-Ok language, they elaborate their mythico–historical priority, centrality, and uniqueness in the area and mark the conceptual boundedness of the "central place" as their domain. Yet, networks of trade, alliance, warfare, intermarriage, and ritual relations bring them into more or less sustained contact with other tribal groups of the Mountain-Ok region and beyond (see Barth 1971). They have known something of Europeans at least since the Kaiserin-Augusta-Fluss Expedition (1912–14) penetrated the Telefomin area to the west. But first direct contact was experienced by a very few individuals in 1957. With the opening of the Oksapmin patrol post to the north in 1961, patrols began to probe the periphery of their territory from time to time. On the eve of fieldwork (1971), however, such contact remained markedly limited. Most of the population had not seen a European; some stone tools were in regular use; little European paraphernalia was in evidence; and familiarity with mission and government custom was slight.

Much of the daily round is spent in sexually segregated subsistence activities. Men do all initial clearing and fencing of all gardens, but then largely abandon sweet potato gardens as the realm of *wanengamariin* ("people of women's houses"),[17] who may transport taro but not enter the taro gardens of initiated men. The primary cultigens are (male) taro and nut pandanus and (female) sweet potato, although other indigenous and some European food plants are grown in low sweet potato gardens on valley floors. Here are grown reeds from which women's skirts are fashioned. Here too are buried tubes of menstrual blood that are used in the ritual fertilization of female crops. Various semicultivated crops (for instance, banana, fruit pandanus, sago) are tended only by initiated men. Taro, in high male gardens on lower mountain slopes, is the paramount cultigen in ritual significance and perception of food value, but the female sweet potato predominates in the daily diet. In taro gardens are grown phallocrypt gourds, and here are placed tubes of semen to strengthen the agnatic *finiik* spirit (see section on "Procreation and substance") within the tubers. Only *waneng aiyem ser* are associated with both taro and sweet potato gardens.

Semidomestic dogs and cassowary chicks are few and are owned and tended by initiated men. Pig herds are tiny by Highlands standards and are replenished by capture of feral piglets. Both men and women have rights in pigs by virtue of ownership (usually male) or custodianship (male and female). Domestic boars are castrated so that women and children may eat them without fear of pollution, but feral boars are the food of only initiated men and *waneng aiyem ser*. There is extensive, regular gathering of wild foods in forest and stream by women and children, and most of these flora and fauna are "female food." Initiated men, through hunting and trapping, provide considerable meat sporadically – only some of which is "male food." Adult women are permitted to hunt some large game on certain occasions, but are denied access to male implements of the hunt and use crude clubs and small (female) stone axes.

Bimin-Kuskusmin social structure (see Poole 1976:384–703) is conceived in an agnatic idiom with overt recognition of significant cognatic, uterine, and affinal links. Patrilineages and cognatic kindred categories are traced in terms of shared "agnatic blood" through the procreative transmissions of men and of men *and* women, respectively. Patriclans, ritual moieties, and initiation age groups, however, are reckoned in terms of shared *finiik* spirit through strictly patrilineal transmissions of semen.

Lineages are of variable size and genealogical span as cultural categories, but are restricted to segments rarely including agnates more distantly related than father's father's father's brother's son's son's son (hereafter FFFBSSS) in local organization. They become focal in numerous transactions, cooperative labor groups, and the ethnohistorical identity of particular hamlets. The conceptual identity of lineage and hamlet is related to the fact that segmentary processes within a lineage may lead to fission and the founding of a new hamlet by a lineage segment (recast as a distinct lineage). In fact, the new hamlet soon attracts shifting congeries of diverse agnates, affines, and others, who usually come to outnumber the lineage "core." Men may seek residence near choice garden land, lineage shrines, or clan cult houses, and among friends, supporters, and kin. But women (married or unmarried) and children have little autonomy in choice of hamlet residence and usually follow spouses and parents.

Lineage and clan relations are linked in marriage transactions, which are arranged by men but can be refused by women. Ideally, lineage brothers ought to exchange sisters (and bridewealth) with men of a particular lineage (but not mothers' lineage) of their mothers' clan. To the degree that lineage wives in previous generations have been drawn from the same lineage (within generations) and clan (across generations), lineage and clan relations are interwoven. The actualization of the ideal pattern, always partial and most common among close lineage agnates, establishes much overlap in the kindreds of lineage agnates. Of course, prior divergence from the ideal, demographic imbalance, variations in the number of lineages in a clan, interlineage hostility, and personal factors, may lead to a rupturing of the ideal pattern. Hence, segmentary fault lines (based on divergence in marriage exchange) within the lineage may appear and be ignored, remedied in succeeding generations, or recognized as a precursor of fission. Despite actual exigencies, however, the obstinacy of women is commonly blamed for failures in the ideal pattern of marriage exchange.

Rights in all types of land are conceptually vested in the clan, ritual moiety, and tribe of all Bimin-Kuskusmin and are mediated almost entirely by men. Most types of land, however, are in abundance, and rights of usufruct are granted generously to both men and women. The ritual sites and esoterica associated with clan, moiety, and age group are forbidden to all women except *waneng aiyem*, although ordinary women may visit lineage shrines on occasion. In fact, only initiated men and *waneng aiyem ser* are associated with one of the four cyclical age groups that are formed during successive performances of the male initiation cycle. Yet, the exogamous *unum* kindred category is conceived in the idiom of agnatic blood transmissions through *both* agnatic *and* uterine links. Although those who trace *unum* relationships to one another may claim rights and obligations that are seen to flow from that relation, these claims are asserted dyadically in most instances; and the *unum* does not form a social group. The uterine links that articulate the *unum* kindred, however, are also considered to be "joints" of the social body (and natural body) through which female "black blood" illness, *tamam* witchcraft, and ancestral vengeance may flow.

Aspects of contrast between male and female seem to permeate all man–woman relations. Residential segregation is strict, with men's houses dominating the crest of a ridge and women's houses strung out below. After the inception of initiation, no male may enter a woman's house under any circumstances; and no female (except *waneng aiyem*) may approach a men's house too closely. Much social space is similarly segregated. Most women (except *waneng aiyem ser*) do not participate directly in the (male) public arena of negotiation, transaction, ritual, and warfare. Yet, they are considered to have some sense of social responsibility, are directly liable for their actions in some contexts, and may receive compensation (including male valuables) for certain personal injuries or insults. In the female association with birth, death, menstruation, and *tamam* witchcraft, however, it is the alien wife from another tribe who is the polluting woman par excellence. But the fertile powers of women – as represented in the image of the mother and the *waneng aiyem ser* – are a matter of positive emphasis among men. As wife and mother, daughter and sister, female relatives are of central importance to men. And certain husband-wife bonds, as well as those of brother-sister, father-daughter, and mother-son, are seen to be close and nurturant in many cases. In the intricacies of gender and male–female relations, Bimin-Kuskusmin possess a highly elaborate exegetical tradition. It is to this heritage that I shall now turn to unravel various facets of gender and of the persona of the *waneng aiyem ser*.

Procreation and substance

In this section, the foundation of gender and social identity in natural substance is explored. In matters of procreation, Bimin-Kuskusmin maintain that males and females transmit to offspring separate, distinctive, and asymmetrically significant, yet basically complementary substances. The exegesis on such matters is more detailed among adult males than among females, with the exception of *waneng aiyem ser*. It is held to be part of the relatively distinct content of male knowledge, although women are clearly aware of its major outlines (cf. Faithorn 1976). Each substance is believed to have a distinct function in the formation of the body, of sexual characteristics, and of more subtle aspects of "spirit" and "heart." The last are related intimately to such phenomena as may be associated with personality, patrilineal identity, moral character, responsibility, loyalty, trustworthiness, and so on.

In the female, during menstrual flow, a gelatinous, whitish mass (*yemor*) forms in the uterus. It consists of a mixture of various vague and undifferentiated vaginal and other secretions (fertile fluids), menstrual blood, and the agnatic blood of several lineage categories. This agnatic blood, carried by and effective in the formation of females and males, is thought to have originated in males. The agnatic blood within the body of a woman that she may transmit to her offspring is believed to include precisely the blood of her own lineage and of the lineages of her mother, father's mother, and mother's mother. The various categories of agnatic blood are thought to be transmitted in increasingly weakened form and effect in direct relation to the degree of ascending generational distance between the female ego and the focal female links of her future child's bilateral, exogamous *unum* kindred category. As a result of the parental transmissions that have defined her own *unum*, she is believed to carry within her body, as are her brothers, the agnatic blood of the lineages of her FFM, FMM, MFM, and MMM as well. However, neither she nor her brothers are believed to transmit this agnatic blood to their offspring. In the ideology of reckoning the *unum*, it is said that agnatic blood, once transmitted through a female, remains "active" in progressively weakened and less effective form for only three descending generations from that focal female, and is not transmitted into the fourth descending generation so reckoned.

Thus, through the multiple acts of sexual intercourse deemed necessary for conception to occur, the male transmits semen that is infused with the agnatic blood of his own lineage and of the lineages of his mother, father's mother, and mother's mother. The agnatic blood of the lineages of his FFM, FMM, MFM, and MMM are merely contained within his body. The male procreative contribution is believed to form a whitish covering that envelops the reddish "skin" formed of menstrual blood, which, in turn, covers the whitish *yemor* mass.

At one end of the white, ovoid *yemor*, there is said to be a tiny hole in the enveloping, white male contribution, which leaves the underlying red aspect of the female contribution (menstrual blood) uncovered. The orientation of that hole toward either the vagina or the "interior" of the uterus is believed to be a determinant of female or male sex, respectively.[18] The orientation itself is not believed to be under human control in any very predictable manner. It is said that private supplications to recently deceased ancestral spirits are occasionally effective. Further increments of semen through increased sexual intercourse are said to shift the balance in favor of a male child. Yet, such acts are severely depleting for males, and the intended effect of further semen can be offset by increases in the antithetical substance of menstrual blood, which weakens the semen in complex ways.

The orientation of the *yemor*, however, is believed to change repeatedly during the course of pregnancy. The critical influences on this change are associated with the travels of the woman near numerous sites of mythological significance that are linked with notions of maleness and femaleness. The visitations of male or female ancestral spirits with the two spirit aspects (*finiik* and *khaapkhabuurien*) of the woman in dreams, certain reflections and shadows, and certain kinds of spirit possession, may also influence a change in orientation. Ultimately, the orientation of the *yemor* body at birth is said to be determined by the last such influence prior to the seclusion of the woman in a birth hut at the first indication of the onset of sustained labor contractions.

Sexual differentiation, then, occurs rather late in Bimin-Kuskusmin conceptions of prenatal development. Men sometimes suspect, and women often claim that females have more control in the matter. Women do practice a secret ritual in the birth hut that is said to have some influence on the sex of the child, but men suggest that such ritual is probably too late in the course of events and is altogether too weak in efficacy. Even women admit that such ritual is weak and contaminated by the residues of the birth hut. Thus, in recognizing some arbitrariness in whether a baby is born male or female, or in emphasizing the importance of female agnates, men sometimes claim that "we must treat our sisters well, for they might have been born our brothers." Such ideas may be transformed into more negative declarations in the course of affinal disputes when husbands not uncommonly remind their wives that they are truly the agnates of their obnoxious brothers and sisters, or the brothers of wives that they are behaving like the women that they should have been. Of particular importance, however, is the fact that conceptions of prenatal gender foreshadow later features of gender mutability, but show them as largely uncontrollable in contrast to the ritual transformations of gender that occur later in the life cycle.

The transmission of all agnatic blood through both mother and father is said to determine – insofar as genealogical reckoning is supportive – the *unum* kindred of the child. This category, founded on a recognition of the importance of uterine links, provides a significant network of supportive cognatic kin for the child. On the one hand, he or she can rely on them more or less for food and shelter, refuge in times of trouble, rights of usufruct in garden and hunting land, and support in certain disputes. On the other hand, these uterine links are critical in the vulnerability of the child, for it is through these connections that the attacks of "black blood" illness (associated with menstrual contamination), the vengeance of female ancestors (as well as male ancestors related through uterine descent), certain debilitating kinds of possession by female spirits, and the dreaded *tamam* witchcraft, which is lethal only when embodied in and wielded by females (see Poole 1974), may descend on the person, male or female. Thus, although female forebears may receive positive ritual attention in some contexts (especially if they were *waneng aiyem ser*), they or the uterine ties that they represent inevitably carry the potential of malevolence (see Goody 1970 and Harris 1973).

Yet, the relative "strength" of the agnatic blood of the lineage categories of the child's mother and father is a subject of detailed commentary in many contexts. Both males and females insist upon the primacy of the father's lineage category agnatic blood in the determination of the child's lineage (and clan) identity, whether male or female. The patrifiliative bond of agnatic blood is held to be the strongest and most active and to be immutable in an ethnobiological sense. It is said to be altered in no conceivable way by residential attachment through cognatic or affinal ties, although it can be transformed in one's descendants through the consumption of certain taro, pandanus nuts, meat, and fat associated with the agnatic *finiik* spirit of another clan. Only in rare cases of moral horror (for example, witchcraft or incest) may the patrifiliative bond be "cut" by ritual procedures. Because the matrifiliative bond of agnatic blood is weaker by cultural definition, however, certain prestations to matrilateral kin are required to insure the actualization of important exchanges between mother's brother and sister's son. Although further prestations to matrilateral kin are required on behalf of both male and female children, they are regarded as strengthening (or compensating for injury to) a bond of substance that is "naturally" weak. They are required for the establishment of a socially enduring bond with matrilateral kin, and *not* for offsetting matrilateral claims in matters of recruitment to social groups. Beyond the conceptualization of identity with respect to the lineage and the kindred, however, the transmission of agnatic blood per se performs no further significant function in the formation of the body and noncorporeal identity of the child.

The various categories of agnatic blood from both parents are thought to be present and to persist in corporeal, as well as symbolic form in the veins and arteries and heart of the child. In addition, a large number of separate, but complementary aspects of the "anatomy" are said to be the result of parental contributions of male semen and female fertile fluids in the child. In offspring of either sex, the semen of the father is said to form the following:

teeth	tendons, ligaments,	ear aperture	eyes
nail	veins, arteries	ear lobe	liver
cartilage, bone	lymphatic system (?)	"external" nostrils	kidneys
upper palate	hair (not facial or	"internal" nostrils	heart
muscle	pubic)	nasal septum	brain
Adam's apple	intestinal mesentery	nasal bridge and	lungs
	bone marrow	tip of nose	frontal cranial sutures

In offspring of either sex, the fertile fluids of the mother are said to form the following:

feces	anus	small intestine	pancreas
urine	rectum	large intestine	abdominal navel
saliva	urinary bladder	stomach	umbilical cord
perspiration	nipples	spleen	skin
nasal mucus	flesh	gall bladder	fat

On the one hand, the corporeal effects of the fertile fluids are said to be "weak," "external," and "soft." They are assumed to be the first anatomical elements to decompose on burial platforms and are, therefore, soft and weak. They are also soft and weak because they are not believed to contribute to the fundamental strength of the body (or its noncorporeal aspects) in either domestic labor or ritual activity. They are said to be external either in a literal sense of being on or close to the surface of the body, or in the sense of having a direct connection with the surface of the body. The latter connections are through some form of ingestion, excretion, or proneness to the effects of certain illnesses that are assumed to enter the body through passages that are associated with ingestion or excretion. All such fleshy parts of the body are associated with the female contribution, with certain exceptions that are associated with the male contribution. All passages involved in breathing, hearing, and seeing (all associated with bony structure and key ritual "senses"); the accumulation of "sacred male knowledge" (transmitted through the frontal cranial sutures); and the flow of both semen and fertile fluids (but not menstrual blood), are believed to emanate from the paternal procreative contribution. Thus, the female anatomy (and the female foods that sustain it) is considered temporary, illness-prone, and weak. It is associated with the more contaminating of human wastes and is largely antithetical to ritual efficacy. Embodied in the postmenopausal *waneng aiyem ser*, female fertile fluids are important to male ritual control of powers of fertility, birth, maturation, and so on, when they are appropriately separated from the pollution of menstrual blood (with which they are bound up in all other women). But these fertile fluids are a male procreative contribution – the power of which is relinquished to daughters in procreation and is reclaimed in the ritual figure of the *waneng aiyem ser*.

On the other hand, the corporeal effects of semen are said to be "strong," "internal," and "hard." They include most of the anatomical elements that are emphasized in male ritual contexts in a positive manner. The contributions of the father are assumed to be the last elements to decompose on burial platforms and to include the only elements that are subsequently incorporated as ritual *sacrae* in *katiam* cult and *am yaoor* initiation performances. In these senses, they are hard and strong. They are also hard and strong because they are believed to contribute centrally to the strength of the body in both domestic labor and ritual activity. They are said to be internal in several senses. They are of central importance in the durability and functioning of the body. They are concerned with surface features that possess "roots" within the body. They are concerned with passages that are either enclosed within the body; are unidirectional and unconnected (unlike the perceived connection between ingestive and excretory passages) in the instances of breathing, hearing, seeing, and acquiring male knowledge; or are associated with the transmission of both semen and fertile fluids.

In regard to such sexual fluids, all of which are considered powerful and dangerous, men commonly claim that women (that is, wives) are highly irresponsible in their conservation. Such women are said to be careless during intercourse and to spill both semen and fertile fluids on the ground of the forest where such activities occur. There these fluids are highly contaminating to both humans and nonhuman creatures and spirits involved in human welfare. There they can be collected by sorcerers and witches for nefarious purposes. Irresponsible wives are said to be particularly wanton in their disregard for conserving and containing menstrual blood (as well as postpartum discharges that are associated with menstrual blood). In this regard, the "promiscuous woman" (*waasop waneng*) and the "female witch" (*tamam*) are the most dangerous, for they intend to injure men with their menstrual substance.

Men neither generate nor have biological connection with the production of menstrual blood, and it is the most dangerous of all female substances to them. Yet, they firmly believe that they alone and by ritual means have the power to control it in most circumstances. However, both semen and fertile fluids are held to be male procreative contributions and, therefore, sacred, as opposed to the ordinary but polluting contributions of the mother. Thus, although menstrual blood is highly ambiguous and threatening, the fertile powers of women, which are of such ritual concern to men, are naturally male in origin. The male anatomy (and the male foods that sustain it) – in both men and women – is considered enduring, ideally invulnerable, and strong. It is associated with the most powerful of natural human essences (with the ambiguous exception of menstrual blood) and is intimately bound up with ritual efficacy.

In offspring of male gender, the father's semen is said to form the following: facial hair; pubic hair; penis; testicles; and semen. In daughters, the male semen is said to form both fertile fluids and breast milk, which are seen as complementary manifestations of a single female fluid that functions in the development of unborn and unweaned children of both sexes. The semen of the father also is said to produce the pus that is exuded in the suppurating sores of both sexes. The substance pus is, then, a manifestation of semen and is associated with semen in males as an aspect of the general category of "male fluids." In females, it is a manifestation of fertile fluids, which are produced by semen, and is associated with fertile fluids in females as an aspect of the general category of "female fluids." Loss of semen and pus in males, and of fertile fluids, breast milk, and pus in females, is considered to be weakening. Such depletion is usually most severe and uncontrolled, however, in the loss of pus in sores. It can kill both men and women, or cause barrenness in women (male sterility is not recognized) or ritual impotence in men. It is of interest to note that the most debilitating of such sores are thought to be caused by female *tamam* witches, who consume male substance (including pus) and primarily produce only the most contaminating of female substances, namely, menstrual blood (see Poole 1974).

Both male and female sexual fluids are believed to be located, in various tubular systems, throughout the bodies of the respective sexes. Normally, the male fluid is manifested entirely as semen, which funnels through various tubes into the penis on ejaculation. Female fluids, however, are manifested as both fertile fluids and breast milk, which are supposed to be temporally discrete and complementary substances. Thus, it is said that the prolonged postpartum sex taboo is necessary, in part, to insure that female fluids are extruded entirely as breast milk and are not transformed into fertile fluids by acts of sexual intercourse. Such transformation would diminish the unweaned child's vital supply of nutrients. Nevertheless, breast milk builds female substance, and it is noted that unweaned children are remarkably fat. Consequently, it is said that the unweaned (male) child who consumes breast milk almost exclusively should not enter the initial phase of male initiation, for the continued direct influence of female fluids in this form would tend to counteract the intended effects of ritual socialization. There is an apparent ambiguity here. Breast milk is a male contribution. Yet, it is a special manifestation of semen that can appear *only* in females, but that is normally ingested by male children.

In daughters, the fertile fluids of the mother are said to form the following: breasts; uterus; vagina; clitoris; pubic hair; ovaries; and small tubes or "cords" in the female reproductive area. Some of these elements possess special characteristics. Thus, breasts are considered to be a powerful manifestation of female substance, for both the breasts and the onset of menses suggest a rapid and "natural" maturation in girls that is not apparent analogously in boys. The clitoris is sometimes said to be an "embryonic penis" that was formed in the womb when the fetus was temporarily in the male orientation. The female pubic hair is said to be soft and weak, in contrast to the stronger, coarser pubic hair of males.

The menstrual blood of the mother is assumed to pass to all offspring. In daughters, it exists throughout the body before puberty and the onset of first menses. It will be the subsequent cause of their own menstruation. It is said to form the placenta at conception and to diminish at menopause. Hence, the postmenopausal *waneng aiyem ser* undergoes a ritual removal of the remaining residues of menstrual blood by deliberate bleeding induced in the region of the head during her special initiation. The menstrual blood of the mother also is transmitted to sons and is believed to be strengthened somewhat in infancy by the ingestion of breast milk. At the inception of the male initiation cycle, however, ritual bleeding, symbolic extrusion of breast milk, segregation of initiates from all associations with "people of women's houses," abstinence from female foods, and so on, all are said to "remove" or "make die" dangerous and debilitating female influences, especially menstrual blood.

Menstrual blood remains an ambiguous substance. It originates in females and is perpetuated by uterine descent. It is somehow essential to natural (female) fertility, yet is inimical to the growth of all but weak, soft female substances. It is strengthened by other female substances. It is often described as "black" and compared to the effluvia of illness, wounds, decay, and death. In this regard, it is contrasted with "red" agnatic blood, yet many red flora and fauna are classified as utterly taboo or as restricted female foods in part on account of their coloration, which then is associated with menstrual blood. Contact with it is debilitating to both men and women, for it weakens the agnatic *finiik* spirit and other aspects of male substance. But such pollution is especially dangerous to initiated men, who may experience lethargy, shortness of breath, bodily weakness, anorexia, irrationality, stupidity, poor hunting and gardening, ritual ineffectuality, and even death as a consequence. Yet, its apparent power and relation to (female) fertility makes it of great ritual interest to men, who claim to control it by ritual means. Thus, at the highest stage of male initiation, actual (and symbolic) menstrual blood, an ambiguous substance, is brought into sacred male ritual contexts by an ambiguous androgyne, the *waneng aiyem ser*.[19] This woman, without menstrual capacity but with fertile fluids, becomes the paramount symbolic medium through which men approach and assert control over this anomalous substance. Without her, it seems only to be inimical to ritual efficacy.

The respective paternal and maternal procreative contributions of the "frontal cranial sutures," glossed here as "male navel," and the "abdominal navel," glossed here as "female navel," are of special importance in both ritual and the complex conceptualization of gender. In brief, it is believed that during pregnancy, through the association of placenta and umbilical cord in vaguely linking mother and child, menstrual blood and other polluting "unknown female things" are transmitted to all children. Such female influences are the focus of ritual extrusions in the initiations of both males and *waneng aiyem ser*. These substances are also contaminating to females, who are noted to become ill during menses; yet, they must be endured as an essential element in childbearing. At the birth of a child of either sex, women invariably cover the male navel with mud. They claim that they do so in order to protect the child from injury to the interior of the head through inadvertent penetration of the soft, weak skin over the cranial sutures. Men, and significantly *waneng aiyem ser*, however, offer an alternative explanation and suggest that the explanation of women is a deliberate lie. In contrast, they claim that the female navel is a "road" of both pre- and post-natal transmissions of dangerous and uncontrolled female influences and substances and "evil, worthless female knowledge." Consequently, women are said to clean the female navel secretly with leaves to permit the entrance of such malevolent influences. It is also said that women may secretly wash the female navel of unweaned children with menstrual blood when they are secluded with the children in menstrual huts.

The female knowledge is said, by men, *waneng aiyem ser*, and sometimes other women, to be of little value. It is conveyed through a fleshy navel. It is associated with polluting ingestive and excretive processes that are focused in the abdomen. It disappears with the decay of the corpse and is not represented in the ancestral underworld. Yet, it is claimed that women strengthen such influences in order to cement the bonds between themselves and their children (especially sons), which then can be severed only by the ritual intervention of men. Men claim that women deliberately cover the male navel with mud to prevent the transmission of male knowledge, which is antithetical to their own, and to bind the child to the female domain. In this context, it is noted that the mud used by women is the yellow mud associated with the bodily adornment of those who mourn the recently deceased. As one informant observed, "The woman's mud comes like death, the 'male navel' it almost goes away."

Yet, the "sacred male knowledge" is considered to be essential to the formation of the gender and social identity of all normal males and all *waneng aiyem*, especially *waneng aiyem ser*. It is conveyed through a bony navel. It is associated with the ritually significant skull. It tends to remain despite the decay of the corpse and is present exclusively in the ancestral underworld. Consequently, during the initiation of both males and *waneng aiyem ser*, the area of the male navel is shaved and cleaned. In contrast, the female navel is covered with the yellow mud that is associated with death and mourning.

In prior discussion of the Bimin-Kuskusmin ideas about agnatic blood, it was noted that the transmission of such blood through females diminishes its strength and activity, whereas the transmission of such blood through males does not. The explanation of this difference focuses on variations in the functioning of male semen with respect to the (male) heart in males and females. In the female, agnatic blood merely collects in the heart and partially decomposes over time. There are several reasons given for this gradual decay. Women do not possess semen, for the paternal contribution is converted into other substances in daughters. Men, of course, do possess semen. Semen contains and transmits the dual spirit entity *kusem* – manifested as *finiik* and *khaapkhabuurien*. The *kusem*, particularly in its *finiik* aspect, is believed to make the agnatic blood strong and active. Semen, containing *finiik*, exists throughout the tubular system of the body, which includes the heart. Thus, it strengthens and increases the agnatic blood which collects in and passes out of the heart (an "arterial logic"). The rituals of males and *waneng aiyem ser* are important in this rejuvenation. During such ritual, when (normal) heterosexual contact is forbidden, the heart is said to become "hot"; and semen flows into it. Furthermore, certain ritual taros, which are infused with actual semen and are believed to be infused with ancestral *finiik* spirit, are consumed in several of these ritual contexts. The *waneng aiyem*, who are not yet (the *seib aiyem*), not presently (the *waneng imok aiyem*), or no longer (the *waneng aiyem ser*) sexually active, are required to consume such ritual taro during these performances. In normal females, however, agnatic blood is neither rejuvenated nor increased. Thus, they transmit a weaker contribution to their children than their husbands do.

The agnatic blood (of his own lineage), semen, and *finiik* that are received from the father create a perduring bond with a series of agnates, deceased, living, and not yet born, of both genders. The agnatic blood, fertile fluids, and menstrual blood that are received from the mother, however, create a more fragile link to a network of matrilateral or uterine relatives. Agnatic blood in its strongest form becomes the idiom of lineage identity. The sharing of *finiik*, by strict patrilineal logic, however, becomes a vehicle for expressing enduring clan and ritual moiety identity. It is through consumption of certain ritual taro containing only the *finiik* of all ancestors of a particular age group that the unity of initiation age groups is articulated. Thus, by also consuming such taro, *waneng aiyem ser* (and other *waneng aiyem* in some contexts) are linked to certain age groups in a manner that does not pertain to all other women. It should be noted that lineages, defined by shared agnatic blood that can vary in strength and mode of transmission, are *recognized* as being subject to processes of segmentation and fission. Clans, moieties, and age groups, however, are viewed as immutable categories over time. In turn, they are all defined by strictly patrilineal transmissions of *finiik* (through semen) that link past, present, and future generations through males exclusively. The *waneng aiyem* may be bound to clan, moiety, and age group through *finiik*, but they are incapable of "naturally" transmitting these bonds of substance.

The *finiik* and the *khaapkhabuurien* are distinct, yet complementary aspects of the generic category *kusem*. All "proper" humans possess both aspects. Certain nonhuman entities also possess *finiik* and are thus endowed with aspects of personhood. They sometimes represent humans in various mythological and ritual contexts. Only human beings, however, possess the aspect *khaapkhabuurien*. The *khaapkhabuurien* is located rather vaguely throughout the body in life. During moments of severe anger or suicidal depression, when it does battle with the antithetical *finiik* aspect, it may reside in the heart. It can be detected as a congealed mass of "black" agnatic blood near the diaphragm through divination at the time of death. In general, it represents the unpredictable and rather idiosyncratic aspects of personality that differentiate individuals per se from one another. In this sense, it contrasts with the moral and jural aspects of personhood that are associated with the *finiik*. In implying the potential for individuation among humans, however, the concept of *khaapkhabuurien* also distinguishes them from animals. That potential, if it is to be jurally appropriate and morally good, must be developed in relation to the strengthening of the *finiik*. As the image of the idiosyncratic individual, the *khaapkhabuurien* is associated with the disordered, compulsive, wild aspect of personality. It bears the imprint of personal experience and is the locus of individual peculiarity and resentment as a consequence. The early experiences of all children in the female domain are instrumental in its formation; for, although it is sometimes said to be a male procreative contribution in substance, it is initially *tabula rasa* in character.

The *finiik* represents the social dimensions of personhood – the ordered, controlled, careful, thoughtful, proper aspect of personality. It stores collective knowledge and experience and becomes the conscience and the valued intellect of the person. Unmodulated behavior, as exemplified in the *atuur kunum* ("man of perpetual anger"), *waasop waneng* ("promiscuous woman"), or *tamam* ("female witch"), is held to be a sign that the *finiik* is weak and the *khaapkhabuurien* is becoming dominant. The erratic behavior of the infirm, the insane, or the uninitiated boy, however, may be viewed as a temporary imbalance of these two aspects of *kusem* – an imbalance that sometimes can be remedied by ritual means.

In general, the *khaapkhabuurien* is held responsible for the somewhat more unruly behavior in women than in men. It is considered to be inferior to and less powerful than the *finiik* in principle and usually to be under the control of the latter. Thus, in men and *waneng aiyem ser* the *finiik* dominates the *khaapkhabuurien* as a consequence of their possession of semen (through procreation and ritual taro) and their endurance of initiation. In women, however, the *finiik* is weakened and the *khaapkhabuurien* is strengthened by pernicious female influences, notably menstrual blood. During life, the *khaapkhabuurien* affects others only through the person in whose body it remains more or less contained. It may sometimes become detached in dreams, shadows, reflections, spirit possession, and illness, but it rarely causes harm independently as long as the person lives. At death, however, it emerges from the corpse to become a wandering, capricious ghost that lingers near the haunts of the deceased. It appears in the form of mist or smoke or a bird suddenly taking flight. Sometimes it is recognized as a wizened, red-skinned figure crouching near gardens or settlements. Almost always, it possesses recognizable and idiosyncratic characteristics of the deceased. It may attack any passers-by at whim, but more often attacks those who have inherited from, or are known to have injured, angered, or maligned the deceased. It often attacks mourners. Eventually, it wanders into the forest where it preys on unwary travelers or frightens away game. On occasion, it may return to garden or settlement, but there are ritual techniques for driving it away. As a wandering ghost, the *khaapkhabuurien* may enter and affect another person temporarily during its attack; and diviners (both male and female) can detect its presence in the reflection of the victim in a pool of pig's blood, where it appears as a ''tiny red worm.'' It is the ghost *khaapkhabuurien* of adult women (not *waneng aiyem*), however, that is the most likely to seek victims, for such women have the strongest *khaapkhabuurien* of all. And the victims that they are most likely to choose are affines (primarily male), that is, such women are seen largely in their identity as wives.

On the other hand, the *finiik* is responsible for the moral and ordered behavior of initiated men and *waneng aiyem ser*. In them, as a consequence of prolonged initiation and frequent consumption of ritual taro, as well as the ritual removal of antithetical female substances, it is in control. It is the essential, noncorporeal substance that links all ancestors, from Afek and Yomnok to the most recently deceased elder or child, to the living in terms of clan, moiety, and sometimes age group identity. Virtually all of the inhabitants (human) of the ancestral underworld are manifested as fully initiated *finiik* of the Bimin-Kuskusmin. The *finiik* of all females (except *waneng aiyem ser*) who possess ''female names,'' and of males who have been named but have not begun or completed the initiation cycle before death, are initiated after death at one of the mythological passages to the ancestral realm. These posthumous rites of passage, however, are conducted by female *finiik* and are said to be very painful and brutal. This image refers to the notion that male and female *finiik* possess roughly similar ritual powers in the ancestral underworld because they have become equivalent in exclusively male substance (that is, *finiik* spirit).

Because the time frame of the ancestral realm is also the time of the primordial ancestors before the advent of death, this image also refers implicitly to the idea that living women once held ritual powers identical to (or perhaps even greater than) those of men (see Bamberger 1974 and Murphy 1959). Having irresponsibly brought menstrual pollution, strong *khaapkhabuurien*, and death to humans, however, women largely lost the strength of their *finiik* and ritual powers. The only contemporary vestige of this heritage is to be seen in the identity of the *waneng aiyem ser*.

The nonnatal *finiik* of deceased immigrants, war captives, alien wives, and so on, are believed to enter peripheral areas of the ancestral abode through different mythological passages. The center of the ancestral underworld, which resembles the ideal conditions of eras before the fall from grace, is the exclusive domain of Bimin-Kuskusmin *finiik*, male and female. The *finiik* of "people of women's houses" enter the ancestral realm more slowly and with greater difficulty than those of initiated men and *waneng aiyem ser* because of their weaker state. The *finiik* of warriors, whose battlefield deaths remain unavenged, are transformed into *aiyepnon* spirits who attack male agnates of the deceased until vengeance is taken. Then, they again become *finiik* and enter the ancestral underworld.

Unlike *khaapkhabuurien*, the *finiik* never attack capriciously through agnatic links when they punish jural, moral, and ritual indiscretions. Through uterine links, however, they are known to attack for no apparent reason, and are then said to have been made somewhat irrational and uncontrollable by the absence of connections of semen and to have a female character. Among the living, neither *finiik* nor *khaapkhabuurien* are localized in particular (male or female) organs, although both (especially the *finiik*) possess some affinity for the (male) heart. Rather, the *finiik* is usually associated with male procreative aspects of the body, whereas the *khaapkhabuurien* is generally linked to the female anatomy.

There are two final aspects of substance that appear anomalous in that they are the *combined* procreative contribution of males and females – the "body shadow or reflection" and the "joints." Although the corporeal body largely decays on the burial platform or thereafter, a body shadow or reflection persists after death. It is entirely androgynous in appearance and character. It is most often manifested in dreams, reflections, and shadows of agnatic and cognatic kin of the deceased, where it is fused with or appears behind their own living reflections or shadows. On occasion, it may appear embodied spontaneously in the smoke of sacrificial fires. It may be induced to appear in the pools of pig's blood that are used for various divinations. Although it tends to be fused with the *khaapkhabuurien* immediately after death, it ultimately joins the *finiik* in the ancestral underworld. When ancestral *finiik* are sacrificially summoned to enter the ancestral skulls in ritual contexts, the body image often accompanies them. It is a generalized "human" image, having neither distinct gender nor individual characteristics. As one informant put the matter, "The great ancestors were both male and female. Fetuses are like that. So are body images. All men and women have them."

The joints are utilized metaphorically to refer to a relation among parts in various ways. They articulate the skeleton, a male contribution, but they are neither male bone nor female flesh. They are more interstitial points than anatomical areas (see Ellen 1977: 366). An analogy is commonly drawn between the joints of the body and the uterine links that articulate the *unum* kindred. These links are seen to have both male and female aspects. On the one hand, they relate a person to a set of lineages through uterine connections (M, FM, MM, FFM, MFM, FMM, and MMM), and to a set of non-agnatic male ancestors (such as MB, FMB, MMB, and so on) through uterine links.

As previously noted, non-agnatic males ancestors related through uterine links can be capricious and malevolent. On the other hand, they relate a person to a set of non-agnatic female ancestors (such as M, MZ, MM, and so on) through uterine links. The latter are particularly dangerous, for they possess the ability to transmit *tamam* witchcraft attacks (see Poole 1974).

The pattern of the transmission of *tamam* capability is the inverse of that of the transmission of agnatic blood. Agnatic blood, once transmitted through a *female* link, flows in increasingly weakened form for only three descending generations, and is not transmitted into the fourth. When transmitted through successive *male*, *agnatic* links, it continues undiminished over the generations. The *tamam* capacity, however, once transmitted through a *male* link, flows in increasingly weakened form for only three descending generations, and is not transmitted into the fourth. When transmitted through successive *female*, *uterine* links, it continues undiminished over the generations. Thus, males can be *tamam* and bring illness, but only females can launch lethal *tamam* attacks (usually against men). Uterine (and agnatic) links relate ego directly (through F, vis-à-vis lineage and *unum* kindred, and M, MM, and MMM vis-à-vis *unum* and *tamam*) or indirectly (through FM, FFM, MFM, and FFM by means of mediating male links) to a set of lineage categories. Non-agnates of these focal lineages are neither kindred supporters (such as MMMBDS) nor *tamam* attackers (such as FFMZDD) in the most common modes of reckoning.

The *unum* and *tamam* patterns overlap in that *tamam* lethal capability is transmitted through uterine links of females (like menstrual blood), but *tamam* attacks can be launched only through links of agnatic blood that connect witch and victim. The phenomenon of *tamam* is said to have originated among Oksapmin women to the north and to have entered the Bimin-Kuskusmin community through intermarriage. Hence, the alien wife, most of whom come from the Oksapmin, is most feared for her mystical powers. The *waneng aiyem*, however, cannot be a *tamam*. In fact, the *waneng aiyem ser* and the *tamam* contrast as almost polar images of females. On the one hand, the social persona of the *waneng aiyem ser* is the antithesis of the polluting woman. She has ritual authority related to her special clan identity as an agnate and ritual leader. She has transformed female fertility (with menstrual capacity) into children (notably sons) as a former mother, and now transforms female fertility (without menstrual pollution) into male ritual power and toward valued male ends. On the other hand, the asocial persona of the *tamam* is the epitome of the polluting woman. She has hidden magical power related to her uterine identity in a line of *tamam*. She transforms male fertility (with menstrual pollution) into female magical power and toward nefarious female ends. She gobbles up male substance through excessive depletion in intercourse and cannibalistic incorporation of male substance, and menstruates incessantly. She becomes fat with the male procreative elements that she has transformed into female substance, yet she is either barren or produces only equally fat monsters (often with genital malformations) or only daughters.

If the lethal attacks of *tamam* are seen to flow through the metaphorical joints or uterine links of the *unum* kindred, they are also seen to enter the victim's body through a set of more corporeal joints, which are classified with respect to gender. The male joints involve the fingers, wrists, elbows, shoulders, and neck. The female joints include the toes, ankles, knees, groin, and waist. Thus, it is said that men are damaged by *tamam* in their vital organs and head – the male procreative basis of their strength and ritual powers. Females, however, are injured by *tamam* in their reproductive capacity – the male procreative basis of their fertile powers. The related contrast of higher–lower is a common encoding of male–female difference in many contexts. Thus, men's houses and taro gardens are "higher" than women's houses and sweet potato gardens, topographically, ritually, and structurally. Men can be polluted by women (usually non-agnates) standing above their heads, whereas women can be polluted by men (usually non-agnates) being lower than their genitalia. In contrast, men's "love magic" amulets are secreted so that women will step over them, whereas those of women are hidden so that men will pass beneath them. The *tamam*, however, places menstrual residues in her love magic bundles and, thereby, entices men to destruction. Once again, ideological or symbolic constructions are anchored in natural substance, lending the former an "aura of factuality" (see Geertz 1973b; see also Turner 1966).

The Bimin-Kuskusmin model of procreation and its entailments are constructed on the basis of reckoning the flow of substance *to* and *through* persons. Male semen and female fertile fluids and menstrual blood form the basic elements from which the essential, psychobiological nature of the person is built. Gender is an invariable part of this foundation. The nature of males and females differs not only in terms of morphological characteristics, but also in terms of capacities to receive, transform, and transmit the very substances that form them, as well as to achieve distinct balances among these substances. Nevertheless, male and female siblings are united also in the sharing of substance. They are one another's agnates, although their gender differences will affect the social reality of this equivalence as they progress (not always "together") through the life cycle. The social differences that emerge, however, will also be encoded, in part, in their divergent natural characteristics as founded in the procreative model of gender. Yet, these natural constructs are also played out to some extent as models of and for social action, which may leave its imprint on their contextual formulation. Thus, I shall examine some implications of procreation, substance, and gender at a few selected points of the female life cycle among Bimin-Kuskusmin.

Birth

In this section, I shall show how ritual, taboo, and prestation are linked to a recognition of the flow and strength of natural substances as the baby first emerges into the social world and is incorporated in social terms. As the fetus matures and the pregnancy comes to full term, the mother is secluded in a birth hut, which also serves for menstrual seclusion. This hut, usually on the periphery of her hamlet or virilocal residence, should be located on the land of her husband's clan. Associated with residues of birth and menstruation, contact with the birth hut is highly polluting to both initiated men and, to a lesser extent, all "people of women's houses." The former must avoid the vicinity of the birth hut entirely, and the latter must undergo minor rites of purification upon emergence. The *waneng aiyem ser*, unlike initiated men, are permitted to approach the exterior of a birth hut (of their clan), but, unlike all other women, they are forbidden to enter it. In her seclusion, the expectant mother is considered highly polluted and highly polluting. The newborn child, the mother, and the women who assist her in childbirth must all undergo various washings and other rites of purication when they emerge. And the infant's father must also cleanse himself ritually when his "couvade" observances cease (see Poole, forthcoming "a").

The mother is accompanied by two women – a lineage father's sister or sister of her husband, who assists in delivery; and a *waneng aiyem ser* of her husband's clan, who advises in matters of midwifery from outside the hut. These women are seen to represent the interests of lineage and clan agnates, for whom the mother bears agnatic offspring. They must insure that the course of delivery is proper, that the child is shielded from excess menstrual blood that is thought to flow copiously at parturition, and that the child is normal in appearance. It is their duty to remove stillborn infants from the mother, and to insure that certain congenitally deformed infants (usually with malformed genitalia), infants of certain abnormal deliveries, and the firstborn of twins are killed immediately. Both breech presentations and firstborn twins are considered to be "forest spirits," who only appear to be human. There is some ambiguity about the significance of the birth order of twins, for some people insist that the physical appearance of the newborn – whether firstborn or secondborn – is crucial in determining which twin is to be strangled. Yet, men sometimes fear that a vengeful wife may offer such explanations for the strangulation of a child (especially male) of normal birth without reliable supervision by their agnates.

At birth, the father's sister (or sister) of the husband cuts the umbilical cord with a ritual bamboo knife that is supplied by the *waneng aiyem ser* and is a male ritual implement. The chant that accompanies this act makes clear that the child is an agnate of the husband and that the uterine link is more or less being severed. The father's sister then discards the blood-soaked moss and placenta in an enclosed pit at the rear of the birth hut to insure that pigs and dogs, which men eat to strengthen their *finiik*, will not consume the residues. Subsequently, the father's sister undergoes purification by rubbing herself with medicinal leaves, and then hands the newborn infant to the *waneng aiyem ser* outside. It is the latter who will examine the child and announce to its agnates its sex and normal birth. The father's sister also pretends to discard the umbilical cord. In fact, it is wrapped in protective bark cloth and placed in a bamboo tube, which the *waneng aiyem ser* will store in her house until the subsequent naming ceremonies. The mother (and sometimes mother's sister or own sister) of the woman is also present, but only in a supportive role. In this sense, her presence contrasts with the jural responsibilities vested in the husband's father's sister and the *waneng aiyem ser*.

While the woman is secluded, she must abandon certain female foods (such as sweet potatoes) and female food taboos, and must consume certain male foods, notably taro and pork. The *finiik* contained in these foods is said to counteract somewhat her highly polluted state and to strengthen and protect the child. In contrast, upon her entrance into the birth hut, her husband is subject to a special set of taboos (see Poole 1980a). For example, he may not enter a men's house, taro garden, or cult house, and must sleep in the forest or a garden hut. His male name, which he received at first initiation, may not be used. He is forbidden to hunt or to touch a bow. While the abdomen of his pregnant wife is covered with white pigment, his head must be so covered. He must avoid taro and pork (and other *finiik*-bearing male foods) and consumes only "soft" and "cold" female foods. In contrast, the father of the woman, who is responsible for her fecundity, is required to eat an abundance of male, *finiik*-bearing foods. In part, the husband's quasi-female identity at this time suggests the fact that the pregnancy is a consequence of his multiple acts of intercourse, which both polluted and depleted him. The husband's restrictions are lifted almost immediately after the birth of a daughter, but continue for a full lunar cycle in the case of a son (and longer for a firstborn son). There is little question that Bimin-Kuskusmin (both men and women) prefer sons among the firstborn, although daughters are highly valued thereafter. When the numerous taboos are removed, however, the new father is required to make certain prestations.

These prestations are specific and several. To the child's mother's brother, a female piglet and sweet potato cutting are given in the case of a daughter. With a son, a male piglet and taro stalk are presented. These entities are thought to signify the male involvement of the woman's lineage in her fecundity. To the child's mother's sister, a "female" pandanus axe is given in the case of either a daughter or a son. This valuable is said to represent the female involvement of the woman's lineage in her proper socialization and premarital virginity that enabled her to produce normal offspring. To the child's mother's mother, a "female" or "male" netbag is presented in the case of a daughter or son, respectively. Both are made by women and are said to represent the uterine contribution of the womb (see Schwimmer 1973 and A. M. Strathern 1972). As one informant noted, "Women carry the child in the belly and then in the netbag. It is all the same when children are small and without names." The child's mother's father receives both taro and pork (raw) in acknowledgement of his observance of critical food taboos and his responsibility for the woman's fecundity through his procreative contributions. The *waneng aiyem ser* and the husband's lineage father's sister (or sister) both receive male valuables for their participation at birth in the capacity of agnates. The mother herself often receives a valuable – male for a son, and female for a daughter.

In some senses, these prestations may be seen not only to acknowledge the gender of the child and those procreatively responsible for it, but also to position the child minimally with respect to the social milieu into which it has emerged. The child is not fully weaned for three to four years. While lactation continues, a postpartum sex taboo is rigidly in effect. Furthermore, the unweaned child is particularly contaminating to fully initiated men and *waneng aiyem ser*. Both avoid direct contact with young children. For men, such contact is dangerous for reasons of *both* female pollution *and* the lack of sacred status of the child. For *waneng aiyem ser*, however, the threat pertains *only* to her high sacred status vis-à-vis the child (see Note 6). At first, all children are nursed on demand. After the appearance of deciduous teeth, gradual weaning will commence. This early phase of weaning is more pronounced with boys, for it is said that they must become stronger than girls and more able to endure deprivation. Already, the image of the strong, restrained, brave, stoic Bimin-Kuskusmin male is being fostered. It is the appearance of deciduous teeth, nevertheless, that also marks the time of naming ceremonies for both boys and girls.

Female naming

In this section, I shall show how early, generalized initiation involves a focus on natural substance and process in marking the early social identity and rather ambiguous (female) gender of the child. All persons who are not initiated in the male *am yaoor* cycle or the special rite of passage of *waneng aiyem ser* possess *only* female names and are said to be essentially female. Unlike male initiation, the ceremonial bestowal of female names, female initiation, and the special initiation of *waneng aiyem ser* focus on individuals. Also unlike male initiation, these ceremonies are coordinated with a recognition of natural cycles, that is, first deciduous teeth, first menses, and menopause. The appearance of deciduous teeth is an auspicious time for the naming ceremony because the child is now held to be less vulnerable to fatal illnesses of the newborn. The ceremony generally takes place near the child's natal hamlet. Like birth, it should occur on the land of his or her clan.

The bestower of female names is invariably one of the two *waneng aiyem ser* of the child's clan. Ideally, it should be the *waneng aiyem ser* who presided over the birth of the child who now officiates. The names themselves, which she creates, are entirely individual. Yet, all are marked by a female name suffix or by no gender suffix, which also distinguishes them from male names, which always possess a male suffix. Often these names will refer to circumstances or characteristics that mark the individuality of the child.

At the time of the ceremony, the *waneng aiyem ser* retrieves the umbilical cord that she has kept since the child's birth. If the child is male, she plants the umbilical cord in *her* male taro garden. If the child is female, she presents it to the child's father's sister, who, in turn, plants it in *her* sweet potato garden. It should be noted that the child's father's sister is said to "own" the sweet potato garden in which the child's mother works and holds rights of usufruct. If a girl, the child will eventually inherit rights in this garden. The child's father presents valuables to his sister and the *waneng aiyem ser* for these services. The former generally receives a female valuable, but the latter always receives a male valuable.

The child's mother's sister or MFZ receives pork for the umbilical cord; but they must distribute some of the meat to their male agnates, who are procreatively responsible for the mother's fertile fluids that formed the umbilical cord. The mother of the child, however, *must* receive no prestation because the "natural" bond of the umbilical cord between her and the child has been severed at birth. It is said that the mother possesses no vestige of the umbilical connection, but that the child possesses an abdominal ("female") navel. Thus, the child, whether male or female, is attached to clan land by the planting of a "natural" female aspect of substance that has been produced by female fertile fluids. In turn, these female fertile fluids have been produced by male semen. Yet, gender is distinguished. Boys are attached to male taro garden land, which they are forbidden to enter prior to male initiation. Girls are attached to female sweet potato garden land, which they may enter at will.

Upon the planting of the umbilical cord, the female name is given. Both MB and FZ are present, and each will present an equivalent gift to the child. Girls receive a digging stick (a female item, not a valuable, that is made locally by individual women), and boys receive a string of *Cowrie* shells (a male valuable that comes from external trade by collectivities of men). Subsequently, the mother's brother will clean and shave the boy's head, leaving only a topknot – the sign of male "people of women's houses." This act is performed to clean the forehead that the mother previously covered with mud, and to expose the male navel to male influences. The father's sister, however, will gird the girl's loins with her first grass skirt, while the boy remains naked. Already, it is considered necessary to cover the genitalia of the female infant, who is said to be inherently more polluting than the boy. The boy will not wear the male phallocrypt until the beginning of male initiation or the appearance of substantial pubic hair.

When the female names have been bestowed, important attributes of personhood appear to have been imposed in a minimal sense. For example, both patrilineal and matrilateral ancestors are now thought to take an interest in the child. Childhood illnesses can be formally diagnosed through divination. If the child is injured, compensation must be given, but only in female valuables and only to the child's mother. If the child is killed, however, some prestations must also flow to both male and female agnates; for the child's *finiik* spirit has escaped. Yet, the bodily substance of the child is primarily female. Only children with female names are buried and are associated with formal mortuary observances. None of these phenomena, however, exhibit any differentiation between male and female children. As social persons, they are inherently female in substantial ways; and this notion is implied in their designation as "people of women's houses."

Although the naming ceremony marks important changes in the social persona of both boy and girl, they remain highly dependent on their mother, are carried between house and garden, and interact little with other children (except older female siblings who care for them). Upon full weaning, however, children are allowed more freedom, and differences in male and female activities rapidly emerge. Girls tend to remain with mothers and unmarried sisters close to hearth and garden. They may develop friendships with other girls of the hamlet, but one rarely sees groups of very young girls abroad. While still quite young, they learn the rudiments of tending babies, pigs, and sweet potato gardens. From father's sister, they may receive rights to tend a small plot in the gardens where their mothers labor. There is much praise and pride associated with the tubers that they harvest. With this tiny crop, they are sometimes jokingly said to "feed" their brothers and to be their brothers' "wives." In fact, young boys soon learn that brutal demands to younger sisters to fetch food often bring quick results and only occasional obstinacy.

In contrast, boys more commonly band together in peer groups to play, gather forest foods, hunt with tiny bows and arrows, engage in mock battles, or explore. They can often be seen watching adult male activities from afar, but with rapt interest. Yet, they are rarely to be found working in sweet potato gardens with their mothers and sisters. Within about a year of weaning, they will receive a piglet from a mother's brother, and their mothers and sisters will be obliged to look after it while they continue to romp with their friends. This piglet from a mother's brother, however, is very significant, for, upon initiation of the boy, it will launch a series of transactions between mother's brother and sister's son that will continue over the years.

Boys ideally enter male initiation at about nine or ten years of age. The *dramatis personae* of such rites include the three categories of *waneng aiyem*: the unmarried, premenstruous *seib aiyem*; the married, sexually mature (often with children) *waneng imok aiyem*; and the postmenopausal, no longer married *waneng aiyem ser*. All are selected by paramount male and female ritual leaders of their natal clans, and most are lineage agnates of the latter. Although the unmarried *seib aiyem* is ideally already coresident with her agnates, the *waneng imok aiyem* (temporarily) and the *waneng aiyem ser* (permanently) are formally returned to their natal clan areas for purposes of their participation in male ritual. In the cases of both *waneng imok aiyem* and *waneng aiyem ser*, prestations to their affinal kin insure the legitimacy of their return. It is claimed that those who are chosen to become *seib aiyem* and then *waneng imok aiyem* gain the potential of succession to the paramount "office" of *waneng aiyem ser*. The *seib aiyem*, however, is often a young girl, rarely more than twelve or thirteen years old. Her selection removes her rather abruptly from the realm of her mothers and sisters, for she must reside with a *waneng aiyem ser* and avoid contact with all other women until her ritual functions are completed. Like the *waneng imok aiyem*, she must undergo rites of purification that are intended to rid her of various female pollutants, notably the menstrual blood that is thought to be enclosed in her premenstruous body. Her rites, however, are rather less severe than those of the menstruous *waneng imok aiyem*. Both relinquish a multitude of female food taboos and assume a more limited set of male food taboos. Both are required to consume taro and pork to strengthen their *finiik* spirit. Both are involved primarily in male initiation.

Their ritual duties are several. For example, they bring pandanus leaves at the inception, and hearth clay and firebrands at the completion of the initiation house. These duties, however, are also allocated to women in the construction of ordinary houses. They weave and present to the novices special bark-fiber netbags, but the weaving of netbags is also women's work. They bring sugarcane and cucumber to the initiates, who are denied water. Although these are sacred foods, grown in special gardens and normally denied to women, women are permitted to eat the usual varieties of male cucumber and sugarcane. Their only utterly male activity involves the bearing of cassowary-bone daggers for the sacrifice of marsupials. All other activities, however, do take place in an exclusively male context, and all are said to have been the ritual activities of the androgynous ancestor Afek at the first of all initiations. In reciprocity for their ritual services, both *seib aiyem* and *waneng imok aiyem* are presented with sacred ancestral taro from special ritual taro gardens and which other women may not consume. Their participation has required, however, that the balance of their natural substances (as expressed in menstrual blood, *finiik* spirit, and food) be shifted ritually through purification and consumption toward the male attributes of lack of menstrual pollution, strength in body and *finiik* (through ritual and food), and sacred qualities. These qualities are permanent attributes of the *waneng àiyem ser*. Nevertheless, a *seib aiyem* cannot become a *waneng imok aiyem* until she has been initiated and married and, preferably, borne a child.

Female initiation

In this section, I shall demonstrate that the genesis (natural) and the control (ritual) of the ambiguous substance menstrual blood is central to all (natural and social) reproduction and to the potential of marriage and motherhood. Among Bimin-Kuskusmin, female social puberty is marked by the onset of first menses at about seventeen to eighteen years of age. A *waneng aiyem ser* of the girl's clan is held responsible for the proper ritual performance of her initiation at this time, which must occur on her clan land. Here, her lineage brothers build a temporary hut ("first blood menstrual hut"), which will be destroyed after her initiation is complete. This structure is immensely polluting to *both* men *and* women, for first menses is rather special in character. It is said that menstrual blood has gradually accumulated in the girl's body since birth, and that some has decayed and turned "black." Although all menstrual blood is held to be black, as opposed to red agnatic blood, in most contexts, the blood of first menses is somehow more so. The girl is both polluted and polluting, severely and to everyone (except to *waneng aiyem ser* in some senses), as a consequence. It is claimed that she would die without the natural release of first menses and the ritual protection of initiation. Unlike the month-long first of ten stages of initiation for boys, however, the sole female initiation (except that of *waneng aiyem ser*) involves only a single girl and requires less than a day, with a week to heal.

The girl is brought to the initiation hut by her mother, who is procreatively responsible for her menstruation. She is stripped naked and sits on a pandanus mat in the center of the hut. With little formality, the *waneng aiyem ser*, using a male cassowary-bone ritual dagger from the clan cult house, pierces her nasal septum. The procedure is similar to the piercing of the boy's nasal septum in the first stage of male initiation. She then pierces the lobe of the left ear, whereas the lobe of the boy's right ear is pierced at a later stage of male initiation. It should be noted that in *some* contexts left–right contrast is used metaphorically to encode female–male difference, but this analogy does not appear to flow from the Bimin-Kuskusmin model of procreation. These ritual wounds are allowed to bleed in an explicit attempt to drain menstrual contamination away from the male skull. The exegesis is virtually the same in the boy's case. Finally, because first menses is said to produce considerable menorrhagia and pain, inch-long incisions (often over a hundred) are made over her entire abdomen, from below her breasts to below her abdominal navel. The incisions encircle the female navel in an oval pattern, which is thought to be efficacious in ridding her of pollution while preserving her fertile powers – a general paradox of female gender among Bimin-Kuskusmin in the ambiguous relation between menstrual blood and fertile fluids in fertility. The incisions are said to ease the pressure and pain of first menses. These final incisions are made by a father's sister with an ordinary bamboo knife. During the first phase of male initiation, however, it is only the head and forearms, covering important male bones, that are incised to remove female contamination.

With these several acts, female initiation is formally complete. The *waneng aiyem ser* withdraws to destroy the ritual implements and to undergo purification (from contact with nonsacred persons, not for sexual pollution). Later, the girl's father will present several strings of *Cowrie* shells (male wealth) to the *waneng aiyem ser*. In myths of the androgynous ancestor Afek, with whom the *waneng aiyem ser* is identified, the *Cowrie* shell is explicitly said to be the 'vagina', through which the menstrual blood, and later the fertile fluids and offspring of the girl will pass after her initiation. The father's sister remains to instruct the novice in how to shield men (and women) from her menstrual flow and in matters of sexual intercourse. Nearby, her lineage brothers conduct a brief rite to insure the cessation of menstruation. She is given water from this rite to drink. Although menstrual flow is a consequence of procreative transmission through only uterine links, its control is thought to be vested entirely in the ritual performances of male agnates. Without the latter, it is said, pollution would be uncontrolled, and mature women would bleed to death. These lineage brothers receive no compensation for their acts, which are performed for an agnate. Neither does the father's sister, who gives the girl a new ritual skirt. The girl's mother also gives a new skirt to her daughter, but it is an ordinary variety that all women wear. All of these several acts involve the moral and jural obligations of kin in the initiation of the girl.

In female initiation, it is interesting to note that control of menstrual capacity shifts from natural genesis to ritual constraint, and from female non-agnate (mother) to female (father's sister and *waneng aiyem ser*) *and* male (lineage brother) agnate. In male initiation, however, the shift from natural to ritual control is paralleled by a movement from female non-agnate (mother) to male non-agnate (mother's brother) to male agnate (father and *kunum aiyem ser*) in the implantation of female substance, the removal of female substance, and the strengthening of male substance (see Poole 1980b). Once boys are born and weaned and enter initiation, men feel strongly that they can achieve more or less complete control over males. Hence, the shift from female to male, and from non-agnate to agnate, is thought to signify this marked control. The dilemma of male versus female control over female reproductive capacity, however, is never quite resolved. Here the shift is from non-agnate to agnate, but from female to *both* male *and* female. Thus, the girl's father presents a female piglet to her mother's brother for the ritual injury to her female substance in initiation, but this substance is actually the procreative contribution of the mother's brother's female agnate. Yet, the father also presents a female piglet to her mother's sister for insuring a strong flow of menstrual blood (as a sign of fertility). In turn, the girl's mother's brother and mother's sister both present male taro (containing *finiik*, which is antithetical to menstrual blood) to her father on behalf of her mother for ritually insuring the containment and cessation of menstrual flow.

The female initiate remains secluded until her scars have healed. She then returns temporarily to her mother's house. She is now considered to be marriageable, and her abdominal scars are a sign of this state. Any attempt to have intercourse with an unscarred (uninitiated) girl is considered to be the most heinous of crimes. For the offender, no support by kin is likely, and no compensation is possible. One can flee to an uncertain future in another tribe, or stand and face certain execution. Ideally, a newly initiated girl should be married quickly and most commonly is, with her consent and with betrothal having been arranged by male *and* female lineage agnates. If she should not marry quickly and take up virilocal residence beyond her clan land (at least at first), she will be sent to live with matrilateral (or other cognatic) kin elsewhere. It is important that her subsequent menstruations do not occur on natal clan ground. This concern is largely based on two considerations.

First, menstrual blood is inherently polluting, and there is virtue in avoiding it whenever possible. Furthermore, there is a general tone in the image of the supportive, generous, ritually significant female agnate that is incompatible with a discussion of menstruation – not to mention a lack of etiquette in juxtaposing these two characteristics. Men are quite willing to discuss more or less openly their ritual modes of control over menstrual process, but become rather upset at the mention of those toward whom such ritual is directed.

Second, and more explicit, it is believed that, with the sole exception of first menses, menstrual blood is mixed with at least some agnatic blood. Thus, women lose agnatic blood regularly and continually deplete themselves of this vital substance. Men, however, lose it only through accident and occasional ritual acts, in which they are otherwise strengthened through the effects of ritual and the *finiik* contained in male ritual food. But the shedding of agnatic blood by any means on one's clan land may provoke the wrath of agnatic ancestors. Thus, one should neither fight nor menstruate on clan ground. Once married then, female agnates are said not to reside in their natal area or to visit at times of menstruation. When they do reside there in some cases of separation, divorce, widowhood, or unusual postmarital residence, or visit at inappropriate times, they are secluded from other (non-agnatic) women in a remaining (or specially constructed) initiation hut. Thus, even in menstruation female agnates are distinguished from female non-agnates, who are secluded in a normal menstrual hut. The *seib aiyem* and *waneng imok aiyem* are unambiguously lineage and clan agnates par excellence; yet, the former is resident in her natal area, and the latter is not. It is only the premenstruous, uninitiated, virginal, unmarried maiden who can become a *seib aiyem*. To become a *waneng imok aiyem*, a woman must be menstruous, initiated, married, sexually active, and usually of proven fertility (that is, a mother), but generally should dwell beyond the pale of clan land.

Marriage and motherhood

In this section, I shall show the implications of ideas of substance in perceptions of a woman as wife, mother, and sister. I shall note the significance of rights *in uxorem, in genetricem,* and *in rem* in relation to substance and to the natural aspects of social identity. It is important to note, however, two general characteristics of Bimin-Kuskusmin marriage (see Poole 1976: 384–569). First, neither marriage nor motherhood alters the identity of a woman as an agnate of her natal group. She may change residence at marriage, and her reputation as wife and mother may affect her identity among her affines. But these factors are held to be irrelevant to her immutable, natural identity as an agnate. Second, more than 80 percent of all marriages are intratribal where fighting among affines is quite restricted, and where affines are embedded in a wide range of interlocking transactions. There is no unambiguous sense in which affines are "enemies" to one another (see Meggitt 1964; cf. Brown 1964). But when one focuses on intertribal marriage and alien women, it becomes apparent that inmarried wives from other tribes are almost always from groups with whom Bimin-Kuskusmin have fought, are fighting, or may well fight in the future. These wives are the most feared for potential betrayal, poisoning, or pollution. The overwhelming majority of these alien wives come from Oksapmin groups to the north, and represent the origin of female *tamam* witchcraft.

Immediately before and after initiation, a young woman is considered to be sexually attractive as her breasts develop. She is constantly chaperoned in hamlet and garden by male and female siblings. There is great value placed on virginity before marriage, which is mandatory for selection as a *waneng aiyem*. All *waneng aiyem* are associated with the mythologically original Bimin-Kuskusmin clans and have been (*waneng aiyem ser*), are (*waneng imok aiyem*), or usually will be (*seib aiyem*) married to men of other natal clans. Often they also are of and marry into senior lineages of these clans. In contrast, the *waasop waneng* ("promiscuous women") of these clans are much stigmatized and usually must marry "down" (into immigrant or war captive clans) or "out" (into other tribes). With a very bad reputation, they may not marry at all in rare cases. Whatever their fate, the negotiable aspect of bridewealth for such women is always relatively small.

Premarital virginity is significant to both agnates and (intended) affines, and is more than a matter of bridewealth and sister exchange. For agnates, the sister is ritually important, especially as a *waneng aiyem*, in terms of her fertile powers. Male ritual control of female fertility is predicated, in part, on social control of the contexts in which it is expressed, and that control is through marriage as the only legitimate context of sexual activity. This value applies to men too, and with considerable force. Premarital dalliance and adultery are remarkably rare and wreak havoc when publicly recognized. There is no custom of courting per se. For affines, the wife is important, in part, as a bearer of children who are unambiguously their agnates. Because multiple intercourse is required for conception, pre- or extramarital affairs can contaminate the natural agnatic identity of children. Thus, it is considered improper and suspicious if a woman conceives too early in marriage, for sufficient sexual contact with the husband is less probable. Given recent first menses and announcement of pregnancy at rather late term, however, such suspicions are rare.

Betrothal is often arranged before first menses when the breasts begin to develop as a sign of impending maturity. Female agnates of a young man usually make the first inquiries within the limits of desired exchange (or beyond). If such inquiries are promising, the negotiable aspect of bridewealth (*bas kunum wanengkariik*) is formally discussed *only* by male agnates of the focal lineages. This aspect of bridewealth consists *entirely* of male wealth (and now some money). Both men (more) and women (less) may give and receive male valuables in this context. In fact, this transaction is one of the few in which women (except *waneng aiyem ser*) may receive such wealth. Cognatic male kin of the bride or groom may also receive or give such valuables in lesser amounts, but female non-agnates cannot. The valuables that women accumulate may be used to support a variety of other transactions, but such wealth must usually be channeled through men in these exchanges. Although women have far less wealth than most men and may be pressured by men into parting with valuables, they do hold rights of disposal over their male wealth and commonly exercise them (although not in public transactions other than bridewealth in most cases).

The consent of groom and bride is essential to betrothal and marriage, and either can refuse. Although social pressure can be placed on the young woman, it is recognized that to ignore an adamant refusal is to court misfortune for all concerned. Marital discord can lead to a multitude of disasters for agnates and affines, males and females. There is much concern to insure that a female agnate's postmarital residence not be too distant, for it is important that she be able to visit her natal area easily. Hence, marriage into other tribes (especially those that are distant) is anathema to both men and women under most circumstances.

Sister exchange between two local lineages, however, is seen as advantageous by both men and women. For men, the advantages are seen largely in extending and reinforcing important exchange relations between particular lineages and clans. For a woman, however, the ideal pattern of sister exchange with particular lineages (other than mothers') of mothers' clans implies that at least some of her close female agnates will be coresident with her after marriage as a support group. Furthermore, it implies that her mother-in-law, with whom friction is almost inevitable otherwise, may be her clan agnate (a father's sister). Despite exigencies of actual marriages, this fiction is sometimes maintained. In addition, her husband may be a clan agnate (a brother's son) of her own mother. Hence, although her mother and father's sister may disagree violently about details of betrothal, they will usually concur on the value of implementing an ideal sister exchange when possible.

Ultimately, if all parties agree, the signal of an accepted betrothal is given by the prospective bride. She takes a male taro tuber, given by her father, and roasts it in the hearth of her mother's house. It should be noted that women do not usually cook taro in a female hearth. She brings the taro to the groom's hamlet, where she breaks the tuber and gives half to her future husband. She then departs to consume her portion in her mother's house. The future husband, in turn, is expected to eat his taro in his father's men's house. If he does, the betrothal is considered complete. To accept broken, cooked taro from a woman (especially a female non-agnate) is a sign of great trust, for the remaining portion could be used for various witchcraft and sorcery attacks. Upon betrothal, the *bas kunum wanengkariik* aspect of bridewealth is exchanged at the bride's natal hamlet (or at least on her clan land) within a few months.

Shortly after this aspect of bridewealth is given, however, a second bridewealth transaction (*kikiis wanengkariik*) occurs at the natal hamlet of the woman. Until this transaction is completed, the couple is not properly married. The *kikiis wanengkariik* involves an ordered series of twelve specific, invariable elements. They represent certain aspects of the relationship that is forged in the transaction. They also indicate something of the rights vis-à-vis women that are transferred at marriage. In relation to natural substance, the woman's agnatic social identity and her (social) productive and reproductive value is clearly labeled in the symbols of the transaction.

The father (or father's brother) of the bride receives nothing in either aspect of bridewealth transactions, although he directs the order of recipients in both. There are two reasons given for his special position. First, it is not quite proper or moral for a man to receive wealth for certain attributes of his child in this regard. He must always leave an ''open road'' for the child's support, protection, and possible return. Second, he represents the child's agnatic identity (through his procreative contribution), which is never transferred or lost. What is being transferred at a daughter's marriage are rights in the external (female) body in terms of labor, companionship, sexual access *in uxorem*, and childbearing *in genetricem*. The male procreative substances of male anatomy and fertile fluids are his natural contribution and remain under his (and his male agnates') ritual control. Note that at the birth of her children, he must observe special taboos and receive compensation, for he is responsible for her fecundity. He has given her semen to produce this capacity, and *finiik*-bearing male foods to strengthen it. As a *waneng aiyem*, she will return to her male (and female) agnates, temporarily or permanently, to bring her fertile powers into contexts of male ritual control. Her agnates retain the right to claim her in this capacity, for they have retained control over her fertility (fertile fluids and even menstrual blood). At death, her agnates will finally claim her in the form of bone (an idiom for the male procreative contribution) to be placed in sacred clan ossuaries or cult houses. And they will speed her *finiik* spirit on its way to the ancestral underworld, where it will become their agnatic (female) ancestor.

Similarly, a father (or father's brother) should not personally receive injury compensation for a child if the wound has been divined in the male anatomy. He will not receive death compensation if the mortal wound or illness has afflicted male substance, and otherwise will delay its reception until the *finiik* (from semen) has come to rest in the ancestral underworld. In a more mundane realm, a similar logic is applied to the notion that a man who is *both* owner *and* custodian of a pig should not eat its flesh. Pigs possess *finiik*, and their custodians give the cooked taro (containing *finiik*) from their male taro gardens. Here, however, a brief rite will allow one to condone the roasting of (merely) female flesh and quickly savor the pork.

The new wife comes to live with her husband and to bear his agnatic children, yet retains her agnatic identity elsewhere. But aspects of her rights and duties are altered or newly constructed in her identity as a wife. Such rights and obligations have subtle associations with natural substances of both gender and other social identities. Sexual rights *in uxorem* are held exclusively by the husband and may pass through the levirate to his close lineage agnates, but her consent is necessary for any remarriage (by levirate or bridewealth). Rights *in genetricem* are held by the husband throughout marriage and his agnates thereafter in the levirate. Rights in control of (and ritual, but not reproductive use of) her fertile powers are held exclusively by her male agnates. Yet, neither divorce nor death will alter the agnatic identity of the children she bears within a particular marriage.

Rights *in rem* are held by both husband (and his male agnates) and agnatic and uterine kin of the woman for injury and liability resulting from her actions, for which she bears personal responsibility. Ritually, she comes under the protection of her agnates (living and dead), but can be possessed by both agnatic and cognatic *finiik*. Otherwise, her affines are responsible for her everyday protection. For injury by members of a third lineage (or clan), her husband (and his agnates) receives all compensation directly. If the injury relates to her working, sexual, or childbearing capacities, he may retain some of it for his loss. Yet, most injury and all death compensation must be given by the husband to her lineage agnates (male and female). In turn, they retain valuables for injury to male substance, but compensation for injury to female substance must flow to matrilateral and uterine kin. Compensation for injury by a husband's agnates (lineage and clan) is given directly to her lineage agnates, who distribute it further for injury to female substance. All such prestations involve only male wealth. For injury to paternal substance, the woman herself receives no formal compensation, but may formally receive male valuables for injury to maternal substance.

The married woman must compensate others for consequences of some of her own actions, although she also represents her kin and draws on their wealth. Thus, for menstrual pollution (of men only), she must give male wealth from her female uterine kin, who are responsible for her menstrual powers. Should she damage the sweet potato gardens in which she works, she must compensate her husband's sister (or female affines) with female valuables; for the latter "own" and fertilize (menstrually) the gardens. If a wife subverts male affinal undertakings through fertile fluids or menstrual blood, some compensation may be given by her male agnates and female uterine kin, respectively. For ritual pollution by menstrual blood, her matrilateral male kin often participate in compensation; for her menstrual powers emanate from her mother (their agnate).

Receipt of the *bas kunum wanengkariik* aspect of bridewealth by a woman's agnates (male and female) entails some liability, for she must fulfill her duties as spouse and childbearer (symbolized in the *kikiis wanengkariik* aspect of bridewealth). Otherwise, they may be unable to retain it. Because *bas kunum wanengkariik* bridewealth is often committed to other exchanges, the possibility of divorce (and its return) is a serious economic matter. Yet, her duties as a wife in loyalty, labor, and companionship are ambiguous. Should her husband place too·many burdens on her in the early, childless stage of marriage, she may suffer *maarmaar* possession by her agnatic ancestors. She is then returned to her natal area to recuperate, and her agnates demand compensation and better behavior from her husband.

Yet, if she is lazy or treacherous by public consensus, she may be beaten without fear of retribution. If divination presents "proof" that she has poisoned her affines, they may kill her if any should die. Deliberate damage to gardens and pigs is more common, but compensation usually remedies the matter. As a childbearer, however, her barrenness is proven by divination after several childless years; and unless a ritual remedy is possible, it usually leads to divorce and complete return of *bas kunum wanengkariik* bridewealth. But it may be a matter of either menstrual capacity (incurable) or fertile fluids (sometimes curable). Some barrenness is divined as a lack of *finiik*-bearing taro and pork, which a husband must provide. Unless he gives divinatory evidence that his wife's pollution or depletion of his *finiik* (or semen) incapacitated him in gardening and hunting, he is at fault. Male food is then prescribed, with the ritual strengthening of her fertile powers by her male agnates. Soon she is considered able to bear children. Of course, if she is a *tamam* witch, there is no hope of normal children, or for the longevity of her husband. She will deplete his male foods and semen, transform them into female substance, kill him through pollution and depletion, and finally devour the male substance of his corpse (see Poole 1974).

When the wife becomes a mother, her social position among her affines is much enhanced. Although the capricious *khaapkhabuurien* spirit adapts tenuously to local circumstances, and thus female attachment to affinal local groups is also fragile and capricious, motherhood brings the woman under the benevolent protection of her husband's agnatic ancestors. Since marriage, she has eaten affinal pork and taro containing their *finiik*. Now she bears their clan *finiik* as represented in her children. At first pregnancy, she is given male wealth by male affines. Female affines weave new netbags for her to carry the child and new skirts to ward off the child's urine and feces.[20] With a child, the bond to her husband is said to be stronger and more amicable and affectionate. It is with respect to the wife *qua* mother that people refer to "good marriages" that exceed marital rights and obligations. If the affinal (male) ancestors continue to protect her in the local group, it is said that "forest spirits" will not possess her, and that she will never have twins. If she bears many normal children who survive to be named, her husband's genealogy may be recited to show that she is increasingly *primus inter pares* among her co-wives and the other wives of her male affines.

The mother of many sons is much admired by both affines and agnates, male and female. She is "strong" in childbirth in a way that differs from the more mundane strength of women who walk long distances, carry heavy loads, and labor in gardens, but that is similar to "male strength" in enduring initiation. Further exegesis reveals that she has used her fertile fluids (male) to produce strong male substance (in sons) and has controlled her menstrual flow (female) toward this valued end. In fact, the images of the mother of sons, the female *tamam* witch, and the *waneng aiyem ser* are often compared. In contrast to the mother, the *tamam* witch is feared and despised. She has misused and subverted her fertile fluids (male) to produce only exaggerated female or highly deformed substance (in both her body and her children), and has deliberately allowed her menstrual flow to run rampant. Rituals of her male agnates to stem the flow and promote fertility are to no avail. Her perpetually polluted (and polluting) state has so weakened her *finiik* and agnatic blood that the strength of her natural relation to them is insufficient for ritual intervention. In contrast to the *tamam*, the *waneng aiyem ser* has been a proper mother (ideally of sons) and now is no longer menstruous (or sexually polluting), yet has retained her fertile fluids in the increasingly male and sacred vessel of her body that has been wrought by natural process and the special initiation rites of her agnates. Her natural and social bonds to her male agnates are strong, and she assists them (in body and ritual praxis) in gaining control over female substance and fertility. The *waneng aiyem ser* and the mother are both women who make proper use of male and female substance. Yet, these images of females are also in contrast. The mother has used her male substance (*with* menstrual blood) to produce non-agnatic children (male and female) naturally. The *waneng aiyem ser*, once a mother, now uses her male substance (*without* menstrual blood) to produce agnatic power (male and female) ritually. In many ways, she is the female agnate par excellence.

The Waneng Aiyem Ser

In this section, I shall note how natural and ritual transformations of male and female substance make sense of the gender and social identity of the *waneng aiyem ser*. Those chosen to become *waneng aiyem ser* by paramount male and female ritual leaders of their clan *ideally* possess certain social characteristics. They have been virtuous female agnates of their lineage and clan, although their identity as *waneng aiyem ser* is reckoned in the context of their clan. They are no longer married or marriageable, and have been married only once or by the levirate.[21] They have remained in their hamlet of postmarital residence.[22] All are past menopause. All have been *seib aiyem* and *waneng imok aiyem* in their youth. All have been prolific mothers, especially of sons. Most have been *waneng kusem* ("curer–diviners"), who diagnose and treat female black-blood illnesses among both men and women. Most are agnates of senior lineages of their clans, from which the single paramount male ritual leader (*kunum aiyem ser*) of the clan is also selected. In each of the mythologically original clans, and only in these clans, there are ideally two *waneng aiyem ser*. Normally, there are only two, or one and another in the process of installation.[23] Occasionally, when a *waneng aiyem ser* becomes feeble, senile, or severely ill, a third woman is initiated to assume her duties and to replace her at death.

The functions of the *waneng aiyem ser* are several. As *waneng aiyem ser*, she is involved in birth, female naming, male and female initiation, male cult, and death rituals most significantly. In the linked identity of *waneng kusem ser* ("paramount female curer-diviner"), she is involved in midwifery, diagnosis and treatment of black-blood illnesses, purification of pollution, *tamam* witch hunting, and ritual autopsy and divination at death primarily. For these services, she receives male valuables; and, despite her short tenure in "office" before death, she may become wealthy even by male standards. She has rights of disposal over this wealth similar to those of men, and may use it publicly to support exchanges of her (male) agnates. Like other women, however, she may never (or almost never) exchange this wealth publicly herself.

Upon selection of a neophyte *waneng aiyem ser*, her senior male lineage agnates and clan male ritual leaders arrange for her formal return to the single hamlet associated with her clan *katiam* cult house.[24] This arrangement is made with their counterparts in the lineage and clan of her former husband.[25] The transaction takes place in the hamlet of her postmarital residence.[26] Here certain prestations (the *waneng aiyem traiyakhaabey*) are given by her senior male lineage agnates and clan ritual leaders to senior men of her affinal lineage. With the exception of the final element (symbolizing her lack of natural reproductive capacity), all prestations of the *waneng aiyem traiyakhaabey* are identical in character and order to those of the *kikiis wanengkariik* aspect of bridewealth (see the section on "Marriage and motherhood"). The locus and direction of the transaction, however, is reversed. Also, the oratory in *waneng aiyem traiyakhaabey* indicates that the significance of the prestations is altered, although they suggest some of the rights transferred in this transaction. In relation to natural substance, the neophyte *waneng aiyem ser*'s agnatic social identity and her (ritual) reproductive and productive value, in contrast to the (social) reproductive and productive value of a wife, is clearly labeled in the symbols of the transaction, which in many ways reflects a reclaiming (by her clan) of those rights relinquished (by her lineage) at her marriage in the *kikiis wanengkariik* transaction.

These prestations suggest that the neophyte *waneng aiyem ser* has become devalued (socially) to her affines and more highly valued (ritually) to her agnates. She has lost not only the range of her obligations *in uxorem* and *in genetricem*, but also the natural capacity to produce and nurse children; for she retains her fertile fluids (male) without either breast milk (female) or menstrual capacity (female). After the *waneng aiyem traiyakhaabey*, she is escorted by male ritual leaders to the hamlet of her clan *katiam* cult house. Here initiated clansmen build a special house (*waneng aiyem am*) for her.[27]

She will live here alone and store her ritual *sacrae*. With the exception of other *waneng aiyem*, all "people of women's houses" are forbidden to enter or even approach this house, but "people of men's houses" – or initiated men – are not so restricted.

The neophyte *waneng aiyem ser* is also given a taro garden, which otherwise is the domain of initiated men. She may not enter the garden during its male ritual consecration, but thereafter may plant, tend, and harvest the taro. In fact, her initiated male lineage agnates usually perform these tasks and place tubes of semen in the garden, which is sacred. No people of women's houses may eat its tubers, although *seib aiyem* and *waneng imok aiyem* are permitted to do so in male initiation contexts. Unlike ordinary taro gardens, stalks are planted twice (or more) in succession in the same garden. She is said to own this garden. Similarly, she owns a sweet potato garden, which otherwise is the domain of people of women's houses, but it too is sacred. Unlike other women, she is said to work the sweet potato garden that she owns. In fact, her uninitiated female lineage agnates plant, tend, and harvest the sweet potatoes. With the exception of *waneng imok aiyem* of her clan, who place tubes of menstrual blood in the garden, neither menstruous women, male people of women's houses, nor initiated men (except in certain ritual circumstances) may enter the garden or usually eat the tubers. These sweet potatoes are largely reserved for her and for premenstruous girls in most contexts, and men may eat them only during male initiation. With the exception of paramount ritual leaders (male and female), mature men and women can pollute her in most contexts. Such pollution, however, is not sexual, but rather a matter of difference in sacred status. Nonetheless, she must avoid such persons in both garden and hamlet, and she must live alone.

When she has harvested and eaten the first tuber from her new taro garden, she is instructed by other *waneng aiyem ser*, male ritual leaders, and curer-diviners of the clan in the esoterica of male and female ritual, divination, and curing. In life, she will have limited access to male ritual domains and to contact with male substance in curing, divination, and initiation. She alone will bring otherwise highly polluting female substances into male ritual contexts. At death, her skull will be placed among male *sacrae* in the *katiam* cult house of her clan. Her ancestral *finiik* will become a focus of male cult sacrifice. During her reign, she alone, through sacrifices in her special house, is deemed capable of communicating with an equal range of agnatic, cognatic, and uterine ancestors. Yet, she is ultimately denied access to much of the highly secret "sacred male knowledge" of myth and ritual.[28] Unlike other women, she will have knowledge of fertility plants and magic that otherwise only initiated men know. Yet, like all women, she will know of secret contraceptive plants and magic that men despise, and will never comprehend the significance of the "totemic" ancestor of her own clan.

When her instruction is complete, she is secluded in a newly constructed hut ("sacred woman forest house") in the forest of her clan land. Here only the other clan *waneng aiyem ser* attends her special initiation. She is bled at the temples to remove menstrual blood from the female substance (flesh) adjacent to her skull (male). On her forehead, her male navel is shaved and cleaned to permit the entrance of that limited sacred male knowledge that she is entitled to learn. This ritual bleeding also strengthens her skull appropriately for future placement in the clan cult house, and her *finiik* for formal ritual participation and ancestorhood. Thus, *waneng aiyem ser* possess strong *finiik* and rather weak *khaapkhabuurien*. They are not capricious like other women, especially wives. In contrast, her female navel is covered with yellow mortuary mud. It is said that she will acquire no further female knowledge, but may retain what she has already learned, as one informant noted, ''when she was a woman.''

When the neophyte emerges from seclusion, she is a full *waneng aiyem ser*. She receives a male name and a sacred name and is granted other special rights by the paramount male ritual leader of her clan. All of her various rights and regalia, however, are distributed among *different* degrees of male initiation status and do not form a coherent pattern of male attributes. Thus, she receives a male name, as do men in the *ais am* phase of initiation. She may wear the *siriik* headdress, as do men in the *ning siir ben*. She places the *ket farong* bamboo cylinder in her pierced left earlobe, as do men in the *en am* (but in their right earlobe). She may never wear in her pierced nasal septum the wild boar tusk, as do men in the *kidikairiin ben* and *en am* phases. Yet, as men do in the *kidikairiin ben*, she may wear the carved limestone *kondus* in her septum. The *kondus* of men are carved from stalactites, but the *kondus* of *waneng aiyem ser* are carved from stalagmites! The sexual significance of this contrast is as obvious to Bimin-Kuskusmin as to a Freud or Lévi-Strauss. Like all initiated men, the new *waneng aiyem ser* may smoke tobacco, which is denied to other women. Her food taboos, however, become unique to her identity – an amalgam of both male and female foods and food taboos, with a few unique prescriptions and proscriptions.

In ritual, divination, and curing, she sometimes appears largely female, representing her (usually male) agnates, yet is never wholly male. She removes, transforms, or implants male and female substances ritually in the bodies of females and males, respectively. Sometimes, she seems to control the balance and flow of both male and female substances in the bodies of either females or males. In her own body, she represents an ideal agnatic female of fertile powers (male) and without menstrual flow (female). But she has lost her ''natural'' reproductive capacity; and when she resumes ''reproduction'' metaphorically as a ''male mother'' (*auk kunum imok*), with male initiates passing beneath her genitalia, she is controlled by male ritual leaders as an almost inanimate vehicle for subtly constructing an analogy between female natural (physiological) birth and male ritual (spiritual) rebirth. She is not only a specialist in ritual matters, but also a complex ''meta-statement'' on matters of birth, genesis, decay, and death; fertility and pollution; male and female. Thus, when she appears in male initiation contexts, she is a transvestite, an androgynous being, and an image of the hermaphroditic ancestors Afek and Yomnok, with whom she is identified. She can bring female substance safely into male ritual contexts for male ritual control. Yet, she cannot be polluted by semen and menstrual blood like all men and women (except paramount leaders, but see Note 6). When her ritual participation is finished, she must undergo rites of purification; but these rites pertain to contamination (nonsexual) by those of lesser "sacred" status.

The *waneng aiyem ser* is indeed an anomaly, but one that may be "good to think" among Bimin-Kuskusmin. She is the female agnate par excellence – isolated, controlled, compliant, strong, fertile, and nonpolluting (menstrually). Her fertile powers are brought back into the agnatic fold to be harnessed ritually. She wears male regalia, but *in toto* it is an odd assemblage, a caricature of natural males. She owns male valuables, but must dispose of them largely through males. She owns both taro and sweet potato gardens, but both are sacred and restricted by male ritual. She is no longer embedded in the domestic domain, but her political-jural identity as agnate and "quasi-male" is expressed largely in male ritual contexts. Yet, as a consequence, she is sacred and can pollute (and be polluted by) virtually anyone who is not sacred. No one else can be possessed by both male agnatic and female uterine *finiik* simultaneously. But this form of possession is the antithesis of *tamam* witchcraft powers. While so possessed, it is only the *waneng aiyem ser* who can destroy *tamam* witches who attack her (usually male) agnates. Having destroyed her female "mirror image"(the *tamam*), however, she finds most of her remaining reflections in the male realm; but they distort her into a being of ambiguous, androgynous gender. Beyond the ritual domain, she is effectively isolated from the flow of ordinary social life by the myriad taboos that she must observe. In some ways, she is a tragic, lonely figure – a splendid ritual artifact.[29]

Only in death does the *waneng aiyem ser* appear to have approximated an almost male identity. Her corpse decomposes on a high burial platform, with most of the full panoply of adult male funerary ritual. Her agnatic mourners are legion, for the entire clan must observe her passing. Her skull is placed eventually in the *katiam* cult house of her clan. Her male name appears at the ascending limits of genealogical reckoning, disguising her gender, and her sacred name passes to her successors. Yet, when her female uterine kin depart from the burial platform, they may remark on the parts of her female substance (uterus and interior part of the vagina) that they must bear away and partially consume. Her successor soon divines through ritual autopsy that her agnatic ancestors have indeed led away her *finiik* to the ancestral underworld, entitling her to significant ancestorhood and sacrificial attention. But the diviner may also intimate that a large *khaapkhabuurien* may have been seen lurking near the burial platform to attack the emerging *finiik*. Thus, when her skull is placed among male *sacrae* in the clan *katiam* cult house, a gaping hole is broken in the male navel to admit the sacred male knowledge that she was denied in life. At the end, in the ragged hole in her skull, she retains an indelible emblem of the gender that another *waneng aiyem ser* long ago attributed to her at birth.

Conclusion

The *waneng aiyem ser* is anomalous, but with metaphorical deliberation. For Bimin-Kuskusmin men are entrapped in a dilemma. Mature, fertile women possess a highly valued power essential to human procreation and ritual creation. Yet, such power has sacred value only when it can be contained and controlled, and it becomes dangerously polluting when it cannot be properly channeled. Men suspect that women (as wives) are not morally prone to control this power, and have no clear jural duty to do so among non-agnates unrelated by substance. But male agnates of these women (as sisters) avoid pollution largely through shared *finiik* spirit and agnatic blood and the substantial, social bonds of siblingship.[30] In turn, brothers hold substantial control over fertile fluids and ritual control over menstrual blood.

Because one can neither marry agnates nor quite trust affines, however, this control is rather abstract. Agnatic women "naturally" reproduce non-agnates beyond the natal area (and clan) and for those with one has no strong substantial tie. Hence, control is to no avail where it matters most – within the lineage or clan. The bonds between males and females must be strong for control to be effective. Beyond the agnatic fold and within the kindred, control over (and protection from) female fertility and substance is founded on weak female (uterine) ties, and diminishes as the circle of cognatic kin radiates outward (from ego). Beyond the kindred and the clan, the shields and controls in substance are shattered, and pollution is rampant. But the woman (as wife) must come from this social periphery, bringing danger and perhaps *tamam* witchcraft. It is socially best if she is from mother's clan (but not mother's lineage); yet such origin implies no bonds of natural substance. The *waneng aiyem ser*, however, as a fertile, nonpolluting female agnate among agnates and encompassed by male agnatic (ritual) power, provides several substantial advantages in partially resolving this dilemma and, thereby, in illuminating aspects of gender.

Ideally, throughout her premenstruous (*seib aiyem*), menstruous (*waneng imok aiyem*), and finally postmenopausal (*waneng aiyem ser*) life cycle, she has always been under at least partial ritual control by her male agnates. Now she is transformed (both naturally and ritually) in social identity and gender and is almost totally encompassed by such control. Her image combines the virtues of virgin (purity), mother (fertility), and agnate (strong, shared *finiik* and agnatic blood), and contrasts with the uncontrolled, polluting aspects of the dreaded *tamam*, the wanton *waasop waneng*, and the alien wife. She becomes a living symbol of the notion that embodied substances, initially laid down in procreative process, may be naturally and ritually altered in structure and balance to permute not only gender constellations, but also the social relations that are articulated with a fundamental differentiation of male and female.

The *wanang aiyem ser* has lost both (female) menstrual capacity (through natural process) and (female) menstrual blood (through ritual extrusion), yet has retained her (male) fertile fluids – as demonstrated in her former motherhood and present ritual efficacy. But her lack of menstrual blood and thus the capacity to be sexually polluting (and polluted) are significant for the strength and the ritual potential of her fertile fluids. Fertile fluids, menstrual blood, and semen must be combined and embodied in the female for natural reproduction, but the *waneng aiyem ser* is asexual and nonmenstruous, neither incorporating semen nor extruding menstrual blood. Thus, she can neither bear children nor contaminate her fertile fluids. In her body, fertile fluids (a male procreative contribution) become like semen (their procreative origin). Fertile fluids interact with agnatic blood and *finiik* spirit in the heart in a (male) manner that strengthens all three substances. Male foods and participation in male rituals increase this strength. Thus, the *waneng aiyem ser* becomes strong in male substance. Her powerful agnatic blood and *finiik* enhance her agnatic lineage and clan identity and enable her to enter male ritual contexts without harm (to them or to her). Her strong *finiik* dominates her *khaapkhabuurien* and allows her to be behaviorally "like a man." Her strong *finiik* enables her to be possessed by a range of ancestral *finiik* and then to destroy the *tamam* witch. Her strong *finiik* quickly enters the ancestral underworld at death to reemerge as a significant ancestor in the *katiam* cult house within the sacred vessel of her skull (the male procreative contribution of bone). Thus, she is called a "male mother," is remembered by a male name, and is held to be sacred in male ritual contexts.

The strong, uncontaminated male substance of the *waneng aiyem ser* allows her not only to participate in male ritual contexts of curing, divination, initiation, and purification against pollution by female (and male) substance, but also to act on behalf of her (male and female) agnates in the more contaminating female contexts of birth, female naming, initiation, curing, divination, and purification against pollution by male (and female) substance. In these instances, however, her more androgynous gender emerges. Semen and menstrual blood are antithetical and are polluting (to both males and females); yet, the latter destroys growth and promotes *only* fertility, whereas the former affects *both* growth *and* fertility positively. Unlike all other persons, the *waneng aiyem ser* possesses neither substance, but only fertile fluids (a female manifestation of male substance); and she can promote *both* fertility *and* growth ritually. She can be polluted by neither semen nor menstrual blood, but only by persons of lesser sacred status. Hence, in rites of curing, initiation, and purification, when semen and menstrual blood must be symbolically separated or joined, she becomes a ritual mediator, using her own body (containing only fertile fluids) to separate and articulate these substances, to promote both fertility and growth, and to remedy pollution. She alone may manipulate *both* actual semen *and* actual menstrual blood in ritual contexts.

As the *waneng aiyem ser* combines male and female substances (nonpolluting) in her body, so she may mediate male and female phenomena (polluting) in other realms. Even her taboos and ceremonial regalia indicate a special androgynous quality. Thus, she may have contact with umbilical cords (female) at birth and female naming, and corpses (male and female) – through divinatory autopsy – at death. At birth, she insures against the treachery of female non-agnates (wives as mothers) for her male agnates, yet presides as a midwife over a woman's childbearing. At female naming, she bestows a female name on behalf of her (male and female) agnates, yet bears a male name and plants the umbilical cord (female) of a boy in her (male) taro garden. At female initiation, she gives the initiate (female) water that has been consecrated in the menstrual control rite of her male agnates. At male initiation, she brings menstrual blood (female) into a male ritual context as a transvestite, wearing a red pandanus fruit as a "penis-clitoris" (*maiyoob-mem fuun*) and representing the hermaphroditic ancestors Afek and Yomnok. At death, her skull (male) is enshrined among male *sacrae* with a distinctive mark (a ragged hole in the male navel) of female gender, yet her funeral approximates that of initiated men. Only she has *both* taro (male, fertilized by semen) *and* sweet potato (female, fertilized by menstrual blood) gardens. But these are sacred gardens, and her fertile fluids (a female manifestation of male substance) are strengthened by *both* ritual taro *and* ritual sweet potatoes. Only she can be possessed simultaneously by ancestral *finiik* (male and female) through *both* agnatic (male) *and* uterine (female) links, and can use this unique form of possession to destroy the female *tamam* witch, who destroys male substance and transforms it into female substance. If the *tamam* becomes the focus of "the myth of feminine evil" (Hayes 1972) among Bimin-Kuskusmin, then perhaps the *waneng aiyem ser* becomes "the image of androgynous good."

If the dilemma of marriage and motherhood, of male agnate and female non-agnate, cannot be resolved directly, it can be articulated metaphorically in the persona of the *waneng aiyem ser* and expressed through her appearance in various ceremonial contexts. The *waneng aiyem ser* may be seen as a sealed, purified vehicle of maleness *and* femaleness, a complex artifact symbolizing the polysemy of gender. Thus, as a ritual specialist, she removes, transforms, or embeds male and female substances in the bodies of females and males, respectively. On occasion, she is instrumental in the control of the dynamic balance and flow of both male and female substances in the bodies of either men or women (especially in initiation and curing rites). Thus, she represents the male-in-female and the female-in-male in everyone, the ancestral legacy of the androgynous Afek and Yomnok. But she is also a complex "meta-statement" on matters of birth, growth, decay, and death; of strength, fertility, and pollution; of male, female, and androgyne, in complex, metaphorical articulation. The aptness of Bimin-Kuskusmin gender ideas as a source of metaphorical elaboration is built upon natural substances (and their structures) and the possibility of partial similarity and partial difference between male and female, which can be focused differently in different contexts, although particular constellations of gender may contrast sharply. This possibility facilitates the construction of analogies between male and female that can be implemented to classify diverse phenomena, but that are ultimately anchored in natural substance. Yet, a symbolic focus that cannot bear the conviction of reality is sterile and impotent. Indeed, it must be realized repeatedly through constant metaphorization in a variety of contexts of shared experience. As the *waneng aiyem ser* follows her male and female agnates through the panoply of rites that mark their life cycle, she provides, in her strikingly anomalous social identity and gender, that focus on (male and female) natural substance and process upon which Bimin-Kuskusmin ideological constructions of gender are founded.

Notes

1 The data on which analysis is based are from fieldwork among the Bimin-Kuskusmin from 1971 to 1973. Research was supported by the U.S. National Institutes of Health, the Cornell University Humanities and Social Sciences Program, and the Center for South Pacific Studies of the University of California, Santa Cruz. Above all, the Bimin-Kuskusmin people are owed the primary debt of gratitude. This analysis draws on aspects of a paper presented elsewhere (see Poole 1975). On that paper, I appreciate the comments of R. C. Kelly, L. L. Langness, J. L. McCreery, M. J. Meggitt, R. A. Rappaport, P. R. Sanday, W. R. Sangree, R. Wagner, and J. B. Watson. On the present version, I thank G. G. Harris, M. E. Meeker, M. E. Spiro, A. M. Strathern, J. M. Taylor, and D. F. Tuzin for criticisms. I am especially grateful to S. B. Ortner and H. Whitehead for thoughtful comments and generous encouragement.

2 The notion of ''embeddedness'' is drawn from the Bimin-Kuskusmin view that ''proper'' procreation – conception, prenatal development, and birth – endows a child with certain minimal and malleable, yet relatively unambiguous sexual characteristics. Thus, the obviously anomalous monorchid is thought not to be a proper person and is destroyed at birth. The rare pseudohermaphrodite (male), however, is considered at first to be a more or less normal girl and only later to be a case of delayed male development once the complete genitalia have descended. The hermaphroditic qualities of these boys are linked to those of *waneng aiyem ser* and certain androgynous ancestors, and these boys have special privileges in male ritual contexts. Throughout the culturally recognized course of normal maturation, however, aspects of gender may be augmented or diminished, lost or gained, or otherwise altered by means of ''natural'' growth and decline, consumption or elimination, pollution, illness, ritual modification, etc.

3 In the social sciences literature, the term *gender* has been used in a variety of ways (e.g., see Bernard 1971; Chafetz 1974; D'Andrade 1966; Green 1974; and Stoller 1968). For present purposes, my perspective is as follows: Gender refers to ideological constructs that ''produce'' male, female, and androgynous categories on the basis of selective cultural perceptions of ethnopsychological characteristics deemed natural and significant. This concrete naturalness invests gender constructs with an aura of factuality (see Geertz 1973b) and renders them fertile for metaphoric (symbolic) elaboration and extension vis-à-vis a diversity of more or less ''sex-linked'' sociocultural phenomena. They pertain invariably, but not exclusively to the conceptual differentiation of men and women. Gender constructs then are systems of meaning, vehicles for a multitude of apparently diverse ideas and values, that are anchored in (cultural representations of) ''nature'' and are implemented in diverse aspects of sociocultural life (see A. M. Strathern 1976, 1978b).

4 For example, see Allen 1967; Aufenanger 1964; Brown 1964; Brown and Buchbinder 1976; Feil 1978; Guidieri 1975; Langness 1967, 1974, 1976; Meggitt 1964; Read 1954; Stagl 1971; A. J. Strathern 1970a; and A. M. Strathern 1972.

5 Because she no longer retains her menstrual capacity, engages in sexual intercourse, becomes pregnant, or gives birth, the *waneng aiyem ser* cannot pollute others with sexual effluvia. Perhaps due to her androgynous gender, she is also not vulnerable to sexual contamination by others (male or female). Hence, she can touch semen and menstrual blood in ritual contexts and preside over rites of purification without harm. In her sacred capacity, however, she is highly vulnerable to pollution by those (male and female) who are less sacred. The same is true

of paramount male ritual leaders, who offer no threat to *waneng aiyem ser* in this respect, but who can be polluted by female (not male) sexual discharges (unlike *waneng aiyem ser*).

6 The sacred name of *waneng aiyem ser* is unique to them and highly secret. This name is identical for all *waneng aiyem ser* of all clans and is an emblem of their common identity, set apart from all others. It is one of the many secret, sacred names of the great, hermaphroditic ancestor Afek, whom all *waneng aiyem ser* are said to represent in male ritual, and no other Bimin-Kuskusmin names are inherited in this manner. But each such name has an individuating suffix.

7 Although much of the conceptual information on gender substance and procreative process is considered to be sacred male knowledge, it is not held to be highly secret. The exegesis of adult men and women is remarkably similar (although men excel) and is often acknowledged to be so in private contexts. With the exception of *waneng aiyem ser*, who often speak in a male *genre*, however, women are often far less detailed, systematic, and articulate in exegesis than men (cf. Ardner 1975: 3). And women have more restricted rights to speak on such matters in public. My most important female informants for these data, therefore, are those considered to possess esoteric knowledge and "to be like men," i.e., the *waneng aiyem ser*. Indeed, as a male ethnographer, my access to other women as informants was often severely restricted.

8 Cf. Allen 1967; Berndt 1962; Langness 1967, 1974; Lindenbaum 1972; Meggitt 1964; Newman 1965; Read 1965; Salisbury 1962, 1965; and A. J. Strathern 1970a.

9 A. M. Strathern (personal communication). Cf. Buchbinder and Rappaport 1976; Lindenbaum 1976; Meggitt 1976; and A. M. Strathern 1972.

10 For example, see Buchbinder and Rappaport 1976; Faithorn 1975, 1976; Herdt 1980; Kelly 1976; Meigs 1976; and Strathern and Strathern 1971.

11 For example, see Allen 1967; Bulmer 1965; Guidieri 1975; Herdt 1980; Langness 1969, 1974; Lindenbaum 1976; Poole 1980b; Read 1952, 1965; Salisbury 1965; A. J. Strathern 1970a, 1970b; A. M. Strathern 1978b; Weiner 1976; and Whiteman 1965.

12 For example, see Berndt 1962; Glasse 1968; Kelly 1976; Meggitt 1965; Meigs 1976; Reay 1959; Salisbury 1962; A. J. Strathern 1971, 1972; and Wagner 1967, 1970.

13 For example, see Herdt 1980; Kelly 1976; Schieffelin 1976; A. J. Strathern 1972, 1973; van Baal 1966; Wagner 1967, 1977; and Williams 1936.

14 For example, see Berndt 1962; Glasse 1968; Langness 1967; Lindenbaum 1975; Meggitt 1965; Newman 1965; Read 1965; Salisbury 1965; A. J. Strathern 1972, 1973; Wagner 1967, 1972a, 1972b, 1977; and Williams 1940–2. See also J. F. Weiner 1977.

15 In male *am yaoor* initiation and *katiam* cult ritual contexts, this threat is by no means idle. Several women were badly scarred as a consequence of minor intrusions into highly sacred contexts, and at least one woman (from another ethnic group) was probably killed for a major indiscretion.

16 Afek and Yomnok are generally identified with the "cassowary" and the "spiny anteater," respectively. These creatures are not considered to be sexually dimorphic in appearance, but are said to be androgynous. In primordial times, Afek and Yomnok descended from the original ancestor Goowpnuuk or Daarkhru (a giant lizard), who was also androgynous and reproduced by some ambiguous kind of bodily fission. Afek and Yomnok were siblings who mated with each other, as well as with their children and grandchildren, to produce the "totemic" ancestors of the original Bimin-Kuskusmin clans. Both of these "great ancestors"

produced offspring. Both possessed a "penis-clitoris" (*maiyoob-mem fuun*) and breasts. Afek, the more female of the pair, gave birth through a vagina in each buttock. The ancestors of the Bimin ritual moiety issued from the right buttock, and those of the Kuskusmin emanated from the left buttock. Thus, an androgynous, but somewhat more female ancestress provides a mythological foundation for conceptually distinguishing between the moieties. It should be noted, however, that the common Bimin-Kuskusmin analogy male: female::right:left is *not* applied in this context and does not affect moiety identification. Yomnok, the more male of the pair, gave birth through the single aperture of the "penis-clitoris." The ancestors that issued from this "vagina" were parallel lines of nonhuman creatures (all possessing critical attributes of personhood) who often symbolically represent the agnatic unity of all Bimin-Kuskusmin (as well as the links among the original patriclans). Thus, an androgynous, yet slightly more male ancestor provides a mythological foundation for conceptually uniting all Bimin-Kuskusmin (see Poole 1976: 487–569, *passim*).

17 The term *wanengamariin* ("people of women's houses") is commonly used to refer to all women except *waneng aiyem ser*, all female children, and all uninitiated males (primarily children). It contrasts with the term *kunumamariin* ("people of men's houses"), which is commonly used to refer to all initiated men. In fact, all initiated men do dwell in men's houses, which are either collective (most men) or individual (paramount ritual leaders). With the exeption of *waneng aiyem ser*, all others live in women's houses in which one often finds a woman, with perhaps a co-wife, widowed mother of husband's mother, or other elder woman, and un-initiated, unmarried children (male and female). The *waneng aiyem ser*, however, is considered to be neither *wanengamariin* nor *kunumamariin*.

18 It is interesting to note that the more exterior exposure (toward the vagina) of the red aspect of menstrual blood is said to be determinant of female gender. The female, until menopause, will thereafter be restricted by her publicly acknowledged menstrual capacity in many ways. This capacity will become a focal attribute of her gender. The orientation of the red aspect of menstrual blood toward the interior of the womb may be seen as somewhat analogous to the more hidden menstrual contamination of male children, which must be remedied in male initiation. Menstrual blood is utterly antithetical to the major attributes of male gender.

19 In this phase of male initiation, the central ridgepole of the initiation house is smeared with menstrual debris (actual), and initiates ritually masturbate over this artifact after passing beneath the genitalia of *waneng aiyem ser* (disguised as male transvestites), who drip "menstrual blood" (actually pig blood) on their heads (see Poole 1975: 32–5).

20 Urine and feces are female procreative contributions, but are said to be polluting to women (and men). Minor postpartum illnesses are often attributed to such contamination. The bodily wastes of older children and adults do not pose a similar problem, for they can control elimination and carefully dispose of such substances, unless very ill or very old.

21 In fact, although most are widows, a few *waneng aiyem ser* were separated or divorced from living husbands at the time of their selection. One, married to a living paramount male ritual leader, was rather anomalous in that her extant marriage (although ritually dissolved as a fiction) was held to be auspicious for her status. Most extant marriages of such women are ritually dissolved and/or publicly ignored.

22 Many have already taken up residence in their natal areas with their agnates.

23 A few extant, but very small original clans, however, had no living *waneng aiyem ser*. Men of these clans claimed a variety of circumstances for this situation, but all were certain that a *waneng aiyem ser* soon would be chosen.

24 The fiction of her ''return'' is maintained regardless of her actual place of residence at the time of her selection.

25 If the former husband is living, he may neither participate in nor even be present at such transactions.

26 If her postmarital residence is unusual (e.g., uxorilocal), a more ideal and fictional hamlet of residence may be selected for the transaction.

27 This special house, isolated in a separate compound of the cult house hamlet or in the adjacent forest, is larger than and elevated above all women's houses (but not men's houses).

28 It is said that the *waneng aiyem ser* of the Watiaanmin and Imoranmin clans, the ranking clans of the Bimin and Kuskusmin ritual moieties, respectively, have quite full knowledge of such secret male esoterica. They are said to insure against the inadvertent loss of such knowledge in the male domain. This assertion is difficult to affirm with certainty, given a great elaboration of secrecy in such matters.

29 Despite the apparent prestige of the ''office,'' the *waneng aiyem ser* is said to become severely depressed and even suicidal at times. No male informant ever admitted this characteristic, but many women attested to it in private. The *waneng aiyem ser*, however, denied that this suspicion was true. Some did admit that they missed some aspects of their ''former lives.''

30 The inadvertent pollution of brothers (male agnates) is usually attributed to accidents of imprecise female ''natural'' rhythms.

References

Allen, M. R. 1967. *Male cults and secret initiations in Melanesia*. Melbourne: Melbourne University Press.

Ardner, E. 1975. ''Belief and the problem of women and the 'problem' revisited.'' In *Perceiving women*, ed. S. Ardener, pp. 1–27. London: Malaby Press.

Aufenanger, H. 1964. ''Women's lives in the Highlands of New Guinea.'' *Anthropos* 59: 218–66.

Bamberger, J. 1974. ''The myth of matriarchy: why men rule in primitive society.'' In *Women, culture, and society*, ed. M. Z. Rosaldo and L. Lamphere, pp. 263–80. Stanford: Stanford University Press.

Barnett, S. 1976. ''Coconuts and gold: relational identity in a South Indian caste.'' *Contributions to Indian Sociology* (N.S.) 10: 133–56.

Barth, F. 1971. ''Tribes and intertribal relations in the Fly Headwaters.'' *Oceania* 41: 171–91.

   1975. *Ritual and knowledge among the Baktaman of New Guinea*. New Haven: Yale University press.

Bernard, J. 1971. *Women and the public interest*. Chicago: Aldine-Atherton.

Berndt, R. M. 1962. *Excess and restraint*. Chicago: University of Chicago Press.

Brown, P. 1964. ''Enemies and affines.'' *Ethnology* 3: 335–56.

Brown, P., and Buchbinder, G., eds. 1976. *Man and woman in the New Guinea Highlands*. Washington, D.C.: American Anthropological Association.

Buchbinder, G., and Rappaport, R. 1976. ''Fertility and death among the Maring.'' In *Man and woman in the New Guinea Highlands*, ed. P. Brown and G. Buchbinder, pp. 13–35. Washington, D.C.: American Anthropological Association.

Bulmer, R. N. H. 1965. "The Kyaka of the Western Highlands." In *Gods, ghosts, and men in Melanesia*, ed. P. Lawrence and M. J. Meggitt, pp. 132–61. London: Oxford University Press.

Chafetz, J. S. 1974. *Masculine/feminine or human?* Itasca, Ill.: F. E. Peacock.

D'Andrade, R. G. 1966. "Sex differences and cultural institutions." In *The development of sex differences*, ed. E. E. Maccoby, pp. 173–203. Stanford: Stanford University Press.

Douglas, M. 1970. *Natural symbols*. New York: Pantheon Books.

Ellen, R. F. 1977. "Anatomical classification and the semiotics of the body." In *The anthropology of the body*, ed. J. Blacking, pp. 343–73. London: Academic Press.

Faithorn, E. 1975. "The concept of pollution among the Káfe of the Papua New Guinea Highlands." In *Toward an anthropology of women*, ed. R. R. Reiter, pp. 127–40. New York: Monthly Review Press.

    1976. "Women as persons: aspects of female life and male-female relations among the Káfe." In *Man and woman in the New Guinea Highlands*, ed. P. Brown and G. Buchbinder, pp. 86–95. Washington, D.C.: American Anthropological Association.

Feil, D. K. 1978. "Women and men in the Enga *tee*." *American Ethnologist* 5: 263–79.

Firth, R. 1973. *Symbols*. Ithaca, N.Y: Cornell University Press.

Fortes, M. 1962. "Ritual and office in tribal society," In *Essays on the ritual of social relations*, ed. M. Gluckman, pp. 53–88. Manchester: Manchester University Press.

    1968. "Of installation ceremonies." *Proceedings of the Royal Anthropological Institute for 1967*: 5–20.

Geertz, C. 1973a. "Ideology as a cultural system." In *The interpretation of cultures*, ed. C. Geertz, pp. 193–233. New York: Basic Books.

    1973b. "Religion as a cultural system." In ibid., pp. 87–125.

Geertz, C., ed. 1973. *The interpretation of cultures*. New York: Basic Books.

Glasse, R. M. 1968. *Huli of Papua*. Paris: Mouton.

Glasse, R. M., and M. J. Meggitt, eds. 1969. *Pigs, pearlshells, and women*. Englewood Cliffs, N.J.: Prentice-Hall.

Goody, E. 1970. "Legitimate and illegitimate aggression in a West African state." In *Witchcraft confessions and accusations*, ed. M. Douglas, pp. 207–44. London: Tavistock Publications.

Goody, J., ed. 1973. *The character of kinship*. Cambridge: Cambridge University Press.

Green, R. 1974. *Sexual identity and conflict in children and adults*. New York: Basic Books.

Guidieri, R. 1975. "Note sur le rapport mâle/femelle en Mélanésie." *L'Homme* 15: 103–19.

Harris, G. 1973. "Furies, witches and mothers." In *The character of kinship*, ed. J. Goody, pp. 145–59. Cambridge: Cambridge University Press.

Hayes, H. R. 1972. *The dangerous sex*. New York: Pocket Books.

Herdt, G. H. 1980. *Guardians of the flutes*. Vol. 1. New York: Macmillan.

Kelly, R. C. 1976. "Witchcraft and sexual relations: an exploration in the social and semantic implications of the structure of belief." In *Man and woman in the New Guinea Highlands*, ed. P. Brown and G. Buchbinder, pp. 36–53. Washington, D.C.: American Anthropological Association.

Langness, L. L. 1967. "Sexual antagonism in the New Guinea Highlands: a Bena Bena example." *Oceania* 37: 161–77.

1969. "Marriage in Bena Bena." In *Pigs, pearlshells, and women,* ed. R. M. Glasse and M. J. Meggitt, pp. 38–55. Englewood Cliffs, N.J.: Prentice-Hall.

1974. "Ritual, power, and male dominance in the New Guinea Highlands." *Ethos* 2: 189–212.

1976. "Discussion." In *Man and woman in the New Guinea Highlands,* ed. P. Brown and G. Buchbinder, pp. 96–106. Washington, D.C.: American Anthropological Association.

Lawrence, P., and M. J. Meggitt, eds. 1965. *Gods, ghosts, and men in Melanesia.* London: Oxford University Press.

Lindenbaum, S. 1972. "Sorcerers, ghosts, and polluting women: an analysis of religious belief and population control." *Ethnology* 11: 241–53.

1975. "Sorcery and danger." *Oceania* 46: 68–75.

1976. "A wife is the hand of man." In *Man and woman in the New Guinea Highlands,* ed. P. Brown and G. Buchbinder, pp. 54–62. Washington, D.C.: American Anthropological Association.

Meggitt, M. J. 1964. "Male-female relations in the Highlands of Australian New Guinea." *American Anthropologist* 66: 204–24.

1965. *The lineage system of the Mae-Enga of New Guinea.* London: Oliver and Boyd.

1976. "A duplicity of demons: sexual and familial roles expressed in western Enga stories." In *Man and woman in the New Guinea Highlands,* ed. P. Brown and G. Buchbinder, pp. 63–85. Washington, D.C.: American Anthropological Association.

Meigs, A. S. 1976. "Male pregnancy and the reduction of sexual opposition in a New Guinea Highlands society." *Ethnology* 15: 393–407.

Murphy, R. F. 1959. "Social structure and sex antagonism." *Southwestern Journal of Anthropology* 15: 89–98.

Newman, P. L. 1965. *Knowing the Gururumba.* New York: Holt, Rinehart and Winston.

Ortner, S. B. 1973. "On key symbols." *American Anthropologist* 75: 1338–46.

1974. "Is female to male as nature is to culture?" In *Woman, culture, and society,* ed. M. Z. Rosaldo and L. Lamphere, pp. 67–87. Stanford: Stanford University Press.

Poole, F. J. P. 1974. "*Tamam:* the ideology and sociology of a species of witchcraft in Bimin-Kuskusmin society." Paper presented at the 73rd Annual Meeting of the American Anthropological Association.

1975. "*Waneng Aiyem:* 'sacred' and 'polluting' dimensions of female identity in Bimin-Kuskusmin Society." Paper presented at the 74th Annual Meeting of the American Anthropological Association.

1976. *The Ais Am.* Ph.D. dissertation, Cornell University.

" 'Couvade' and clinic in a New Guinea society: birth among the Bimin-Kuskusmin." In *Medicalization of life and patient compliance,* ed. R. Berg and M. deVries. Cambridge, Mass.: Harvard University Press (forthcoming a).

"The ritual forging of identity: aspects of person and self in Bimin-Kuskusmin male initiation." In *Rituals of manhood,* ed. G. H. Herdt. Berkeley: University of California Press (forthcoming b).

Read, K. E. 1952. "Nama Cult of the Central Highlands, New Guinea." *Oceania* 23: 1–25.

1954. "Cultures of the Central Highlands, New Guinea." *Southwestern Journal of Anthropology* 10: 1–43.

1965. *The high valley.* New York: Scribner's.

Reay, M. 1959. *The Kuma.* Cambridge: Cambridge University Press.

Rosaldo, M. Z. and Lamphere, L. eds. 1974. *Woman, culture, and society.* Stanford: Stanford University Press.

Salisbury, R. F. 1962. *From stone to steel.* Cambridge: Cambridge University Press.

1965. "The Siane of the Eastern Highlands." In *Gods, ghosts, and men in Melanesia,* ed. P. Lawrence and M. J. Meggitt, pp. 50–77. London: Oxford University Press.

Schieffelin, E. L. 1976. *The sorrow of the lonely and the burning of the dancers.* New York: St. Martin's.

Schneider, D. M. 1968. *American kinship.* Englewood Cliffs, N.J.: Prentice-Hall.

Schwimmer, E. G. 1973. *Exchange in the social structure of the Orokaiva.* New York: St. Martin's.

Stagl, J. 1971. *Der Geschlechtsantagonismus in Melanesien.* Vienna: Institut für Völkerkunde der Universität Wien.

Stoller, R. J. 1968. *Sex and gender.* Vol. 1. New York: Science House.

Strathern, A. J. 1970a. "Male initiation in the New Guinea Highlands." *Ethnology* 9: 373–9.

1970b. "The female and male spirit cults in Mount Hagen." *Man* (N.S.) 5: 571–85.

1971. "Wiru and Daribi matrilateral payments." *Journal of the Polynesian Society* 80: 449–62.

1972. *One father, one blood.* London: Tavistock Publications.

1973. "Kinship, descent and locality: some New Guinea examples." In *The character of kinship,* ed. J. Goody, pp. 21–33. Cambridge: Cambridge University Press.

Strathern, A. J. and Strathern, A. M. 1971. *Self-decoration in Mount Hagen.* London: Gerald Duckworth.

Strathern, A. M. 1972. *Women in between.* London: Seminar Press.

1976. "An anthropological perspective." In *Exploring sex differences,* ed. B. Lloyd and J. Archer, pp. 49–70. London: Academic Press.

1978a. *Self-interest and the social good: some implications of Hagen gender imagery.* Unpublished manuscript.

1978b. "The achievement of sex: paradoxes in Hagen genderthinking." In *The yearbook of symbolic anthropology I,* ed. E. G. Schwimmer, pp. 171–202. London: C. Hurst.

Turner, V. W. 1966. "Colour classification in Ndembu ritual. A problem in primitive classification." In *Anthropological approaches to the study of religion,* ed. M. Banton, pp. 47–84. London: Tavistock Publications.

Van Baal, J. 1966. *Dema.* The Hague: Martinus Nijhoff.

Wagner, R. 1967. *The curse of Souw.* Chicago: University of Chicago Press.

1970. "Daribi and Foraba cross-cousin terminologies: a structural comparison." *Journal of the Polynesian Society* 79: 91–8.

1972a. *Habu.* Chicago: University of Chicago Press.

1972b. *Misreading the metaphor: 'cross-cousin' relationships in the New Guinea Highlands.* Unpublished manuscript.

1977. "Analogic kinship: a Daribi example." *American Ethnologist* 4: 623–42.

Weiner, A. B. 1976. *Women of value, men of renown.* Austin: University of Texas Press.

Weiner, J. F. 1977. *Substance, siblingship and exchange: aspects of social structure in New Guinea*. Unpublished manuscript.

Whiteman, J. 1965. "Girls' puberty ceremonies amongst the Chimbu." *Anthropos* 60: 410–22.

Williams, F. E. 1936. *Papuans of the Trans-Fly*. Oxford: The Clarendon Press.
1940–2. "Natives of Lake Kutubu, Papua." *Oceania* 11: 121–57, 259–94, 374–401; 12: 49–74, 134–54.

Self-interest and the social good: SOME IMPLICATIONS OF HAGEN GENDER IMAGERY

Marilyn Strathern

Introduction

In 1976 in the Papua New Guinea Highlands, I was roundly criticized for taking two Hagen women friends for a drive. My critics were men, who said that women should not sit in the front of the vehicle – it was not their place. I shall use implications of this incident to comment upon some issues in gender analysis.[1]

Consider for a moment some of the remarks made by men and women in the discussion surrounding the incident. One of the vehicle owners was the man whose scathing views about women in general I had recorded twelve years before: "They are little rubbish things who stay at home simply, don't you see!" (M. Strathern 1972: 161). On this occasion, talking about the car purchase, he added a rather different observation: "Some women are rubbish, they do not think of earning money. [But] some women are strong and help their husbands by taking food to market; they earn money and contribute to buying a car or to bridewealth and they help their husbands." Wives of the vehicle owners gave an account of themselves in similar terms. "I may give the money to X [her husband] or Y [her son] or buy things for the children – some I put aside for myself and this I don't eat. I don't buy things for myself, I just put it by. Later if the men need money, if they are in trouble [and have to pay compensation], I help them." One woman spoke of how she and her husband always pooled their resources. "The coffee we pick together and sell together. When we get money some R [the husband] gets and some he gives to me . . . . R picked a first lot of coffee and earned K100 which he put towards the car.[2] This was R's coffee, we just picked it together and I helped him. It is our car. R didn't take the money and drink beer, it was our car [which he spent our money on] and I felt it was all right."

I choose this incident for the way in which it highlights certain issues in the understanding of gender concepts. There has always been an implicit contrast in Hagen men's statements between categorical denigration of females and contextual evaluation of particular women. The women's remarks quoted here hint as well at a perspective on their involvement in men's affairs that is not unlike the perspective of the men. Much has been written on how men have captured the anthropological imagination and imposed their worldview on the resulting ethnographies. Is it simply the case that Hagen men have managed to impose their view on Hagen women?[3]

On the anthropological analysis of male–female relations two points are generally separated: (*a*) gender stereotypes, the symbolic representation of the sexes, and the way these often underpin formal relations of authority or power; (*b*) how women adapt to their position, the maneuvers and stratagems to which they resort, their informal power and interpersonal influence. These may be set against one another. Rosaldo and Lamphere comment that ''although the formal authority structure of a society may declare that women are impotent and irrelevant, close attention to women's strategies and motives . . . indicates that even in situations of overt sex role asymmetry women have a good deal more power than conventional theorists have assumed'' (1974: 9). Faithorn's conclusions about the ethnography of the Papua New Guinea Highlands is that Highlands women have been ''neglected'' and characterizations of male–female relations ''over-simplified'' (1976: 86). Her essay, taking to task the emphasis of reporting relations between the sexes as antagonistic and women as restricted to the domestic domain, is entitled ''Women as Persons.''

Hageners' own definitions of male and female, and of persons, suggest that we should, however, be particularly careful of our levels of analysis. They lead me to make three points.

First, dissatisfaction with an androcentric bias in anthropology, with constructs such as ''political power'' or (male) ''group,'' cannot be met by concentrating on women as actors in the system, as persons ''in their own right,'' individuals outside the formal male/anthropological model. No doubt Weiner is right in saying that ''any study that does not include the role of women – as seen by women – as part of the way the society is structured remains only a partial study of that society'' (1976: 228). But I would question her ensuing comments: ''Whether women are publicly valued or privately secluded, whether they control politics, a range of economic commodities, or merely magic spells, they function within that society, not as objects but as individuals with some measure of control. We cannot begin to understand . . . why and how women in so many cases have been relegated to secondary status until we *first* reckon with the power women do have, even if this power *appears* limited and seems outside the political field'' (1976: 228–9, her italics). An analysis of individual action can surely not *compensate* for a cultural bias in gender constructs. It can only show us the extent to which this impinges upon action.

I do not wish to ignore the many questions associated with the nature of ideological construction (cf. Asad 1979); nevertheless, there is a sense in which any understanding of the meaning with which action is endowed must consider the symbolic structure as it is. Bias in the reporting of events is one thing; but a remedy of bias in this area cannot compensate for bias in the symbolic order. A closer look at interaction between men and women is likely to reveal only the organizational impact of people's models. The models themselves are already constructed at a distance from behavior. Certainly we should not simply reproduce people's own symbols in our analysis of events and behavior. But neither can a symbolic antithesis between male and female

somehow be readjusted by taking up one of its terms – characteristics associated with femaleness – and showing that actual women do not fit the image.

A concentration on "the individual" as a unit of analysis brings into focus
the nature of interpersonal power. For example, Faithorn seeks to show that
Kafe women exert considerable power in broad areas of their daily lives,
while Weiner talks of the kinds of decision-making control that Trobriand
women have. (She also makes the point that women's power is not to be
valued simply in relation to men's, but is a domain in its own right.) All this is
very proper in terms of our overall understanding of society. Because a
male–female antithesis is of symbolic importance we should not therefore
imagine that it governs all that men and women do, or that there is a simple
identity between the ideal and the actual. Yet we cannot turn to "the individual" as a self-evident analytical category to rescue us from the conceptual
bias of the symbolic order.

My second point concerns conceptualizations of personhood. In the previous citations, Weiner talks of individuals, Faithorn of persons. There is
tremendous rhetorical force behind the exhortation to consider women as
"individuals" or "persons." To my mind the rhetoric is suspect. It draws on
cultural obsessions of our own, which view the person as a political entity
("in his/her own right") with interests opposed to those of society. When
"society" is identified as a male construct, women's strategies can thus be
taken up on the basis of their being "individuals": people set apart from the
social system, actors manipulating structure. The "real" state of affairs is
thus revealed. To endow the "individual" with such superior reality (Evens
1977) is mistaken concretism. At the least attention should be given to the
ideological status of such an entity in the society being studied, and to the
cultural presuppositions about behavior based on this. In Hagen the individual as a "person" stands in a specific relationship to ideas about gender
that cannot be preempted by the kind of antithesis suggested by Faithorn
and Weiner.

The terms "person" and "individual" are used in a number of ways,
sometimes as synonyms, sometimes diacritically, sometimes in antithesis. In
this essay I shall argue that we can usefully talk of Hagen ideas of the person,
in an analytic sense, provided we do not conflate the construct with the
ideological "individual" of Western culture. This latter is best seen as a
particular cultural type (of person) rather than as a self-evident analytical
category itself. The point can be made from Dumont's (1977) formulations.
He takes "individual" as his key word, and distinguishes two meanings. First
is the "subject of speech, thought, and will, the indivisible sample of
mankind," and I retain "individual" for this. His second definition refers to a
culturally constituted moral entity, one defined by its potential autonomy and
independence from others like it. For this, I shall use the term "person."
Dumont's own formula in fact fuses a general description (the autonomous
moral being) with a particular case (the "nonsocial" being "as found primarily in our modern ideology of man and society" (Dumont 1977: 8)). In
Western notions of personhood, bounded units of the species are seen as *ipso
facto* morally self-contained, and further are set in opposition to nature and

society. Social science notions of personhood that emically oppose "the individual" to "society" are best understood as flowing from this specifically Western conception. But in other cultures, the ethical entity, the person, may be conceived along rather different axes. Certainly Hagen notions of the person are embedded in neither a mind/matter nor an individual/society contrast insofar as these presuppose some kind of relationship between nature and culture (cf. M. Strathern 1980).

In concentrating on the concept of "person" as an ethical entity, I refer back to Read (1955) who also wished to make "person" stand for just such an ethical category, although he argued that it was not to be found in the Gahuka Gama moral system. [4] My usage also fits Poole's description of personhood in Bimin-Kuskusmin, as the "attributes, capacities, and signs of 'proper' social persons that mark a moral career" (1979: 3). He specifically sets this conception of the person apart from the western "individual." Expectations about how people behave as persons enter into Hagen calculations and evaluations of others. It remains to be seen how far Hagen ideas of the person share elements of our folk concept "the individual."

The final point is that we need to distinguish interests and viewpoints that identify particular sections of society from models that set up such categories in symbolic opposition. The issue here is raised by Reay's observation that besides the perspective of women, New Guinea Highlands ethnographers have neglected the perspective of rubbish men (1976: 13). Yet not all potential positions offering a particular perspective on events are likely to receive the same symbolic emphasis. Thus Hagen old people certainly share characteristics that mark them as a category, but as the basis of a contrast with youth or middle age these are of little metaphorical value.

We are led here to what I believe has been an underappreciated dimension of Papua New Guinea "sex antagonism" – that the male–female opposition *is* of metaphoric value (see Buchbinder and Rappaport 1976; Kelly 1976). And where metaphor exists, we must be clear about its function. We should not *assume* for cultures that make heavy symbolic use of the antithesis between male and female that it literally divides men and women into social classes – so that we then have to account for each class having its own model. This may well be true for certain ideological structures. But insistence on looking for alternative models entails the premise that ideologies are exclusively about dominance and power relations, and that the symbols they employ are to be understood in their own terms. Thus (so the argument goes) images of maleness and femaleness refer only to men and women, and a model with a male "bias" must be about men's control of women. Hence, there must be a woman's version of equal validity.

As a medium through which the activities of men and women are perceived, models that focus on male and female may indeed misrepresent or mystify modes of interaction. They may obscure the bases of production and trivialize women's contribution. They may support men's (actual) domination over women in some contexts. Yet even in doing all of these things, male–female models often do something else as well. If I tend to concentrate on gender as a mode of creating symbolization, at the expense of its other dimensions, it is to underline a single significant point. Our understanding of gender constructs in Hagen cannot stop at what they tell us about men and women. Through the imagery of sexually based differences is ordered a wide range of values.[5] In what they sometimes set up as a "problem of women," Hageners – of both sexes – are also spelling out certain implications of personhood, of the alignment between self-interest and group action, in short, what is to them a "problem of people."

The Case of the Appropriated Landcruiser

The car over which I caused so much trouble belonged to a subclan of the Kawelka tribe who have settled away from their former territory in a lucrative cash cropping area. Spouses usually see themselves as working together in growing coffee (the chief cash crop), although as in the case of food production much routine care falls on women. Men are energetic at the height of the harvest season and in the subsequent processing of the bean. They also plant most of the coffee, which is therefore in their "name," but the division of proceeds goes generally by quantity. When more than about K5 is being sold, men take the bulk. The significant fact is the division into large and small sums. Householders vary in their arrangements. If the wife is selling she may hand the total sum to her husband, or hand over most and keep a small amount for herself; if he sells, he may keep it all, or give some to her. This figure also represents the ceiling of what women expect to earn at market (K2-4 per trip). The marketing of vegetable produce, planted by themselves, is almost entirely in their hands. Normally the wife keeps all this money herself.[6]

Money figures in transactions where traditional valuables are employed (A. Strathern 1976). The ideal is to produce money off the land or raise it through finance; wage labor tends to be denigrated (M. Strathern 1975), for the laborer must consume a high proportion of what he earns. Investment is valued over consumption. Money of any significant amount should be channeled into ceremonial exchange or some productive enterprise such as vehicle purchase, productive both of prestige and further financial enterprises. "The people with cars are able to travel around, and they taunt others – 'You haven't bought anything [big] with your money: you have eaten the money yourselves at home. You don't do anything good with what you earn!' " (male driver of the Kawelka car).

THE DISPUTE

The vehicle (a Landcruiser) cost K6000, purchased in the name of ten men. It was seen as enabling them to travel to exchange partners, transport pigs, take women to market, and earn money from fare-paying passengers. The designated driver was a man; typically some men would accompany him in the cab, while their wives sat with others in the back.

The ten owners were proud they had bought it before the 1976 coffee season was underway, for this indicated the strength of their resources. Through contributions raised on their personal networks, each man had donated the substantial sum that marked his "ownership." By no means their first car, it was also further proof of their prosperity as pioneers in this area; and a politically precious object, for the money had been raised in rivalry against men of the pair subclan.

As a minor contributor and a driver I had a lien on the vehicle.[7] I had gone to visit a friend in another tribe, taking with me Ann and Lucy (pseudonyms) who were married to two of the owners. We all sat in the cab. We returned to a crowd at the roadside, and to a quite virulent attack. Two men rushed up, one of them demanding heatedly of my companions who they thought they were to ride in the front, and insisting that the proper place for women was in the back with the netbags and produce – they would endanger the vehicle. He protested over and again that the car had only been recently purchased, and what were the women doing in the men's place. Other men pressed around, and the affair escalated into an altercation.

The attack was not just about the women. The chief accuser belonged to a faction within the subclan that was highly critical of the general way the car was deployed. The basic criticism in such situations is always that the car is being used for consumption rather than investment. The point of course is that one person's investment is another's consumption. A driver who attends exclusively to the fund-raising affairs of one set of people will be looked upon by those left out as gadding around for pleasure. What began as an object of group prestige will seem to have degenerated into one of personal benefit for some.

The two factions comprised Lucy's husband, Michael, the subclan's regular driver, along with his close associate who had originally planned the purchase, and Edward, an aging minor big-man whose chief followers were dependent sister's sons living with him. It was one of the sister's sons who led the attack. As the driver whose personal agreement was inevitably involved in the daily journeying, Michael felt himself much put upon. Now he became the main object of Edward's recriminations. Their open argument quickly reached the point of Michael saying that they would return Edward's money. Then Edward and his cronies could go and buy their own car – Michael would even give them some extra money to start them off! If, after the money was returned, Edward forgot himself and begged a lift, why he would be no better than a dog! Edward demanded the withdrawal.

Some interesting issues came to light when money was indeed returned the following day. Lucy and Ann were no longer participants in the dispute, their actions neither defended by their menfolk nor the basis for further public recrimination. But others of their sex were very much involved. Edward's contribution had included money given him by women. His adult son, an owner in his own name, was treated as a separate person, it being up to him whether he withdrew his share (he did not). It was assumed that the sister's two sons – whose names were subsumed under Edward's – would go along with Edward. But also involved were Rachel, the mother of these men, and Katherine his wife. Between them, sister and wife had privately provided at least the equal of Edward's personal share. Two very different interpretations were made of this by men of the other faction.

Edward was said to have been shamed by the revelation of how little was his "own" money. He had claimed to have put in K400 in his own name, but only K70 was discovered to have been raised independently of his household. To show self-sufficiency is to be "strong"; if dependency on others is made a public matter, one is displaying "weakness."[8] Thus females who are categorically dependent upon males are "weak." Here the rubbishing of Edward was bound with bringing into the open his dependency on women. Edward suffered a diminution of personal status both from the publication of the fact and because his actions were ultimately against his own enduring self-interest. Others could imagine a time when there would be conflict within himself – between his wanting to use the car and this emphatic withdrawal. If he ever lost awareness of the social consequences of his actions and gave in to petulance, he would be something less than human – a dog, Michael said.

Rachel and Katherine themselves had turned upon Edward and said they did not want to take back their money. This was acknowledged as a feasible course of action; they were treated, like Edward's son, as autonomous persons with a self-interest in the matter. Their claims to the car were never made in terms of ownership but of usufruct. Rachel stressed that she relied on it to take produce to market, for she was an old woman now and the netbags heavy. Both of them also underlined their right to independent action in terms of specific social relationships. Rachel noted that it had been her own decision to reside on her brother's land where she could plant cash crops (earn money to help him among others), and she was not going to forfeit her position. Katherine said she had had her children (not just her own offspring but the junior generation in general) in mind when she contributed to the car and refused to make them argue by withdrawing her money. The women's autonomy was respected; only Edward and his sister's sons were given back their shares, and Edward received much less than he had originally given in his name.

Edward's association with females was thus used to show up his own weakness, a device that rested on categorical attributes of "femaleness." His wife and sister, by gender "weak," were symbols for Edward's lack of personal strength. Yet when it came to considering the consequences of Rachel's and Katherine's contributions in the matter of returning the money, the men organizing this dropped these symbolic equations and put in their place certain assumptions about women as persons. This switch in attitude reveals something of the connections Hageners themselves make between the categorical use of gender attributes ("male" and "female" behavior) and reference to the actor as a person, whose sex may or may not be relevant.

Women as persons

The male owners of the Landcruiser had, like Edward, almost all received money from women – wives, mothers, sisters, a mother-in-law.[9] One or two such contributions exceeded or equaled those of some men. Money the owners initially put forward as their "own" would have included earnings based upon women's labor, but this prior appropriation is done in the name of the household as a joint unit. The cash women in addition gave specifically for the car came from further tiny amounts earned and kept by themselves.

Contributing money did not make a woman an owner: She had no independent claims on financial returns from the vehicle, her relationship to the enterprise being mediated through the son or husband who had counted her money in with his. From the man's point of view her support was in the nature not of transaction but domestic production, money raised as food and pigs were raised from home resources (M. Strathern 1972: 133–42). Nor did the women make any claims to be considered among the owners, although they regarded themselves as entitled to particular attention when they wanted to use the car.[10]

Women save money, then, and contribute it toward group enterprises. The expectation of this is an element in men's calculations of the support they can give other men. Women whom I spoke to were proud of their contributions; several stressed their self-sufficiency – it was specifically money they themselves had earned (na nanemnga-ko, "myself my own"). Another of Michael's wives told me she had secretly saved cash that her husband assumed she was spending on herself and the children. She and her co-wife,[11] she said, wanted to provide substantial sums because it mattered to them what others, especially the older wives in the subclan who were also contributing, would think of them.

Her colleague corroborated this. "Our husband did not help in the gardens and it was hard work earning the money. Now the money is gone on the car we feel bad. But if we didn't give to the car then other women would gossip about it. They would say: 'All the time you take food to the market [i.e. earn money] yet you don't help your husband . . . ' The other women would wonder what we did with our cash, and if we did not contribute to a big thing, would talk against us." There are three assumptions here: (a) women should assist in group enterprises; (b) they do so through individually helping their husbands; (c) money is ideally invested in "big" things. Wives do not simply aid the husband in the attainment of his goals, but make these goals theirs.

Men encourage this and accord prestige to women whose interests are demonstrated to coincide with their own. Michael praised these two wives (privately to me) for working hard and promoting his welfare. Lucy, the third wife, had yet to prove herself: Would she eat all the money she earned, throw it about, spend it on food and clothes, or would she also save and contribute toward important things? He will wait, he told me, and see how she behaves, what she does with her money.

Both sexes are evaluating women's behavior in terms of personal volition. A wife cannot be coerced: She must be motivated from within to identify her interests with her husband's. Hageners express this by saying that the noman is set on a particular road. Noman is mind, consciousness, conscience, desire, the capacity to translate wishes or intentions into action. It spans the individuality of decision making and the social nature of a person's orientations (see the discussion in A. Strathern, in press). Behavior is under its control. Observable actions are explained by the state of an individual's noman, and there need be no reference to anything else other than that he/she is behaving "as him/herself" (elemnga noman-nt). If people are persuaded to do something, then, it is seen as the product of internalization. Women, like men, are amenable to persuasion, comprehend general social values, and have the opportunity to incorporate such values within a personal framework of action. Indeed, Rachel and Katherine both gave voice to a self-image as "social persons," bearers of a configuration of statuses. They reminded Edward that they were not only *his* wife and sister, but were attached to others of the subclan whose concerns they were also thinking of. They thus implied the contrast between acting for the sake of wider social ends and for the narrow personal ends that men so often attribute to women. Although their recognized efforts were not of the same order as the men's, and did not bring them owner status, the women contributors to the car were perceived as having behaved in a socially responsible manner, evidence of good *noman*.

Here we have something of a Hagen theory of "the person." Individuals act under volition in the acquisition of prestige; corporate effort is seen to arise from the combining of people's several self-interests.

But if women have wills subject to influence they also have wills of their own. A person is autonomous precisely because the *noman* is within. Ultimately, aims, values, and interests are accessible only to him or herself. The *noman*'s orientation has to be judged from external behavior, as Michael said of Lucy. The positive side of this is self-sufficiency, that people strive on their own. In treating women as persons Hagen men demand of them commitment, loyalty, the capacity to perceive "social" interests, in short an active engagement of their volition and purposefulness. But on what may sometimes be regarded as a negative side, self-interest also provides a reference point independent of other people's goals. Men and women alike may follow aims of their own.

Edward's autonomy in getting his money back was seen by his opponents as an exercise in futile self-interest. Had the sum been larger it would have threatened group solidarity; as it was his motives were obscure, judged in the light of his history of unreliable participation in subclan matters now joining in, now swearing never to join again. His self-interest had ends only of its own, leading to behavior not only irresponsible but ultimately self-destructive. His wife and sister, on the other hand, exercised autonomy very much at his expense and through an appeal to wider issues. They had a choice of roles before them: their self-interest, in maintaining use rights to the car, was explained by reference to attachment to the land or their position within the whole subclan as against a particular relationship to Edward. It is in such situations of choice that "the person" is made visible – it has been shown that there is nothing automatic about the role the actor is playing.

One aspect of Hagen ideas should be made clear. What I gloss as "autonomy" comprises self-sufficiency, privacy, the person as a self-governing agent, to the extent that behavior can on occasion be assessed independently of those statuses and roles that also define the actor. There is an ethical dimension here insofar as such elements are taken into account in the way behavior is evaluated. Yet these ideas do not incorporate a contrast between the naturally constituted biological "individual" and the conventional, culturally contrived constraints of society. Rather, personhood is shown in the engagement of the mind in enterprises, in purposefulness (A. Strathern, in press). The dual connotations of the Hagen *noman* is aptly paralleled in Rosaldo's description of the way Ilongots speak of "hearts": "to indicate those aspects of the self that *can be alienated – or engaged –* in social interaction" (1980:43, my italics). When Hageners consider the nature of purposeful action, men and women emerge as persons.

The person is made visible, then, when an actor draws attention to the volitional, self-governing aspects of his or her socially acceptable role behavior. When he/she does not consider alternative social interests, and discards one set of such interests without reference to any others, then self-interest alone emerges, and the person is seen to go against social concerns. Here the person is no longer a manifestation of social values (as were Rachel and Katherine) but acts in contradistinction to them. Edward was judged by Michael in these terms.

Although men and women may equally subscribe to social goals or be judged as antisocial, from the stereotyped behavior of males and females Hageners draw certain symbols for these same possibilities. Unaligned self-interest is portrayed as typically female. Hageners also posit that constitutionally females are not the same kind of "persons" as males. This moves us into another realm of symbolism.

WOMEN AS FEMALES

I use "female" rather than "woman" when I wish to draw attention to gender constructs.

The *noman* may be classified by gender. Thus through the different ways it works, females are held to be less capable than males of pursuing rational goals. This contrast is one of many tied to that of male–female. The most salient and embracing is between the prestigeful (*nyim*) and the rubbish (*korpa*). Prestige is particularly to be gained through ceremonial exchange but in general is associated with public matters in which men play the major part. A man is able to both enhance his own status and contribute to that of his clan or subclan, so that his acquisition of prestige has a moral dimension. The big-man is the successful transactor, skillful in deploying wealth and influencing others. Males as a category have an aptitude for big-manship. Females, on the other hand, carry out worthy and necessary tasks, attaining prestige only when their activities are seen as contributing to male enterprises. In themselves they may be called "rubbish."

There is a concomitant distinction between investment – males put their resources to social use – and consumption – females want to eat the fruits of their labors. Consumption is waste, spending on oneself for items that do not carry the prestige that gives a social dimension to individual behavior.

If males can usually claim some "social" benefit from their use of resources, females who demand clothes, tradestore food, school fees for their children, are "eating" money all the time. They are archetypical consumers because they spend money on domestic concerns.

Both men and women may situationally apply gender images (for example, the symbolized male or female) to persons of the other sex without implying that such a classification is totally encompassing. To consume or to be weak may be female characteristics, but do not thereby completely define women. The car-owning husbands who subscribed to the belief that females cannot do anything for themselves but are dependent upon males also solicited money from the women, relying as much upon women's sense of commitment as upon their independent earnings.

Yet when men think of themselves and not their wives as the owners of a vehicle, it is because males are investors. They (it is stressed) have planned and negotiated the purchase and now drive the car. Drivers in Hagen are invariably men, and although in the case of the Landcruiser there was only one regular driver, the cab is a marked male area. Wives, on journeys to market or to see relatives, sit in the back, benefiting from the men's enterprise, and are also encouraged to use the car for small enterprises of their own. Only prostitutes are said to sit in the front of vehicles. Whereas wives consume what their husbands give them (the husband initially cleared the land they grow their food on), prostitutes are seen as extractive, making a man squander his resources and turning him into a consumer like themselves. It so happened that the reputations of my two companions were already somewhat at risk on this last count.

Buchbinder and Rappaport consider the male–female distinction as summating a host of other oppositions; they write, "in taking gender to be a metaphor for the conventional oppositions they impose upon the world, people establish forever these oppositions in their own bodies" (1976: 33). The attack on the women in the car was a clear example of this. Whatever incidental justification we had for being there, I chose an unfortunate moment, when men were arguing among themselves in terms of consumption and investment, to present to them actual living women sitting in the front of the car, returned from a private visit. This sight provided the most perfect symbol Michael's critics could have wished for, a switch between back and front, female and male, between rubbishness and prestige itself.[12] The ensuing dispute did not, of course, turn only on our actions.[13] Rather, where my companions sat was used to reveal the car's general misuse.

In their evaluation of types of behavior as sex-linked, Hageners construct a set of symbols they can apply to other areas of behavior. Thus the domains male–female and *nyim-korpa* (prestige and rubbishness) are brought together into a metaphorical relationship (cf. Kelly 1976: 51). Each "symbolizes" the other; but neither signifies the totality of the other. It is certain *contrastive* elements in *nyim-korpa* that are imaged through the male–female distinction, and vice versa. Here the relationship is mutual: A dismissal of a rubbish man as "like a woman" entails also the equation of being female and rubbish. In the case of self-interest, an element itself ambiguous is differentially evaluated by reference to male–female. Autonomy expressed in some ways is typically male, in others female.

The contrast between "wider" and "narrower" goals, even between what is of "social" and what of "personal" concern, is largely contextual, contingent on an actor's standpoint. The differing interests of some may be brought together under the rubric of common goals, whereas the divergence of others may be branded as "antisocial." However, Hagen political units, tribes, clans and their subdivisions are seen to operate *ipso facto* on the basis of solidarity and the meeting of interests; and these units are to some extent defined through their male membership. When they act as bodies it is in activities where men are predominant. Hence men appear to have a vested interest in a type of corporate action that women cannot fully share. The demands of clan morality give a further shape to the use of gender symbols and, in the equation of "collective" concerns with male, attribute to the female goals of an emphatically "personal" nature.

It is in this context that I return to the original issue of how in analyses of other societies we tend to oppose the individual as actor to the kinds of cultural definitions involved in gender designations.

The logic of Hagen gender symbolism has been treated in other recent articles (M. Strathern 1978, in press). In the present account I am concerned with the accommodation Hageners make between these constructs and their notions of personhood, and in particular how this affects women – whose femaleness is denigrated, and who are less than men able to align "personal" with ostensible "social" goals. That Rachel and Katherine's socially oriented decisions contrasted nicely in this case with Edward's selfishness should not blind us to the way in which Hagen stereotypes are frequently used by both sexes to presuppose that males generally have a somewhat larger and females a narrower social horizon. But my argument is that in a situation that denigrates femaleness, women nevertheless have a position of some substance and maneuverability, and this is inherent in the cultural categorizations Hageners themselves make.

The Problem of People

As a preface to further discussion, let me summarize features of Hagen constructs that turn upon differences betwen male and female.

Gender imagery faces two ways. On the one hand it affects the identity individuals claim, and influences the evaluation of men's and women's activities; on the other, notions of maleness and femaleness receive input from specific cultural concerns (such as the acquisition of prestige) and in turn can be used to evaluate other ideas and activities. Insofar as the latter is true, gender is not just "about" men and women but "about" other things as well. I have already noted that in Hagen the contrast between success (being *nyim*) and failure (being *korpa*), and a contrast between public and private orientations, are both linked to an antithesis between maleness and femaleness.

The attachment of these other ideas to gender employs gender as a ranking mechanism. It is essential to such a mechanism that one sex should carry connotations of inferior status. Men's and women's affairs are frequently classified in terms of a distinction between the public and private (e.g., Rosaldo 1974) or the large scale and small scale (Langness 1976: 101). The way in which women's power is thus *valued* in respect of men's draws on a model of cross-sex ties in which a significant component is the relative position of male and female to one another. Ortner (1974: 71) has asked how we are to explain the universal devaluation of women. She suggests that women everywhere have come to symbolize a realm, "nature," which is in opposition to the higher order "culture." My point is that the object of denigration may be less crucially women themselves than what they *stand for*. That a contrast between male and female is used to symbolize a disjunction of values does not *ipso facto* imply an antagonism between men and women.

Hagen females are represented as wayward, individualistic and antisocial. Those who value integrative, universal concerns are going to devalue socially fragmenting, particularistic ones and thus devalue the "female" (cf. Ortner 1974: 79). But who are the "those"? Although the relationship between social and personal concerns, as well as the antithesis between the prestigious and the rubbish, are symbolized in stereotypes based on gender, the values themselves are held across the sex divide, by men and women alike. Women can dissociate themselves from the handicap of being female, as men have to prove they can utilize the potential of being male, because these gender markers do not totally encompass the person. An individual Hagen woman is not entirely identified with the stereotypes of her sex. In using gender to structure other values, then, Hageners detach posited qualities of maleness and femaleness from actual men and women. A person of either sex can behave in a male or female way.

The substance of the symbols – that it is "male" to have higher-order interests at heart – perhaps makes us think we are dealing only with men's models. This would be an illusory concretism, for the same prestige values also separate the rich from the poor, the energetic from the lethargic, the intelligent from the stupid, adults from children, and so on. Indeed in terms of capacity for prestige such categories are more realistically distinguished than are actual men and women.

Yet insofar as maleness is on the superior side of the equation and insofar as these values are realized most fully in activities in which men take the most active social roles, this model of the relationship between gender and prestige appears to have a marked male bias. I believe most Hagen men and women take these associations for granted. It is true that in certain contexts men use these equations to bolster their power in relation to women, and that women perceive the equations as favoring men. At the same time, the ranking of the sexes in terms, for example, of *nyim-korpa* primarily concerns the allocation of public prestige, and although men attempt to generalize this model and use it to represent power relations between the sexes (cf. M. Strathern 1978), such relations are not their central focus, and men are not very successful in their endeavor. Men use the notion in a rhetorical manner to support situational power, but the concept itself is predicated on the idea of achievement, rather than simply on the idea of male control over females.

Nevertheless, we are left with the question of why women allow "female" to have connotations of inferiority. The acceptability of the model rests on three notions: that women agree with the basic social values at issue, which involve matters other than the relations between the sexes themselves; that all that is put on the female side is not in fact negative, even though it may appear antisocial; and that as persons women can free themselves from the gender stereotype.

GENDER AND THE PERSON

As a formal entity in Hagen structure, the person is both symbolically linked to and differentiated from gender. Far from revealing an alternative cosmology, the way in which Hagen women act and are perceived of as persons turns out to uncover one basis for their apparent acceptance of the kinds of public models men also hold.

"Women" can be distinguished from stereotypes and symbols of "females" not simply as the theoretical "social actors" of the anthropologist's framework, but as "persons" within the Hagen worldview. The "self-interest" of persons in Hagen is seen not merely as a maximization of individuality, but as a mechanism through which individuals, male and female, may be committed to socially oriented roles (cf. Wagner 1972b). Indeed women do make such commitments, and their behavior can be calculated accordingly. At the same time, such commitments tie women into the very structure of cultural expression that uses the male–female antithesis to conceptualize commitment to as against divergence from social goals, ability as against inability to attain success. This is only apparently paradoxical. To become *nyim* ("successful") has to be seen as within the reach of all men and women, for it is the medium through which common aims are presented; it underlies group (clan) morality and (as I shall argue) relations between big-men and others. At the same time, *nyim* must be marked off from its opposite, *korpa* ("rubbish"); and the sex contrast, established at a general level by the contrast between men's and women's spheres of activity, provides an image of boundary.

One result of this is that certain orientations of self-interest come to be labeled "male" and others "female." The autonomous big-man projects male success though merging group interests with personal ones (and gets away with it), but the willful wife and the recalcitrant clansman show equally a "female" irresponsibility ultimately destructive of the self. Obviously, when private interests can be aligned with social goals, they are cloaked under the rubrics of collective action. Women, whose actions are classified under fewer "social" idioms than those of men accordingly more often appear autonomous in the negative sense. And men, failing to align a personal with a collective interest, appear as women. Thus gender comes to classify types of autonomy in relation to social goals.

But the point is that the sex stereotyping of modes of orientation is in many ways the precondition for the visibility of the "person" as a genderless locus of orientation. Individuals of either sex can be seen to act in a manner typical of the other. The weak, dependent man is "like a woman," a divergence from the male ideal; the strong, committed woman is "like a man," congruent with it. The deviation of individuals from their gender type makes the "person" visible. Women commit themselves to the attainment of prestige as persons setting their self-interest in an approved direction (positive autonomy); men flying in the face of corporate concerns are following their self-interest to destruction (negative autonomy). The Landcruiser dispute shows people switching from one frame of reference to another in their evaluations: The men and women involved are seen by other men and women to act out gender stereotypes, to exemplify self-interests of particular kinds, and to behave as autonomous persons. It is the point at which the frame of reference is shifted, the issue that selects one evaluation over another, that reveals the moral imperatives behind the symbols.

Hagen men's and women's ideas about the person are not just a set of residual notions dealing with aspects of individuality and personality that social categories leave out. They amount to an ideology of personhood, and give a special place to the factor of self-interest in social interaction. This is both a source of morality – the process by which individuals acknowledge the values held by others implies a specific orientation on their part – and a problem – for the self also has its own goals. When men switch from deriding women as weak and dependent females to urging them as persons to consider rational, long-term aims, they are not simply playing tricks to extract the best out of those they keep down. In the imagery of cross-sex relationships are symbols for the bases upon which people as such interact – coercion, persuasion, and the threat of indifference.

THE "PROBLEM OF PEOPLE" IN RELATIONS OF PRODUCTION

There is a more general issue at the back of gender symbols in this society. Among Hageners the problem of aligning individual interest to social goals takes the particular form of reconciling striving for achievement, differential prestige, and inequality between individuals with a positive emphasis upon egalitarianism and autonomy. Achievement in social terms is seen by Hageners to rest on the bringing together of multiple personal interests: This is the essential skill and technique at the heart of big-man systems. It entails a high evaluation of individual autonomy, and Douglas has pointed to the paradox. "A society so strongly centred on a structure of ego-focussed grid is liable to recurrent breakdown from its inherent moral weakness. It cannot continually sustain the commitment of all its members to an egalitarian principle that favours a minority. It has no way of symbolising or activating the collective conscience" (1970: 139).[14] In Hagen this is precisely what the symbols of gender provide. Douglas's point is that in such societies questions about the identity and value of the self are only soluble in manifestations of success and only the few can be successful. By linking the capacity for success to gender, Hageners sustain an image of the person in which the *orientation* and not just the results are a reward. People's intentions and endeavors are seen to be set on certain ends, and these are symbolized as "male" or "female."

Egalitarianism and solidarity are represented in same-sex images (the bond between clansman is that of fraternity); differential achievement, in cross-sex images (not everyone has the same potential for success) (see Forge 1972: 536). Another kind of differential is also encompassed in these metaphors, I have suggested, for collective action is held to spring not from solidarity alone but also from the alignment of disparate interests. The male–female contrast is used to point up potential disparity in the differing orientations that individuals are bound to have, and provides something of a model for crossing the gap.

I want to bring out two points: (*a*) insofar as male–female is used to symbolize achievement differential, men have an interest in keeping domestic and political relations on a qualitatively contrasting basis, to separate labor and wealth; (*b*) at the same time cross-sex relations within the domestic unit, between husband and wife, are to some extent modeled on and provide models for intraclan and interclan relationships between men. That male–female can provide such symbols I take to stem from particular relations of production between the sexes. Gender ideology is anchored primarily in the husband–wife dyad; in the relationship of spouses are mirrored issues to do precisely with the meeting of autonomy and collective action.

Gender is the chief axis of the economic division of labor in Hagen – not between males and females working as teams but within the household between spouses. The domestic dyad is the primary unit of stock raising and gardening; yet not the sole source of wealth. Through their exchange partners men traditionally had access to shell valuables (which Western money has to some extent replaced). This source of wealth is of singular importance to their self-definition as males (A. Strathern 1979). The circulation of shells is interlocked with that of pigs, which are, from a man's point of view to be gained partly from transactions with others and partly from the pig-raising efforts of his wives at home. Vegetables, produced mainly by women, and the foodstuff of pigs as well as people, are not valuables and are not objects of public exchange.

Women regard their labor as entitling them to some control over the disposal of pigs, for they own no counterpart to men's shells.[15] Whereas a wive converts garden produce into pork, but has to relinquish some control over animals entering the exchange system, the husband, through his shell exchanges, brings other pigs into the household. Nevertheless, men are dependent on women, both for personal daily sustenance and for the tending of pigs, for they replace those kept by their wives with those kept by other women.

The problem of production is not so much that of resources as of labor, and the problem of labor is its effective mobilization – the degree of work women are willing to put into producing a surplus of foodstuff necessary to maintain the stock. The ultimate problem, then, is people's motivation. A husband sees himself as having to encourage his wife to work for their mutual benefit. In precisely the same way, big-men can carry their personal aspirations only so far as individuals. Men's deployment of pigs in transaction converts produce into wealth, but it takes group-based collective displays to convert wealth into prestige. Although individual exchange transactions enhance a man's reputation, ultimately personal success lies in the success of the clan or subclan of which he is a part. Thus clan members have to be *encouraged* to join in group enterprises. Hagen men see a parallel between the management of persons within the clan and within the household.

I am here extrapolating from various remarks made by men and women rather than reporting a systematic symbolism. Nevertheless, it is significant that the wife who ''listens'' to what her husband says is described in the same terms as the clan brother who takes his mates' interests to heart. One Kawelka man told me how men became *nyim* (important) in two ways. "Those who have talk [are public orators, planners] and those who have things [wealth] – they are both *nyim* . . . A man who has few things but good talk, we don't blame him. And a man who has no talk but owns something, *he helps us too* [my emphasis]. But a man who owns nothing, has no talk either, doesn't help his brothers, he is *korpa* ('rubbish'). He doesn't contribute to anything. He hides his things. A man who doesn't help others [to him they say], 'You have no feelings for your brothers or your fathers, you are rubbish' . . . A woman who looks after pigs and gardens, who doesn't round and decorate [like a potential prostitute], she is *nyim* . . . She thinks of her work and her gardens and her children, she is *nyim* even if she has no talk. The woman who gives no heed to things, her children, she has no name. But a strong woman who works in the gardens, *she helps her husband* [my emphasis] so they will both have a reputation, this kind of woman is *nyim*." Earlier he had said, "Women who humbug, who don't hear the talk of men, they are *korpa*, they don't listen to what their husband says, don't give food or valuables to people . . . they don't have good thoughts . . . Some men, too, they eat things, they lie, they don't return their debts, we say they are rubbish . . . The men who are *korpa* ('rubbish'), they don't make *moka* ('ceremonial exchange')."

The implicit presumption here is that husbands and wives cooperate as clansmen do: They have interests in common, and the husband directs these interests as big-men influence lesser men. It is a presumption of mutuality and hierarchy, providing a context for women's labor and effort; when women assist their husbands they are engaged in a "social" enterprise. Wives are thus made out to be dependent upon men to give this value to their work. But a crucial second factor is the degree of influence actual men have over their spouses, and women's willingness to perceive things their way. It is the *husband-wife* relationship, and not other male–female pairing, that provides a particular combination of mutuality and separateness, in terms of the division of labor, for it is only over the labor of their own wives that men have a controlling voice.

A big-man haranguing his followers treats them as persons, acknowledging their autonomy but hoping to set their minds on a particular course of action. In putting pressure upon the lazy or uninterested, the would-be leader is likely to use a symbolic antithesis between male and female. However he uses only one side of the contrast. He is not likely to use the image of wives helping their husbands, for such help can be appealed to on the more immediate basis of fraternal solidarity. He may well however use the second image: Those who do not contribute to joint enterprises are like socially irresponsible females, interested only in "eating" and in their own petty concerns. Here again we find the antithesis between investment and consumption.

Hagen political structure is acephalous, leadership being a matter not of office or administration but interpersonal influence. Big-men see themselves as manipulating others. They are supremely autonomous in Read's (1959) sense, in that they strive to create a situation in which clan enterprises and their own ambitions are reciprocally enhancing. But their autonomy to act in the light of their own interests can be preserved only at the cost of attributing this autonomy to others also. The price in fact raises their own value. It is *because* individuals have their own selves to consider that influence over others is an achievement. The renown of a big-man rests on his being seen to have engineered solidarity. We might say it is in his interest that such action should not be perceived as mechanical but as the combining of multitudinous self-governing individuals: It is he who has drawn them together. (One term for big-man is *wua peng mumuk*, ''the head man who gathers [everything] together – A. Strathern 1971: 188, 190.) The problem is that only an individual can commit himself. In intraclan relations (as opposed to those mediated by exchange or hostility) collective action must be based on a perceived *mutuality* of interest. If men are making an effort to involve women by setting themselves (men) up as agents of social transformation, they also use a disjunction between the sexes to symbolize problems of joint action among themselves.

Let me give an example: Hagen men and women agree that one cannot force a girl to marry against her will. For the marriage to succeed, her own commitment is important – to some extent the arrangement must be presented as in her self-interest also. Yet at the prospect of an impending breakup they will point to the wife's wanting to run away as an example of a heedless and typically female pursuit of self-interest in the face of responsibility. They may agree post facto that her mind had been averse to the match from the start, but once the marriage relationships had been set up the woman was in a situation that demanded that she take notice of the interests of others. Someone who goes his or her own way is not behaving illegitimately (a person has a ''right'' to follow his/her self-interest). Rather, spouses, like clan members, should also take other people's interests into account. Females are regarded as specially prone to acts of irresponsibility.

Men who do not join in clan enterprises are criticized for staying at home, being interested only in sex and other forms of consumption, giving in to short-term desires rather than pursuing long-term plans. By succumbing to such gratification (*kum*) they are seen as dependent upon comfort and domesticity; they are ''like woman.'' Female dependency on males, in men's view, both expresses their subordinate position and integrates them into ''society'' (through the mediating husband); male dependency upon the female, on the other hand, deflects men away from wider social concerns. Economic dependency is one thing (both sexes privately acknowledge that it is wives who make their husbands *nyim*); whereas an exaggerated social dependency is seen to detract from other commitments, and is actually set up in symbolic antithesis to them. Men who spend all their time with women are rubbish. Autonomous insofar as they go against the wishes of their clansmen, by ignoring group interests they ultimately destroy themselves. *Kum*, the greed that leads to loss of reason (*noman*), forces one to eat and in the end, Hageners say, itself eats one up.

It is possible for an ambitious man to bring his group prestige through a selfish manipulation of relationships; a woman cannot bring prestige to anyone by pushing her own interests exclusively, because she cannot thereby bring prestige to herself. Females much more frequently than males are seen to pursue idiosyncratic and personal goals. This representation is not a simple devaluation of *women*, but an ideological comment upon self-interest. In its association with the unprestigious, uncommited female, strong controls are put on the direction in which men are made to see their personal interests as lying. Converting personal interests into social ones is a matter of trying to influence other people's self-orientations. The power of the male–female symbolism is to suggest that the contrast between social and antisocial orientations is axiomatic and self-evident, not the matter of context an outsider might see it as. In fact wives may be cast into the role of ally or enemy as well as helpmate. Sometimes they are kept sweet with gifts, sometimes coerced, sometimes urged to help. In their individual lives particular couples may make any of these terms dominant. In men's imagery of the female, and specifically the female as wife, all three are run together. The wife-as-enemy is classified as untrustworthy, liable to succumb to hostile impulses, as treacherous as male enemies are, to be beaten into submission; wife-as-ally can be counted upon most of the times, but must be flattered, complimented, given the generous attention that will make her feel good; wife-as-clan-member is appealed to as a rational person who can see where long-term interests lie, who acknowledges the significance of group affairs and is bent upon common goals. All three involve notions of females as persons with orientations of their own; they differ in the degree of disjunction between husband and wife and the method of coping with this. Do cross-sex relationships mirror some of the alternatives that men are faced with in their dealings with others? If there is a mutual symbolization here, the husband–wife dyad is the crucial locus, for it is the chief relationship in which the sexes come together on the basis of their differences.[16]

MEN'S AND WOMEN'S MODELS

Shirley Ardener (1975) has found useful the distinction between dominant and muted models. A society may be dominated or overdetermined by models generated from a particular group within it. For that group there will be a fit between their perception of surface events and the underlying structure, whereas the muted group is faced with problems of accommodation. In the case of Hagen I argue that we should not take the focus of the model – men defining themselves as prestigious "social" beings in contradistinction to unfortunate females – in terms of its own apparent value hierarchy. That "female" is not given positive value in this instance does not imply that women are to be defined as subscribing to values forever in antithesis. On the contrary, I think I have shown the extent to which Hagen men and woman do share common goals. My concern has been to demonstrate that one of the enabling conditions – by which men and woman may share goals and yet notions of male and female be used to differentiate expected orientations – lies in the idea of person. People, of either sex, can act independently of the stereotypes that define their gender.

Nonetheless, one can detect some difference in emphasis in the way men and women make use of gender symbolism. My companions were told to get down because of the gender associations of the driver's cab. They complied rather resentfully. Such equations are louder in the mouths of men than women, although women also give them voice. But what do women think of some of the assumptions, that, for example, to be female is to be spendthrift? There was an element of glee in the way Michael's wives explained how they would surprise him by revealing what they had actually managed to save. This would show: (a) that they were acting responsibly; (b) as far as their own behavior was concerned, they were not going to conform to this particular female stereotype, but present rather the more role-grounded image of the "good wife." From the men's point of view, such attitudes are already accommodated in their models: Women can be treated as persons, or if they show exemplary devotion to male affairs are regarded as behaving "like men."

When women talk of other women as "like men" it is with less approval and more insinuation of presumptuousness. They use the terms *nyim* and *korpa*, readily enough to brand their personal enemies in the derogatory idioms men use of females in general. I suspect that women think of themselves as "persons" in subjective assessment of their own worth, applying symbols of female to others as appropriate. However, they do not operate a symbolic system that apportions connotations of male–female in any radically different way.[17] If they use the ideology of autonomy more than men do, this is to assert particular counter interests, and is a maneuver that concepts of the person take into account.

Wives grumble that their husbands do not help enough, do not buy them clothes, make exchanges with their kin. Yet they concur in the view that large sums of money should not be frittered away but allocated to collective enterprises. They accept it as the order of things that when coffee is sold any sum of magnitude will be appropriated by the man. Their minor share is "for eating," separated conceptually from the resources men will feed into ceremonial exchange, compensation, bridewealth, and so on. In fact, they may save their share, only to contribute it at a later stage. The contrast is between money for personal and for wider purposes. Women become bitter when husbands use money in the pursuit of what they interpret as narrow interests, as when it is consumed in gambling and drink. If men interpret the "social good" as evinced in transactions that will bring them renown, perhaps women find it in the benefits that flow back from the men's involvement in collective action – exchanges with their kinsfolk, a car on whose journeying they have claim, a successful bridewealth for their children, pigs they will eat.[18]

It is men who seem to be put on the side of morality, to represent the "social" dimension of commitment, to be rewarded when their self-interest coincides with the public good. But that is precisely the appearance that the images of gender assume. Qualitative differences in the spheres of action between men and women are used to symbolize values shared by both sexes and to differentiate the prestigious of either sex from the nonprestigious. These formulations also support activities such as clan affairs and the major institutions of ceremonial exchange and warfare in which men play leading roles; they justify an exclusion of women from cult performances and other spiritual matters. It follows that women may well have a perspective on the matter, but not necessarily countermodels or a definitive domain of power. Indeed, I have suggested that the autonomy that defines persons as beings with wills of their own opens up the way for women to be subjectively involved in some of men's affairs.

At the same time, insofar as an extremely high cultural value is put upon autonomy, people are not, as it were, only social creatures. The point is that which is socially oriented is not the only good, and a high valuation of autonomy may override contextual evaluations of the "inferior" female. Whereas prestige must rest upon the opinions of others, self-interest has its own ends, and the exercise of autonomy, whatever others may think, is a payoff in itself. This social versus personal antithesis, to the extent that it is developed, is much more fraught with ambivalence than the *nyim-korpa* ("prestige–rubbish") one. But it is certainly not completely obvious that male is, in this case, always on the preferred side.

To be true to Hageners' representation of themselves, one cannot reduce group interests to a matter of transactions between individuals (Evens 1977: 588–9; Cohen 1977). Gender imagery is, among other things, a symbolic mechanism whereby "collective" and "personal" interests are made to seem to be of different orders. Yet I have suggested that this distinction is not to be equated in an unexamined manner with the Western opposition between "society" and the "individual." Hagen notions of autonomy, for example, do not conceive it as a "natural" condition upon which the artifice that is society has to work. A study of situations in which people display autonomy could not thus yield an analysis in some privileged sense more true or more real than those presented in the rhetoric of collective action. When Hagen women are seen to act autonomously they are, quite as much as the socially oriented men, providing exemplars of ideologically constituted behavior.

I have followed the Hagen definition of the person to show how notions of autonomy mesh with sexual symbols. These are not themselves simply statements of power. Prestige is also at issue, and it is through the possibility of women as well as men acquiring a measure of prestige that they can both demonstrate their personhood as purposeful beings with interests of their own, and at the same time accept the equation male equals social equals group enterprise. We certainly need to ask also why men accept that women often go their own way, and why they feel it necessary to engage their commitment as well as their labor. Are they seeking evidence of volition behind the action, the person behind the role? The effort of "social" achievement paradoxically rests in this society upon a high evaluation of the person as an autonomous entity. But to be visible it must also be set apart. The autonomous female is as crucial to men's values as hardworking wives are to their success.

We may surmise that women themselves have an interest in promoting men's sense of the "social." In their everyday lives they are much concerned with focusing men's attention upon their status as wives, mothers, sisters, and so on. A polygynist's wives demand that he manage their separate relations with scrupulous fairness – men say ruefully that a polygynist never rests, for whichever house he sleeps in he always has to remember the others. Another

stereotyped dilemma points to the hapless distributor of pork who in satis-
fying all the demands upon him can keep none for himself. Keeping numerous
ends in view is a burden the manager places upon himself, and one that
women encourage insofar as they demand that they be taken into men's
calculations. Perhaps indeed it is the very image of female as consumer as
well as producer that anchors men's affairs to women, making women the end
as much as the beginning of their endeavors.

Indeed, Van Baal wonders if women's self-selected role of care giving has
not led them to invent politics, putting men into debt with one another over
their marriage contracts, creating a mythical need for protection ''to lure men
into marriage, into willingness to submit themselves to their loving cares''
(1975: 113). He suggests that among the Nalum of the Star Mountains (West
Irian) men feel themselves encapsulated by women's cares, and the netbags in
which children are carried become a threatening symbol of embrace.[19] If
Hagen women encapsulate men it is within a domesticity that lies conceptually opposed to the domain of public affairs. Yet at the same time
women may also be considered as socially responsible persons whose own
orientations include the goals men pursue. Not only food and children but also
wealth is carried in their netbags, and wealth is inevitably destined for some
man. Women's productive capacities do not belong in some alternative social
cosmos with its own scale of values, but are regarded by both sexes to have a
value contingent upon other aspects of social life. Where women themselves
perhaps differ from men is less in having a model that obliterates the distinction between private and public worth, than in rating their domestic chores
and personal enterprises more highly. This is largely seen as a matter of the
different interests that are bound to affect people. In itself it does not point to
some structural inconsistency, nor even a classlike cleavage between men and
women. On the contrary, for all that Hageners use gender stereotypes to
represent a contrast between social and personal goals, every woman, as well
as every man, is visibly a person in the way she or he works out his or her own
accommodation between self-interest and the social good.

Notes

1 I have received fieldwork assistance from several institutions in the past, including
   Cambridge University and the Australian National University. In 1976 I was
   making some inquiries on my own account. I am very grateful to Andrew Strathern
   and Jerry Leach for their detailed comments, to Peter Gow, and to Marie Reay for
   remarks on another paper, which stimulated me to write this one. I thank the
   Women in Society study group in Cambridge, and members of anthropology
   departments in Cambridge, London, and Oxford for their helpful criticisms; the
   editors of this volume have made several constructive points. Finally I should
   acknowledge my debt to Gillian Gillison for general discussions on gender that
   have influenced my presentation here.
2 K = Kina (Papua New Guinea currency); K1 is worth roughly $1.20 Australian.
3 Women's accommodation of the ''male world'' is the theme of Strathern (1972).
   My perspective has since shifted. The present essay does however illuminate this
   original formulation – that in spite of Hagen women's own viewpoints and in-

terests, there is no "female world." It reiterates some of the material found in Strathern (1978), to which the reader is directed for fuller information on gender stereotypes, although again I have moved on from the standpoint taken there.

4 Among the early writings on the Papua New Guinea Highlands was an article by Read, which specifically explored the difference between "Western" and Gahuka Gama notions of self. These Highlanders, he argued, have an idiosyncratic sense of self without the higher consciousness of person – by which he meant an ethically discrete entity of intrinsic worth. Behavior is judged according to an individual's social status rather than his worth as a "person." Hageners have specific ideas about people's behavior that are to be understood independently of their roles or statuses, and that are taken into account in the assessment of actions and may constrain or modify any reaction. In this sense I talk of "person." Two further points should be made. First, I have not elsewhere been consistent in my usage of the terms "person" and "individual." Second, although it will be clear that the Hagen "person" is constituted with a social orientation, I am not referring to person in the sociological sense of an ensemble of statuses (cf. Fortes 1969), nor on the other hand the "oneness" of the person that Cohen (1977) describes as selfhood. The self is only one referent of the Hagen person.

5 Ortner made this general point when she insisted that we should sort out "levels of the problem" (the relationship between women's subordination and specific ideologies): "it [would be] a misguided endeavour to focus only upon women's actual though culturally unrecognized and unvalued powers in any given society, without first understanding the overarching ideology and deeper assumptions . . . that render such powers trivial" (1974: 69). La Fontaine applies a similar idea to the study of initiation (1977: 422–3; see also 1978: 1–2). It should be clear that my concern is with "gender" as a set of ideas constructed in reference to male and female, and not with the process of self-definition by which individuals make sense of their genital characteristics.

6 It was pointed out (by both Hagen men and women) that men get the major proceeds from coffee even if women's labor has gone into weeding and tending as well as the picking. Women claim the proceeds from vegetable produce, even if men's labor has gone into clearing the gardens.

7 Hagen women do not drive. I fall myself into the stereotype of the "strong" woman (resolutely set on my work) with something of the ambiguity of "waywardness," a reputation stemming from 1964 when I first set up house apart from my husband.

8 "Dependency" on clansmen or allies in a positive light is glossed as common solidarity, friendship, contract, etc. The small amount Edward was shown to have actually contributed himself was picked on by seniors of Michael's faction as evidence that he could not be considered a true "owner." Many other men had in fact been "helpers," like the women. What differentiated them from the owners was that (a) they had not taken part in the basic planning but were approached for assistance afterwards; (b) the amounts they gave were relatively small; and (c) they gave to specific members of the owning core in personal transactions. Men who helped in this way claimed rights to the use of the car. The denigration of Edward was largely internal to Michael's faction; I was not present when the money was returned, but was told that the men saved his face by giving him K100 (and K130 to his supporters) because they did not want to make his shameful situation too intolerable.

9 In a subsequent quarrel within his faction, Michael was himself accused in the same idiom of having no money of his own and having to depend on his womenfolk. The total amount from women was 20–25 percent.

10 In other purchases women occasionally claim to have contributed substantial sums
    in their own name; A. Strathern (1979) gives an example of a money *moka*
    (exchange) in which a woman is given token donor status. This account of gender
    ideology in money transactions was written about the same time but quite indepen-
    dently of the first draft of the present essay, and I regard it as corroborating my analysis.

11 Michael had three wives, Lucy being the most recently married and much less
    established than these two. The pair had both received gifts from their brothers,
    which they also put toward the car.

12 Possibly an example of symbolic innovation (Wagner 1972a: 8). I had not pre-
    viously heard categorical statements that women should never ride in the front,
    although it is a well-established custom. The only exception – apart from the case
    of prostitutes, which is the idea stated in reverse – is made for dignitaries such as
    the mother of a Council President. Once voiced the other men did not dispute it
    (there was no argument as to whether the women did have the right).

13 Many other social issues not mentioned here also involved the men at the time. For
    example, Edward's sister's sons had been involved in recent disputes with out-
    siders in which the Kawelka had refused to support them. They also originated
    from a clan that happened to be an enemy of Lucy and Ann's clan of origin (they
    were classificatory sisters).

14 She illustrates this class of society by Papua New Guinea examples. ''In New
    Guinea a leader's dependence on his followers creates a sensitive feedback system.
    Everyone who transacts with others subscribes to the respect for reciprocity, and
    feels as sensitive to shame as to glory. These moral restraints are generated in the
    competition itself. Though they inform the concept of the upright man, the honest
    broker, they do nothing further to relate the individual to any final purposes of the
    community as such'' (1970: 135).

15 Pigs are an ambiguous category, both food and valuable. Husbands and wives
    clashing over their disposal can each use the idioms of consumption and trans-
    action. A husband whose wife wants to send a particular animal to her own kin may
    regard this either as a legitimate transactional claim or as her wanting to ''eat'' it
    herself – i.e., not dispose of it in some more ''productive'' way (in light of his own
    interests). Women support their claims by pointing to the hard work they had done,
    in return for which they want to ''eat,'' i.e., consume it themselves, or else to the
    pressures they are under from their kin as partners of the husband. Note that pigs
    are only part of men's strategic resource, not the whole.

16 Barth (1975: 206) suggests that the Baktaman contrast between male and female
    metaphorizes transactions between men and ancestor, and in-group versus out-
    group. In Hagen it is not simply that females are outsiders, but that male–female
    interaction may carry analogies for either internal or external actions among men.

17 Any role or status position will afford a particular ''perspective'' upon events. I
    would restrict the term ''model'' to concepts and structures that are to some extent
    objectified, that is, given voice by a self-conscious segment of society.

18 Pork is consumed primarily in the context of exchanges, being distributed widely
    through personal ties after public events involving an initial group prestation (as at
    bridewealth, *moka*, or funeral). Opportunity thus depends upon the scope of one's
    network, for this potentially brings in meat all year round. When meat is finally
    divided up for consumption, women receive the bulk and receive first. (Men hope
    to eat later from pieces their wives will have saved for them.)

19 Van Baal's account is based on Hylkema's analysis (S. Hylkema 1974: *Mannen in
    het Draagnet*. Verhandelingen van het Koninklijk Instituut voor Taal-, Land- en
    Volkenkunde vol. 67, The Hague, Nijhoff).

References

Asad, T. 1979. "Anthropology and the analysis of ideology." *Man* (N.S.) 14: 607–27.

Ardener, S. 1975. Introduction to *Perceiving women*, ed. S. Ardener, pp. vii–xxiii. London: Dent.

Barth, F. 1975. *Ritual and knowledge among the Baktaman of New Guinea*. New Haven: Yale University Press.

Buchbinder, G. and R. A. Rappaport. 1976. "Fertility and death among the Marin." In *Man and woman in the New Guinea Highlands*, ed. P. Brown and G. Buchbinder. pp. 13–35. Washington, D.C.: Special publication American Anthropological Association, No. 8.

Cohen, A. 1977. "Symbolic action and the structure of the self." In *Symbols and sentiments*, ed. I. Lewis. New York: Academic.

Douglas, M. 1970. *Natural symbols*. London: The Cresset Press.

Dumont, L. 1977. *From Mandeville to Marx*. Chicago: University of Chicago Press.

Evens, T. M. S. 1977. "The predication of the individual in anthropological inter-actionism." *American Anthropologist* 79: 579–97.

Faithorn, E. 1976. "Women as persons: aspects of female life and male-female relationships among the Kafe." In *Man and woman in the New Guinea Highlands*, ed. P. Brown and G. Buchbinder, pp. 86–106. Washington, D.C.: Special publication American Anthropological Association, No. 8.

Forge, A. 1972. "The Golden Fleece." *Man* (N.S.) 7: 527–40.

Fortes, M. 1969. *Kinship and the social order*. Chicago: Aldine.

Kelly, R. C. 1976. "Witchcraft and sexual relations: an exploration in the social and semantic implications of the structure of belief." In *Man and woman in the New Guinea Highlands*, ed. P. Brown and G. Buchbinder, pp. 36–53. Washington, D.C.: Special publication, American Anthropological Association, No. 8.

Langness, L. L. 1976. "Discussion." In *Man and woman in the New Guinea Highlands*, ed. P. Brown and G. Buchbinder, pp. 96–105. Washington, D.C.: Special publication, American Anthropological Association, No. 8.

LaFontaine, J. S. 1977. "The power of rights." *Man* (N.S.) 12: 421–37.

    1978. Introduction to *Sex and age as principles of social differentiation*, ed. J. S. LaFontaine, pp. 1–20. ASA Monograph 7. New York: Academic.

Ortner, S. B. 1974. "Is female to male as nature is to culture?" In *Woman, culture and society*, ed. M. Z. Rosaldo and L. Lamphere, pp. 67–87. Stanford: Stanford University Press.

Poole, F. J. P. 1979. "The ritual forging of identity: aspects of person and self in Bimin-Kuskusmin initiation." Paper presented to Association for Social Anthropologists of Oceania meetings.

Reade, K. E. 1955. "Morality and the concept of the person among the Gahaku-Gama." *Oceania* 25: 233–82.

    1959. "Leadership and consensus in a New Guinea society." *American Anthropologist* 61: 425–36.

Reay, M. 1976. "The politics of a witch-killing." *Oceania* 47: 1–20.

Rosaldo, M. Z. 1974. "Woman, culture and society: a theoretical overview." In *Woman, culture and society*, ed. M. Z. Rosaldo and L. Lamphere, pp. 17–42. Stanford: Stanford University Press.

    1980. *Knowledge and passion: Ilongot notions of self and social life*. Cambridge: Cambridge University Press.

Rosaldo, M. Z. and L. Lamphere. 1974. Introduction to *Woman, culture and society*, ed. M. Z. Rosaldo and L. Lamphere, pp. 1–15. Stanford: Stanford University Press.

Strathern, A. 1971. *The rope of moka*. Cambridge: Cambridge University Press.

1976. "Transactional continuity in Mount Hagen." In *Transaction and meaning*, ed. B. Kapferer, pp. 277–87. Philadelphia: Institute for the Study of Human Issues.

1979. "Gender, ideology and money in Mount Hagen." *Man* (N.S.) 14: 530–48.

in press. "*Noman*: representations of identity in Mount Hagen." In *The structure of folk models*, ed. L. Holy and M. Stuchlik. ASA Monograph. New York: Academic.

Strathern, M. 1972. *Women in between*. London: Seminar (Academic) Press.

1975. *No money on our skins: Hagen migrants in Port Moresby*, New Guinea Research Bulletin 61, Canberra: Australian National University.

1978. "The achievement of sex: paradoxes in Hagen gender thinking." In *The yearbook of symbolic anthropology I*, ed. E. Schwimmer, pp. 171–202. London: Hurst.

1980. "No nature, no culture: the Hagen case." In *Nature, culture and gender*, ed. C. MacCormack and M. Strathern, pp. 174–222. Cambridge: Cambridge University Press.

in press. "Domesticity and the denigration of women." In *Women in Oceania*, ed. D. O'Brien and S. Tiffany. ASAO Monograph.

Van Baal, J. 1975. *Reciprocity and the position of women*. Amsterdam: Van Gorcum.

Wagner. R. 1972a. *Habu*. Chicago: University of Chicago Press.

1972b "Incest and identity: a critique and theory on the subject of exogamy and incest prohibition." *Man* (N.S.) 7: 601–13.

Weiner, A. B. 1976. *Women of value, men of renown*. Austin: University of Texas Press.

5

Sexuality and gender in Samoa: CONCEPTIONS AND MISSED CONCEPTIONS

Bradd Shore

Introduction

In anthropology, sexuality and gender have emerged as a "problem." More specifically, the issue appears to focus on the feminine, its nature and culture, and we are led to believe that if we could clarify the status of woman, the problem of sexuality and gender itself would be resolved. That the nature of the feminine is taken to be significant and problematical is not to say that the feminine is understood as the primary aspect of gender. In some sense, the opposite view seems to prevail. In our own culture, at least, "man" or "the male" is linguistically and genetically implied to be generic to gender itself, with "woman" or the "female" as a second sex, an afterthought in creation, a derivative class, but a primary problem for analytical attention.

Ortner (1974), in a thoughtful and provocative essay on what she claims to be the universally subordinate evaluation of women in relation to men, suggests that the problem involves the tendency to associate women with a conception of "nature" and men with a complementary conception of "culture." More precisely (and importantly) Ortner stresses that women are "seen merely as being *closer* to 'nature' than men" (italics in the original) (1974: 73). Specifically, it is through her reproductive physiology and the social roles associated with it that woman comes symbolically to represent nature. Man, on the other hand, not doomed to "mere reproduction of life . . . must (or at least has the opportunity to) assert his creativity externally, 'artificially,' through the medium of technology and symbols" (1974: 75). Such enduring artifice, according to this view, links man, through his productions, to culture, just as her natural capacities link woman, through reproduction, to nature.

Ortner's treatment of the female "problem" takes her on two distinct analytical paths. Insofar as women are distinctive because they are identified with nature, they are condemned to a devaluated, secondary status. To the extent that women are distinctive, however, because they *mediate* nature and culture, they become of special rather than simply secondary importance. Rather than opposing female to male in the nature–culture dichotomy, this more powerful vision of the female dilemma sees women as bridging nature and culture. Here, women are understood to be made of the same stuff as men, and yet also different, both more and less than man. If it is in the perfect opposition with man, as nature to culture, that woman is culturally devalued, it is equally in her imperfect separation from man, her double dealing in things natural and cultural, that the female is specially empowered. It is perhaps true, but nonetheless too simple and incomplete a truth, that women are universally open to devaluation in relation to men. Implicit in the power to mediate culture and nature is the distinctively female capacity to become at once both more and less than man, to suggest in her dual aspect a dialectic of purity and pollution, of divinity and defilement. It is to this dual aspect of woman's nature that Ortner refers in discussing the ''propensity toward polarized ambiguity – sometimes utterly exalted, sometimes utterly debased . . .'' (1974: 86), which characterizes feminine symbolism. It is, finally, to this bridging role of women in conceptions of nature and culture, that one may point in elucidating what Ortner has called ''those cultural and historical 'inversions' in which women are in some way or other symbolically aligned with culture and men with nature.''

In using the familiar nature–culture dichotomy, two things must be clarified. First, as Ortner herself has pointed out, we are dealing with cultural *conceptions* of nature and culture, rather than with culture and nature in any simple, ''objective'' sense. To argue that women are associated with nature is therefore to suggest something about how they are categorized, not to suggest that women are in fact more ''natural'' or less ''cultural'' than men. As symbols, nature and culture are both artifacts of culture and of human thought. Second, there is no ethnographic evidence that all societies will elaborate an explicit dichotomy between nature and culture, or even that binary opposites will be characteristic of the symbolism of every culture (for example, see Barth 1975). On the other hand, there is ample evidence that many cultures do indeed elaborate such binary symbols and that the nature–culture dichotomy is implicit in a great deal of this symbolism. Where it is, Ortner argues, we can expect the female to be associated with a conception of nature.

This essay is an attempt to explore within a particular cultural context the implications of the symbolic intermediacy of women in relation to nature and culture.[1] In the Samoan case, at least, the symbolism of woman, and of gender itself, it importantly framed by the double valence of the feminine. Although, as Ortner suggests, this state of affairs may well originate in certain facts of nature, in the physiology and psychology of reproduction, it is equally true that any particular *conception* of the feminine is the handiwork of culture and must be interpreted as such. Thus, whether we are to treat systems that associate women with culture rather than nature as ''historical inversions'' of a more basic vision of the feminine or as somehow anomalous is an issue for ethnography to arbitrate.

Reproductive sexuality, psychological sexuality and gender

In recent years, with the increasing public and scholarly attention given to such phenomena as changing sex roles, transsexuality, homosexuality, and medical sex-change operations and their psychological and social implications, traditional understandings of the relations among biological, psychological, and social aspects of sexual identity have been challenged. In the process dictinctions have proliferated, and categories have become simultaneously more precise and less clear-cut. Clearly, sexual identity is a particularly complex phenomenon. To help clarify and illustrate something of this complexity in a Samoan context, I propose an analytical distinction among three aspects of sexual indentity, which may be separated for analytical purposes: biological, psychological, and sociocultural. The first of these dimensions we call *reproductive sexuality*, limiting it to the biological and reproductive aspects of sexual dimorphism. Whatever the significance of the cultural and purely idiosyncratic aspects of sexual identity, human beings are importantly differentiated by primary and secondary sexual attributes and functions. Until the successful development of cloning techniques, or some other form of parthenogenesis, human beings are dependent for biological reproduction on sexual dimorphism and the conjunction of complementary opposites. In this sense, reproductive sexuality defines a relatively ''objective'' or ''natural'' aspect of sexual identity.

The second of the three domains we may label *psychological sexuality*, and limit to the psychological and subjective aspects of sexual identity. Rather than focusing on body, psychological sexuality draws our attention to mind, and includes the subjective apprehension of sex drives, sex-object preference, erotic arousal, and a personal perception of one's own complex sexual identity.

Third is a domain more clearly social and cultural. This is what we may call *gender*, for it suggests conventional categories of greater or lesser generality for the appropriation of experience, categories that are part of a shared social environment and cultural heritage. *Gender* in this sense includes certain functional distinctions, sex roles, as well as sets of cultural symbols and meanings that link conceptions of sexual dimorphism with other aspects of experience.

Sexuality, in its reproductive aspect, focuses attention on shared functions, whereas gender stresses shared meanings. In other words, reproductive sexuality links humanity concretely (in both space and time) through metonymy (contiguity of differences) while gender links experiences more abstractly, through metaphor (similarity of form). Reproduction connects parents to children through the nature of biological conception, a fertility of body and a bridge between generations. The latter perspective, gender, provides a metaphoric linkage through cultural conceptions of nature, a fertility of thought, and a union of disparate experience.

To make these associations is not, however, to argue in a simple sense that reproductive sexuality and gender are manifestations of the dichotomy between nature and culture. For although it is fair to suggest that gender in this usage is clearly a cultural artifact, reproductive sexuality is inevitably ambiguous, bridging nature and culture. We may understand sexuality to refer to natural distinctions, but they are inevitably apprehended as conceptions of nature, mediated by cultural and social forms. We may only approach a pure perception of such natural facts, but the conceptual apparatus that enables us to grasp such facts is always partially cultural. In the end, the pure perception of nature is denied to us.

Nature and culture in Samoan thought

Although there is in Samoan no abstract term corresponding to the English "nature," Samoans do classify human behavior according to its motivation in a way that does suggest our own nature–culture dichotomy. The key concepts employed in these classifications are *āmio* and *aga*. *Aga* refers to social norms, proper behavior, linked to social roles and appropriate contexts. *Āmio* describes the actual behavior of individuals as it emerges from personal drives and urges. In describing an individual's behavior, *aga* suggests the degree to which the behavior conforms to the expectations of others in relation to correct social behavior, whereas *āmio* suggests the extent to which the behavior was personally motivated by self-gratifying urges. *Aga* thus links behavior to society, while *āmio* links it to self, to what we call "motivations." That one's actual *āmio* may conform to *aga* on any particular occasion is understood as a reflection of proper teaching (*a'oa'oina*) or socialization, and the ability to "think" (*māfaufau*) properly.

Most compound terms derived from aga (for example, *agalelei* "good *aga*"; *agaali'i* "chiefly *aga*"; *agavaivai* "humble *aga*" and *agaālofa* "generosity") suggest social virtue. *Agaleaga* "evil *aga*" is also possible, suggesting that some forms of evil are socially conditioned, part of certain roles or contexts, and thus encompassed by culture.[2] *Aganu'u*, the *aga* or conduct of human settlements, is the Samoan term for culture. *Āmionu'u*, the *āmio* of a settlement, does not exist as a word or a concept in Samoan thought because it is a kind of contradiction of terms. *Āmio* appears in a number of compound terms (*āmio pua'a* "piggish behavior"; *āmio inosia* "disgusting behavior"; *āmio leaga* "bad behavior" and *āmio lē māfaufau* "thoughtless behavior"). Most of these compound terms associated with *āmio* suggest socially undesirable forms of behavior. On the other hand the forms *āmio lelei* "good behavior" and *āmio tonu* "correct behavior" exist, suggesting that personally motivated behavior may have socially beneficial consequences. In general, the use of the term *āmio* focuses attention on the personal qualities of an act, whereas *aga* emphasizes its social dimensions.

Although the term *āmio* does not refer explicitly to any specific acts, stressing instead their source, *āmio* is sometimes used as a euphemism for impulsive, self-gratifying behavior, most commonly sexual in nature. *Fai le āmio* "to do the *amio*" is a colloquial way of expressing the youthful impulsiveness associated with the gratification of appetites. Stealing food at night and sexual behavior (also a kind of stealing for the unwed) are perhaps the quintessential forms of *āmio*.

In this opposition of *āmio* and *aga* there is something approaching Western conceptions of nature versus culture. One only has to limit nature to human nature, and permit it the status of a residual category, a reservoir of personal impulses that precede the acquisition of culture, remaining latent even where cultural controls have been imposed. Although these Samoan categories of nature and culture do suggest our own, they are not understood by Samoans in the same way. There is a crucial difference of value. To the externally derived aspects of behavior, those derived from social roles and associated with *aga*,

Samoans attribute a centrality and primacy in the definition of self. This Meadian "social self" is suggested by the term *agāga*, a term that probably derives from the nominalization of *aga* by the suffix *ga*, and that means "soul." As one Samoan pointed out, one's soul may be understood as the totality of one's *aga*.

That Samoans are concerned with the elaborate symbolization of this dichotomy between *aga* and *āmio*, socially controlled and uncontrolled aspects of human existence, is suggested by an elaborate symbolic dual organization manifest in Samoan social institutions. Elsewhere (Shore 1976, 1977, 1978) I have examined in detail the manifestations of this dualism in Samoan thought in Samoan language, social structure, and aesthetic forms. In each case, one term of a complementary opposition corresponds generally to *aga* and suggests social constraint, dignity, and subordination of personal impulse to cultural style and social control; the other term corresponds to *āmio*, implying lack of social restraint or form, and the expression of personal impulse and spontaneity.

In the opposition between *aga* and *āmio* we do not have a perfect realization of the culture–nature distinction. *Aga* does indeed suggest culture, explicitly for Samoans. *Āmio*, like reproductive sexuality, only approaches nature. Insofar as *āmio* and its associated symbols represent precultural forces, they do suggest human nature. However, insofar as these are symbols, manifest in social institutions and coopted by culture, framed in an elaborate dual structure that is itself part of culture, *āmio* is a cultural representation of nature and not quite nature itself.

Sexual relations

There are few polite terms in Samoan referring to sexual relations. *Fai'āiga* ("to make a family") is one more or less euphemistic expression for connubial sexuality. Sex is a concept that would seem to belong to the realm of nature for Samoans, associated strongly with those aggressive, private impulses classified as *āmio*. Sexuality suggests the antithesis of culture.[3] Among the young, sexual relations are sometimes referred to as "play," "wrestling," "fighting." "Doing bad things" (*fai mea leaga*) also describes sex play. It is also significant what sexual relations are not. They are clearly distinguished from *alofa* (love or empathy) and *fa'aaloalo* (respect), both of which are often invoked as the proper reasons for avoiding sexual relations or sexual reference at the wrong time.

The Samoan attitude toward sexuality is complex and suggests neither the thorough prudishness of missionary morality nor the casualness and erotic abandon reported for traditional Marquesan or Tahitian society (Linton 1939, Danielsson 1956). On the one hand, there is in Samoa the traditional cultural stress on virginity for unmarried girls, particularly for daughters of high-ranking chiefs or (nowadays) pastors' daughters. That this attitude is no simple missionary innovation is suggested by the traditional institution of the *taupou*, a ceremonial "princess" bearing a title attached to that of an important chief. The *taupou*, also called the *sa'otama'ita'i* ("straight/correct lady'') was the leader of the *aualuma*, the organization of village ''girls'' (girls and women belonging to the village by birth rather than by marriage). She was expected to dance and make kava at formal occasions when representing the village as host or guest with outsiders. In addition to her status of ''high birth'' as daughter, sister's daughter or other close relative to a high chief, the *taupou* was expected to remain chaste, her virginity intact until formal marriage. The term *taupou* means ''virgin'' as well as referring to the specific holder of a title. Traditionally, the marriage of a *taupou* was an arranged and highly formal relationship marked by elaborate exchanges of goods between the descent groups of bride and groom. An important part of the marriage ceremony was the formal assay of the bride's virginity, either by the groom himself, or by an orator representing the groom's side. The *taupou*'s hymeneal blood, staining a white piece of tapa, was considered a sign of her virtue. Her proven chastity reflected not only upon her own honor, but also upon that of her village, her family and, most of all, her brothers. Representing a Samoan ideal of feminine status, the *taupou*'s chastity suggested the state of purity to which all unmarried girls should aspire. Should the *taupou* fail her public test, she and her family and those of her village were shamed, the girl herself being subject to severe verbal and sometimes physical abuse.

Despite the persistence of many of the attitudes associated with the *taupou*, attitudes supported by the local church, Samoans are not in fact particularly prudish. Virginity for unmarried girls remains an important value in Samoan society, but its realization is far from universal. Although discouraged by public morality and church teaching, premarital sex play is part of growing up for many Samoan boys and girls. Certain attitudes toward sexual adventure appear to contradict the stress on chastity implicit in the *taupou* complex. Privately, at least, many Samoan youth see sex as an important part of youthful adventure. Nobility, normally representing models for ideal behavior, are sometimes conceived to have voracious sexual appetites, as well as a certain licence to gratify them. This appetite is associated with noble*men*, but not with their sisters. Sexuality is associated with vitality and power, and with the political advantages that accrue to any man by virtue of spreading his seed far afield and thereby creating many branches of his descent line, through different sets of children. Serial monogamy and the tolerance for and acceptance of illegitimate offspring fathered by one of high rank are both understandable in terms of these fundamentally political considerations.

Finally, the traditional *pōula* or night dance, largely discontinued under missionary influence, seems to have involved a freedom from the normal sexual inhibitions of the daytime. This ''daytime morality'' is suggested by the existence of a complementary *ao siva* or daytime dance characterized by formal constraint and separation of male and female dancers (Stair 1897, Turner 1884). Not only was dancing between visiting men and girls of the host village encouraged in the night dance, but the dancing is reported to have been explicitly erotic.

These apparently contradictory attitudes toward sexuality are not accounted for in terms of a simple ''double standard'' or ''hypocrisy.'' Samoans appear to subscribe to both attitudes, each in its own set of contexts. The expression of sexuality for both the married and the unwed is contextually restricted to the night time, to the "bush" or areas away from normal social life, and to women conceived of as "wives." Its control is linked to the daytime, the village or other public place, and to "girls" thought of as "sisters." There is also an association of sexual expressiveness with high-ranking males, but not high-ranking females. Among distinguished families, which in modern Samoa might refer to possession of wealth, church status, education, part-European parentage as well as traditional rank, female chastity is stressed, a reflection of the enduring power of the *taupou* ideal.

Control

The Samoan word for blood is *toto*. It is a symbol for biological kinship as in the expression *toto e tasi* ("of one blood"). *Toto* is often used to suggest the difference between agnatic and uterine links, the former often designated as *toto mālosi* ("strong blood"), the latter as *toto vaivai* ("weak blood"). A central symbol for both biological and social continuity, blood is for Samoans as for many other peoples an important nexus for the interplay of natural and cultural aspects of experience. In chiefly respectful address, blood is referred to as *palapala* (literally "mud") or *'ele'ele* ("dirt"), *but only when it flows uncontrolled from the body*. Thus, blood flowing from a wound accidentally contracted or menstrual blood may be called "dirt" in respectful address. On the other hand, blood transfused in a hospital, blood spilled in the process of childbirth or tattooing, and blood flowing within the body remain *toto*, with no linguistic implications of pollution. Distinguishing blood proper from pollution is social control, the regulation of its flow from the body. This distinction is implicit in the opposition between menstrual blood (over which society has relatively little control) and hymeneal blood of the new bride (which may symbolize the power of society to regulate its flow).

This opposition between menstrual and nuptial flows of blood suggests Samoan conceptions of the different potentials of female sexuality. On the one hand, there is the female degraded by sexuality uncontrolled, at the service of *āmio* rather than *aga*. Should a brother discover his sister in a compromising situation with a lover, both the sister and her lover are subject to stoning and a severe beating by the girl's brothers. At issue is not simply the girl's honor, but that of her family, most particularly her brothers. At the other extreme is the *faletautū*, the carefully arranged political marriage between a high-ranking chief and the daughter—presumably the *taupou*—of an important family. These marriages, contracted in traditional times by groups of orators, represent female sexuality subordinated to the demands of political alliance and social prestige. The contrast between the purely personal and the political uses of female sexuality is paralleled by a distinction between the offspring of such matches. The *tama a le pō* ("child of the night") is the illegitimate child, a child of passion, who may be accepted into either the father's or mother's households, recognized by both families, but who has few political hopes. On the other hand, the *tama a le fuafuataga* ("children of the arrangement"), children born to a couple whose union was carefully negotiated by the families and villages of the pair, are accorded special prestige, and have superior claims to succession to their father's titles.

Highest of all is the rank of the paramount chief's eldest sister whose status *as sister* confers upon her and her descendants the status of *tamasā* ("sacred child") to the title. Marriage for her is a secondary consideration in her power. In the absence of a sufficiently high-ranking match to whom she is not already related (often a dynastic marriage with a Tongan or Fijian nobleman), her status is better protected through her remaining unwed. Such, for example, is the case with To'oā Salamasina Malietoa, sister of the present Head of State of Western Samoa, and usually considered to be the premier lady of Samoa. By contrast to the sister of a royal chief, his wife has the status of *masiofo* ("royal consort"), and has status and prestige as befits a royal wife. Her status is, however, clearly eclipsed by that of her sister-in-law. One might represent the difference in terms of *mana*: The chief basks in the glow of his sister's *mana*, his power a reflection of her status; the *masiofo* basks in the *mana* of her husband, the chief.

From culture to nature: transformations of female status

In Samoan thought, the transformation of what are understood as facts of nature to artifacts of culture suggests the imposition of cultural and social controls on natural processes. Women, through their sexuality, represent the potential for effecting such a transformation. As *sisters*, their reproductive sexuality controlled (by their fathers and brothers), women symbolize the pinnacle of *aganu'u* or culture. A calculus of control over female sexuality suggests for female status a set of important transformations between nature and culture. As "girls," they are virgins, sisters but not wives. To remain a virgin under the pressure to lose control is to triumph over nature. Such control is not understood as self-control, but rather as the control exerted by brothers over their sisters. The *taupou* represents the public recognition of brothers' control over a girl's sexuality. Through the *taupou* institution, the girl, her brothers, her descent group, and her village group are honored.

The arranged marriage of a girl suggests an intermediate status: woman as sister to be given in marriage and as wife to be received. Sexuality remains controlled here not by simple denial, but by elaborate economic arrangement. Such arranged marriages are marked by careful negotiation and elaborate exchanges of *toga*, "female" exchange items comprising fine mats and other largely decorative goods, and *'oloa*, "male" gifts consisting traditionally of food and implements of practical value. Today, *'oloa* remains a kind of male product, being represented by payments of money.

With the birth of children, marriages initiate two politically significant forms of descent link. The one, focusing on the relation of husband to wife (or, from the point of view of a child, the relation between mother and father), distinguishes paternal and maternal "sides" with the agnatic links receiving an emphasis as the "strong side" or the "strong blood." The uterine links are also recognized formally as an important "side" or "part" of an individual's social identity, but these links are devalued as "weak blood" indicating a patrilateral bias in the transmission of political status.

The other form of descent link established through marriage and childbirth focuses on the relation between brother and sister. The children of the marriage become "sister's children" or *tamafafine* in relation to the wife's brother and any titles he may bear, and *tamatane* "brother's children" in relation to their father's sister and her offspring (their patrilateral cross-cousins). We may reduce both sorts of descent link (matrilineal and patri-lineal on the one hand, and sororal and fraternal on the other) to the key relations that define them. Where husband-wife links are the basis of the descent idiom, female status is devalued, becoming "weak blood." On the other hand, where the focal relation underlying the descent idiom is the brother-sister, the female is accorded higher status and honor than the male as *tamfafine, tamasā* ("sacred child"), and *ilāmutu* (a kind of sacred advisorial position of sister, backed up by a cursing power). Moreover, the power that a husband has over a wife is not the same quality as that which a sister has over her brother. "Masculine" power, associated with husbands, chiefs in general, *tamatane* and orators as a political class is *pule*, a secular authority backed up by secular sanctions (violence, banishment, fines). *Pule* (a term with fascinating cognates throughout Western Polynesia) is power associated largely with utilitarian activities. "Feminine" power, on the other hand, is associated with the roles of sister, father's sister, *ali'i* ("nobility") and (since missionization) with God. Such sacred power is *mana*, a kind of negative power to *fa'asā* ("forbid, make sacred") by preventing improper activity, and backed up by largely supernatural sanctions embodied in curses. *Pule* and *mana* together constitute two complementary aspects of power, a secular and sacred pairing, uniting active and passive energies into a vital *feagaiga* or bond.

The third status of women is that of common law wife, whose marriage was not arranged, and received little in the way of public regulation. Most marriages fall into this category. Frequently, marriage is initiated by the elopement of a couple who run off to live with distant relatives with the intent of evading the brothers of the girl. Such elopements are dangerous to the couple and embarrassing to the girl's family because they are equivalent to a kidnapping of the girl from her brothers and suggest a failure on the part of a family and its men to protect the chastity and fertility of its women. Obviously, however, families must come to terms with the necessity of accepting such marriages, because they constitute the most convenient, least expensive form of marital union. Brothers must also come to terms with the fact that they will need wives as well as sisters. Thus, despite an initial tension and hostility between brothers-in-law, the relationship is eventually given tacit acceptance by both families, particularly once a child is born. In this case, the girl's status as sister has been superceded, at least temporarily, by that of wife. In the Samoan idiom, one *feagaiga* or bond has replaced another. The brothers having had little to do with the transmission of sexual rights and the fertility of a girl, the relation between husband and wife is marked by the ascendancy of personal impulse (*āmio*) over social arrangement (*aga*). Female status is correspondingly degraded.[4]

Table 1. *Nature and culture: transformations of female status in Samoa*

Culture (Sister) ◄-------------------------------► Nature (Childbearer)			
Taupou (Virgin)	Arranged marriage	Elopement	Promiscuity
+sister	+sister	+wife	+"wife"
−wife	(+wife)	(+sister)	−sister

The last stage of the transformation of female status is that of the unmarried girl, the sister, who is caught while sexually promiscuous. This situation would include being caught with a lover, the discovery that a *taupou* was not a virgin, and the pregnancy of an unwed girl. The implications of each of these situations are a total lack of control over a girl's sexuality by her brothers, and the complete triumph of personal desire. In cases like these, the usual norms that brothers must respect and avoid close contact with their sisters are reversed, and girls are subject to violent beatings at the hands of their brothers.

In the progression from *taupou* to unwed mother, there is a schematic representation of Samoan understandings of the transformations to which female status is subject. These transformations are represented in Table 1. It is clear from this figure that in the Samoan view, the cultural potential of woman is linked to her status as "sister," whereas her natural (and less culturally valued) potential is tied to her status as wife and childbearer.

The concern over sexual control and the proper allocation of reproductive potential is focused on the female and not the male in Samoa. There is thus a strong double standard in regard to sexual control, men being accorded considerably more freedom in sexual matters than are women. *Pule*, and maculine power in general is understood to be active, productive, and aggressive. Such potency is consistent with the Samoan concept of sexual activity. Thus, although premarital sexual activity is generally discouraged for all, it is tacitly approved of, even encouraged, for males. At the least, it does not matter if men are sexually active in the way that it does matter for women. Men are thus free to pursue sexual interests, with incestuous liaisons and discovery by a lover's brothers as the major limiting factors.[5]

This lack of concern over male sexuality per se is linked to the fact that there is for males no parallel of the female opposition between the statuses of wife and sister. In several important senses, there is an indentification of husband and brother that makes male status very different from female. The relative continuity between roles of husband and brother as contrasted with the discontinuities between those of wife and sister becomes clear when we examine the traditional divisions of labor and ceremonial categories – a conceptual moiety system based on division of labor. The "village of men" (*nu'u o ali'i*) comprises all of the men's organizations within the village: the chiefs' council (*fono matai*) and its associated committees and the untitled men's organization ('*aumaga*). The "village of women" (*nu'u o tama'ita'i*) includes a somewhat more elaborate organization: The Women's Committee, the village girls' association (*aualuma*), the Organization of Chief's Wives

Table 2. *"The village of men" and "the village of women"*

Group	Membership	Functions
The village of men		
Chiefs' council (*Fono matai*)	All holders of village titles; Male residents of village holding titles from other villages.	Basic legislative and judicial body for village affairs.
Chiefly committees	Various village chiefs.	Administration of specific village projects and regulations (i.e., water pipes, agriculture, land boundaries, village school, village laws).
Untitled men's group (*Aumaga*)	All males past puberty residing in the village, and not possessing a chiefly title.	"The strength of the village"; Carry out orders of chiefs in large scale projects such as planting, building and maintenance. Young men practice oratorical skills.
The village of women		
Village girls' organization (*Aualuma*)	All daughters and sisters of the village; open to all girls who were born into families belonging to the village.	Hosting guests to the village; performing *kava* ceremony and dancing for visitors.
Chiefs' wives (*Faletua ma tausi*)	All wives of village chiefs, whether they are also members of the village by birth or not.	Overseeing the work of the young women of the village.
Village affines (*Fafine laiti*: junior women)	Wives of untitled men, residing virilocally.	Eat together on Sunday; may have their own "weaving house."
Weaving house *Fale lalaga*	All village women and girls; often subdivided according to *aualuma, faletua ma tausi* and *fafine laiti*.	Cooperative weaving of fine mats ("women's goods," decorative and valuable in exchange only) Teaching of weaving skills from old to young.
Women's committee (*Komiti fafine*) (Subdivided into specific committees)	All females residing in the village.	Village sanitation; inspection of households for cleanliness and maintenance of proper supplies for hosting visitors; nutrition, health, hygiene.

(*Avā Matai* or *Faletua ma Tausi*), the Wives of Village Untitled Men (*Fafine Laiti* – literally, "little women") and the weaving organization (*Fale Lalaga*). Village cooperative work is associated with these organizations, suggesting a general sexual division of labor. In Table 2, these groups, their membership criteria, and associated functions are summarized.[6]

It is apparent from Table 2 that there is for Samoans a general distinction between male and female work. In general, males are associated with work that is "heavy," dirty, instrumental, and linked with the peripheries of the village (the bush and the open sea). Furthermore, men's work is associated with the direct transformation of the natural world (planting, clearing of bush). Women, by contrast, are linked with work that is "light," clean, largely decorative rather than instrumental and associated with the centers of village life (the household, the protected lagoon, and the village proper). Public health and sanitation are closely associated with the labor of women. In contrast to male transformations of the natural world through planting and clearing of bush, women are responsible for the maintenance of a received order through weeding the gardens and keeping the village presentable for outsiders. This concept of public presentability is closely connected with women's roles, and with their meaning in a Samoan context.

A closer look at Table 2 reveals several other interesting patterns. Women's functions appear to be more finely differentiated by group membership than are men's. Furthermore, whereas men's jobs are differentiated only by age and possession of a chiefly title, women are allocated to social groups in a village through the chiefly status of their husbands, and, more important, through their statuses as wife or sister to the village. For instance, one is a member of an *aualuma* only as a sister (or daughter) to the village, but a member of the Wives of Chiefs or the Junior Women through an affinal link. Nowhere is the parallel distinction for men made between status as husbands to the village and as brothers or sons. A holder of a chiefly title may be a member of a village by birth (a brother/son) or by marriage to a "girl" of the village (husband). The same is true for membership in the 'aumaga, for the untitled.

Thus, where reproductive sexuality is the primary distinguishing feature of a status (wives versus sisters; husbands versus brothers) the distinction is marked for women exclusively. Women are unambiguously differentiated by social group membership into wives and sisters. The one exception is membership in the Women's Committee. In this case the exception underscores the rule, however, for of all the groups discussed, the Women's Committee alone is of postcontact exogenous origin. Not only does group membership distinguish sisters from wives, but it also suggests a difference in their functions, and thus in their meaning to a village. Women as sisters (*aualuma*) have a largely decorative role in presenting a dignified face for the village in relations with outsiders. The *aualuma* is responsible traditionally for looking after guests, making kava for the chiefs, dancing and entertaining village guests. Women as wives, by contrast, and women as mothers, are associated with the more utilitarian aspects of sanitation and cleanliness, and their roles are thereby less clearly differentiated from men's.[7]

Sexuality: male and female status

Female identity, as we have seen, pivots about reproductive sexuality and the public and private uses to which it is put. The female statuses that are accorded the highest cultural value are those in which reproductive sexuality is either completely suppressed (*taupou*), or in which it is transformed from a fact of *āmio* ("personal, natural drive") to one of *aga* ("conventional arrangement") through an elaborate arranged marriage. The transformations are held to be the responsibility largely of males – brothers, husbands, or orators – who are given control over the sexuality of women. This conception of female status makes woman a kind of symbolic bridge between nature and culture in Samoan thought, and is the basis of the extreme bifurcation of female value, the susceptibility of women to the extreme valuations of purity through total control (*taupou*) and pollution through total loss of control (*pa'umutu*: "wanton," "promiscuous").

I have suggested a kind of calculus through which Samoans evaluate female status ranging from extreme honor and purity through total defilement and disgrace. It is significant that each of these statuses that directly involve reproductive sexuality is understood in terms of simple binary oppositions, classifying females unambiguously as one status or its opposite. We have noted that such simple binary discriminations distinguish sisters from wives in membership of women's organizations in a village. In parallel fashion, females are accorded one of two statuses when they are classed either as *teine* ("girl") or *fafine* ("woman"). *Tama'ita'i* is a third term, bridging the two, respectfully referring to any "lady." Categorization as *teine* or *fafine* is based on a number of criteria: virginity, marital status, reproductive status, and residence. A *teine* is a female who is (*a*) a virgin, (*b*) unwed, (*c*) has not borne children or conceived, and (*d*) is residing in her natal rather than her affinal village. Ideally, all four conditions coincide and reinforce one another, making a distinction among them unnecessary. When they do not, however, it appears that it is the virginal status of the girl that is most important. Polite usage, however, does not permit an unwed mother to be called *fafine* in public, although people will sometimes privately allude to the fact that she is obviously not a "real girl" (*teine mo'i*), that is, a virgin. Similarly, even a married woman with many children is commonly referred to as a *teine* when she visits her own village, in keeping with the fact that her connection to the village is as sister/daughter rather than as wife.

Although there is some complexity in the categorization of a female as *teine* or *fafine* when the criteria do not all coincide, it is interesting that each of these criteria involves a simple binary discrimination focusing on the oppositions married/unmarried, nonvirgin/virgin, own village/husband's village.[8] Between *teine* and *fafine* there is no intermediate status. One is no less a virgin than another for having had more sexual experience. Similarly, having given birth to a child is sufficient to make a woman a mother, and her maternal status is not increased through having many children. As I have said, it does appear that virginal status is the focal criterion for classifying females as *teine* or *fafine*. Young men are often anxious in Samoa to enhance their prestige among their friends not simply by having many sexual relationships, but specifically by deflowering virgins. The *taupou* complex in Samoa revolves about physiological virginity, and the traditional public defloration of a newly married *taupou* to assay her status as a "true girl" is the supreme Samoan manifestation of this obsession with virginity.

By contrast, male sexuality is far more ambiguously related to male status. Male status does not involve any kind of clear-cut double valence pivoting on the male reproductive function. There is no clear calculus of sexual purity and pollution for the male. Moreover, where male sexuality is relevant in determining social prestige and status, the criteria for these discriminations suggest a logic of degree rather than simple binary discriminations. For instance, young men will commonly and only half-jestingly comment on the relative size of each other's genitals. One is presumed to be "more male" through having a larger penis. Likewise, males will boast among themselves about the number of girls they have slept with, the number of virgins ("first-breaks") they have conquered, the number of children they have sired, and the number of villages to which they have made *faiā* or connections through women.[9]

Virginal status is recognized for boys, who may be called *tama mo'i* "real boys," but such status has neither important physiological nor social implications and is more a source of embarrassment than pride for boys. Any male prestige that accrues through reproductive sexuality comes through active expression of sexual impulses rather than their repression or suppression. Males may, through sexual prowess, earn prestige and even political power, but sexuality for males has none of the potential for the extremes of sanctity and pollution that it does for females.

The distinction between *tama* ("boy") and *tamāloa* ("man") is generally parallel to that between *teine* and *fafine* for women. It suggests the difference between a male who is virginal and one who is not, as well as the difference between a bachelor and a married man. But in contrast to the relatively clear-cut discriminations that the terms suggest for women, the male discriminations are far less precise. In fact, sexual activity does not appear to be the primary criterion distinguishing boy from man, because many unmarried youth, called *tama*, are presumed and admitted to have an active sexual life. Marital status appears to be far more important for classifying males as *tamāloloa* (the plural of *tamāloa*). An older bachelor, with some social standing, however, is likely to be called a *tamāloa* rather than *tama*, whereas in the analogous case with a female, the term *teine* or "girl" would always be stressed. Calling an older bachelor a *tamāloa* is to honor him. Calling an older spinster a *fafine* would be an insult.

In summary, what I have called "reproductive sexuality" has a different value for male and female status. For females it provides a crucial pivot for an important set of binary discriminations between high and low prestige, and at its extremes, between purity and pollution. What I have called the double valence of the feminine in Samoan thought focuses on the potential for social convention to coopt and control the power inherent in female sexuality. This double valence is associated with sets of social categories for women that are simple binary discriminations, with reproductive physiology providing a focal point for the discriminations. For males, on the other hand, sexuality provides a far more ambiguous and less precise vocabulary for social classification. Discriminations of "maleness" in terms of reproductive sexuality tend to employ less categorical discriminations involving factors at once biological and social. Sexually, at least, only males come of age gradually. Samoans appear to permit no such intellectual sloppiness for the classification of their women.

Gender: male and female status

This study has focused thus far on social status as defined through reproductive sexuality and its social control. We have stressed the distinctions for females between sisters and wives, and between girls and women. The male analogies to these discriminations are neither as precise nor as culturally emphasized as are those for females.

In this section we turn from reproductive sexuality to gender. While an analysis of cultural elaborations of "male" and "female" discriminations in Samoa would take us into some very complex aspects of Samoan culture and society, dealing with cosmology, dance styles, linguistic distinctions, and an array of social institutions all involving a system of dual organization, we will limit our discussion here to several of the more important ways in which gender discriminations are involved in cultural symbolism. A more complete analysis of this dual cognitive schema for Samoa may be found in Shore (1977).

Samoans elaborate an extensive set of oppositions that may be shown to involve "Male" and "Female" gender discriminations. (I shall capitalize Male and Female when referring to cultural gender associations, as opposed to biological males and females.) I have already alluded to the general distinctions in Samoa between Male and Female work, and to the associations between Male work and an active, pragmatic orientation and between Female work and a more passive, honorific orientation.

Dress styles are also well defined for males and females, particularly in the way in which the wrap-around *lavalava* is tied. Although men and women may use the same material and colors for their garments, men are careful to leave a large and suggestive end of their *lavalava* flopping over in the front. Women, in contrast, do not let any end "hang out," but tuck the ends of the *lavalava* smoothly inside the waist.

Speech styles are also implicitly marked for gender. The sociolinguistic implications of these styles have been explored elsewhere (Kernan 1974, Shore 1977). For our purposes, it is important to point out that the formal pronunciation has a Female association, whereas the intimate or colloquial style is Male in Samoan thought. More specifically, formal speech is that of "girls" (as opposed to "women"), whereas colloquial speech is associated with both boys and men. Despite these associations, almost all Samoans speak the intimate forms most of the time and are far more comfortable using them than they are using formal speech. Women, girls, men, and boys are all users of "k" speech. On the other hand, the Female nature of formal speech and the Male nature of its colloquial counterpart are important symbolic and psychological facts for Samoans. Formal speech is "good speaking" (*tautala lelei*), associated with dignified and controlled occasions in which personal impulses (*āmio*) are subordinate to proper social necessity (*aga*). Intimate speech, associated with *āmio*, is "bad talking" (*tautala leaga*), and with either intimate contexts or roles, or the unrestrained expression of personal feelings and thoughts.

In addition to these gender attributes, gender distinctions include dance styles (a formal *siva* dance complemented by an uninhibited clowning style), bodily comportment, eating styles, division of food and eating implements, and a variety of other customary distinctions. Even more abstract is the gender aspect of the distinction between two types of chief, the *ali'i* or "high chief" and the *tulafale*, his orator. In dress, dance style, general demeanor, and passive power, the *ali'i* is a Female status. In contrast is the Male orator, associated with intimate pronunciation, the clowning *'aiuli* dance and utilitarian power (*pule*) rather than passive potency (*mana*). "Gender" clearly moves our perceptions from concrete to abstract, from perceived differences to conceived categories. The more abstracted the associations, the less likely they are to refer to biological males and females, but rather they cross-cut our perceptions to show us the "masculine" potentials of biological females and the "feminine" potentials of biological males. Ultimately, these gender distinctions come to mark aesthetic tone of social contexts and roles, and the tenor of personal moods. Thus most chiefs (*matai*) are men because political power is normally a male prerogative. On the other hand, within the category of *matai* is a Male–Female split between two types of chief, or two aspects of political power, one embodied by the *ali'i*, and another embodied by the *tulafale*.

Another example of the distinction between "*sexuality*" and "*gender*" is implicit in the distinction between *tamatane* and *tamafafine* – the descent categories based upon descent from a chief (or one of his brothers) and descent from any of that chief's sisters. These descent categories embody clearly a gender component, linking *tamatane* status with Male power (*pule*: the power to effect change), and *tamafafine* status with Female power (*mana*: a supernatural or sacred power, a negative force counterposed against *pule*). Although based on a gender distinction between Male and Female power, and between an original brother and sister, membership in *tamatane* and *tamafafine* groups at any gathering of kin includes both males and females, and does not distinguish between them.

The complexities of such an embedded, context-bound logic of gender attribution are particularly apparent when we examine the shifting symbolic associations that define the various statuses of a female. Initially, she is a sister, defined through her *feagaiga* or sacred bond with her brothers. Here her feminine qualities are set off against those of her brothers, and provide a primary and for Samoans generic definition of the male–female relationship. At marriage, she adds a second *feagaiga*, a marital bond, setting her off as woman (*fafine*) and wife against her husband. This bond is also a model of the male–female bond, but is secondary to that of brother–sister because the female element is defined in marriage through reproductive sexuality. In some important psychological and symbolic sense, therefore, the primary male–female model for Samoans (brother–sister) does not provide a model of an erotic relationship.[10] In both bond relations, the sister and wife are paradigmatically Female. When we examine the relations between sister and wife, however, there is a weak replication of the Female–Male dichotomy, in which "wife" is symbolically a more "Male" status than is sister, which remains quintessentially Female. The role of any wife in a village is far more active, productive (reproductive), and instrumental than that of sister. Thus the opposition between brother and sister remains a kind of perfect paradigm of the Male and Female, whereas that between husband and wife is only partial, and remains ambiguous. After all, in Samoan terms, husband and wife come together, become one; brother and sister remain clearly apart and distinct. They, and they alone, maintain respect through distance.

Such contextualization of Male–Female associations does not lead to a simple mapping of (Cultural) gender onto (Natural) sexual identity. The notion of person implied by this complex skein of relations does not identify biological and sociocultural classifications in any direct or simple sense. A person is, rather, a complex of discrete "sides" or "parts," some of which are seen as infracultural, and others of which belong to the social aspect of existence, to what we call social roles and Samoans know as *aga*. Some of these parts or sides are linked to gender concepts, as either Male or Female in nature. Samoans refer to the psychological or personal aspects of identity as a person's *'uiga*, a term that may be translated as "trait" or "characteristic" but that also signifies "meaning" in a more general sense. Male and Female *'uiga*, potential aspects of anyone's identity, are both psychological and sociological. Psychologically, Samoans believe that every person contains both a passive or dignified aspect and a more aggressive and active side. *Aga* and *āmio* are equally human capacities. Sociologically, every person is understood to be an aggregate of a number of different "sides," a constellation of links to descent groups, to villages, to titles, and to ancestors. Some of these sides are Male, such as one's "father's side" (any patrilateral connection), or one's status as *tamatane* in relation to a particular title, or, more abstractly, status as an orator. But everyone also has certain Female sides, links to one's mother's people, maternal villages, *tamafafine* connections, and rights to *ali'i* status. Biological sex is one important aspect of a gender identity, but is not unique, nor even, necessarily, the most significant aspect.

Fa'afāfine: male gender and the transvestite

Clearly, psychosexual identity is a complex set of associations including both reproductive sexuality and gender identity. In Samoa as elsewhere, there are inherent ambiguities and ambivalence in this identity, contradictions partially accounted for by the fact that Male and Female gender associations embedded in a cultural context do not map directly onto biological distinctions between male and female. In their social identity, at the very least, all men have Female gender attributes, and all women are part Male. Some men are recognized to have particulary well-developed Female *'uiga* in their personal identities. An *ali'i*, though usually a male, represents a Female principle, and Samoans sometimes say that certain males are temperamentally more suited to an *ali'i* status than to *tulafale* status. Such congruence between personal temperament and social status is, however, no prerequisite for holding that status. Conversely, women are understood to have Male as well as Female *'uiga*. Women may assume chiefly titles, and become either *ali'i* or *tulafale*. It is commonly held, however, that *ali'i* status is more appropriate for a female, although an aggressive and politically astute woman might well be identified as suitable to hold an orator title.

Although Samoan assumptions about the faceted nature of the person permit, even require, such multivalent gender attributes, it is nonetheless clear that there is a difference between males and females in the degree of gender ambiguity that is permitted expression. We have already identified for women in Samoa a split between the statuses of sister and wife, a split that sets a quintessentially Feminine aspect of the female against a more Male aspect. This is why, I think, the *taupou*, a ceremonial village maiden, a prototypical model of the feminine for Samoans, loses her *taupou* status upon marrying.[11]

For men, however, no such formal recognition of a Female aspect is made in terms of the brother–husband relationship. Neither is significantly more "male" than the other. Both are associated with *pule* (secular authority) – whether as *tamatane* in relation to a title, as husband in relation to a wife, as father in relation to children, or, finally, as protective brother. It is only at an abstracted level of Male–Female relations, as an *ali'i*, or as member of a *tamafafine* side that gender ambiguities in males are expressed. At the more concrete levels of dress, speech styles, and in terms of the division of labor, males are more strictly held to Male behaviors and signs than are females to the Female aspects of gender attribution. A woman wearing her *lavalava* tied in male fashion would probably not be noticed. A male, however, who forgets or fails to leave an end dangling would risk humiliation and public censure.

The specific control of male encroachment on female domains is the fear of being called *fa'afāfine* – transvestite. Any male who shows too much interest in Female activities, or fails to maintain a proper Male style of dress, speech, or deportment is open to the accusation that he is a transvestite. *Fa'afāfine* means literally "like a woman" and stresses not the fact that a person *is* a female, but rather that he is similar in appearance to a woman. It is perceived behavioral style that is at issue. *Fa'afāfine* does not mean *homosexual* in that it makes no direct claim about the erotic preferences of an individual. There is in Samoan no clear term for homosexual. The focus in Samoan interests is on the gender classification of an individual, the symbolic and sartorial aspects of gender attribution in terms of more general codes of Male and Female.

A male who accepts the attribution of *fa'afāfine* status represents not a female but rather a derivative third gender class. *Fa'afāfine* is a distinct gender class because it is normally not confused with either Male or Female. But it is derivative for it represents a kind of caricature of the feminine, an exaggeration and distortion of Female behavior and aesthetic style. The *fa'afāfine* represents for males a negative role model, and such individuals, either by temperament or socialization unsuited to the normal Male role, are a part of the social environment of almost every Samoan male. Transvestites serve to demonstrate what Male gender attributes should be by a presentation of failure, a powerful lesson by distortion or contrast. Few taunts have the power of this one to check inappropriate gender behavior in males. Males are thus formed in Samoa through a system of negative feedback. By avoiding inappropriate gender signs, and thereby evading the taunts they would bring, Males are created by default. Undesirable traits are punished and thus avoided. Every male is thus assumed to have certain *fa'afāfine* potentials. By keeping them at bay, a boy becomes a man.[12]

A focus on gender definition rather than on reproductive or psychological sexuality underlies the *fa'afāfine* institution. Men may have casual and occasional relations with a transvestite without themselves being accused of transvestism. Men may even cohabit with a transvestite, and, so long as they remain socially Male, are not open to accusation. Even casual homosexual relations between nontransvestite males lead to no accusations so long as the relationship does not violate the gender code of proper social presentation.

Because there is so little stress on reproductive sexuality and sexual activity in the definition of the transvestite, there is no analogous status to *fa'afāfine* for females. Although females may be noted to have certain Male characteristics in appearance or interests, there is no summarizing label for such a condition, nor is there any significant social stigma for the female who violates the gender code. In some important sense, such female violations of the gender code do not matter for Samoans in the way that male violations do. Women are permitted considerable flexibility and scope in relation to gender definition whereas men are not. Indeed we have seen this very scope built into the distinction between the statuses of sister and wife. Men, on the other hand, are permitted no such free play when it comes to the expression of gender attributes.

Conclusion

No simple distinctions linking male with a concept of culture and female with nature will illuminate the complexity of sexual identity in Samoa. Samoan sexual identity involves both what I have called sexuality and gender. They are closely linked, just as human biology and human culture are always linked in some way. At each level, male is distinguished from female. At the level of reproductive sexuality, these differences are relatively clear and elaborate. There are physiological and anatomical differences between the sexes, differences that, in Bateson's phrase, make a difference. Women and men possess significantly distinct anatomies. Women menstruate; men do not. These differences are, not surprisingly, recognized in Samoan thought. Women *fānau* "give birth"; men help *fofoa* "conceive" and *fa'atō* "impregnate" a woman. Female physiology creates for Samoans an important set of binary distinctions: girl/woman, virgin/nonvirgin, mother/not-mother, women who menstruate/girls (and old ladies) who do not menstruate. Male roles in reproduction lead to gradual rather than categorical oppositions.[13] In relation to sexuality, boys become men gradually and only ambiguously; girls become women suddenly and unambiguously.

There is also a second-level difference between male and female in terms of reproductive sexuality. For males, there are no crucial variations in social status that focus specifically on reproductive sexuality. For females, however, reproductive sexuality represents a crucial axis distinguishing wife from sister. We have analyzed a set of transformations to which the female is subject in Samoan thought, transformations from sister to wife. Following Bateson (1973), we can recognize that sexuality carries for the female a greater load of information than it does for the male. Not only does reproductive sexuality permit us to distinguish male from female, but it permits a distinction between sisters and wives that is central to a Samoan concept of the feminine.

Male and female have also been shown to be significantly distinguished at the level of gender attribution, through analogous sets of symbols involving increasingly abstract and diffuse associations. In its most general form, these gender distinctions associate females with control, dignity, grace, negative action (reaction), and *mana*, a sacred power, and link males with complementary notions of movement, disorder, growth, positive action, and *pule* (secular authority). The feminine is linked with culture and the masculine with nature. The problem for analysis is the lack of clear fit between these gender categories of Male and Female, and biological males and females. Only in certain of their ''parts'' or characteristics do males and females realize Male and Female gender.

Gender ambiguity is more pronounced for females than for males in Samoa, at least partly because of the internal contradiction in the feminine between the statuses of sister and wife. The statuses of brother and husband do not reveal a parallel gender contradiction for males. In their primary sociological statuses, males are permitted little expression of their Female side. Samoans stress for males a fairly rigid control of gender display and attribution, a control partly carried out through the institution of the transvestite. The male fear of losing control of his gender display, of being called a *fa'afāfine* is analogous to the female's fear of being caught in a sexual liaison by a brother. For females, that is, public control is over her sexuality. For males, public control is over his gender definition. Just as reproductive sexuality distinguishes for women *pa'umutu* (''wanton woman'') from wife from sister, so the gender system focuses on men, distinguishing male from *fa'afāfine* from woman. Male status is marked for ''gender''; female status is unmarked. These relations between male and female status are summarized in Table 3.

It is evident from Table 3 that there is an important parallel between the transformations about which female identity clusters (sister/wife/whore), and those that are focal for male identity (male/*fa'afāfine*/female). In both cases, one term represents a failure, a loss of control both personal and social in significance. For the female, this failure involves a misappropriation of reproductive sexuality for personal satisfaction. The failure is the whore. In the male case, the failure involves control over gender definition and a confusion of the categories in terms of which culture itself is predicated. The failure is realized as the transvestite, an institutionalization of a cultural anomaly. For the female case, however, the stress is on a positive model, the *taupou*. For the male case, the emphasis is instead on failure, on the transvestite.

Table 3. *Marked aspects of sexual identity in Samoa*

Biological male	Biological female
Reproductive Sexuality (Nature)	*Reproductive Sexuality (Nature)*
Unmarked	Marked
	Control through fear of brothers
	Sister/Wife/Whore
	Taupou:
	Positive model
Gender (Culture)	*Gender (Culture)*
Marked	Unmarked
Control through fear of being	
called *fa' afāfine*	
Male/*Fa' afāfine*/Female	
Fa' afāfine:	
Negative model	

In the Samoan scheme of things, the female articulates with the Feminine, precisely where her natural reproductive potential is controlled. "Sexuality" is thus the key axis around which her identity is articulated. Her cultural identity is a kind of glorious negative achievement, maintained through cultural control of natural capacities. The male, on the other hand, articulates with the Masculine precisely where human nature, his *āmio* is expressed. Expression of sexuality is, thus, no "problem" for males. On the other hand, Male gender attributes, the cultural expressions of Maleness, represent a conventional model of nature, a rendering of *āmio* in terms of *aga*. Gender definition is for males what reproductive sexuality is for females, a key axis on which sexual identity turns. If it is through the control of her natural capacities that the female achieves the fullest expression of what Samoans mean by culture, it is equally through the control of cultural capacities that the male comes to represent a cultural rendering of what Samoans mean by nature.

Notes

1 For helpful comments and discussion of an earlier draft of this essay, I would like to express my thanks to Shelly Errington, David Schneider, Wender McKenna, Sherry Ortner, Harriet Whitehead, and Penelope Meleisea. The essay was enriched considerably by the detailed comments that Penelope Meleisea made on the earlier draft, particularly concerning the relations of sister and wife in Samoan thought. The essay also reflects a number of discussions I have had over the past few years with Robert Levy. The influence of his work on Tahiti will be obvious throughout the essay. Naturally, all of the conclusions and analyses are, in the end, my own responsibility.

2 It is possible that the term *leaga* ("evil" or "bad") is itself derived from the negation (*lē*) of *aga*, suggesting that evil is a kind of residual state associated with the absence of social norms.

3 The fact that Samoans conceive of sexuality, particularly socially unregulated (premarital) sexuality, as antithetical to culture may shed some light on Samoan's dislike of M. Mead's *Coming of Age in Samoa*, the one work on Samoa by an anthropologist that educated Samoans are likely to know. The typical Samoan reaction to the work is that Mead lied. And perhaps, in Samoan terms, any discussion of premarital sexuality in a book that is understood to portray Samoan culture (*aganu'u*) does constitute contradiction. Sexuality does not for Samoans lie within the realm of their culture, nor would a statement suggesting that Samoan culture is characterized by relatively free premarital sexuality be acceptable as a characterization of Samoan culture by Samoans.

4 Today, with formally arranged marriages relatively rare, the distinction between the *faletautū* ("arranged match") and the *āvaga* ("elopement") has been transformed into that between mere cohabitation (*nofo fa'apōuliuli*, literally, "cohabiting in darkness") and church marriage (*fa'aipoipoga*). Both distinctions share the opposition of *āmio*, relations based on personal impulsiveness, and *aga*, socially regulated behavior.

5 Although the incest prohibition defines an important constraint over both male and female sexual activity, it is important to distinguish male and female perspectives here. For men, the incest prohibition focuses attention on proper and improper objects of sexual attention, rather than on their own sexuality. Failure to confine sexuality to nonkin brings only temporary disgrace to the male, but permanently damages (*fa'aleaga*) a female. In other words, women may be "polluted" permanently through improper sexual activity, whereas men are only temporarily disgraced, a distinction that Yalman (1963) has discussed for Ceylon and South India.

6 Although the distinction between the village of men and the village of women is general throughout Samoa, the precise composition of these categories appears to vary considerably from village to village. Table 2 includes the particular divisions made in the village where I did my major field work.

7 In the case where a chief holds a title in his wife's descent group and the couple resides in the wife's village, the woman may participate in both the *aualuma* (as a "girl" of the village) and the Wives of Chiefs (as an affine to a village *matai*). These two statuses remain institutionally separate, however, and at any given time, a woman must participate as *either* sister or wife, and never as both.

8 In this context, it is interesting to note the strong preference in Samoa for village exogamy. Samoans assume and fear that they are probably related to any co-resident of their own village.

9 For a woman, the number of offspring she bears is not nearly so important as the fact that she has given birth. Sexual barrenness is usually blamed on the woman rather than on the man, and defines her status more distinctly than it does her husband's. Moreover, the male stress on the relative numbers of offspring he sires helps to explain why men commonly object even more than women to government programs of birth control.

10 The fact that it is brother-sister rather than husband-wife that serves as the generic paradigm for cross-sex relations implies a powerful dilemma for Samoans in terms of sexual relations. Every potential lover for a Samoan male is in several senses also a potential "sister." First is the fact that incest prohibitions extend ideally to all cognatic relations. Samoans are aware that in a small society such as their own, with a relatively closed, inbreeding population, everyone is potentially related. It only remains for two people to trace links back far enough to discover their kin tie. In such a context, the distinction between a "wife" and a "sister" (Samoan kin terminology being the basic Hawaiian type) is a function of *knowledge* of

genealogy rather than of genealogy itself. It is a distinction of degree rather than of kind. Samoans often stress their ignorance of kinship links as an excuse for any liaison discovered to be incestuous (Shore 1976). All lovers are also potential sisters in a more direct sense because a girl's brothers will react violently to any discovered violation of her chastity. For a male, these brothers represent both a fear and also a reminder that this would-be wife is also a sister to someone. Finally, the initial cross-sex relation for any child other than that with a parent is the brother–sister relation in which a child learns the correct way to respect someone of the opposite sex. The brother–sister relation involves avoidance of intimacy, and a respect that precludes any suggestion of sexuality. This relation carries with it strong association for any other cross-sex relation in which a young Samoan will engage. The difficulty that Samoan men have in transforming cross-sex relations into sexualized ones, from moving from the perception of girls as sisters to women as wives is suggested by (a) the male tendency to rely on alcohol to dispel shyness and encourage aggressive overtures to potential lovers; (b) the avoidance of all signs of sexual familiarity with females while in the public eye, thus treating all girls as sisters; (c) the practice, known by most youths if not universally carried out, of violently forcing a new lover into sexual submission. This last practice, a kind of institutionalized rape, is far from rare in Samoa and suggests what may be psychological difficulties in transforming a brother-sister relationship into one admitting of sexuality.

11 The male status parallel to the *taupou* is the *mānaia*, a kind of chief over the untitled men, and official head of the *'aumaga*. I am not sure, but it is my impression that a *mānaia* does not lose his title upon marriage, but rather upon his assumption of a true *matai* title.

12 Levy (1973) makes a similar observation about the role of the transvestite (*mahu*) in Tahiti.

13 In popular Samoan belief, the male role in conception underscores this distinction between categorical and gradual transformations. Women are believed to become pregnant by an accumulation of semen from a single lover. It is the male's role in conception that stresses the gradual and quantitative contribution to the creation of a child.

References

Barth, Fredrik. 1975. *Ritual and knowledge among the Baktaman of New Guinea*. New Haven: Yale University Press.

Bateson, G. 1973. *Steps to an ecology of mind*. St. Albans: Paladin.

Danielsson, Bengt. 1956. *Love in the South Seas*. New York: Reynal.

Kernan, K. 1974. "The acquisition of formal and colloquial styles of speech by Samoan children." *Anthropological Linguistics* 16:107–19.

Levy, Robert. 1973. *Tahitians*. Chicago: University of Chicago Press.

Linton, Ralph. 1939. "Marquesan culture." In *The individual and his society*, ed. Abraham Kardiner, pp. 137–250. New York: Columbia University Press.

Mead, Margaret. 1969. *The social organization of Manu'a*. 2d ed. Honolulu: Bishop Museum Press.

Ortner, Sherry. 1974. "Is female to male as nature is to culture?" In *Women, Culture and Society*, ed. M. Z. Rosaldo and L. Lamphere, pp. 67–87. Stanford: Stanford University Press.

Shore, Bradd. 1976. "Incest prohibitions and the logic of power in Samoa." *Journal of the Polynesian Society* 85:275–96.

1977. *A Samoan theory of action: Social control and social order in a Polynesian paradox*. Unpublished doctoral dissertation, Department of Anthropology, University of Chicago.

1978. "Ghosts and government: alternative structures of conflict resolution in Samoa." *Man*. N.S. 13:175–99.

Stair, J. 1897. *Old Samoa, or flotsam and jetsam from the Pacific Ocean*. London: The Religious Tract Society.

Turner, George. 1894. *Samoa: A hundred years ago and long before*. London: Macmillan.

Yalman, Nur. 1963. "On the purity of women in the castes of Ceylon and Malibar." *Journal of the Royal Anthropological Institute of Great Britain and Ireland* 93: 25–58.

6

Like wounded stags: MALE SEXUAL IDEOLOGY IN AN ANDALUSIAN TOWN

Stanley Brandes

Y los hombres avanzan
como ciervos heridos.

And the men push forward
like wounded stags.

—Federico García Lorca, *Yerma* (1934)

Introduction

To most people, the term "ideology" denotes a more or less consistent, systematic, and interrelated set of beliefs. Moreover, ideologies are usually considered to be conscious and explicit, in that we generally expect the individuals to whom they are attributed to be able to explicate them in orderly fashion. Ideologies, in other words, are popularly portrayed as the products of reflection, of concerted intellectual effort. They are also supposed to guide or otherwise underlie action. Born of particular socioeconomic circumstances, ideologies are thought to become transformed into motivating forces in their own right, at once promoting and justifying certain types of behavior. Ideologies presumably provide people with a rationale for their own way of life.

Of course, as Karl Mannheim long ago pointed out (1955), ideologies are often attributed to people who in little or no way recognize an ideological component to their own thinking. Mannheim posited the opinion that the quest to understand ideology is born of group conflict and distrust: Political opponents, in the effort to make sense of one another's utterances, try to reconstruct from disconnected bits and pieces the coherent set of beliefs that is supposed to underlie their adversary's thought and behavior. Similarly, the anthropologist, when confronted by people who are guided by different presuppositions from his own, may seek to fashion some comprehensive ideology out of the temporally disjointed statements of his informants. Recognizing that his informants may be totally unaware of the principles behind what they say, the anthropologist – like Mannheim's political man – may nonetheless attempt to ferret from their apparently random, unrelated beliefs and speech patterns some larger, more comprehensive meaning.

In this essay,[1] I undertake this type of ideological reconstruction, specifically for the sexual domain. The people whose ideology I try to represent are the men of San Blas, a rural town of some eight thousand inhabitants located in southeastern Spain, within the borders of the vast and distinctive region known as Andalusia. San Blas is typical of eastern Andalusian settlements. Its economy rests almost entirely on the production and processing of olives, and its groves are concentrated in the hands of a relatively small, highly educated elite. Unlike the homogeneous, egalitarian pueblos of Castile described elsewhere (e.g. Brandes 1975a, Freeman 1970, Kenny 1966), agrotowns like San Blas are internally divided by deep conflict between social classes, as well as between men and women. My main concern here is to describe how men perceive sexual conflict, and why, in the face of obvious economic and social advantages, they feel so threatened and powerless in their self-proclaimed confrontation against women.

The men of San Blas are a highly diverse group in occupation, political sentiments, and educational background. This diversity, when coupled with the rapid economic and social changes that Andalusia as a whole is currently undergoing, makes it difficult to speak of ''male ideology,'' as I purport to do. Nonetheless, it is fair to say that, regardless of the socioeconomic circumstances in which men find themselves, they are all consciously pre-occupied with the basic fact that they are men, and that this condition presumably differentiates them radically from members of the opposite sex. They also frequently engage in the open, assertive display of behavior that is considered to be masculine, indeed, that is male prerogative. American social scientists would label this social posture as *machismo*, although the men of San Blas themselves never use the term, nor does there seem to be a native equivalent for it. Despite this lexical void, men, in a variety of ways, constantly assert the privileges automatically accorded them as males.

In San Blas, as in towns of Portugal (Riegelhaupt 1967) and Greece (Friedl 1967), women are much more secluded from public view than are men. Upper-class women, to be sure, enjoy a degree of freedom unknown to those of the working class. But, still, women from all social strata are restricted in comparison with men. Men, whether singly or in groups, are allowed – even encouraged – to lounge in taverns, plazas, and other public locales. The times and places where they can display their leisure are virtually unlimited. Women, in contrast, have only begun to enter the bars in the past decade, and even now are severely criticized if unaccompanied by either their husbands (in the case of working-class women) or groups of relatives and friends (in the case of upper-class women). Except during the Sunday *paseo*, or formal stroll, women should refrain from loitering in the street; and, when strolling, they should invariably be escorted by other women or by male relatives.

Just as the public domain is dominated by men, so the domestic domain belongs to women. Women are supposed to stay close to home, where they work at housekeeping and occasionally entertain female relatives during free afternoon hours. Women can regularly leave home for shopping or attending church, but in either case their domestic role is reinforced: Marketing is necessary for the upkeep of her household, while the Mass and Rosary place her in the presence of the Holy Family, the psychological equivalent in many ways of her earthly family. This equivalence is undoubtedly one reason why men who frequently attend church are criticized severely, as if they were somehow deviating from the appropriate masculine spatial domain. To San

Blas men, "The home is for eating and sleeping; otherwise a man belongs out with his friends."

These distinctive sex roles are learned in childhood, and reinforced through a variety of informal sanctions. Young girls are given a good deal of domestic responsibility, which requires that they lead a more home-bound life than their brothers. As they grow older, strict curfews are imposed upon them, and their appearance and demeanor in public are closely monitored. They must remain neat and modest, and refrain from being overly spontaneous or demonstrative, lest this attitude be interpreted to carry over into the sexual domain. Young men, on the other hand, are expected to lead an unshackled existence, to remain out as late as they wish, to drink with friends and seek female company. Throughout life, men initiate conversations and greetings, while women are placed in the position of merely responding. Girls who appear flighty, forward, or aggressive severely limit their chances for matrimony. Later in life this type of behavior evokes accusations of sexual promiscuity and eventually results in ostracism from normal social relations.

The curious paradox is that, even though women in San Blas are restrained and restricted by their society, men nonetheless feel severely threatened by them, or at least they are encouraged by the ideology to feel so. The male ideological posture accords women considerable superiority. It is an ideology that reverses the state of affairs that exists in the realm of actual behavior: Women are portrayed as dangerous and potent, while men suffer the consequences of female whims and passions. Male fears and fantasies are codified in and expressed through cultural formulae, which form the elementary units out of which an ideological stance may be constructed.

How can a sexual ideology be identified and constructed, when no systematic set of beliefs is expounded by the men of San Blas themselves? In this situation, we can draw upon at least three devices. First, there exist explicit informant statements bearing on the perception of masculinity and femininity. Men embrace certain opinions regarding their intrinsic sexual nature and their relationship to women, and these opinions are frequently articulated. The problem with relying too heavily on testimonies of this kind is that they seem to vary from one individual to another, particularly according to the informant's educational level. For this reason, I have tried in my analysis briefly to specify the social background of the people whose statements I directly cite. Nonetheless, as I have already stated, virtually all San Blas men assume the same general tone and posture when trying to explicate sexual relationships. It is mainly the refinement of the language in which their opinions are couched, and the supporting examples they draw upon, that vary from class to class.

The second device consists of codified folkloristic items, like proverbs, jokes, and legends. San Blas men consistently quote traditional sayings to support their opinions regarding the nature of masculinity and femininity. The utilization of proverbs is an effective appeal to time-honored sources of authority; hence, whenever talking about sexual matters, men will resort to them as a conscious means to buttress and legitimize their own point of view. Jokes and legends are not usually used in this sort of overt manner to explain certain beliefs, but they certainly reveal and reinforce sexual stereotypes. They are therefore also valuable in the formulation of a people's ideology.

Finally, we have recourse to idiomatic expressions, which are like jokes, proverbs, and legends in that they are culturally shared and transmitted, but are unlike them in that they operate largely as unconscious vehicles for the transmission of sexual attitudes. Idioms often as not are metaphoric; they reveal symbolic equivalences between two domains that, on the surface, seem totally disconnected. In the case of San Blas, animal names and qualities are used to describe human sexual attributes, and genital properties are associated with particular emotional states. Usually, the metaphoric relationships codified in speech remain unrecognized by the people themselves. The anthropologist, however, may identify them and use them as building blocks in the construction of a native ideology.

My main purpose here is ethnographic. I wish to draw upon these three devices to outline how San Blas men perceive the sexes and sexuality. The ultimate origin of this male perception is beyond the scope of my discussion. In the conclusion, however, I hope briefly to explore why men should portray themselves as utterly powerless and vulnerable, when in reality they seem to exercise such vast power and prerogatives over women. A consideration of this paradox is fundamental to an understanding of San Blas culture and society.

The moral dichotomy between the sexes

The first step in analyzing male sexual ideology in San Blas is to understand an essential moral dichotomy: Men believe themselves to be inherently more virtuous than women. They justify this opinion primarily on religious grounds. "Women are of the Devil," a butcher once explained to me, as three of his friends listened and nodded in agreement. "God created the world in seven days. Let's say that the first day He made the earth and plants, the second day the sun, the third day . . . well, I don't quite remember it all. But the fifth day He made man. And from the ribs of man He made woman on the sixth day. That's why women have one more rib than men. If you have the chance to see a human skeleton, you'll find this out for yourself."

The butcher then went on to explain that the original man and woman were called Adam and Eve and that they lived together in Paradise. God told them that they could reside there as long as they did not eat an apple. Then one day the Devil appeared to Eve in the form of a serpent, and he tempted her to eat an apple off a tree. Eve, in turn, tempted Adam to eat the apple. "And that is why woman is of the Devil," said my informant, continuing his rendition of the Fall. "She was that way from the very beginning, and she has been trying to tempt and dominate man ever since." As for man, he "is of God because he did not sin and he remained pure. He only sinned after he was tempted by woman to sin. He was and still is closer to God than is woman."

Referring to this Biblical legend, men frequently state that women "dress like serpents" (se visten de serpientes) in order to create harm and dissension among men. Female iniquity is particularly evident in sexual matters, about which it is asserted contemptuously and assuredly that all women are seductresses and whores (*putas*), possessed of insatiable, lustful appetites. When women wield their powers, men cannot resist temptation and are forced to relinquish control over their passions. This is why men believe that:

Pueden mas dos tetas que cien carretas.
Two breasts can do more than a hundred carts.

Women who are determined to get their way will always win in the end; thus there is no alternative, men claim, but to capitulate to them from the start.[2]

But it is not solely in sexual matters that women rule. Women are also blamed for perpetuating the San Blas class system, and for being much more exclusivist than men. It is said that women of the elite refuse to associate with commoners, and that they urge their husbands, who are thought to be more egalitarian by nature, to act likewise. Female exclusivity also manifests itself in discrimination against "outsiders" (*forasteros*), people who are not San Blas born and bred. Wives who have married into San Blas from elsewhere complain that they are forever rejected by women from long-established San Blas families. Lengthy residence in San Blas, complain these outsider women and their husbands, does nothing to alter native female attitudes. Men who marry in, however, are said to be integrated rapidly within town society. No wonder, then, that the men of San Blas proclaim:

La mujer es de pelo largo pero intentamento corto.
Women have long hair but few good intentions.

Or, alternatively,

La mujer es de pelo largo y sentimiento corto.
Women have long hair and little feeling.

Whether describing a woman's goals or emotions, San Blas proverbs never portray her in a favorable light. Man is good, woman evil.

Similarly, the men of San Blas unconsciously express a binary opposition consisting of two distinct metaphoric chains: God is associated with men and sheep, while the Devil is linked to women and goats.[3] Sheep, like men and God, are good; goats, like women and the Devil, are evil. It is said that God was the original shepherd and the Devil the original goatherd.[4] God and the Devil one day decided to have a race to see who would get to the river with his animals first, so they could drink. To win, God sent a curse (*echó la maldición*) on the goats and the Devil, forcing them high up in the hills, in the opposite direction from the water supply. Ever since then, goats have been destined to graze in the hilliest, poorest terrain, just as women are forced to accept a formally subordinate niche within the human domain.

People claim that at night, when it is perfectly dark, if you run your hands along a goat's back it will emit sparks – the fire of the Devil. They also state, by way of proof, that if a goat eats the tips off an olive branch, the branch will remain forever stunted; but if a sheep nibbles at the tips, the branch will regenerate. These phenomena occur despite the fact that olive trees are a natural and appropriate food supply for goats, which subsist on trees, shrubs, and bushes, while sheep prefer to eat grasses and other herbage from the ground.

Men further assert that goats, as punishment for their association with the Devil, were banished from Christ's manger at the time of his birth, while sheep were permitted to flock there in great numbers. Again in order to demonstrate their claim, they point out that Christmas creches always contain sheep but never goats. Indeed, Spanish artistic representations of the Nativity – from medieval retablos all the way to contemporary greeting cards – almost invariably exclude goats from among the flock of animals in attendance. The Spanish image of the goat, by contrast, is nowhere more accurately portrayed than in Goya's painting, "Escena de Brujas" (usually translated as "The Witches' Sabbath"), dominated by a gigantic horned goat representing the Devil, who is surrounded at the base of the painting by countless female witches.

In San Blas, the association between humans and animals is more subtle than is reported, for example, among the Sarakatsani shepherds of northern Greece, among whom "Women and goats are conceptually opposed to men and sheep" (Campbell 1964: 31), and whose sexual division of labor is in effect determined by this conceptual opposition (1964: 31–5). Nonetheless, in San Blas the symbolic associations between people and animals emerge in unexpected ways. When men speak of sexually promiscuous women, for example, they are likely to say:

La cabra que es de monte siempre tira al monte.
The goat from the woodlands always heads toward the woodlands.

That is, once a woman begins to sleep with a series of different men, she will forever continue doing so. Although it would be possible to generalize from this proverb in other ways, I have never heard it applied to any other context. Similarly, when several men depart from a gathering in order to conduct private business, the ones who are left behind state, by way of explanation,

Deja la oveja mear.
Let the sheep piss.

In other words, men should be left to conduct their affairs undisturbed. Women, in my experience, are never referred to metaphorically as sheep. Spanish literary tradition, I might add, embodies the same associations between animals and the sexes as is found in San Blas.[5]

An important expression of the metaphoric chains linking animals and humans is the evil eye, a destructive, invisible, and often involuntary emanation causing illness or death.[6] Because of their inherent wickedness and close association with the Devil, certain females, and females alone, are accused by the people of San Blas of being possessed by the evil eye (*mal de ojo*). And certainly it is more than coincidental that animal victims of the evil eye in San Blas, as throughout Mediterranean Europe (Blum and Blum 1965: 131; Campbell 1964: 338), are often sheep and rarely goats. In one particularly interesting case, a woman nicknamed Culona ("Big-Ass") is believed definitely to have the evil eye, which she regularly, though unconsciously, uses to destroy sheep. "Only last year," a shepherd confided,"she was staring at a perfectly healthy, well-fed sheep. 'What a beautiful sheep!' she remarked. The next day the animal died."

We may surmise, in anticipation of the forthcoming analysis, that the female destruction of sheep through the evil eye is a symbolic projection of woman's destruction of man. Furthermore, in the case of Culona's evil influence, we have a clue to one important source of man's downfall: the *culo*, referring variously to the buttocks or the anus. It is significant that a woman who has been dubbed by the community with the nickname Culona should also be perceived as destroying sheep.[7] For, as we shall presently see, men believe themselves to be threatened as much by their attraction to women – an attraction that centers primarily on the female buttocks – as by their potential anal penetration by other men.

Serpents and human sexuality

In the attempt to uncover some of the important ways in which women seem threatening and dangerous to men, I wish to explore further the symbolic connection between women and serpents. We have already noted that in San Blas men say that women "dress as serpents"; because, in standard Spanish, the word *serpiente* is often used as a synonym for the Devil (Real Academia Española 1956: 1194), there is a clear implication that women become transformed conceptually into the Devil through their symbolic metamorphosis into serpents. In this respect, it is noteworthy too that the word *serpiente* is feminine in gender (*una serpiente*),[8] which is consistent with a strong artistic tradition in southern Europe of portraying the serpent in the Garden of Eden with a woman's face (Rowland 1973: 144). Overall, the San Blas symbolic system suggests an identification of serpents as female. Here, at least, it is decidedly wrong to apply the usual psychoanalytic link between this creature and the phallus, a connection that Ernest Jones once termed "one of the most constant and invariable symbols" (1949: 101).[9]

Besides the serpent in the Fall of Man, serpents have two other important sources of reference in San Blas. The first is a well-known local rendition of the Holy Family's journey to Bethlehem. The pregnant Virgin, it is said, was seated on a mule, which was plodding along the road. A serpent suddenly appeared in front of the mule, scaring the beast so greatly that it tossed the Virgin onto the ground, nearly causing death to her unborn child. In those days the serpent still had its legs. But as a punishment for endangering the Virgin and child, God deprived it of its legs and forced it to crawl along the ground forever after. God also punished the mule – referred to in the legend as a *mula*, the female of the species – by making her permanently barren, the price for scaring easily and hurling the Virgin to the ground.

The significance of this story becomes understandable only if we recognize that the two culprits, the serpent and the mule, both represent females. They endanger the lives of another female, the Virgin, and her male child. We have here one of the clearest possible expressions of the intense, indissoluble bond between mother and son, which is characteristic of San Blas, just as it has been of the entire northern Mediterranean world at least since ancient Greece (Slater 1968: 3–74). The son's fate is bound to that of his mother, who is an idealized, pure version of womanhood. To the pure Virgin, we can contrast the dangerous serpent and the disruptive *mula*, who represent negative manifestations of the feminine character, and who embody the potential destruction of family well-being. Indeed, according to San Blas men, it is women in their role as Devil who pose the greatest threat to family unity, just as it is women, in their role as mothers, who solidify the family bond. The legend of the journey to Bethlehem is a superb reflection of male ambivalence toward women.

The second significant reference to serpents is a folk medical belief concerning infants, which is now confined to the poorer and older residents of San Blas but which, until the early 1960s, was quite widespread among all but the educated elite. It is said that at night a serpent may crawl surreptitiously into the bedroom where an infant and its nursing mother are sleeping. When the child awakens from hunger and begins to cry, the serpent suckles the mother's breast and inserts its tail into the infant's mouth. In this manner, the serpent draws nourishment from the mother's body at the expense of the infant. This deception continues for a period of several weeks, until the child finally withers and dies. The mother remains unsuspicious throughout this period, because the tail acts as a soporific to the infant, while the sucking motion of the serpent's mouth exactly replicates the child's. It must be noted that the efficacy of this belief depends in large measure upon the assumption that breast milk is a "limited good," in George Foster's sense of the term (1967). If it were not, the child could simply compensate for lost nighttime nourishment by nursing more during the day. What happens, however, is that the serpent consumes so much milk at night that it completely exhausts the mother's restricted supply, leaving nothing for the infant.

This belief, as I said, is fast disappearing. It no doubt arose as a culturally shared and codified projection of anxieties concerning infant mortality and the availability of an adequate supply of mother's milk, in the days when as many as half of all infants died and wetnurses or, later, bottled formulas were available only to the wealthy elite. However obsolete, the belief still represents a powerful symbolic portrayal of masculine attitudes toward women.

Let us note, at the outset, the structural parallel between this folk medical belief and the legend of the Virgin's journey. In both, the serpent plays an aggressive, destructive role, which is directed toward the death of an infant. In both cases, too, the infant is masculine. The gender is clear in the instance of the baby Jesus, while in the medical belief, the comprehensive masculine term *niño* is always used when referring to the victimized nursing child. Furthermore, the medical belief, like the legend, incorporates contrasting portrayals of females, the serpent representing the evil dimension of womanhood, the mother representing the positive one. In both folkloristic references, the disruptive aspect of women threatens to or does destroy their creative, productive side (giving birth, providing milk). In both, too, the strength and well-being of the mother-son bond are also endangered. Overall, the two folklore references may best be viewed as expressions of the ambivalent attitude toward women that prevails in San Blas.

There is one critical element appearing in the medical belief alone, however, that we cannot afford to overlook: the *leche*, or milk. The milk is at once denied to the nursing child and incorporated within the serpent, to the beast's immediate benefit. To recognize the full significance of the serpent's thievery, we must realize that in San Blas, as throughout Spain, the term *leche* means semen as well as milk; it is, in fact, the most universally and commonly employed word to refer to male sexual fluid. Moreover, the linguistic association between milk and semen is not merely incidental, but rather is codified in and popularized by jokes, which turn on puns for the term leche.[10] It is not surprising that semen and milk should be so closely linked when we consider that both substances, besides being white fluids, are connected with the creation or sustenance of life. (In English, cream, rather than milk, is given the dual connotation.) Just as a man in infancy depends on milk to survive, so too he relinquishes *his* milk in adulthood in order to produce children. And just as the people of San Blas consider a mother's milk to exist in limited supply, so too do they perceive semen as a finite substance, permanently depleted with each ejaculation.[11] Because people consider semen to be an essential ingredient for maintaining a man's vigor, energy, and youth, its dwindling supply, they believe, can only lead to his more rapid demise.

We can finally understand how the medical belief of the suckling serpent relates to the sphere of adult sexuality in San Blas. Just as the serpent deprives the child of milk, woman deprives man of his semen. Just as the serpent benefits from the nourishment of the milk, it may be supposed that woman benefits from incorporating semen into her body. In both cases, man is victimized by woman. The serpent's role, in other words, replicates that of the wife, and mirrors one of the most critical feminine threats to masculine well-being: the destruction of life.

Body substances and bodily strength

For the men of San Blas, women are inherently evil, and on this account alone pose a serious threat to their very existence. But it is also women's sexuality that men fear, primarily because it threatens in various ways to rob them of their masculinity and convert them symbolically into females. The men of San Blas believe that they must constantly guard and defend their sexual identity against potential assault. This assault may take one of three principal forms, each of which we shall discuss in turn: (*a*) the wife's attempt to drive her husband to a premature death; (*b*) the wife's adultery, which feminizes her husband; and (*c*) the man's enforced adoption of a feminine, passive role.

To explain the first point, let me begin by summarizing how a San Blas man views sexual relationships. From the time women are in their early teens, they begin to use makeup and dress provocatively, so that they will attract men and be able to capture them (the usual verbs here are *atrapar*, "to trap," and *cazar*, "to hunt"). While the prospective husband is courting, a woman acts submissive, shy, and compliant, but this is just part of her overall plan of attack. Once the man is bound by an official, indissoluble wedding ceremony, the woman begins to demonstrate her true ambition, which is nothing less than to dominate completely, to rule her husband and children, and above all to sap her husband's strength, by forcing him to engage in heavy sexual activity and physical labor, until he utterly expires and dies. Her ultimate goal, it is believed, is twofold: to live from her husband's social security or insurance premiums, without having to share the income with him; and to satisfy her voracious, indiscriminate sexual appetite, without the restrictions imposed on her by marriage.

I have heard a variety of opinions regarding the period of life during which women actually begin to desire the death of their husbands. Some men claim that the woman's attitude changes abruptly upon marriage; for others, the change occurs after the women give birth to all the children they want; and for still others, it does not come until the children are grown and able to contribute to the upkeep of the household. Regardless, the general male opinion is that women want and need husbands as a temporary security measure, or as a means of legitimizing their children. Once these functions are fulfilled, they say, women feel they are better off as widows.

It should be noted that, even without the feminine advantage in marriage, men consider women to be constitutionally much the stronger sex. In the short run, to be sure, men – especially young men – are demonstrably stronger than women. They can run longer and faster, lift and pull heavier objects, and do more strenuous labor. But men lack the long-range bodily resistance and durability of women, and therefore die at a much younger age. Especially in matters of sex, women are said to have superior strength and drive to that of men.

The main reason given for this female corporal superiority is that women have "clean" blood. The menstrual flow, men believe, freshens the blood supply every month, by divesting it of.impurities. Like most Mediterranean peoples (e.g., Blum and Blum 1965: 33–4, 138, 170; Blum and Blum 1970: 20, 46; Campbell 1964: 31), as well as some from other parts of the world (Douglas 1966: 121, 147, 151, 186; Schieffelin 1976: 67), the people of San Blas consider menstrual blood to be polluted, for the specific reason that it carries away the filth that inevitably accumulates over the course of a woman's cycle. As one informant put it, a woman is like a bottle of water that receives periodic washing and refilling. Her blood supply remains fresh and renewed. Man, on the other hand, is like a bottle of water that becomes stagnant. The impurities of his body continuously build up with no means of release. He therefore naturally becomes weaker over time than does woman.

To compensate, however, men have one great source of strength that women lack: semen. Semen, as we have already noted, is said to be lifegiving and beneficial. Given the inability of male blood to regenerate and cleanse itself, semen is without doubt man's single most important bodily substance, the one upon which his very existence, as well as his continued enjoyment of sexual pleasure, depends. In fact, one could almost say that just as a man's genitals are the locus of his strength and will – a notion we shall examine in the following section – so, too, his semen, which is located within the genital region, *is* his strength and will.

Considering this point of view, it is understandable that men are greatly preoccupied by the allegedly debilitating aspects of sex, which deprives them of valuable semen after each ejaculation. In San Blas, I have observed no concern among men that coitus or sexual contact of any kind with women is immoral or contrary to religious standards. Nor do men seem to fear that their sexual relationships will cause them to be punished in the afterlife. In other words, men are totally unconcerned that women will lead them into sin. What does worry them, however, is that their wives will, through sexual activity, deprive them of their strength and youth, and drive them to an early grave.

I became aware of this male preoccupation soon after my arrival in San Blas, when I visited a tavern where there hangs a prominently displayed glazed tile, upon which is written the following rhymed proverb:

Agua de pozo y mujer desnuda
Llevan al hombre a la sepultura.
Well water and a naked woman
Lead men to the grave.

I asked the three or four men who were gathered at the counter to explain the saying to me. The first part of the proverb, concerning well water, they dismissed as self-evident; anyone knows that well water is bad for you, they said. As for the reference to the naked woman, one of them opened his eyes wide, furrowed his brows in a knowing sort of glance, and began moving his outstretched arm and tightly closed fist back and forth to and from his chest, in the typical Spanish gesture depicting coitus. By way of further explanation to the perhaps untutored foreigner, the men simply said, "*Debilita*" – "It weakens."

Although the tavern tile was manufactured elsewhere than San Blas, and in fact does not bear a traditional town saying, the proverb accurately reflects the San Blas male point of view. Townsmen grow up hearing their own proverbial wisdom to the same effect:

Si quieres llegar a viejo
Guarda la leche en el pellejo.
If you want to reach old age,
Keep your semen within your skin.

Because semen, the life-giving element, exists in limited supply, men should be careful to preserve it as much as possible. This means, for male youth and unmarried men of all ages, that self-control should be exerted against masturbation. After marriage, when intercourse becomes the main avenue of sexual release, abstention is the best way for a man to conserve his vigor, especially as he grows older.[12]

Men are on the constant lookout for cases that demonstrate their perception of women's ultimate goals. In one instance, a fifty-nine-year-old widower eloped with a forty-year-old widow, who, it was said, had been trying to seduce him for months. Within days after the elopement, word was out that the man had left her, with the complaint that she had a voracious sexual appetite. Every time he would turn over to sleep, she would try to arouse him into another encounter. It was more than he could take, and all the men I knew seemed to sympathize with the man's lot. It was assumed that the woman was after his money, and was trying to do him in.

Men claim that widows immediately gain weight and acquire a lustrous glow after their husbands die, which demonstrates their happy state. They also are likely to become sexually promiscuous. Pitt-Rivers's data from elsewhere in Andalusia confirm my own observations:

It is a matter of popular consensus that women uncontrolled by men will throw caution to the winds and indulge in the most abandoned love affairs; no matter how improbable on account of her age, the widow, it is thought, is likely to take on the predatory male attitude towards sexual promiscuity. I have often been astounded by the amatory conquests credited to septuagenarian peasant ladies. [Pitt-Rivers 1977: 82]

Widows with whom I have discussed the matter explain that it is only after their husbands have died that other men can begin to notice them openly, without fear of reprisal. I know at least one widow who is deeply hurt by the constant implications that she and others like her wanted their husbands to die. Yet despite these and similar protestations, the male popular opinion of heightened sexuality in widowhood persists in San Blas.

Horns, super-goats, and the preservation of masculinity

For men, women are dangerous not only because they try to sap their husbands' strength, but also because their intense sexuality creates the constant threat that they will enter into an adulterous union. Men operate in daily affairs on the assumption that their wives want to deceive them, and in fact will deceive them if given the least opportunity. José Cutileiro's description of male attitudes in southern Portugal holds equally true for San Blas:

A man enters marriage hoping that he will not become a cuckold. The bride's virginity and the wife's fidelity are the basic moral assumptions on which the family is built. The ideal state for a woman is a state of purity, but purity is only part of her nature: her *vício* (vice), the predisposition responsible for the potential social dangers attached to her active sexual life, is also part of it. [Cutileiro 1971: 99]

A wife's infidelity threatens the moral reputation of her entire family. But it affects no one so profoundly as her cuckolded husband, who is charged with the responsibility of harnessing her rampant sexuality and confining it within the secret walls of their bedroom.

In San Blas, as throughout Spain, the predominant symbol of the cuckold is the *cabrón*, or super-goat, and its *cuernos*, or horns. The term *cabrón*, in fact, has become so purely synonymous with cuckold that it is no longer usefully applied to the actual male animal, who is referred to instead as a *macho cabrillo* ("little male goat") or simply, where conversational context permits, *macho* ("male"). And the goat's horns have become so representative of the cuckold, as well, that the word *cornudo*, horned one, is employed interchangeably with *cabrón*.

Interestingly, in the techical use of the term, the *cabrón* is not simply a cuckold, but rather a cuckold who is aware that his wife is engaged in extramarital affairs and continues to live with her despite this knowledge. According to the San Blas male view of the world, any woman is capable of sexual deceit; in fact, as I have already pointed out, men commonly state that "All women are whores" ("*Todas las mujeres son putas*"), and then, if this remark is greeted with surprise, emphatically repeat the word "All ("*Todas*").

What is shameful for a man is not so much that his wife should suddenly adopt her natural role. The true humiliation comes, first, from having been unable to control her, and second, from tacitly tolerating her behavior by continuing to reside with her. In fact, this type of conscious cuckoldry, for all I can determine, is extremely rare. Close informants of mine could name only two known cases in 1975 and 1976.

Nonetheless, no man in San Blas is anxious for his wife to have an affair, even if he never learns of it. The specter of a wife's infidelity haunts men daily, for they know full well that:

El cabrón es el último que se entera.
The cuckold is the last one to find out.

For this reason, I believe, men seem completely unashamed to admit that, *so far as they know*, their wives have been faithful, but that they can never be one hundred percent certain. By stating this repeatedly, men advertise their total ignorance of their wives' behavior, should the latter actually have betrayed them. In this manner they demonstrate at least a technical disqualification from the category *cabrón*, and they announce to their friends that they are ready to hear the worst.

In matters like this, however, technicalities are hardly satisfactory. Men worry constantly that people might be pointing to them behind their backs, pitying them for their wives' infidelity and yet embarrassed to confide the truth to them. For this reason, the people of San Blas are hesitant even to state that a child, especially a newborn, looks like the mother, for this is an indirect way of raising the question of paternal identity. In San Blas, no matter what their actual appearance, the vast majority of newborn infants are said to resemble their legal fathers. Such a statement is, at the very least, a correct and polite opinion to express to an infant's parents and kinsmen, despite what might be said privately.

Throughout the course of a year in the field, I was told countless times that because of my coloring it would not be unusual if my wife gave birth to a blond baby. What most of the dark-haired men of San Blas fear, however, is that this fate shold happen to them. Everyone cites the curious case of a married couple from a nearby town who emigrated several years ago to work in northern Europe. The woman became pregnant and returned some time before her husband to give birth among family and friends. Her progeny, however, turned out to be a pair of black twins. It is said that when her husband returned to town, he took one look at them, and left that very day. She later was also forced to leave in disgrace. The story, which is likely legendary, clearly projects male anxieties about the actual paternity of their children. (It has nothing whatever to do with race relations.)

Men scrutinize all the available evidence to assure themselves that their wives have remained faithful, for it is said that if a woman is having an affair, she will do anything to prevent her husband from discovering it. Her best means of disguise, claim the men of San Blas, is to be overtly affectionate toward her husband, in order to dispel his possible doubts. The social consequence of this view, of course, is that husbands and wives display little open affection for one another. Wives know they if they cling with too much frequency to their husbands, they not only place their despised and threatening sexuality on display, but also arouse the suspicions of their husbands. Men, too, refrain from embracing their wives in public too often, lest they encourage the women to act similarly, and thereby endanger the family's reputation.

But we have yet to ask the critical question of why men should feel so threatened by the prospect of female infidelity, especially considering that such infidelity is actually rare. To answer, we must reconsider the meaning of the metaphors by which the cuckold is described. Julian Pitt-Rivers, who first introduced this matter into the anthropological literature nearly a generation ago, is still the only Hispanicist to have given it serious thought. One passage from his now-classic *People of the Sierra* is crucial:

> The word *cabrón* (a he-goat), the symbol of male sexuality in many contexts, refers not to him whose manifestation of that quality is the cause of the trouble but to him whose implied lack of manliness has allowed the other to replace him. To make a man a cuckold is in the current Spanish idiom, "to put horns on him." I suggest that the horns are figuratively placed upon the head of the wronged husband in signification of his failure to defend a value vital to the social order. He has fallen under the domination of its enemy and must wear his symbol. He is ritually defiled. [Pitt-Rivers 1971: 116]

Here, as in another passage (116), Pitt-Rivers implies that the horns themselves symbolize the masculinity and virility of the cuckolder – indeed that they are the emblem of the cuckolder, who places them symbolically on the head of the cuckold.

Although Pitt-Rivers's interpretation of Andalusian symbolism is appealing and has been uncritically accepted, it needs to be challenged. For, if we continue to rely on this interpretation, the reason behind the male preoccupation with being cuckolded will forever elude us. In San Blas, as in Pitt-Rivers's community, people commonly use the expression "to put horns on him" as meaning "to make a man a cuckold." But it is not the male rival who puts on the horns, as Pitt-Rivers implies; it is the wife! Thus, one man will say of another, *"Pobrecillo, que no sabe que su mujer le está metiendo los cuernos"* ("Poor guy, for he doesn't know that his wife is placing the horns on him"). Men also wonder aloud of their wives, *"No sé si me habría meti'o los cuernos"* ("I don't know if she ever put horns on me"). In these as in countless other expressions, it is clear that it is the cuckold's wife, not his rival, who bears primary responsibility for the horns on his head.[13]

It is only by clarifying this seemingly minor, yet critical, point that we can explain why men fear being cuckolded: To be cuckolded is to be transformed symbolically into a woman. The horns, originally associated with or belonging to the woman, are placed upon the head of a man, thereby feminizing him. The cuckold not only wears horns but also simultaneously becomes symbolically converted into a *cabrón*, or super-goat. And the goat, as we have seen, is closely associated with womankind. Here it is perhaps significant that female goats, unlike female sheep, have horns. It is, in fact, safe to extrapolate and say that goathorns in San Blas, and probably throughout Andalusia, represent the harmful, devilish dimensions of the feminine character. The cuckold, who suffers the consequences of his wife's uncontrolled sexuality, becomes forever branded with this female symbol.

But it is necessary to state, too, that goathorns are sometimes said to grow from within the cuckold, as well as being placed upon him from without. The men of San Blas are careful never to rub their foreheads, lest people begin to wonder whether horns are beginning to disturb them. "I wouldn't touch myself on the forehead too often," advised one close friend. "I don't even like to *think* of touching myself there," stated another, "much less actually do it." I remember, in particular, one uncle's campaign to try to get his nephew to leave his girlfriend because she was reputed to have slept with a string of other men. After private conversations proved to have no effect, the uncle and some of his friends resorted to public ridicule. In the marketplace, the bars, and wherever else crowds were gathered, they would call out to the young man, "¡*Cabrón*! After you marry her, let me have a turn with her, will you? She's a real piece! The horns are already sprouting from you! (¡*Ya te están saliendo los cuernos*!)"

The thought of goathorns is especially horrible to the men of San Blas when they are said to emerge from within the body, for this indicates that the man not only wears a symbol of feminity but also to some extent actually becomes a woman. No wonder, then, that men are so fearful of their wives: By an act of infidelity, an act toward which women are in any case naturally inclined, a wife can deprive her husband of his precious masculinity, and even go so far as to convert him into a member of her own sex. This potentiality, of course, invests her with an awesome power.

Male genitalia and masculine behavior

In order best to understand the third threat to masculine identity – the enforced adoption of a symbolically feminine, passive role in the sexual act – we need to examine further some masculine notions of how the male body relates to the male being. We will begin with an incident that occurred while I was collecting a genealogy from a young, highly educated member of the land-owning elite, a native of San Blas and at the time town judge. During the course of the interview, I found out, to my surprise, that one of my informant's brothers was married to an English woman. "To a Spaniard it's not important who he marries," said the judge jokingly, "not even if she's from England!" With that, a San Blas bureaucrat, who was listening in, quickly interjected, "Didn't you know? Spain conquered America not by the sword, but by the prick (*polla*)." Eager to better the bureaucrat, the judge then recalled that one of his professors at the University of Madrid used to say, "America was conquered by Spaniards who were carrying the cross in one hand and the prick in the other."

These ideas, to be sure, were stated in typical San Blas jest. Nonetheless, they reveal an important component of the masculine self-image throughout Andalusia: The locus of power and will, of emotions and strength, lies within the male genitals. Men speak as if they are impelled to act according to opinions and desires that originate in their testicles or penis. In this particular speech pattern, the most common colloquial expressions for penis – *chorra, polla, pijo* – and those for testicles – *cojones, huevos* (literally, "eggs") – are employed interchangeably. Thus, if a man impulsively decides to miss a day's work and is asked to justify himself, he will most likely say, "*Porque me sale de los cojones,*" literally, "Because it comes to me from the balls." Similarly, if a man's wife should ask why he did not come home earlier the previous evening, he will answer, "*Porque no me salió de la chorra*" ("Because it didn't come out of my prick"). In all such cases, the speaker proclaims total freedom from obligations and responsibility on the grounds that conformity to the rules is contrary to his will, which emanates in some fashion from his genitalia. To rationalize one's actions by reference to the penis or testicles is, above all, to assert one's complete individuality. It is an extreme, yet very common, expression of the obstinate refusal to comply with ordinary behavioral expectations. And just as this particular manifestation of the human will is somehow related to the male genitalia, so too is it perceived as being especially characteristic of men. For nonconformity of any kind requires the fearlessness and sense of abandon that only men are thought to possess and that, with a single exception to be cited shortly, they alone are permitted to express.

This is why a man who is considered especially assertive, aggressive, and fearless in San Blas, is called a *cojonudo*, a "big-balled man." His extreme masculine behavior is projected linguistically onto his genitals, as if normal-sized testicles were not large enough to accomodate the full force of his personal strength and will. There is also the rare woman who is called a *cojonuda*, a "big-balled woman," because she is courageous and determined, especially in business affairs, and shows herself willing to work alongside her spouse for the greater financial benefit of the household. Of such female entrepreneurs it is said that "they have balls inside," and that "God made a mistake, for they should have been born as men." A *cojonuda* is equipped with a highly desirable personality trait ordinarily reserved to men, and therefore she is similarly associated metaphorically with masculine physical attributes.

Sometimes, however, even the strongest of human beings is overwhelmed by life circumstances beyond his control. To act *por huevos* or *por cojones* ("by the balls") is to do something out of force or necessity. Thus, if one has to pay an outstanding bill lest his property be attached, the payment is made *por cojones*. Similarly, to flatter a potential employer, a detested member of the elite, is to act *por huevos*, for if one were wealthy and independent, he would certainly not stoop to such demeaning behavior. A woman may also speak of being forced into an action by circumstances beyond her control, but she will employ the euphemism *por papas* ("by potatoes") or *por pantalones* ("by the trousers"), instead of openly saying "by the balls."

Let us now turn to the question of the degree to which the people of San Blas actually believe that the penis and testicles are repositories of masculine personality traits – of force and will and determination – in the manner, say, that we in the United States locate these characteristics in the brain. For the people of San Blas, does masculinity actually reside within the male genitalia, or is it only spoken of *as if* it resided there?

On the one hand, men justify some of their speech patterns by making an explicit analogy between their emotions and bodily processes. When a man becomes angry and is at the height of fury, just before lashing out with a punch, he shouts at his opponent "¡*Me sudan los huevos de tí*!" ("My balls sweat from you!"). By way of explanation, men claim that this is said only when a person is so furious that his emotions, rather than physical labor or the heat of the day, are enough to make his testicles sweat. Similarly, when a man is fearful with what seems to be good reason (in one such case, a man was trapped inside a truck that was perched over a cliff), he can say that he has *cojones en la garganta* – "balls in the throat," the equivalent of our "heart in the mouth."[14] Men claim that even though this is the standard way of expressing legitimate fear, a man might just as well say that his testicles are anywhere in his body other than the place they belong. The critical metaphoric message is that the testicles are displaced from ordinary position, as is said actually to happen, through the shriveling of penis and testicles, when a man is afraid.

Of course, these examples demonstrate a conceptual link between emotions and their effect on the male genitalia, not that the genitalia are themselves repositories for the emotions. Regarding the latter issue, a fortuitous circumstance allows us to assert that the people of San Blas almost certainly speak *as if* masculine attributes reside in the genitalia, rather than believing that they actually do. It is well known that the former mayor of San Blas, a man who held that post for nearly thirty years, lost one of his testicles in combat, and for this reason was believed unable to have children. The man ruled with the tight political control required of mayors by the Franco regime in the years immediately following the Civil War (1936–9), and was decorated by that regime for his valiant service in the Blue Division, the volunteer unit that Franco deployed to Germany during the Second World War to assist Hitler. This man is detested by some, revered by others. But all say that "even though he is missing a testicle, he has acted in this town as if he had seven or eight of them." Reference to the genitals in matters of masculinity is clearly metaphoric.

So is the following popular joke, which arose in San Blas several years ago, when the town acquired (through appointment by the provincial governor) its first woman mayor. "In San Blas, we're going ass backwards. First we had a mayor with two balls, next we had a mayor with one ball, and now we have a mayor with *no* balls!" It is difficult, given the overweening importance of the personality attributes associated with the male genitals, for men to understand how a town can hope to function and survive under such circumstances.

The threat of anal penetration

We have been forced, in the previous section, to digress from our main discussion of how women threaten men in order to demonstrate a stark contrast between the biological imagery of masculinity and that of femininity, to which we now turn. If masculine behavior, for the men of San Blas, has its conceptual locus in the male genital region, then feminine behavior is concentrated linguistically on the anus. Men show themselves to be constantly aware that the anus can be used in homosexual encounters, in which case the passive partner is perceived as playing the feminine role, and indeed of being converted symbolically into a woman. It is this sexual transformation that men fear. As a defense, male speech forms reveal a constant attempt to force masculine rivals into the feminine role, in a never-ending quest to avoid adopting this role themselves.

Perhaps the most common expression along these lines is *tomarlo por culo*, literally "to take it by the ass," which has more or less the same meaning as the colloquial "Shove it up your ass" in American English. The important difference, however, comes with usage rather than meaning. In San Blas I have never actually heard one man insult another by telling him to "Take it by the ass." This would be an uncommonly grave attack, in which the rival would in effect be transformed symbolically into a woman. Instead, men who are angry at one another commonly state behind each other's back that they are going to *mandarlo tomar por culo* – "order him [the rival] to take it by the ass." When women are present, the euphemism *saco* ("sack" or "bag") is substituted for the word *culo* ("ass"), a clear example of symbolism by analogy to biological function.

Men generally think of strategic weakness in daily affairs, be they economic or political, in terms of potential anal penetration. To *bajar los pantalones* ("lower your trousers"), for example, implies being forced into readiness for phallic attack by a male rival. On one occasion, two wealthy landowners were discussing the recent labor shortage in the olive harvest, made all the more serious by their inability to mechanize. In disgust, one of them blurted out, "We're fed up with having to *bajar los pantalones a los obreros*" ("lower our trousers for the workers").

But again, as with the male attitude toward horns, we have to ask whether speech patterns regarding the anus are merely metaphoric or whether they reflect an actual fear of playing the passive role in a homosexual encounter. Here, medical beliefs and practices can lead us to the answer. Throughout Spain, suppositories are one of the most widespread forms in which drugs are administered, and they are regularly prescribed for both children and adults. In San Blas, men and women differ radically in their views of suppositories: Women accept this form of treatment readily and without complaint, while most men categorically refuse ever to permit a suppository to be inserted into their anus. The male fear – sometimes expressed jokingly, sometimes seriously – is that through consistent use of suppositories, a man can become accustomed to having objects placed there; he may then begin to derive pleasure from it, and will become transformed into a homosexual and, worse, one who is relegated to the female, passive role. "There's a plague of suppository prescriptions here in Spain," complained one bank employee. "Can't they find some other way of curing disease?" I know of several cases in which men suffered fever and sore throat for weeks before their wives could convince them to follow the doctor's advice and use suppositories. "They think it's only for homosexuals," explained one woman, whose husband stubbornly refuses this form of medication, and whose seventy-year-old father has done likewise throughout his entire life.

Interestingly, men in San Blas, as throughout the Mediterranean (Dundes and Falassí 1975: 189; Dundes, Leach, and Ozkok 1970), are unafraid to joke about playing the phallic, "male" part in homosexual intercourse. This role, at least, is consistent with masculine notions of genital assertion and aggression. It is, rather, the dread of assuming a feminine posture – of being the victim of sexual attack, instead of the perpetrator – that preoccupies the men of San Blas.

Conclusion

To conclude the discussion, I wish to turn briefly to the problem posed earlier in this essay. If, as is the case, men are socially superior to women, and throughout all stages of life actually enjoy a good deal more freedom of action than do women, why do they portray themselves ideologically as potentially vulnerable and weak, and women as hostile and aggressive? Why do they assume a psychologically defensive position, when their appropriate behavioral role is assertive?

Although I can offer no definitive answers at this time, a number of speculative ideas present themselves. The first, and least satisfactory when standing on its own, is the historico-geographical explanation: Male ideology in San Blas is simply the local variant of ideas found throughout the Mediterranean. It is true, as I have tried casually to demonstrate with comparative remarks sprinkled throughout the text, that male ideology in San Blas has its counterparts in southern Italy, Portugal, Greece, and elsewhere in southern Europe. It also bears striking resemblance to Muslim sexual ideology, as presented most recently and effectively by Fatima Mernissi (1975), who emphasizes the awareness and fear of women as active sexual beings in traditional North Africa, and the consequent seclusion of women, which that awareness and fear entail. Actually, if we had to seek a native explanation for San Blas attitudes, we would find it to be historical, specifically based on the centuries-long Moorish occupation of Andalusia. Men and women in San Blas believe that they carry "Moorish blood," and that this racial heritage accounts for their reputedly passionate disposition. They are like the Moors, they claim, in practically everything except religion – and, of course, in the fact that they lack the institution of the harem, a void about which the men of San Blas lose no opportunity for joking.

There, of course, exists a retrievable history behind the spread of similar sexual attitudes throughout the Mediterranean, but the precise lines of influence have never adequately been traced. Nor, in any case, would such a history explain the persistence of a particular ideological configuration, or its meaning in the specific context of San Blas. Alternatively, we may consider a vastly different type of explanation, one based on the psychoanalytic principle of projection. If we could demonstrate that men attribute to women motives that they (the men) themselves hold, then we might at least have some dynamic explanation for their sexual ideas.

Projection is appealing at least as a partial explanation because, even through it cannot be proved, it seems to fit a number of the facts. For instance, men constantly and openly covet woman; men believe that women constantly crave after men, even though there is little in female words or deeds to confirm their opinion. Similarly, men complain about being tied down to a single wife and to family obligations; they believe that women secretly work to free themselves from these obligations, when all the evidence indicates that women are unfailingly devoted to house and home. I believe that the men of San Blas do project their own feelings onto their wives and other women, thereby helping to alleviate whatever guilt those feelings might evoke. Yet, short of actually psychoanalyzing a large number of men, the validity of this explanation must remain in doubt; the explanation has to be assumed, taken on faith. And in any case there is a preferable alternative that we can call upon from among the overt features of San Blas culture itself.

The alternative is to suggest that, in limited but important ways, San Blas women really are hostile and powerful. Their hostility is born of legitimate protest against and frustration at the restrictions imposed upon them. To be sure, most women love their husbands and have a right to feel hurt when men insinuate that they want their husbands to die; after all, the vast majority of women spend countless hours devoting themselves to meeting their spouses' needs, and to providing them an affectionate, nurturant home. Yet some widows, in retrospect, admit that they are better off alone and quote the popular San Blas saying,

Te casaste, te cagaste.
You got married, you shit on yourself.

In fact, in one conversation between a group of married women concerning the topic of widowhood, not one could think of a widow whom she regarded as worse off, economically or otherwise, than when she was married. In part, this may be explained by the fact that married men invariably spend a good portion of the family income in treating their friends to drinks in the bars. In part, too, women are resentful of the vast amounts of time that husbands spend away from home. If men feel trapped by marriage, then women can legitimately consider themselves even more so, and transmit their complaints through means both subtle and overt to their husbands. It is hardly surprising, then, that men occasionally become aware of their wives' frustration and anger, and that they should try to absolve themselves of responsibility by placing these female sentiments in the framework of a male-oriented sexual ideology.

But we have yet to explain why women should be attributed not only with unkind motives, but also with the power to make them matter. There is no doubt that, given certain premises of San Blas culture, the attribution of female power is at least partially valid. Women may not exert formal influence over the course of most daily affairs (the female mayor, a special instance, was obviously appointed to her post because of her superconservative frame of mind, not out of any desire to change the position of women); but, in their sexual behavior, they have ultimate control over the fate of their families. Pitt-Rivers has provided a pithy and wholly accurate formulation of how family and individual honor are closely intertwined in Andalusia: "There is a near-paradox in the fact that while honour is a collective attribute shared by the nuclear family it is also personal and dependent upon the will of the individual; individual honour derives from individual conduct but produces consequences for others who share collective honour with this individual'' (Pitt-Rivers 1977: 78).

In San Blas, a family's honor is probably more dependent on the sexual conduct of its women than on any other single factor. Female purity and fidelity must be maintained at all cost, lest the entire family's reputation be tainted. Women with blotched sexual records destroy chances for their daughters to secure a good marriage; in a single unguarded moment, they can transform their husbands into laughingstocks. The fact that personality attributes are considered to run in the blood, and to be inherited, means that virtually all of a woman's consanguines are affected by her behavior as well. A woman, therefore, is imbued with a good deal of power, insofar as she is the repository of her family's good name.

Considering that San Blas women, like those described by Mernassi in North Africa (1975), are thought to be possessed of a seethingly active sexual nature, the husband's prime responsibility is to control the conduct of his wife and daughters. If these females should go astray, their behavior reflects more on him than on themselves. It is no wonder, then, that men try to restrict their wives' and daughters' activities. Male sexual ideology in San Blas cannot be dismissed as a mere rationalization for the political and economic exploitation of women. Rather, it must be understood on its own terms as a strong motivating force in determining relationships between the sexes.

Notes

1 This essay was written on the basis of information collected in 1975–6, and in the summer of 1977. The research was supported by generous grants from the National Institute of Child Health and Human Development and from the American Council of Learned Societies. An earlier version of the essay was presented at the Social Anthropology Faculty Seminar at the University of California, Berkeley, and at a colloquium sponsored by the Latin American Studies Center at California State University, San Diego. I am grateful to Tom Davies, David Ringrose, and other friends and colleagues who attended these functions for their instructive comments. I also wish to thank Alan Dundes, Sulamith Potter, and Judith Brandes for their assistance, though I, of course, assume full responsibility for the data and interpretations expressed herein. San Blas is a pseudonym. Large segments of this essay originally appeared in Chapter 5 of *Metaphors of masculinity: sex and status in Andalusian folklore* (Philadelphia: University of Pennsylvania Press, 1980). They are reprinted here with permission.

2 There are similar proverbs in Old Castile, where there exists a more egalitarian relationship between the sexes than in Andalusia; however, these proverbs are employed to describe the great power of a woman's love (Brandes 1975b: 177) rather than the scheming nature of females in general.

3 I have refrained in this essay from analyzing binary oppositions per se, although it should be clear from the discussion that they are an important structural feature in San Blas male ideology. Henry Schwarz has carried out a binary structural analysis for a town in Extremadura (Schwarz 1976: 115–40).

4 In Christian symbolism, of course, sheep are of extraordinary significance, sometimes being associated with Christ himself. One scholar asserts that ''sheep are

accorded a larger share of attention in the Bible than any other animal and their names – ewe, lamb, ram, sheep, and flock – are found seven hundred and forty-two times, in seven hundred and three verses, which exceed one forty-fifth of the whole number of verses'' (Wiley 1957: 370). An important segment of the Roman Catholic Mass is entitled ''Lamb of God.'' Interesting discussions of animal symbolism in Christianity can be found in Ferguson (1954), Rowland (1973), and Wiley (1957).

5 In Lope de Vega's *Fuente ovejuna*, for example, Laurencia addresses the men of her town as *ovejas* or ''sheep'' (1969: 120). Bernarda, in Lorca's *La casa de Bernarda Alba*, refers critically to the women who have come to pay their respects at her husband's funeral as ''*una manada de cabras*,'' ''a herd of goats'' (García Lorca 1960: 1361).

6 Bibliography on the evil eye is vast. See Gifford (1958), Meerlo (1971), and the references contained therein.

7 For extensive discussions of nicknaming in Spain, see Brandes (1975c) and Pitt-Rivers (1971: 160–9).

8 Despite the usual assumption that the gender of Spanish (and other Latin-derived) words is arbitrary, many Spanish speakers have told me that serpents must be female because the term *serpiente* is feminine. Death (*la muerte*) is also considered to be feminine for the same reason. The issue is complex and obviously cannot be resolved here. I merely report that there is supporting evidence from informants for my interpretation.

9 This is not to suggest that all psychoanalytic thought conforms to Jones's formula. Roheim early recognized that the snake's infamous tendency to devour, i.e., incorporate, makes it analogous to a ''dangerous vagina'' (Roheim 1924: 408). More recently, Slater has offered a sensitive and subtle analysis of the bisexual symbolic qualities of the serpent (Slater 1971: 75–122). Here the serpent is portrayed as particularly feminine in nature, for it is the ingestive, incorporative function of the beast that receives primary emphasis.

10 One joke, for example, tells of a Spanish emigrant working on a German farm. Among all the laborers, he was the only Spaniard. One day they held a contest to see who could get the most milk out of the cows, but they assigned to the Spaniard the only bull on the farm. When the laborers presented their results, they each had milked eighteen to twenty liters, except the Spaniard, who brought in only half a liter. Said the foreman, ''Aren't you ashamed to show up with only this small quality of *leche* [milk]?'' ''But, sir,'' the Spaniard replied, ''you gave me a bull to milk and I had to jerk him off to get even this much *leche* [semen]!''

11 In parts of Nigeria, too, a man's lifetime supply of semen is considered to be finite (Foster 1967: 309).

12 Most San Blas men, in fact, do not abstain from sexual activity, despite their undeniable fear of its long-term consequences.

13 Occasionally the people of San Blas speak as if it is the illicit couple who together put the horns on the cuckold, but this speech form is not as common as the one in which the wife alone puts horns on the husband. Never is the husband's rival spoken of as the sole source of the horns.

Very rarely it is also said that a man has put horns on his wife by engaging in an extramarital affair. This usage, I suspect, is a recent introduction into Spanish sexual ideology, but, because of its rarity, I have not investigated this notion thoroughly enough to speak of it with authority.

14 In San Blas, as throughout the Western world (Firth 1973: 231), the heart is also considered an important repository of emotions, though this organ has not found its way into popular speech nearly to the degree that the genitalia have.

References

Blum, Richard, and Blum, Eva. 1965. *Health and healing in rural Greece: a study of three communities*. Stanford: Stanford University Press.

—— 1970. *The dangerous hour: the lore and culture of crisis and mystery in rural Greece*. London: Chatto and Windus.

Brandes, Stanley. 1975a. *Migration, kinship, and community: tradition and transition in a Spanish village*. New York: Academic Press.

—— 1975b. "The selection process in proverb use: a Spanish example." *Southern Folklore Quarterly* 38: 167–86.

—— 1975c. "The social and demographic implications of nicknaming in Navanogal, Spain." *American Ethnologist* 2: 139–48.

Campbell, John. 1964. *Honour, family, and patronage: a study of institutions and moral values in a Greek mountain community*. Oxford: Clarendon.

Cutileiro, Jose. 1971. *A Portugese rural society*. Oxford: Clarendon.

Douglas, Mary. 1966. *Purity and danger: an analysis of concepts of pollution and taboo*. London: Routledge and Kegan Paul.

Dundes, Alan and Falassi, Alessandro. 1975. *La terra in piazza: an interpretation of the Palio of Siena*. Berkeley and Los Angeles: University of California Press.

Dundes, Alan; Leach, Jerry W.; and Ozkok, Bora. 1970. "The strategy of Turkish boys' verbal dueling rhymes." *Journal of American Folklore* 83: 225–49.

Ferguson, George. 1954. *Signs and symbols in Christian art*. London and Oxford: Oxford University Press.

Firth, Raymond. 1973. *Symbols: public and private*. Ithaca, N.Y.: Cornell University Press.

Foster, George. 1967. "Peasant society and the image of limited good." In *Peasant society: a reader*, ed. Jack Potter, May Diaz, and George Foster, pp. 300–23. Boston: Little, Brown.

Freeman, Susan Tax. 1970. *Neighbors: the social contract in a Castilian hamlet*. Chicago: University of Chicago Press.

Friedl, Ernestine. 1967. "The position of women: appearance and reality." *Anthropological Quarterly* 40: 97–108.

García Lorca, Federico. 1960. "La casa de Bernarda Alba." In *Obras completas*, pp. 1349–1442. Madrid: Aguilar. (First published 1936.)

Gifford, Edward S., Jr. 1958. *The evil eye: studies in the folklore of vision*. New York: Macmillan.

Jones, Ernest. 1949. *Papers on psychoanalysis*. Baltimore: Williams and Wilkins.

Kenny, Michael. 1966. *A Spanish tapestry: town and country in Castile*. New York: Harper and Row.

Lope de Vega. 1968. *Fuente ovejuna*. Ed. William E. Colford. Woodbury, N.Y.: Barron's Educational Series. (First printed 1619.)

Mannheim, Karl. 1955. *Ideology and utopia*. New York: Harcourt Brace Jovanovich.

Meerlo, Joest A. M. 1971. *Intuition and the evil eye: the natural history of a superstition*. Wassenaar, The Netherlands: Servire.

Mernissi, Fatima. 1975. *Beyond the veil: male-female dynamics in a modern Muslim society*. Cambridge, Mass.: Schenkman.

Pitt-Rivers, Julian A. 1971. *The people of the Sierra*. 2d Ed. Chicago: University of Chicago Press.

—— 1977. *The fate of Shechem, or the politics of sex: essays in the anthropology of the Mediterranean*. Cambridge: Cambridge University Press.

Real Academia Española. 1956. *Diccionario de la lengua Española*. 18th ed. Madrid.

Riegelhaupt, Joyce. 1967. "Saloio women: an analysis of informal and formal political and economic roles of Portugese peasant women." *Anthropological Quarterly* 40: 109–26.

Roheim, Geza. 1924. "Totemism and the fight with the dragon." *International Journal of Psychoanalysis* 5: 407–8.

Rowland, Beryl. 1973. *Animals with human faces: a guide to animal symbolism.* Knoxville: University of Tennessee Press.

Schieffelin, Edward L. 1976. *The sorrow of the lonely and the burning of the dancers.* New York: St. Martin's Press.

Schwarz, Henry F., III. 1976. "Modelos dualísticos en la cultura de una comunidad tradicional española." In *Expresiones actuales de la cultura del pueblo*, ed. Carmelo Lison-Tolosana, pp. 115–40. Madrid: Centro de Estudios del Valle de los Caidos.

Slater, Philip E. 1971. *The glory of Hera: Greek mythology and the Greek family.* Boston: Beacon Press.

Wiley, Lulu Runsey. 1957. *Bible animals: mammals of the Bible.* New York: Vantage Press.

7

Pigs, women, and the men's house in Amazonia:
AN ANALYSIS OF SIX MUNDURUCÚ MYTHS

Leslee Nadelson

This essay is an exploration of Mundurucú concepts of sexual identity.[1] Rather than approaching this topic through a general consideration of the relevant ethnography (Murphy 1954, 1956, 1957, 1958, 1960; Murphy and Murphy 1970), I have chosen to focus on a set of myths.[2] My analysis will show that these texts contain basic statements of Mundurucú concepts of the nature of men and women and the consequences of their interaction. In particular, the myths are concerned with the creation of a symbolically, socially, and biologically viable male identity.

Although this analysis is intended primarily as a contribution to our understanding of Mundurucú culture, it also contains ideas that have wider application. In dealing with material that is concerned with sexual symbolism, a central task must be to assess the culturally specific content of notions of "maleness" and "femaleness." These general notions, though often basic to a cultural system insofar as they seem to recur constantly, are often *not* basic in the sense that they are not unitary, consistent ideas. On the contrary, as I will illustrate with the Mundurucú material, the idea of maleness may subsume notions that are opposed and mutually exclusive. For the Mundurucú, one mode of "maleness" is achieved by shunning women, while another mode consists in seeking them. Because this is a conceptual opposition that is not unique to the Mundurucú, an understanding of its full implications in one culture will aid in understanding systems with similar social and symbolic organization.

In this essay, I suggest the usefulness of thinking about male/female distinctions as emanating from an underlying dichotomy of homosexual and heterosexual structures. By these terms I mean to indicate a very general range of social, conceptual, and possibly but not necessarily, sexual patterns.[3] In the Mundurucú case, the importance of the men's house and the extensive separation of the sexes, make the model of two parallel social systems, one homosexually composed and the other heterosexually composed, relatively easy to detect. Whether this conceptualization significantly illuminates and organizes the data, the reader must judge after considering the analysis in its entirety. However, some general advantages of this approach may be pointed out.

Because of the necessity of considering "maleness" and "femaleness" as symbols to be analyzed rather than natural categories to be taken for granted, the sheer simplicity of the homosexual/heterosexual opposition has the appeal of elegance. In the realm of sexual interaction (social, verbal, or physical), the most basic distinction we can make is between same and mixed term interaction.

Furthermore, when the "shun woman"/"seek woman" motifs that emerge in the Mundurucú material are tied to homosexual/heterosexual counterparts, we are better able to understand culturally created manifestations of conflict within individuals, for the demands of one system must violate the demands of the other. Any cultural system that imbues its male homosexual structures with a strong "shun woman" imperative and fails to compartmentalize this system adequately, must place individuals in a serious cultural bind. Because social systems generally require that men reproduce (except for those providing celibate roles), there is always potential conflict. For the Mundurucú, where the homosexual structures are pervasive and serve to organize the majority of traditional life, the common complaints of impotence are not inconsistent with such a model of sociosexual organization. Or, to take a more geographically distant example, among the Mae Enga of New Guinea, where all male bachelor ritual is accompanied by a strong "shun woman" ideology (in the form of pollution beliefs), men approach marriage and any heterosexual contact with the greatest anxiety and reluctance (Meggitt 1964).

Finally, viewing sexual symbolism as arising from two subsystems that have very different implications makes it possible to see how any symbolic formation may lead a sort of double life. From the point of view of a man adopting a "homosexual" stance (as would be the case in male-only ritual activity), that which may be categorized as "female," may also be thought of as an aspect of his other, "male heterosexual," self. The reproductive symbolism commonly found in male-only initiatory ritual in the form of rebirth imagery is often imbued with a seemingly "female" quality. Such symbols may well refer more to the appropriation of the reproductive power of heterosexuality and less to a ritual reverence for women.[4]

The myths dealt with in this essay constitute the basic Mundurucú creation cycle and feature the major culture hero, Karusakaibö. The explicit accomplishments that the texts narrate are the creation of wild pigs (the most important game animal) and women. We will see that this explicit creation is accompanied by the disguised and implicit creation of a key (if not the key) Mundurucú social institution, the men's house.

Among the Mundurucú, men tell myths and women listen to them. This plus evidence internal to the myths convince me that the myths are best understood as expressing specifically male formulations. Thus, this essay is essentially about men and the creation of male identity. The myths encourage and embody culturally informed fantasy because of their ability to posit a world in which the constraints of real life may be suspended. The mythic form invites a man to think about how life *might* look . . . were it not for reality.[5] When reality intrudes as a limiting factor, the myths become a bargaining process in which a compromise between fantasy and reality must be reached. The narrative line displays an evolutionary process in which a dilemma, posed at the outset, is explored and overcome through the construction of a solution acceptable to the demands of Mundurucú fantasy and the exigencies of the Mundurucú image of nature. That solution is the men's house, the covert subject of the myths.

In discussing Mundurucú culture and the symbolic world that infuses these stories with meaning and vitality, we will be referring to a "conservative" group of Mundurucú who are least affected by the general involvement with the Brazilian rubber trade. This group, numbering around 360 in 1960, live in the traditional setting of mixed forest and savannah between the Cururú River and the Das Tropas River and continue the traditional economic activities, hunting, fishing, and slash and burn horticulture.

Although the garden and its products exact long hours of labor from the people and contribute the staple food, manioc, nothing that comes from the garden is endowed with notable status. The men perform the heavy tasks of clearing the land but the women do most of the daily chores. In addition, the women must convert the manioc into edible form by ridding it of poisonous prussic acid. The endless and arduous task of making palatable manioc flour, "farinha," is performed by the women in the village farinha shed.

The chief occupation of the men, both in terms of importance and time, is hunting. This is done in cooperative groups and is considered the only truly prestigious male occupation. So, too, meat is considered the only truly "good" food. Men also fish, but although fishing may contribute importantly to the diet, it does not compare with hunting in prestige. Both men and women almost always perform their economic duties in cooperation with others, but this cooperation is confined to single-sex units. The continuation of rigidly separated male and female labor is one of the crucial patterns that set the conservative savannah villages apart from more acculturated Mundurucú settlements. In the latter, much to the horror of traditionally oriented males, the men regularly help in manioc processing.

Although descent is determined through a patrilineal system, the Mundurucú practice matrilocal residence. Therefore, the majority of married men of a village are not connected through formal lineal ties.

The village consists of from three to five dwelling houses and the men's house. Because of the matrilocal preference, each dwelling house consists of a core group of consanguineally related women. Their young children, including boys not old enough to live in the men's house, live with the women. All the adult males, both married and unmarried, reside in the men's house and are in contact with the dwellings of their wives or mothers in a visitor capacity only. The acculturated villages, in contrast, have no men's houses.

The traditional men's house is not merely a gathering place for men. It is their primary residence, where they eat, sleep, make tools, and so on. The structure consists of a lean-to where all the men of the village hang their hammocks. Attached to the lean-to is a small enclosure housing the three sacred flutes of the village. These three instruments are thought to house ancestor spirits and are nominally connected to the patrilineal clan system. They must be properly played and "fed" with a meal brought into the flute chamber. Some food taken from the men's communal meal is offered nightly to the mouth of each instrument. The playing and feeding of the flutes constitute the main ceremonial activity. Formerly, an elaborate ritual system that involved the taking of trophy heads and an initiatory system existed.

The Karusakaibö creation cycle consists of six myths. The first two, which are long and complex, will be presented individually, each text followed by analysis. The last four myths are much shorter and will be presented together. The section of analysis that appears with the texts is intimately related to the developmental aspects of the myths and is thus quite concerned with the "plot."[6] The next section of analysis addresses itself to more strictly structural features and includes an examination of the men's house in the context of wider village organization.

Myth text I. Karusakaibö and the wild pigs[7]

In times long past, Karusakaibö lived in the village of Uacuparí. This settlement was not at the site of the modern Uacuparí, but was nearby.

During one dry season Karusakaibö and all the people of the village were out hunting in the forest, where they lived in temporary lean-tos. That of Karusakaibö was separated from those of the other people, and he stayed there alone with his son Korumtau. The people killed a great deal of game, but in that time there were no tapir, wild pig, or veado capoeira; the only equivalent of the wild pig was the catitú. Karusakaibö, however, hunted the nambú bird to the exclusion of all other game, and every day he sent Korumtau to the lean-tos of his sisters to trade his kill for game that their husbands had taken. On the fourth day the aunts became angry with the boy and said to him, "Your father hunts only nambú which is no good to eat, and we always have to give you food. We do not have any." Korumtau began to cry and went away. The sisters called him back, offering him food, but he would not return.

The boy returned home crying, and Karusakaibö asked him what had happened. He replied that the aunts had scolded him because the nambús did not please them. Karusakaibö said, "They will pay for this," and sent his son outside to gather the feathers of the parrot, the mutúm, the jacú, and the nambú and to bring them back to him. There were many feathers outside, for Karusakaibö had killed many birds, and the boy gathered them and brought them back. The father transformed his son into a small bird, the taukörenjujut, and sent him out to surround the lean-tos of all the other people with the feathers. In this disguise, Korumtau flew around the lean-tos and planted the feathers in the ground, quills first. As he went about his task, he sang the song of the bird. He was nearly out of feathers when someone in one of the lean-tos called out, "Who is that singing out there," and threw a piece of burning firewood at him. The boy flew away and returned to his father.

Karusakaibö asked the returned son, "Did you put all the feathers in the ground?" The boy said that he had not finished, and his father sent him out for more feathers. He replenished his supply and finished his task in two more days.

Upon completion of his chore, Korumtau reported to Karusakaibö, and the latter told him, "Now go back and tie the feathers together at the top." For this purpose he transformed the boy into a frog and made the feathers grow to a great size. The boy, in the disguise of a frog, returned to the encircled lean-tos and climbed a tree, singing the song of the frog, "pök, pök, pök . . . " as he tied the tips of the feathers together. When he finished, the lean-tos and their environs were covered by a huge dome of feathers. He had almost completed his work when a man from one of the lean-tos hit the tree in which he was seated with a piece of firewood, causing the boy to fall to the ground. He was not hurt, however, and hopped home to his father.

Korumtau reported the successful completion of his mission to Karusakaibö who said, "We will take care of your aunts now." He then began to blow smoke in the direction of the encircled lean-tos, and it entered under the feathers in great clouds, making the people dizzy. At this point, Karusakaibö shouted at his prisoners, "Eat your food, people of Uacuparí." They misunderstood him and thought that he meant for them to have sexual intercourse. They proceeded to have coitus and made the usual grunting sounds while doing so. Gradually, these noises turned into the grunts of wild pigs and the cries of the children into the squeals of sucklings. The dense tobacco smoke choked the people, and Karusakaibö then threw husks of the fruit of the taurí tree into the pen. The people put these husks up to their noses to avoid breathing the smoke-filled air, but the husks grew onto their noses, transforming them into pig snouts. The prisoners then turned completely into wild pigs, but without hair. Karusakaibö did not like the pigs in their hairless state and asked a frog to gather hair for them. The frog said that he had none, but sent him to an anteater named Radjerapšebö. The latter gave him a quantity of anteater hair which Karusakaibö threw among the wild pigs, saying that it was for them. He then returned to the nearby village of Unacuparí.

The people who had remained in Unacuparí suspected that Karusakaibö had done something with their fellows. He denied this, saying, "No, they will come. They are still out hunting."

Karusakaibö then went back to the pigpen and planted a tacumá palm immediately outside the gate. He went there every day, opened the gate, and threw a tacumá fruit in front of it. When a wild pig came out to eat the fruit, Karusakaibö shot it. He then closed the door and went back to the village with the pig. He told no one where he was getting the animals.

After many days of shooting wild pig, Karusakaibö ran out of arrows and had to go away to replenish his supply. He was afraid, however, that a cunning and scheming armadillo named Daiïrú would induce Korumtau to tell the secret of the wild pigs. To avoid this Karusakaibö instructed the boy the refuse to talk to anyone. He covered him with white tapioca and told him, "Stay in your hammock. If Daiïrú comes, tell him that you are sick and cannot get up." He then went in quest of the arrows.

As soon as he had left the village of Uacuparí, Karusakaibö turned himself into a tapir and directed himself toward Wasappí (Savannah of the Home of the Little Birds), a village between the sites of the modern villages, Arö and Cabitutú. He walked near the men's house of the village at night, while everyone was sleeping, and left many tracks. In the morning the men of Wasappí saw the tracks and set off to hunt the tapir. The tracks were very clear, and they followed them to the place where Karusakaibö, in his tapir form, was sleeping. The dogs ran up to him barking, and the hunters sent many arrows into his body. The tapir got up and ran off, but he chose a trail where he knew other hunters were waiting in ambush. He passed them slowly and received many more arrows and did the same thing at another ambush place. He then ran away from his pursuers and retransformed himself into a man, pulled all the arrows out of his body and set off for home with a good stock.

In the meantime, all was not well in Uacuparí. Shortly after Karusakaibö had left the village, Daiïrú arrived. He went to Korumtau and asked, "Tell me, where is your father killing the wild pigs." The boy refused to tell him but Daiïrú was persistent. Finally, Korumtau said to the armadillo, "I would show you only I am sick and have to stay in my hammock." Daiïrú replied, "Oh, you are not sick. Come out of the hammock." Korumtau gave in to the repeated requests and descended. Daiïrú then blew smoke all over him, in the manner of the shaman, and stamped his feet heavily on the ground, causing all the tapioca to flake off his body. He then said, "Good. Now you are well." But Korumtau still refused to tell his father's secret to the wily armadillo. After long and persistent questioning, the boy finally wearied and decided to fall back on a ruse that his father had devised before leaving. He had prepared for this eventuality by building three small hunting lairs, like those made by the Mundurucú; one was under a piquí palm and the other two were under uchí palms, and on the wall of each little straw hut, Karusakaibö had placed a piece of wild pig hide to convince the curious that it was here that he shot the animals.

Korumtau took Daiirú to the first of these and said, "We get them here. You have to wait." A band of catitú came along, and Korumtau said, "Here come the wild pigs. Shoot!" Daiirú was not so easily fooled and said, "No. These are not the animals that your father kills. These have short black hair mixed with white. Here on the wall are the long black hairs of your father's game." He let the catitú pass. Korumtau then took Daiirú to the second false hunting lair and then to the third. At both places the same conversation took place.

Daiirú became even more insistent that he discover the secret. The boy realized that he could not hope to fool the armadillo and consented to bring him to the pen and show him what to do. He ended his instructions with the admonition to be careful that the pigs did not all escape. The irresponsible Daiirú ignored this warning and, instead of throwing one tacumá fruit in the opened doorway, he pulled a whole cluster off the tree. This attracted many pigs, and when the first came out, Daiirú shot it. Unfortunately he did not know how to shoot wild pigs and the arrow fell out. Another pig and then another came out and the same thing happened. Korumtau, seeing what was happening called out, "Shut the door and keep the rest in." On hearing this, all the pigs made a rush for the door and ate Daiirú. Korumtau fled, but the wild pigs set off in pursuit of him. As he ran through the forest, he called to his father for help.

Karusakaibö was returning through the forest at the time his son called. He was still some distance away when he first heard the shouts for help, and he was unable to intervene directly. Instead, he magically changed the boy into an ant which crawled into an anthole, then into a grasshopper which hid under the blades of grass, and finally into a cricket. None of these transformations tricked the vengeful wild pigs and they continued the chase. In desperation Karusakaibö threw up a chain of hills between his son and the pursuing pigs. (These are the same high hills which one can see today at the headwaters of the rivers which drain the Mundurucú country.) The pigs were very clever, however, and passed around the sides of the hills, catching Korumtau and making off with him. The pigs, with Karusakaibö following, reached the banks of the Tapajós River, and the culture hero threw a hill over part of the herd, imprisoning his captive son, also. They are still there today.

Those pigs who were not caught within the hill that Karusakaibö created went to the banks of the Tapajós but were unable to cross the river because of its great width. They then magically made an anaconda and stretched it from one bank to another. The giant constrictor tightened his coils and drew the banks together, making the river very narrow at that point. The pigs crossed over safely and spread out into the forests on the west bank of the Tapajós. Their descendants are the wild pigs which are hunted in the forests today.

Karusakaibö had lost his only son and returned to Uacuparí, crying as he went. On the path he stopped at the now empty pigpen, looked around at all the tracks and noted some blood on the ground. This, of course, was the blood of Daiirú, but Karusakaibö thought that it might be that of his son. He gathered the blood together, blew on it, and stamped on the ground, but, instead of producing his son, he returned Daiirú to life.

Disappointed and enraged, Karusakaibö began to beat the armadillo and to berate him for causing his son's death. Daiirú begged forgiveness, and the culture hero relented. He then continued his return journey to Uacuparí, still weeping for Korumtau.

Karusakaibö is presented to us as a man who functions at an unusual level of isolation. His distance from his own community is expressed spatially, for his house is separated from the others, and socially, for he apparently has no wife, and thus lacks the usual affinal obligations and prerogatives. His only companion is his son, Korumtau. Such a father/son residential group represents a striking departure from the actual Mundurucú pattern. A basic dwelling unit normally consists of a group of matrilineally related adult women and their children, including boys too young to live in the men's house. Karusakaibö's patrilineal group, consisting entirely of males, thus represents the polar opposite of the real Mundurucú pattern.

Karusakaibö's separation from normal social life is additionally manifested by his idiosyncratic hunting. He has removed himself from the important nexus of mutual economic obligations by hunting only for inedible birds. The importance that the Mundurucú attach to a man's ability to hunt and thus his ability to provide meat, makes Karusakaibö's anomalous choice of prey especially meaningful. Karusakaibö is not an inept hunter. On the contrary, he is a skillful hunter who is able to capture many birds. Rather, he *chooses* to be a bad provider.

This perversion of the role of hunter becomes even more laden with implications when we consider how Karusakaibö attempts to utilize his catch. Under normal circumstances a man brings his day's kill to his wife, who distributes the meat, generally sharing it with other family units who may be short of meat that day. Presenting this food to the wife embodies the central symbol of being married. The first such presentation is tantamount to a marriage ceremony. When a man stops giving meat to a woman, or she refuses to take it, the marriage is over. Because Karusakaibö has no wife, he must present his kill, which is nonfood, to his sisters, and expect to receive food in return. It is their refusal to participate in this exchange that touches off all the ensuing events in the myth cycle.

Karusakaibö's isolation produces some unusual results. He has a son but no wife, so he has reproduced seemingly without the aid of a sexual partner. He hunts successfully but produces no food. Until his sisters object, he has, however, gotten food. Note that he has not traded his male-produced nonfood for female-produced food like manioc flour or other horticultural products. Rather, he has used his male offspring as an intermediary to his sisters, who are yet another link in the chain connecting him to his real aim, the meat that is hunted by his brothers-in-law. He has created a situation in which he has the results of sexual union, a son, without engaging in sex and has the satisfaction of hunting without implying that he is a viable husband, because he does not provide any food. Yet he still manages to get food from other men. He has, in other words, suggested the possibility of living in a world that does not include women and the economic and social obligations that come with them. This is the crux of Karusakaibö's dilemma. The myth asks how men can successfully cope with women and the problems and responsibilities they imply. How can they remain apart from women in a world that insists on men and women being together?

Reality, in the form of a demand for normal reciprocity, intrudes and destoys Karusakaibö's isolation. The vulnerable spot in his system is, not surprisingly, the sisters on whom Karusakaibö has depended. Despite their sexual neutrality in relation to their brother, they are women nonetheless and thus agents of downfall. Karusakaibö begins a course of revenge.

After gathering many feathers, he transforms his son, Korumtau, into a bird. The bird plants these feathers in strategic places. The women and those men who have affiliated themselves with women are trapped by the feathers, which grow to enormous size.

The people caught within these spectacular magic feathers are ordered by Karusakaibö to "eat their food," but the command is misinterpreted as an order to copulate. The trapped couples begin to have intercourse, the activity that epitomizes the sexual interaction that Karusakaibö had so successfully avoided. Herein lies their punishment; their human sexual noises turn into animal grunts and finally they are totally banished from the world of humanity and are turned into pigs.

This episode brings together several symbols. Two animals are present: birds (with the associated images of feathers and the sky in general) and pigs. Two action domains are explored and linked: eating and sexual intercourse. We have already seen that the question of eating and the provision of food is a sensitive one for Karusakaibö, recognizing as he does that he needs food, but being unwilling to get it for himself. He tells his enemies to "eat" but they respond by having sex, a strangely appropriate response because the phrase for sexual intercourse among the Mundurucú is "eating penises." This symbolic equation of food and penises makes Karusakaibö's reluctance to provide food more complex. We may think of his refusal to supply food for consumption as a refusal to supply his penis for consumption. Not giving food can thus be understood as an act of self-preservation. The events of the myth thus far tell us that the realm of food and sex is a dangerous one, full of potential conflict. Karusakaibö will not hunt for food, and his sisters will not give it. When the trapped people follow the command to eat, the men lose their pensises (because they are metaphorically eaten), and the sexuality they display transforms them into pigs.

This myth accomplishes the creation of wild pigs, which are the main and most desirable objects of Mundurucú hunting. The negative association of pigs with bestiality is clear enough and Karusakaibö's transformation of his fellows is obviously a punishment, yet these same animals are the most highly valued creatures in the forest. They are thus truly ambivalent symbols, simultaneously very good and very bad.

The pigs also serve, in the myth, to contrast with birds. Pigs are the descendants of men and women who have committed the ultimate act of interaction, interdependence and sexuality. Karusakaibö, who hunts only for birds, Korumtau in the form of a bird, and the punitive, phallic feathers are the agents of retaliation. Their symbolic opposition to the pigs stems from their association with Karusakaibö's stance of isolation, autonomy, and his implied asexuality. The myth tells us that there are two kinds of people in the world; those who distance themselves from food production and sex are associated with birds, and those who produce food and have sex are associated with pigs. We will examine the nature of pigs and birds in more detail later.

The transformation of Karusakaibö's enemies into pigs accomplishes his revenge. But a viable compromise between his ideal of male autonomy and the world of social and sexual interaction has not yet been reached. The events of the latter half of the myth still show Karusakaibö in an adversary relationship with reality.

After creating the pigs Karusakaibö's role as a hunter changes. He now goes every day to shoot a pig, thus placing himself in a more normal, indeed a privileged, position as a provider of meat. His refusal to share this bounty, however, an unthinkable act among the Mundurucú, significantly blunts the importance of his new role. In addition, his insistence on hunting *alone*, which is in sharp contrast with the actual pattern of communal hunting, serves to emphasize his inability to cooperate successfully. His step into productive reality is thus quite limited; it is nutritious but not social.

Moreover, although his prey has become normal, his hunting technique has become anomalous. The method he employs reveals the consequences Karusakaibö thinks must accompany his concession to socioeconomic reality. In order to replenish his stock of arrows he first transforms himself into a tapir. This animal is said by the Mundurucú to symbolize the male sexual drive because of its prominant genitals. This symbolic linking of food production and sexual activity is consistent with our earlier association of the realms of food and sex. The fact that Karusakaibö becomes a tapir in order to hunt pigs proclaims that to be a true hunter, that is, one who kills animals and *also* provides food, he must admit his sexuality. Although this is a radical change, it is made clear to us that Karusakaibö has not lost his distaste for sexuality. He must go in his tapir form to be shot in order to collect his arrows. By thus making the tapir a target, he combines the symbols of male sexuality and male food producer with the image of the *hunted* animal. He characterizes an acknowledged Mundurudú symbol of male sexuality as a being who is vulnerable to attack.

While Karusakaibö is away, Daiïrú the armadillo manages to get the secret of the pigs from Korumtau. The incident represents more than simply Daiïrú's powers of persuasion; it represents a breach of faith between father and son. It is this "infidelity" that deals the final blow to Karusakaibö's attempts at isolation. The pigs escape and chase the faithless son over the countryside. Karusakaibö transforms Korumtau into various insects to elude the pigs, but to no avail. Finally, he is trapped under a hill, and lost forever. The myth closes with Karusakaibö returning to his village, still weeping for his son.

The various transformations that Korumtau undergoes are microcosmic of the overall pattern of this myth. It is no accident that Karusakaibö changes him into an insect instead of a bird at a point when the ability to fly away would have been most useful. Korumtau's first transformation is to a bird and it takes place at a point in the myth when the father-son, male-male tie is strongest; both are working together to punish the aunts. It is a point at which the affirmation of male solidarity and separation from women is crucial. Next, he is transformed into a treefrog, a creature able to climb high into the air, thus bridging the gap betwen sky and earth, male fantasy and hetero-sexual reality. The next transformation consists of a set of three insects, creatures who crawl on the ground. Korumtau has become earthbound while trying to escape from the pigs. The secret is out, the pigs are lost, the strong tie between father and son, male and male, has been broken by the son's inability to maintain secrecy and isolation. This makes it impossible for Korumtau to be a bird anymore. Indeed, the whole basis for bird symbolism is gone; he must now crawl on the earth. Finally, he is trapped *under* the ground. The fall from the world of the sky is complete and Karusakaibö's isolation is de-stroyed. He must return to a village filled with men *and* women. His last action before continuing his journey is significant; he reluctantly revives his future son-in-law, Daiirú.

Myth text II. Karusakaibö punishes the seducers of his son

After Korumtau had been stolen by the wild pigs, Karusakaibö returned to his house in Uacupurí.He went out to his garden one day and, when returning, heard the voice of his son calling, "Father, Father." He looked around, but saw no one. Some days later, Karusakaibö went to his garden again, and the same thing happened. He looked again and saw only two trees standing near the path. The next time he went to the garden, he heard the voice calling "Father, father," and thought, "Could that tree be my son?" He turned back and cut down one of the trees and brought it home. Out of the wood of this tree he fashioned a doll upon which he blew tobacco smoke. He left the doll in a corner of his house and after a few days went to inspect the results. The only human development that had taken place in the doll, however, was that it had grown ears—and these were orelhas de pau, the fungus growth that grows on logs. He threw the doll out saying that it was no good and was obviously not his son.

The next time he went to the garden he heard the same voice and forthwith cut down the remaining tree. He again fashioned a doll out of the wood, repeated the same operations, and left it in a corner of the house. The next time he looked at the doll, it had turned into a beautiful boy, all painted and decorated. He took this boy as his son and was consoled.

Karusakaibö kept his new son concealed from all the women of the village. The boy's only food, however, was the jurití bird, and the father had to go out every day to hunt some. In order to guard the son, he kept him in a small enclosure within the house and told an old woman of the household to guard the child and to keep everybody away from him. He then set off for the forest.

In Karusakaibö's house were several sieves which the women of the village always borrowed when they made beijú. Shortly after he had left his new son for the first time to hunt the jurití, a woman came to the house to borrow a sieve. The boy was inside his enclosure, but the woman heard the buzzing of a disk-and-string toy with which the lad was playing. She asked the old woman, "What is that?" "Go away," replied the boy's guardian. "Leave him alone." The woman listened more and then said, "I will go." That night, Karusakaibö came home, roasted the jurití, and called the boy out to eat. The son came right out, for he did not have coitus and thus was not ashamed. On the next day and the one after that, different women came to the house and the same things transpired. On the fourth day, another curious woman came, and was also sent off by the old woman. She left, but slipped in by another entrance and entered the boy's chamber. The boy was very beautiful and the woman desired him immediately. She asked him for his penis and he gave it [i.e., they had sexual intercourse]. His penis remained enlarged and erect, however, after the conclusion of the act.

When the father came home that night and called his son, there was no response. He called again, and the ashamed boy still did not come out. Karusakaibö wondered what was wrong and he went into the chamber. He saw the lad's enlarged penis and knew immediately what had occurred. Going to the old woman, he asked, "What happened? I told you to watch him and to keep the women away but you did not!" "But I told them," replied the woman. "It is just that they would not listen." Karusakaibö returned to his son's room and pushed his thumb against the head of the boy's penis, saying "Šikiriú" three times [the šikiriú is a small bird with a short beak – the magical association here is obvious]. The penis grew very small, and the boy then came out to eat his juriti. After finishing he returned to his chamber.

On the following day, Karusakaibö went to the forest to hunt, leaving the same instructions with the old woman. A short time later a woman entered the house, ostensibly to borrow a manioc sieve, and inquired as to what was inside the closed chamber. The old woman repeated the same warning to leave the boy alone, but the woman, who had heard of the boy from his lover of the previous day, entered surreptitiously and offered herself to the boy. After completing the act the boy's penis grew even longer than it had the day before, and he was afraid to leave the chamber when his father returned to the house. Karusakaibö discovered the son's wayward behavior immediately and again chided the old woman for her negligence.

Karusakaibö became disgusted with the son and determined to get rid of him. He seized him by the nose and yanked, giving him a long snout, then stretched the boy's ears and banged the sides of his head to make the head narrow. He next grabbed him by the back of the neck so as to produce a hump, and stretched his penis to enormous size. He then took a large wooden pestle and rammed it into the boy's anus, shouting. "Go away." As he ran away, Karusakaibö threw a piece of tauri bark over him, and it turned into a thick hide. In essence, the boy had been converted into a tapir. From this moment on this particular tapir became known as Anyocaitche.

The tapir ran off in the direction of the nearby stream where the women gathered every day to bathe and draw water. The women learned that he lurked in this neighborhood, and, subsequently, when they came for their bath they would jump into the water and call, "Anyocaitche," whereupon the tapir would emerge from the forest and have intercourse with them.

One day a man of the village was near the stream, engaged in making a basket. His attention was caught by a young woman who came to bathe, but who, upon entering the water called, "Anyocaitche, come bathe." The man was amazed to see the tapir jump into the water and perform coitus with the woman and all the others who followed her into the water. The man thought, "Is it possible that my own wife will do the same thing!" His fears were quickly confirmed.

He went back to the village and announced to the other men, "It is not we who have been making our women pregnant," and described what had transpired. They thereupon resolved to kill the tapir. The next day Karusakaibö ordered all the women of the village to work in the gardens. The men prepared a supply of arrows but first sent one of their number ahead to lure the tapir so that they could kill him from ambush. The decoy suspended a gourd on either side of his chest to simulate breasts and set off. As he left he called back, "Do not delay, for if you do, that tapir will get me in the anus."

Upon reaching the stream he dove in and called Anyocaitche. The tapir appeared and was immediately shot by the concealed archers. They then cut the tapir up and made from its blood an armadillo, whose proper name was Nembukarare, which they left in the place of the tapir. The meat was brought back to the village and cooked and eaten. All traces of it were eradicated before the women came home, and they suspected nothing.

When the women left the village for the gardens on the following morning, one left her child, who was still nursing but was able to talk, with her husband. The child was hungry when the mother returned and cried for the breast. The mother, however, was in a hurry to receive the attentions of the tapir at the stream, and she took a gourd water container and hurried out of the village. The child followed her, crying angrily for the breast. Finally, the little boy cried out in vexation, "It was a good thing that we ate your husband." The mother wheeled upon the boy and said sharply, "What was that?" The child became frightened and answered, "Nothing, I only asked for the breast." She slapped him lightly on the head and the boy immediately turned into the tekerú, a small bird, and flew off. The mother tried to grab it but got only a tail feather.

The woman went on to the port and called for the tapir. In its place came the armadillo, who attempted to have intercourse with her. Since the women customarily had coitus with the tapir in the position of animals, it was only as the armadillo was mounting her that she realized that it was not Anyocaitche. She returned to the village weeping for the loss of the tapir, but pretending that the tears were for her lost child. All the village women went to the port and had the same saddening experience. Upon learning of the remark made by the child, the women realized what had happened and resolved to avenge the tapir's death by jumping into the water and turning into fish.

Karusakaibö's wife, who was also enamored with the tapir, went to the men and told them all to hunt the next day. They did so, leaving only one man, whose wife had given birth the night before. The women then congregated and painted each other ornately. The mother of the newborn child was reluctant to leave it, but the women were determined not to leave a single female behind so they finally persuaded her to join them. They then started out in single file for the stream, the youngest woman in front, the oldest bringing up the rear. As they marched, they sang, "We are going to fall into the water for we are angry because of our men." One by one they jumped into the water and turned into fish.

In the meantime, the one man who had remained in the village began to wonder at his wife's absence. He went to the port and upon seeing what was taking place ran back to give the alarm. Placing the baby under an overturned pot for protection, he ran into the forest blowing on a signal horn and calling to the other men, "Your women are all jumping into the water." The men heard him only indistinctly, but ran to see what the trouble was. Just as they reached him, the man turned into a jacú bird. The men hurried back to the village; those who did not hear the alarm were transformed into japín birds.

The men, however, were too late. When they reached the stream, there were only three old crones left, and Karusakaibö made them into alligators and crabs. The little boys who were abandoned on the beach by their mothers turned into birds and flew away. The Mundurucú tribe was then composed only of men.

The opening episodes of Myth I reveal Karusakaibö's isolated nature. As the myth progresses, this desire for isolation and separation is opposed to the realm of heterosexual interaction. The opening episode of Myth II reaffirms this opposition and enlarges its meaning by portraying Karusakaibö's desire to reproduce asexually. He leaves his tree, just as birds leave their eggs, to incubate and become his son. The use of a tree as raw material in this asexual "birth" is interesting. Trees may be thought of as connecting, and in this case embodying, the male asexual sky and the fecundity of the earth. In addition, the "ears" that grow in the form of fungus on the first, unsuccessful attempt to create a new son are notable. The use of fungus is a particularly appropriate symbolic formulation, growing, as it does, quickly and spectacularly out of seemingly inert material.[8]

We find that Karusakaibö feels it necessary to keep his new son hidden specifically from women, in a special compartment of his house. The boy's only food is a kind of bird that Karusakaibö must hunt for every day, and that he himself prepares and serves to the boy (these tasks in reality are exclusively reserved for women). In addition, Karusakaibö demands complete sexual reserve from his son. This list of conditions under which the boy is "born" and with which he is nurtured represents a new, very explicit statement of Karusakaibö's notion of an ideal existence. It is as though, after making his first tentative move, in Myth I, toward cooperating with economic and sexual reality and having these attempts result in the loss of his son, he has retreated to an even more rigid position. Asexual reproduction, absolute separation from women, food only in the form of birds and no sexual activity are the imperatives for the new son.

But as in Myth I, there is a vulnerable spot in Karusakaibö's plan. Earlier we saw that his sisters, their female sexual danger apparently neutralized by their close consanguineal tie, prove to be the ones who destroy Karusakaibö's neatly closed system. In Myth II a woman, her sexuality dimmed not by incest avoidance, but by age, occupies the same position. It is through her negligence that the son is "contaminated" by sex. His father, forced to repudiate him, transforms him into a creature who we will see embodies the menace Karusakaibö has tried to escape.

The perfect son proves to be fatally flawed when, given the appropriate stimulus, he cannot help but reveal his sexual nature. I use the term stimulus quite deliberately because the unfolding of the second son's sexuality is treated in the myth in almost classic "stimulus–response" terms. He is not cajoled into having sex with the women who come to his enclosure. Unlike the first son who is badgered by Daiïrú into breaking faith with his father, the second boy needs only to be presented with a woman to instantly consent to have sex with her. After the first sexual encounter, Karusakaibö shrinks the boy's enlarged penis to acceptable size by invoking a bird that the ethnographer notes in the text as having a short beak, thus explaining the magical association. But there is more at stake here than simply the size of penises or beaks. Karusakaibö is telling the boy to remain a bird, which in this case is symbolic shorthand for being sexually inactive, isolated from women, and capable of reproducing asexually.

But the boy who himself was born asexually from a tree cannot perpetuate this mode of existence. When he again has sex with a woman, Karusakaibö throws him out and transforms him into a tapir. A closer examination of the boy's behavior and his subsequent metamorphosis will reveal in stark terms what Karusakaibö most abhors.

As I have noted, the boy's sexual response is immediate, and I would venture to say, instinctual. Furthermore, after his first two sexual encounters his penis remains enlarged and erect; a strange condition, because we might assume that a successful sexual interaction would result in climax and a return to a nonexcited state. The myth is telling us that heterosexual desire, once "turned on," does not naturally turn itself off. The son thus represents, with his ever erect penis, a state of continual instinctual arousal, continually unfulfilled desire. It is a violent and pessimistic assessment of heterosexuality because it regards this form of desire as both uncontrolled and incapable of producing satisfaction.

The son is changed to a tapir. Previously we saw that male sexuality and vulnerability were linked when Karusakaibö became a tapir. The son-tapir offers us an amplified version of this important connection between the male heterosexual mode and exposure to attack. The father-tapir activates his heterosexuality in a relatively disguised manner. Killing a pig makes him heterosexual in the sense that by producing meat he is starting to behave like a viable husband. However, he must be wounded in the process. The son-tapir, on the other hand, far from offering a subtle hint of heterosexual symbolism, presents us with its most blatant form: constant, indiscriminate intercourse. For this he is not simply wounded, he is killed. Thus, males operating heterosexually have ample reason to be both fascinated and afraid. This image is not inconsistent with what has been reported of aspects of Mundurucú sexuality; the men are interested in amorous pursuits but are also bothered by impotence (Murphy 1954, Murphy and Murphy 1974: 108–9).

We note that the sense in which man is portrayed as vulnerable when heterosexually "on" cannot be understood as a simple manifestation of "fear" of women or female pollution. (The Mundurucú do not have extensive pollution beliefs.) A crude worldview of warring male and female principles is not at work here for in both the instances of attacks on tapirs, the "attacks" are launched by *men*, not women. I suggest that what is being expressed is not that women are dangerous, but rather that they are capable of triggering dangerous and ultimately unsatisfying (remember the son's permanent erection) impulses in men. Although the myths certainly exhibit a symbolic level that tends to oppose "male" and "female" as inimical categories, this simple contrast, with its concomitant cultural manifestations of sexual antagonism (which the Mundurucú certainly have, see Murphy and Murphy 1974, chapter 5 passim), is not sufficient to decipher the complex events of the myths. I argue that along with the crude "male/female" split, there is a systematic development of opposing types of male sexuality: "bird" maleness, which is *exclusively* male, shuns women and sexual activity, is economically unproductive, and aims to reproduce asexually, and "tapir" maleness, which in its Anyocaitche form represents unbridled libidinous drive, a magnetic attraction to women, accompanied by the element of indiscriminate and uncontrolled sexual reproduction. In the form of maleness symbolized by birds, male and female are conceptually opposed because, by definition, they are antithetical and must function only in separate spheres. In the maleness symbolized by tapirs, male and female are conceptually opposed because of their inherent *complementarity*. This is an important point. Because heterosexuality is always a "mixed-term" relationship, the maleness of the tapir only exists in the context of femaleness. It must always imply femaleness, either because it is actively seeking or actively engaged with women. Further-more, the choice is presented as an all-or-nothing proposition. One either remains totally isolated or one is exposed to women and is led down an inevitable path. Thus in the context of forging a coherent male identity, the problem for a man is not so much whether women are good or bad, but which set of conditions he will conform to.

The myth values "bird" maleness and murders "tapir" maleness, thus portraying the men as eliminating an aspect of themselves. But although the killing of heterosexuality is a mythic possibility, in reality it can never happen. Mundurucú men are not free to rid themselves entirely of women, and their own heterosexuality. The impulse to avoid women can only be partially realized. The myth sets about to construct a partial solution, a compromise. The last episode of Myth II provides a major symbolic resolution. As a result, the character of the remaining myths changes dramatically. Let us carefully review the events of this episode to see how this is accomplished.

The tapir is lured to his death by a decoy who suspends two gourds from his chest to attract the animal. Again we see here the emphasis on the mindless "stimulus–response" quality attributed to Anyocaitche; just seeing two spheres is enough to trap him into sexual arousal. In fact, the decoy, sure of the success of the ruse, even fears the tapir will be so indiscriminate in his response as to "get him in the anus" if the other men do not shoot the animal swiftly. He is shot in time, an armadillo is made of his blood, and the meat is brought back to the village and consumed by all the men. The women, still unaware of this, are anxious to meet their lover. But the child of one of them, angry at her neglect, for she has not suckled him sufficiently, tells what has happened and when slapped by his mother, turns into a bird.

The women soon fully realize what has happened. All of them including the mother of a newborn baby (who no doubt would die without her milk) and Karusakaibö's wife, who now makes a sudden and surprising appearance, decide to leave the human world and become fish. The men try unsuccessfully to stop them. Some of the men turn into birds. Only three "old crones" are prevented from jumping into the river and these Karusakaibö turns into alligators and crabs. The little boys, abandoned by their mothers, turn into birds. Now only men exist in human form.

The men kill the tapir, an emblem of unacceptable desire and action. But they do not do away with him entirely. Rather, they transform his blood into an armadillo and they consume the meat that remains. This development is crucial because it reveals the men's willingness to incorporate within them-selves an aspect of the tapir they have just murdered. Let us investigate the qualities of the meat consumed by the men.

The "blood armadillo" is a particularly compact symbolic formulation. That it arises from the remains of the tapir indicates that the constituent parts of the tapir's body are not only blood and meat, as we might assume from the text, but include bones as well. The armadillo, characterized by a hard shell, an "external skeleton," thus implying bones, is shown in the myth as devoid of meat, for the meat of the tapir is specifically not used in its creation. The notion that armadillos are "empty" is confirmed by the fact that the Mundurucú never eat them although they contain edible meat (Murphy and Murphy 1974: 63). The opposing categories of blood and bones are clearly mediated by the symbol of meat on a purely formal level: dry solid versus liquid mediated by a moist solid. I suggest that its position as a mediator, a uniter of opposites, allows the meat to function in this episode as an analogue of heterosexuality, which is also a mediating relationship, a uniter of opposites. And indeed, the armadillo, deprived of the meat that is the essence of the tapir's heterosexuality, is unable to successfully mount the women.

By consuming the meat, the men put heterosexual libido in its proper place, deep inside. Although this act symbolically buries the tapir's sexuality, it also indicates a true incorporation. What the men ingest and thus symbolically claim as a part of themselves, is the viable fertility thus far lacking in Karusakaibö's all male organization, for he has by now lost both of his sons. The killing of the tapir, although it eliminates any overt manifestation of unregulated libidinous drive, also conveys the idea that the men who manage to control their heterosexuality may appropriate its reproductive power.

While Karusakaibö and the other men are in the process of accomplishing this remarkable symbolic feat, the women of the myth are moving in a different direction. There is the surprising appearance of Karusakaibö's wife. We should note that the revelation that he might engage in such a relationship comes only after he and the other men are fortified by having eaten the tapir's meat. Her appearance is an important foreshadowing of how women will be treated in the coming myths.

Significantly, as the men are in the process of simultaneously controlling heterosexual drive and incorporating its reproductive potential, the women are doing the complete opposite. In this episode they become ever more sexually active with the tapir; so active, so aroused in fact, that they forget to be properly nurturant mothers. One woman is in such a hurry to meet for a sexual encounter that she neglects to feed her child sufficiently and then strikes him when he complains. Another abandons her newborn to die. Thus, as the men come symbolically closer to being able to reproduce on their own, the women relinquish their claims on motherhood.

The final sentence of this myth represents the complete fulfillment of the essential aim of the myths so far: "The Mundurucú tribe was then composed only of men." This is the ultimate expression of a fantasy that can only be realized in symbolic form. The striving to create and preserve a world free of the economic, social, and biological realities of heterosexual interaction has, until now, always ended in failure. But with women eliminated, and the men *symbolically* capable of reproduction, the problem is solved.

This total separation from women, combined with the implication that the men, left alone, are not doomed to extinction, forms the ideological basis of the Mundurucú men's house. We will explore this institution in greater depth later, only noting for the moment that the male desire for separation expressed in the texts is accomplished insofar as it is possible by the men's house. Yet despite its obvious relevance and its centrality to Mundurucú life in general, it is mentioned only rarely in the myths. What we do find, however, is a systematic development within the narrative of all the social and physical properties of the men's house, until, at the end of Myth II, the concept of the men's house is brought to its logical (though unrealistic) conclusion. It is this development that constitutes the ultimate, though covert, mythic resolution.

The first indication of the men's house is the form of the primary residence group in Myth I. It is composed only of males, the essential attribute of the social structure of the men's house. The only way in which a father and son live together, as they do in Myth I, is as coresidents of the men's house.

In Myth II the properties of the men's house are dealt with in more specific ways. The most revealing element of the myth is the actual structure of Karusakaibö's house when he acquires his second son. The son is placed in a secluded enclosure within the house and no women are allowed to go inside. In reality, the traditional dwelling houses of the Mundurucú are completely uncompartmentalized. The only structure in the entire village that is analogous in form to the house described in Myth II is the men's house, which has a special enclosure attached to it for the purpose of housing the sacred flutes. Moreover, it is this particular enclosure that is absolutely forbidden to women. Women are not ordinarily allowed into the men's house, but the prohibition against entering the flute enclosure is much stronger. The punishment for such an act is gang rape of the female offender by the entire male population. In the myth, the women who succeed in entering the forbidden chamber, do so for the specific purpose of having intercourse with Karusakaibö's son, indicating that the result of entering his enclosure is similar to the consequences of entering the flute chamber. In addition, Karusakaibö brings food to his son every day in his secluded chamber, a practice identical to the daily ceremony of ''feeding the flutes'' in their secluded chamber.

To summarize, what has been introduced in the first two myths is a residential group with an exclusively male composition, and a physical structure that conforms to the requirements of the traditional Mundurucú men's house, this structure being forbidden to women. The result of a breach of this prohibition is sexual intercourse. Included also is the concept of a daily feeding of whatever (in the myth a boy, in reality, the sacred flutes) is hidden in the special enclosure. In short, the men's house has been completely described without it ever being mentioned. The last line of Myth II embodies the logical outcome of the whole concept of the Mundurucú men's house and finally provides, in symbolic, mythological form, the very condition that reality will never permit to exist. ''The Mundurucú tribe was then composed only of men.''

We have now reached the critical turning point of the myth cycle. The situation at the end of Myth II represents the fulfillment, on a symbolic level, of Karusakaibö's ambition; there are no women in Mundurucú society. The events of the myths have also established, in subtly disguised terms, the basis for the men's house, an institution that is a compromise between a social reality composed of male and female and a social fantasy composed of only males.

The first hint of the new treatment of social and sexual reality is the sudden appearance of Karusakaibö's wife in Myth II. Her existence has very little significance in terms of the concrete events of the myth; what occurred could easily

have happened without her. However, her introduction into the cycle provides an important foreshadowing of what is to follow in the subsequent myths.

The four remaining myths, all much shorter than the first two, will be
presented and discussed together. Viewed as a sort of epilogue to the drama of
the first half of the cycle, Myths III–VI face a new reality. Now that
Karusakaibö's "demands" have been symbolically met, he is free to face the
world with a new assurance and candidness. I will point out briefly how this is
achieved, leaving discussion of some selected episodes for a later section.

Myth text III. How Karusakaibö and Daiirú caught the women

On the day after the women had jumped into the water and turned into fish, Karusakaibö sent all the men of Uacuparí out to hunt. He then went to the garden and dug up
some sweet manioc, which he brought back to the house. After this he went to the
forest and killed a jacú, whose thin leg bone he used as a hook. The meat was left on the
bone as bait, and he tied the hook to a length of sipó (jungle vine). He then collected
some leaves of the tacumá palm and set out to the stream into which the women had
jumped. The women, all transformed into fish, were lying at the bottom of a deep hole
where the stream had undercut the bank, and there Karusakaibö could hear them
talking and laughing.

He dropped his line in the water and immediately hooked one of the fish, which he
yanked out of the water and left flopping behind him. He refrained from looking over
his shoulder at the fish and proceeded to make a basket out of the tacumá palm leaves.
Finally, the fish stopped flopping, and he felt someone come up behind him and
laughingly tickle his ribs. He then turned around and beheld his wife, transformed
again into a woman. He blew smoke on her and passed his hands over her body to
remove all the scales and fish slime. Bidding her fill a container with water and follow
him, Karusakaibö returned to the house. Back at the house, he ordered her to make the
traditional sweet manioc drink, werú, and then concealed her in her hammock, which
he hung above the storage platform. But the presence of the sweet manioc drink
indicated the work of a woman, and Karusakaibö thrust the arms of his pet coatá
monkey into the beverage, intending to tell the men that it was the monkey who had
prepared it.

Among the returning hunters was Daiirú, the trickster companion of Karusakaibö.
The other men were easily misled by Karusakaibö's allegation that the monkey had
made the drink, of which they had all imbibed upon returning. The wily armadillo,
however, sniffed upon entering the house and remarked, "There is something here."
"No there is nothing at all," replied Karusakaibö, "take some manioc drink." Daiirú
lifted the half-gourd to his mouth three times, but he did not drink. He only sniffed and
repeated his suspicion. He then began to sing a song at the conclusion of which he
wiggled his hips in an amusing manner. Each time that he sang the song he looked
around but saw nothing. On the third time, the wife peeked from her place of
concealment to see who was singing. She saw Daiirú and began to laugh and was
thereby discovered.

The armadillo immediately cried, "I told you that there was something there," and
asked for "first preference," that is, for the hand of the first daughter born to
Karusakaibö and his wife. Karusakaibö granted the request, and Daiirú then asked him
to tell how he had gotten his wife back. The culture hero did not wish to tell him for he
knew that Daiirú lacked the necesary patience, but he finally gave in to the insistent
questioning.

Daiirú secured the requisite equipment and went to the stream in which the women were swimming. He caught one of the fish, pulled it out of the water, and left it flopping on the ground behind him while he commenced work on the basket. The fish finally stopped thrashing about and was on the point of turning into a woman when Daiirú grew impatient and turned around to look. He saw only a jacundá pintada. Exasperated, he had intercourse with the fish and threw it back in the water. Until this day, the jacundá pintada (called "wife of the armadillo" in Mundurucú) is inedible and does not ever serve for bait.

The armadillo returned to the village and made the sweet manioc drink in an effort to convince Karusakaibö that he had been successful in his fishing venture. The culture hero tasted the drink and knew immediately that Daiirú had made it. He then went down to the stream and created an otter, which he placed in the water to frighten the transformed women from the hole in which they were hiding. The fish then scattered up and down the river.

Myth text IV. How Karusakaibö and Daiirú pulled the people out of the ground

Now it came to pass that a child was born to Karusakaibö and his wife. When the child had learned how to walk Dairú came to claim her as his wife in accordance with his agreement with Karusakaibö. He brought the little girl home and slept with her every night, but for some time he refrained from violating her. Finally he had intercourse with the infant and, in so doing, killed her.

Karusakaibö determind to avenge the death of his daughter. He brought Daiirú to the forest and shot arrows high into palm trees, ordering the armadillo to retrieve them in the hope that he would fall down. When this did not happen, Karusakaibö shot an arrow high into a thorny-trunked tacumá palm. The wily armadillo climbed up the palm tree by pushing his paws up the trunk instead of climbing hand over hand. By this device he bent the palm thorns down, and they did not wound him.

Finally Karusakaibö made a huge garden clearing in the forest and, when the time for burning off the felled vegetation came, he ordered Daiirú to build a fire in the middle of the clearing. He then ignited the perimeter of the clearing and left Daiirú trapped by the advancing flames. But the resourceful trickster dug deep into the ground and escaped.

When the fire had cooled, Karusakaibö returned to the garden to look for the ashes of the armadillo. He found only the hole and thought, "Could it be that he is still alive?" He blew tobacco smoke into the hole and stamped his foot, whereupon Daiirú issued from the ground.

The still angry culture hero began to beat Daiirú, but the armadillo cried, "Do not do that! Do not do that! There are people down in the earth where I was." Karusakaibö sent Daiirú for some cord and then sent the armadillo down the hole with it with instructions to tell the people to grab the cord securely. Daiirú did as he was told, and Karusakaibö began to pull the people out of ground. First came the "savage Indians," who tried unsuccessfully to kill Karusakaibö. These dispersed throughout the forests. The next people to be pulled out of the ground were the "peaceful Indians," or people like the Mundurucú. They too scattered over the land and, with the "savage Indians," are now the tribes of the region. The last to emerge to the terrestrial level were the Mundurucú, for immediately after their appearance, a maracaná flew past and cut the cord with his beak. The remaining people, who were the most beautiful of all, fell back down the hole. The underworld in which these people live, said Daiirú, is a replica of the world in which terrestrial people live. The hole through which the people were drawn was at Uacuparí, the village of Karusakaibö.

Myth text V. Karusakaibö makes more women

After drawing the people from the ground, Karusakaibö decided to make more women, since he was the only man to have a wife. He made many women out of clay, but they lacked vaginas, and these were made by various animals, who formed the vaginas by having intercourse with the clay figures. Some were made by the agouti, and because of the shape of his penis, the women had a long thin vagina. More were made by the paca, and these were nice and round. Finally, the squirrel made the best – round and pretty. After the vaginas were made, Daïirú dabbed a bit of rotten Brazil nut on the mouth of each one. It is because of the animals who made the vaginas that they are of different shapes and sizes today, and it is because of the armadillo that the female organ smells as it does.

Myth text VI. How Karusakaibö made the sky and finally avenged himself against Daïirú

Now Karusakaibö resumed his plans to rid himself of the armadillo-trickster, Daïirú. One day he invited Daïirú to accompany him to bathe. On the way, Karusakaibö told him, "Carry a flat stone." The armadillo picked up a flat stone and carried it in his hands. "No," said Karusakaibö, "carry it on your head." As soon as Daïirú had placed the flat stone on his head, Karusakaibö caused the stone to grow in diameter. It grew and grew, and, in order to support it, Daïirú braced his hands beneath it. As it grew larger Daïirú cried out, "It is heavy." When the armadillo could no longer support it, Karusakaibö caused both him and the stone to rise high into the air. This great, flat stone is now the sky.

Karusakaibö then made roots grow from Daïirú's nose and implant themselves in the earth; the armadillo thus became transformed into the apoi, a tall tree of the jungle. It is this tree which to this day supports the sky, although nobody knows where it is.

The essential message that emerges from these texts is that women, for better or worse, are here to stay on this earth. But Karusakaibö's acceptance of heterosexual reality is implemented specifically within the boundaries of marriage. He makes women for the express purpose of providing *wives* for men. The heterosexuality of this new world will not be enacted by adulterous women and uncontrolled tapirs! In addition, the sexuality that is now embraced with such openness is not without echoes of ambivalence; vaginas may be "round and pretty," but they are made by intercourse with animals, and they smell rotten.

Be that as it may, there is no doubt that Karusakaibö has now definitively entered reality. The most apparent change of attitude that emerges from this myth is Karusakaibö's close association with a sexually active female. His first action after recreating his wife is to bring her to their home, thus establishing for his first time a heterosexual household.

Upon Daïirú's discovery of the concealed wife, Karusakaibö makes an open acknowledgement of the sexual bond existing between his wife and himself by promising Daïirú their next daughter. Not only has Karusakaibö admitted to an open sexual union, but he has presented himself as a potential producer of female offspring. Clearly there has been a complete turnabout in attitude.

The creation of female genitals in Myth VI represents the completion of the development of sexuality in the cycle. Recognizing the indispensability of women, Karusakaibö provides wives for all Mundurucú men. In his almost craftsmanlike modeling of vaginas, we see a demystified and candid acceptance of heterosexual reality. It is a curiously cheerful and affectionate embracing of femininity . . . bestial and smelly though it may be.

The last myth deals especially with Daïirú, a character who has become progressively more active in the cycle. Because we will be having a closer look at him in a later section, we will merely note that in ending this cycle he provides us with a final cautionary commentary: the asexual male world of the sky and the sexually active male and female world of the earth must be kept apart.

We have seen a variety of themes emerge from the myths. There is the presentation of an existential problem, the "dilemma" I referred to earlier, namely, how can men separate themselves from women in a world where women must exist. This problem was "solved" by the narrative evolution of the myths, which offers two complementary solutions. The "overt" solution operates by literally eliminating women on a metaphorical level, that is, the women turn into fish in a mythic world. The "covert" solution operates by metaphorically eliminating women in the literal, real world, that is, the men's house is created, thus defining an area of life that exists without women. Having looked at the symbolic formulations while embedded in the narrative structure, we will reexamine some of them, specifically the relevant animals, without being constrained by the narrative development.

We have been presented with four recurrent animal symbols: birds, pigs, tapirs, and armadillos. When understood as a system of meaning, the symbols map out the problems dealt with in the myths. Let us enter this system on the bird versus tapir axis.

Birds function as the embodiment of a valued mythic ideal: men are self-sufficient. Now if we know anything about this proposition, we know it is untrue. At the very least, men need food and women to live and reproduce. It is thus the task of birds to symbolically challenge and deny what is conceived of as a natural exigency: a reality filled with eating, excreting, birth, and death, the total continuity of life.

By merely defying the laws of gravity, birds present themselves to man declaring that there is a way out of natural reality. The egg-laying "external" reproductive cycle of birds permits men to speculate on the possibility of their own ability to reproduce without sex, pregnancy, and lactation. The powerful imagery of anal birth is also involved and linked to notions about food and sexuality. Whereas men in the "natural" world take food in their mouths and excrete feces (useless decay, because Mundurucú horticulture does not utilize manure), birds excrete eggs, which are miraculously purified food and the begining of new life. If we view feces as the alimentary analog of death (food-feces = birth-death), birds and their mode of reproduction suggest that death may be turned into life. In this symbolic formulation, life processes turn back on themselves, the "end" always transformed to a "beginning." The mythic world in which men are birds is a world in which there is no constant march toward decay and death. Thus the set of ideas projected by bird imagery is a Mundurucú version of a "steady state" free of the tension of change and development. Thus, in the beginning of Myth II, when we find Karusakaibö refusing to hunt for edible food despite his clear ability to do so, we are being confronted with a man who is refusing to take the crucial step into adult maturity that admits that man must produce food, give it to a woman, marry her, have children, and die.[9]

As has been demonstrated many times, symbols have a peculiar tendency to generate their opposites. Karusakaibö's second son, born asexually, isolated, fed only on birds, has within him a tapir, a volcano of unrestrained libido. This being, first in human, then in tapir form, with his constantly erect and thus never satisfied penis, is the embodiment of temporal lineality and ongoing process. His nature is fully realized by unendingly seeking out women. Karusakaibö's final act of repudiation, putting a pestle in the tapir's anus, defines the animal's sexuality. By recognizing the anus as a "feminine" organ we see that the tapir has both male and female parts that are actively engaged. He is heterosexuality incarnate. The myth portrays this sexual mode as instinctual, for the women cannot resist him and he cannot resist them; endless, for it is never fulfilled, and destructive, for it impregnates the women promiscuously and leads to the abandonment of children.

We have before us two unacceptable alternatives. On the one hand, there is the mode of living proposed by the bird motif, which is homosexual in composition and doomed because it is *excessively controlled* sexually and is therefore sterile. On the other hand, there is the mode of living proposed by the tapir motif, which though heterosexual in orientation, is doomed because it is *insufficiently controlled* sexually and therefore destructive and thus ultimately sterile.

What is emerging here, is a system of ideas concerning the relationship between rule bound, that is, structured and controlled, behavior, and levels of sexual expression. Birds, whose level of control precludes sex, and tapirs, whose lack of control allows sexuality to burn itself out, are two members of a four-part system:

	unstructured/uncontrolled	*structured/controlled*
nonsexual	armadillos	birds
sexual	tapirs	pigs

The compromise between birds and tapirs is worked out in the men's house. We have seen already that through the incorporation of the tapir's meat, the symbolic premise of this institution reflects a subtle blending of the imperatives of birds and the demands of tapirs. We will examine the complexities involved in that synthesis in more detail later. For the moment, however, we can easily acknowledge that a sociocultural system based *only* on an exclusively male social, economic, and ritual unit is out of the question – no matter what its symbolic premise.

Because it cannot work alone, it must be linked to an *acceptable, controlled* heterosexual subsystem. In other words, the practical compromise that emerges really has two parts: a social system dominated by the bird ideal but informed by man's tapir nature, and a social system dominated by the tapir but tempered by the control of birds. The former is the men's house, the latter is the system of marriage and ongoing life that takes place in Mundurucú dwelling houses. It is the dwelling-house system that we can see symbolically elucidated by pigs.

To begin, we must examine the behavior of wild pigs and the method the Mundurucú use to capture them. Although individual men often hunt alone (Murphy 1960: 54–5) and small hunting parties of up to three men are frequently formed, these techniques, which require no or only a low level of organization, are employed only for hunting animals other than pigs. Pigs, which always travel in herds of twenty to a hundred, are only profitably hunted by a team composed of the entire male population of one or two villages because an individual hunter could only shoot one or two pigs before frightening away the herd. As Murphy notes, this collective technique requires a very high level of knowledge, skill, and cooperation on the part of the hunters for each man must adjust his own actions to be consistent with a collective goal. This ethos of collectivity and cooperation is what Murphy terms the ''keynote'' (1960: 66) of Mundurucú economy in general and indeed of every aspect of their social life (Murphy and Murphy 1974: 66–8). It is a characteristic that the Mundurucú specifically attribute to themselves and that serves explicitly as a way of distinguishing themselves from all other people. That is, according to their own conscious self-image, the Mundurucú share and cooperate, others do not. Thus the collective pig hunt emerges as the activity that epitomizes their culture. In it the energy of each hunter is harnessed to promote the general good. A man unable or unwilling to perform the task allotted to him or to gear his behavior to the context of other men's actions will reduce the success of the hunt.

Thus Karusakaibö's creation of the pigs and the fact that they are subsequently scattered to the forest, brings into existence the activity that is the highest expression of Mundurucú culture, an activity that demands that each individual be controlled by an overriding organizational structure. Merely creating the pigs and keeping them in a hidden enclosure is an act of control but it is Karusakaibö's individual control. The pigs must escape his personal control, for it is by roaming as organized groups in the forest that the pigs create the necessity for rules of organization and collectivism. As the only herd animal known to the Mundurucú, they represent rule-bound human society. As objects of the collective hunt they bring that society into being.

It is clear then that pigs are symbols of order and cultural control in general. My argument, however, demands that the symbolic value of pigs embody control of a special nature, namely, the restraint (but not obliteration) of heterosexual impulse; the channeling of sexual energy into viable fertility. A hunter who allows his desire for game to overcome the rules of the collective hunt will lose, not gain, his prey. So too, the unbridled desire for sex displayed by the tapir is too strong for successful reproduction. Indeed, the sexual frenzy of the tapir and his mistresses is quite antithetical to proper parenthood because it induces the women to mistreat and abandon their children. The result of such intense sexuality is the disappearance of the women altogether. Their reproductive potential is, of course, lost with them.

The adulterous nature of the tapir's sexuality is, in itself, destructive and sterile. Apart from the socially disruptive aspects of adulterous unions, the Mundurucú belief that pregnancy requires repeated sexual intercourse over a period of time makes them skeptical of the fertility of sex outside of marriage. Adultery is generally thought of as isolated sexual encounters. Thus in the Mundurucú conceptual scheme, only marriage produces children. They acknowledge, however, that exceptions may take place and so as though to make certain that reproduction exists only in the context of marriage, infants thought to be the product of adultery are the most frequent victims of infanticide (Murphy and Murphy 1974: 101, 102, 166). Similarly in the myth, although a man asserts that the tapir has made the women pregnant, these children are never actually born.

Although many of us may feel justified in assuming that the equation sex + cultural control = marriage has an intuitive correctness about it, it is possible in this case to uncover evidence internal to the structure of the myth that the connection between pigs and marriage is justified.

In order to see the relationship between pigs and marriage we must recall the circumstances of the pigs' creation. The myth tells us that it takes place in the dry season when the people are away from their village and living in temporary lean-tos in the forest in order to hunt. According to Murphy (1960: 56–7) the actual dry season pattern does entail moving from the main savannah village but not in the manner described in the myth. Rather, when the rainy season floods have subsided and the water and fish are confined in the river beds, the Mundurucú leave the savannah and head for the river banks where they stay temporarily in order to fish. In modern times this pattern has been intensified because people go to their "rubber avenue" homes, which are located on the river banks during the dry season. While tapping rubber, they are able to take advantage of the good fishing. Thus, the dry season is associated with fishing and the rubber trade, while the myth asserts an association between the dry season and pigs. Because there is an important connection between the dry season economic activities and marriage, by setting the creation of pigs in the dry season, the myth associates them with marriage.

For various ecological and economic reasons (see Murphy 1968: 139–43, 155–77, and passim), the rubber trade has served to isolate and enhance the nuclear family and the husband and wife "working team." I will not go over how this occurs since Murphy's account is so clear and accessible. Suffice it to say that from the perspective of a man from a conservative savannah village there are two versions of rubber involvement: his own, the "weak" version that entails only dry season part-time rubber collection and the "strong version" of the assimilated Mundurucú who have taken up permanent residence along the rivers and are heavily involved in the rubber trade. For this man, his weak involvement has resulted in a rather subtle emphasis on his economic, social, and emotional ties to his wife. But even more importantly, the image of the assimilated villages must have tremendous impact, seeming as it does to be a triumph of marital obligations and the women who symbolize them.

The men of the permanent rubber villages rarely hunt, routinely help with manioc processing, and *have no men's house*. They really live with their wives.

Fishing is also associated with marriage in the sense that a man who is good at and enjoys fishing (as opposed to hunting) earns the reputation of being a "good provider," a title that is only significant in the context of marriage. The connection of fishing and marriage is reaffirmed when we examine the key episode involving fishing in the myths. This occurs when Karusakaibö "fishes" out his wife after all the women have jumped into the river, thus providing the symbolic turning point of the cycle. This "creation of a wife" and the creation of pigs prove to be structurally analogous events, and I suggest that they are, in a sense, equivalent creations. What follows is a sketch of the major parallels and inversions connecting the two episodes. For the sake of brevity, I will point out only some of the aspects of some of the corresponding elements.

Creation of pigs	*Creation of wife*
Karusakaibö surrounds people with feathers.	Karusakaibö drops bird leg bone into midst of fish.

The obvious point of identity between these two elements is that Karusakaibö is employing bird fragments to begin his act of transformation-creation. But although traps of bird origin are employed in both elements, in the case of pig creation, the part used is the most distinctively birdlike part of a bird, whereas in the case of the wife creation it is the most anthropomorphic because birds are bipedal. The change in character of the transforming agent from "most bird-like" to "most humanlike" is consistent with the tone of the two events. Both are impositions of control brought about by the symbol of perfect control and order: birds. But as we can see from the parts chosen, birds may have a strong or weak manifestation. The strong manifestation appears in the creation that is also a punishment. It appears in the cycle before the main conflict resolution while Karusakaibö is still looking for a way out of reality. The weak version appears after the compromise with male autonomy has been made and participating in a marriage can be viewed as a positive act.

The feathers grow, the people have sex.	The fish takes the bait.

The command to "eat food" is mistaken for "eat penises." Thus the intercourse of the humans turning into pigs is a kind of metaphoric eating. The wife puts her husband's "hook" inside of her. This "eating" is metaphoric sex. But there is more than a simple inversion at work here because the quality of the sexuality involved is also inverted. The active sexual symbols in the pig creation are the growing, punishing feathers. This is a phallic and coercive image. The fish, on the other hand, willingly takes the bait that calmly sits there waiting to be eaten. This contrast of phallic sadism and unthreatening heterosexuality is consistent with the issues discussed in the previous elements.

Concealed from view there is a general morphological transformation into pigs. Karusakaibö gives hair.	Karusakaibö refrains from looking while there is a general morphological transformation into a woman. Karusakaibö takes off scales.

└─Use of smoke to aid transformation.─┘

The parallels and inversions here are obvious.

Karusakaibö lures pigs out with tacumá fruit.	Karusakaibö orders wife to bring water in tacumá leaf basket.

Karusakaibö in effect turns the pigs into food via the tacumá palm and reaffirms the woman's status as his wife by having her perform a wifely task, also via the tacumá palm.

Pigs provide meat.	Wife provides manioc drink.
Karusakaibö conceals son in dry manioc and tries to trick Daiirú by placing son in hammock.	Karusakaibö conceals wife in hammock and tries to trick Daiirú with wet manioc.

The several inversions involving tricking, concealing, and the wet/dry contrast should be apparent. I would, however, draw attention to the son/wife contrast. The use of the son as the key image here, on first glance does not enhance a heterosexual or marriage-oriented interpretation because he exists without any mention of Karusakaibö's wife. But it must be recalled that from this point forward in the myth the son is doomed. The wife, on the other hand, is here to stay. In addition, starting at about this point, Daiirú seals Korumtau's fate by making him tell the secret of the pigs but he anticipates the birth of Karusakaibö's daughter by claiming "first preference." Marriage apparently means that someone loses a valuable son but gains a daughter. This is a fairly good reflection of reality for the patrilineal but matrilocal Mundurucú.

The next few pairs are so transparent that I will simply list them.

Trick doesn't work.	Trick doesn't work.
Son is discovered.	Wife is discovered.
Daiirú tries to get a pig.	Daiirú tries to get a wife.
Daiirú fails.	Daiirú fails.
Daiirú is eaten (i.e. becomes food).	Daiirú makes food.
Pigs are scattered.	Fish are scattered.

In short, I think we can safely say that there is good reason for understanding these two fragments of the myth cycle as mirrors of each other.

Pigs then, for many reasons, represent sexuality tempered by control. Sexual appetite thus filtered through culture is no longer the destructive force it is when embodied by the tapir. The tapir's sexual drive, springing directly from instinctual impulse and never undergoing a taming, plunges along, never fully satisfied, leaving destruction in its wake. In the end it too is destroyed. The sexuality of pigs, in contrast, is domesticated in the full sense of the word.

The animal still requiring explanation in the four-fold table is the armadillo. Whereas the birds, tapirs, and pigs we have discussed each make a positive statement concerning human potentialities, the armadillo serves as an object lesson in failure. We saw that when the tapir is murdered and reduced to his constituent elements, blood, bones (in the form of the armadillo's shell) and meat, the armadillo is symbolized as devoid of meat and thus empty. This is consistent with the fact that the Mundurucú refuse to eat them, despite their edible meat. Lacking in the element that acts as a mediator, a uniter of opposites, the armadillo image projects a quality of fragmentation and disjunction. Thus handicapped, he is unable to relate to others even on the most basic level; his one attempt at intercourse is unsuccessful.

The other instance of armadillo symbolism is in the character of Daiïrú the trickster. His behavior is also filled with disjunctive elements that impair his ability to function adequately as a competent social being. Situations requiring relationships and connections with other beings are impossible for him, and he consistently sabotages the relationships of others.

When we first encounter Daiïrú, his activites come between Karusakaibö and his son Korumtau, eventually resulting in the boy's death. We then find that although he wants to hunt, he doesn't know how to shoot (the appropriate way of relating to an animal in the context of hunting). He turns the proper hunting relationship inside out by being so inept as to allow the pigs to kill *him*. Karusakaibö unintentionally regenerates him from the drops of blood that remain, thus confirming that beneath the armadillo's shell there is only blood. In Myth III, Daiïrú attempts to catch a wife out of the water the way Karusakaibö caught his. Again, he does not know how to do it; unable to fish properly, his efforts yield only an inedible fish that the Mundurucú call "wife of the armadillo." The inedible nature of this fish, which the Mundurucú spurn even as bait, carries the symbolic message that it is devoid of meat. The "empty" armadillo has an "empty" and useless wife. Undaunted by his failure, Daiïrú attempts to frighten the fish women out of hiding but again only succeeds in losing what he had sought to gain.

In Myth IV we have a quite graphic instance of Daiïrú's inability to make successful relationships. He takes Karusakaibö's daughter as his wife but is unable to wait until the proper time to have sex with her. His premature advances kill her, an unsuccessful liaison if there ever was one.

Of course his final fate in Myth VI embodies his essential nature. He prevents connections.

The "wily armadillo" then is not wily at all. He is able to put parts of a puzzle next to each other but is unable to provide an organizing principle that would make them interact to form an integrated unit. Just as the tapir's lidibinous energy goes haywire in the absence of a controlling principle, the armadillo's actions result in failure because both he and his actions are insufficiently structured. His behavior is uninformed by the skills and knowledge that are a result of adequate socialization. Unable to fish, hunt, or even have sex properly, he has not acquired the most basic abilities to appropriately regulate his behavior.

In the analysis of these myths we have seen the symbolic process operate in step with the narrative, achieving the expression and resolution of conflict internal to the logic of a cultural system. Through analysis of four of the major animals that appear in the myths we have seen that issues concerning the structuring and control of sexual energy form a backdrop against which the action of the myths must be understood. This done, I want to explore more fully the connections between the ideas we have seen develop in the myths and the Mundurucú men's house and associated cult.

The men's house is a key, if not the key, institution that structures Mundurucú life in general. Its totally male character combined with its position as *primary* residence for men certainly serves to facilitate and express the extreme physical, economic, and psychological separation of Mundurucú men and women. But as I have pointed out, the simple opposition of male versus female does not go very far in helping us understand the complexities of the Mundurucú (or any other) case. The men's house, it is clear, segregates men, but in so doing, rather than implying that the individual dwelling houses are "female" as we might at first glance suppose, it imbues the dwellings with a decidedly *heterosexual* character. Women are barred from the men's house, but men are not barred from the dwellings. Indeed, a common reason for a man to spend time in his wife's house is to have sex with her. This is in line with my argument that the homosexual/ heterosexual opposition has more explanatory potential than the simple male/ female dichotomy. But the total picture is even more complex because there is an area of Mundurucú life that is almost totally female and that Murphy and Murphy refer to as the female "equivalent" of the men's house. This is the "farinha shed," a village structure where women collectively process the bitter manioc, extract its poisonous acid and turn it into flour. It seems we have several structures to interconnect: men's house, farinha shed, and dwelling.

In discussing the "architecture" of Mundurucú villages, Murphy and Murphy comment (56–7) that the open lean-to style of the Mundurucú men's house is a bit puzzling. The place where men spend most of their time tends to be cold, wet, and full of mosquitos. Most other Amazonian cultures that have men's houses build them with walls. However, we should note that the Mundurucú men's house is not completely open because the enclosure containing the sacred flutes is attached to it. If we think of the men's house as *two* structures, one open and one closed, we will be able to understand the farinha shed (open) and the dwelling houses (closed) and the men's house as forming a structured set.

The open lean-to segment of the men's house does not appear to be of particular ritual significance. The activities that take place there generally are sleeping, eating, talking, and preparations for hunting, all in full view of the women. Although it is rare for a woman to enter the lean-to, it is not unheard of and does not constitute a crime punishable by gang rape. It is such a crime if a woman enters the flute enclosure. Whereas the men's house is, of course, attributed great symbolic and ritual importance, its lean-to portion seems to be a rather mundane, work-a-day place. The only exclusively male activity that takes place there is related to the economics of hunting.

The farinha shed is a female counterpart of the men's house *lean-to*. It is totally public and open and is a place for female economic activity. Men rarely enter it.

These two structures mirror each other in form and function. The remaining structures, the flute enclosure and the dwelling houses, do so as well.

The most significant activity that takes place in the dwelling houses is the reproductive cycle: sex between married couples and birth, in other words, from the male perspective, the privileges and rewards of marriage. The house is the place where raw sexuality is domesticated and made fruitful.

The activities of the flute chamber mimic through ritual this cycle of fertility. Although no longer a focus of initiatory activity, in which the symbolism of birth through men would no doubt be relatively obvious, the playing and feeding of the flutes in which ancestral spirits reside is still self-consciously concerned with fertility: the multiplication of game.

But there are other factors that encourage us to understand the flute chamber as the place where a homosexually constituted subunit of society mimics the functions of its "real world," heterosexual counterpart.

We note that although the flutes are phallic in gross design, they are hollow and contain a reed, thus showing that the instruments have both a male and female component (see Murphy and Murphy 1974: 92–5). In addition, we are told in another myth that the flutes were originally in the possession of the women who were coerced into giving them to the men (see Murphy and Murphy 1974: 87–92).[10]

We will recall too that the moment in the myth when the men rid themselves of women, thus metaphorically creating the men's house, is marked by their consumption of the tapir meat. This act allows them to absorb the hetero-sexual fertility embodied by the tapir.

Moreover, as I have shown earlier, the predominance of birth symbolism in formulations concerning exclusively male units and autonomous male repro-duction is consistent with a fantasy of miraculous anal birth. This theme of anal birth leads us directly back to the flutes, for as Dundes (1976), following Jones (1974), has recently shown, ritual instruments emitting low roaring sounds are commonly associated with intestinal flatus and excrement, which often signify male fecundity and anal birth. Dundes' demonstration concerned itself with the symbolism of the bullroarer, but his argument seems even better suited to flutes, which emphasize blowing and excreting characteristics even more than bullroarers. We will recall too that Karusakaibö's second son, who I have shown to be analogous to flutes, is discovered in his hidden chamber by the village women because the noise of his "disk-and-string toy," that is, *his bullroarer*, gives him away! This myth, it seems, has left no symbolic avenue unexplored.

Thus the flute ritual, although performed only by men, is imbued with symbolism that has decidedly heterosexual and reproductive implications.

Mundurucú village architecture then looks like this:

I	II	III FARINHA	IV
FLUTE CHAMBER	LEAN-TO	SHED	HOUSES
Closed	Open	Open	Closed
Concealed (secret)	Public	Public	Concealed
Homosexually constituted *but* heterosexual symbolism	Homosexually constituted	Homosexually constituted	Heterosexually constituted
Locus of ritual reproduction	Locus of male labor	Locus of female labor	Locus of real reproduction

Although it is clear that this system exists, the question of why this particular set of activities is organized with this particular open/closed pattern remains. Because it seems that each of the structures makes an assertion about the world, it would be well to examine them in detail. The assertions are:

I: Men can, through ritual, reproduce.
II: Only men hunt.
III: Only women process manioc.
IV: Heterosexual intercourse is necessary for reproduction.

Only women bear children.

How "true" are these propositions?[11]

I. *Male reproduction*. It will never be. Men can play the flutes forever, but they will never bear children, anally or otherwise. Let us say this is an obviously false statement.

II. *Only men hunt*. This is problematic. Although it is, of course, the case that only men *do* hunt, we are all aware that the question of whether it is feasible for women to hunt is controversial. No one can deny, however, that it is physically possible for a woman to learn to shoot and kill animals. It is possible that it may be extremely inconvenient to organize an economy based on female hunting, less inconvenient if hunting were shared between men and women. But this speculation is neither here nor there. It is simply not obvious that women are, *by nature*, incapable of hunting. Let us say this statement is questionable.

III. *Only women process manioc*. This is obviously false as any visit to an acculturated Mundurucú village will show.

IV. *Heterosexual intercourse is necessary for pregnancy. Only women bear children*. I think we can all agree that this is true.

The open/closed structure of the village is arranged such that attention is drawn to the first three propositions. The rituals of male reproduction are spotlighted by being mysteriously hidden and their secrecy is protected by ritual sanctions. The "economic" nature of the sexes is in sharp focus because these activities are so public. The business of reproduction is, in contrast, tucked away, but not hidden. It is simply given no special advertising.

The three propositions whose objective veracity we have every reason to doubt are precisely the ones that Mundurucú culture has gone to great lengths to enhance. The most impossible statement is thus completely ritualized and mystified. The assertion of the flute chamber is so grossly false that it must be concealed and forbidden so as to make it unverifiable. The final and only obviously true statement is not denied, for who could deny that women give birth? It is simply "not seen." The men manifest a studied lack of concern and interest when an actual birth takes place (see Murphy and Murphy 1974: 164–5).

It appears that a process of cultural "one-upmanship" is taking place. From the point of view of a Mundurucú male, his ability to control the world via ritual that increases available game stems from his assertion that he can reproduce with other men. This assertion however cannot be brought to full consciousness or made public because it is outrageously false. It would never hold up under scrutiny and no woman would ever believe it. Indeed on a very conscious, mundane level, Mundurucú women are not fooled by any of the mystery surrounding the flute ritual. They are aware that their husbands and not their ancestors are producing the sounds emanating from the men's house. Although they publicly play along with the ritual requirements, privately they are not impressed. The women joke about the flutes while the men play them in dead earnest (see Murphy and Murphy 1974: 18, 101, 141).

But the assertion of male homosexual reproductive capacity, protected as it is by ritual secrecy, equalizes the capacities of men and women. If men and women both reproduce, each in their own way, there is nothing of *importance* that a woman can do that a man cannot. The manioc flour that women produce for all to see in the farinha shed, may, in our nutritional categories, be the staff of life, but in the Mundurucú conceptual scheme, it is not valued. Real food, important food, is meat, which only men may provide. Thus the role of hunter, loudly proclaimed as the hallmark of manhood, is the key to male superiority. By elevating meat to superior status and reserving its capture for men, it tips the "balance of power" – economic, political, and ritual – toward men. In a male-dominant society such as this (Murphy and Murphy leave no doubt that this is so, see Murphy and Murphy 1974: 87 and passim), it is not enough to postulate a male reproductive mode equal to the reproductive role of women. The men elevate themselves by glorifying a role they must claim as exclusively theirs, Hunting is the ultimate activity, not merely because men do it, but rather because women *do not* do it.

A Mundurucú man lives his life with his commitments split between two systems. In his role as householder he allows his libidinous drive to be regulated by marriage and thus puts this drive in the service of his wife's body, in order to produce children by her. He commits himself to use his hunting ability to provide food for his family (and secondarily all other families through sharing). He enters the inevitable cycle of mortality.

But with his men's house identity, there is an escape, if only an illusory one. Separated as they are from the realities of meat distribution and cooking, the men have placed themselves in a situation that dulls the connection between hunting and providing for a family because the family is not a relevant unit. The men's house emphasizes that aspect of hunting that Karu-sakaibö portrays at the beginning of the myths: hunting as pure, glorious male activity, not the chain that connects him to husbandly obligations. And while the women jokingly dismiss the possibility of an afterlife (Murphy and Murphy 1974: 140) the men regularly resurrect their ancestors by playing the flutes. Those people who seem dead and gone truly live in the men's house. And, of course, new generations of this miraculous breed are ritually born there as well. In the men's house we are not dealing with a zero sum game as we must in the "real world." Life is continually renewed but no one must truly die in payment.

Symbolic formations that embody and express notions of sexual identity must straddle these systems. They must encompass reality and fantasy. The myths we have examined do just that by reflecting the various facets of Mundurucú thinking about the nature of sexuality and the essence of manhood. In this regard they are indeed "creation" myths, for although men are born into a world already populated by pigs and women, the Mundurucú image of male sexuality is a complex entity that must be re-created in each man.

Notes

1 I would like to thank the editors of this volume, Harriet Whitehead and Sherry Ortner, for their helpful comments and suggestions.

2 I have not done fieldwork in Amazonia. My interest in the Mundurucú derives from my commitment to comparative research. The present analysis is based on the exceptionally rich material provided by Robert and Yolanda Murphy. Considerations of length prohibit me from incorporating a great proportion of relevant ethnographic detail into the analysis itself, but I think I can safely say that my omissions have not misrepresented the total picture. In addition, the interpretation of Mundurucú culture offered here is consistent with the more psychoanalytically informed account in Murphy and Murphy, 1974.

3 I considered substituting a less (for us) culturally marked term for "homosexual." I rejected this idea because I think this dichotomy has significant cross-cultural potential and represents a way of conceptualizing the similarities between cultures that, like the Mundurucú, do not have a system of institutionalized *physical* homosexuality and those that do. I thus wanted a term appropriate to the whole range of possible behaviors.

4 Clay makes a similar point about the symbolic permutations of male and female among the Mandak of New Britain (1977: 135–7 and passim).

5 I must point out that there is nothing contained in this analysis that is not touched on in some way by Lévi-Strauss in *Introduction to a Science of Mythology* (1970, 1973, 1978). It is, however, far beyond the scope of this essay to systematically explore the relationships between my understanding of these six myths and Lévi-Strauss's analysis of the whole of South American mythology. The influence of structuralist thought on my treatment of the myths will be apparent.

6 See T. Turner, 1969, for a discussion of temporality and narrative development in myths in the context of structural analysis.

7 All the myths are quoted verbatim from Murphy, 1958, pp. 70–80.

8 The "ears" are significant too, because as Jones (1974) has shown, the symbols of ears and hearing are commonly associated with the theme of miraculous birth.

9 Needless to say, these ideas are not the exclusive property of Mundurucú thought. The logic that for them connects bird symbolism with desires to overcome the death that is a consequence of life is the same logic that makes eggs an appropriate symbol of resurrection during Easter and allows the phoenix to arise from its ashes.

10 See Bamberger, 1974 for a further consideration of myths of this nature.

11 I offer my apologies for talking about "truth," but in the interest of brevity I will refrain from any long-winded discussion of assessments of ontological status. I think my point is clear from the text.

References

Bamberger, Joan. 1974. "The myth of matriarchy: why men rule in primitive society," in *Women, culture and society*, ed. M. Z. Rosaldo and L. Lamphere, pp. 263–80. Stanford: Stanford University Press.

Clay, Brenda. 1977. *Pinikindu*. Chicago: University of Chicago Press.

Dundes, Alan. 1976. "A psychoanalytical study of the bullroarer." *Man* NSII: 220–38.

Jones, Ernest. 1974. "The Madonna's conception through the ear," in *Psycho-myth, psycho-history, Volume II*, pp. 266–357. N.Y.: Hillstone.

Lévi-Strauss, Claude. 1970. *Introduction to a science of mythology: I, the raw and the cooked*. New York: Harper and Row.

1973. *From honey to ashes, introduction to a science of mythology: II*. New York: Harper and Row.

1978. *The origin of table manners, introduction to a science of mythology: III*. New York: Harper and Row.

Meggitt, Mervyn. 1964. "Male-female relationships in the highlands of Australian New Guinea." *American Anthropologist* 66: 204–24.

Murphy, Robert. 1954. "The rubber trade and the Mundurucú village." Unpublished Ph.D. dissertation, Columbia University.

1956. "Matrilocality and patrilineality in Mundurucú society," *American Anthropologist* 58: 414–34.

1957. "Intergroup hostility and cohesion." *American Anthropologist* 59: 1018–35.

1958. *Mundurucú religion*. University of California Publication in American Archeology and Ethnography, Volume 49.

1960. *Headhunters heritage*. Berkeley: University of California Press.

Murphy, Yolanda, and Murphy, Robert. 1974. *Women of the forest*. New York: Columbia University Press.

Turner, Terence. 1969. "Oedipus: time and structure in narrative form," in *Forms of Symbolic Action*, ed. Robert Spencer, pp. 26–68. Proceedings of the American Ethnological Society.

PART II
The political contexts of gender

8
Politics and gender in simple societies

Jane F. Collier & Michelle Z. Rosaldo

This essay provides a model for the study of gender as a cultural system.[1] Our strategy is at once comparative and programmatic. Building from the observation of unexpected regularities in the gender conceptions of several societies, we propose a model that shows how inequalities between the sexes figure in and can be understood with reference to structural inequalities that organize particular forms of social and economic life. Differences in gender systems become intelligible, we claim, when understood in terms that relate gender to society.

A cross-cultural sampling of gender reveals both similarities and differences. Women in all cultures mother, but cultures vary considerably in the extent to which they associate femininity with nature, fertility, maternal widsom, or motherly love. Most people engage in heterosexual relations; yet again, cultural variation runs the gamut from sex-as-polluting to sex-as-transcendence, sex as the loss of vital substance to sex as a model creative act. Finally, men, of course, differ: Some are thought to need sex while others resist and abhor it; some see women as valuable complements while others are fearful of mothers, or certain that men, through their knowledge and prowess, can virtually give birth by themselves. Some form of sexual asymmetry is probably a cultural universal. But the varieties of male preeminence are, we suggest in this essay, both as various and as patterned as all human social and cultural forms. We will particularly argue that cultural conceptions of the sexes are intimately and systematically linked to the organization of social inequality. Gender is part of society, and our purpose in this essay is to outline how, for one particular type of society, the organization of maleness and femaleness can be understood in relation to the organization of society at large.

More narrowly, our concern here is with the organization of gender in what we commonly regard as the simplest human societies. Readings on Australian Aborigines, American, Asian, and African hunter-gatherers and hunter-horticulturalists[2] led to the discovery that themes of motherhood and sexual reproduction are far less central to such peoples' conceptions of "woman" than we had assumed. Contrary to our expectation that motherhood provides women everywhere with a natural source of emotional satisfaction and cultural value, we found that neither women nor men in very simple societies celebrate women as nurturers or women's unique capacity to give life. Rather, Man the Hunter, which we thought to be *our* myth, turned out to characterize *their* conception of maleness. By contrast, Woman the Fertile,

Woman the Mother and Source of All Life was, quite remarkably, absent from all available accounts.

In simple societies, Man the Life Taker is not balanced by Woman the Life Giver, nor is male "culture" readily opposed to a "natural" and distinct women's world. Instead, men and women both are defined by a system opposing uni- (male–male) and heterosexual models of reproduction and social relationship. Men are celebrated for their skills as providers, and providing – especially through hunting – is characteristically associated with men's ability to order, energize, and nurture both social and natural worlds. Women's rituals, by contrast, have much less to do with the creation of life than with health and sexual pleasure. It is not as mothers and nurturers that women win ritual status, but rather as sexual beings; cultural conceptions of women acknowledge their role as participants in the heterosexual relationships through which adults organize and manipulate mundane cooperative bonds.

Our goal in what follows is to make sense of these views of the sexes, by relating recurrent conceptions of gender to the social systems in which they are used. In trying to understand why, for example, gathering never achieves the ritual acclaim earned by hunting, we found it inadequate to look first to protein needs, masculine strength, or the masculine psyche; nor could we grasp women's concern for their sexual vitality through appeal to the flexibility, autonomy, and equality common in descriptions of hunter-gatherer groups. Instead, we have pursued an analysis that links ritualized notions of gender to practical social relations. People celebrate those very self-images that they use when creating relationships, promoting cooperation or conflict, articulating desires and claims. Gender as an aspect of personhood should, we suggest, be understood in terms of its place in a social system, wherein inequalities in status and privilege determine the goals people fight for, their motives for politics, and the conditions they seek to explain.

Our essay is divided into four parts. After a brief theoretical section outlining the concerns guiding our research and presentation of results, there is a longer section on economic and political processes, followed by a discussion of core cultural conceptions. Because productive and political processes cannot by analyzed apart from the cultural understandings people have of such processes, the section on political economy focuses both on what people do and on cultural understandings underlying action. The section on cultural conceptions, by contrast, examines core symbols underlying and uniting understandings associated with different fields of endeavor. A final section summarizes our results and discusses their implications for creating an anthropology capable of understanding *both* men's and women's lives.

Theoretical considerations

Simple societies of hunter-gatherers have long held a privileged place in the anthropological literature as living examples of social systems based on a technological adaptation presumably followed by "cultural man" for 99 percent of "his" time on earth (Lee and DeVore 1968: 3). In their questionable status as ancestors, modern hunter-gatherers have been analyzed to

discover elementary social forms and/or basic human nature, uncontaminated
by disparities in wealth and power that result from food-producing adaptations. Feminists, in particular, have recently turned to hunter-gatherers to
discover a lost primitive egalitarianism in which both women and men
enjoyed autonomy and freedom from arbitrary constraints. The well-known
fluidity of hunter-gatherers' social organization, which makes them difficult
to analyze in terms of traditional social-structural categories, has contributed
to a view of hunter-gatherer behavior as determined by biological and ecological needs rather than socially constructed rules.

Our knowledge of all human societies is, of course, shaped by our questions and theoretical predispositions, but because hunter-gatherers have been
treated as presumed ancestors, our knowledge of their social forms has been
particularly skewed. Most investigators have been less concerned with understanding the organization of meaning and obligation in hunter-gatherer life
than with discovering how and why hunting peoples are, or are not, like
ourselves. Thus, different ethnographers have wondered: "Do simple peoples have families?" "Are they aware of men's role in procreation?" "Do
they maximize economic advantage?" "Do they have political as well as
domestic organization?" and, more recently, "Do they, like modern capital-
ists, subordinate women to men?" Not surprisingly, the often unstated
assumption that hunter-gatherers act out innate drives has colored debate over
relations between the sexes in such groups. Whereas investigators of more
complex societies have had no trouble finding social or economic causes for
instances of male aggression or female power, similar instances among
hunter-gatherers are treated either as proof of universal male dominance or as
proof that women are naturally the equals of men. As a result of the context of
contemporary discussions, scholars on both sides have failed to reckon with
data that seems inconsistent with the interpretations they propose. Thus, we
hear all too rarely about threats of rape among the "harmless" and egalitarian
Bushmen, much as we read far too little about old women like the Pygmy
Balekimito whose death led to Turnbull's (1961: 51) discovery that she was
"a mother to us all." At the same time – and from our point of view, even
more serious – the arguments concerning hunter-gatherers have done little to
illuminate the relationship between experiences of limitation and opportunities for exercising power; whether or not women are, in some places or tribes,
men's true equals, we have yet to understand just what, substantively, the
relations of the sexes consist in, and how these, in turn, are connected to other
features of the organization of social existence in hunter-gatherer worlds.

The alternative proposed in this essay requires a suspension of earlier,
evaluative questions in favor of an approach that treats gender as a particularly salient aspect of social personhood, and assumes that personhood
itself is intimately bound up with economic and political processes that give
rise to and help reproduce social relationships and inequalities. A model
adequate to understanding gender is then, we suggest, a model showing the
connections between productive relationships, political processes, and folk
conceptions of human nature; plausibly, such a model should permit the
delineation of structurally significant similarities and differences in the con-

struction of gender in diverse social groups. The account we propose here represents an effort in this direction; in order to come to terms with Man the Hunter, we need to grasp his significance in relation to recurrent patterns in hunter-gatherer life.

Anthropologists have long recognized kinship and marriage as critical points of access to the organization of cooperative relationships in nonclass societies. Marriage and descent – figuring differently in different theories – are recognized continually in ethnographic reporting as providing the terms in which people organize productive relationships and construe their obligations and rights. More narrowly, because marriage is a concern of both sexes, requiring some representation of gender difference, it has been suggested that the organization of marriage provides a privileged clue to the organization of gender-relevant productive relationships in all classless social formations (see Siskind 1973, Rubin 1975). In marrying, people ''make families,'' but they also contract debts, change residence, stir enmities, and establish cooperative bonds. A typology of nonclass societies in terms of the organization of marriage would seem, then, an important first step for the analysis of gender. The different ways in which tribal peoples ''make marriages'' are likely to correspond, on the one hand, to important differences in economic and political organization, and, on the other, to salient variations in the ways that gender is construed.

Thus, we suggest here that the analysis of gender in hunting societies should be grounded in a characterization of how marriage works in such groups. Briefly, we would characterize marriage in nonclass, nonrank societies in terms of an analytical distinction between groups in which gifts of labor by the groom to his in-laws are the expected form of marital legitimization and groups in which the groom presents gifts of valuables acquired through the labor of someone other than the groom himself. The first, here called ''brideservice'' societies, are groups in which all adults control the distribution of their produce, and so, ongoing relationships depend upon free and continuing gifts and services through which cooperating persons organize the distribution of food. These can be contrasted with the generally more complex class of ''bridewealth'' societies in which goods given on marriage are seen as payment for rights to a woman's labor, sexuality, or offspring; in such groups, the acquisition of marital prestations typically places the groom in a relationship of debt to senior kinfolk who provide young men the prerequisites for launching their adult careers. In bridewealth, but not brideservice societies, gifts can be given in lieu of labor, and indebtedness is often repaid by work; failure to give gifts may be seen as negating a marital arrangement; and social offenders – including grooms with inadequate resources – may be required to pay, through prestations or labor, in order to rectify wrongs. Generally speaking, most hunter-gatherers and some horticulturalist-hunter groups organize marriage in a manner consistent with the expectations of brideservice; bridewealth, by contrast, seems to characterize most horticultural tribal groups.

At the same time, however, because we are concerned to characterize systems of social relationship – rather than ecological adaptations – it is important to stress from the outset that the distinction between bridewealth and brideservice corresponds only roughly to more conventional, technologically based typologies, in terms of which hunters and horticulturalists have, traditionally, been opposed. Brideservice describes not only most extant hunter-gatherers but also such horticultural peoples as the Philippine Ilongots (whom we discuss here), the tropical forest peoples of the Amazon, and probably many lowland New Guinea horticultural groups. All of these differ in predictable and systematic ways from bridewealth peoples familiar in the ethnographic literature (such as Kaguru, Ibo, Mae Enga); all share certain gender conceptions; all reveal similarities in the shape of productive relations; and all are characterized by a style of political process not found in bridewealth groups.

Bridewealth peoples, for instance, tend in their rituals and cosmology to display a preoccupation with female reproductive capacities; women are valued as mothers, but feared for their polluting blood. Characteristically, men in their rituals stress the rejection of feminine qualities; femininity is threatening to maleness, and male adulthood requires rejection of childhood ties to a feminine world. For brideservice peoples, by contrast, there is little to fear – or respect – about mothers; birth rituals are virtually lacking; women celebrate sexual prowess; and adults of both sexes acknowledge that men, through their knowledge and skill as providers, are the people who nurture and order a problematically heterosexual world. Brideservice, unlike bridewealth, societies stress affinal bonds in the organization of productive relations. No person works for another, and although predictable patterns of local cooperation grant men considerable freedom, there is an enduring assumption that young men, on marriage, will share a good part of their produce with members of wives' natal groups. Finally, where bridewealth peoples conduct legal disputes in idioms concerned with debts, rights, and remunerations, the politicking in brideservice societies seems consistently to give rise to contests. Brideservice gifts are not payments but proofs of equality in status, and what people readily negotiate has less to do with obligation than the recognition of others as peers.

Brideservice/bridewealth appears, in short, a scheme of classification that unites aspects of gender, social relationship, and politics. But, as with any typology, the analysis of any one type depends on its implicit or explicit contrasts with the types to which it is opposed. Limitations of space and the requirements of coherent exegesis have led us, however, to concentrate only on brideservice societies in this essay. Our goal is to suggest a strategy for the sociological analysis of gender by tracing internal relations, and so explicating the logic of what seem significant correlations within the class of brideservice groups. The kind of understanding developed here is ultimately circular: Social relationships of production, marriage, politics, and gender are construed not in linear fashion but as mutually determining aspects of a complex social whole. We begin our analysis of brideservice societies by characterizing an asymmetry that seems to obtain in the social relations of the sexes in the process of production, in order then to show how brideservice relates to an organization of labor wherein affinity underlies cooperation, marriage is a male achievement and the logic of social relations permits men, as "achievers" of women, to attain a public position not generally enjoyed by their wives. The political strategies and self-images typically associated with the sexes are then made intelligible with reference to the organization of cooperative relations in the contexts of everyday life.

The connections we trace here between personhood, politics, and production are seen as characteristic of *all* brideservice societies. Without denying that brideservice societies differ, our claim is that *all* are constrained by the kinds of relationships, images, and social processes that we seek to describe. Brideservice societies are seen to represent, in short, a qualitatively distinctive social configuration, amenable, we suggest, to initial analysis and description in terms of its typical form. Any real group will differ, of course, from the ideal type in ways determined by the particulars of history and environment. Each will display unique sociological arrangements, differences in cultural foci, and distinctive capacities for change. Equally, it is clear that in certain contexts bridewealth and other types of more complex societies may exhibit some of the features we associate with brideservice groups. Our argument, however, is that both similarities and differences are to be understood not as isolated facts but as aspects of social configurations that determine, in every instance, the implications of particular courses of action and the kinds of social consequences that are most likely to obtain. Thus, for example, apparent commonalities among certain bridewealth and brideservice peoples – in terms of polygyny, gerontocracy, exclusive male ritual practice and so on – are here seen as the product of distinctive processes in what are, at base, radically different social formations. And, correspondingly, when we find that brideservice societies differ – in degrees of stratification, technological adaptations, the prevalence of polygyny, or dominant ritual concerns – our view is that these variations are best seen as the product of cultural and historical contingencies that have interacted, over time, with recurrent processes and patterns characteristic of brideservice societies as a type.

The static qualities of our model and the fact that it disregards important differences between what are, of course, quite different groups will be distressing to those who are, quite rightfully, distrustful of a prevalent analytical tendency to operate with stereotyped impressions that negate ethnographic detail. But such violence is necessary to progress. Brideservice, like patrilineality, is a theoretic construct enabling the discovery of connections. Inadequate to the analysis of any given example, it is, first and foremost, a model that tells where to look for determinants and how to describe interrelations that – empirically – seem to obtain. Ultimately, the proof, as it were, of our argument, will not lie in statistical testing but, rather, in the ability of our model to reveal intelligible relations among what once appeared as unrelated, or even contradictory, ethnographic observations. What we seek is a generalization that will permit us to return, with new insight, to hitherto unilluminated descriptions. Our act of cross-cultural violence is ultimately justified by its ability to encompass, in new ways, the ethnographic riches with which we began.

In order to concretize our ideal account, and to display its range of application, we concentrate in our discussion on evidence from three historically and geographically specific societies – !Kung Bushmen of the Kalahari Desert,[3] Australian Aborigines of Northeastern Arnhem Land (Murngin), and Ilongot hunter-horticulturalists of Northern Luzon, Philippines. Differing both in the extent of male dominance (relatively egalitarian Bushmen versus more asymmetrical Aborigines) and in their technological adaptations (foraging Bushmen and Aborigines versus Ilongot hunter-horticulturalists), the three societies were chosen to show that what, superficially, appear as quite distinctive social formations can be analyzed in similar terms.

The Bushmen have occupied a central place in recent discussion of hunter-gatherers. The fluidity of their social world, and the leisure of a form of economic life concerned with little more than the needs of day-to-day consumption, have made them a primary example of "primitive egalitarianism" (Draper 1975). By contrast, Australian Aborigines are typically pictured as living in a relatively harsh environment (either the fertile but densely settled forests of Arnhem Land or the Central Australian desert), in which women, even as they enjoy certain prerogatives, are nevertheless clearly subordinated to men through the dynamics of a marriage system that gives rise to polygyny and gerontocracy. The Ilongots of the Philippines contrast with both societies in depending for subsistence on rice, a cultivated staple; but, as of the late 1960s, they continued to complement their diet with a rich supply of forest products – game, fish, birds, honey, ferns, and tree crops – foraged almost exclusively by men. They, like many hunter-gatherers, appeared to their investigators as relatively egalitarian, and Rosaldo's (1975, 1980) work on their gender organization was central to the development of our model of how brideservice societies work.

Economic and political organization

SOCIAL RELATIONS OF PRODUCTION
"Sexual asymmetry" – a basic imbalance in the nature and organization of obligations and the availability of public reward – is in the base of productive relations in very simple societies.[4] It is, however, a particular form of asymmetry, neither universal nor biologically determined, associated with a particular organization of productive roles. This asymmetry lies in the fact that although women's gathering or gardening and men's hunting both contribute needed foods to the diet, women are required to feed families, whereas men distribute their meat through the group according to rules favoring members of the senior generation. These rules, associated with brideservice, permit *all* adult men to appear as the forgers of social relationships. Furthermore, among seniors, the organization of productive obligations permits men but not women to hope to be free of obligations, and, in this limited sense, to be dominant – not in their rights to labor but in their ability to distribute meat freely, creating cooperative connections in the interests of a social whole. Thus, although adult men and women in very simple societies may work apart

and produce different things, the social relations of the sexes are not created from equal or balanced exchanges of male and female products, nor are men and women simple commodity producers who enter into exchanges for the mutual satisfaction of biologically determined needs. Men's game and women's gathered foods are not equivalents because they acquire their values from socially determined obligations that precede and underlie possibilities for exchange.

Among the !Kung of Nyae Nyae, for example, "every able, adult woman is responsible for gathering for herself, her family and her dependents. She may give to others as she wishes, but custom and expectation in !Kung society do not require that plant food be shared in a general distribution as meat is shared. This means that every able, adult woman must gather regularly" (Marshall 1976: 97). Men do not hunt every day, and Marshall notes that only very large animals are divided according to formal rules. Middle-sized animals are shared among the hunters and given to kin and friends, while very small animals are eaten within the family (1976: 133). Marshall describes three "waves of sharing" when a big animal is killed. "The first distribution the owner (of the animal) makes is to the hunters and to the giver of the arrow, if the arrow was not one the owner made himself" (1976: 297). On the second distribution "certain obligations are compulsory" (1976: 297). The first obligation of a man who has received meat in the primary distribution is to give to his wife's parents. "He must give to them the best he has in as generous portions as he can, while still fulfilling other primary obligations, which are to his own parents, his spouse, and his offspring" (1976: 298). On the third wave of sharing, those who received meat give to "his or her parents, parents-in-law, spouse, offspring, siblings and others." Members of the senior generation, particularly parents-in-law, thus have privileged access to meat hunted by others.

A Murngin wife, like her !Kung counterpart, also "has few commitments to meet, beyond providing vegetable foods, fruit, shellfish, damper and so on for her children, her husband and herself." If she has any food left over, she gives it to "co-wives and their children or to her parents if they are nearby" (Berndt 1965: 97). Men, on the other hand, have extensive obligations to others. Although Berndt states that "a man's major responsibility is to provide meat, and fish where it is available, for his wife or wives and children," he later notes that due to men's heavy obligations a man's family may, in fact, eat none of his meat on some occasions. The greater part of a man's catch, particularly when he is young, "goes in settlement of other kin obligations or is eaten by men with whom he has ritual ties, or given to older men to whom he is religiously indebted" (1965: 97). Similarly, for the neighboring Gidjingali, "A man had responsibilities to provide for his wife and young children and to make gifts of food regularly to the mother and MBs of his wife or betrothed," whereas the wife's primary obligations are those of "obtaining daily nourishment for the hearth group, and assisting her husband in fulfilling his obligations to others" (Hiatt 1965: 68).

Finally, among Ilongots, women pound and cook rice every day – a point on which Ilongots often remark when contrasting the hard work their women do to the sexual cooperation in rice preparation expected among Ifugao and Ilocano peasant settlers in their area. Ilongot women daily prepare at least two major meals for their families, while men's hunts are at once more intense and more erratic. Trips to the forest depend in large part on social pressures and moods. Game is often committed to storage for sale, gift, or the sponsoring of communal rituals, and the obligation of pan-settlement distribution means that men rarely give meat to the members of their households alone. Young hunters may know how to butcher game, but seniors typically supervise its distribution. And, significantly, men's stories about both hunting and headhunting almost always begin with a routine statement of their claims in women: Men, before leaving, tell their wives, mothers, or sisters, "pound me rice for I am going off." Finally, generosity in the distribution of game is characteristically associated with male seniors. Conscientious young men, like their hardworking wives, are seen as fulfilling their reasonable social obligations, but only old men are remembered for never roasting so much as a tidbit of game in the solitude of their own homes.

In all cases, then, a woman is obliged to provide daily food for her family, whereas a man is expected to distribute his meat according to predetermined rules favoring seniors. And although adult women must fulfill daily obligations that change little throughout their lives, adult men do not hunt every day, and more of their meat becomes available for exchanges, gifts, and the manipulation of social relations as their seniors grow old and die.

MARRIAGE

Men's obligation to distribute meat widely while women feed families causes marriage to have very different implications for women and men. A newly married man is sharply distinguished from bachelors by having direct, privileged access to both female sexuality and the products of female labor; marriage, to the bachelor, is a necessary and desirable attainment. A newly married woman, on the other hand, appears to have no more privileged access to male products than her single sisters,[5] and sexual access to a husband often fails to compensate her for the loss of personal and sexual freedom she enjoyed when still unattached. It is this difference that underlies the fact that men, but not women, in brideservice societies, are apt to think and talk about their marriages in terms of the achievement of rewards and claims.

Male youths approach their adult lives in need of a partner. Once they are old enough to leave parental homes, bachelors begin courting their future spouses, but this is a slow process. Before and after initiation, Murngin youths are sent out for several years of visiting in the homes and settlements of distant "kin" who may at some time give them daughters. And Ilongot youths may spend periods ranging from weeks to several years working as "followers" or almost-adopted "sons" in homes of senior relatives who themselves have maiden daughters or who show promise of supporting the youths in future suits. In almost all cases, boys old enough to know of sex are required to sleep apart from the main camp. Young boys are expected to do very little work, but adolescents camping near the parents of girls they hope to wed are subjected to demands for labor – even if they respond to such demands by moping (see Marshall 1976: 173).

Because they are attractive, free, and often ready to approach desirable girls at will, these bachelors tend to be viewed as sexually aggressive, and, consequently, they are likely to be blamed for causing trouble. Young children in brideservice societies apparently enjoy considerable sexual freedom and are often described as engaging in quite explicit sexual play (Shostak 1976; Berndt and Berndt 1951). But as boys and girls reach adolescence, their actions acquire social consequences, and so are accompanied by more serious constraints. Because adolescent girls are either married or have recognized suitors, adolescent boys' and girls' attempts to continue youthful sexual play are usually interpreted as young men's infringing on older men's socially recognized rights.

In short, the organization of sexual privilege, together with the more strictly economic need of all men for a wife and hearth, means that marriage marks a critical transition in the life career of a man. From being a wanderer and troublemaker, he becomes a settled and responsible adult. Once he has a wife to keep his fire and build his shelter, he acquires a place in the camp. With a wife to sleep beside him at night and provide sexual services on demand, a man need no longer live apart with bachelors, and other married men no longer regard his presence as threatening. As long as his wife feeds him, a man need never ask for food, and he can be seemingly free from obligations to others after distributing the meat from each hunt.[6] Furthermore, marriage enables a man to become an effective social actor. He can play the role of host and invite others to share the hearth, food, and, in some cases, sexual services, provided by his wife. As a man with recognized interests to protect, he can speak up and expect to be heard in public gatherings. And, as an individual whose basic needs are provided, he can devote his time to building the exchange networks that enhance social influence and prestige.

The contrast for women is striking, because marriage marks, in general, a decline in female status and autonomy[7]–a fact made clear by numerous accounts of young girls who declare themselves too young to marry, flee husbands, take lovers, and even kill unwanted offspring in order to avoid marital constraints.[8] There is even considerable evidence of parents and siblings who virtually force unwilling girls into marriage: Shostak writes of !Kung girls pressured by their parents to accept the intrusive demands of unwanted and elderly husbands (even if only temporarily!); and Ilongot parents recall times they hit, or watched new husbands beat, their lazy daughters in order to teach them the duties appropriate to wives. Girls in brideservice groups are taught that they need husbands in order to bear children (whether, as in the Australian case, one needs a man to "dream" them, or, as with the South American Sirionó, babies are left to die in the absence of fathers who are the only persons licensed to cut a child's umbilical cord).[9] And, of course, it is largely in anticipation of grown children that marriage acquires a positive significance in most of these women's lives. Men become adults upon marriage, but it is only with age that conjugality gives women new privilege. As the mother of daughters, an older woman enjoys special access to the labor and products of sons-in-law, who, of course, are sexually taboo.

Our analysis of marriage in brideservice societies is thus rooted in the observation that at the same time that young men need wives, young women do not perceive themselves as needing husbands – and so marriage is cast, overwhelmingly, as a matter of a man's establishing claims to the moral commitment and daily services of some particular bride. Furthermore, men establish these claims, not by providing for wives and children, but, rather, by distributing produce to senior in-laws, so as to win support and commitment from those who most influence wives.

Thus, even though prestations and services by sons-in-law do not "buy" them spouses – and the evidence shows that young wives have considerable freedom to reject an unwanted spouse – it is nevertheless clear that the characteristic ways men create claims to women involve transactions in which future wives have no role. Future husbands and wives may give each other little presents, but the features that distinguish marriages from more flexible and egalitarian lover relations are precisely the transactions that occur between a man and his wife's kin. Lovers are related as equals (a point to which we will return), but inequality is built into the relationship of spouses, precisely because of the fact that young men have need of wifely providers – a fact that gives rise to the fiction that men, through their gifts or exchanges, "win" something to fight for and value, in coming to live with a wife. Of course, it is also true that a wife may give presents to her husband's kin, but such presents tend generally to follow on, and be subordinated to, her husband's prestations, and so are more aptly viewed as an acknowledgment of her status than as a means of establishing claims in the hunting accomplishments of her spouse. The basic obligations of men and women already decree that a husband gains more from marriage than his wife. And a man's dependence on in-laws for help in controlling his bride combines with rules of meat distribution that consistently favor seniors to create a situation in which parents-in-law have first rights to the labor and products of young married men.

Marriage emerges, then, as a relationship that binds specific people together in a particular, hierarchical system of obligations, requiring that women provide services for husbands, young grooms enjoy privileges not available to bachelors, and husbands owe gifts and labor to wives' senior kin.[10] The fact that young men need wives in a way that young women do not need husbands grants power to those (men and women) able to influence women's behavior, and casts women as the desirable prize of male competition. Specifically, it permits men to "achieve" women by assuming productive obligations vis-à-vis senior persons in their wives' natal groups. Thus, the only married people free from direct obligations to specific others are senior men whose parents-in-law are dead. And, at the same time, senior men are privileged in that they tend to have the largest number of specific others (wives and sons-in-law) obligated to provide for them.

It is significant, in this regard, that hunter-gatherer/horticulturalists do not have elaborate wedding ceremonies. In fact, Hoebel's observation about the

Eskimo that "marriage is entered into merely by bedding down with the intention of living together; divorce is effected simply by not living together any more" (1954: 83) appears true of many other groups, particularly for women's second and subsequent marriages. Girl's first marriages may be celebrated by simple rites (usually symbolizing a wife's duty to feed her family and a husband's duty to feed his in-laws), but ethnographers writing on hunter-gatherer/horticulturalists seem most impressed by the lack of ceremony (particularly striking when one contrasts accounts of ceremonial negotiation in bridewealth societies) surrounding what they regard as an important change of status (see Thomas 1959: 159).

What ethnographers of brideservice groups report, instead, is that marriage is a gradual process, through which both young women and their kinfolk come to find themselves "accustomed to" the would-be groom. Among Ilongots, for instance, hopeful men may first visit and work in their would-be brides' households, and then begin, as their efforts are acknowledged, to avoid the names of future affines in anticipatory respect of conventional taboos. Over time, a man begins sleeping regularly with the woman he hopes to marry; he may give gifts to calm recalcitrant and "angry" in-laws, and, perhaps, encourage one of his "sisters" to enter an "exchange" transaction and marry a "brother" of his wife. Some Aboriginal men (see Goodale, 1971) initiate marriages by becoming "sons-in-law," who offer gifts of game and service to the senior kin of future spouses. And !Kung men, much like Ilongots, typically establish a marriage by distributing game to kin of their wives.

More generally, we can say that ethnographic accounts record four ways in which a man may create socially recognized claims to a specific woman for his wife. First – and apparently most commonly – some form of brideservice or uxorilocality is practiced. Second, a man may inherit a wife or be given one of the wives of a polygynous older brother. Third, and more often, some form of direct exchange – sister exchange, bilateral cross-cousin marriage, exogamous moieties, or section systems – is mentioned as the preferred transaction among hunter-gatherer and hunter-horticulturalist groups. Finally, often combined with the methods already cited, men may establish claims by giving gifts, which ethnographers sometimes label bridewealth.[11] It is important to note, however, that these "bridewealth" payments among hunter-gatherer/horticulturalists are fundamentally different from those called by the same name in Africa and Highland New Guinea, where marriages are validated through an exchange of goods that the young and poor have difficulty acquiring. Among hunters, what analysts call bridewealth is more aptly viewed as brideservice, because the meat or trade items a young man gives his parents-in-law are things he can obtain on his own, without having to borrow from an elder.

Thus, as already noted, for Ilongots, marriage by "exchange," uxorilocal residence, and gift giving are all common and they may combine in the establishment of a single marriage. Men say they take wives "in exchange" for the insult suffered when other men take their sisters; and, depending on the immediate political context, exchange marriages may dampen requests for prestations, or, at some times, increase them – for brothers object to the use of *their* sisters as objects in male-male exchange. Furthermore, much as Thompson (1949) reports for the Murngin and Marshall (1976: 272) hints for the !Kung, Ilongots recognize a number of named prestations, varying from the gift of an animal to recalcitrant in-laws to the sponsoring of feasts that are accompanied by gifts of cloth, ornaments, and tools purchased, for the most part, from game caught by the husband himself.

The important point here, however, is that gifts and prestations among Ilongots, as in all brideservice groups, are not used to ''buy'' rights or privileges vis-à-vis women but, rather, to dramatize and enact new commitments. An Ilongot father or brother may dislike and ''be angered'' by an undesirable suitor; he may choose to move and encourage his newlywed daughter to follow, in hopes of annoying her husband and ultimately, perhaps, undermining their developing affective bonds. But no man can, in fact, ''sell'' another a claim to his daughter or sister, nor can he, in lieu of required prestations, insist on his right to take back a kinswoman associated with an apparently unworthy groom.

Thus, the services young men perform in affines' homes are not the equivalent of payments, as is the brideservice performed by poor men in what we call bridewealth societies. Rather, the services young men perform are enactments of patterned obligations that are likely to be of significance throughout the man's marital life. !Kung men, for example, never escape the obligation to ''provide for'' wives' parents. Even if a man's wife should die, he must continue to ''support'' her parents and young siblings if they decide to accompany him when he performs brideservice for a new wife (Marshall 1976: 384). Similarly, R. Berndt reports that a Murngin man, ''throughout his life . . . is expected to give his actual father-in-law presents of food and other goods'' (1965: 83); Hiatt claims for the neighboring Gidjingali that a groom ''began making gifts . . . from the time of bestowal and continued as long as the woman remained his betrothed or his wife'' (1965: 81). Writings about ''patrilocal hordes'' among Aborigines and hunter-gatherers generally show limited appreciation of the importance of these enduring affinal connections. [12] And yet, not only did Murngin grooms reside with future in-laws for years leading up to the culmination of a marriage but Hiatt (1965) and Peterson (1970) both report that affinal ties were often central to the organization of cooperative residential groupings in Australia; similarly, Lee (1974) has observed that !Kung bands are often woman centered, by which he means that women often live near their mothers, and that affinity (rather than lineal connection) typically organizes cooperative bonds among men. Finally, Ilongots are explicit in opting for uxorilocal postmarital residence and associating this with the requirement that grooms ''feed'' the parents of their wives.

One consequence of these arrangements is that in brideservice societies the bonds linking husband to wife involve much more than simple ties between spouses and that the obligations assumed upon marriage make the existence of nuclear families dependent on cooperative relations that encompass a much larger group. Many scholars report that the nuclear family is a ''building block'' (see Service 1979: 5) in hunter-gatherer societies, but our analysis suggests, on the contrary, that "the family" is not a particularly strong or autonomous unit and, in fact, that its very existence is always dependent on men's active affinal bonds. We alluded in our opening remarks to the relative absence, in simple societies, of public cultural stress on the role of the mother. Whatever her affective import, the mother is not (as she so often is in bridewealth societies) the focus of lineage division, the object of stereotyped nostalgia, or the source of nurturant but dangerous substances that inhibit the growth of young men. Very young boys in brideservice societies eat at mother's fire and breast, but after weaning, boys are described by most ethnographers as roaming in gangs and either eating irregularly or at the fires of various "mothers" in turn. No matter how strong their affective bonds, parents and their male children are ultimately separated by the fact that marriage is a requirement of social adulthood, and neither mothers nor fathers can provide wives for unmarried sons. Parents can make arrangements for a son to marry, and, should a suitably aged daughter be available, they can put considerable pressure on her to marry as her brother wishes; but because the most important privileges enjoyed by a husband depend on the day-to-day behavior of his wife, a husband is ultimately most dependent on those most able to influence his wife's actions. As a result, he is more likely, in adult life, to find himself actively involved with her parents than with his own. We regard it as no accident, therefore, that Lorna Marshall, for instance, reports that nuclear families among Bushmen can be found only among extended ones (1976: 168), or that a recent discussion of the very fluid residential groupings among some hunter-gatherers stresses that familial units are always interdependent, and that local cooperation is, characteristically, organized in terms of affinal ties (Morris 1979).

It is, in short, because of the ways that marriage involves the establishment of these enduring (and socially and economically crucial) affinal connections that we have decided to use the label "brideservice" to characterize the organization of productive relations in the societies considered here. If, as we believe is the case, kinship organizes production in nonclass societies, then the marriages that give rise to kinship must determine, in large part, the shape of productive bonds. Our point can be illustrated briefly by exploring the contrast, established earlier, between brideservice and bridewealth societal types.[13] In bridewealth societies, where marriages are validated through exchanges of goods the young and poor have difficulty acquiring, young men work for those who provide their marriage payments, and relations between husbands and wives are shaped by men's need to acquire the goods that enable them to participate in others' marriages, and thus to acquire rights in the labor and products of the young. In such (bridewealth) societies, a wife's domestic services may be far less important to her husband than his rights to appropriate the products of her labor, to collect bridewealth for her daughters, and to demand compensation from her lovers. His bridewealth payments constitute a claim in the future, a stake in the outcomes of activities in which a wife may or may not be engaged. By contrast, in the brideservice societies we are discussing, the only benefits a husband derives from marriage are the daily services of his wife. Because young men create claims to women by performing services for in-laws, goods have no real value, in the sense that they cannot be converted into the kinship ties that structure productive obligations. And because goods have no transcontextual value, a husband can enjoy the privileges of his married status only so long as his wife acknowledges their bond. Finally, it is this dependence of husbands on wifely compliance that ensures husbands' performance of services for those most able to influence the behavior of wives.

Stated otherwise, brideservice is critical to understanding social relations in simple societies because it provides both the foundations for, and the limits on, what inequality exists in such groups. On the one hand, young men's need for wives grants power to those able to influence the behavior of marriageable women, but, on the other hand, the fact that men earn wives through their own labor puts limits on the amount of power available to leaders.[14] Brideservice, in other words, provides the analytical link between productive obligations and political processes. To explore this link, we turn now to a consideration of the characteristically "sexual" politics found in all brideservice groups.

POLITICS
Descriptions of hunting societies – be they polygynous Australians or relatively monogamous Bushmen – generally agree upon one point: These are egalitarian social systems in which no adult can command the labor or obedience of any other; all control (to a considerable extent) the distribution of the foodstuffs that they, as individuals, acquire; and all experience considerable freedom to withdraw or flee from undesirable social relationships, commitments, and demands. Aging men and women in these groups do not enjoy the right to rule or make demands of junior fellows. And although one reads of a diffuse respect for senior persons recognized as "parents" of cooperating kinfolk, one does not hear of elders who can command labor, shape political decisions, or make choices that their children are expected to obey.

The status of respected senior kin lies not in rights that they enjoy to persons or to goods but, rather, in the things they know, their histories of cooperative endeavor, and their ability (at a time of life when needs and obligations are minuscule at best) to act generously, in the interests of the social unit as a whole. In societies that typically place strict taboos on the naming of the dead (see Thomas 1959: 249; Maddock 1972: 170; Berndt and Berndt 1964: 389; Turnbull 1961: 106; Wallace and Hoebel 1952: 123; Chagnon 1968: 10; Rosaldo 1980a: 158), kin ties are themselves most likely to be reckoned and invoked with reference to these living seniors. And so, as foci for the solidarity of cooperating junior kin, respected elders may enjoy a somewhat special place, while at the same time, children whose marriages are secure will display the independence that tends ultimately to undermine whatever power aging parents once could claim.

Stated otherwise, at the same time that people of both sexes can look forward to an old age of respect and real centrality in relation to new generations of cooperating young, the egalitarianism of brideservice societies resides precisely in the fact that wives are the only things that individuals must work for and then fight to keep, so that once a man is married he needs nothing. Thus, no adult individual is apt to be dependent on another's will for long nor can anyone look forward to commanding resources necessary to oblige others to accede to his demands. For aging women and men alike, the privileges and statuses associated with a successful adult life are, unlike men's marriages themselves, things to be enjoyed but not "achieved."

Adult women and men, through their exchanges among kin and friends, may establish cooperative networks that will open doors when they need help and create bonds likely to be realized in concrete coresidential groups when they are aging. But what they do not win are powers, rights, or goods that might enable wealthy and successful persons elsewhere in the world to enforce their wishes and make regular claims. Because no son-in-law owes ongoing debts to his wife's kin, but rather, hopes to win (and then maintain) their sympathy for his suit through the establishment of a long-term relation, it turns out that whatever benefits his parents-in-law enjoy are ultimately dependent on the youth's good conscience and productive skill.

Father- and mother-in-law alike are often recognized as statuses fraught with privilege and esteem. But although the mother-in-law, for instance, often holds a special claim to her daughter's husband's goods, and parents-in-law and children-in-law may find taboos constraining the development of intimate relations, it remains (in general) the case that senior adults rarely have the power to demand more than a daughter's husband wants to give in dramatizing his marital claims. Thus, once a man knows that his marriage is secure (a sense likely to follow the birth of children who, of course, constrain his spouse's movements), there are no future powers or statuses to seek, no elevated roles demanding proof, subordination, and competition for their ultimate attainment. Indeed, securely married men, much like their wives, are apt to find themselves less interested in prestige or fame than in the love, companionship, and far-reaching sorts of bonds that will secure a life with "children" to attend them in old age.

Thus, it is hardly surprising to discover that brideservice peoples do not, in general, argue and compete for rights to lead, because the leader has no special powers. Rather, much as one might expect, disputes in public contexts are overwhelmingly concerned with the wives that all men need and all can fear to lose: Theirs is a politics of sex. Male adulthood is predicated on men's claims to the spouses who attend their equal hearths, and men compete and fight for the attainment of a secure marital status.

Thus, Fried's useful observation – that men in egalitarian societies do not display a desire for dominance but do display a considerable drive to achieve parity, or at least to establish a status that announces, "Don't fool with me" (1967: 79) – emerges both as a description of the stance of a successful married man and of the kinds of actions apt to be required before his marital independence is achieved. Because the equal status all men hope to earn is based on marriage, men must be able to assert, and to defend, their claims to women. And so marriage, by defining what men in brideservice societies can desire, shapes what men are apt to fight for, and how they enter into and resolve disputes. Socially organized life goals for men thus determine political processes by shaping the arenas in which claims are made and contested. And political processes, in turn, have consequences for relations between the sexes because they provide a framework for social action. In what follows, we will begin to relate idioms of conflict to the strategies and goals associated with men and women in brideservice groups, by seeing how these both reflect and, at the same time, shape the quality of social relationships and their legitimizing ideologies.

In a world where acquiring a wife is the most important – and most problematic – goal to which one can aspire, social relationships among adults will have a good deal to do with claims to women. Furthermore, in a world where marital claims are realized in the daily ways a wife attends her husband's needs, sexual contact is virtually indissociable from marriage – and sexual intercourse can readily become a matter of political consequence. Thus, we find that in brideservice societies polygyny, though limited, testifies to high status,[15] cooperation among men is expressed in the giving of women (sisters, daughters, wives), and enmity is expressed in competition for women. Men fight other men because affronts impugn their claims to women, while women may take lovers in order to manipulate and constrain their husbands' or their brothers' plans. Finally, because their claims to women are so central in men's lives, men will, in Fried's terms, seek to establish a status that announces "don't fool with me" (1967: 79) in order to assert at once their independence and their willingness to fight.

Sexual intercourse is thus central to political relations in brideservice societies for two reasons. First, sex is, in actual fact, the form through which men forge relationships with one another. We have already indicated the significance of affinity for the establishment of cooperative relations and of peership among men. But second, sex can operate metaphorically, permitting men to express claims to women whose marriages they may at some time wish to influence – or to enjoy themselves. Potential claims like these may prove especially important at a time when men have cause to fear either the illness, death, or disloyalty of their wives. As a result, a man's guarantee of continued independence lies in creating claims to other women; for example, by enforcing incest taboos that delimit the sexual prerogatives of other men.

Korn criticized Lévi-Strauss's equation of incest prohibitions with the obligation to marry out on the grounds that "the former refer to sexual relations, the latter to marriage" (1973: 16). But in brideservice societies, it is precisely such a confusion of sex and marriage that gives incest and/or avoidance rules their power for organizing social relations. Where sexual intercourse symbolizes the possibility of marriage, and where marriage is the basis of social inequality, rules about who may and may not sleep with whom provide a framework within which individuals can make legitimate claims on others. For a man to renounce sexual access to a woman *is* equivalent to giving some other man a wife, and it is politically significant in that it is consequential for subsequent relationships between "givers" and potential recipients. We would stress, however, that the observed "scarcity" of women in "primitive" societies, which Lévi-Strauss attributes to men's "deep polygamous tendency" (1969: 38), results neither from men's sexual voracity nor from their desire to accumulate working wives but from a wider structure of social relations. Although sexual and psychological needs, ''brute'' physical experience, aggressive tendencies, and social forces may interact in influencing the quality of male–female interactions, it seems that, in important ways, it is the significance of sexual access for the establishment of both male autonomy and adult cooperative relations that turns wives into valuables to be exchange and guarded – rather than the reverse. Furthermore, it is this social and political significance of sexual contact that leads sexual encounters to have very different meanings in the lives of men and women, and supports a recurrent association between sexuality and violence, both in the relationships of men and women and in competition among men.

Data on sexuality among non-Western peoples is, for obvious reasons, difficult to come by and even more difficult to interpret. This said, it is particulary striking to discover, first, how much *is* said about sex in ethnographies of brideservice peoples and, second, that ethnographic accounting tends, consistently, to highlight two (seemingly contradictory) themes.

Recurrently, sex emerges as a subject for both play and violence. Rituals around women's puberty celebrate their sexuality, young adults often engage in forms of playful sexual contest,[16] and love and courtship are often occasions for cultural elaboration and stylized gender display. Women, who often resist attempts to marry them to persons older than themselves, tend happily to display their prowess, health, and skill in hope that adult sexual ties (in marriage as in more casual affairs) will incorporate the sense of equal, free exchange found in relationships with lovers. In fact, for them, good husbands are like lovers, in that most women seek in husbands men who share with them and bring home gifts of game.

But if, for women, sexual bonds are associated with an ideally balanced and even intimate relation, men know wives are not lovers. A young man's interest in creating marital ties is apt to have much less to do with a desire for female partnership in life than with emergent claims to adult status among men. Thus, while the world of pleasurable and playful sex can easily give way to jealousy and fights for adults of both sexes, it seems clear that when men claim a wife (or quarrel with a wife's lovers) their deeds acquire a political and explosive cast absent from female marital claims or quarrels over men. Because a man's public status rests on his access to women, a wife's adultery becomes a direct challenge to his claim for adult independence. And such challenges are often met with violence. Furthermore, the very fact that wives are all men need in order to be equal to their fellows makes it likely that whatever the precipitating cause of struggle, their conflicts will be seen in sexual terms.[17] Ilongots, for example, claim that most intratribal killings in the past were occasioned by fights over women, and Murngin seem to recognize only three causes for war: revenge for the death of a kinsman, retaliation for the stealing of a woman, and (less frequently) execution of men who viewed totemic emblems under improper circumstances (Warner 1937: 159).

In short, we find that, characteristically, men's conflicts have sexual interpretations and that these tend, in turn, to lead to escalating threats of force. Whether such force is feared, as is the case with !Kung Bushmen, or enjoined, as it occasionally seems among Ilongots and Aborigines, the important point is that we find a tendency in all brideservice societies to think that conflicts, if expressed, will lead inevitably to violence. "I didn't want to kill him," Ilongots will report, "so I decided to forget that I was annoyed." Violent protest emerges recurrently in the ethnographic literature as the only perceived practical response to wrong or insult in a world where leaders lack power to enforce submission, and where exchanges of goods cannot create such rights in people as might compensate a man for the loss of his wife. The amount of force actually displayed may vary from mild to extreme in different cultures, but what matters is that people perceive no alternative means to resolve their unrepressed disputes. Elders cannot act as mediators. They cannot play the positive role of suggesting solutions to conflicts between men because they lack the power to reward compliance and because they cannot suggest that wrongs be compensated in goods. As a result, elders and others who interfere are reduced to such strategies as physically separating fighters or evoking kinship in order to urge peace. Such negative strategies, of course, only highlight the central role of violence in political actions, and the lack of viable alternatives to it.

The !Kung, for example, "have no mechanisms in their culture for dealing with disagreements other than to remove the causes of the disagreements" (Thomas 1959: 22). So when a husband found out his wife had eloped with her lover, he became "wildly angry, taking up his spear and sharpening it . . . the headman of the band set off after the elopers to preserve the peace" by urging the woman to return home (Thomas 1959: 85). In another instance, two !Kung women stopped a fight between men by holding one of the fighters down (Marshall 1976: 282). Similarly, among the Murngin, for whom "the conception of wergild . . . is very poorly developed and seldom solves the problem of terminating a feud" (Warner 1937: 179), men fighting over adultery rely on kin to hold them back and prevent them from getting hurt or hurting others. As Warner notes, it is "by remonstrating with their friends and struggling to get free from them [that] they are able to vent their outraged emotions and prove to the community that no one can infringe upon their rights without a valiant effort being made to prevent it" (1937: 167). A similar description holds true for Ilongots, for whom shows of violence are seen as inevitable in lieu of – or whenever individuals forget – their kinship. Ilongot husbands have been restrained from killing their wives' lovers in the past only (contemporary commentators insist) because of senior figures who were able, first, to separate and, then, to calm the opposed parties, by establishing that apparent enemies and competitors were really kin.

It is hardly surprising – when fights among men (for whatever cause) are characteristically linked to sexual offenses, and when men perceive these fights as leading, necessarily, to shows of force – that heterosexuality, however pleasurable, comes to take on conflict-laden connotations and that views of male adulthood tend to associate masculine creativity with men's use of force. In fact, we find recurrently that some sort of violent potential is symbolically associated with the independence that productive relations make available to securely married male adults. The violence through which men attempt to guarantee their independence and display their very real capacities to defend marital claims, is often taken to explain the married man's prerogatives. And so, successfully married men are said, characteristically, to have "earned" their wives through success in hunting, killing, or some ritual feat that proves their potency and force. Man the Hunter is thus celebrated because men have good political cause to boast about the skill and prowess in terms of which they first assert and then defend their claims to wives.

Thus, although it is not, in fact, through violent deeds that men acquire wives but, rather, through the assumption of obligations toward in-laws, it may appear, at times, that the equality enjoyed by independent men is actually achieved through willingness and ability to use force. And although the fact that women cannot marry wives is ultimately what underlies their peripheral role in public negotiations of male status, their limitations are typically explained by the absence of those very qualities believed to typify the process through which men apparently earn a spouse. So, a !Kung woman told Lorna Marshall that women left decisions to men because "men can do everything, they can shoot and make fire" – the two activities that women are, of course, specifically barred from performing (1976: 176). And, similarly Ilongot women explained their fear of husbands and their willingness to obey them by referring to men's accomplishments as killers and to the fact that only men pollard trees – both activities associated with a predominantly male form of "energy" or "anger" that is said also to make babies, and to be required of bachelors who would display their worth as grooms. Real experience, of course, supports these views of the significant achievements of male prowess, because men *do*, in fact, "make marriages" and fight to defend them, and because loss of a wife, if she is an only wife, significantly undermines the independent status of a would-be adult man.

What is more, the experiences and ideas that link marriage, male independence, and the threat of violence also underlie the use of contests as the formal means through which brideservice peoples manage their disputes. Because equality is the highest status available to men, and because such equality is symbolically achieved through willingness and ability to use force, contests in which both sides demonstrate their capacities for violence provide the most appropriate means for affirming the equality that allows adult men to make peace. Chest pounding, club duels, song contests, debates, and regulated spear throwing ideally allow *both* sides to demonstrate strength, intelligence, and bravery. Western ethnographers may interpret such contests as having victors (see Hoebel 1954: 92), but it seems clear that although individual contestants may get carried away, saner heads work to ensure a draw. Were someone actually to win a contest, peace would be impossible, because inequality is precisely the denial of independence that breeds strife.

In short, we are suggesting that the place of marriage in men's lives gives conflict its distinctive form, combining sexual idioms with dyadic contests among men who must display the equal forcefulness that alone can testify to their status as independent adults. The idioms through which claims are articulated and equality achieved mean, furthermore, that violence is a constant threat. All men recognize that their fellows can, as equal men, defend *their* claims to women and that independent married men, who in important ways need nothing, cannot readily be coerced by leaders to obey. It seems no accident, therefore, that men in brideservice societies seem reluctant to assume authority over others. Lacking power and at the same time fearing violence, they are hesitant to make excessive claims. The equality of independent men thus becomes a public virtue and even women may enjoy considerable autonomy at the same time that their lives are constrained by men's willingness to fight over them.

POLITICAL PROCESSES

The associations just traced between sex, violence, and men's marital autonomy, provide an initial sketch of the parameters that define political action in brideservice societies. In what follows, we try to trace the implications of this description for actual strategies and relationships in which individuals are likely to be involved, in order, then, to talk about the links between political action and recurrent stereotypes in terms of which the sexes are perceived.

In brideservice societies, it is in the interest of all adults to build networks of cooperative bonds with fellows who, eventually, may come to visit or reside with them and, in times of trouble, offer welcoming homes to which the victims of unhappy circumstances can escape. Both men and women thus forge trading partnerships with distant friends and kin, distribute produce beyond obligatory bounds and may, when free from mundane pressures and demands, seek lovers. For women, in particular, ties like these provide the residential mobility necessary for them to reject unwanted suitors and influence selection of a spouse.[18] Furthermore, for senior adults of both sexes, broad supportive networks help them shape other people's residential decisions and constrain children's marital designs.

But if most women can, like men, build adult networks of support and hope in old age to enjoy considerable influence vis-à-vis their children, the organization of marriage in brideservice societies also dictates that men (and not women) will be seen as the creative forgers of ongoing relational bonds; women are most likely to be cast as objects of men's grander plans or, perhaps, as persons who should passively accept but tend, instead, to undermine the alliances made by men. To begin with, in brideservice societies women appear to be the objects of male-male exchange because men reap the political benefits of marriage. Even though men, rather than women, move at marriage, and even though marriage may actually involve an exchange of sons between old women (who are thus able to enjoy considerable power),[19] men look like the makers of marriage because it is as husbands that individuals acquire the independence that makes them equal to other adult men. Men's perceived willingness to fight over women serves, furthermore, to ground women's status as objects in real experience. Because of fears that men will fight other men, women cannot share food and sex as freely as they might please. Because of fears that women who lack protectors endanger not only themselves but the tenuous social bonds of potential lovers, women cannot choose to remain unmarried. And because of fears that a husband might have to fight other men, husbands are justified in beating errant wives.[20]

What is more, just as everyday experience may exaggerate the sense in which married men's independence is determined by their violent feats, so fears of violent consequences may come to support the view that it is women who make trouble and are responsible for the fights of men. Clearly, insofar as a man's status in the world of men *does* rest on his immediate claims in women, it is always possible to find a woman on whom his fears and conflicts can be blamed. Furthermore, the very fact that in brideservice societies women feed families and are unable to marry wives, leads them to engage in behaviors that are readily labeled "selfish," "nagging," or "greedy." Women's productive obligations, like young men's, prevent women from displaying the generosity exhibited by mature men whose senior kin are dead. And yet women are unlike young men, in that they often have good cause to selfishly hoard food for their own families. Similarly, the very structure of husbands' and wives' obligations makes women seem more demanding than men. Because wives perform daily services for husbands, men seldom need ask for food and shelter, but because husbands perform only occasional services for wives, women must tell men when they want tools, meat, or clothing – and perhaps, as with the Sharanahua, threaten to "go and eat penis" if husbands fail to bring them game (Siskind 1973). Men, who must strive to be equals, dare not beg for fear of demeaning themselves, but women can and do ask for food and assistance from others and so may be seen as unreasonable persons, with never-satisfied demands.

These derogatory interpretations of women's behavior affect women's lives by supporting a tendency to cast them as scapegoats for unwanted trouble. By appearing to know too little and want too much, women are readily condemned for provoking the loud marital quarrels that disturb others' sleep, for seducing men into adultery, and for disrupting intergroup relations by refusing to marry suitors chosen for them by kin. The interpretation of women's behavior as "selfish" and "greedy" thus provides daily proof of the idea, derived from men's political competition, that women cause trouble among otherwise peaceful men. And so women, as well as men, turn against women when men fight with one another. Ethnographers report cases of women telling men of other women's transgressions, approving of wife beating, and even beating other women themselves. In contrast, we can think of no recorded instance in which a man was penalized for causing fights among women.

Finally, cultural conceptions that make women ready scapegoats for unwanted trouble simultaneously suggest to people that the most effective strategy for achieving peaceful relations among men is to control trouble-causing women.[21] And this idea may undergo an even further transformation, suggesting that men would not fight if left by themselves. This transformation permits a symbolic division between the "harmonious" world of men and the conflict-ridden world of heterosexual relations (see Nadelson, this volume), and it also underlies the ugliest aspect of male–female relations in brideservice societies: gang rape. Whether or not rape actually occurs – and evidence indicates it is extremely rare – rape has symbolic importance, and ethnographers report that women fear it. Rape is such a powerful symbol because it unites three culturally salient themes: sexual intercourse, male violence, and male solidarity. Gang rape is a peculiarly appropriate sanction for women who wander beyond male control – through promiscuity, assertions of undue independence, and/or refusals to marry – because it simultaneously reveals (in a particularly brutal way) women's inability to forge social relationships through the use of their sexuality, asserts the controlling and even creative power of male prowess, and affirms male solidarity in the face of women who disrupt their bonds.[22]

Ironically, however, the same fears of violence and perceived lack of alternatives to it that limit women's freedom to avoid men or choose partners on their own are also responsible for women's reported autonomy within the family.[23] Public confrontations between men provide contexts for celebrating men's willingness and ability to fight, but the requirements of local cooperation elicit a deep fear of the "anger" that is celebrated in public. And so, it is not only "harmless" people like the !Kung but also Ilongot headhunters who find it embarrassing to press claims or abuse others in ways that could undermine the kinds of cooperative assumptions necessary to daily life. Turnbull's classic observation (1968) that hunters would rather separate then quarrel has particular relevance for relations between the sexes because husbands, aware of this possibility, are justly reluctant to abuse, and so alienate, their wives.

The pervasive fear that conflict breeds either violence or dispersal thus leads men, in particular, to avoid any actions, such as demands or assertions of will, that might provoke resistance. In fact, it is in this context that we understand the lack of marriage rituals in brideservice societies. No one wants to dramatize the inequities that underlie marital unions in a world where all must recognize that force inevitably undermines the mutual accommodation that alone can make marriages succeed. Accounts of brideservice peoples make it clear, in fact, that husbands (once they are married) are reluctant to make extreme demands of spouses[24] and that kinspeople only rarely force unmarried daughters into an undesired match. Thus, women's will is recognized at the same time that men may speak in terms of male-male marital exchanges, because marriages, like all social relationships in brideservice societies, depend, ultimately, on the cooperative commitment of potentially autonomous individuals, whose ongoing connections require acknowledgement of one another's independent needs.

Furthermore, just as fear of conflict shapes the quality of marital bonds, and sustains an aura of mutuality, so a reluctance to engage in violence among kin limits possibilities for significant accumulation of goods in brideservice groups and make it meaningful to share. Sahlins has attributed hunters' observed lack of avarice to their having made a virtue of the necessity forced on them by ecologically determined nomadism (1972: 33). We, on the other hand, suggest a social cause for why even sedentary brideservice peoples show little interest in accumulating material possessions. In a world where inequality occasions conflict, and conflicts are thought to lead immediately to violence, people are reluctant to provoke others by refusing requests for goods. Furthermore, in a world where "ability to possess [is] nine points of the law" (Hoebel 1940: 66), and the unwilling loss of possessions is seen to reflect upon an individual's ability to sustain his equal status, men, in particular, are reluctant to lay claims to more than they are able to defend. As a result, all recognized valuables (except those that are never requested, either because everyone has them or because they are kept hidden) tend to pass from person to person, usually along lines of reciprocal gift giving. (See, for example, Thomson 1949; Sharp 1952; Stanner 1933, for Australia, and Wiess 1977, for Bushmen.)

Not surprisingly, then, we read that men in brideservice groups seem to be very generous because it is much easier to maintain a "don't fool with me" stance if there is little for others to take away. Not only would an excess of personal possessions condemn a man to a lonely life of perpetual fighting but the theft or unauthorized use of his possessions might reveal his ultimate inability to keep others from appropriating what he claimed as his (namely, his wife). It is in this context that we understand men's reported "laziness," their "reluctance" as hunters (Siskind 1973), and their lack of concern for taking care of their belongings (Sahlins 1972: 13, 19). Although we read that shows of force and hunting skill are what win bachelors wives, young men do not, in fact, appear to hunt or kill with anything of the energy of married adults – at least in part because they realize that *until* they have a wife more than a minimal display of worth can have no meaning. But even married men are understandably reluctant to invest heavy labor in producing or maintaining objects they are unlikely to be able to keep for personal use.

It is in this context, too, that we understand reported limits on polygyny. Men may dream of, or work toward, acquiring several wives, but men who actually accumulate women tend to pass all but two or three on to "younger brothers," or, as in Australia, either to "lend" wives to younger men or turn a blind eye toward adultery.[25] It is by passing women on, in fact, that senior men forge positive political ties with the "brothers" who, because of incest rules, are all too likely to become their enemies and competitors in the search for wives.

Although men are unwilling to invest labor in objects for personal use, they seem quite willing to invest labor in objects for exchange (Thompson 1949). There is limited demand for such objects, however, because people are reluctant to accumulate things, and because goods can be exchanged only for other goods.[26] There is no way to convert accumulated goods into the marriages that create the inequality between youths and adult men so fundamental to brideservice societies. As a result, all exchanges of goods appear to be balanced. This fact has two consequences. On the one hand, balanced exchanges give material expression to the parity Fried sees as the object of male achievement in egalitarian societies (1967: 79). But, on the other hand, the equation of balanced exchanges with parity provides the cultural rationale for destroying or seriously damaging generally valued objects of contention in situations where balanced exchange becomes impossible. It is in this context that we can begin to make sense of the otherwise puzzling reports that

Australian Gidjingali (Hiatt 1965) and the Yanomamo (Biocca 1971) of tropical South America either mutilated or killed women when men's fights concerning them appeared recalcitrant to peaceable resolution; that even among the generally nonviolent Pygmies, girls whose preferences disrupted the marital exchanges of men might find themselves brutally beaten (Turnbull 1965); and, finally, that Northern Australian brothers (but, we would stress here, not fathers) were wont to throw spears at their sisters if they heard these women abused by other men (Warner 1937: 109–12; Hiatt 1965: 112–18). Brutality against women in a world where wives are what men need would seem a self-defeating show of purposeless and exaggerated male drives for dominance. But whatever men's immediate psychological motivations, our point is that in social and cultural terms activities like this make sense because of the ways in which a woman *can* disrupt men's peerlike stance of balance in exchange.

We suggested earlier that blaming women for fights among men provided the cultural logic for a division between the "harmonious" world of men and the "conflict-ridden" world of heterosexual relations – a division symbolized, for example, in the contrast between men's solidarity songs during the Pygmy *molimo* ceremony and the "battle" between the sexes that emerges both in women's puberty rituals and on the rare occasions when women join with men in singing and calling on the forest (Turnbull 1965). We would now like to suggest that balanced exchanges provide material expressions of the harmony men celebrate. In other words, men's harmony is not a mere absence of conflict; it is positively created through the balanced exchanges by which men declare themselves and each other equal. Although ethnographic evidence makes it quite clear that men, women, and children *all* engage in balanced exchanges, women's and children's exchanges do not have the same cultural significance as men's because women, in particular, have no chance to acquire the wives that make adult men independent.[27] Thus, Ilongot men, but not women, exchange gifts in peacemaking ceremonies, as do the Yanomamo of South America (Chagnon 1968).

The most culturally significant balanced exchanges are, of course, exchanges of women between men. We have put off discussing such exchanges until this point, however, for two reasons. First, we think that exchanges of things (and the vast amounts of time people spend making things for others) are more important than exchanges of women for expressing the mutual respect and concern that permit *daily* cooperation. And second, we disagree with Lévi-Strauss's (1969: 62) view that women are merely the most valuable of things, and have therefore postponed full discussion of exchanges of women until we had established the context for exchanges of things. In our view, it is precisely because things in brideservice societies are unlike women in having no long-term consequences for social inequality that they can move so easily between people and thus serve so effectively to mark relations of cooperation. And it is precisely because women are producers, whose marriages do establish relations of inequality between bachelors and married men, that exchanges of women can provide the basic metaphor for social order in brideservice societies. It is in this context that we understand the almost universal preference for some form of direct-exchange marriage in the groups we are discussing. (See, for example, Siskind 1973: 60; Turnbull 1961: 206; Marshall 1976: 262; Rosaldo 1980a: 211).[28]

Although there are societies far more complex than those discussed here that also prefer direct-exchange marriage (such as South India, Tiv), direct exchange provides a particularly salient model in brideservice societies because balanced exchanges of women turn out to be the ultimate expression of men's ability to create harmony, and hence social order, in the face of apparently conflict-ridden heterosexual relations. We deliberately refer to direct exchange as a model, however, because in brideservice societies (unlike what we imagine happens in more complex groups), the exchange of women is usually accomplished by moving men around. Ironically, the fact that it is (characteristically) men who move comes to support a view that men, far from being passive pawns of women who remain at home, are the initiators of affinity. Because men, on marrying, assert their independence by approaching foreign households and establishing separate hearths, their circulation acquires an active cast, and they are seen as the people who "make marriages," by forging new relationships with other men.

Of course, the regular practice of direct-exchange marriage tends to be based on a fiction of ascribed status, wherein certain categories of women are identified, from birth, as the rightful wives of certain men. As such, direct exchange may seem incompatible with the notion that men achieve wives through personal demonstrations of violence and hunting prowess (and with the fact that men actually acquire wives by fulfilling obligations to wives' kin). But there are two senses in which direct-exchange marriage complements the cultural logic inherent in emphases on male achievement and male violence. First, direct exchange has meaning for individuals because if a man needs a wife and nothing else to become independent then the only thing that can be exchanged for a woman is another woman. In giving a sister to his wife's brother, therefore, a new husband affirms his independence from, and his equality with, his affines. He simultaneously frees himself from debt and obligation (even though he continues to give meat to his in-laws) and strengthens his claim on his own wife by giving her brother a vested interest in seeing his sister fulfill her obligations. Understandably, the relations of brother and sister are given special weight in such a system,[29] and women, if they are said to "belong" to any kinsman, are apt to be more closely linked to brothers than to fathers. Fathers may receive meat and services from daughters' husbands, but a brother's command over his sister's marriage may be the foundation of his own claim to adult independence – his basis for acquiring the wife who will make him the equal of mature men. Thus, among Ilongots, for instance, unmarried brothers are likely to experience an approaching groom as a potential source of challenge. Far more frequently than fathers, they will respond with "anger" to a suitor's first petitions. And "anger" when a "sister" weds may well give rise to a demand for "sisters" in exchange, or else a gift of goods, or (in the past) an opportunity to take a victim's head—all of which, of course, may then help the brother when he seeks a wife.

Second, direct-exchange marriage has meaning on a social level as the basis for cooperation and order, because it can be interpreted as a prototype of men's socially creative powers. If, in cultural logic, men achieve their independence through feats of violence, it is also the case that male potency (which leads to marriage) is what brings men together in peace and cooperation. Thus, Ilongots will shout out "let our children marry" as a symbol of projected cooperative relations after completing (far more tenuous) ritual exchanges to forge peace. Marriage *is* what creates lasting bonds, and insofar as men "make marriages," the social order that exists stands as a proof that men, in fact, are endowed with an extraordinary and valuable sort of force. Tellingly, among the Sharanahua of tropical South America, sister-exchange marriage is recognized in traditional myth and lore as the foundation of social order, and Sharanahua myths distinguish between men whose marriages to supernaturals create social "brothers-in-law" and women whose similar marriages create freaks (Siskind 1973).

Finally, characteristic forms of political leadership in brideservice societies, like the balanced exchanges through which men declare themselves equal, provide visible proof of men's ability to create harmony among themselves. We have already noted that men in brideservice societies seem reluctant to assume positions of authority or to give direct orders. Rather, leaders apparently prefer to make suggestions or to direct activity by performing desired tasks themselves (Fried 1967: 83). It is striking that even among such "fierce" people as the Yanomamo, a village headman cannot command his fellows' labor; at best, he may encourage others to pull weeds from the communal plaza by initiating the activity himself (Chagnon 1968: 108). Indirect leadership patterns are, of course, quite practical in a world where the mature men who are natural foci of group cooperation both lack the power to obtain compliance from securely married men and are culturally barred from making assertions of will that might provoke resistance. Nevertheless, such leadership patterns have their positive side. In the first place, they give leaders the appearance of being selfless and thus may promote the view that men (in contrast to women) are capable of completely altruistic behavior. Second, because leaders usually phrase their suggestions for activity as being for the general good, or "because it has always been done this way," their pronouncements suggest the existence of moral imperatives beyond human control. It makes experiential sense, then, that Pygmy men, but not women, secure the transcendent support of the forest (Turnbull 1961), that Ilongot men's headhunting rituals provide the spiritual basis for human renewal, and, most vividly, that Australian men create harmony among themselves by following the "law" of the Dreaming that is and always was.

Cultural conceptions

In the introduction to this essay, we suggested that men and women in brideservice societies are culturally defined by a system opposing uni- (male-male) and heterosexual models of biological reproduction and social relationship. Man the Hunter, who both kills and nourishes, is not balanced by

Woman the Gatherer or Woman the Mother. Nor is male "culture" readily opposed to a "natural" women's world. Rather, community and men's rituals celebrate men's abilities to order, energize, and nurture the social world of both sexes in the context of all-male activities, whereas women's rituals seek to promote social and sexual relations between women and men. Female rituals are designed to enhance such qualities as beauty, health, and sexuality – qualities that permit women to engage as actors in the heterosexual relations through which adults organize and manipulate ongoing cooperative bonds.

Images of Man the Potent or Man the Hunter, and of Woman as his Sexy Partner – motivated, we suggest, by the facts of political and economic organization – are elaborated in the cosmology and ritual of brideservice societies in terms so various that it is difficult to perceive their underlying commonalities. First menstrual rites are, for example, more important in some Bushmen groups than in others; the same can be said for rituals surrounding the hunt. Equally, among Australian Aborigines, the contrast between Central and Northern groups in terms of the relative stress on female sexuality in male ritual has been the focus of a good deal of analytical concern. Ilongot headhunters, Aboriginal ritualists, and !Kung huntsmen are, of course, engaged in different projects. Our analysis leads us to suggest, however, that a grasp of their distinctive meanings depends on an adequate diagnosis of *both* commonality and contrast: Cultural details become more intelligible through a recognition of their common sociological anchoring and the patterns they share. Thus, in the section that follows, we describe the content and context of specific rituals among the !Kung San, Arnhem Land Aborigines, and Ilongot hunter-horticulturalists, in order, first, to illustrate their similarities and, then, to provide the basis for a discussion of relations between culture and polity, as these explain both the silences and the ritual claims voiced by women and men.

!KUNG SAN

Community and men's rituals among the !Kung celebrate Man the Hunter, whose prowess as a provider enables him to nurture others, forge marriages, and heal the sick. Women are excluded from all aspects of hunting by the belief that "femaleness negates hunting prowess" (Marshall 1976: 177) and so cannot participate in either men's hunting rituals or in "the extremely important initiation rite for boys, the Rite of the First Kill, which is based on hunting and which must be performed before a boy may marry" (Marshall 1976: 178). The Rite of the First Kill is performed twice for each boy, once after he kills a large male animal and again after he kills a large female animal, and it is designed to enhance his hunting prowess. During the ceremony, the boy is scarified. A gash is cut in his chest, which is then filled with magical substances to insure that he will not be lazy and that "his heart will say to him, Why am I sitting here at my fire? Why am I not out hunting?" (Marshall 1976: 131).

Marshall notes that "hunting is ritually linked with marriage" (1976: 270), and the form of their association clearly suggests that men acquire wives through demonstrations of hunting prowess. Informants told Marshall that "a boy who has never killed any large meat animal would not be given a wife"

(1976: 270). At the time of a wedding, the groom must kill a large animal for his wife's parents (1976: 270), and !Kung believe a groom wins his bride's cooperation by "feeding" her when she is young (1976: 169). Finally, !Kung myths and games equate marriage with hunting; men "chase," "kill," and "eat" women just as men chase, kill, and eat animals (Marshall 1976; Biesele 1975; McCall 1970).

Marshall also suggests that male hunting prowess is linked to male sexual prowess (1976: 270), but she provides no data on cultural conceptions of male sexuality. She states that "with bride service, the bride's people can capture at once the sexual and hunting powers of the young man" (1976: 270), but gives no indication of what tangible benefits male sexual powers might convey. Men are clearly associated with wives' children, however, through their "duty and right . . . to name their sons and daughters" (1976: 223). Naming not only gives a spirit essence to a child but also reflects, in part, genealogical positions that determine patterns of joking, avoidance, and sexual access. Thus men, as namers of children, are, in important ways, the creators of children as social beings and so creators of children's social relations. Men's hunting prowess enables them to marry, and their sexual prowess shapes marriages in the next generation.

Men's ability to create and maintain social order is also expressed in men's (but not women's) right to make the ritual fires that are kindled at each new camp, after a death or misfortune, and for all rituals, including curing dances (Marshall 1976: 83). But because such ritual fires are kindled by the oldest capable man, fire building dramatizes the inequality between old and young men at the same time that it dramatizes differences between men and women. This threefold social division is made particularly obvious by male initiation rites and curing dances. At male initiations, senior men forge relations with juniors in the absence of women; at curing dances, where men dance and women sing, age and sex differences are dramatized by the fact that senior men help junior men achieve trance states while women urge them all on by singing in an undifferentiated group (Katz 1976).[30]

Whereas men's rituals and community rituals appear to stress what we call the unisexual model of reproduction and social relations, women's (much less well-documented) rituals appear to celebrate women's capacities for creating heterosexual ties with mature men. In particular, women seem to celebrate the beauty and sexual attractiveness that create social relations by arousing men's sexual passion. Marshall reports that all !Kung women have scars on their faces and buttocks, "for beauty,"and that girls are scarified around the age of twelve (1976: 41) – a time when they are attracting husbands but have probably not yet menstruated (see Howell 1976). In playful dances, girls enact a variety of sexual pursuits (McCall 1970). And finally, a girl's first menstruation is celebrated with a rite involving her seclusion and the staging of the sexually suggestive Eland Dance by other women. At the Eland Dance, sexually mature women remove their clothes and dramatize the power of their sexuality for energizing and rejuvenating adult men. Girls' puberty rituals do not seem to stress women's capacity for bearing children, and this lack of elaborate *ritual* concern for female fertility or maternity is reflected in the fact that women give birth in the bushes apart from the encampment, either alone or with their own mothers (Marshall 1976: 166).[31]

Silberbauer (1963) gives a detailed account of a girl's puberty ceremony that he observed among the G/wi Bushmen. Although the ceremony did not include an Eland Dance, it did include other activities that can be interpreted as celebrations of women's "sexual" abilities to create ties with men and bring good fortune. After five days of strict seclusion, the pubescent girl was joined by her husband and both were washed, decorated, and scarified by older women. Later, the girl was "introduced" to food plants and a "rainstorm" to bring her good fortune and to attract rain, which would benefit those who lived with her. Finally, in a joyful conclusion, the girl was accompanied by her father, who "introduced" her to each member of the band. Silberbauer notes that "it is an indication of particular favor to be the first so introduced . . . to a man, it brings especially good fortune in hunting, and a woman is helped by this in her searches for food and in bearing and rearing children" (1963: 21). Although themes of nurturance may figure loosely in rituals of female puberty, Silberbauer makes it clear that there was no aspect of the ceremony that suggested a fertility rite. "The G/wi give little thought to fertility – their concern is more with ease of childbirth and success in rearing the child" (1963: 25).

The cultural definition of men in terms of hunting prowess and of women in terms of sexual attractiveness is reflected not only in boys' and girls' initiation rites but also in sanctions for breaking sitting taboos and in parental statements about desirable qualities in children's spouses. Neither men nor women are supposed to sit where adult members of the opposite sex have sat, but a man who violates this taboo destroys his hunting prowess, whereas a woman "suffers disorders of her urinary tract" (that is, we would suggest, becomes incapable of enjoying sexual intercourse) (Marshall 1976: 249). Sterility, the common sanction for taboo breaking by women in most African bridewealth societies, is not even mentioned. Similarly, parents of girls, when asked about desirable qualities in daughters' husbands, say they want good hunters, whereas parents of boys hope the girls to whom their sons are engaged will grow up to be "good looking" (Marshall 1976: 267). Boys' mothers, more realistically, also hope that sons' wives will fulfill their obligations and not cause trouble: that they "will not be lazy or wander about visiting at night at other people's fires" (Marshall 1976: 267). Marshall's account, however, contains no suggestion that boys' parents care about a girl's capacity for bearing children – a common, if not the most common, concern of boys' parents in most African bridewealth societies.

!Kung rituals seem to stress, in short, the very qualities that daily life marks as socially and politically most desirable: the transcendent skill of men who hunt (a skill related to men's marriages and to the claims of knowledgeable adults), and the sexual, and perhaps, nurturant capacities of these men's future wives.

PEOPLES OF NORTHEASTERN ARNHEM LAND
Warner's conclusion that Murngin men are to women as sacred is to profane has been criticized by scholars who focused on women's experience (Kaberry

1939). Nevertheless, few would disagree with Maddock's very similar statement that men's cults, which, "despite their secret core, require the active
participation of the community at large" and "express broad, cohesive and
impersonal themes such as fertility and continuity of nature, the regularity of
society and the creation of the world," whereas "women's cults are centered
on narrow, divisive and personal interests, such as love magic and reacting to
physiological crises" (1975: 155). Our interpretation of the Australian material leads us to suggest, by contrast, that Maddock, like Warner and Durkheim
before him, has misconceptualized Aboriginal ideas of women because of an
inclination to think dualistically and thus cast women as opposites of men. If
men are associated with the rainy season, so – these analysts infer – women
are linked to the dry season. If men are associated with death, women are
thought to be associated with fertility and life. And, paradoxically perhaps, if
men's cults are integrative, then women's cults must be – as indeed Aboriginal
men probably view them – disruptive of social life. The paradox dissolves
when one realizes that men's cults are associated with *both* violence and
fertility/well-being and that women's rites are concerned not with fertility but
with sex.

Hunting is not a major focus of Murngin men's rituals. A boy's first kill
receives some ritual attention, and hunting is ritually linked to the birth of a
man's first child (Warner 1937: 128), but ritual knowledge, not hunting
prowess, is the recognized basis of male status. Murngin men "provide" for
others less through hunting, per se, than by ensuring "the fertility and
continuity of nature" (Maddock 1975: 155). For them, circumcision is a
more important marker than a boy's first kill. There is some evidence,
however, that killing humans, as opposed to killing animals, does confer
ritual power. The spirit of a dead man is believed to enter the body of his killer
and give the killer strength (Warner 1937: 163).

Murngin men's cults are elaborate, complex, and symbolically rich, but for
our purposes it is most important to note that all dramatize differences
between young and mature men, even as they are about world continuity and
order. In Warner's words, "All the ceremonies are associated with age
grading, as being participated in by men initiated into certain age grades, or
serving to initiate a man into a higher status" (1937: 259). Ritual age grades
are "closely correlated with a man's family position" (Warner 1937: 125).
Circumcision occurs when a boy leaves his mother's fire to live in the
unmarried men's camp. A man sees the (low) python totem for the first time
when he has a moustache and beard – both markers of his eligibility to marry.
And finally, men released from food taboos through the birth of a child
become eligible to view the higher and more sacred totems that ensure the life
of the group (Warner 1937: 125–37).

The ritual dramatization of male age-grades occurs against a background of
absent, undifferentiated, sexless, or controlled women. Women are absent,
of course, from men's most secret rites, and when present on certain occasions, they dramatize their exclusion by hiding under mats. But women's
most frequent form of participation in men's and community rituals is to
dance and/or sing in an undifferentiated group, usually within the camp or on

a "women's dancing ground." Older women, near or past menopause, may be invited to play parts in rituals from which other women are excluded. But when sexually active women are to be dramatized, men play the parts. The fact that female founders in myths are not portrayed by sexually active women in either men's or women's rituals suggests that the imaging of female fertility, to the extent that it occurs is more a metaphor for men's life giving capacities than a statement about women.

Finally, women may participate in men's rituals in ways that dramatize men's control over their sexuality. Young girls may lie under mats with initiates while adults sing over them – dramatizing elders' prerogatives in bestowal. And sexual license occurs after the Gunabibi ceremony, when men ceremonially exchange wives or lend wives to tribal "brothers." Women (and men) who show reluctance to participate in such license are threatened with death. Murngin are quite explicit in viewing sexual license as a means of preventing fights among men. Warner was told that "It is better that everybody comes with their women and all meet together at Gunabibi and play with each other, and then nobody will start having sweethearts the rest of the time" (1937: 308).

Although Warner saw masculinity and femininity as organizing principles of Murngin social organization dramatized in rituals, he had a hard time characterizing femininity. His assertion that women were "profane" in contrast to "sacred" men has been criticized (see Kaberry 1939), and his attempt to link male and female to wet and dry seasons, respectively, ends up equating the female principle with what everyone regards as the best season of the year (1937: 395). Warner went wrong, we think, in trying to apply Durkheimian dualities too quickly. Murngin rituals dramatize differences among men and the problematic potencies associated with uncontrolled female sexuality. They are not concerned with female fertility per se. Thus, for example, when Murngin boys are initiated, they may indeed be physically separated from women and uninitiated boys; yet, the ritual does not dramatize the leaving behind of an old status but, instead, the acquisition of a new one, through the incorporation of female potencies in association with knowledgeable older men. In being circumcised, Murngin boys do not lose a "feminine" part of themselves, as boys are said to do in many bridewealth societies (see Beidelman 1971: 104). Indeed, the circumcised foreskin, far from being discarded, is preserved in an effort to enhance the boys' growth (Warner 1937: 277), and circumcised youths, far from *losing* their feminine attributes, are said to *acquire* the masculine and/or androgynous totemic affiliation, known as the "mark of the snake" (Warner 1937: 126). Again, Murngin ritualists induce bleeding, not as a purge but as a mime of ancestral "menstruation." "Male menses" – a symbolic conglomerate of female menstrual substance and heart blood, associated with souls and with masculine violence – is smeared on practitioners as a sign of transcendent, life-giving strength (Munn 1969: 189, 195). Rather than enacting envy of, or ambivalence toward, women's "natural" reproductive powers, Murngin rituals display men's unisexual capacities for creation, and their ability to incorporate feminine associations in an all-male ritual context, and so to give life by themselves.

Many brideservice societies have myths in which women's initial creative endowments – which we read as having less to do with fertility than with their stimulating sexuality – prove disruptive, occasioning the ritual practice and cultural transcendence of men. The well-known Murngin myth of the Wawilak sisters, whose exploits provide a charter for men's Gunabibi ceremonies, exemplifies these general themes (see Warner 1937: 240–9; also Munn 1969). The myth portrays two young women alone, who discover and name sacred animals, the capacity for naming suggesting creative potentials claimed presently by adult men. The girls come, eventually, to the well of the sacred python, where the animals they gathered desert them, and uncontrolled menstrual bleeding leads the python to rise from his confines, his water flooding their ground.

Because, as Warner tells us, the onset of menstruation is believed to be "due to the sexual act" (1937: 64), it appears that the sisters, in menstruating, are not polluting a sacred place but exhibiting uncontrolled sexuality. The response they elicit is then, appropriately, a symbol of the ritual and sexual domination of men. Whether or not the rising snake is declared a male figure, phallic masculinity is generally recognized as one of its senses (Munn 1969: 185). In fact, commentators, focusing on the way in which the snake both swallows and then vomits up the women, come close to expressing what one might expect of brideservice symbolic structures: that the snake/ penis is also a vagina capable of giving birth.

The snake vomits the women, waters recede, and finally their brothers dream of the songs and the rites men will need to control things. The mythic initiatives of women thus give way to a contemporary ritual order men alone will be able to regulate and reproduce. Ultimately, then, in governing female sexuality, adult men not only win ritual control of their women but also, of course, of the seasons and – perhaps most importantly – of as yet uninitiated men.

Less is known about women's rituals in Northern Australia.[32] Their rites occur only rarely, yet the scant evidence suggests, again, that investigators have been misguided in seeing them in simple opposition to the collectivizing rituals of men. Women's rituals do not concern the themes men celebrate. Where men are concerned with fertility, women practice "love magic" and celebrate physical well-being. Catherine Berndt reports that women's love magic rituals stress "certain specific wishes and desires – of obtaining lovers, the retention or recovery of a husband's affections; and they abound in references to phallic symbols and sexual intercourse" (1930: 26). But even though love magic "is the most striking and obvious feature" of women's rituals, "it does not represent their sole content and purpose" (C. Berndt 1950: 26). Women's rituals are not just "centered on narrow, divisive and personal interests" (Maddock 1975: 155). Rather, women's rituals invoke supernatural beings, and the power unleashed in their songs can be used for healing the sick and injured (C. Berndt 1950: 26). In contrast to their concern for sexuality and health, however, women show little ritual interest in female biology. Women of Northern Australia "have few songs connected with such physiological crises as birth, the growing of a girl's breasts, and menstruation" (C. Berndt 1950: 26). In fact, songs to hasten the onset of puberty in women "are considered to be the men's province" (C. Berndt 1950: 26). Among the Murngin, a girl's first menstruation was apparently marked only by seclusion (Warner 1937: 75), and Warner reports no birth rituals for mother and child.

Thus, while Northern Australian rituals differ from those of the Bushmen, they conform to the brideservice model in at least the following respects: (a) men are celebrated as nurturers/creators, although in this case ritual knowledge rather than hunting skill is associated with male adulthood, marriage, and sexuality, and the healthy reproduction of human society as a whole; (b) men's capacities involve, not the rejection, but the incorporation of a set of symbols that bespeak their ties to mothers and to female biological endowments; and (c) the powers women claim have less to do with reproducing life or nurturing their sons than with their sexual vitality and skill.

ILONGOTS

"Man the Hunter and Woman" was the title Rosaldo and Atkinson gave their 1975 article on the gender conceptions portrayed in Ilongot hunting and horticultural magic. The title reflects their conclusion that although rice and game are, in many ways, symbolic equivalents, Ilongots equate hunting with headhunting and so with men's valued and life-taking violence, but do not associate women's cultivated produce with life-giving fertility and birth. Although the terms of Rosaldo and Atkinson's discussion are somewhat different from those developed here, they do suggest that Ilongots contrast with certain bridewealth groups in the same area in that the latter *do* oppose life taking to life giving, and identify life giving with feminine productive and reproductive concerns.

Among Ilongots, men's hunting spells use metaphors and magical plants found also in spells women perform in their gardens. Both invoke images of sociality, well-being and "concentration," which apply equally to men's foraged and women's cultivated produce, because – as Ilongots put it – "it is the same food that we eat." Women's spells, however, appear to highlight competitive aspects of production: They describe the fact that healthy gardens grow through "thefts" of "rice hearts" from neighbors, and that successful cultivators may win both their neighbors' guests and envious esteem. Men's hunting spells, by contrast, elaborate on the very different cultural preoccupations that link male foragers in the forest to young men in search of heads. Young headhunters, in oratory, are equated with young hunt dogs; and hunt dogs, in spells, are described through invocations of an imagery associated with violent natural forces – lightning, wind, and crashing branches – and with duels, gongs, and hornbill ornaments that celebrate men who kill. The equation of hunting and headhunting is also reflected in myths where valiant men at once fetch game and "cut down" enemy bodies; it is revealed in the fact that a single deity attends at once to headhunters and hunters; and most importantly, it emerges when men describe their marriages and recall wives' brothers who required that suitors not only bring them game but lead them on raids in search of heads. Universally, young men hold hopes of taking heads before they settle into marriage; and the "anger" or "potency" proved through beheading is confirmed when suitors "answer" their affines' demands for grooms who can drink rivers, climb on clouds, and walk on knives – or, in more practical terms, present them with such proofs of "potency" as festive meals and valued goods.

Headhunting is, then, for Ilongots, an act ideally preceding marriage. It is associated with valued male "anger" that is established and displayed at once in murders and in men's successful hunts. Although men kill for various reasons and at different times in their lives, few Ilongot men in this century have accomplished more than one beheading; additional proofs of violent prowess are more likely to be associated with untoward aggressiveness than social recognition and prestige. This is because Ilongots view headtaking as overwhelmingly the concern of restless bachelors who, though taught of killing by the boasts of older men and led on raids by seniors, are described as "anxious" and "distracted" in the years before they "find" a victim and a bride. Marriage itself and, in particular, the birth of children are said to deplete youthful "anger" and vitality in both sexes, and Ilongots say that married men are unlikely to plan killings because they are too preoccupied with their children's cries.

But at the same time that they think adult bonds "diffuse" one's youthful violence, Ilongots believe that "anger" realized in bachelor years is a vital source of life. Thus, Ilongots say that children's names reflect the anger of their fathers, and babies are, in the Ilongot view, created from male anger concentrated as sperm. The equation of hunting and killing thus identifies productive pursuits with an "anger" that provides for social reproduction. And the celebration of killing is itself a moment of collective well-being and transcendent joy.

The rituals for beheading bring a wide circle of kin and friends together for a night of feasting celebration. A pig is slaughtered to appease the spirits, who in turn, ward off the curses sent by victims' kin. After these propitiatory rites, successful killers and their guests engage in endless rounds of boasting, dance, and choral singing. The ritual process at once unites the group and yet distinguishes among significant classes of participants: (a) young boys, who have not taken heads, may playfully behead a chicken while their elders kill the pig but do not themselves participate in choral singing; (b) one or two senior men will stab the pig and otherwise direct proceedings; (c) the head-taker himself must sit on the pig as it is stabbed in order to acquire strength and, after all his guests are gone, perform a ritual that echoes one performed upon his first successful hunt; (d) a group of adult men, all killers, daub their faces with the sacrificial blood and then enter the house to dance and join in choral songs they punctuate with boasts of past beheadings; and finally, (e) the women are treated as a group and are kept separate from the men until a ritual "rubbing" guarantees their health and safety. Women neither eat nor touch the pig "belonging" to the killers, and yet they will encourage men to sing when, in a huddle on the floor, they initiate their choral counterpart to the standing men, who sing and boast in the celebratory song. Some women may join men in individual dancing, but Ilongots feel that women's dances are much "vaguer" and less "concentrated" or lovely than the quite similar dances of men.

Persons are thus grouped in terms of age, accomplishment, and sex, but the general aura of enthusiasm makes clear that all can share in what they see as a rejuvenating celebration. And so, although headhunting is clearly recognized as grounds for the generalized authority of men, women do not discourage the headhunting exploits of their bachelor friends. Instead, they taunt young boys to prove their "anger." And men say they are particularly ashamed to return from unsuccessful raids when maiden voices bid farewell.

Men are, then, defined through violent deeds, performed primarily by youths, that make for social reproduction. But then again – in terms of labor men and women both perform, the glamour of unmarried years, their love of emulation and display – the contents of Ilongot magic, song, and lore suggest that men and women are, for many purposes, construed in similar terms.

Finally, however, elaborate representation of distinctively *feminine* concerns are virtually absent in Ilongot life, and those representations that do exist highlight not women's reproductive role but a concern for her productive skill, her health, attractiveness, and sex. Thus, Ilongot houses often have as decorations on their roofs two arms called "headhunting knives," declaring the ferocity of male residents; and inside, on the beams that hold these "knives," Ilongots have in the past portrayed the female complement to men's violent knives and carved two lumplike "breasts." The "breasts," they say, are not indicative of a mother's love and care but, rather, of nubile sisters whom fierce brothers will defend. Similarly, in harvest rituals, which individual women perform almost entirely alone, no idioms link new rice to babies, but women may dress up "flirtatiously" in glamorous clothes in order to entrance the spirits who protect their crops. Menstruating women should not sit on pillows, but, aside from this, no rituals or restrictions mark a woman's puberty or menstruation. Women may be assisted at birth by any man (or woman) whom they do not see as "brothers," but again, aside from spells to ease delivery of the infant, no ritual celebrates the event of birth. And finally, upon birth itself, people seem much less concerned with the condition of the newborn than with expulsion of the placenta and the mother's health. There are a series of short rituals optionally performed in early months to guarantee the health of the new child, but, significantly, these focus less on the new offspring than on fears that children will deplete their mothers' strength. Men are usually excluded from these rituals for fear that they will "become infants" and lose their skill in hunting; yet a parallel exclusion, separating women from beheaders, does not concern a woman's luck in gardening or reproduction but, rather, threats of pimples, ugliness, and poor health.

As with the Bushmen and Northern Australians, Ilongots clearly see something rejuvenating and creative in male prowess. They link male skill in hunting and killing to the proof of self deemed necessary for marriage. And the rituals in which male feats become the source of a renewed sense of collective life are also rituals that dramatize the differences between men and women and between old and youthful men. Finally, Ilongots seem, in part, to think of women in terms of things like nurturance, health, and feeding; but they do not celebrate biological reproduction or the specialness of mothers.

Instead, what is important about women is that they are lively, energetic, sexually attractive and – as such – both stimulants and complements to men.

INTERPRETING CULTURAL REPRESENTATIONS

In our introduction, we suggested that gender conceptions in any society are to be understood as functioning aspects of a cultural system through which actors manipulate, interpret, legitimize, and reproduce the patterns of cooperation and conflict that order their social world. In other words, we view gender conceptions not as simple *reflections* of biological or social reality but as aspects of wider conceptual systems that arise from, and contribute to, social action. Obvious biological and material facts may constrain possible gender conceptions, but in order to understand how people interpret the world they are given, we must study the social *relations* of men and women in terms of patterns of cooperation and stratification in complex social wholes. Ideas have meaning in interaction – in contexts where people explain their predicaments, voice challenges, and make claims. And so, it is only by examining the kinds of claims people make on one another that we will understand why people in brideservice societies celebrate Man the Hunter when it seems that hunting skill does not, in fact, account for socially significant differences between seniors and young men or between men and women, and why women themselves are apt to celebrate not fertility but sexuality.

Briefly, our argument is that the organization of social relations in brideservice societies gives rise to particular forms of political action and that idioms derived from these forms of alliance and conflict underlie both the ''uni-sexual'' model of reproduction and social order displayed in male and community rituals and the ''heterosexual'' model celebrated by women. Thus, we claim, the potency celebrated in rituals where senior men pretend to energize their social world by transmitting their powers to juniors is but one expression of the force and potency highlighted in all of men's politics. And the powers that bind men to gods are recognized as powerful, we suggest, at least in part because they are related to forces invoked in the articulation of difference and the establishment of peace. Inequality among men is attributed to differences in hunting ability, ritual knowledge, or ''anger,'' and these same qualities are invoked in political contexts when men declare themselves their fellows' peers. For just as conflict is resolved by allowing both sides to display their equal competence, so mature men ritually make equals of youths by teaching them hunting skills, esoteric knowledge, and bravery. Similarly, although in very different terms, women celebrate the *sexual* attributes they invoke when forging relationships with men.

In short, our interpretation of ritual life assumes that ritual elaborates upon politically salient themes. Correspondingly, ideas expressed in rituals must be understood by examining their placement in political contexts. In particular, it appears that the social groupings dramatized in rituals derive from groups defined by different kinds of obligations and that the qualities assigned to such groups are likely to reflect qualities individuals invoke when making claims on others. The qualities assigned to groups, therefore, will not reflect "real" relations between groups but, rather, qualities made salient in situations in which people talk and fight about these "real" relations. The "real" difference between mature men and youths in brideservice societies is that mature men have wives and youths do not; but the situations in which youths acquire wives and mature men defend claims to women are ones in which individual men demonstrate hunting prowess/ritual knowledge and/or the capacity for violence.[33]

Our claim, then, is that relationships of cooperation and obligation shape consciousness by shaping the world in which people live. The idioms used in political action are constrained by the kinds of claims people can make on one another and by the situations in which it is relevant to articulate such claims. Thus, although there are obvious differences among !Kung, Murngin, and Ilongot concerns with hunting, ritual knowledge, and headhunting, respectively, we would argue that these idioms are structurally similar in three ways. First, they all differentiate senior men from junior men and so are appropriate for articulating the publicly most salient form of inequality in brideservice societies. Second, they all refer to exclusively male activities. Third, they are concerned with sexual imbalance, in that all involve activities seen (by members of both sexes) as beneficial to women as well as men. As a result, hunting, ritual knowledge, and headhunting are particularly appropriate idioms for interpreting and manipulating relations in brideservice societies because they make sense of relations between the sexes at the same time that they make sense of inequalities among men.

Our view that ritual idioms are not, in any direct way, a picture of the social world, prescribing forms of action, but, rather, a description of the ways that people rationalize and defend the things they claim, also helps us understand why people in brideservice societies do not follow their own rules for getting ahead. Functionalist theories of stratification (Davis and Moore 1945) as well as Dahrendorf's rewriting of such theories (1968) suggest that people who perform valued behaviors receive social rewards.[34] Yet, we find that among brideservice peoples, who accept as reasonable the notion that virile hunters exchange meat for sex, young men who are presumably most in need of sex are unlikely to be avid hunters. If hunting or killing really were the way to get a wife (as rituals seem to claim), then we might expect to find bachelors combing the bush for game or eagerly setting out to conquer enemies, steal their women, and win the prestige of a kill. Instead, we read that !Kung adolescents do even less work than children (Draper 1975: 213); that when young Murngin kill, "everyone speculates on who did the 'pushing,' for it is always assumed that an old man is really responsible" (Warner 1937: 169); and that Ilongot elders yell headhunting boasts to taunt young men into "anger." In short, ethnographers make clear that it is not bachelors, eager for wives, who do the most hunting and killing,[35] but mature men who, in fact, provide most of the meat and who go on raids against enemies to keep young men from turning back. The relationship between rewards and behavior is thus almost the opposite of that postulated by Dahrendorf and the functionalists. It is not the performance of a behavior that elicits the reward but, rather, the achievement of a desired status that makes repeated performance of these behaviors meaningful to individual men. It is not hunters who receive wives but husbands who hunt.

Thus, our analysis of values allows us to explain why natives tell ethnographers that hunters earn wives without suggesting that elders deliberately mystify the bases of their privilege or that ideological distortions come from the bad faith of elites. Ritual statements of value are elaborations of commonsense idioms and claims that people use to rationalize the privileges they already have. Low-status persons rarely wear themselves out performing valued behaviors because, although failure to perform such behaviors may lead to denial of rewards, everyone knows that rewards do not automatically follow performance. Thus, it is no accident that young men in brideservice societies spend only as much time chasing wild animals and enemies as they have to. An Ilongot boy fortunate enough to take a head at the age of twelve must still wait ten or fifteen years before he can move in with a wife. Excess zeal in performing valued behaviors, moreover, not only does *not* bring extra rewards but can lead to a reputation for boorishness. Among Ilongots, for example, overly successful hunters are said to make others sick because the meat they distribute has been ''poisoned'' by overuse of magical spells.

Our view that rituals elaborate politically salient ideas also allows us to understand why Man the Hunter is not balanced (or opposed) by Woman the Gatherer and why ideas of male potency have not evoked a corresponding stress on female fertility.[36] In the first place, although women may attract or discourage young suitors, and unhealthy or lazy women may undermine their husbands' hopes to entertain guests, women's activities are not relevant to understanding why one man has a wife and another does not. Wives are, of course, very important, but differences among women do not explain politically salient differences among men.

A related point is that in brideservice, as against bridewealth, societies, the relations of production do not create situations in which men could benefit from defining women as inferior. In the latter, but not the former, men's marital and political careers often depend on surplus produce, acquired, in large part, through wives' labor. But in brideservice societies, by contrast, goods cannot be used to create or dissolve obligations, and so the men who eat women's food are not taking from the women anything women could use in other ways. Sexual antagonism in brideservice societies typically takes the form of ritual and/or playful contest concerning initiative among (real or potential) sexual partners. But with no goods to fight for control of, men have no cause to deny that their wives have legitimate desires nor do women have reason to define their prerogatives and interests in absolute opposition to men's.

In fact, our reading of the data would suggest that when women in brideservice societies boast of economic activities, sexual prowess, or reproductive powers that men lack, it is not to claim privileges men cannot share but merely to assert their equal value as social persons. Side by side with the dominant stress on male activities in brideservice societies, we find a much less elaborated view that men and women engage in balanced exchanges to supply each other's equal needs. Such balances, of course, are most likely to be enjoyed by lovers, but established married couples may come equally to see themselves as people who "care for" one another, especially as husbands come to be concerned for the provision of their children and as maturing children help relieve their mother in her daily work. Thus, Ilongots will urge a widowed mother to rewed because her children need a father; !Kung women hail men as "providers"; and among the Murngin, women are appreciative of men's efforts to protect them from the dangerous powers unleashed by male activities. Lorna Marshall captured the essence of a pervasive way of thinking about relations between the sexes when she noted, for the !Kung, that although men are dominant, women are not subjugated and that "instead of being domineering, the men's role is one of protection and support" (1976: 177). Similarly, among Ilongots, although men may demand services from their wives on the basis of their established force as killers, women and men both agree that men are "fearful" that their wives may leave them; and women will respond to men's claims, based on violence, with the reminder that even killers have hungry stomachs, requiring that *both* men and women share the fruits of their work.

Finally, we would attribute the observed lack of stress on motherly care or female fertility to the fact that in contrast to bridewealth societies, children in brideservice societies are unlikely to obey or to work for parents or other adults who can claim to have given them support. Children in brideservice societies, in fact, do very little work at all. Thus, there are apt to be very few contexts in which it makes sense for mothers or mothers' kin to stress how much mothers have done, or suffered, for their children. And the ritual marking of fatherhood that is found in brideservice societies (see the section on marriage) has, we suggest, less to do with establishing claims to children (although men do invoke fatherhood when claiming rights to participate in children's marriages) than with reinforcing a man's claim to his child's mother.

What, then, of positive views of femininity? Rather than relating women's puberty rites to such vague notions as "female status," our view that rituals elaborate politically salient ideas allows us to explain why women's rituals in brideservice societies celebrate the creative, energizing powers of female sexuality. In our discussion of political processes, we noted that sexual intercourse is a core metaphor for social relations. Politics are sexual politics because, whatever else they may concern, relations among men are organized through men's claims to women. And if men say they hunt and kill in order to gain sexual access to women, then women turn the idiom around and use their sexuality to make claims to men (see, for example, Warner 1937: 83; Shostak 1976: 250; Siskind 1973: 12). Women expect meat from lovers, and women invoke their sexuality when urging men to kill the enemies who would steal women away from familiar kin. In brideservice societies, therefore, women's sexuality *does* energize men, and so the onset of sexual maturity in a girl is, in a very real way, an occasion for joyful celebration.

Conclusion

We began this essay with a puzzle. Why, in the simplest human societies, do we not find such a basic and profound fact as maternity highlighted in cultural conceptions as the center of women's lives? An answer to this question required exploration not only of gender conceptions but also of the place of beliefs about men and women in a particular kind of society. One implication of our analysis should be obvious: We believe there are *no* facts about human sexual biology that, in and of themselves, have immediate social meanings or institutional consequences. Mothering[37] is a social relation, much like fathering, judging, or ruling, whose meaning and organization must be understood with reference to a particular configuration of relationships within a complex social whole.

For this reason, our account of gender conceptions in brideservice societies is rooted in a model that relates personhood, economics, and politics. Having noted a recurrent pattern – Man the Hunter/Provider and unisexual reproducer of human social relations is ritually opposed to women, heterosexuality, and conflict – we asked what, in the social experiences of people in brideservice societies, could account for commonalities in the structure of their beliefs. A contrast with more complex bridewealth societies, in which women *are* conceptualized in terms of their reproductive powers, made it clear that the sort of understanding required could not be gained by appealing to universals. Instead, we would have to link conceptions of gender to a system of social relations of a particular *kind*.

Here, traditional anthropological accounts were of little value. Because of a tendency to assume the universality or invariance of women's position in systems of kinship and marriage, anthropological discussions of social structure do not help us to identify *differences* in the social meanings and consequences of such facts as marrying and mothering. Descent theorists, for example, tend to assume the invariance of the mother-child bond. In their view, men lack such natural connections and so must attach themselves to potential mothers to build ties with the descendants men are assumed "naturally" to want. Thus, even though descent theory can help us understand how men's jural ties create households of different sizes and shapes, descent theory cannot tell us anything about differences in what it takes as given – the bond between a mother and her child.

Alliance theory is not much better. For if descent theorists root family life in invariant facts of reproduction, Lévi-Strauss's exploration of the ways in which family and society mutually define one another assumes the invariance of sex. For alliance theorists, it is "man's deep polygamous tendency" (Lévi-Strauss 1969: 38) that turns women into objects whose exchange creates relations of alliance, equality, or hierarchy among men. Lévi-Strauss's attempt to cast kinship and marriage as social and cultural processes marks an important advance over those who root kinship in natural reproductive processes. But in describing the *forms* of exchange, Lévi-Strauss pays scant attention to *contents* (Bourdieu 1977: 1–30); he assumes that relations between men who get wives and women who become wives are everywhere of the same kind. Different styles of exchange may give rise to new orders of male-male relations, but because heterosexual bonds are assumed to be natural, invariant, and universal, alliance theory suggests no ways in which differences in social structure can influence relations between women and men.

Varying patterns of male–female cooperation, dominance, and independence cannot be explained, therefore, by either descent or alliance theory because each treats as invariant and natural a relationship that is, in fact, variable and social. Both theories mask problematic assumptions as unchanging natural law. For theorists of both camps, the problem lies in the ease with which they link contingent facts about gender to biological assumptions. In discovering such supposedly universal facts as marriage and motherhood, they failed to note the qualitative differences in the social context and significance of what are, of course, social bonds. In assuming the functional logic of both sex and reproduction, they treated as secondary the question of their social uses, and so failed to explore the ways in which relations between women and men are conditioned by a social order. They failed to ask how the facts of marriage and motherhood organize responsibility and privilege in *particular* ways.

Our task in this essay was to develop just such a characterization. We suggested that gender in very simple societies is best understood through an examination of how marriage organizes obligations, and of how such obligations shape political life. In nonclass societies, where social relations of production are articulated in idioms of kinship, marriages create not only families but also those patterns of cooperation, obligation, and expectation that organize productive activity. Therefore, we began our analysis of gender conceptions in simple brideservice societies by noting that marriage creates an asymmetry between wives and husbands and between husbands and wives' kin. Not surprisingly, *given* the organization of production, women in brideservice societies are reluctant to take on obligations of marriage, whereas men willingly assume obligations to in-laws in order to acquire the wives who make them independent. Ultimately, we suggested, the political significance of sex and marriage, as experienced by both sexes, derives from the critical place of marriage in the life careers of men.

Our conceptualization of political relations in brideservice societies is thus based on our understanding of the ways in which productive relations figure in the typical life cycles of both sexes. Men, we found, leave their maternal homes early in life and spend much of their teenage years as relatively unanchored bachelors who must attach themselves to senior men in order to enjoy the services of women, achieve symbolic proofs of creativity and prowess, and ultimately, of course, win a wife. In particular, they must establish a relationship with future in-laws, who accept them as the husbands of their daughters, in order to secure desired conjugal ties. Marriage for a man is a prerequisite to adult autonomy and status; and although conflict surrounding this status makes it seem that wives are earned through shows of force, adult autonomy depends, in fact, on the assumption of obligations and responsibilities vis-à-vis those affines best equipped to influence potential wives.

Only when marriages are secure do men begin to appear free of such obligations. And so it is that only older men are likely to be seen as generous providers who, through gifts of game, can guarantee the welfare of their households and coordinate cooperative bonds. These older married men, identified with the territory where they live and generally respected for such qualities as wisdom and generosity, are apt, as well, to benefit from the support and services of newly married young couples. But unlike the division between married and unmarried men, the contrast between young husbands and the seniors they respect is unlikely to be elaborated in political or symbolic forms, because the senior's status is itself a function more of age than of the resources or authority he commands. In fact, the only power any man can claim is an ability to influence another's actual or wished-for wife; thus, a man whose marriage is secure need obey no other. And without the possibility of power over other men, adults are understandably reluctant to compete in the pursuit of what is ultimately an unwieldy authority. At best, accumulated goods and powers claimed are a reassurance to the insecure; at worst, they often prove a pretense demanding challenges by less accomplished men that are likely to lead, in turn, to loss of face and outright violence.

In short, within a world where men need only wives in order to be independent of and equal to their fellow men, men's need of women combines with leaders' lack of power to make sex and violence the most salient aspects of conflicts between men. But furthermore, because parity is all a man can desire, and because the denial of parity is readily associated with violent conflict, equality itself becomes a virtue (to be achieved by potent men), and excessive shows of dominance are abjured. Women's freedom and autonomy is, as we have seen, a function of the violent politics that also, of course, constrain them. But because women are assured a share of game by virtue of their membership in *any* group of kin, they have little cause to assert claims either in husbands or in sons or otherwise to engage as men's competitors in predominantly male politics. Instead, women are most likely to use sexual skills in an attempt not to win power from men but, rather, to escape constraining marital bonds and build the networks of affection and support that will assure them considerable freedom throughout life.

Ultimately, it was this characterization of contrasting strategies in political life that provided us with an account of gender. Political action, shaped by the social relations of production – which, of course, *include* and presuppose cross-sex alignments – was seen as consequential for core cultural conceptions that define women and men. In particular, we have argued here that the organization of political life provides the material basis for a cultural contrast between a unisexual world of potent, solidary, and occasionally violent male hunters and a heterosexual world associated with women, sexuality, and conflict. In making marriages, men make peace among themselves at the same time that their relationships with women are a recurrent source of conflict. Thus, real experience confirms ritual statements that male potency organizes and maintains the world – because men *do* articulate their claims to wives in terms of hunting skills and violent feats – even though, as we have shown, men do not get wives through public proofs of individual prowess but, rather, by fulfilling obligations toward those adults able to influence desired brides.

In conclusion, we would then reassert our claim that gender conceptions do not reflect, in any simple sense, a set of social facts but, rather, that gender conceptions grow from, even as they shape, social and political processes. Beliefs about the dangers and virtues of each sex do not arise simply to rationalize the unjust powers certain people claim, reinforce unchanging order in the world, enjoin commitment to collective norms, or celebrate something like women's "status." Even though people can do lots of things with shared ideas – mock or worship leaders, dull the consciousness of the oppressed, escape the world or fight to change it – the ideas people use for such purposes are themselves shaped by the system of relations within which they pursue their goals. The feminist insight that sex is ultimately a political and therefore a *social* fact holds true not only for the Western world (where women are, we think, oppressed) but also for the qualitatively different worlds of hunters. And so, it is only by understanding men and women as actors in specific social and political spheres that we can understand their self-conceptions and thus come to terms with the social processes that determine what is, after all, society's creation: the way gender is construed.

Stated otherwise, this essay builds from the belief that the relations between the sexes in all human societies are shaped by and contribute to such other inequalities as pervade the organization of political and economic life. And because we are convinced that social inequalities differ in much more than *quantity*, we would insist, as well, that an understanding of sexual asymmetry requires an ability to discriminate among its qualitatively different forms. Thus, women in the societies discussed in this essay are not men's equals in terms of life possibilities or opportunities to enforce their wills upon others, but women are not dependent in the manner of unmarried bachelors nor do they appear to be "exploited" by husbands in ways that occur in certain more complex societies. Such qualitative differences cannot, we claim, be quantified as so many degrees of women's status nor can we grasp qualitative difference through a mere enumeration of women's prerogatives and rights.

The things women fight for, criticize, and perhaps achieve are all dependent on the things they want, and desires themselves are products of social systems that already specify relationships and include presuppositions about individual capacities. Analyses of gender, therefore, must be rooted in analyses of social wholes. And so, having come to recognize hitherto slighted facts about the lot of women and the organization of their lives, our need is now for models that help us to characterize the relationships between women and men, discriminating among various forms of "sexual politics."

Notes

1 This is the third version of a paper that was presented first at the 1975 meetings of the American Anthropological Association, and later at the conference on Hunters and Gatherers held in Paris, June 1978. Because this paper has had such a long history, the numbers of people whose suggestions, insights, and criticisms have

shaped our thinking are too numerous to list. We are very grateful, however to everyone who took the time to comment on earlier versions of this paper, and we particularly want to thank Richard Abel, Gregory Accaioli, Kathleen Adams, Jane Atkinson, Ellen Basso, Keith Basso, Elsie Begler, Barbara Bender, Nancy Chodorow, Bette Clark, George Collier, Donald Donham, Shelley Errington Duncan Foley, Helene Foley, Ernestine Friedl, Esther Goody, Jean Jackson, Nan Keohane, Richard Lee, Lynn Levine, Karen Mason, Brian Morris, Fred Myers, Bridget O'Laughlin, Sherry Ortner, Susan Philipps, Renato Rosaldo, Judith Shapiro, Janet Siskind, G. W. Skinner, Carol Smith, Eleanor Sosne, Kathrine Verdery, Harriet Whitehead, Beatrice Whiting, Barbara Yngvesson. Jane Collier's contribution to the research and writing of this paper was supported by a grant from the National Science Foundation (No. BNS 76–11651) to study "Stratification and Legal Processes." Part of Michelle Rosaldo's contribution was supported during her period as a Fellow at the Center for Advanced Study in the Behavioral Sciences, through a grant from the National Endowment for the Humanities. In addition, both authors are grateful to the Ford Foundation for supporting their trip to the Conference on Hunters and Gatherers in 1978.

2 Our readings on Australian Aborigines included C. Berndt 1950 and 1965, R. Berndt 1965, Berndt and Berndt 1964, Elkin 1938, Gale 1974, Hiatt 1965, Goodale 1971, Hart and Pilling 1960, Kaberry 1939, Maddock 1972, Meggitt 1962, Munn 1973, Roheim 1974, Thomson 1949, and Warner 1937. Our readings on North American Aborigines included Balikci 1970, Briggs 1970, Burch 1975, Chance 1966, Giffen 1930 and Kjellström 1973 on the Eskimo; Leacock 1954, Lips 1947, Rogers 1972, Speck 1935 and Strong 1924 on the Montagnais-Naskapi; Landes 1971 on Ojibwa; Hoebel 1940 and Wallace and Hoebel 1952 on Comanches; Steward 1938 and Whiting 1950 on Basin-Plateau peoples; and Downs 1961 and 1966 on the Washo. Our readings on South American Aborigines included Biocca 1971 and Chagnon 1968 on the Yanomamo; Holmberg 1969 on the Sirionó; R. Murphy 1960 and Murphy and Murphy 1974 on the Mundurucu, and Siskind 1973 on the Sharanahua. Our readings on African groups included Turnbull 1961 on the Pygmies; Woodburn 1968a, 1968b, 1970 and 1972 on the Hadza; Lee and DeVore 1976, Marshall 1976, and Thomas 1959 on the Kalahari Bushmen.

3 Our primary Bushman source in what follows is the material on the !Kung San, only one of the so-called Bushman groups. Although ethnographers have recently been concerned to eliminate misunderstandings generated by nonindigenous ethnic classifications, we use the word "Bushman" interchangeably with "!Kung" throughout the text in an effort, first, to indicate the kind of scope we think appropriate to our argument, and second, to facilitate reading by a nonspecialist audience.

4 Whether or not one can produce a cross-culturally valid definition of sexual asymmetry (see, e.g., Tilly 1978, Rosaldo 1980b), our purpose here is the narrower one of isolating a set of relationships that seem central to understanding gender in simple societies; women elsewhere feed husbands, but the significance of this fact for an understanding of gender hierarchies and prerogatives is not likely to be the same as that described in this account.

5 The fact that married women have no more privileged access to male products than their single sisters is made obvious when women with one husband are compared to women with two, for contrary to popular anthropological opinion (see, e.g. J. Steward 1938: 245), women with two husbands do not have more meat than women with one husband; they have only more work. See Collier, n.d., for a discussion of this point with reference to Plains Indian societies.

6 Compare C. Meillassoux: "The hunters, once they share the common product, are free from any further reciprocal obligations or allegiance" (1972: 99). Unlike Meillassoux, however, we attribute this freedom not to a technology of "instantaneous production," but to a system of social relations wherein hunters on distributing game are free of obligation because married men need nothing from one another: They do not find themselves in relations of ongoing obligation because all married men have equal access to desired rewards. Thus, our discussion treats systems of social relations as equally causal with brute material constraints.

7 One seeming exception to our generalization is R. Berndt's account of Murngin girls as disobeying parental wishes and going to live with their much older husbands "because being a married woman means extra status, even though it involves added responsibility" (1965: 85). In this case, it seems likely that, at marriage, girls acquired the economic services of same-age or older "sons-in-law," and that marriage actually meant more, rather than less, sexual freedom, because a married woman's adulteries caused fewer fights among men than did unmarried girls' liaisons. The Murngin are thus an exception to our generalization that *marriage* marks a decline in women's status, but they are not an exception to our more general claim that what women want is not marriage but egalitarian exchange relationships with men and sexual freedom.

8 Turnbull's account of Yambabo's reluctance to marry the brother of a woman *her* brother desired (1961: 106) is a good example of the kind of situation we have in mind; see also Thomas (1959) and Shostak (1976) (on Bushmen), Siskind (1973) (on Sharanahua), Murphy and Murphy (1974) (on Mundurucú) and Goodale (1971) and Cowlishaw (n.d.) (on Australia), for evidence of women's active role in seeking lovers, as well as their willingness to engage in infanticide and abortion, as, it appears, a strategy for avoiding marital constraints.

9 Among Bushmen, death of the father during pregnancy is seen as cause for infanticide (Lee 1972). Ilongots mark the importance of the father by saying, first, that male "anger" concentrated as sperm is what makes babies, and second that the names of children (of whatever sex) are, in effect, the realization of paternal "anger." Finally, Holmberg writing of the Sirionó, recounts a number of ways in which the life of a newborn depends upon the actions of its father: Postpartum restrictions constrain parents of both sexes; fathers hunt when wives begin their labor, and the child is named after the animal the father kills; additionally, fathers are required to cut the umbilical cord of the child (1969: 177–97). A likely hypothesis we have not been able to explore is that so-called couvade rituals will be concentrated in brideservice groups.

10 Because marriages create not only families but also extraconjugal obligations and social ties, people in simple societies never face one of the major problems posed by Western bourgeois ideology. Our ideal of marriage – as an egalitarian and self-sufficient relationship of husband and wife – would seem to provide no grounds for forging wider social networks. But although lovers may, in simple societies, enjoy a self-sufficient bliss, their bonds are not long lasting. It is only by establishing bonds of obligation and dependency toward their in-laws that men in brideservice societies can create stable marital ties.

11 Wallace and Hoebel, for example, imply that Comanche men paid for wives when they describe Comanche suitors as sending a messenger "to make an offer to the parents or brother (of the bride) as compensation for their daughter or sister" (1952: 135). The "horses or other goods" given as "compensation" by Comanche grooms, however, were things they obtained by themselves (see also Collier, n.d.). Similarly, Woodburn reports for the Hadza that "long strings of bridewealth

beads should be, and usually are, given by the bridegroom to his parents-in-law"
(1968: 109). "Bridewealth beads," however, are things a man can obtain on his
own without having to borrow from seniors. Hadza men obtain the beads from
outsiders in return for hunted meat or honey.

12 Friedl's (1975) suggestive discussion of why humans marry, with its stress on the
importance of affinal bonds for organizing economic cooperation is one of the few
exceptions to a general trend in the theoretical literature.

13 The differences between brideservice and bridewealth societies are further explored
in a yet unpublished book by Collier that contrasts "brideservice" Comanche,
"equal bridewealth" Cheyenne, and "unequal bridewealth" Kiowa. Bridewealth
societies have more complex political systems than brideservice ones because
goods can be converted into rights in people, but both brideservice and bridewealth
societies are far less complex than societies where women bring dowry goods into
marriage (Goody 1973). In brideservice societies, only fathers of daughters can
acquire young men's services, but in bridewealth societies, even men without
daughters can acquire the services of young men by providing young men's bridewealth payments. As a result, there is more inequality in bridewealth societies, although this inequality is manifested in sizes of "estates of production," not in
styles of consumption (see Gluckman 1965). The contrast between brideservice
and bridewealth societies is vividly illustrated by Turnbull's account of the differences between Pygmies and Bantu villagers (1961), and we suspect that the contrast is equally vivid between some lowland and highland peoples in New Guinea.

14 Power, in this analysis, is understood as a function of followers' needs (Emerson
1962). Although Emerson used his formulation to analyze dependents' strategies
for minimizing power differentials, Collier (1979, n.d.) has found his formulation
useful for analyzing the stratification processes that link the forces and relations of
production to political and legal structures. If, as Emerson suggests, the power
available to superiors depends on the degree of inferiors' dependence, then the
amount of power generally available to leaders in a socioeconomic formation
should be directly related to the efficiency of those mechanisms that recruit people
into positions of dependency on the bottom of a social hierarchy. Hence, young
men's need for wives in brideservice societies grants power to those able to
influence marriageable women, but securely married men's lack of needs severely
limits the amount of power available to leaders.

15 Of course, the extent of polygyny is extremely various in the societies we are discussing, reaching a high in the North Australian groups (where we imagine, slaving
and trading have had a considerable impact on the shape of marital politics). By
contrast, Ilongots would appear to constitute a partial exception to our remarks in
that polygyny is extremely rare, and few married men and women celebrate or engage in sexual relationships with lovers. However, the tendency of widowers but
not widows to remarry skews age-sex ratios in a way that tends to make wives
younger than husbands and to create a class of somewhat troublesome aging bachelors, who do in fact compete with other men for women and have affairs.

16 The rituals in which Sharanahua exchange meat for sex, accompanied by cross-sex
nettle throwing, are, of course, a prime example (Siskind 1973). Ilongot bachelors
and maidens engage in cross-sex water-pouring contests and the Pygmies are
reported to have all-male and all-female teams oppose one another in a ritual
tug-of-war at the time of gathering honey. In addition, puberty ceremonies for
Pygmy girls require them to chase and catch the boys they want as lovers; the boys
so designated are then required to prove themselves as men by fighting their way
into the girls' puberty enclosure (see Turnbull 1965).

17 "Sex" is widely recognized as the major "cause" of conflicts among men in simple societies. Fried, for example, concludes that "sexual tensions are the cause of much of the conflict (ethnographers) saw or heard about in Bushmen and Eskimo society" (1967: 75), because of the threat that the female's normal roles in the division of labor will be upset by attentions paid to her lover or lovers (1967: 78). It is important to note, however, that we disagree with Fried's causal explanation: The "value" of women is determined through political processes and not economic contribution alone.

18 The autobiographical account, *Yanoama* (Biocca 1971), of life among the South American Yanomamo, provides numerous examples of the fact that women can and do flee to distant groups where they have relatives or friends when local relationships (and, in particular, the actions of a domineering spouse) prove intolerable. See Rosaldo (1980a: 200–1) for comparable Ilongot materials.

19 Perhaps the clearest instance of this point comes from the Tiwi of Northern Australia, among whom women will, on husbands' death, acquire rights in allocating daughters (Hart and Pilling 1960) and, according to Goodale (1971), a girl at puberty becomes affiliated with a "son-in-law" of her own age, whose services then constitute a marital claim to her, as yet, unborn daughters. See also R. Berndt (1965: 86) for Murngin, and Marshall (1976: 272) on Bushmen.

20 Begler (1978) cites evidence of the legitimacy of wife beating among the Australian Aborigines and claims that the Pygmies, by contrast, do not accept the use of force as legitimate in husband–wife relations. Although Pygmies may find wife beating problematic (and recognize that brutality by a husband may well occasion the violent response of his wife), its importance as a legitimate threat emerges in Turnbull's report of a young husband who reports that his wife is so obedient he does not have to beat her (1965: 205). Among Bushmen, mothers of sons voice hopes that their daughters-in-law will prove sweet tempered and not lazy "like a bitch," suggesting that a young wife's obedience is seen as problematic and may well require violent sanctions (Marshall 1976: 167). And Ilongot men, although never observed by the Rosaldos to beat their wives, are said to teach wives to respect them by threatening force (1980a: 101–2).

21 A concern to control "trouble causing women" as the most effective strategy for achieving peaceful relations among men makes it likely that the amount of male violence against women in brideservice societies is a function of the amount of aggression among men. We think it no accident, therefore, that male aggression against women appears most extreme in those modern brideservice groups living in areas where, during the last century, agents of capitalist expansion wittingly or unwittingly caused members of some brideservice groups to exterminate others (Australia), enslave them (Amazon Basin and western rim of the United States Great Plains), or steal their furs (northern North America). In contrast, male aggression against women appears mildest or nonexistent in those modern brideservice groups that have long been surrounded by, and partially integrated into, bridewealth or peasant societies (e.g., Ilongot, Bushmen, Pygmies, Hadza, Semang).

22 The use of violent and sexual sanctions against women who resist marriage and/or witness secret ceremonies of men is alluded to in Maddock's (1974) discussion of marriage in Australia; among the Murngin, rape and incest are associated with moments of mythic creativity (Warner 1937: 328); and Roheim, writing of the Western Desert, comments, "it frequently happens that a group of men will drag one woman into the bush, where they force her to have sexual intercourse with all of them" (1974: 241). Again, threats of gang rape as a sort of "punishment"

toward the woman who wanders out of bounds are widely reported for South America (e.g., Siskind 1973: 14; Murphy and Murphy 1974: 94). Hadza women (Woodburn 1972: 6) are threatened by rape; and Richard Lee (personal communication) tells that threats of rape are known among the Bushmen.

23 Ilongots, for example, say that husbands will, in most contexts, ignore rather than address their wives' deviations, because as one man put it, "I didn't want to kill her so I had to forget that I was angry."

24 Stated otherwise, whatever "surplus produce" men are able to command is not likely to be based on "exploitation" of their wives, but on their extramarital exchanges. Among Australian Aborigines, for example, men apparently did consume food prepared by women at exclusively male rituals but we suggest that this food was not obtained by husbands from wives, but rather by young men from sexually taboo women. Such an inference is partially supported by Thomson's (1949) account of ceremonial exchanges in Arnhem Land, which describes young men as obtaining the cooked food they had to present to senior men during rituals from sexually taboo women (mothers, sisters, mothers-in-law) in direct exchange for hunted meat.

25 Gerontocratic societies of Northern Australia represent the inegalitarian extreme of our brideservice type, and, as such, they have more inequality than many egalitarian bridewealth groups, such as the Ndendeuli of Tanzania (Gulliver 1971). We argue, however, that although Australian societies may differ from other brideservice groups in the *quantity* of inequality, Australian societies are *qualitatively* more similar to brideservice than to bridewealth groups. This is true not only on the level of gender conceptions, but also on the level of productive and political relations. Thus, for example, Murngin bachelors and married men alike control the products of their labor and distribute those products to create ties with others. Young men in bridewealth societies by contrast do not control the products of their own labor, for their labor (obedience) already belongs to seniors who support them in the quest for wives. Again, among Australians, as in all brideservice societies, bachelors wander from group to group, performing little productive labor. In bridewealth societies, young men tend to be firmly incorporated into household production units where they are characteristically assigned the heaviest male tasks.

Finally, Northern Australian societies share the political processes common to brideservice groups in that they lack "big men" (Sahlins 1963) and settle disputes through contests rather than moots. Tiwi elders can sponsor ceremonies by giving away the produce of their own wives (Hart and Pilling 1960: 50) but they lack the capacity of Melanesian "big men" or African elders for giving away the produce of others men's wives. Similarly, Tiwi settle disputes over adultery by staging confrontations between cuckolded husbands and wives' lovers (Hart and Pilling 1960: 80–3), not by having elders negotiate restitutive damages. Most importantly, however, Tiwi politics center on men's claims to wives: Politics in bridewealth societies characteristically revolve around seniors' claims to juniors (see Turner 1957).

26 There are two major brakes on development of the productive forces in brideservice societies. First, persons with rights to appropriate the products of others' labor have no means of either forcing or persuading those others to increase production. And, second, people are reluctant to acquire goods others do not have, even if those goods are useful tools in production. Warner reports that Murngin who knew how to make dugouts with outriggers, nevertheless made frail bark canoes for ocean crossings because such canoes could be discarded after a single use (1937: 459). And, Chagnon, in a paper delivered at the 1967 meetings of the

American Anthropological Association, told of a Yanomamo headman who destroyed the canoe he could not keep others from using without his permission, and of men who destroyed entire plantings of such introduced crops as watermelons, papayas, and sugar cane when others stole the fruits of their labor.

27 Rubin's (1975) formulation of the relationship between the "exchange of women" and male dominance makes a similar point concerning the fact that the social organization of heterosexuality cross-culturally makes women inferior by virtue of the fact that they cannot engage in the same kinds of exchanges as men. It is relevant, however, that in bridewealth, as opposed to brideservice, societies, where marriage is a matter of the acquisition of rights in persons through gifts of goods, women *can*, in some cases, "purchase" wives of their own.

28 Note too that Lévi-Strauss's work (1969) not only documents the importance of direct "exchange" in "elementary" kinship systems, but shows in particular the relationship between Australian "section systems" and an orientation to "sister exchange" (Greg Acciaioli, in an unpublished paper, suggests that "direct exchange" as a model probably fits the Murngin, whom Lévi-Strauss discussed in other terms). The elaborate regulations on joking and seating arrangements among the Bushmen (Marshall 1976) probably operate in a similar fashion, as indicators of sexual access and opportunities for "direct exchange."

29 Among Ilongots, use of obscene words and allusions to sexual and reproductive functions are taboo among cross-sex siblings but not, for example, among fathers and daughters. In addition, Warner (1937) and Hiatt (1965) both report the special marking of sibling relationships as revealed in the fact that Northern Australian brothers spear their sisters when the latter are insulted by another man.

30 Katz (1976) states that about one-third of adult !Kung women also learn to trance, but his article says nothing about either the occasions on which women enter trance states or how women learn to trance.

31 Nancy Howell, though she thinks she is saying the opposite, supports our sense of a relative lack of cultural concern for female fertility when she says of the !Kung, "the costs of gonorrhea to particular women who were left sterile have been very heavy . . . women's lives are geared to childbearing and rearing; the childless woman is unemployed in the most serious business of life . . . you can always tell the infertile women when you enter a new village because they are the ones with the clean faces . . . better dressed and more careful of their appearances than heavily burdened mothers" (1979: 187). Howell goes on to report that these infertile women "specialize in beautiful beadwork . . . become involved in the new women's drum dance . . . some are active in *hxaro* ("gift giving") relations, and others may carry on their sexual liaisons and romances with style and enthusiasm." Childbearing and rearing may be the most serious of !Kung women's activites, but they hardly seem the most culturally valued or desirable. Judith Shapiro (personal communication) reports a similar bias among the Yanomamo, as do Murphy and Murphy (1974: 165) in discussing childbirth among Mundurucú.

32 Contemporary researches by such persons as Diane Bell and Annette Hamilton lead us to hope that this gap in the literature will be redressed in the near future. In the traditional literature, Catherine Berndt's writings (1950, 1965) remain the best source on women's ritual life in Arnhem Land. And Kaberry's (1939) classic account of Aboriginal women (concerned not with Arnhem Land, but the Kimberleys) provides additional testimony to the centrality of sexual concerns in women's life crisis rituals and secret corroborees. Birth, Kaberry claims, is a ritually important moment; yet ritual attention seems more concerned with ejection of the placenta and health of child and mother than with the celebration of fertility per se.

33 Althusser's (1971: 158–77) discussion of the nature of "ideology" as an institution that at once alludes to and misrepresents or distorts people's "real conditions of existence," was the source of many of our first insights into the relationship between gender conceptions and political economy in very simple societies. Our approach differs from his, however, in that, rather than write of "misrepresentation," we suggest that beliefs that purport to "describe" reality are often best understood as idioms in terms of which people make claims on their fellows; the social practices that give belief (or "ideological") systems their compellingness and vitality are always *political* practices, and politics are shaped, in large part, by the organization of productive life.

34 Dahrendorf and the functionalists agree that people who perform valued behaviors are rewarded, but they disagree on how behaviors become valued. Dahrendorf seeks the genesis of value in the interests of elites, whereas more conventional functionalists such as Marvin Harris, locate value in survival needs. Thus Harris, for example, has argued (1977) that in contexts of protein scarcity, men are motivated to seek out all available game by a humanly induced shortage of women, which means that only successful hunters will be able to reproduce.

35 Siskind's (1973) book on the Sharanahua documents the fact that bachelors are "reluctant hunters" in a world where ideology clearly postulates an exchange of meat for sex. The Yanomamo case is even more striking. In a world where a reputation for "fierceness" is supposedly all a man can desire, young men turn back from raids against enemies "because of" stomach cramps or sore feet (Chagnon 1968: 130). The point, of course, is that youths rarely get anything out of raids, because senior men appropriate all the captured women. It is only after a bachelor marries that he must become "fierce" in order to keep others from seducing or stealing his wife.

36 The elaboration of pollution beliefs and symbolic representations of female reproductive processes in bridewealth as against brideservice societies has to do with several of the factors previously listed: the political importance of offspring in bridewealth societies; the fact that men gain bridewealth goods at women's expense; the consequent structural bases for sexual antagonism; and so forth.

37 The tendency to see mothering as more natural, universal, and constant a role than fathering is reflected in much of the anthropological literature on kinship (e.g. Barnes 1973; for critiques see Yanagisako 1979, Boon 1974, Drummond 1978, and Rosaldo 1980b).

References

Acciaioli, Gregory L. n.d. "Descent and alliance in Arnhem Land: the underlying structure of exchange." Unpublished manuscript.

Althusser, Louis. 1971. *Lenin and philosophy*. New York: Monthly Review Press.

Balikci, Asen. 1970. *The Netsilik Eskimo*. Garden City, N.Y.: The Natural History Press.

Barnes, J. A. 1973. "Genetrix: genitor:: nature: culture?" In *The character of kinship*, ed. J. Goody, pp. 61–73. Cambridge: Cambridge University Press.

Begler, Elsie B. 1978. "Sex, status and authority in egalitarian society." *American Anthropologist* 80: 571–88.

Beidelman, T. O. 1971. *The Kaguru: a matrilineal people of East Africa*. New York: Holt, Rinehart and Winston.

Berndt, Catherine H. 1950. "Women's changing ceremonies in Northern Australia." *L'Homme* 1: 1–87.

1965. "Women and the 'secret life.' " In *Aboriginal man in Australia*, ed. R. M. Berndt and C. H. Berndt, pp. 238–82. Sydney: Angus and Robertson.

Berndt, Ronald M. 1965. "Marriage and the family in north-eastern Arnhem Land." In *Comparative Family Systems*, ed. M. F. Nimkoff, pp. 77–104. Boston: Houghton Mifflin.

Berndt, Ronald, and Berndt, Catherine. 1964. *The world of the first Australians*. London: Angus and Robertson.

Bettelheim, Bruno. 1962. *Symbolic wounds: puberty rites and the envious male*. Glencoe, Ill.: Free Press.

Biesele, M. 1975. "Folklore and ritual of !Kung hunter-gatherers." Unpublished Ph.D. dissertation, Harvard University.

Biocca, Ettore. 1971. *Yanoama: the narrative of a white girl kidnapped by Amazonian Indians*. New York: E. P. Dutton.

Boon, J. A. 1974. "Anthropology and nannies." *Man* 9: 137–40.

Bourdieu, Pierre. 1977. *Outline of a theory of practice*. Cambridge: Cambridge University Press.

Briggs, Jean. 1970. *Never in anger: portrait of an Eskimo family*. Cambridge, Mass.: Harvard University Press.

Burch, Ernest S., Jr. 1975. *Eskimo kinsmen*. St. Paul: West Publishing.

Chagnon, Napoleon A. 1968. *Yanomamo, the fierce people*. New York: Holt, Rinehart and Winston.

Chance, Norman A. 1966. *The Eskimo of North Alaska*. New York: Holt, Rinehart and Winston.

Collier, Jane F. 1979. "Stratification and dispute handling in two Highland Chiapas communities." *American Ethnologist* 6: 305–27.

n.d. "Marriage and inequality: a comparison of three nineteenth century Plains tribes." Unpublished manuscript.

Cowlishaw, Gillian. n.d. "Infanticide in Aboriginal Australia." Unpublished manuscript.

Dahrendorf, Ralf. 1968. *Essays in the theory of society*. Stanford: Stanford University Press.

Davis, Kingsley, and Moore, Wilbert E. 1945. "Some principles of stratification." *American Sociological Review* 10: 242–9.

Downs, James F. 1961. "Washo religion." *University of California Anthropological Record* 14: 349–418.

1966. *The two worlds of the Washo*. New York: Holt, Rinehart and Winston.

Draper, Patricia. 1975. "!Kung women: contrasts in sexual egalitarianism in foraging and sedentary contexts." In *Toward an anthropology of women*, ed. R. Reiter, pp. 77–109. New York: Monthly Review Press.

1976. "Social and economic constraints on child life among the !Kung." In *Kalahari hunter-gatherers*, ed. R. Lee and I. DeVore, pp. 199–217. Cambridge, Mass.: Harvard University Press.

Drummond, L. 1978. "The transatlantic nanny: notes on a comparative semiotics of the family in English-speaking societies." *American Ethnologist* 5: 30–43.

Elkin, A. P. 1938. *The Australian aborigines*. London: Angus and Robertson

Emerson, Richard. 1962. "Power-dependence relations." *American Sociological Review* 27: 31–40.

Fried, Morton H. 1967. *The evolution of political society*. New York: Random House.

Friedl, Ernestine. 1975. *Women and men: an anthropologist's view*. New York: Holt, Rinehart and Winston.

Gale, Fay, ed. 1974. *Woman's role in Aboriginal society*. Canberra: Australian Institute of Aboriginal Studies, no. 36.

Geertz, Clifford. 1973. *The interpretation of cultures*. New York: Basic Books.

Giffen, Naomi. 1930. *The roles of men and women in Eskimo culture*. Chicago: University of Chicago Press.

Gluckman, Max. 1965. *Politics, law and ritual in tribal society*. Chicago: Aldine.

Goodale, Jane C. 1971. *Tiwi wives*. Seattle: University of Washington Press.

Goody, Jack. 1973. "Bridewealth and dowry in Africa and Eurasia." In *Bridewealth and dowry*, ed. J. Goody and S. J. Tambiah, pp. 1–58. Cambridge: Cambridge University Press.

Gulliver, Philip. 1971. *Neighbours and networks: the idiom of kinship in social action among the Ndendeuli of Tanzania*. Berkeley: University of California Press.

Harris, Marvin. 1977. "Why men dominate women." *New York Times Magazine* 46, November 13, 1977: 115–23.

Hart, C. W. M., and A. R. Pilling. 1960. *The Tiwi of North Australia*. New York: Holt, Rinehart and Winston.

Hiatt, L. R. 1965. *Kinship and conflict*. Canberra: Australian National University Press.

Hoebel, E. A. 1940. *The political organization and law-ways of the Comanche Indians*. American Anthropological Association, memoir no. 54.

1954. *The law of primitive man*. Cambridge, Mass.: Harvard University Press.

Holmberg, Allen R. 1969. *Nomads of the long bow*. New York: Doubleday.

Howell, Nancy. 1979. *Demography of the Dobe !Kung*. New York: Academic Press.

Kaberry, Phyllis M. 1939. *Aboriginal woman: sacred and profane*. London: Routledge and Sons.

Katz, Richard. 1976. "Education for transcendance: !Kia-healing with the Kalahari !Kung." In *Kalahari hunter-gatherers*, ed. R. Lee and I. DeVore, pp. 281–301. Cambridge, Mass.: Harvard University Press.

Kjellström, Rolf, 1973. *Eskimo marriage*. Nordiska museets Handlingar 80.

Korn, Francis. 1973. *Elementary structures reconsidered*. Berkeley: University of California Press.

Landes, Ruth. 1971. *The Ojibwa woman*. New York: Norton.

Leacock, Eleanor. 1954. *The Montagnais 'hunting territory' and the fur trade*. American Anthropological Association, memoir 78.

1978. "Women's status in egalitarian society: implications for social evolution." *Current Anthropology* 19: 247–76.

Lee, Richard B. 1972. "The !Kung bushmen of Botswana." In *Hunters and gatherers today*, ed. M. G. Bicchieri, pp. 327–68. New York: Holt, Rinehart and Winston.

1974. "Male-female residence arrangements and political power in human hunter-gatherers." *Archives of Sexual Behavior* 3: 167–73.

Lee, Richard B., and DeVore, Irven, eds. 1968. *Man the hunter*. Chicago: Aldine.

1976. *Kalahari hunter-gatherers*. Cambridge, Mass.: Harvard University Press.

Lévi-Strauss, Claude. 1969. *The elementary structures of kinship*. Boston: Beacon Press.

Lips, Julius E. 1947. *Naskapi law*. Transactions of the American Philosophical Society, NS 37(4).

Maddock, Kenneth. 1972. *The Australian Aborigines*. Australia: Penquin Press.

Marshall, Lorna. 1976. *The !Kung of Nyae Nyae*. Cambridge, Mass.: Harvard University Press.

McCall, Daniel. 1970. "Wolf courts girls: the equivalence of hunting and mating in Bushman thought." *Ohio University Center for International Studies Papers for the International Studies Africa Series*. no. 7.

Meggitt, Mervyn. 1962. *Desert people*. Sydney: Angus and Robertson.

Meillassoux, C. 1972. "From reproduction to production." *Economy and Society*. 1: 93–105.

Morris, Brian. n.d. "Group structure and affinal ties among the Hill Pandaram." Unpublished manuscript.

Munn, Nancy. 1969. "The effectiveness of symbols in Murngin rite and myth." In *Forms of symbolic action*, ed. R. Spencer, pp. 178–206. Seattle: University of Washington Press.

Murphy, Robert F. 1960. *Headhunter's heritage*. Berkeley: University of California Press.

Murphy, Yolanda, and Murphy, R. 1974. *Women of the forest*. New York: Columbia University Press.

Peterson, Nicolas. 1970. "The importance of women in determining the composition of residential groups in Aboriginal Australia." In *Women's role in Aboriginal Society*, ed. F. Gale, pp. 9–16. Canberra: Australian Institute of Aboriginal Studies.

Rogers, Edward S. 1972. "The Mistassini Cree." In *Hunters and gatherers today*, ed. M. G. Bicchieri, pp. 90–137. New York: Holt, Rinehart and Winston.

Roheim, Geza. 1974. *Children of the desert*. New York: Basic Books.

Rosaldo, Michelle Z. 1980a. *Knowledge and passion: Ilongot notions of self and social life*. New York: Cambridge University Press.

1980b. "The Use and Abuse of Anthropology." *Signs*. 5: 389–417.

Rosaldo, M., and Atkinson, J. 1975. "Man the hunter and woman." In *Interpretation of Symbolism*. ed. R. Willis, pp. 43–75. London: Malaby Press.

Rubin, Gayle. 1975. "The traffic in women: notes on the 'political economy' of sex." In *Toward an Anthropology of Woman*, ed. R. Reiter, pp. 157–210. New York: Monthly Review Press.

Sahlins, M. 1963. "Poor man, rich man, big-man, chief: political types in Melanesia and Polynesia." *Comparative studies in society and history* 5: 285–303.

1972. *Stone Age economics*. Chicago: Aldine.

Service, Elman. 1979. *The hunters*, 2d ed. Englewood Cliffs, N.J.: Prentice-Hall.

Sharp, L. 1952. "Steel axes for Stone Age Australians." In *Human problems in technological change: a casebook*, ed. E. H. Spicer, pp. 69–90. New York: Russell Sage Foundation.

Shostak, Marjorie. 1976. "A !Kung woman's memories of childhood." In *Kalahari hunter-gatherers*. ed. R. Lee and I. DeVore, pp. 246–77. Cambridge, Mass.: Harvard University Press.

Silberbauer, George B. 1963. "Marriage and the girl's puberty ceremony of the G/wi Bushmen." *Africa* 33–4: 12–26.

Siskind, Janet. 1973. *To hunt in the morning*. London: Oxford University Press.

Speck, Frank G. 1935. *Naskapi*. Norman: University of Oklahoma Press.

Stanner, W. E. H. 1933. "Ceremonial economics of the Mulluk Mulluk and Madngella tribes of the Daly River, North Australia." *Oceania* 4: 156–75.

Steward, Julian. 1938. *Basin-Plateau Aboriginal sociopolitical groups*. Bureau of American Ethnology Bulletin 120.

Strong, William Duncan. 1924. "Cross-cousin marriage and the culture of the Northeastern Algonkian." *American Anthropologist* 31: 277–88.

Thomas, Elizabeth Marshall. 1959. *The harmless people*. New York: Knopf.

Thomson, Ronald F. 1949. *Economic structure and the ceremonial exchange in Arnhem Land*. Melbourne: Macmillan.

Tilly, Louise. 1978. "The social sciences and the study of women." *Comparative Studies in Society and History* 20: 163–73.

Turnbull, Colin M. 1961. *The Forest People*. New York: Simon and Schuster.

1968. "The importance of flux in two hunting societies." In *Man the hunter*, ed. R. Lee and I. DeVore, pp. 132–37. Chicago: Aldine.

Turner, Victor. 1957. *Schism and continuity in an African society*. Manchester: Manchester University Press.

Wallace, Ernest and Hoebel, E. A. 1952. *The Comanches*. Norman: University of Oklahoma Press.

Warner, W. Lloyd. 1937. *A black civilization*. Rev. ed. 1958. New York: Harper and Brothers.

Whiting, Beatrice B. 1950. *Paiute sorcery*. Viking Fund Publications in Anthropology, no. 15.

Woodburn, James. 1968a. "An introduction to Hadza ecology." In *Man the hunter*. ed. R. Lee and I. DeVore, Chicago: Aldine.

1968b. "Stability and flexibility in Hadza residential groupings." In *Man the hunter*. ed. R. Lee and I. DeVore, pp. 103–10. Chicago: Aldine.

1970. *Hunters and gatherers: the material culture of the nomadic Hadza*. London: The British Museum.

1972. "Ecology, nomadic movements and the composition of the local group among hunters and gatherers: an East African example and its implications." In *Man, settlement and urbanism*, ed. Peter J. Ucko, R. Tringham, and G. Dimblely, pp. 193–206. London: Gerald Duckworth.

Yanagisako, Sylvia J. 1979. "Family and household: the analysis of domestic groups." *Annual Review of Anthropology* 8: 161–205.

9
Women, warriors, and patriarchs

Melissa Llewelyn-Davies

I am extremely rich. Look at my cattle – they're mine and no one else's . . .
The sheep – they're mine. You see this village – there are young people in it
and there are old people – they're mine. Children, elders, women, old
women, little boys – all mine. It's I who control (*a-itore*) them all. This is how
I come to be an important person . . . I do not share with anyone . . . I am the
owner who is in charge (*a-itore*). I control people and I control cattle.
—*Boasting recorded in an interview with a prosperous elder*

Introduction

In this essay I shall describe how, among the Maasai of the Loita Hills,
Kenya, the relations of material production and reproduction are organized by
notions of "property."[1] I hope to demonstrate that the elaboration of difference between male and female is fundamental to the property system as a
whole. The overall status of Maasai women is inferior to that of men. But it is
my assumption that inequality between the sexes can never be taken for
granted in any particular society; it is a social construct and as such related to
other features of social organization and in particular to the relations of
material production.

Maasai is an age-graded society and the social construction of gender
cannot be considered in isolation from the social construction of age. Indeed,
I hope to make it clear that the "age organization," as it is generally known in
the literature on the Maasai and other East African societies, should more
properly be called the "age/gender organization." It not only defines relations between members of the same sex on the basis of formal age status but
also relations between the sexes. Relations with women are important in the
age hierarchization of men. Moreover it is within the workings of the age/
gender organization that notions of "male" and "female" are primarily
constructed.

Material production, as Engels has pointed out, has a twofold character: the
production and reproduction of the means of subsistence and the production
and reproduction of human beings (Engels 1972: 26). In Maasai, both aspects
of production are organized by concepts of "ownership" (*enkitorria*) or
"property," and rely upon an opposition between dependents in whom others
have property rights and propertied persons on whom others depend. Rights
in property include rights in human beings as well as rights in livestock and

inanimate objects, as we shall see. Productive labor, legitimate sexuality, and childbearing all take place in the context of dyadic relationships in which one party has property rights in the other. The propertied and the dependent are not absolutely discrete groups of persons because, for example, it is possible for a man to acquire dependents of his own while still formally dependent upon his father's livestock. Similarly, women who are dependent upon their husbands have certain property rights in their daughters. The distinction does not, therefore, coincide with the boundary between the sexes. However, provided they live long enough, all men grow out of their dependent status and into the potential acquisition of full property rights in themselves, livestock, and human beings. Women are permanently and inherently dependent; they never acquire full rights to themselves and their rights in livestock and in their children are always contingent. In the first part of this essay I shall analyze the system of property rights in more detail and hope to demonstrate that the social construction of women as dependent or ownable is fundamental to that system.

In a discussion of slavery, M. I. Finley has remarked that "one may speak of a spectrum of statuses between the two extremes of absolute rightlessness and of absolute freedom to exercise all rights at all times . . . The latter has never existed, nor has the former" (Finley 1968: 308). Maasai women, like Maasai men, possess sets of rights and responsibilities that change at different stages of the life cycle. As social persons they. are engaged in a variety of relationships, many of which do not include property rights between parties. Even as wives and daughters, their status as property is only one aspect of their relationships with their husbands and fathers. And they are not without support: They may call upon the appropriate kin if their rights are infringed in particular circumstances. They are not, in other words, reduced to the "thinglike" status of pure chattel slaves. Nevertheless, together with children and livestock, they are said to constitute the wealth of an individual man and they are given away in marriage as if they were passive objects of property to be transacted between men; the payment of bridewealth, for example, is referred to as the act wherein a husband "buys" his wife.

The idea of people as property, which lies at the heart of the organization of material production, is thus an important and meaningful one to Maasai even though it does not exhaust the description of any one person's status. It is also limited in its acknowledgment; women who are happy to speak of their husbands "buying" them do not usually refer to their fathers "selling" them. But it is an idea that has far-reaching implications for the general status of women; the inherent ownability and transactability of women distinguishes them from adult men in whom property rights cannot be acquired by other Maasai.

In an important and stimulating paper (Rubin 1975) Gayle Rubin draws attention to the widespread existence of property rights in women and suggests that such rights are a clue to womens' almost universal subordination. She writes:

Exchange of women is a shorthand for expressing that the social relations of a kinship system specify that men have certain rights in their female kin,

and that women do not have the same rights either to themselves or to their
male kin. In this sense, the exchange of women is a profound perception of
a system in which women do not have full rights to themselves. [Rubin
1975: 177]

However I feel she overstates her case when she goes on to say that, insofar as
kinship and the incest taboo are crucial to social integration, the *economic*
oppression of women is everywhere "derivative and secondary" (Rubin
1975: 177). Property rights in women are not universal; they are present in
some socioeconomic systems and not in others. In Maasai moreover, as in
many small-scale societies, the structures of kinship and the structures of
economic life are not easy to disentangle from each other. Property rights in
women are important to both spheres because they include rights to labor
power as well as to sexuality and fertility.

If we look at the wider context of rights in persons in general, there is often
a connection between a lack of rights to the means of (non-human) production
and political or jural inferiority. Thus in preindustrial Europe it was generally
held that a lack of rights to the means of (nonhuman) production (land, tools,
and so on) entailed dependence upon others which in turn entailed a status of
political or jural minority (see Kant 1974; Edelman 1977; Finley 1968). This
assumption was relevant to the status of women and children as well as to the
poor. In Maasai the ideas of ownership and authority are similarly allied. To
make sense of the Maasai system and to elucidate Maasai notions of male and
female I believe therefore we must look at the *pattern* of rights in *all* persons
from the political, kinship, and economic points of view without assigning
causal priority to any of these and without distorting the material to fit our own
notions of property, work, and the family.

In fact, the status of ownability is not confined to females: Rights in young
males ("boys") may also be owned. Only"moran" (youths or warriors) and
"elders" possess full rights to themselves. Essentially, Maasai property
rights in a person consist in the right to enjoy, or to alienate to another, certain
rights in the dependent's physical person: his or her labor power, sexuality, or
child-bearing potential. These rights imply the moral superiority of the
possessor to whose will the dependent ought to subordinate him or herself.

Among the Maasai, dependence is a function of age and sex status; the
opposition between the propertied and the propertyless cannot be considered
in isolation from concepts of gender that are, in turn, structured by the age
organization. Age and sex status, although based upon biological characteristics, are defined by formal criteria.[2] Women pass through two formal age
categories ("girlhood" and "womanhood"), whereas men pass through
three ("boyhood," "moranhood" [or "warriorhood"] and "elderhood").
During moranhood, men are formally extruded from the elders' villages in
which they lived as dependents during boyhood and they become associated
with the nonsocial world outside. As moran, they have their own quasiauton-
omous organization and from the point of view of other Maasai they are, to
some extent, marginal to secular social life. However, it would be hard to
exaggerate the importance of the institution of moranhood to Maasai. Moran
constitute the army, which, in the past, was responsible for the defense of the

villages and for raids on neighboring peoples. But moranhood is also fundamental to the way in which Maasai think about themselves as Maasai and to
the way their neighbors think about them. The past is referred to in terms of
the age set that was serving in moranhood at the time; elders look back upon
their own period of service with pride and nostalgia; women ostentatiously
express admiration for the courage and beauty of the young men and compare
them favorably, as lovers, to the elders to whom they are married.

In the second half of this essay I argue that the paradox of moranhood (it is
simultaneously central to and marginal to social life) is illuminated if considered as a period of transformation during which propertyless boys, in
whom others have property rights, become elders, in whom no individual
may have property rights but who hold such rights in others. As such,
moranhood has some of the features of a "rite of liminality" (Van Gennep
1960) and the young men may be seen as novices in a prolonged rite of
passage. In this light, the semisacred aura that surrounds them (perhaps best
described as a sort of glamour) in spite (or because) of their many anti-social
activities, becomes somewhat less surprising.

Production and reproduction

It's men who control (*a-itore*) the cattle. The only animal you get is the one
which has been specially slaughtered for you [when you give birth] or one
that has died from disease. You can dispose of (*a-itore*) that one. And you
can dispose of milk because it is you who do the milking and the storing of
the milk. You can give it to anyone you want to. But there is a big "right of
ownership" (*enkitoria* – a noun form of *a-itore*) in your husband's stomach
because if the time comes when he wants milk and you've given it all
away, he beats you because after all he has authority over you (*a-itore*).
[From an interview with a young married woman]

Looking at the Kenyan Rift Valley as a whole, the Maasai can be considered specialists in animal husbandry. They obtain a variety of nonpastoral
goods and services from cultivating groups, hunter-gatherers, smiths, and
diviners, in exchange for livestock or, nowadays, cash. Indeed, to be Maasai,
as the Loita Maasai see it (or did until very recently), is to depend upon
livestock – cattle, sheep, and goats – for subsistence and the acquisition of the
products of one's neighbors.

Pasture lands, salt deposits, and water resources are administered in common by local users but the crucial element, livestock, is owned (*a-itore*) by
individuals. There are several words in Maasai that refer to different aspects
of the notion of possession, but for purposes of this essay that two most
important terms are *a-itore* and *a-itodol*. *A-itore* (v.t.) may be defined as
follows: "to have rights of disposal in," "to be in charge of," "to be
responsible for," "to command," "to control, " (v.i.: "to be in charge").
A-itore thus expresses the idea of authority as well as the idea of property
rights. *A-itodol* (v.t.) means "to point out," "to allocate"; it is used to
describe the gift to an individual of limited rights in a domestic animal, such
as milking rights or rights to its eventual inheritance.

A-itore may be used in the contexts of rights over inanimate objects, livestock, or human beings. With respect to inanimate objects and animals, *a-itore* discriminates between rights of alienation (the right to sell, to give away, or in the case of an animal, to slaughter) and the more limited rights of use or inheritance implied by *a-itodol*. With respect to human beings, *a-itore* means the right to the direct enjoyment or disposal of a person's labor power, sexuality, or child-bearing potential. These rights are *in rem* or "rights . . . as against the world," that is, they impose duties on all other persons in respect of that particular person (or thing) (Radcliffe-Brown 1965). But such rights must also, inevitably, imply the right to the obedience, the subordination of the will, of the person in whom these rights are held. *A-itore* may be used in contexts where rights *in rem* over persons are fairly minimal, for example, to describe the rights of moran in relation to the uncircumcised girls over whom they have rights of sexual access and who are obliged to run errands for them, as well as in contexts where such rights are much greater, for example, the rights of a husband over his wife. It may be understood as expressing an idea that varies, also according to the context, along a continuum between the English notions of authority and ownership. However, it is possible for a Maasai to hold authority, of a moral or spiritual kind, over a person in whom he or she has no rights of property. There is, by contrast, no property relationship between persons that does not also involve authority. I have therefore used property rather than authority in my shorthand translation of *a-itore* because the authority involved is of a particular kind associated with rights *in rem*. These ideas are usually referred to in Maasai by the use of the verb form *a-itore*, but for convenience and to avoid complicated circumlocutions I shall refer to property, the propertied, the ownable and so on, even though these are not always literal translations of Maasai constructions in common use. (For example, I may write "women have no property" when in Maasai this would be rendered as "there is nothing which women own" [*meeta ene-itore inkituaak*].)

When she marries, a woman is allocated (*a-itodol*) a number of animals from the household herd. Rights implied in the notion of *a-itodol* are of great importance but they are limited in comparison with the full rights implied in the term *a-itore*. A woman has milking rights to the females of her herd and the right to the sale or use of the hides of all stock that die or are slaughtered. She may also dispose of the flesh of animals that die from natural causes (as opposed to those that are slaughtered) as well as those slaughtered by her, or on her behalf, at births and circumcisions. These animals constitute the nucleus of the herds and flocks her sons will eventually come into possession of. She alone is responsible for the reallocation (*a-itodol*) of specific animals to them, and she can decide to give nothing at all to a particular son. But she never has rights of alienation (*a-itore*) over any living animal; these rights pass through her from her husband and settle on her sons when they come of age.

The pattern of entitlement to *a-itore* rights in livestock and human beings is *structured* by the formal age-organization but such rights are largely *realized* within the dependency units of individual men. And the aspiration of a man is conceptualized as being the indefinite increase, not merely of his herds and flocks, but of the number of his human dependents. In this way a man becomes "rich" (*karsis*). A rich man is one who lives to a leisurely old age surrounded by wives, children, and grandchildren who together tend and subsist upon his flourishing herds and flocks. The idea of wealth also implies the good fortune to live through all the formal stages of maturation and it has spiritual as well as material consequences. A rich man is believed never to die but merely to go to sleep. His death will be acknowledged by the anointing of the corpse with fat (prior to its consumption by scavengers), a procedure that takes place after the other two great rites of passage in an individual Maasai life, birth and circumcision. The deaths and even the previous lives of lesser men are formally ignored. Their corpses are hurried outside the village fences to be consumed, unanointed, and their names should never again be spoken out loud in front of their kin and friends. Men pray for "life" (*enkishon*), a life that "potters slowly through them, full of the circumcisions of sons and daughters."

The Maasai ideal of wealth is achieved only by a few and only in old age; a man is formally considered rich only when he has survived the circumcision of some grandchildren. But every man's life is conceptualized as progressing toward this goal and virtually all men succeed in taking the first step: the establishment of their own patriarchal units. There is no Maasai word for this most basic social group that consists, as I shall use the term, of a (male) herdowner and his dependents. The Shorter Oxford English Dictionary gives as its principal definition of "patriarch": "the father and ruler of a family or tribe." I agree with recent writers that this term has been overused, but I would argue that it is specifically appropriate to describe the structure of the Maasai family because the power of its head derives from his property and authority rights over his wives, children, herds, and dependents.

All men are potential heads of patriarchal units. But to be socially and economically autonomous, a man must acquire property rights in sufficient livestock to feed a number of human dependents in different age/sex categories because roles in material production are, like a person's entitlement to property rights, determined, at least ideally, by sex and age status. To understand the structure and development of the patriarchal units, then, we must briefly discuss the age organization.

The age organization ranks all males and females into separate but interlocking hierarchies. The male hierarchy consists of three age categories: uncircumcised boys (*olaiyoni*), circumcised young men known as moran (*olmurrani*), and elders (*olpayian*). Men are further differentiated into age sets (see the section on "Moran"). The female hierarchy consists of only two age categories: uncircumcised girls (*entito*) and circumcised women (*enkitok*). The hierarchies may be schematically drawn as follows:

superordination ↑

elders	
moran	circumcised women
uncircum-cised boys	uncircum-cised girls

subordination ↓

Circumcision for both sexes takes place in early adolescence (in the case of a girl, a year or so after her breasts have begun to develop) and for both it marks the formal end of childhood. A woman's social maturity is unequivocal after her circumcision. She is considered ready for childbirth and most women are married about a year after the operation. Men, on the other hand, are not likely to take their first wives until about ten years later when they are in the process of becoming full elders.

People should respect (*a-anyit*) all those who are placed above them in the formal hierarchy, and junior age sets of elders should respect more senior age sets of elders (Llewelyn-Davies 1978). In contrast, *a-itore* relationships do not exist between members of the same age category, for example, between junior elders and senior elders. An age set of elders has collective moral or spiritual authority over their alternate junior age set (the firestick relationship; see Jacobs 1965). But neither as individuals nor as an age set do they have rights *in rem* over them. The only exception to this rule is in the case of a father who has sons who are also elders. Elder sons do not formally acquire rights in their own livestock while their father lives and they are in a somewhat ambiguous position with respect to him.

A-itore rights are structured as follows. Elders may have rights in the sexuality and fertility of circumcised women, while moran have rights in the sexuality of uncircumcised girls; boys have sexual rights in no one. Furthermore, elders have potential rights in the labor power of women and boys, while women have right in the labor power of girls. Moran are entitled to demand that boys and girls run errands for them, but because they are not directly involved in material production, rights to labor and fertility are largely irrelevant to them.

If these various rights *in rem* over persons are infringed by, for example, the adultery of a wife with a moran or through the laziness of a son, the owner of the rights may be entitled to compensation, in the form of fines or other ritual payments, from the person who has usurped his or her position. Alternatively he may physically chastise the person in whom the rights are held and who has effectively denied their existence by his or her disobedience. Women and men sometimes explain the rule of men over women in terms of their supposedly superior physical strength; women say, for example, that they could not stand up to their husbands and that they do not beat even their uncircumcised sons because they would not be physically capable of overpowering them. But this view is not, I believe, founded upon empirical observation; it should be seen as part of the moral and ideological system of property rights as a whole. The beating of a dependent expresses the legitimacy of the idea of property in the moral and physical subordination of the person beaten. Women do most of the heavy work in Maasailand; they chop wood, build houses, and draw water. So an elderly husband is not relying on his physical strength alone when he exerts his right to chastise a vigorous young woman; he is also drawing on the moral strength that derives from the acquiescence of all the age and sex categories in the basic principles of the property system as a whole.

The age organization thus has crucial implications for relations within the patriarchal units. With the significant exception of moran, all the terms for the age categories are also kin terms. Thus, *entito* = "uncircumcised girl" and "daughter"; *olaiyoni* = "uncircumcised boy" and "son"; *enkitok* = "circumcised woman" and "wife"; and *olpayian* = "elder" and "husband." Elders have no rights of sexual access to girls and the prohibition against incest between a father and his daughter, or the daughter of any of his fellow age-set members, is made much of in Maasai culture. The transgression of this prohibition is the only case of incest that is a matter for public concern and the only one that is sanctioned by formal punishment. Fathers also have no right to the labor of their daughters, except indirectly insofar as the girls help their mothers. A daughter must never cook for her father nor hand him his milk-calabash; after the age of eight or nine she may not sleep in the same house; nor may she ever be beaten by him. Instead, fathers have rights in the disposal of their daughters in marriage. Indeed, this right of disposal is so highly valued that the right itself may be given away as a gift to a friend or relative. In this case, the man who gives away the bride becomes the affine of the husband; he has responsibilities regarding the welfare of the young couple and he shares the eventual bridewealth payment with the bride's father.

A husband does, obviously, have rights of sexual access to his wives. These are to some extent shared with other members of his age set; sexual relations with the wife of an age mate do not constitute adultery. But a husband has exclusive rights to any children born to his wives. Thus he has rights to the use or disposal of the labor of his uncircumcised sons. And a man may send a boy to live with a friend or kinsman to help with the herding because it is considered inappropriate for an elder to take the animals to pasture, particularly on a regular basis. This work should be done by boys. Women, aided by their uncircumcised daughters, see to the milking and to the welfare of the youngest animals. They decide how much milk to take for the human population and how much to leave for the calf. Women and girls also build and maintain the houses, fetch water and firewood, and, in addition, take care of the babies. It is believed that a circumcised man might fall sick or die if he performed certain household tasks for himself while there were able-bodied females in the village.

Elders, as I have described, have overall responsibility for their dependents. They make all the important decisions involving the disposal of resources, the sale, slaughter, or gift of livestock, and the marriage of daughters. They decide alone, or with other elders of the village, where the animals will pasture, and where and when they will be watered or taken to the salt licks. They are also jointly responsible for the construction of the village fence, which is expected to protect the inhabitants from the untamed world outside, that is, from animal and human predators and from cattle diseases. Moran, on the other hand, are formally extruded from the patriarchal units and they are not normally expected to labor on the family herds. But in the driest areas, or in times of drought, they may be called upon to escort the livestock over long distances to available pastures. Their role in material production has been, until recently, mainly that of defending the animals against attack as well as augmenting their own herds through raiding.

As they become elders, men are expected to begin to acquire sufficient dependents in the appropriate age and sex statuses to perform all the pastoral and household tasks necessary for the reproduction of the patriarchal unit, even though a man does not formally come into full formal control of his livestock until the death of his father. Broadly speaking, the control of a father over his sons gradually diminishes, in spite of his titular ownership of their animals, when they reach moranhood and, even more so, as they approach elderhood.

Male circumcision and moranhood mark, as I have said, the transformation of boys in whom men have *a-itore* rights into elders who have such rights in themselves, livestock, and women. Sons who are also elders are in an ambiguous position because their autonomous public status conflicts with their status as dependents within the patriarchal units. Most fathers ease this problem and avoid overt disputes over the allocation of resources by gradually granting their sons *de facto* management of their mothers' herds. Thus as they take wives of their own, groups of uterine brothers begin to disengage the administration of their own stock from that of their father's and to behave in almost all respects as the heads of patriarchal units themselves. But the increasing independence of the younger men does not mean that the family will be physically broken up. It is common for uterine and nonuterine brothers to live together even after their father's death. And although they strive toward theoretical self-sufficiency, men almost invariably prefer to live with others, affines, agnates, or friends, pooling their herdsboys and herding their animals as one unit.

There is no simple relationship between the number of a man's wives and the size of his herds. Poor men may obtain wives if the fathers of marriageable daughters believe them to be assiduous in their efforts to become richer. But expanding herds do facilitate marriage because a father or guardian is anxious to give his daughter to someone who will be able to look after her and at the same time be a useful friend to himself. Men build up their herds partly through natural increase, fostered by careful and thoughtful husbandry on the part of themselves, their wives, and their children. But the creation and exploitation of formal friendships with kin, neighbors, and affines are also important. Formal friendships are initiated by a gift from one party to the other and must be honored by further, or return gifts when one's friend is in any sort of need. Thus a man of good character who is down on his luck turns to his friends for help. One non-Loita herdowner, who had lost all but one cow through drought, moved to the area specifically because he had several sisters and cousins married to prosperous Loita men from whom he eventually hoped to obtain stock. So it is not surprising that the rate of polygyny dramatically increases with age: The herds of older men tend to be more numerous and they have also acquired more friends to whom they can apply for wives. And elders never give up trying to marry. The richest man in the area I censused took his fourteenth wife at the age of over seventy having, the previous year, married off a daughter to his own father-in-law by a previous marriage, a man even older than himself. In this census the oldest age set of elders possessed an average of just over three wives each, compared with less than one each for the youngest age set of elders.

There is no absolute standard for measuring the requirements of individual patriarchal units. Men say that with twenty to thirty head of cattle they can support a wife, assuming that, as the children grow the cattle will increase; around forty cattle is the ideal. Cattle are normally pastured in two or three units, according to age. Each of these units should have two herdsboys. The sheep and goats that are browsed together should also be handled by two boys. It would seem, then, that a man needs six or eight uncircumcised sons to tend his property. But in practice, as I have said, men almost invariably live and herd together. They also compromise on the ideal labor arrangements. Boys may be sent out alone; it is said that an experienced herdsboy can manage five hundred head of cattle in the worst conditions of the dry season. An elder may send a daughter with the sheep and goats and go herding, on occasion, himself. Furthermore, deficiencies in personnel are often made up by the fostering of children; boys are lent to friends to help with herding; girls may be sent to a grandmother or aunt to help with childcare or household tasks. Men who find themselves without sufficient animals to feed their dependents usually go and live with better-placed kin or friends, obtaining milking rights for their womenfolk over a number of animals, while they hope to build up their own herds.

It should be clear that the pursuit of wealth by individual men is fundamental to the Maasai social system. Control of the production and reproduction of livestock, as well as the production and reproduction of human beings, is increasingly concentrated in the hands of elder patriarchs as they progress through the age set system. But this concentration contains the seeds of its own dissolution; the birth of grandchildren heralds simultaneously the apotheosis of the grandfather and the inevitable breakup of the patriarchal unit into new centers of growth around the sons.

However, the working of the system depends upon the general acceptance of the notions of property described above. Property is of course "only" an idea, but it actually organizes the processes of production and reproduction because it is on the basis of their claims to different forms of property that elders set their wives and children to work and marry off their daughters. The system works so long as the principle that elders have full rights to themselves and to livestock and that property rights may be held in women and their progeny (that is, that women and children are 'ownable') is unchallenged by those concerned in it.

A woman's aim is to bear sons to take over her allocated herd so that she will continue to "consume her own cows" as a member of the patriarchal unit of one of her own children, usually her youngest son. As mother-in-law to her sons' wives she is much respected; she is also relieved from some of the more arduous tasks by the younger women. Women who have given birth prolifically may be called rich like their husbands and their corpses are annointed with fat like the corpses of rich elders. Indeed, elderly mothers may claim if they are drunk (when Maasai tend to become boastful) that they have become equal to their husbands and that they are the female "owners" of the village (*enopeny enkang'*). But this assertion of equality in successful old age does not alter the basic vulnerability of a woman's position: Her right to livestock is always contingent upon her relationship with a male herd owner. If she has produced sons she must hope that they will be of good character and acknowledge their responsibilities to their mother. A woman with no sons, by birth or adoption, will almost certainly lose her rights to her allocated herd. On the death of her husband, her animals will be divided up among the sons of her co-wives or other male relatives of her husband. Such widows must persuade their own or their husband's kin to give them temporary milking rights over some unallocated animals from the men's residual herds, or they must depend directly upon their hospitality.

Thus, when widows are driven away from their husbands' herds and when sons neglect the needs of their mothers, women lament their lack of stock. Indeed, women tend to identify the root of their dependence and vulnerability as their lack of rights of disposal over livestock. One purpose of this essay is to show that this economistic diagnosis is only a partial one. But to the women involved in the system it appears to make sense. Women, as we have seen, have a measure of control over the distribution of milk. But this control is contingent upon their possession of milking rights to animals over which their male guardians have ultimate control. A husband may give away or slaughter (for friends or ceremonies) any of his wife's allocated animals, including any that may have come from her own kin. And women are excluded from most important decisions that relate to the welfare of the herd (that is, decisions that relate to pastures, salt, dipping, and so on). Even a widow with sons who is left caretaking her allocated herds and flocks must be appointed a male guardian to administer her animals until her sons come of age. The guardian will manage the animals without seeking her advice. One informant said: "A woman controls (*a-itore*) nothing. Because the cows in the village, she just looks after them. She can't say: 'I shall sell one today because I have a purpose in mind,' because she cannot dispose of it (*a-itore*)." But animals also appear to women to enter into the relations of production and reproduction of livestock and human beings and, in the form of bridewealth, to buy them out of their rights to their own persons. They say: "We are 'bought' (*a-inyang'u*)[3] with cattle"; and they justify the beating of a wife by her husband in a rhetorical question: "Didn't he buy her with cattle? Doesn't he therefore own her/have authority over her (*a-itore*)?" In this case, women overestimate the role of livestock in their subordination. Women, as a socially constructed category of persons, are *inherently* transactable and their lack of property rights in animals is *irrelevant* in this respect. Livestock certainly *marks* the circulation of women but the payment of bridewealth presupposes the conditions for that circulation, namely the existence of property forms in human beings. When a woman is formally "bought" with cattle (a payment that does not take place until the circumcision of her eldest child) the bridewealth animals are a return gift to the man, normally her father, who gave her away to her husband. But this gift should not be seen as an exchange of equivalent value to the original gift of a woman, but rather as expressing a commitment to a relationship in which the transactability of women is taken for granted. Thus, the husband of a woman who has proved barren, must include an extra animal in the bridewealth in spite of the fact that his wife has failed to provide the services which he had hoped for. The extra animal affirms his commitment to the relationship with his in-laws in spite of the disappointment caused by the woman's failure to produce children.

So the status of women within the patriarchal units cannot be accounted for solely in terms of their lack of rights of disposal over livestock. Of equal importance is the fact that they do not have rights of disposal over themselves. It is illuminating in this context to consider the position of the category of elders (*ilkiriko*) who have no property in animals or human dependents. *Ilkiriko* are men without substance. They are usually said to have lost their herds, and consequently their wives and children, through restlessness, alcoholism, or an excessive desire for women that has led them to neglect their responsibilities. (Men of good character who lose their herds through drought or other misfortunes are believed capable of recovering their positions through gifts from kin and friends.) *Ilkiriko* are anomalous figures, alternately regarded as comical or dangerous, being possessed of a powerful curse if hospitality is refused them. But they never do women's work and they never lose rights in the disposal of their own persons. They wander around Maasailand surviving on the sometimes grudging hospitality of their age mates and other men with herds. Although they are in fact dependent upon others for subsistence, they never acquire the status of dependents in whose labor power or sexuality others may acquire rights.

Ilkiriko are anomalous because they are elders with no property or authority. Childbearing women without husbands are also anomalous, but for the opposite reason: They do not constitute property for an individual man and thus no one holds direct authority over them. Circumcised women who remain unmarried are thought to be in a vulnerable position even though they too have a powerful curse. Such women, usually kept at home to bear sons to inherit the allocated herd of another woman who has failed to produce sons, are known as ''daughters of the village.'' They are under the protection of the male guardians of the livestock to which they have milking rights (often their fathers) but these men have no authority over their sexual behavior. (Interestingly enough, however, such men are highly liable to imputations of incest with their daughters.) As women point out, no one is entitled to beat a ''daughter of the village'' and men characteristically complain that they are ''spoilt'' (-*pashipasnut*).

The anomalous positions of *ilkiriko* and the daughters of the village confirm, I suggest, that implicit in Maasai thought is the notion that elders should own and that women should be owned. I shall now examine the process that re-creates, in every generation, the social categories of non-ownable owners and ownable dependents that makes elders out of boys, and leaves females in a state of perpetual jural minority. This transformation, as it takes place in the lives of men and as it fails to take place in the lives of women, is the pivot of the property system and of the cycle of social reproduction.

The moran: elegant rebels

Once men and women were equal. There were no (male) "elders" in the land, but only women, known as *ilpongolo* (women-warriors), and "moran" (young men; warrriors). The women were braver than the men. At that time, they had no vaginas, but only tiny holes for urine to pass through. One day they accompanied the moran to war because the men needed assistance. That night, as they were sitting round their separate fires, the moran crept up behind the women carrying bows, things which the women knew nothing of. The moran pushed the sharp ends of their bows into the women's bodies and created vaginas. The women and the moran lay down together. In the morning, the moran got up and said "Ahah! These are only women after all!" So they took them and married them. Women lost their bravery, and life/fertility (*enkishon*) began. ["secret" women's myth]

In the myth of the women warriors quoted at the beginning of this section the females of the past are described as equal partners with males in the enterprise of war. Their loss of equality coincides with the creation of their sexuality and fertility, which leads to their being passively taken as wives. This event also transforms the males from moran into husbands and elders. If the status of women as dependents or as property is inherent in the social construction of womanhood, this in turn is inextricable from the formal age organization. For girls, circumcision marks the acquisition of fertility, which is transactable as soon as it is acquired. Circumcision for boys, on the other hand, marks the acquisition of the fullest rights in his own person (*a-itore kewan*, literally, "to be in charge of oneself"); no individual is entitled to chastise a circumcised man and his status in this regard is irrevocable. From moranhood men subsequently reemerge into patriarchal society as potential heads of the patriarchal units, entitled to rights of disposal over livestock and to property rights in women and their children.

The transformation of boys into elders is more disruptive to existing social relationships than other changes in age status. When a girl becomes a woman, for example, her relationships with her father and mother are not fundamentally or formally altered. And although her fertility will bring her certain property rights in her children, her own status within the property system is fundamentally unchanged. In contrast, when a boy becomes an elder, he begins to take charge of his share of his mother's herds and she may begin to live under his protection as a dependent member of his patriarchal unit. His new status, in fact, affects his relationships with everyone in the community and, moreover, his position within the property system is reversed. The contradiction between ownable dependents and nonownable owners lies, as I have argued, at the heart of the processes of material production. But for the social system to be regenerated, some individuals must cross the boundary between the two statuses; some of the ownable dependents must become nonownable owners. And the cultural importance of moranhood, which constitutes this process of regeneration, is related to the structural importance of the contradiction itself.

The transformation begins with the ceremonies that lead up to a boy's circumcision and ends in a series of rituals that start about seven years later and reincorporate the men into secular social life. In fact, the rituals that surround circumcision (*emurata*) differ in only minor ways for boys and girls. The ceremonies that lead to and include the circumcision are organized when boys are about fifteen years old; for girls, shortly after their breasts have begun to develop. These ceremonies mark the separation of the individual from childhood. The circumcision operation involves, for boys, the partial removal of the foreskin and, for girls, the excision of the clitoris and the *labia minora*. Boys' circumcisions are performed by elders from the hunting-gathering Dorobbo people; girls' are performed by skilled elderly Maasai women. In both cases circumcision is said to remove ''the dirt of childhood.'' But the two- or three-month period of semiseclusion that follows circumcision completes the formal transformation of girls into women. There are no further rites of passage held directly on behalf of women, although as wives and mothers they have important roles to play in some of the men's rituals. But for men, the seclusion period following circumcision heralds not their entry into full social maturity, but their entry into an age set that is currently in moranhood.

A man belongs, automatically, to the age set that is open at the time of his circumcision and each age set recruits for about fourteen years. Age sets are organized on a sectionwide basis, but they are coordinated across all of Maasai. A man remains a member of the age set into which he was initiated throughout his life. It moves as a whole through the various rituals and its members change status together. When all its members have died, the age set itself is considered to be finished. Some of the rituals are held by the age set as a whole, some by parts of it, and some on behalf of individual members. The different territorial sections of Maasai manage the age set and initiation rituals slightly differently; what follows refers to Loita section.

The ceremonies have many different elements. But they all celebrate the age set on whose behalf, or on whose members' behalf, it is held. And almost all the ceremonies contain elements that call attention to the changing status of the initiate or initiates. There is no space here to go into the details of the individual ceremonies. But, for our purposes, they may be grouped into two categories: those leading up to moranhood and those leading out of it. The first three rituals in the cycle establish the existence of a potential age set before any of its future members have been circumcised. They are followed by the individual circumcision ceremonies. *Eunoto*, the fourth group, celebrating the glory of moranhood per se, is regarded as the most splendid of all Maasai ceremonies. At the same time it marks the beginning of the end of active moranhood. *Eunoto* is held by the whole age set (or one of its two subsets) but it is not performed until several years after the last members of the age set (or, more commonly, one of its subsets) has been circumcised. It should be preceded by the ritual called ''the ox of the earplugs,'' which is held separately for every individual member. The main feature of this ceremony is the hilarious and obscene joking between the moran and four of their mothers in which the two sides accuse each other of intergenerational incest. The ceremony is said by moran to demonstrate that they can henceforth stand up to their mothers. Much of the meat of the ox that is slaughtered is given to the mothers and it is described as a "thank you" (*enashe*) to them for having reared them as boys. At the same time, the ritual feeding of the mothers calls attention to the fact that henceforth the young men will start to provide for them. *Eunoto* itself ends with the shaving off of the men's pigtails, the most visible attribute of moranhood, although the men are not permitted to cut their hair again until a year or so later at the ritual called "drinking milk."

The remaining rituals take another fifteen years or so to complete. Those called "drinking milk" and "eating meat" relax the commensality rules that express the solidarity of the age set and its separation from women and the elders' villages. The former permits a man to drink milk, the staple food, when there is no other member of the age set present; the latter permits him to eat meat that has been seen by circumcised women (to eat meat in the elders' villages). "Drinking milk" marks the return of a man to his father's village and the first step in the process of individuation and reincorporation into the patriarchal units. Two remaining communal rituals also emphasize, in a variety of ways, the increasing individuation and patriarchal status of the age set members. At the one called "village of the thong," for example, a long leather strip cut from the hide of an ox slaughtered at *eunoto*, is divided into small pieces that are distributed to every member of the age set participating in the ceremony. Each man then ties his length around the neck of one of his own calves. And after the ritual called "the village of stools," a man may claim the privilege of playing *enkeshui* ("African chess") in the villages and he may place the various sticks and clubs carried by elders (as opposed to the spears of the moran) on the roofs of the houses he visits. He also acquires for the first time his own personal stool, which no female, nor any man junior to him in the age organization, may sit upon. This stool is important in the assertion of social paternity: In the various ceremonial shavings surrounding childbirth and circumcision, the hair of his wife and child must be placed upon it. After "the village of stools," the age set is said to "rule the country" together with the age set senior to it, while the age set senior to them both begins to take a back seat. The ceremonies end with "the ox of wounds," which is held individually and which permits a man to hold a circumcision ceremony for his eldest child.

Thus although a man's entry into moranhood is clear, his exit from it is much more difficult to pinpoint. In some contexts, men may be referred to as elders as soon as they have been through *eunoto*, whereas in other contexts they remain moran much longer. Indeed the initiate in "the ox of wounds," the last rite of all, dresses, with an age-mate companion, in the formal clothing of moranhood. Most men begin to marry between "drinking milk" and "eating meat" and thus establish embryonic patriarchal units. But, as I have briefly outlined, many of the specific privileges of elderhood are only gradually obtained and not fully so until the last ritual of all.

Until they have ritually "drunk milk at home," moran have no formal homes in the elders' villages although they frequently visit them. Instead the young men of each locality have their own special encampment (*emanyata*), which is built and inhabited by the mothers (and uncircumcised siblings) of some of the moran (especially those whose fathers also have younger wives to look after them). The *emanyata* serves as the ceremonial and political head-quarters of the age set of moran and is said to be important as the place where moran can always be found by members of the territorial section in case of trouble. The alternate senior age-set acts as the moral guardian to the young men and its members supervise the ceremonial cycle. But moran organize their own affairs on a day-to-day basis and their social organization is focused upon the *emanyata* and not upon the villages.

Moran are, first of all, warriors. In the event of an attack upon a village, all able-bodied men present will attempt to defend it. But the responsibil-ities of moran in this regard are greater than those of others. In the past, moran would have been responsible for punitive and offensive raids, organ-ized in the *emanyata*, against non-Maasai villages. And they are always the first to be called upon for the execution of dangerous tasks such as dealing with the wild animals that sometimes harass people and livestock; indeed lion hunts are an important and highly ritualized feature of moranhood. A moran who dies in battle is greatly honored in songs that directly invoke his name, contrary to the usual practice of forgetting the death of a man who has no grandchildren. Those who succeed in killing a human enemy or a lion are distinguished at *eunoto* by a particular pattern of body painting. Thus moran are associated with death and the killing of enemies, both human and animal. They are indeed identified, in a general way, with the untameable world that lies outside the circular fences built for protection around the villages by the elder patriarchs.

Following Van Gennep's classic analysis of rites of passage (Van Gennep 1960) I argue that moranhood, as a transitional stage between the two statuses occupied by males within the patriarchal units, may be seen as the "liminal" rite in a rite of passage that makes elders out of boys.[4] In Van Gennep's scheme, circumcision and its attendant ceremonies may be regarded as a rite of separation, both from childhood and from the patriarchal units, and the ceremonies that lead out of moranhood (which begin with "the ox of the earplugs") may be regarded as rites of reincorporation, which reintegrate the young men back into the patriarchal units as full adults. Moranhood itself is the period of waiting or transition that constitutes the middle, liminal stage.[5]

Liminal stages, in general, are characterized by their location outside the structures of ordinary social life, the marginality of the initiates being ex-pressed through symbols that deny their participation in mundane social relations. They may be veiled, masked, or spatially segregated and they are commonly associated with features of the asocial world. However, ideas about the asocial are inevitably derived from ideas about the social; "nature" is, to a large extent, a negative image of what is believed to be "culture." And in Maasai, the marginality of the moran is appropriately expressed in their association with the space that lies beyond the elder patriarchs' control and in behavior that seems to be disruptive to social order and to be in opposition to some of the most important values of that order: respect for property and self-disciplined livestock husbandry.

Maasai have no linguistic categories that correspond to the English opposition between nature and culture or the tame and the wild. But they are very conscious of the distinctions between three areas: the order and safety of the area inside the village fences (*boo*); the area within sight of the village fences (*auluo*); and the area beyond this, which in Loita is mainly forested (*entim*). The safety and danger of the three zones is seen partially in terms of their accessibility to nondomestic animals. The livestock go out every day toward the forest but return at night to the security of the villages where the gates are shut behind them. At night the wild animals travel down from the forest and graze outside the fence, in the *auluo* area. *Auluo* is consequently regarded as safe, human territory in daylight but dangerous in the dark.

Women in particular express great fear of the "enemy" animals (*olmang'-atinta*) that are capable of attacking human beings (that is, carnivores, elephants, rhinos, and buffalos). When a child is born, the women are expected to sing in the house of the new mother, for several evenings. In the wet season, on a moonless night, the paths from house to house become too muddy to negotiate and such expeditions become burdensome because the women believe it is dangerous to venture even a few paces outside the fence in the darkness. So they hurry round the perimeter within touching distance of it.

The fence and the village gateways are, indeed, frequently encountered elements in ritual and in Maasai thought. It is inauspicious, for example, for deaths to occur inside the fence (*boo*): The dying are carried a few yards outside the fence and corpses are carefully laid in *auluo* for scavengers to dispose of. The slaughter of animals does not normally take place inside the fence and the knife should be wielded, not by elders, but by those "outsiders," the moran: Elders should not be directly involved in the shedding of blood.[6]

Moran, on the other hand, are associated with killing and they sometimes live closely with the "enemies" of the forests, the wild animals. For example, all moran belong to an *olpul* group of a dozen or so men that periodically takes an ox or a succession of oxen into the forest. They kill and eat the animal at a permanent campsite (*olpul*). They remain there between a week and three months until the entire carcass or series of carcasses is consumed (apart from certain cuts of meat that must be sent back to the formal "owner," the father of the moran who gave it to the group). In the forest camps, moran compose and sing songs that glorify the age set and its slain heroes. The songs also express a fellow-feeling with the forces of the wild. For example, the singer may claim a kind of friendship with the lion; a conventional image is the sharing of a communal meal of ox flesh:

> Oh lion with coloured patches, you who live where the rivers meet in the dense black forest. Tell me what delayed you yesterday? I waited for you till nearly midnight. There is water here and I had laid out meat for you on the leaves, ready to eat. With you alone I share the good fatty meat of the oxen we slaughter in the black forest. [part of a song]

Sometimes, a whole *olpul* group descends upon a village after dark, after they have finished their ox. Such a visit is heralded by the sound of distant shrieks and cries from the direction of the forest. The people in the village speculate as to the origin of the noises; at first it is not clear whether they come from birds, animals, or moran. Eventually the first moran reach the gateways of the village where they call attention to the boundary between the patriarchal villages and the outside world by going into paroxysms (*olokirikiri*) of shaking, fainting, and moaning.[7]

Moran do not always acknowledge their visits to the villages in this way. Like the animals, they may use the cover of darkness to prowl around the fences out of sight of the inhabitants. The young men do this particularly when they are visiting their female friends and hoping to find one of their mistresses alone. This nocturnal wandering is known as *dooro*. The mistresses of moran may be uncircumcised girls to whom the young men have legitimate rights of sexual access. But they also have love affairs with married women to whom they have no such rights. In the latter case, the utmost secrecy must be preserved, because a wife discovered in a liaison with a moran is liable to a severe beating by her elder husband. In addition, the whole age set of moran may be collectively fined. However, these sanctions do not prevent such relationships from occurring and the topic of adultery between the wives of elders and moran is a theme constantly dwelt upon by men and women alike.

Such adultery violates the integrity of the system of property rights because, first, it disrupts the pattern of entitlement to rights of sexual access according to which circumcised women are the legitimate partners of elders. Appropriately, men and women both refer to the act of adultery between women and moran as stealing (*a-puroo*). Secondly, if women exercise choice and dispose of their bodies as they please in sexual relationships, they deny the principle that rights in women's sexuality are transactable between men.

Moran are also apparently disruptive of property rights over livestock. The young men are, in any case, in an anomalous position with regard to rights of disposal over animals. As moran, they are required to contribute meat to the *olpul* camps and to slaughter at various rites of passage. Formally, however, as I have said, a man's livestock remains part of his father's herd until the death of the senior man, regardless of the age status of the son. During moranhood, even the fatherless must leave their animals to be administered within the patriarchal units of elders because herd management is deemed incompatible with the responsibilities and irresponsibilities of moranhood. When moran need an ox to slaughter at *olpul*, they may steal one from a fellow Maasai (*enyamu*), an act of theft that is conceptually distinguished from raiding. Even if they take an animal, for the same purpose, from their "own" stock within their father's herd, they must ritually "snatch" it at dawn and hurry it through the village fence before the gateways are opened by the women. If a man has no suitable ox to slaughter for the ritual of "the ox of the earplugs" he must snatch a heifer to exchange for an ox, an action considered even more profligate.

From the point of view of the villagers, then, moran are associated with intemperate and disorderly behavior. They appear to be aligned with the uncontrollable forces of death, violence, and the wild and to stand in opposition to the patriarchal values of responsible livestock husbandry and respect for property.

They have, of course, their own orderly internal organization but they are always more or less outsiders with respect to the structures of patriarchal village life. However, I would suggest that this marginality appears to elders and to women in somewhat different lights. Elders are sentimental about their own moranhood. They refer with pride to the brave deeds of their age sets and hint broadly that they too were thieves of women in their day. However, they compare the current age set of moran unfavorably with their own youth. And, as elders, they express vehement disapproval of moran attitudes toward property. To them, the disorderly activities of the existing moran are most apparent. They complain that the young men lack "respect" (*enkanyit*) and that they destroy property when they "snatch" livestock and women. As one elder put it: "They destroy all the wealth of men . . . You have to beat your wives so that they don't keep on loving them. Elders resent the moran because they bring trouble to the villages."

But women have no property of significance and their response to moran is, for this reason, different in its emphasis. To women, I suggest, the moran appear less as disorderly than as glamorous, semisacred figures. Although they are in the process of becoming owners of livestock and women, the temporary extrusion of the young men from the property system manifests itself in apparently rebellious anti-elder behavior. I believe that this aspect of moranhood appeals to women who in general express some dissatisfaction with their position as wives. In their determined love for the moran, they even make use of the young men's disrespect for property to assert their right to dispose of themselves in sexual relationships of their own choice and to carve out an area of limited autonomy from the system of property relationships in which they themselves constitute the property.

Moreover, moran are expected to cultivate their charm and their physical beauty. They should plait their hair in the latest fashion, wear sweet-smelling herbs around their necks and in their armpits, and adorn themselves with ochre and with jewelry made of beads and leather. In doing so, they hope to make themselves attractive to the wives of other men. But they are also displaying to their fellow Maasai and the outside world, the elegance of masculinity and the aesthetic excellence of Maasai culture in general. This reveals the paradox that these often troublesome outsiders are expected to embody the culture at its most splendid.

Moranhood, as we have seen, is part of the most fundamental transformation in Maasai social reproduction. Moran exist outside the parameters of ordinary social relations and they are seen by those in the elders' villages as sometimes dangerous, sometimes sacred outsiders (see Douglas; T. Turner; V. Turner). They display a kind of undifferentiated masculine potential that is tied neither to the exploited nor to the exploiting male status within the patriarchal units. It is a masculinity that transcends the statuses of boy and elder but that appears in paradoxical and apparently antisocial forms. I write "apparently" because, although moran *appear* to be in opposition to patri- archy, the qualities they are supposed to show are by no means irrelevant to the system of property rights as a whole. Indeed moran must cultivate some of the very characteristics that, in another context, are thought necessary to responsible property ownership.

For example, moran are expected to be very brave. They live in the forests, hunt lions, and face death on raids. Opportunities for the display of courage are, indeed, actively sought. For example, moran hunt buffalo for sport because raiding is very difficult to organize. A cowardly moran is utterly despised by his fellows and although he will acquire a wife if his economic prospects are good enough, he is unlikely to find any girlfriends. The importance of bravery to the moran may be demonstrated by the use of the word *osuuji*. *Osuuji* describes bad qualities in persons. In the case of a girl or a woman, it implies that she is slovenly or a poor housewife; in that of an elder, it usually means that he is poor. But in the case of a moran, it almost always means that he is a coward. I have personally never heard a man referred to as cowardly, except in jest. The insult is too serious to be used lightly and the imputation of cowardice to any member of an age set would disgrace the age set as a whole. Physical courage is thus an important element of moranhood and mothers exhort their small sons to be brave "like little moran."

In the context of the patriarchal units, men and women both tend to say that women could never take charge of the herds because they are too cowardly. If, for example, an animal is found to be missing on return from pasture, they dare not go into the forest to search for it in the dark. In a recorded interview with some young married women, I asked if women preferred to bear sons or daughters. One said: "They prefer sons." Another broke in with a question: "What if raiders came to your village and took your cow – a lovely large fat cow – would you dare to follow it?" I said I thought not and she said, "That's because you are a woman. You dare not because you'd be beaten up. The raiders would beat you up. Now a man, if his cow is stolen he would follow it – even as far as Nairobi – because he dares to do so." "Because he's a man," said another. "And he'd go on his own if necessary," finished the first speaker. "That's why men are a good thing."

Another quality thought necessary to pastoral management is the ability to cooperate with others, to place the common good before one's own immediate interests. In moranhood, men organize themselves into a solidary age set. As patriarchs, they will be differentiated in terms of their relative wealth, but from the point of view of the age set men are formally equal. At age set councils, every member has the right to voice his opinion and decisions are made on the basis of consensus. Offenses against the rules regulating relations between the age sets (such as the seduction by moran of elders' wives) are punished by collective fines levied against the age set as a whole or by curses that are thought to affect all members equally. But the principle of collective responsibility is most dramatically expressed in the organization of raiding. After a raiding party has seized the livestock from the village under attack, a group of moran are supposed to remain behind to protect those who are going ahead with the animals. This is thought to be the most dangerous aspect of raiding; the moran of the rearguard (*oltim*) risk their lives in the interests of the enterprise as a whole.

Women are believed to be incapable of such selfless organization and a myth told by both sexes, but mainly by women, makes explicit the connection in Maasai thought between the men's ability to exploit their herds and their ability to cooperate with each other:

> Elephants used to move the houses of women; buffaloes were their cattle; Thomson's gazelles were their goats; warthogs were their sheep; zebras were their donkeys. Those were women's herds before. And then one morning, they got up early to slaughter an ox. And there were many women in the village. And there was not one who did not say, "My child is not going herding because he will stay to eat some kidney." One said, "My child is not going." And another said "Neither is mine" . . . So the cattle went off on their own. They went into the forest. The zebra became wild; the gazelle became wild; the buffalo became wild. But they were our cattle before. We let them go on account of a kidney . . . So we no longer have cattle. These cows all belong to men. We have become the servants of men because we let our cows go off into the forest and become wild beasts . . . We no longer have cattle that we can dispose of . . . It was us who put the herds in danger through putting our own individual interests first, so off they went. So we are not in charge of anything any more. All we have is calabashes to milk into.

Implicit in the contentions that women are cowardly and unable to act in the interests of the common good is the idea that they have less self-control. There is no general Maasai term for this concept, but it is nevertheless a significant one that appears in many contexts.

Its importance is related to the fact that herds and flocks, as F. Barth has pointed out, are very easy to destroy (Barth 1961). A pastoral community that loses its herds has little basis for recovery; it is forced to take up another mode of subsistence. And men who have no property, the wandering *ilkiriko*, are almost always said to have destroyed their herds as a result of a general weakness of character or an inability to control their appetites for meat, liquor, or women. In practice, the steps that lead a man to the status of *olkirikoi* may be more subtle than this but the important point is that a man's control of livestock is thought to be associated with his control of himself. Patriarchs are, furthermore, said to need self-control in order to deal magnanimously with those in their power, their dependents. An elder argued to me that women are unfit to rule because their notorious cowardice would undermine their mastery of themselves. If a woman started to chastise another person, he said, she would carry on until he was dead for fear of his subsequent anger.

Moran do not display self-control in the patriarchal sense of respecting property; they steal women and snatch livestock for food. But in other ways, the quality is stressed during moranhood. Men are proud of their ability to survive more or less without food or sleep for long periods, as they journey to or from raids outside Maasailand. And magnanimity in battle is greatly admired; there is a semilegendary Loita hero of whom a famous story is told. In the war against the Laikipiak agricultural Maasai, at the end of the last century, the Loita man came face to face with the bravest Laikipiak warrior. The two men fought and the Loita moran eventually had his rival on the ground and at his mercy. But instead of killing him he merely speared him in the thigh, saving his life but at the same time demonstrating his power to kill him if he so chose.

The most public opportunity for a man to display his self-control is during the ritual that constitutes his entry into moranhood: his own circumcision. Male initiates are said to be utterly shamed if they so much as blink an eye during the ordeal; their parents will be beaten by onlookers and the incident will never be forgotten. I never heard of a disgrace of this kind but moran sometimes arrange for boys who are expected to cry out (those who are circumcised particularly young and those who are mentally backward) to be initiated after the formal period of recruitment to the age set is closed. This device is designed to preclude the disgrace of the age set as a whole should the boys fail to withstand the ordeal. It is hoped that girls will also be brave during circumcision but this is not an important matter. No lasting stigma attaches to the many who do cry out or even try to escape. I would suggest that because girls are destined to have little control over livestock or other human beings, their self-mastery is of little public significance.

Moran, then, display the qualities of a responsible property owner in military and ritual contexts and in the wild, in setting, that is, that are far from the property relationships that organize the production and reproduction of material necessities and human beings. They are put to use, furthermore, in the service of the age set or on behalf of the community as a whole, rather than in the selfish pursuit of riches by individual men. These qualities are thought to be, to some extent, immanent in boys. I witnessed an incident in which a group of women found a poisonous snake near a village. They at once called to some boys to come and kill it. The women showed no fear and instructed the boys in the best method of dispatching the snake. When I asked why they had not killed it themselves, they explained that "males (*ilewa*) are braver."

At the same time, however, the qualities of masculinity are thought to be created in moranhood. A moran explained: "You know only a few things when you are a child. When you are a moran you become very clever ... a moran sees many things; he goes to steal cattle for food; he can go about at night and he can go raiding; he can fight enemies and survive on maize [when he is far from home] ... If you are circumcised and then immediately 'drink milk' then you are nothing." Thus in 1974, when local government officials insisted that *eunoto* be held before the moran were considered to be ready for it, there was some reluctance on the part of the Loita people. Women, in particular, complained that the moran were still "mere children" because they had not spent enough time in the forests "becoming strong." The moral inferiority of the boy is perhaps best summed up by the use of the word *enkorrok*, which may be used to refer to the typical qualities, or "essence" of a category of persons. It is most commonly heard in compliments. Thus an elder who is said to embody the "essence of elderhood" is likely to be noted for his wealth, generosity, and wisdom. The "essence of moranhood" connotes the qualities of bravery and elegance. The phrase "the essence of boyhood'' is linguistically possible but it is not used; asked to explain why, male informants would laugh and say that the phrase would imply nothing but laziness and disobedience.[8]

Boys and elders thus possess their own supposedly typical characteristics that are consistent with their relative positions within the property system. I am arguing that the *idea* of masculinity is constructed, in the abstract as it were, in moranhood, a setting that is marginal to the pragmatic concerns of the patriarchal units but that constitutes, at the same time, the very process on which the regeneration of the property system depends. Hence the paradox that moranhood is simultaneously marginal to social life and crucially important to masculine identity.

Females never become moran and they are seen as lacking in the desirable qualities of masculinity. Indeed to some extent, femininity is thought of as an absence of masculinity. When asked to account for the differences in the respective positions of men and women, informants of both sexes would tend to describe women in negative terms: they are ''not brave,'' ''not clever,'' they ''don't own anything.'' Circumcision for girls defines them as fertile women. It does not change their positions within the property system in any fundamental way and it is not supposed to alter, fundamentally, the way they behave. Women are thought to be both wiser and calmer (*medala elukunya*) than girls. But the phrases ''the essence of girlhood'' and ''the essence of young womanhood'' (*esiankiki enkorrok*) connote in each case the qualities of beauty, grace, and sexual attractiveness. Women are thought to possess certain special characteristics of their own, associated with their role as childrearers. The most important of these is that they are expected to be kinder, more quickly moved to pity for helpless creatures (*keibor oshoke*) than men.

The importance of fertility to the positive valuation of women may be seen in the fact that the phrase ''the essence of postmenarchal womanhood'' (*entasat enkorrok*) like ''the essence of boyhood,'' is not used. Informants said it would be rude to refer to a person in terms that imply wrinkles, gray hair, and a general loss of good looks. But it would be wrong to see the high value placed, by both men and women, upon motherhood and women's maternal qualities as ''balancing'' the stress on masculine bravery, self-control, and so on. Female fertility is directly associated, in Maasai thought, with women's inferiority. In the myth quoted at the beginning of this section, the acquisition of fertility coincides with the loss of women's courage, one of the most important of the pastoral virtues as we have seen. It also coincides with the women being passively ''taken'' as wives. With the advent of sexuality and fertility women become ownable; the subordination of women is seen as necessary to the continuation of human society.[9]

Some further considerations

The idea of ''nature'' as opposed to ''culture'' has appeared in different guises in different parts of this essay. This issue has been discussed theoretically, by some recent writers in connection with the opposition male: female (see

Ardener, Mathieu, Ortner). These writers tend to assume that a distinction between nature and culture exists and is important in all systems of thought. An opposition between what is regarded as social or cultural and what is regarded as not social or not cultural is certainly frequently encountered (as we have seen, it appears in various contexts in Maasai) but I would question whether it is a universal preoccupation and thus able to account for some of the cross-cultural similarities in the position of women, as these theorists suggest.[10] The content of "nature" is, in any case, variable, because what is perceived as "not cultural" must depend upon what is perceived as "cultural." Thus, to the Bakweri described by Ardener, nature is essentially "the wild" whereas to Ortner it includes such items as social atomism and female reproduction. Moreover, the elements of the "not cultural" are not always linked together in a single concept, "nature," but may be independent constructs relevant to specific contexts. This is the case, I would argue, in Maasai.

In Maasai, it is males rather than females who are most obviously identified with the wild; the asocial setting of moranhood is, as we have seen, an integral part of the young men's transformation into property holders. And I would suggest that "the wild," which is one of the more common components of "nature," together with such supernatural constructs as "the world of the spirits," are highly appropriate to the symbolism of marginality characteristic of social transformations: They are obvious "places" for novices to "go" in the middle phase of a rite of passage and from which to return as new social persons. Where these constructs appear in transformations that involve one sex and not the other they are likely to be used in the social construction of gender.[11]

Ortner puts forward the view that it is women's biology that places women conceptually closer to nature than men. But in Maasai, women's fertility is not particularly associated with the nonsocial world. On the contrary, it is asserted to be the artificial creation of men and of ceremonial. In the myth of the women warriors it is the male warriors who bring fertility into existence by "opening up" the women with their bows.[12] Similarly, in real life, girls are believed to be unable to develop breasts, and hence to mature physically as women, until "the path has been opened up" by the moran, with whom they engage in sexual relations. Conception should not take place until they have been further opened up in a rite of circumcision: Pregnancy in an uncircumcised girl is regarded as highly unpropitious. This denial of the naturalness of female sexuality and fertility is associated, I suggest, with the transactability and ownability of these functions.

Ortner also suggests, however, that women's social role is seen as closer to nature because women tend to be confined to the "lower levels" of social and cultural organization, to "socially fragmenting, particularistic sorts of concerns, as opposed to interfamilial relations representing higher-level, integrative, universalistic sorts of concerns" (Ortner 1974: 79). I should like to suggest that, in this sense, Maasai women are indeed less "cultural," less "Maasai" than men even though I do not believe that they are seen as correspondingly more "natural" in any of the English senses of the word.

In Maasai, as we have seen, the "traffic" in women (to use Rubin's term) between the heads of the patriarchal units creates relationships between families and between age sets (as does also the traffic in livestock). Women as transactable assets, as the objects of the traffic, are pawns rather than partners in the integrative links thus established.[13] They are excluded from membership of the age sets whose structures define the widest limits of the Maasai polity and that have ties with the corresponding age sets of, among others, the Samburu, Baraguyu, and Arusha peoples. And their exclusion from moranhood further excludes them from direct participation in the "highest" levels of culture.

The age-set rituals that surround moranhood are the most important social events in the calendar, attracting visitors from all over the territorial section and beyond, from other sections and even from neighboring non-Maasai peoples. Furthermore, they are important to Maasai, who have little in the way of plastic or pictorial art, as aesthetic events, and they are evaluated by the audience of women and elders in terms of the splendor of the performance and the good looks and dancing skills of the participants. Moranhood thus embodies more than an abstract ideal of masculinity. It also displays Maasai culture at its most brilliant; it is crucial to the image of the culture as Maasai represent it to themselves and to the outside world.

Women are integral to social and cultural life; the property system revolves around the control of their reproductive powers and a major effect of the age organization, as I have argued, is the elaboration of difference between male and female. But property rights are held *in* rather than *by* women. And their role in the activities of the age sets is contingent; where they appear in the great ceremonies, they are cast as the wives, mothers, or mistresses of the main protagonists. Thus despite their centrality to the workings of the social drama, they remain, to some extent, off-stage, spectators in the wings.

Conclusion

The reproduction of the system of property rights turns structurally upon the transformation of boys into elders. But the cycle as a whole depends for its continuance upon the acceptance, by those participating in it, of the validity of the notion of property rights in goods and people, and their belief in the justice of the existing distribution of those rights. If either of these premises were to be successfully challenged, the relations of material production would have to be radically reorganized. In fact women do, on occasion, express resentment of their lack of stock, their relative lack of autonomy and their subordination to the will of others (especially their husbands). In doing so, they are complaining about the current distribution of property rights in goods and people. They do not question the institution of property per se, whether it relates to goods or to people. But within these limits, women are aware that things might be organized differently.

Thus, they do not suggest that girls should be free to choose their own husbands (or that the stock should be shared by all in the same way as the land is shared). But they do sometimes say that they ought to have a say in the marriages of their daughters and that they should receive a significant share of the bridewealth payments. Women would often ask me about inheritance in

Britain and wonder whether they should not be entitled to inherit from their fathers as their brothers do. They particularly resent their inability to slaughter their ''own'' livestock in times of sickness.

But the proposition that women should share more equally with men in the rights of property is, in Maasai, easily disposed of by the argument that men are cleverer, braver, and so on, an argument with which women ruefully, in the end, tend to concur.

I should like to conclude this essay by suggesting that moranhood, which is so important in the construction of these ''truths,'' is in fact a hegemonic institution in the sense developed by Gramsci (1971). Gramsci was interested in people's commitment to the social systems in which they participate and, in particular, in the aquiescence or consent of subordinate groups to the social systems in which they are subordinated. He was concerned with European history and class societies, but I believe that his discussion of the concept of hegemony is relevant as well to nonclass societies. Gramsci pointed out that if the subordinate groups are to be convinced of the justice or inevitability of the social order, the superordinate groups must also believe in its justice or inevitability and in their own fitness to rule. He suggests that neither rulers nor ruled are likely to be reassured by a narrowly self-interested justification of the privileges of the rulers. Instead, he argues that the basic principles that organize the processes of social life are likely to be given expression in such ways that all or most of the participants in that social life can acknowledge and respect them.

Gramsci illustrated his points with a discussion of the French Revolution. Eighteenth-century French society may appear very distant from the pastoral Maasai. But I suggest that, just as the ideas of ''liberty, equality, and fraternity'' expressed the economic and political motives behind the bourgeois revolution at their best, in terms of their own highest ideals, so the Maasai social system, which rests upon the principle of male ownership of livestock, labor, and sexuality, is represented to its members, in terms of its own highest ideals, in the institution of moranhood. Moran display the moral characteristics on which the pastoral way of life is thought to depend. But their bravery and self-control are seen, not in the quest for individual gain, but in their most selfless and splendid aspect. Like ''liberty, equality, and fraternity'' or, in the Western world nowadays, ''human rights'' or ''freedom of the individual,'' the glory of the idea of moranhood is beyond question.

The connection between the brave and beautiful moran and the subordinate status of women is, however, obscure to Maasai. Thus women, who often complain about the autocratic behavior of elders and their own lack of livestock, characteristically express admiration and affection for moran. Older women may refer with tenderness to members of the age set who were moran when they were young, calling them moran long after they have become elders; small boys are addressed as ''my little moran'' by their mothers to encourage them in manly behavior. In their admiration, however, women implicitly assent to their own subordination within the property system because their admiration is an acknowledgment of the jural and moral transformation of men from which they are themselves excluded.

Notes

1 The material on which this essay is based is drawn from research done among a subsection of the Loita Maasai. The research was funded by Harvard University and by The Child Development Research Unit, University of Nairobi, with the aid of a grant from the Carnegie Foundation. My thanks to these institutions and to John and Beatrice Whiting for unfailing help and encouragement during the period of research. I am indebted to the editors and to Liz Brown, Chris Curling, Peter Loizos, Sarone ole Sena, and Keith Tribe for valuable comments during the preparation of this essay.

2 The biological basis of the age/gender organization lends a mien of naturalness or inevitability to the property system even though this system is based upon a biologically arbitrary distribution of rights of alienation over livestock, labor power, and sexuality.

3 *A-inyang'u*, to buy, is also used in the context of commercial transactions in shops. I know of no other contexts in which it is used.

4 Spencer describes the moran of the Maasai-speaking Samburu as the "odd men out in the society ... in a limbo between boyhood and elderhood" (Spencer 1965: 100).

5 As I mention earlier, moran is the only age-grade term that is not also a kinship term.

6 See also Galaty (1978).

7 See Spencer (1965) for a discussion of "shaking" among the Samburu.

8 My approach to the stereotypes of the various age and sex categories is largely anecdotal. For accounts of a systematic investigation into personality trait organization using sociolinguistic methods, see Kirk and Burton (1977) and Burton and Kirk (1978). Among many interesting results, these investigators find that young women are viewed more negatively by women themselves than they are by men. They also find that older girls are viewed very positively by all categories but that women, in particular, see them as different from young women. These findings partially corroborate my own analysis but suggest that circumcision and the acquisition of fertility constitute a more radical break in the moral development of females than is perhaps indicated in this essay.

9 For further discussion of the cultural meaning of motherhood and aspects of women's culture, see Llewelyn-Davies (1978).

10 In a slightly different context (a discussion of cultural vs. biological elements in the makeup of the sexes) Marilyn Strathern points out that "the boundary between nature and culture" is a particularly Western preoccupation. She suggests that we may sometimes use "sex differences to illuminate and talk about, in short to symbolise, the relationship we see between nature and culture" (Strathern 1976).

11 Harriet Whitehead has drawn my attention to the interesting nature – culture distinction between the superordinate elders and the subordinate moran. "The imminent power of the latter colours their "nature" with creative overtones; the imminent demise of the latter makes their "culture" rather pale and stodgy. Women wind up on the side of culture through their identification with their owners and the settled community." She goes on to suggest that the American "Western" is played out along similar lines. "The noble but dangerous gunfighter drifts in from Out There somewhere, he can never really settle down into the domesticated ways of the townspeople (women, children and bankers) but because he is inherently more valorous than they, they must rely on him to do the dangerous work for them ... " (private communication).

12 Bows and arrows are rarely used by Maasai as weapons. Their use is nowadays
    confined to the relatively recent practice of hunting wild animals. But they are
    important in several age-set rituals. I hope to discuss the ritual meaning of the bow
    in a future publication.

13 Similarly, although women are responsible for allocating animals to their sons, the
    livestock never becomes theirs to control; control passes *through* them from father
    to son. Rubin calls attention to the fact that such transactions conform to a common
    pattern. She points out that, in kinship systems, "the relationship of a male to every
    other male is defined through a woman. A man is linked to a son through a
    mother . . . etc." (Rubin 1975: 192). Following Lacan, she suggests that in a
    "male-dominated" culture the phallus "is the embodiment of the male status" and
    that the Oedipal crisis is precipitated by the "castration" of the mother or "the
    recognition that the phallus only passes through her, but does not settle on her"
    (Rubin 1975: 192).

References

Ardener, E. 1972. "Belief and the problem of women." In *The interpretation of
    ritual*, ed. J. S. LaFontaine, pp. 135–58. London: Tavistock.
    1975. "The 'problem' revisited." In *Perceiving women*, ed. S. Ardener, pp.
    19–28. London: Malaby Press.
Barth, F. 1961. *Nomads of South Persia*. Canada: Little Brown (Canada).
Burton, M. and Kirk, L. 1978. "Sex differences in Maasai cognition of personality
    and social identity." Unpublished manuscript.
Douglas, M. 1966. *Purity and danger*. London: Routledge and Kegan Paul.
Edelman, B. 1977. "The transition in Kant's 'Doctrine of Right'." *Economy and
    Society* 6: 145–65.
Engels, F. 1972. *The origin of the family, private property and the state*. New York:
    Pathfinder Press.
Finley, M. I. 1968. "Slavery." In *International Encyclopaedia of the Social Sciences*,
    ed. David L. Sills, pp. 307–13. New York: Macmillan and The Free Press.
Galaty, J. 1978. "Pollution and pastoral anti-praxis: the issue of Maasai inequality,"
    American Ethnologist 6: 803–16.
Gramsci, A. 1971. *Selections from the prison notebooks*. London: Lawrence and
    Wishart.
Jacobs, A. 1965. "The traditional political structure of the pastoral Maasai." D.Phil.
    Thesis. Nuffield College, Oxford.
Kant, I. [1887] 1974. *The philosophy of law*. Edinburgh: T & T Clark.
Kirk, L., and Burton, M. 1977. "Meaning and context: a study of contextual shifts in
    meaning of Maasai personality descriptors." *American Ethnologist* 44: 224–
    761.
Llewelyn-Davis, M. 1978. "Two contexts of solidarity among pastoral Maasai
    women." in *Women united, women divided: female solidarity in cross-cultural
    perspective*, ed. P. Caplan and J. Bujra, pp. 206–37. London: Tavistock.
Macpherson, C. B. 1962. *The political theory of possessive individualism*. Oxford:
    Oxford University Press.
Mathieu, N. C. 1973. "Homme-culture, femme-nature?" *L'Homme*, July-Sept.:
    101–13.
Ortner, S. 1974. "Is female to male as nature is to culture?" In *Woman, culture and
    society*, ed. M. Rosaldo and L. Lamphere, pp. 67–88. Stanford: Stanford
    University Press.

Radcliffe-Brown, A. R. 1965. *Structure and function in primitive society*. New York: The Free Press.

Rubin, G. 1975. "The traffic in women: notes on the 'political economy' of sex." In *Toward an anthropology of women*, ed. R. Reiter, pp. 157–210. New York: Monthly Review Press.

Spencer, P. 1965. *The Samburu*. Berkeley and Los Angeles: University of California Press.

Strathern, M. 1976. "An anthropological perspective." In *Exploring sex differences*, ed. B. Lloyd and J. Archer, pp. 49–70. New York: Academic.

Turner, T. 1977. "Transformation, hierarchy, and transcendence." In *Secular ritual*, ed. S. F. Moore and B. Myerhoff, pp. 53–70. Amsterdam: Van Gorcum.

Turner, V. 1969. *The ritual process*. Chicago: Aldine.

Van Gennep, A. 1960. *Rites of passage*. Trans. M. B. Vizedom and G. L. Caffee. Chicago: University of Chicago Press.

10

Gender and sexuality in hierarchical societies:
THE CASE OF POLYNESIA AND SOME COMPARATIVE IMPLICATIONS

Sherry B. Ortner

Introduction

Since the days of the early voyagers, Polynesia has been famed for its distinctive culture of gender and sexuality. Sensualism, eroticism, and a high level of sexual activity are actively cultivated throughout the area. Homosexuality is unstigmatized. Relations between men and women are relatively harmonious and mutually respectful. Women achieve high public office with some regularity. From a western point of view, the area has appeared as a "paradise" of "liberation," liberation of sex and of women.

This picture is surprisingly accurate as far as it goes, but it is only a partial picture. A more thorough excursion into the ethnographic literature reveals some more problematic features: enforced virginity of unmarried girls, a relatively high frequency of rape, a very marked subordination of wives to husbands within the domestic context.

The purpose of this essay[1] is to develop a general and systematic interpretation of Polynesian society that will account for as many as possible of the salient (and apparently contradictory) features of Polynesian gender culture. I will argue that the sex/gender system (as Rubin [1975] calls it) can be best understood in relation to the workings of the "prestige system," the system within which personal status is ascribed, achieved, advanced, and lost.

For Polynesia the "prestige system" is a system of hereditary ranking.[2] People are born into certain statuses, high or low, that are theoretically unchangeable for life, and that in turn are passed on to their offspring. Polynesia thus belongs to that large class of societies labeled "hierarchical" in Louis Dumont's classic formulation. In modern times the most famous exemplar of the category is India, organized as a system of ranked castes. Dumont argues for the uniqueness of the Indian case, but the organizational principles he identifies for India may be seen as central to a wide range of well-known societies – feudal Europe, feudal Japan, pre-modern China, much of Southeast Asia, and probably the "archaic states" of Egypt, Mesopotamia, and Central and South America. Most recently Irving Goldman has (independently) discussed Polynesia in much the same terms in which Dumont discusses India, and Goldman's superb (in my view) *Ancient Polynesian society* inspired much of my thinking in developing the present essay.

The characteristic features of "hierarchical" societies may be very briefly summarized here. The first is what Dumont calls the "encompassing" status of prestige criteria vis-à-vis other principles of social organization. This means, very simply, that persons and/or categories of persons are ranked or graded according to criteria of social or religious value that theoretically transcend immediate political and economic "realities." Neither great wealth nor great power necessarily generate great prestige, which derives rather from intangible qualities like "purity" (in India) or "mana" (in Polynesia), considered to be largely innate and inherited. The highest social status in the system is the one highest on the scale of such qualities, regardless of actual political or economic power. To put the point slightly differently, doctrines of hereditary purity or hereditary mana are ideologies of aristocratic superiority, and these are the hegemonic ideologies of the society. The Brahmins of India, and the highest-ranking aristocrats of Polynesia, may not in fact be the most powerful group in terms of "real" politics, but it is their values that order society as a whole from high to low, and that must be drawn upon to legitimate more mundane political and economic power.

The second distinctive feature of hierarchical organization is what Dumont calls "holism," which has two interrelated aspects. First, rather than the "strata" being seen as independent units that are then "linked" in various ways, they are seen as differentiated, functionally specialized precipitates of a prior whole. In terms of social practice this means in turn – the second aspect of holism – that social relations between members of the different "strata" are organized in terms of mutual reciprocities and obligations. Inferiors owe goods and services to superiors, but superiors also have reciprocal obligations to inferiors: *noblesse oblige*. Thus notions of "exploitation" appropriate to the analysis of "class" societies are only partially and imperfectly applicable to the analysis of hierarchies.

In the present essay I will attempt to account for features of Polynesian gender and sexual culture by relating them to various aspects of the hierarchical social organization, or in other words, to aspects of the workings of "the prestige system." I must thus begin by justifying the decision to draw this particular set of connections.

The decision partly derives from the fact that, as just discussed, prestige criteria are in fact "encompassing": They provide the largest framework and the ultimate reference point for the organization of almost every aspect of social life. Further, my reading of the general literature on sex and gender over a wide variety of ethnographic cases – and not only in hierarchical societies – suggests that, empirically, the prestige system virtually always seems to have powerful interactions with the gender system. Thus in New Guinea the system of achieving "big man" status seems "key" to the organization of gender (see, for example, Strathern, this volume); in India it appears to be caste ranking (see Gough 1955; Yalman 1963; Leach 1970; Tambiah 1973); and in the Mediterranean it appears to be the system by which men gain and lose "honor" (see Pitt-Rivers 1966, 1977; J. Schneider 1971).

Finally, and perhaps most importantly, there is a more general theoretical reason for looking to prestige. The prestige system of any society is the system that defines the ultimate goals and purposes of life for actors in that society. It defines what men and women are, as well as what they are (or should be) trying to accomplish or to become, and it defines how they can and cannot go about that project. To anchor the analysis in the prestige system, in other words, is to anchor it in *cultural* definitions of personal and social value, rather than in externally defined criteria. This does not mean that we confine ourselves analytically to explicit cultural notions and values; on the contrary, as will be evident in this essay, we must be aware that cultural categories and values themselves constitute interpretations and even distortions of other configurations, which must be brought to light through the application of our own ("external") analytic tools. But we must *start* with the cultural categories, or we will distort the data from the outset.

I begin the discussion then by describing the formal characteristics of the Polynesian prestige ("rank") system. I then move on to a discussion of the primary goals of social action in such a system. Briefly, these include the *maintenance* of status position, which is legitimate, and the *advancement* of status position, which is not legitimate (and theoretically not even possible). I then consider the structurally available means (or, in the jargon, the "strategies") for achieving these goals, and specifically those strategies with the maximum number and widest range of implications for gender relations. Put very simply, I ask first what men (for it is usually their prestige system) are trying to do in these societies, and then how that project hinges on the organization of their relations with women.

The approach I utilize thus entails identifying a particular pattern of action that systematically links male–female relations on the one hand with the largest culturally defined orders of prestige relations on the other. The pattern or strategy in question is often (but not always) "hidden"; identifying it properly is in many ways the hardest part of performing the analysis. Parenthetically it might be noted that, whereas the analysis of "egalitarian" systems entails identifying the hidden *constraints* on prestige-oriented action, the analysis of hierarchies entails locating the hidden *possibilities* for such action.

Finally, in the conclusion, I turn to the implications of the Polynesian analysis for understanding sex and gender patterning in hierarchical societies in general. I try to establish that there is in fact something like a "complex," a coherent set of sex/gender patterns characteristic of such societies, and that this "complex" is best interpreted in relation to certain general structural features of hierarchical social organization. I base the comparative discussion on Goody's and Tambiah's essays in *Bridewealth and dowry*, covering large areas of Europe and Asia. In making manifest the empirical parallels between Polynesia and these more well-known areas, and in critiquing Goody's and Tambiah's interpretations of their data from the point of view of the Polynesian analysis, I try to show that the interpretation developed in the present essay for one fairly exotic corner of the world is in fact of quite wide applicability.

The rank system

STRUCTURE AND FUNCTIONING

Polynesia is the designation for a large number of islands in the south Pacific, including (to mention a few that are familiar to non-specialists) Hawaii,

Tahiti, and Samoa. The populations of the islands are historically related to one another, although all of the historical links have not been fully established. The languages of the various islands are also closely related, and the peoples are racially very similar. Furthermore, there are both general and specific similarities of social and cultural patterning over the whole of the area.

Among the many social and cultural patterns shared, with variations, by all Polynesian societies, perhaps the most prominent is the system of hereditary ranking. I argued earlier that Polynesian rank systems fit Dumont's definition of "hierarchical" societies, and must be kept conceptually distinct from societies organized in terms of "class." It may be noted here, however, that in some Polynesian societies the social organization is more classlike, while in others it is more "hierarchical" in the Dumontian sense. I will use Goldman's terminology to tag the different types, "traditional" being the more hierarchical, "stratified" being the more classlike.[3] In a future essay I hope to look into variations of gender patterning in relation to variations of social organization along the hierarchy-versus-class axis, but such comparative questions are beyond the scope of the present essay.

Rank in Polynesia operates through the kinship system.[4] The primary units of social, economic, and political organization are (internally stratified) descent groups, at the apex of which stand the "chiefs" who collectively constitute the "aristocracy" of the society. Such descent groups are sometimes ranked in relation to one another, with some sort of supreme or paramount chief at the top of this ranking, but such meta-organization is not present in all cases.

Within descent groups all subunits and individuals are ranked through the application of two simple rules. These are: (a) that siblings (I confine myself to males unless otherwise stated) are ranked by birth order, and (b) that descendants of siblings are ranked collectively by the birth order of their respective ancestors. Hence the elder brother is senior to his younger brother, and all the descendants of the elder brother are senior (and socially superior) to all the descendants of the younger brother. An elder and a younger brother thus theoretically produce two related descent lines that are ranked as superior and inferior, respectively, within a single descent group. Within the respective lines, in turn, the same rules continue to apply, and ranking is systematically applied down to every individual, the eldest son of the eldest son (of the eldest son, etc.) being highest in the group, the youngest son of the youngest son (of the youngest son, etc.) being lowest.

Ranking is thus continuous from top to bottom, the principles of seniority of descent producing a gradation of superiority and inferiority that encompasses all members of the group. In addition, however, all Polynesian societies make a categorical distinction between "aristocracy" and one or more nonaristocratic classes. The terminological distinction is clear enough, but the question of who falls into which category is extremely variable from one Polynesian society to the next, and is often rather hazy at the border even within any given society. Best's comment about the Maori is applicable to most Polynesian societies: "Inasmuch as all members of a tribe are connected with well-born families, then it becomes a difficult matter to define the *ware* or *tutua* class, the people of low degree. Never have I met a native who would admit that he was a member of that class'' (Best I 1924: 346).

But the difficulty of stating authoritatively who is "in" the aristocracy, and the vagueness of the border between aristocrats and everyone else, will not affect the arguments in the present essay. A fairly junior member of the descent group as a whole may well be the senior figure in his locality, style himself as a member of the aristocracy, and be treated as such in the local framework of social relations. Insofar as this is the case his family would exhibit the same behavioral tendencies and patterns characteristic of the "aristocracy" in other localities or at higher levels of the structure.

Within the descent group, "the aristocracy" consists of the senior line – the "chief," his senior son, *his* senior son, and so on. From a perspective external to any given descent group, the aristocracy of the society as a whole consists of all the senior lines of all the descent groups. The extent to which they form a society-wide self-conscious "class" is one of the major axes of variation between the most "traditional" (or ranklike) and the most "strati-fied" (or classlike) Polynesian societies. Even in the simplest, most "tradi-tional" cases, tendencies toward class formation are present, particularly with respect to marriage – senior lines of different descent groups tend to intermarry with one another, across the groups, whereas the remainder of the descent group tends to be endogamous, the members marrying within the unit. In the more complex "stratified" systems, this tendency hardens into fixed rules and practices of class endogamy. Tendencies toward aristocratic class formation are also seen in visiting and feasting patterns – aristocrats travel to visit one another, and host one another to lavish hospitality, with the produce supplied by the host's descent group, eager to have their chief put on a good show.

In some of the "stratified" societies, the ruling class is in effect a single kin group, unrelated to the commoners of the society. In most Polynesian societies, however, the aristocrats are senior kin to their own commoners, and this fact places important constraints on true class formation, as well as on class conflict. Chiefs and aristocrats share at least as many interests with their own commoners as they do with other members of their status class. Thus the Maori, a "traditional" Polynesian society organized along lines quite close to the ideal state of affairs outlined here, say that it is impossible for chiefly and commoner interests to diverge (Mishkin 1961: 433). This is surely an overstatement even in a traditional system, but it refers to the fact that although all chiefs belong to "the aristocracy," each is there only by virtue of his kinship position in his own descent group. He is more like a representative of his group within the aristocratic circle, than a member of an exclusive "class" with interests divergent from those of the "class" of commoners.

Polynesian politics, religion, and economics are all best understood with reference to the descent group organization and class tendencies just outlined. Considering politics first, power and authority are fairly directly ordered by the nesting structure of the ranked units within the descent group. Chiefs have both more power and wider power; lesser aristocrats (such as heads of junior lineages) have less power, and over smaller units; and so on down to household heads. Power is a direct function of status position. It is not primarily a function of wealth per se (though chiefs are generally a little richer than everyone else); and it is not, except in the most complex, "stratified" societies, a direct function of control over economic production.

Access to supernatural power (*mana*), and degree of personal sacredness (*tapu*), closely follow the same lines, although tapu tends to be graded along the continuum of graded rank, whereas access to and control of mana tends to be binary – aristocracy has it and commoners do not. The tapu/mana distinction is thus partly intelligible in relation to the contrast between continuously graded kinship rank on the one hand, and the (incipient or overt) class distinction between aristocrats and commoners on the other. The aristocracy's exclusive direct access to or possession of mana is in some cases the most important basis of the class distinction (e.g., in Tikopia [Firth 1963: 314]). The significance of the chief's control of mana for his political authority cannot be overstated: Throughout much of the area the chiefs are believed to control the forces of nature critical to life and death, even where their worldly power over their subjects is quite minimal and circumscribed.

As for economic organization, most observers agree that the key to understanding the system in Polynesia lies in distribution rather than production. Although chiefs have certain regulatory functions in production, and are the ultimate titular "owners" of all the land, they, and the aristocracy in general, do not have actual control over the distribution of the means of production (primarily land), or over the actual execution of production, except in the "stratified" systems. Within the distribution structure, on the other hand, the chief is focal: Surplus in the form of gifts, tribute, first fruits, and the like is channeled up to him from his kinsmen, and he in turn redistributes most of it back down through the structure of the kin group. Redistribution is one of the most fundamental obligations and privileges of chiefship; it displays both his "power," in terms of his ability to command resources from a wide group, and his qualities of leadership, in the sense that his wide distributions appear as generosity, and as concern for the welfare of the whole.

As the chief's political authority is in the simplest cases a function of his kinship seniority, so are his economic functions and capacities. In the absence of taxation and other force-sanctioned surplus extraction mechanisms, which only appear in the "stratified" societies, his capacity to draw resources to himself depends upon normal mechanisms of kinship prestations and exchanges. And by virtue of being at the pinnacle of the kin group, the chief simply has more kinsmen (that is, more active kin ties with more people) than other members of the group (Firth 1975: 235).

I have thus far been using the terms "chiefs" and "aristocrats" somewhat interchangeably. But whereas all chiefs are aristocrats, all aristocrats are not chiefs. The chiefship is an office occupied by a single individual, whereas the aristocracy is a category and, in some cases, a social class. Thus, succession to the chiefship is a somewhat distinct issue. In a large number of cases the seniority principle of prestige ranking is the same principle that produces the chief – the chief is the senior son of the last chief. In other cases, however, this does not apply, and succession to high office operates on different principles. The succession principle must be separately determined for each society.

It is also important to distinguish between principles, or rules, of succession, descent, and inheritance. Throughout Polynesia, succession to high office passes patrilineally (through the male line), whether to the first-born son (primogeniture) or to some other patrilineally related male chosen by some other criterion. In exceptional cases it passes to a daughter or some other patrilineally related female, but always "in trust" for the next patrilineally related male when he becomes available, or after the death of the woman.

Descent, however, passes cognatically, that is, membership in a descent group passes through both men and women. Throughout Polynesia descent groups are preferentially endogamous, that is, it is both normal and preferred for one to marry a member of one's own descent group beyond a certain prohibited degree of kinship. Given these points, a child normally belongs to the descent group of both of its parents. When the parents belong to two different groups, the child's affiliation seems largely determined by residence – by whether the family resides with the wife's or husband's group. Given cognatic descent, however, the child also retains claims of membership in the other parent's group, and can activate that tie if he or she desires, for whatever reason.

Inheritance patterns are similar to descent patterns. By and large, inheritance is bilateral, that is, both sons and daughters inherit rights in their family's real property, mostly land. But a daughter's rights in land are largely usufructory – she and her husband and children can work it and enjoy its produce during her lifetime, but it reverts to her brothers or their children when she dies. Only the brothers can continue to pass land down to their children, unless again the woman's children reside and affiliate with her kin rather than her husband's. There is a general preference for virilocal residence, for the wife to reside with her husband's people, but in fact the rates of uxorilocality, of husbands residing with the wife's people, are quite high throughout Polynesia. Where the rate is reported it seems to be between 30 percent and 40 percent of all postmarital residence (Hecht 1977: 193; Loeb 1926: 80; Mead 1930: 23). Even in cases of virilocal residence, however, women commonly send one or more sons back to be adopted into households of their immediate kin, and thus to retain a stake in the property.[5]

Finally, one should also mention rules of what might be called "breeding." Throughout Polynesia these are somewhat variable. In general, however, it appears that the father is seen as the fixed point of reference, while the mother acts as the variable, that is, all things being equal, one inherits one's father's rank or status, but if there are major divergences of status between mother and father in either direction, the mother exerts the greater pull on the child's status, up or down. Normally marriages are between persons relatively equal in rank, but both hypergamy (women marrying up) and hypogamy (women marrying down) are possible and not uncommon.

WHAT DO ACTORS WANT AND HOW CAN THEY GET IT?

Within the structure and rule system just described, Polynesian men and women pursue lives informed by the values and ideals built into the system, and constrained by its structural constraints. The supreme cultural values are implicit in the claim that issues of status and prestige are culturally encompassing. What every Polynesian wants is, minimally, to maintain the status and prestige given by the position into which he or she was born, and maximally, to improve position and hence gain more prestige.

In theory, of course, status is fixed by birth. Advancement or rise (as opposed to simple maintenance) is theoretically not possible, although some Polynesian societies (those Goldman labels "open") allow for the legitimate rise of exceptional individuals by virtue of extraordinary deeds in special circumstances. In fact, however, there is a "hidden" mechanism of status advancement available, with only minor variations, in *all* Polynesian societies, including the "open" ones, which does not depend on extraordinary personal characteristics or deeds at all. It depends simply on systematically manipulating the descent system in a certain way, and it serves as well for maintaining position (which accounts for its legitimacy) as for advancing or rising. This mechanism, moreover, hinges centrally on the manipulation of women, and on the manipulation of men *through* women, by senior males in positions of authority. The mechanism thus links the organization of gender relations to ultimate cultural goals, and as such it will play a major role in subsequent discussions. I will sketch it briefly here, and return to it in more detail at various points throughout the essay.

We may begin by taking the point of view of a junior aristocrat seeking to rise in the system. It will be recalled that a descent group consists of senior/superior and junior/inferior "lines," theoretically descended from senior and junior siblings. If a junior line can build itself up in size, strength, and wealth, it may arrive at the possibility of either fissioning off and establishing a full-fledged independent group of its own, or of making a bid for the leadership and dominant position in its own group. (This latter is only possible if the senior line is very impoverished in membership, and/or has no appropriate candidate to succeed to the chiefship. But this state of affairs may itself be the result of the building process of the junior line, during which it attracts many members of the senior line to its ranks [see also Biersack 1974].)

Status advancement through descent-line building is explicitly recognized among the Maori (Best II 1924: 24), but something like it must take place in all Polynesian societies. Thus even where it is not explicitly described, there are references throughout the literature to the importance of maintaining large group size, as well as an interest in weakening other groups by thinning their membership (for example, Buck 1932: 29; Linton 1939: 157; Gifford 1929: 30; Mariner I 1827: 82). Even in those (many) Polynesian societies in which warfare is the more visible (if illegitimate) route to mobility, it may be presumed that descent line and/or descent group building is necessarily operating, for a group would have to attain relatively large size before it could undertake a major military campaign.

Descent line growth, as well as decline and deterioration, must often happen "naturally," as a consequence of demographic fluctuations in different lines. It is also, however, highly manipulable, and in ways that are particularly significant for issues of gender. Specifically, it appears that a father may utilize the bilateral inheritance system, the flexibility of cognatic descent line affiliation, and the flexibility of residence rules, to bring new members and even additional land into his orbit. Because daughters can inherit, sons-in-law with less substantial property stakes in their own lines may be attracted into their wives' lines, while at the same time, given the patrilineal bias in the inheritance structure, they can hold on to their own land and bring it into their affinal line's orbit. And perhaps even more important for this process, the children of an uxorilocal marriage would be more likely to affiliate with their mother's than their father's kin, thus adding significant numbers of people to the line. People, even more than land, are the basis of descent line strength.

We have thus far viewed the process primarily from the point of view of an upwardly mobile junior aristocrat, for whom building up a large descent line could result in major status advancement. With a large group there is the possibility of either fission, in which case the leader becomes the top man in the newly independent unit, or of direct takeover of leadership within the natal unit as the senior line withers and wanes. The process is not all that different for commoners. A commoner cannot actually envision becoming a chief in his lifetime, because he is not by birth a member of the aristocracy from which chiefs are drawn. But on a smaller scale a commoner might build his line to a point at which it behooves a chief to take notice of its strength, and thus to make special efforts to retain its loyalty to himself rather than, say, to his presuming younger brother. Thus the chief might marry one of his daughters into the line, and/or give the line special land grants, and/or appoint its leader to special office, and so forth, all of which (but particularly the first) begins a process of "aristocratization" of the line.

Indeed, even for an individual with no personal ambitions for mobility, there is value in playing the same game, in maintaining the size and strength of the unit, however small and low, of which he is the head. Headship of any significance only exists when there is membership of any significance. There is a sense then in which even the littlest man is actually or potentially engaged in this process.

And finally we must consider the high chiefs themselves, who pursue a slightly different though closely related set of strategies. A chief, like everyone else, would hope to attract uxorilocal sons-in-law, and ultimately to retain children of daughters as well as sons, to maintain or augment the strength of his own particular line. But he also has an interest in the well-being of the descent group as a whole – in its internal cohesiveness and its external relations – because the group, and not just his own line, is his political base. Hence at least some chiefly daughters are exported from the group to forge strategic alliances with other groups, while yet others, as previously noted, might be married down into lower internal lines, to reward them for past services and/or to bind them more closely to the chiefly line. Beneath these varying strategies, however, lies the same thread: enriching, enlarging, and solidifying the descent group through retention of female as well as male kin, the females in turn "binding in" additional members or potentially schismatic existing members.

It should be noted for future reference that even the export of chiefly daughters to other groups for purposes of forging political alliances has a significance different from that of the exogamy typically practiced in unilineal systems. Given the cultural emphasis on descent group endogamy in Polynesia, even exogamous marriages are viewed as "incorporative," or at least centripetal. A Maori "tribe," for example, viewed such marriages as "cords" to "pull" other tribes its way when assistance was needed in war (Best II 1924: 235). Thus the retention of the daughter's or sister's loyalty, if not her actual residential presence, remains crucial to the strategies of status maintenance among chiefs, as it is to strategies of both maintenance and advancement at other levels of the system.

Another way of visualizing this process is to realize that, from the point of view of heads of social units (whether of households, descent lines, or full descent groups) cognatic kinship reckoning creates an in-built problem: The units always have the potential for evaporating out from under the top. Given the fact that everyone has dual affiliation, everyone could theoretically disperse to his or her other set of kin, leaving the head as head of nothing. There is thus great cultural emphasis on centripetal processes, on "pulling," "binding," and "concentrating," accounting among other things for the preference for descent group endogamy, and even in some cases for (chiefly) brother-sister marriage, which "concentrates" the "mana" of the line in which it occurs (see Kirkpatrick 1979). Kinswomen – especially daughters and sisters – are crucial to this "pulling in" process, in ways we have already indicated, and on which we will elaborate more fully in later sections.

Before moving on to a consideration of the treatment of kinswomen, however, it is important to reemphasize that manipulations of descent, marriage, and residence are not ends in themselves. They serve the purpose of maintaining or enhancing status, which are the supreme goals of the system. Much of the ensuing analysis will concentrate on the relationship between descent and marriage manipulations on the one hand, and patterns of gender relations on the other, but such manipulations are means, not ends. The significant analytic relationship remains that between status or prestige on the one hand, and gender and sexuality on the other.

Gender relations

SISTERS AND DAUGHTERS

The emphasis on descent for the reproduction of status; the descent group as the most important social, economic, and political unit; and finally the cognatic and endogamous nature of Polynesian descent groups, all combine to make kin relations the most important relations in society. Within the general domain of kin relations, in turn, the cultural emphasis falls upon siblingship. The sibling axis is both the axis of unity and the axis of division in the system. A solidary group of brothers (we will come to the role of sisters in a moment) is the cultural ideal, forming the structural backbone of a solidary kin group. But there is also incipient division in this group: The question of succession to headship of the unit divides one brother (usually the eldest) from all the others. Given high rates of divorce and remarriage, as well as polygyny among chiefs, there are half-brothers as well, whose claims to succession, like those of junior full brothers, are weaker, but who may well have such designs nonetheless. Sibling unity is the ideal, but sibling rivalry, sometimes violent, is documented throughout the area (Best I 1924: 100, 413; Firth 1963: 166, 330; Buck 1938: 155; Rogers 1977: 172; Mariner I 1827: 137; Mariner II 1827: 112; Oliver 1974: 644, 727, 742).[6]

The respect for sisters, also documented throughout Polynesia, "fits" with the general emphasis on the sibling axis, but is not fully explained by it, and must be explored more fully. The sister is in some sense a "key symbol" (Ortner 1973; Schneider 1968; Turner 1967) in Polynesian culture, and like all good key symbols she opens many doors and guides us to important insights into the inner workings of the system.

Brother–sister and father–daughter relations. Goldman points out that the terms of address for opposite-sex siblings (sister, brother speaking; brother, sister speaking) are throughout the area, and with very few exceptions, built on a stem term that is related to the term for "deity": "Throughout all of the area this one concept of the godlike quality of brother and sister to each other stands as a formidable constant" (1975: 460; see also Firth 1970: 272 and passim). Goldman cautions us against reasoning from terminology to behavior, and indeed the brother–sister relationship has a markedly different character in Western and Eastern Polynesia (see Goldman's chart on the distribution of brother–sister "respects" [1970: 579]).[7] In the West the brother–sister relationship is one of great formality of interaction, or of complete formal avoidance. Cross-siblings in such avoidance relationships do not speak to one another, eat together, sleep under the same roof, or even (in some cases) remain in the room when the other one is present. Above all, the subject of sex must never be raised when an opposite sex sibling is about (Huntsman and Hooper 1975: 425; Mead 1949: 34; Gifford 1929: 21; Goldman 1970: 579).

In the East on the other hand the relationship is close and even intimate. In some cases brothers and sisters are active in facilitating the love affairs of their opposite-sex siblings. In Mangaia, for example, "a brother and sister may ease the way for a sibling's partner of whom they approve" (Marshall 1971: 128; see also Loeb 1926: 65 for Niue, and Firth 1957: 180 for Tikopia. [Tikopia is a western Polynesian society with "eastern" brother–sister relational patterns.]). And in Hawaii, "the most suitable partner" for the king was his sister; their offspring were "sacred" and "divine" (Malo 1903: 80).[8] Thus where, as in these examples, the brother–sister relationship is not marked with formal respect and avoidance, it often appears as having particular intimacy.

The Western Polynesian pattern of formal respect between brother and sister has implications for intergenerational kinship relations. Throughout this part of Polynesia, the father's sister stands in a relationship of exceptional authority over her brother's children (in Tonga, an even higher authority than their father), and the mother's brother stands in a relationship of exceptional indulgence to his sister's children (Huntsman and Hooper 1975: 424; Firth 1957: 196, 199; Mead 1930: 18, 136–45; Gifford 17, 18, 23–5; Kaeppler 1971: passim; Rogers 1977: passim). Father's sisters and mother's brothers also often have important ritual responsibilities vis-à-vis their cross nieces and nephews, from which the mother and father may be excluded (Huntsman and Hooper 1975: 424; Mead 1930: 27, 29. See also Handy 1923: 71 and Suggs 1966: 127 for an Eastern case of this).

Concerning the complementary issue of great intimacy between brother and sister carrying into the succeeding generation, it should be noted that although brother-sister marriage is rare, and is restricted to high aristocracy, first cousin marriage is not uncommon throughout the area. Mostly it takes place between cross-cousins, that is, between children of opposite-sex siblings, and so carries the theme of the special relationship between opposite-sex sibling further. In the Marquesas it is the preferred form of marriage, at all levels of the society (Suggs 1966: 127; Handy 1923: 71), but in most cases it is preferred and prevalent primarily among the aristocracy, and optional for members of other strata (Buck 1938: 130–2; Gifford 1929: 16; Oliver 1974: 764; Handy and Pukui 1958: 109). Because cross-cousins are classed with siblings in many Polynesian societies (Goldman 1970: 464), cross-cousin marriage is sometimes culturally recognized as marriage between "brothers" and "sisters," and hence as a violation of the incest taboo (Gifford 1929: 22; Goldman 1970: 464) – which is nonetheless culturally rationalized in various ways.[9]

It will be useful before pursuing the discussion further, to expand our sense of the sister, and to see her as, at the same time, the daughter of her and her brothers' father. The cultural emphasis on her as sister makes sense in terms of the overall emphasis on the sibling unit, as the unit of both necessary solidarity and potential division over time. In fact however the treatment of "daughters" is virtually constant throughout the area, even where (mostly in eastern Polynesia) the special respects, avoidances, and obligations of the brother–sister relationship are not culturally elaborated. It may be tentatively suggested that the sister avoidance complex is a particular variant on the more general pattern of special treatment of daughters. But we need not decide whether the daughter or the sister is the more "basic" figure in this drama. It will simply be useful to be able to shift flexibly between her two aspects as the occasion arises.

It will be recalled that daughters as well as sons normally inherit at least usufructory rights to real property throughout the area.[10] Although there is a general preference for, or at least a tendency toward, virilocal residence, there is also a high rate of uxorilocal residence, mostly for reasons of the wife's property. Uxorilocal residence appears to carry no shame or social disability for the in-marrying husband, nor is he placed in a subordinate or dependent position vis-à-vis his affines, because affinal relations, unlike kin relations, are not inherently hierarchical. Thus uxorilocal residence may often have attractions for the individual male, especially a junior son/brother with no particular prospects of succession in his own line, who can at least better his economic situation if not his status prospects.

From the point of view of his wife's kin, in turn, in-marrying sons-in-law are also highly attractive. Not only do such sons-in-law themselves add strength to their affinal descent lines. They also probably add their children who, because of residing with the mother's kin and working their land, will tend to affiliate with their mother's line rather than their father's. Moreover, the in-marrying sons-in-law may also add land. A woman's land rights generally revert to her kinsmen after she dies and cannot be passed on to her children, unless she and the children remain on the land and affiliate with her father's and brothers' line. Men's rights, on the other hand, are "real" and heritable; even if they move away their claims are stronger on retaining the land and passing it on to their children. The uxorilocal son-in-law may thus add himself, his children and his land to his wife's group. Virilocal residence, the "normal" pattern, maintains the status quo; it neither adds nor subtracts much of significance for the wife's or husband's line. Uxorilocal residence, on the other hand, has very strong building power for the wife's line.

It is thus clear that enlarging a descent line by means other than, or in addition to, natural increase entails holding on to daughters (or, from the brothers' point of view, sisters) and using them to bring in men as in-marrying sons-in-law. [11] It is this dynamic that provides the basis for understanding the peculiar treatment of Polynesian daughters: enforcing their virginity while at the same time beautifying them and making them more sexually attractive. This pattern makes sense if we see the first part, control of virginity, as a symbolic "holding on" to the daughter through close regulation of her sexual behavior, and the second part, the enhancement of her sexual attractions, as an expression of her function as "bait" for her descent line. The two practices, in other words, are really two sides of the same coin, the coin of her role in the descent line building game. Let us now explore some of the ramifications of controlling and beautifying Polynesian daughters.

Virginity. "Holding on" to daughters may begin early, with special affection and indulgence accorded them in childhood by their fathers (see Firth 1963: 154; Kaeppler 1971: 191). But the fullest manifestation of this tendency is seen in the guarding of unmarried daughters' virginity. The most fully elaborated form of the sexually controlled daughter/sister in turn is to be seen in the institutionalized "sacred maid," found throughout the aristocracy of Western Polynesia. I will begin with her, and then show how the principles of her role, minus the full institutional paraphernalia, are to be seen operating throughout the entire area, and through all levels of society.

The "sacred maid" complex has been described by Mead for Samoa. The Samoan sacred maid, or *taupo*, is supposed to be the chief's sisters' daughter, but often in fact it is his daughter (Mead 1930: 26). [12] The *taupo* position is one of ritual responsibility and honor. She heads the organization of unmarried girls and untitled men's wives that has the responsibility of hosting and entertaining visiting parties that come to the village. Her position is actually ritually superior to that of the chiefly heir and successor, the *manaia*, who heads the organization of unmarried and untitled men (Mead 1930: 14). She even receives more respect than the wives of high chiefs (Mead 1930: 184).[13] Her marriage is a village affair (Mead 1930: 27) and all the women of the village make mats and tapa for her dowry (Mead 1930: 70). In a real sense she is symbolically the daughter/sister of the entire village, and its prestige is tied up with her prestige (Mead 1949: 65). *But*: The *taupo* is under strictest sexual constraint. She has to retain her virginity until marriage, and if she is seduced, it is dealt with by the *fono*, the governing council, as a public crime punishable by the drowning or beating to death of her seducer (Mead 1930: 17). Her marriage may be publicly consummated (Mead 1949: 63), but even if it is not, there is public display of the proof of her virginity in the form of a bloodstained mat, after the consummation. If she is found not to be a virgin, she is beaten by her (female) relatives (Mead 1949: 56).

A similar institution is reported for pre-sixteenth-century Tonga (Rogers 1978); in modern Tonga all the chief's unmarried daughters are called *taupo* (the term borrowed from Samoa) and must be chaste (Gifford 1929: 129), but the specially favored figure is the *tamaha*, the chief's sister's daughter (Gifford 1929: 74, 79, 80). A *taupo*-type institution is mentioned for Mangaia (Mead 1930: 93), and one observer notes in modern times that the only virgins and/or "old maids" in the Mangaian village he studied were from a high chiefly family (Marshall 1971: 130). In Mangareva, if the first born of the first wife of a high aristocrat is a female, she is given the special status of *tepeiru*, with very high social rank. She often receives "exaltation by the people of her district, and some *tepeiru* went on to become de facto rulers of their groups" (Buck 1938: 156). Among the (ancient) Maori the institution closely resembled that in Samoa. The *puhi*, or sacred maid, was usually the eldest daughter of a chief of high rank "who was elected or chosen as a person of consequence and made tapu in the sense of prohibited. She had to remain a virgin until marriage" (Best I 1924: 450). She often had ceremonial functions, and was highly respected, even "petted" and deferred to (1924: 351). "Some famous *puhi* became renowned chieftainesses in later life, and commanded respect of their own and other tribes." (1924: 453). But they were "sometimes late marrying because their families were so particular about the choice of mate" (1924: 450). And finally, in Pukapuka, the sacred maid – "an eldest daughter, eldest sister, or even father's sister" – is initiated with special rites and never marries at all, "remaining a guarded virgin for life." She is a fully sacred figure who links the chief to the gods (Hecht 1977: 196–8).

It is important to note first that the sacred maid position is one of high – sometimes very high – honor. This may be taken as, among other things, an expression of the genuine value of the daughter or sister who remains affiliated with her natal group, in line with the arguments presented earlier.

In addition to great public honor, the most obvious aspect of the sacred maid's situation is her virginity, which is culturally stressed and forcefully protected. What is symbolized by her virginity is not her own self-control (as in occasional, usually religious, male celibacy) but the control by her kinsmen over her behavior (see especially Shore, this collection). As a symbol of the structure discussed earlier, the daughter's virginity thus respresents the kinsmen's "hold" on her, necessary for the process of building or simply maintaining descent line size and strength.

The process of descent line maintenance is particularly important for chiefs, whose very position depends upon heading a large, internally cohesive, and externally well-connected group that is his economic and political base. We said earlier that chiefs may deploy their daughters in a variety of ways to achieve this end, including retaining them in uxorilocal marriages, marrying them down into lower lines of the descent group, or sending them out in geographically exogamous marriages. But we also noted that all of these methods (including exogamy) assume the notion of the daughter as a centripetal force. It is vital that she be "held" symbolically even when sent out in marriage for strategic purposes.

Not surprisingly, then, the virginity of chiefly daughters is nearly *universally* required throughout Polynesia, and backed by physical force, even where there is no sacred maid complex at all (Goldman 1970: 564). Among commoners, however, there is also a generally reported tendency to oversee daughters' sex lives more closely than sons' (e.g., Buck 1932: 34; Suggs 1966: 64; Gifford 1929: 21, 191). This would be consistent with the point that status mobility through descent line building is an avenue potentially open to all. In general however, commoner control of daughters' sexual behavior is far less strict than among the aristocracy, because the chances of mobility for commoners are clearly more remote (Goldman 1970: 564).

Sex as theft. Although high-status girls are heavily controlled, and lower-status girls are at least more closely watched than boys, this does not mean that there is little premarital sexual activity in Polynesia – far from it. Boys, as we shall see, are encouraged to be as sexually active as possible, and most of their sexual activity takes place precisely with these same girls, Paternal/fraternal control thus does not actually block premarital sexual activity, but it does mean that sex with an unmarried girl is in some sense "stolen" from her father and/or her brothers. It is in the context of a view of much of premarital sex as "theft" in turn that a fairly wide range of Polynesian sexual practices become intelligible: the semiinstitutionalized form of (quasi) rape called "sleep crawling"; the general interest in deflowering virgins; institutionalized elopement and marriage by capture; and the displays of hymeneal blood and other signals of "triumph" at weddings. Not all premarital sex in Polynesia is construed by the parties involved as "theft," but the proliferation of sexual *patterns* with theft connotations requires explanation. I will say a few words about each.

Sleep crawling, first, entails stealthily and unexpectedly entering a girl's house at night and having sex with her, usually over her protest and resistance. In Mangaia it is called *motoro*, and is seen as a sign of masculinity. A man who gains sexual access to a girl through formal engagement is seen as a weakling. The important thing is to sweet-talk her, rather than to use force, so that she will not scream and wake up her family (Marshall 1971: 129). In

Rakahanga *motoro* is said to be noncoercive, but the emphasis again is on not waking the father, who will beat the boy if he is discovers him (Vayda 1961: 204). Sleep crawling is also common in Mangareva (*motoro* – Buck 1938: 120), in Samoa (*moetotolo* – Mead 1930: 61; Shore, this collection)[14] and in Tahiti (*mafera* – Oliver 1974: 365),[15] in the latter two cases apparently coercive. The institution expresses well the fact that, because unmarried girls are under the control of their fathers and brothers, sex with them must be "stolen." This is the case even when they are consenting, as they sometimes are in sleep crawling, and usually are in other contexts. Indeed the fact that coercion in sleep crawling might range from none to total shows that the girl's personal interest or lack of it is irrelevant, for the practice has more to do with her structural position than with her sentiments. On the other hand, the fact that there *is* often strong coercion, that sleep crawling often approximates rape, will require further discussion, and I will return to this aspect of it later.

The other great sport of adolescent sexual activities is deflowering virgins, the interest in which is nearly universal throughout Polynesia. Deflowering a virgin is a major event for a boy, and boys "count coup" as to how many virgins they have deflowered (see Firth 1957: 519; Marshall 1971: 151; Mead 1930: 95–6). In Tikopia a boy might undergo a private religious ritual for success in deflowering virgins (Firth 1957: 523). Most men also claim to want virgin wives, or at least girls who were virgins when they first got to them (Firth 1957: 514; Loeb 1926: 75). Because girls in fact do not make much effort to retain their virginity, the interest in the conquest of virgins has again less to do with conquering the girl, than in succeeding in taking something that "belongs" to her kinsmen.[16]

Elopement and marriage by capture again carry the same message. In Samoa the great thing is to elope with the *taupo* of the next village, stealing her out from under the collective nose of her kin (Mead 1930: 95). More generally, elopement is the standard form of marriage in Samoa, modern Tonga, and among Tikopian commoners (Mead 1930: 95; 1949: 64–7; Rogers 1964; Beaglehole 1941: 98; Firth 1957: 439). Among the Tikopian aristocracy, on the other hand, virtually all marriage is by capture. The woman is selected by the groom's kin, forcibly taken from her household to the waiting bridegroom, and held down for her first (rape) intercourse with her husband (Firth 1957: 442, 450). It is considered a shame for the bridegroom if the girl is not a virgin (Firth 1957: 451). The capture is often resisted violently, in a more or less pitched battle, by the girl's family (as well as by the girl herself), and later often retaliated in a countercapture (1965: 470).

Finally, in this cluster of patterns expressing the notion of sex as theft from the girl's kin, I would also include the pattern of public display of tokens of virginity at marriage, reported for Samoa (Mead 1930: 95–6), and for Tikopia (Firth 1965: 464). Tongans too expect their women to be virgins at marriage, although they dispense with the public display of hymeneal blood as "indelicate" (Mariner I 1827: 141). Note however that at one Tui Tonga's wedding, a man at the door of the nuptial chamber announced the bedding down of the bride and groom with "three hideous yells (similar to the war-whoop) . . . followed up immediately by the loud and repeated sound of the conch'' (Mariner I 1827: 124). In all three cases the demonstrations appear as ''triumphal,'' expressing *both* the boy's triumph in ''getting'' the girl, *and* her kinsmen's triumph in having successfully guarded her virginity until then.[17]

To recapitulate: A girl has real value to her descent line, particularly if she sustains her affiliation with it and brings in her husband, his land, and their children. There is thus structural motivation for ''holding on'' to a daughter/sister. This ''holding on'' is symbolically expressed through control of her virginity. The virgin both displays her kinsmen's symbolic retention of her and, because virginity is defined as highly honorable, expresses her genuine value to her group. At the same time the control structure means that sex with her must be ''taken,'' ''stolen,'' or otherwise forcefully appropriated, even when she presents herself, as she often does, as a consenting party. Hence the prevalence of various forms of sexual theft – sleep crawling, marriage by capture, triumphal defloration of virgins, and the like.

We have seen that some of these sexual forms are violent, not only vis-à-vis the girl's family, but vis-à-vis the girl herself. In fact the full range of sexual violence has yet to be explored and accounted for. In addition to the various forms already discussed, there is a fairly high incidence of plain rape, both by individual males, and by gangs. In order to understand this, as well as to understand the full significance of the daughter/sister in general, we must explore further the symbolic treatment of this figure.

Beautification. For the full process of building or even sustaining a descent line to work itself out, the girl must not only be retained by her kin but must also bring in a husband. The Pukapukan sacred maid who remains celibate for her entire life is an extreme symbol of the first part of the process, but most sacred maids, and indeed most daughters, however closely guarded they may have been, eventually marry. If one side of the symbolic coin is strong control of the girl's sexual behavior, rendering her remote if not wholly inaccessible, the other side entails enhancing her attractions and her value. Hence the apparently contradictory practice of elaborately beautifying the girl while keeping her under surveillance and control. The daughter/sister is clearly being used as ''bait.''

It should be remembered that her value is already high. Economically she has her inheritance that, if the boy is willing to join her group, becomes more ''real'' and transmissible to her and her husband's children. Ritually too her status is high. Sacred maids have formal status superiority, but all virgins have the honor that derives from virginity itself. In other words the guarding of her virginity is also part of her general social enhancement.

Beyond all of this, however, there are direct and systematic efforts aimed at enhancing a girl's beauty and sexual desirability. In most cases the beautification practices are combined with the restraint and/or seclusion of the girl, thus showing rather conclusively the link between retaining her as a virgin, and treating her as sexual ''bait.'' In Tonga, ''special care [is] taken of the complexion of a girl of rank.'' Her skin is lightened through the use of various preparations, and she is kept sitting in the shade as much as possible. She sits on soft cushions to keep her buttocks and thighs soft and smooth, and sits in such a way as to keep her ankles from being marred, all of which both beautifies and immobilizes her simultaneously. A daughter of a very high chief is bathed and oiled every evening, after which her knees are tied together and she is laid down on her side. The position is said to serve the dual function of keeping her elbows smooth and securing her against sexual attack (Gifford 1929: 129–30). In Mangaia the upper ranks seclude young people (why both sexes are included will be explained shortly) for bleaching and fattening. Mangaian girls also have their clitorises lengthened, and are given instruction by older women in achieving orgasm (Marshall 1971: 110, 124, 122). Tahiti too has both fattening and skin bleaching, and girls are "trained" to be pleasing and charming to men (Oliver 1974: 257, 431, 783; Henry 1928: 274). In the Marquesas adolescent girls are kept at home for skin bleaching (and in some cases tattooing) and for vaginal treatments aimed at beautifying their sexual organs (Suggs 1966: 88, 39–42, 65–6; Handy 1923: 75. See also Hecht 1977: 190 on Pukapuka, and Handy and Pukui 1958: 94 on Hawaii.)

The girl in these cases is almost wholly turned into a symbolic object by her kin. The result is sometimes formally displayed for the appreciation of the young males who are its targets. In the Marquesas there is "ritual display" of the girls' bodies and genitalia (Suggs 1966: 88). In Mangareva there are "beauty shows" at which secluded children are brought out and displayed (Buck 1938: 127–8). And although these cases are somewhat extreme (the Marquesas in particular appear extreme in many aspects of their sexual culture, although clearly within the Polynesian range) the principle of displaying daughters and sisters as passive objectified attractors of men is seen in other cases as well. Among the Maori the sacred maids ("*puhi*") attract "young men, singly or in parties, [who come] from distant parts to see them and try to find favor in their eyes" (Best I 1924: 450). And in Mangaia, according to hearsay information Best picked up among the Maori, "girls of good family stayed in a collective house before marriage. At the age of marriage they were lined up against the wall of the house, and young men of rank would come in and line up and look them over. Each man then picked out one and if she were agreeable... they were... married" (Best I 1924: 453; see also Handy and Pukui 1958: 102 on Hawaii).

Elucidating the consistent cultural tendency to use a daughter or sister as sexual bait to "pull in" (desirable) men also allows us to account for what would otherwise be some rather discordant reports concerning post-contact Polynesian prostitution. In the Marquesas, Tahiti, and Mangaia, girls are reported to be prostituted, mainly to Europeans, by their fathers and/or brothers (Suggs 1966: 64; Oliver 1974: 356; Marshall 1971: 152). Given the overall Polynesian respect for sisters, and the special protection of daughters, this pattern would make no sense at all unless it were realized that the special protection of these girls relates in part precisely to their value as centripetal forces, used to attract men and/or their valuables into the women's families. In the case of European men what is apparently being "drawn in" is the men's superior *mana*, via their insemination of the women (Sahlins n.d.).

Rape. The discussion developed thus far also provides us with most of the pieces necessary to account for the prevalence of rape in Polynesia. I include here ordinary individual rape, gang rape, sleep crawling where it is reported to be typically coercive, and marriage by capture and/or abduction. Rape and gang rape are reported for Tahiti (Oliver 1974: 363, 607), Mangaia (Marshall 1971: 152), Samoa (Shore, this collection), and the Marquesas (Suggs 1966: 63, 96, 120). Samoa, Tahiti, and Mangaia are all reported to have sleep crawling with fairly strong coercion (Mead 1949: 61; Oliver 1974: 365; Marshall 1971: 129). Tikopia has marriage by capture, with rape consummation, and even the reportedly less libidinous (Best I 1924: 450) Maori occasionally forcibly abduct unwilling brides (Best I 1924: 462).[18]

Reported motives for rape include anger at, and retaliation for, rejection, and/or an intention to "tame" a woman who gets out of line. Mead reports anger over rejection as a motive for coercive sleep crawling in Samoa (1949: 61), and it is generally a rejected Maori suitor who forcibly abducts his bride (Best I 1924: 462). In the Marquesas girls "who do not receive the advances of men" are often raped (Suggs 1966: 63). Jealous and "difficult" Marquesan wives may also be raped by their husbands to bring them into line (Suggs 1966: 120). And in Mangaia gang rape is said to be perpetrated "to tame a haughty girl" (Marshall 1971: 152). It should be noted that the cultures treat these actions as semiacceptable and, as it were, understandable. Although a girl's kinsmen may avenge her honor (or their own) by beating up the boy – *if* she reports the incident to them – the *public* sanctions range from light to nil. In Mangaia the penalty is less than that for stealing a pig (Marshall 1971: 152).[19]

In light of our earlier discussions, much of this information is now explicable. Rape presupposes the resistance of the girl (or woman), and it seems reasonable to suggest that girls accept the symbolic value placed by their kin on their virginity, their sexuality, and indeed their persons. They would tend to consider themselves sought-after and valuable objects who may voluntarily withhold sex altogether, and who always at least retain the right to pick and choose their lovers. Because girls and women are in fact genuinely valued by their kin, and in some sense "by society," their stance is consistent with their status, but to men it may appear "stuck-up" and haughty. Hence the "taming" aspects of rape motivation. But a girl's haughty stance might not in itself provoke sexual assault, were it not for the other message the girl is transmitting, a message *also* consistent with her self-perception as encouraged by her treatment in her kin group: enhanced sexual attractiveness. I suggest that it is the combined and contradictory message transmitted by the girl – "come hither/go away" – that is so provoking to the men. The permissive cultural attitude toward rape would moreover seem to recognize the "legitimacy," as it were, of this sort of reaction to this sort of bind.[20]

This discussion of the (non-kin) male reaction to the young woman's presentation and self-presentation now brings us to the question of what young men are up to themselves as this stage of life. As we turn to a consideration of adolescent males, it is important to keep in mind that girls, although more closely watched than boys, are hardly sexually unavailable. Whereas sacred maids and high chiefs' daughters exhibit the extremes of both control and enhancement, other girls are treated with somewhat less of both. Indeed as one moves down the social ladder, the control appreciably diminishes and the availability correspondingly increases. On the other hand, boys and men of all classes are subject to virtually no constraints. On the contrary, they are expected by society – by their seniors, their peers, and the girls themselves – to be as sexually active, skilled, and successful as possible. We must now consider some of the sources and consequences of this pattern.

BROTHERS

Let us return once again to the dynamics of status maintenance and mobility, this time from the point of view of male siblings. We must first distinguish between the select individual who will succeed to the headship (whether of household, descent line, or kin group as a whole), and all the rest of the siblings who will not. The successor is usually, but not always, the first born; I will refer to him as the senior sibling whether he is typically the eldest or not, and to all the rest as juniors. Whereas there is only one senior son per father, there are potentially a large number of juniors, including not only the full brothers of the senior son, but also the sons of secondary wives and/or concubines, and of other marriages of the father. The senior sibling is sometimes the metaphoric "chief" of his juniors, who are his metaphoric "commoners" (Buck 1932: 45; Handy and Pukui 1958:199); in Tonga junior siblings become "virtual servants" of senior siblings (Gifford 1929: 112), and in Hawaii the junior siblings are metaphorically their senior siblings' "slaves" (Malo 1903: 96).

The structural possibilities of, and constraints upon, the life careers of senior and junior siblings are as different as their statuses. The senior son/ brother has an unambiguous position as heir to the headship, and an unambiguous duty to marry and reproduce the line. The junior siblings' situation, on the other hand, is much more ambiguous, both with respect to their prospects for succession, and with respect to their obligation to marry and reproduce. It is these ambiguities that we shall explore in this section.

We have seen that there is a tendency to try to hold onto sisters, for the enrichment of the group and hence for the (potential) advancement of its status. If a sister stays and brings in resources, both human and material, this represents a gain for her kin. However, given the status superiority of husband to wife (which will be explored later), it is considered "normal" for daughters/sisters to reside virilocally, and to merge themselves and their children with their husbands' lines. Thus, if they stay with their kin it is a gain, but if they leave, it is not seen as a loss. Brothers, on the other hand, are the backbone of the group, and their unity is essential. A brother who fissions off with his descendants and followers is taking the very stuff of the group with him. By and large, it appears that full brothers, particularly in families of any substance, normally do stay together and share a concern for the welfare of the unit as a whole, but this outcome is never assured.

The potential for split is obviously situated at the point of marriage and reproduction. An unmarried junior brother has no wife and children dividing his interests between his paternal/fraternal group and his own. He works the paternal land, participates in the work projects of the paternal household, and is simply a contributing member of the group. We thus begin to see some of the systemic "interest" in delaying, if not prohibiting, the marriage of junior brothers. In fact, in Tikopia, the marriage of junior brothers is discouraged altogether. They are expected to remain single (though not celibate) for life, and to form a cohesive body of "executive officials" for the senior brother who has the position of leadership, and who marries and reproduces the next leader and his fraternal executives (Firth 1975: 188). The Maori show the same pattern in less extreme form: "Males seem to have awaited more mature age until marrying. They often took wives when middle aged, sometimes slave-class women, or a widow of a brother . . . " (Best I 1924: 450). And in Tahiti too, as we shall see, junior siblings could join a "society" with a positive ethic in favor of singleness and against reproduction.

Normally however there is an important counterforce that favors eventual marriage and reproduction by junior siblings: the reproduction of the hierarchical structure itself. For it is the junior siblings who produce the junior descent lines, ranked collectively below the senior descent lines, and forming the commoners of whom the chiefs are chiefs. The notion of commoners as descendants of junior siblings of chiefs is culturally articulated. The Tongarevans call the younger brother "the link with the people" (Buck 1932: 45), and the same idea is expressed in most other Polynesian societies (see Mishkin 1961: 434; Firth 1963: 312; Buck 1938: 145; Malo 1903: 96; Gifford 1929: 112; Mariner II 1827: 90). Junior siblings should thus ultimately marry and reproduce not only for the maintenance of the size and "weight" of their descent line, but for the reproduction of the hierarchical structure of "classes" within the group and within society as a whole.

At the same time they (and their descendants) must remain subordinate and loyal to the senior brother and/or the senior line of the group. The actual incidence of junior full siblings fissioning off and making war on senior brothers for the headship is nearly impossible to determine, but was probably, in fact, rare. The incidence of half-brother and cousin "treason" was probably somewhat higher (see Mariner I 1827: 137; Oliver 1974: 742; Rogers 1977: 1072). Most commonly, a junior brother might simply replace the senior brother at the head of the unit if the senior appears less competent. This is always open as a possibility, even in the strictest primogeniturial systems (Goldman 1970: 26). In theory the junior brother should simply hold the headship until a more competent member of the senior line comes of age, but in practice a strong junior can probably arrange things so that succession passes to his own descendants.

All of which explains the fact that sibling rivalry, in the form of suspicion and mistrust, seems to go from senior to junior sibling rather than the other way around as one might have expected. In a hierarchical society, it is "ungrammatical" for a junior to envy a senior; the privileges accorded to the senior are based on a superiority seen as "natural." Seniors, on the other hand, may well suspect the loyalty and subordinate solidarity of juniors, given the juniors' potential for ascent just outlined. Thus both Tonga and

Tahiti have legends of older brothers killing their younger siblings (Mariner II 1827: 112; Oliver 1974: 727). Elder-to-younger sibling rivalry is also documented for Tikopia, where it is apparently encouraged by the fact that fathers tend to favor, sentimentally and materially, their younger sons (Firth 1963: 166). A similar pattern is seen among the Maori, where the youngest son is often spoiled and petted by the father, and tends to be seen as more intrinsically clever and talented than the eldest (Mishkin 1961: 455n.; see also Handy and Pukui 1958: 46 on Hawaii).

Junior siblings then are in a peculiar and ambiguous position within the structure. Particularly in high-ranking families, they are both high (by parentage) and potentially low (as progenitors of subordinate lines), but also low (by birth order) and potentially high (by replacing the senior or by heading their own independent groups). They are, we begin to see, a liminal category in the social structure, and it is the varying and contradictory aspects of their position that provide the key to many features of male adolescent sexual culture.

Polynesian adolescence may be characterized as a period in which boys form cohorts, the primary focus of which, and the primary topic of interest of which, is sex: having a wide range and a large number of sexual relations with girls. Because elite girls are, for the most part, well watched and controlled, it appears that they participate in adolescent activities, if at all, only on a very reduced scale. Similarly, there is good evidence that, in many cases, the most senior elite males, those who will actually succeed to the titles and headships, are often de facto removed from participation. In some cases they, like elite girls, are secluded for fattening, tattooing, or skin bleaching. In other cases they are betrothed in early childhood, or forced as youths into early marriage (see Firth 1957: 440; Best I 1924: 454–5; Malo 1903: 80; Handy and Pukui 1958: 105). The social composition of adolescent cohorts thus primarily includes (*a*) *junior* elite males, (*b*) commoner males, and (*c*) commoner females.

Adolescent social activities include making assignations, having a large number of sexual affairs, and exchanging information on such affairs as well as sexual folklore in general. In addition, boys and girls spend time in same-sex and/or cross-sex groups beautifying themselves, composing songs, poems, and entertainments, and engaging in pleasant sports, games, and amusements. For the most part they do little productive work. In many Polynesian societies they live apart from their parents, either in sex-segregated "dormitories," or in individual separate residences in their parents' compounds; in other cases there are collective houses where young people may congregate and sleep when they wish to be away from home. (See Suggs [1966: 175] for a list of ten cases, in addition to the Marquesas which are his primary focus. See also Firth [1963: 82].)

We may now consider this "complex" of institutionalized sexual activeness for adolescent males in relation to the structural problems of the male sibling bond already discussed. From a purely fuctional point of view, Polynesian adolescence may be seen as both solidifying the sibling bond *and* contributing to the slight downward mobility of junior siblings, thus reproducing correct united-but-hierarchical relations between brothers and their descendants.

In the first place, the marriage and (legitimate) reproduction of the junior sibling is simply delayed, with his happy and voluntary compliance. The junior brother thus remains longer in his subordinate and dependent role in his paternal/fraternal household (although the behavioral freedom and independence masks this dependency to some extent). At the same time, Polynesian adolescent culture emphasizes the importance of large numbers of affairs with a range of girls. Adolescent boys should play the field. Strong attachment to any one girl is antithetical to a proper adolescence, and may have the unfortunate effect of leading to marriage. The pattern of low emotional involvement, particularly with members of the opposite sex, but more generally with any individual, has been reported by some observers to begin in early childhood (Mead 1949: 118; Levy 1973: 496), and is both expressed and reinforced during the adolescent period of playing the field. The effect of this emotional detachment is not only to leave the sibling bond relatively unthreatened by competing attachments during adolescence, but possibly also to establish (or reinforce) a pattern that will continue after marriage as well. As we shall see in the next section, the husband-wife bond is relatively "weak," and there is a sense in which husbands (and wives) remain Polynesian-style adolescents for life, with frequent adultery, divorce, and serial monogamy.

Both delay of marriage and encouragement of a wide range of noninvolving affairs support the cohesiveness of the sibling bond and of kin (as against sexual/marital) relations in general. At the same time the social organization of adolescence encourages the downward social identification and even downward mobility of junior siblings. As already noted, male adolescent cohorts contain both junior elites and commoners. The elite boy is often the leader, formal or informal, of the group, and its social focus (Suggs 1966: 91, 95; Mead 1930: 14; Gifford 1929: 128; Firth 1963: 392; Oliver 1974: 961). As such he gains a sense of prestige and leadership in relation to *his* structural juniors, shifting his sense of himself from one of junior elite to, in a sense, senior commoner, which is precisely the shift that must take place in his orientation in order for him fully to accept his mediating place in the hierarchy, as "link with the people."

There is an analogous effect in his heterosexual relations. Because elite girls are largely kept from participating in the assignations and affairs (which does not fully prevent the young men from trying to court and seduce them, but which makes it all somewhat more difficult), it is the lower-status girls who are more sexually available. The chances are thus reasonably good that a boy will eventually marry a girl of slightly lower status than himself (radical differences in status between husband and wife are generally frowned upon). The slightly lower status of the wife is important for not contradicting the normative domestic superiority of the husband, which will be discussed later.[21] More important for the present argument, lower status of the wife will generally insure lower status of the children because, as noted earlier, the social status of the children appears to be determined more by the mother than the father in the case of status discrepancies between the two. Thus the greater availability of lower-status girls in adolescent activities increases the possibility of a junior elite boy marrying and reproducing in a slight downward direction, which is desirable for the reproduction of correct hierarchical relations between his and his elder brother's descendants.[22]

But enough of functions. There is also a sense in which adolescence is *formally*, as well as functionally, appropriate to the structural situation of junior male siblings. The organization of the cohorts and their typical behavioral patterns, as well as the patterning of the sexual relations themselves, may be seen to encode and express the structural features of the junior sibling position already discussed. Sons and brothers, like daughters and sisters, are simultaneously symbols and actors within their structural positions.

Specifically, just as the junior sibling position may be seen as a liminal one, so too the organization of adolescent activity has typical "liminal" qualities (Turner 1967; van Gennep 1960). First, adolescent sexual activity, or even hints thereof, has to be invisible to society at large. It takes place in special houses or dormitories, or else in the bush or on the beach, and properly at night in the dark (see, for example, Shore, this collection). In many Polynesian societies opposite-sex adolescents, particularly individuals who are having sexual relations with one another, do not mix at all in public and/or during the day (Marshall 1971: 127; Loeb 1926: 88; Buck 1938: 183; Handy and Pukui 1958: 171; Oliver 1974: 613).[23]

In addition to being "outside" the structure, adolescent activity typically has certain *anti*structural qualities. Maori young men show off by "violating minor tapus" (Mishkin 1961: 453). Marquesan and Tongan young men raid people's food storehouses (Handy 1923: 97; Mariner I 1827: 78). Sleep crawling, in which the boy both "steals" the daughter under the father's nose, and has illicit sexual intercourse *inside* the house, surely has the same antistructural quality, as does dramatically eloping with the *taupo* in Samoa, and perhaps eloping with any girl. Modern Tahitian youths even risk "a little incest" for the excitement and virility of it all (Hooper 1976: 235–6). But the fullest development of antistructural forms and symbols is seen in the most fully institutionalized adolescent organization, the (now defunct) Tahitian *arioi*. Its members were "communalistic" with respect to property, they went about giving "lewd plays and performances," during which they might "snatch the tapa clothing off the women in the audience." Their plays involved social satire, including "making jokes of high personages." In some contexts "they broke all the tabus" (Oliver 1974: 225, 913–62 passim; Henry 1928: 230–40 passim).

But it is important to emphasize that, despite the many extrastructural and antistructural qualities of adolescent cohorts throughout Polynesia, *rank is always maintained*. In most, as noted, the elite boys are the groups' informal leaders. And in the Tahitian *arioi*, which had a formal structure of ranks and offices, only elite boys could occupy the upper ranks and higher offices (Oliver 1974: 961). The combination of both structure and antistructure in these cohorts thus expresses faithfully the double aspect of the junior sibling's position, as both (ideally) committed to his hierarchical relations and (potentially) schismatic from them.

Why sex? It could be argued that adolescent male sexual activity functions, socially and psychologically, as a cathartic mechanism for potentially disruptive junior siblings. All but the most elite individuals are encouraged to waste themselves in socially inconsequential but personally absorbing sexual activity, as well as in games and sports that may be seen as having many of the same effects. The Samoans, in fact, classify sex with other forms of "play" (Mead 1930: 84), and Tongans liken it to the sport of pigeon snaring (Gifford 1929: 117). Furthermore, in both sex and sports, with their aspects of "winning" and "triumphing," young men get to play at power and status in ways that have few real-world effects, but yet presumably satisfy desires for prestige felt by all in these status-conscious societies.

The catharsis argument may well be appropriate but hardly tells the whole story. Junior males are potentially disruptive, for various structural reasons, in many societies, but there are alternative ways of controlling them. It must be recalled at this point that the "problem" of junior males centers about their marriage and reproduction, which are both socially motivated (for maintaining the size and strength of the kin group, and for reproducing hierarchical organization) and countermotivated (as potentially schismatic). The "solution" to the problem of junior siblings would thus intrinsically tend to focus, at least in part, on sexual and reproductive behavior. In other words, the first answer to the question "why sex?" is that sex is in fact central to the problem at hand.

It is, however, possible to carry the argument further, through an exploration of the cultural meanings of sex and reproduction. Both sex and reproduction in Polynesia were, in the past, deeply involved in religious notions of the original creation of the cosmos, of ongoing creation and creative power, and of the ongoing fertility of the land.[24] The gods were born from the sexual union between (male) Sky and (female) Earth. All of the gods were male. Humans were begat by a god fashioning a physical female form from (nondivine) earth, then vivifying her with his breath and mating with her. The process of cosmic creation is a continuing process: " . . . creation was not believed to be one series of events accomplished in a distant past, but to proceed continuously in all time through fertilization" (Handy 1927: 24). The *mana*, the "natural" energy or power upon which success and efficacy in all human enterprises depends, was itself in its original essence procreative power (1927: 27). "*Mana* was primarily associated with nature's superior, divine aspect, with male procreative energy, with light, . . . [and with] life" (1927: 35). The Polynesians "made generation, operative through sexual union, a universal principle of their natural philosophy" (1927: 143).

The gods were responsible in an ongoing way for the fertility of the land. It was apparently thought that their divine libido needed to be stimulated and aroused in order to get them to perform their fertilizing function. This was the rationale for the extensive use of erotic chanting and dancing in religious ritual, as well as for sexual orgies in ritual contexts, especially during "the season of abundance " surrounding harvest: "The erotic dancing . . . which was in its origin a form of worship, was designed to stimulate and bring into action the *mana* of the gods who were believed to be animated by the same emotions as men, and on whose procreative activities the fecundity of human beings, the earth and sea depended'' (Handy 1927: 210; see also 307–8). The idea that sexual arousal raises productivity is also seen in modern times in the Mangaian practice of telling obscene jokes to get people to work harder on collective projects (Marshall 1971: 109).

The specific channel of divine *mana* on earth was the chief. ''As the first born male of the tribe, he stood for land and people as the prime embodiment of generative power in nature'' (Handy 1927: 138). ''He was the channel or medium through which the land was nourished,'' and was believed to have ''close rapport'' with the natural elements (Handy 1927: 141, 142; see also Firth 1975: 171 and passim; Hocart 1915: 637; Loeb 1926: 55). Given the chief's association with divine procreation and fertility,'' the generative organs . . . of the divine chief were thought to be particularly potent'' (Handy 1927: 145). Certain sacred and esoteric words, which give power to certain Marquesan spells, ''all had reference to the virile organ of the chief'' (1927: 143), and one modern Marquesan euphemism for the penis is ''chief'' (Suggs 1966: 81). In the past, Hawaii and Tahiti had rituals centering on the loin-cloths of the ''kings'' and of the god-images (Handy 1927: 146–9).

Beyond the sphere of religion, it may be noted that chiefs are associated with exaggerated sexual activity and prowess in ordinary life. Chiefs are typically polygynous (Goldman 1970: 564) and are expected to have more affairs and conquests (e.g., Gifford 1929: 21), as well as to perpetrate more rape (see note 18). They are probably also more visibly fertile, in that with multiple wives, concubines, and passing affairs they probably produce more children than other men. Furthermore, chiefly reproduction is much more highly ritualized – their first matings, and/or the birth of their first children are everywhere surrounded with elaborate rites celebrating the continuation of their lines (Goldman 1970: 522–36 passim).

Several generalizations about cultural notions of sex and reproduction may be drawn from this sketch. First, and most clearly, both sex and reproduction are basically masculine activities. The female principle is conceived as passive (Handy 1927: 12), a receptacle for and a vehicle of male sexual and procreative energy. It is partly no doubt because of these associations that masculine pride in Polynesia is tied up with sexual success in a way that is less true of feminine pride (see Goldman 1970: 564; Best II 1924: 532; Mead 1949: 30, 19; Marshall 1971: 124, 126, 151; Gifford 1929: 21, 117). In Mangaia it is said that ''the name of the island travels on its penis'' (Marshall 1971: 126).

As for fertility and reproduction, the original responsibility of (male) gods for cosmic creation, and the ongoing responsibility of both gods and chiefs for the fertility of nature, mean that fertility too is basically the doing of men.[25] These beliefs thus probably contribute to the notion prevalent in at least some Polynesian societies that the male contribution to human conception is greater than that of the female. Both Maori and Tikopia claim that the woman is merely the ''haven'' for the development of the fetus, which is made from the male contribution (Best I 1924: 406; Firth 1957: 479). Tahitians also attribute at least greater, if not exclusive, reproductive influence to the male than to the female (see Oliver 1974: 410; see also Handy and Pukui, 1958: 54 for Hawaii; Handy 1923: 73 for the Marquesas).

Both sex and reproduction are thus male in general, and chiefly in particular. It may also be noted that married men are metaphoric chiefs, the metaphor referring primarily to their status superiority vis-à-vis their wives, but also clearly describing their sexual situation, as both sexually active and reproductive. It now remains to point out that adolescent males are normatively sexually active *but not reproductive*. The norm against adolescent reproduction is implicit in a variety of cultural rules and practices. Illegitimacy is culturally frowned upon in many parts of the area (see Best I 1924: 474; Loeb 1926: 84; Buck 1938: 120). This fact is surprising in light of the encouragement of active adolescent sex, the absence of indigenous contraceptive methods, and the actual high rate of illegitimate births. But the cultural view makes sense in terms of the unspoken rule that adolescents must not be reproductive. The combination of encouraging intensive sexual activity for the unmarried while prohibiting their reproduction reaches formal expression in the Tahitian *arioi* society, in which many of the implicit norms of adolescence in other Polynesian societies were here formally codified as rules. In the *arioi* society sexual promiscuity of the members was required, but reproduction was specifically banned. A woman (and/or a couple) who bore a child and did not kill it was expelled from the society (Oliver 1974: 940; Henry 1928: 235).

I suggested earlier that the general focus on sexuality and (negative) reproduction is symbolically (as well as functionally) consistent with the nature of the "problem" of junior siblings in Polynesian hierarchical society. The more detailed exploration of the norms of adolescent sexual behavior now allow us to see even more specific symbolic consonances. The active sexual behavior of junior males aligns them with maleness in general, including the maleness of gods and chiefs, as the restraints on girls' participation aligns them with the cultural view of femaleness as passive. But the normative nonreproductiveness or infertility of junior males distinguishes them sharply from gods and chiefs (and married men who are metaphoric chiefs). Once again then junior males are symbolically "in between," affiliated with high status by their sexual activeness, and with low status by their prescribed infertility.

Given the pleasure, excitement, and freedom of adolescence, it is not surprising that young people seek to perpetuate it as long as possible. We have seen that Tikopian junior brothers often never marry at all, and Firth reports that in most cases this is voluntary (1963: 373). Even the senior brother sometimes has to be physically coerced into marriage, because in this case he, along with his junior siblings, is allowed to participate in the adolescent dalliances (Firth 1957: 440). In Tahiti one-fifth of the population is estimated to have belonged voluntarily to the *arioi* society (Oliver 1974: 914). Throughout the area unmarried girls abort, kill, or give away babies in adoption on the explicit motive of prolonging the girls' youth and freedom (Firth 1957: 373, 528; Loeb 1926: 84; Suggs 1966: 44; Oliver 1974: 943). Throughout the area too, both boys and girls express directly their commitment to and enjoyment of adolescence, and their unwillingness to end it with marriage. Their views are echoed by older married people, who look back on their own adolescent freedom with great sentimentality (Firth 1957: 465; Marshall 1971: 142; Handy and Pukui 1958: 167).

Ultimately, however, most people marry *of their own accord*. Because for the most part only the highest elite marriages are arranged (to insure the reproduction of the senior line, as well as its proper breeding) all other marriages are undertaken voluntarily. Why people marry, and what happens when they do, is the subject of the next and final section of the analysis.

SPOUSES AND PARENTS

Husbands and wives. Marriage in Polynesia may be said to be only weakly structurally motivated. Almost all the important social relations are kin relations, and specifically sibling relations and their derivatives – uncles, aunts, and cousins. Affinal relations are of very little social consequence, and throughout the literature one can scarcely find references to them, no less extended discussions.

Part of the "weak" motivation for marriage, and the lack of cultural interest in affinity, derives from the fact that marriage normally takes place within the descent group, between people who are already related to one another by kinship. Not only is this the normal state of affairs, it is preferred. The Maori view is typical: "Marriage within the *whanau* ["tribe"] met with much approval, in that problems in the marriage would not have political repercussions as opposed to intertribal marriage" (Best I 1924: 447; see also Hecht 1977: 193; Firth 1963: 316; Buck 1932: 35; Suggs 1966: 127; Beaglehole and Beaglehole 1941: 77; Oliver 1974: 638). Marriage is thus secondary to or encompassed by kinship as a social organizational principle. It neither expresses nor forges important social or political alliances between groups, nor does it generate any important new personal relationships for the bride and/or groom. It does not tie either husband or wife into extensive affinal obligations with the other's kin, nor alternatively does it bring either husband or wife any special help or cooperation from the affines.[26]

Economically, too, marriage is only weakly motivated. Because both men and women inherit property, neither needs a spouse in order to have the means of self-support. (See Note 10 for exceptions.) As for labor, husbands and wives provide each other with little that they cannot legitimately get from kinspersons, or at least from someone other than a spouse. Although there is (relatively balanced) division of labor by sex throughout the area, there is virtually no productive or domestic work, including child care, that must be performed by a spouse, or even that ought preferentially to be performed by a spouse.[27] Indeed in the Marquesas, there are certain intimate services that can only be performed for a man by a kinswoman, which is one of the cultural reasons given for preferentially marrying one's cross-cousin rather than an unrelated woman (Suggs 1966: 127).

One might at least expect that a wife provides a man with one thing a mother or sister cannot: sex. It is true a man cannot get this from his (close) kinswomen, but a wife is by no means his only legitimate source. Sex is available with widows, divorced women, and with most unmarried girls. In addition there is always the possibility of sex with other men's wives, and although this is culturally unacceptable, it is certainly frequent enough: High rates of adultery are reported throughout the area (Loeb 1926: 48, 79; Mead 1949: 68; 1930: 84; Suggs 1966: 131; Best I 1924: 474–5; Goldman 1970: 566; Malo 1903: 82, 91, 284; Henry 1928: 284; Oliver 1974: 354, 358).[28]

The situation with respect to sexual dependence is somewhat different for women, at least at the formal level. Because unmarried girls are relatively less sexually free than boys, and because, as will be explored shortly, married women are theoretically out of bounds for men other than their husbands, a woman is apparently dependent on having a husband for having legitimate sexual relations. In practice however, we have seen that most unmarried girls are tacitly permitted much more sexual freedom than cultural ideology allows, and married women appear to engage in extramarital sexual relations nearly as often as their husbands. It seems, moreover, that divorced women may have almost complete and legitimate sexual freedom, even in those societies in which premarital female chastity and marital fidelity are strongly emphasized. In Tonga, for example, "when once divorced, [women] may remain single if they please, and enjoy all the liberty that the most libertine heart can desire" (Mariner II 1827: 145–6). Mariner also points out that some Tongan women choose never to marry, and have similar freedom (1827: 145–6).

The relative lack of material mutual dependence between husband and wife, as well as the relative paucity of larger social implications of their marriage, may well account for the widely reported "amiability" of husband-wife relations in Polynesia (Firth 1965: 122; Loeb 1926: 76; Huntsman and Hooper 1975: 422; Mariner II 1827: 148, 226, passim; Buck 1932: 119).[29] Because there is little practical or social necessity for staying together, one may assume that when couples stay married (or for as long as they do stay married) the parties simply like each other.

But the arguments that account for the amiable quality of relations between Polynesian spouses also account for the high rates of adultery and divorce.[30] There is little holding the relationship together either from the outside (structures of affinal obligations) or the inside (mutual dependence), and the relationship is largely sustained (or not, as the case may be) on personal sentiment. Personal sentiment is, of course, a rather shifting business in any society. But it is perhaps particularly so in Polynesia where, as noted earlier, the habit of not getting deeply emotionally involved with other individuals is often inculcated in childhood, and is strongly reinforced during the adolescent period of moving quickly from one lover to the next; such habits probably die hard, if ever. If we then add in the fact that a woman can always return to her kin group, where she has land, and where she and her children are always welcome additions, we see most of the reasons for what Mead called the "brittle" quality of Polynesian marriage (1949: 69). The high rates of adultery throughout Polynesia have already been noted; the rates of divorce are equally high (Buck 1938: 134; Hecht 1977: 192; Mead 1949: 69; Handy

1923: 100; Suggs 1966: 133; Buck 1932: 54; Mariner II 1827: 141; Gifford 1929: 16; Loeb 1926: 78).

At this point, however, it is worth distinguishing between getting married and staying married. Much of the discussion thus far pertains to the weak motivation for staying married; clearly the motivation for getting married is stronger, and remains to be explored. On this issue it is important to distinguish further between male and female "interests." We begin with the men, and specifically with the junior males for whom whether to marry or not is a question.

Young men, as we have seen, are at least ambivalent about getting married. Ultimately however they have a real "interest" in doing so: Only by getting married can they reproduce offspring that are legitimately theirs, and only by producing such offspring can they acquire any independent standing in the status system (as the head of a recognized social unit, no matter how junior and how small), as well as any possibility of mobility within it. This "interest" is culturally codified (or equally, is a precipitate of a prior cultural value) in formal markings of the higher status of the married state as such. In Samoa, for example, only married men may get the aristocratic titles that allow them to sit on the *fono*, the governing council. Men who are divorced or widowed must lay aside their titles and resign from the *fono* in order to go courting again. Unmarried men are grouped with untitled men in a separate and subordinate organization, the duties of which consist of carrying out *fono*-decreed work projects, and serving food and drink to the members of the *fono* when they are meeting (Mead 1930: 14). In Tikopia, too, married men are classed with "elders" and have community authority, whereas bachelors have more freedom but remain social subordinates (Firth 1957: 509; 1963: 335; see also Buck 1932: 51 for Tongareva).

Even where married men do not have higher public status, it is nearly universal throughout Polynesia that a husband/father has absolutely high domestic status. The role of husband/father is generally defined as one of absolute superiority and authority vis-à-vis wife and children, no matter how junior the man may be in the public hierarchy (see Best I 1924: 477; Oliver 1974: 813; Mead 1949: 69). In some cases the relationship is formulated through the metaphor of the husband as "chief" and the wife as "commoner" found in a number of Western Polynesian societies (Loeb 1926: 63; Gifford 1929: 17; Kaeppler 1971: 177; Firth 1963: 80). In Mangareva, an Eastern Polynesian island, wives feed their husbands by hand, as servants feed chiefs (Buck 1938: 224). The metaphor of husband as chief expresses both the actual and potential status benefits of marrying and producing children – the higher status of heading one's own social unit as opposed to being a dependent in another unit, as well as the potential for status mobility inherent in fathering (legitimate) children and thus founding an incipient descent line.

The "chiefly" status of the husband gives him (among other things) the culturally defined right to expect fidelity from his wife, explicitly parallel to the right any chief has to fidelity from his subjects. Thus in Tonga "there was no word for chastity except one which means 'remaining fixed and faithful,'

applied only to a married woman, and also to a warrior vis-à-vis his chief"
(Mariner II 1827: 130). In both Tonga and Tikopia married women are
labeled "sacred" and/or tabu, and should not under any circumstances be
trifled with (Gifford 1929: 16; Mariner I 1827: 124, II 1827: 141; Firth 1957:
474, 1965: 118–19). In fact, sexual fidelity was demanded of wives at all
levels of society throughout the area (see Best I 1924: 450, 474; Oliver 1974:
358), although the more "real" (i.e., the higher ranking) the chief, the more
severely was adultery with his wife penalized (Sahlins 1958: Ch. I passim).

It is in the context of these rules, related to the metaphoric chiefliness of
husbands, that the pattern of intense husbandly jealousy, seen throughout
Polynesia, becomes intelligible. In the Marquesas, for example, jealous
husbands "would beat or even kill their wives," their wives' lovers, or both
(Handy 1923: 100; Suggs 1966: 132). "Most of the murders [in this society]
were motivated by sexual jealousy" (Handy 1923: 56). Among the Maori,
"adultery was very serious . . . The wife was sometimes killed by her husband, or he may have killed her lover . . . Occasionally a man would discard
an adulterous wife, or expose her on a path spread-eagled, with her limbs
pegged down or compose and sing a song reviling her" (Best I 1924: 474). In
both the Marquesas and Mangareva, men commit suicide out of sexual
jealousy (Suggs 1966: 131; Buck 1938: 472. See also Oliver 1974: 54, 826,
and Henry 1928: 230 on Tahiti; and Marshall 1971: 159 on Mangaia).[31]

Such intense jealousy may seem suprising in light of the points made earlier
to the effect that a man does not really "need" a wife for goods, services, sex,
or significant social relations, and also in light of the patterns of low emotional involvement in personal relations described for at least some Polynesian
societies. We can see now, however, that "husband" is not merely a social
role, but a prestige status, as expressed by the metaphor of husband-as-chief.
Wifely infidelity is thus not merely a violation of some sort of "contract"
between the husband and wife, but an offense against the husband's pride of
status. The link between sexual jealousy and other forms of prestige sensitiv-
ity is explicit in the Marquesas and Mangareva, where male suicide may be
motivated by offenses in either category. At issue in male sexual jealousy, in
other words, is not (primarily) either material need or deep emotional involvement, but rather the pride in status culturally associated with husbandhood itself. And given the intensity of status pride throughout the area (see
Best I 1924: 389; II 1924: 225; Firth 1957: 440; Suggs 1966: 134–5), the
intensity of husbands' jealousy makes sense.

We have taken this little detour through the problem of wifely infidelity as
part of establishing the point that marriage provides men with both actual and
potential status benefits, such benefits in turn being among the primary
motives for Polynesian men to settle down and get married. Little of this
applies to women. It is true that in marrying women gain their only legitimate
source of sexual relations. In practice however, the heavy penalties on wifely
adultery mean less sexual freedom for married women than for adolescent
girls, as well as the loss of gratification of being sought after by many men,
which girls have been socialized to maximize and enjoy. It is also true that
some women gain personal mobility from marriage, because a wife shares her

husband's status (but generally not vice-versa), and because most marriages are probably de facto hypergamous (see the earlier discussion that men are more likely to marry down as a result of the social composition of adolescent cohorts). This minor status accretion however, is surely offset by a woman's demotion to "commoner" vis-à-vis her husband as chief. And wifehood *is* a demotion: Throughout much of Western Polynesia the status of sister is formally higher than that of wife (Hecht 1977 passim; Mead 1930: 184; Gifford 1929: 59, 79; Kaeppler 1971: passim). But even where a sister does not have formal superiority, nowhere is she categorically inferior to a brother (although she may be relatively inferior to some brothers by virtue of birth order). As a wife, on the other hand, her inferiority vis-à-vis her husband is categorical and absolute.[32]

It is difficult then to see the benefits of marriage for a woman, and it is easy to see its costs: a loss of both status and freedom. It may thus be suggested that girls marry more at the instigation of their lovers, than out of any overwhelming motive of their own.[33] It may also be suggested, although the data are not available to prove it, that women are probably the prime instigators of divorce. Given the losses of status and freedom; *and* given the freedom of divorced women; *and* given a woman's higher status as a kinswoman; *and* given the interest of her kin group in attracting her and her offspring – it is highly probable that women are less personally committed to their marriages than are their husbands.[34]

The relations of husbands and wives to marriage is thus structurally different, and probably emotionally different as well. These differences continue into parenthood, to which we now turn.

Fathers and Mothers. The social role of parent as we know it – as central supporter, nurturer, and socializer of one's children –is not a highly significant role in Polynesian society. Parenting functions are spread over a wide range of kin of the biological parents (Best I 1924: 361; Firth 1963: 130; Linton 1939: 159; Mead 1949: 22, 32; Handy and Pukui 1958: 90), and children are encouraged to see themselves as belonging to the wider kin group. Tikopians have explicit ideology to the effect that biological parents and children should not be exclusively attached to one another (Firth 1957: 192). Instituionalized adoption and/or fosterage, which are *universal* throughout Polynesia, and at a high rate, implicitly carry the same message (Carroll 1970; Levy 1973: 473–484).

But the general deemphasis on parenthood is differently realized for men and for women. The differences are virtually direct functions of the differential structural relationships of husbands and wives to the marriage. Specifically, a strong paternal role, like a strong husbandly role, is supported by cultural ideology, whereas a strong maternal role is not.

Fathers are granted metaphoric "chiefness" vis-à-vis their children, as husbands are to their wives. Their authority over their children is absolute and unquestionable. They are granted certain privileges symbolic of this status in their households, and are even hedged about with tabus similar to those surrounding a chief (see Firth 1963: 80, 163; Buck 1932: 51; Gifford 1929:

17, 18; see also Handy and Pukui for the reverse metaphor – the chief as father to his people [1958: 198]). All of this provides them with additional personal prestige; it also probably strengthens their "interest" in the paternal role and in the durability of their relationships with their children. The result is that Polynesian fathers do appear to take a strong interest in their paternal roles. Thus, Linton claimed that Marquesan fathers were the sole socializers of their children (1939: 164), and although this was probably an overstatement, it surely reflects some of the tendencies described here. Similarly, a Maori text says, "The salvation of the men of old was the attention they paid to raising children" (Best II 1924: 24). In Tikopia, "In infant nutrition, education, discipline and ritual of adolescence a father is closely associated with his child . . . he is expected to be emotionally concerned in its welfare" (Firth 1963: 118). The metaphoric chiefly status of fathers both fosters this greater investment in the paternal role and expresses its very "paternalism" – its strong authority combined with its caring, nurturing, and protecting qualities.

The pattern of strong fatherhood relates to, among other things, the "political" interest men have in children. Legitimate children, in fact, are the primary raison d'etre of marriage. They are not only a source of greater personal status for a man; they are his social and political "base." We have seen that a chief (or a "chief") is only as strong as the social unit he heads, and that heading a flourishing social unit is also the only potential source of status mobility in the system. Thus children must be not only (legitimately) produced, but raised as loyal adherents to their group. And thus fathers have a structurally induced interest not only in having legitimate children, but in overseeing their development as loyal and adhering members.

All of this is less true, if at all, for mothers. Mothers have little "political" interest in their children, a fact that may well contribute to the high rates of abortion and infanticide throughout the area (*Abortion*: Best I 1924: 257; Firth 1957: 373, 527, 528; Loeb 1926: 84; Linton 1939: 164; Oliver 1974: 63; Malo 1903: 103. *Infanticide*: Best I 1924: 413; Firth 1957: 374; Loeb 1939: 84; Oliver 1974: 63; Handy and Pukui 1958: 79; Goldman 1970: 563). Because women are not directly involved in the processes of maintaining or building descent lines, women do not "need" children for social or political purposes. At the same time, women gain virtually no personal status from motherhood. Birth is not ritualized except in the case of high-status women producing the senior child who will carry on the senior line, and even in these cases the birth rituals are generally conceived as being for the child and not for the mother (Goldman 1970: 522 ff.; Best II 1924: 2; Buck 1938: 510; Henry 1928: 184; Oliver 1974: 414; Malo 1903: 183).[35] And the mother role is not granted any special cultural prestige: The Marquesan mother is "respected but a figure of indifference" (Linton 1939: 159). In Tonga a mother is as much a "commoner" to her children as a wife is to her husband (Gifford 1929: 17). And in Tikopia, "They recognize no unvarying moral obligation; they do not subscribe to the opinion that a son is bound to remain attached to his mother by any filial sentiment *per se*" (Firth 1963: 162; see also Mead 1949: 111 for Samoa).

The mother–child bond is thus much like the wife–husband bond from the wife's point of view. It receives little cultural support and is largely a matter of (variable) personal sentiment. The bond has, like marriage, an optional quality, depending largely on how well the parties get along. Not surprisingly, then, mothers and children do not (somewhat to the chagrin of Western observers like Linton) appear to be strongly committed to one another. Mothers may easily give children up for adoption or fosterage. Even if they do not do so, they do not necessarily take an intense interest in the care, nurturing, and socialization of their children. In both the Marquesas and Hawaii, wet nursing is apparently common practice (Linton 1939: 164; Malo 1903: 94). Hawaiians even have a notion that some women's laps are inimical to their children's health, and that the child of such a mother has to be raised by someone else in order to survive (Handy and Pukui 1958: 48, 49). More generally, it is reported throughout the area that women turn over the care of younger children to older children as early as possible. Children in turn are free to wander off and affiliate with other "parents" if they choose (see Mead 1949: 33; Handy and Pukui 1958: 71).[36]

The parallels for women between motherhood and wifehood (as for men between fatherhood and husbandhood) are systematic, as might have been predicted by the fact that both are metaphoric "commoner" statuses. Just as wives have no great economic or "political" stake in their marriages, so mothers have little in their children. Just as wives gain no prestige from marriage, and indeed lose some, so mothers gain none and perhaps lose some in motherhood. And thus as the wife–husband bond is "weak" and easily broken, so the mother–child bond is weak and, if not easily "broken," then certainly easily attenuated.

At the same time, just as the husband–wife relationship is generally reported as "amiable," so is the mother–child relationship, and doubtless for the same reasons. I said earlier that the fact that husbands and wives did not "need" each other could account in large part for the reported "amiable" quality of marital relations, when those relationships survived, or for as long as they did. The same point may now be made of mother–child relations, which similarly lack structural motivation or "interest." Observers repeatedly remark that, although the mother is not a very significant figure to the child, nonetheless mother–child relations are generally "easy" and affectionate (see Firth 1957: 172; Linton 1939: 159; Kaeppler 1971: 191; Rogers 1977: 159). It may be suggested that such easy affection is possible in part precisely *because* mothers and children do not "need" each other in any structurally significant way. Predictably, on the other hand, father–child (and especially father–son) relations are often reported as "strained" (Firth 1963: 153; Rogers 1977: 159; Oliver 1974: 724; Handy and Pukui 1958: 49).

The differential relations of fathers and mothers to their children may be seen to have effects that link back to the very earliest discussions in this essay, and specifically to the general cultural prominence and particular social dynamics of sibling relations. The father's more active role in the care and socialization of his children manifests itself later in the domestic cycle in the particular protection of daughters with which we began this whole excursion. In addition, his "interest" in the unity of his children as a group, and in their loyalty to his (and his successor's, their brother's) line, would manifest itself in the nonnormative but systematically seen pattern of giving special affection and attention to those of his children whose loyalty is not structurally assured – the daughters and the younger sons. Hence the pattern of babying and petting those other children, which probably does foster their loyalty, but which may also incidentally contribute to the reproduction of the pattern of elder-to-younger sibling envy and mistrust. Potential elder–younger sibling cleavage in turn underlay many of the patterns of male adolescence discussed in the section on brothers. And finally, the mother's relative distance from her children also has important implications for the children's sibling relationships. Here, I would particularly stress the point that when mothers turn over child care to others, as they frequently do, the preferred choice appears to be one of their older children (see Mead 1949: 23; Levy 1973: 456). In other words, it is often siblings themselves who are among each other's significant caretakers and protectors in younger years, and this point is surely consequential for the emotional underpinnings of the sibling relationship.

The "status of women." There is one more important link from the patterns of parenthood back to the patterns of siblingship with which we began this essay. The point may be made by raising the question: If women are not primarily wives and mothers, in terms of cultural emphasis, and apparently in terms of personal commitment, then, what, socially, are they? Where are they socially focused, and what are they doing of social significance? The answer, of course, is that they are continuing to be what they always were – *kinswomen* to their kin, sisters to their brothers, and now that they are in the parental generation, aunts to their brothers' children. As adult kinswomen they may be important as family genealogists, as ritual participants, as economic managers, and even, if their brothers are "kings" (paramount chiefs), as their "queens" (see Hecht 1977: 196; Huntsman and Hooper 1975: 424; Firth 1957: 196; 1975: 105; Gifford 1929: 181, 232; Mariner II 1827: 10). And, as discussed earlier, as aunts to their brothers' children they may also be key ritual sponsors, as well as important authority figures in the children's socialization. If as mothers married women are hardly visible in the ethnographic literature on Polynesia, as adult sisters and aunts they are everywhere. Indeed, the strong continuing participation of women in their natal kin relations is clearly a large factor (as both cause and effect) in their "weak" wifely and motherly roles.

More importantly, it may be argued that women's continuing kinship significance is one of the major sources of their relatively high overall social status throughout the area, despite their "commoner" status in relation to their husbands and children. It may surprise the reader to learn that most observers consider Polynesian women to have quite high social status, and further that I would agree with them (e.g., Loeb 1926: 82; Linton 1939: 162; Mariner II 1827: 95, 119, 211; Oliver 1974: 1132).[37] This assessment is made despite the strong (but not absolute) sexual control of daughters and wives; despite the high incidence of rape and other forms of violence, sexual and otherwise, against women; despite the typical (though not total) exclusion of women from high religious ritual and high office; despite (a certain amount of) cultural ideology of female weakness and pollution; and despite the formal subordination of wives and the lack of marked respect for mothers.

The concept of "the status of women" has been notoriously difficult to pin down. It certainly requires a great deal more theoretical clarification and specification than I have space for here. For present purposes I will use the following indexes of relatively "high" or "low" status: formal cultural ideology concerning women's "nature," quality of male–female relations, access of women to significant public roles, and degree of male control over female behavior. My sense of the relatively high status of Polynesian women, then, derives from at least the following comparative observations: Ideology of female pollution and inferiority is far less elaborated than, for example, in the New Guinea highlands;[38] the occasional sexual violence does not, as in New Guinea, manifest itself in antagonistic gender relations in everyday life; women in Polynesia do occasionally succeed to high office, and more frequently than in many other societies; and sexual control of women is less consistently and less effectively applied than, say, among Muslims or among Indian Brahmins. Among these points the most significant in my view is the relatively low elaboration of cultural conceptions (both formal ideology and general folklore) of female inferiority; Polynesians simply do not express, whether in word or deed, many notions of women as inherently less worthy sorts of persons than men.

The problem then is to account for this (provisionally defined) "high status" of Polynesian women. I would argue that the answer lies in two interrelated points: that *kinswomen* – daughters, sisters, aunts – have culturally defined high status, *and* that kinship is analytically the "encompassing" domain of social relations. I said earlier that marriage is subordinate to kinship in organizing critical social relations – most people marry kin; marriage performs few functions and establishes few relations not already performed or established by kinship; and it is kinship (specifically, descent) rather than marriage that generates rank and prestige. Another way of stating this would be to say, in the Dumontian sense, that kinship encompasses marriage in Polynesia – that the symbols and values of kinship are the hegemonic symbols and values in the system. The high culturally assigned status of women as kin thus encompasses their lower status as wives, and produces an overall *cultural* respect, or at least lack of disrespect, for women in general. Sisters are more respected than wives, *and* women in general appear to be seen more *as* sisters than as wives (see also Shore, this volume).

Thus if we look again at the list of indexes of *low* status of Polynesian women, we see that most of them pertain to sexual and reproductive functions, and thus essentially to wives, lovers, and mothers. The assignment of formal subordination to wives and mothers is straightforward. Much of the violence, as we have seen, is sexual violence, and/or violence stimulated by sexual faults. Notions of pollution and weakness center primarily around sexual relations and/or birth. The bias against succession of women to high office works categorically only against wives; sisters and other kinswomen occasionally do succeed to public office within their kin groups (Best I 1924: 353, 453; Buck 1938: 156; Gifford 1929: 88; Mariner I 1827: 137).

As for the strong control of sisters'/daughters' sexual behavior, which might appear on the surface to signal low status for women *in kinship roles*, it must be recalled that such control is culturally associated with high, and sometimes very high, status. The Samoan sacred maid formally outranks her male counterpart, the successor to the chiefship, and the Tui Tonga's sister's daughter – one of the very women who as a girl must have been oiled and massaged and had her knees tied together every night – is formally the highest-ranking person *in the whole society* (Gifford 1929: 74, 80).

Thus most of the negative ideology concerning women centers upon their sexual and reproductive activities as lovers, wives, and mothers; kinswomen, who are neither sexual nor reproductive from the point of view of their kinsmen, escape the problematic associations of such activities and functions. It is not, however, a matter of simply balancing off one set of cultural evaluations (low status of wives, etc.) against another (high status of sisters) from an external point of view. The culture must provide the weighting, and in the Polynesian case, as I said, kinship has priority over marital role definitions in the hierarchy of cultural ordering systems.

Conclusion: prestige, kinship/marriage, and gender

The reader may well be saying by now, "This is all very well and good, but Polynesia is only one isolated, and possibly quite idiosyncratic part of the world." It remains for me then to place Polynesia in a larger comparative context, in relation to a range of other "hierarchical" societies, to show that this is not the case. The key "texts" for the discussion will be the extremely useful compendia essays by Goody and Tambiah, in their joint volume, *Bridewealth and dowry*.

Goody and Tambiah derive many generalizations about the treatment and status of women in "complex," "stratified" societies, from the fact that women in such societies are given substantial wealth from their families in the form of dowry or inheritance. Goody surveys the world in general, but particularly the area from Western Europe to Sri Lanka. He links dowry to "complex forms of stratification," arguing that dowry functions as a way of preserving the status of daughters as well as sons. From female endowment in turn flow many implications reminiscent of what we have seen in Polynesia: control over the premarital sexual activity of daughters; endogamy and other forms of in-marriage, including brother–sister marriage in some scattered cases; significant patterns of adoption (for purposes of creating "fictitious" heirs); significant patterns of filiacentric unions (in-marrying sons-in-law) for the same reasons. Tambiah confines himself to a smaller area (India, Sri Lanka, and mainland Southeast Asia) and fewer variables, but his data show essentially the same familiar patterns. He finds dowry linked with hypergamy, guarding of female virginity, in-marrying sons-in-law, and certain patterns of institutionalized adoption. Tambiah, unlike Goody, systematically distinguishes between dowry and female inheritance, seeing the latter as a "shift" from the former (I will return to his argument on this point shortly). He then finds the "shift" to bilateral inheritance to be associated with a shift to:

bilateral kinship; higher rates of uxorilocal residence; kin-group endogamy; easier divorce and higher divorce rates; more adoption; and more equal status of women.

Before discussing the (close) parallels between Polynesia and these other areas, it should be noted that Goody considers the kinship/marriage/sexual/ inheritance patterns listed here to be associated not only with "complex forms of stratification," but with "large states," having economies based on "plough and intensive agriculture" (1973: 26). Neither of these latter developments, however, is characteristic of Polynesia. State formation comes quite late (in fact, post-European contact) in its historical development; agriculture nowhere entailed the plough, and in only a few parts of the area did it approximate the intensity of Eurasia (see Sahlins 1958). It would appear, then, in Polynesia at least, that hierarchical social organization historically preceded state formation and economic intensification, and was at least as much a cause as an effect of these other phenomena. Moreover, we have seen that the hierarchical status system alone, without these other aspects, has most of the correlates pertaining to gender discussed by Goody and Tambiah, and is thus clearly the most relevant social structural dimension for the analysis.

We have seen in this essay that Polynesian sex/gender patterns closely parallel those manifested by some or all of the societies covered by Goody and Tambiah. And as noted, both authors consider that the critical factor linking these patterns to hierarchical social organization is female endowment or inheritance, both of which have (analogous) effects on the way the girl is treated before, during, and after marriage, and on the ways in which marriage itself tends to be organized.

But giving daughters substantial wealth is actually itself more of a puzzle than either author notices, and requires some more systematic explanation. Women could easily be construed as social and economic dependents of men, and usually are. There is thus no reason to give them much of anything, certainly not real estate, but not even valuable movables in the form of jewels and money that they may keep for themselves for life and dispose of as they wish. The fact that women in hierarchical societies do systematically get substantial durable wealth from their natal families thus means that some prior factors are already in operation, which need to be brought to light.

I would suggest that both dowry and female inheritance express certain preexisting, general features of the social situation of women in hierarchical societies. It is inherent in the nature of hierarchies that certain nongender-based principles of social organization take precedence over gender itself as a principle of social organization. In these systems social units (castes, ranked lineages, or whatever) that contain both men and women are ranked on the basis of principles such as (in Polynesia) genealogical seniority. The status of the individual in turn is based in the first instance on birth within one or another such unit, and only secondarily (if at all) on any of the following: personal biological characteristics (age, gender); individual talents, skills, or achievements; or functionally defined roles ("hunters," "shamans," "midwives," and so on). Any or all of these other ways of classifying and ordering persons may subsequently enter into further construction of social categories and groups, and the location of individuals within them. But the peculiar feature of hierarchical systems is that the highest level principles of social organization do not divide, but rather unite, women and men in social categories and social units from which both derive their primary statuses, and in which both share common "interests."

There is a sense, then, in which the logic of hierarchical systems inherently tends toward (even if it never reaches) gender equality. At any given level in the system, men's and women's statuses are more similar to one another's than to persons of either sex at other levels.[39] It is in the context of these points then that we can understand why women in such systems inherit or are endowed with property: They are, in varying degrees in various hierarchical societies, full-fledged members of their "classes," and their rights to a share of the wealth of their natal units appear, at one level, as "natural" as the men's.

Having said this, however, one must also hasten to add that there is still an overall male-favoring bias in the system: Within the "strata," men are formally superior to women, have near-exclusive access to positions of social leadership, and dominate decision making on issues of importance to the unit as a whole. It is this point that requires the analyst to continue to take the male point of view, and to look at the ways in which women (as well as junior men) are "used" by senior men in the transactions that reproduce the system as a whole, and the dominance of senior men within it.

Returning to Goody's and Tambiah's arguments, let us agree that hierarchy has "something to do with" certain widespread gender patterns found in hierarchical societies. The real question is, what is the logic of the relationship? Here I diverge from both authors. We have seen in the present essay that the link between rank and gender lies in the organization of the kinship/marriage system. Critical for the Polynesian analysis has been the cognatic-endogamous nature of Polynesian descent groups, and the fact that marriage relations are subordinate to kin relations within such an organization of descent. The cognatic-endogamous type of kinship/marriage organization prevails, with minor variations, from Polynesia, through Southeast Asia and Sri Lanka, to a number of societies of south India (see Tambiah). Most of the "variations" from this pattern are in the direction of matrilineal descent, most famously among the Nayar, but also in many parts of Southeast Asia.

Cognatic kinship organization is not, however, the only type possible in hierarchical systems. In India and China (to take the two most familiar examples) internally stratified kin groups tend to be patrilineal and exogamous. In other words, there appear to be at least two major ways of organizing descent and marriage in hierarchical societies or, to turn the point around, hierarchical systems may be built upon two very different types of kinship systems, a patrilineal exogamous type, and a cognatic-endogamous type with occasionally realized tendencies toward matriliny.

The first lesson to be drawn from this is that the type of kinship system involved is a relatively independently varying factor in the analysis. It is neither a logical precondition nor a logical consequence of hierarchical social organization. Whether a given society is of one or the other type is often largely a function of geographic area, or at any rate, a function of historical factors probably largely beyond our retrieval. I stress this point because I consider it important to see the operation of certain indeterminate cultural factors in the analysis, and not to sustain an illusion of airtight structural determinism. I will return to this point shortly.

The split (whether viewed areally or typologically) between the patrilineal and the cognatic systems in fact lines up neatly with a split between patterns of female property accession through dowry (in the patrilineal systems) and through inheritance (in the cognatic systems). Both Goody and Tambiah obscure both of these splits, although they do so in different ways. Goody, in a drive to make a fully structurally determined argument, simply merges dowry and female inheritance under the rubric of "diverging devolution," seeing both as correlates of "stratification," and ignoring major areal differences as well as the different empirical correlates of the two types. Tambiah, who is more area-conscious, recognizes the break between India on the one hand and Sri Lanka and Southeast Asia on the other, but proceeds to analyze Sri Lanka and Southeast Asia as "weakenings" of the classical Indian system, with Indian patriliny, virilocality, and dowry "weakening" toward cognatic (or "bilateral") kinship reckoning, balanced patterns of virilocal and uxorilocal residence, and equal male and female inheritance. Although Tambiah argues vehemently against some unnamed opponent that the pattern should be viewed in this way, I submit that Sri Lanka and a few south Indian groups are far more straightforwardly seen as typologically (and probably historically) part of the Polynesian/Southeast Asian pattern, rather than as "weakenings" of the classical Indian type.[40]

The concordance between patriliny, exogamy, and dowry on the one hand, and between cognatic descent reckoning, endogamy, and female inheritance on the other, gives radically different significance to marriage in the two systems. In the first, marriage carries an enormous burden in the reproduction of status relations. Daughters will be married into other groups, and unrelated women will be entering one's own group. Seeing that the daughter marries "well," and that incoming women are of suitable statuses, are issues of great importance for both internal "quality" and external "show" of the group, as well as for the quality of intergroup relations. Dowry, which is given at marriage, is generally appropriate to the marriage-emphasis of the system; it also specifically (as most authors have emphasized) aids in procuring desirable mates and marriage connections, and in putting on a good "show" for the group itself. It is further important that dowry almost never involves land. In a patrilineal system, a woman's children will belong to the group of their father. If she obtained land from her kin group, and passed it to her children, it would automatically be alienated from her group. If women are to get wealth in patrilineally organized hierarchical systems, as our earlier logic suggests they should, then they will nearly inevitably get it in the form of dowry, that is, as a set of *movable* goods endowed upon the women *at marriage*.

For reciprocal reasons, female inheritance is equally consistent with cognatic descent and endogamous marriage. As discussed at length in this essay, marriage is not of great significance in such systems, and the absence of any special bestowal of wealth, designated *as a marriage portion*, is consistent with this overall nonemphasis. At the same time, a woman's children in a cognatic system are as much hers as her husband's, their more active affiliation depending primarily on where they live. Thus female inheritance of land and the further devolution of such land to her children does not automatically alienate it from her kin group, and the problems that militate against female land inheritance in patrilineal systems are absent.

The relative deemphasis on marriage in the cognatic-endogamous systems, on the one hand, and the heavy emphasis on marriage in the patrilineal-exogamous systems on the other, in turn may be seen to influence (or at least correlate with) differential patterns of divorce. We have seen in Polynesia that divorce is easy and frequent, and we suggested that this pattern is at least partly explicable in terms of the fact that Polynesian women retain significant roles in relation to their consanguineal kin throughout their lives. In the patrilineal systems, on the other hand, women generally do not retain such roles, or at least not to anywhere near the degree seen in Polynesia. Correspondingly, divorce in these systems tends to be more socially unacceptable (often wholly so), and in practice infrequent.

The descent rules in the two systems feed into these differential patterns. In the patrilineal systems a woman's children belong to her husband's kin unit, and if she leaves she must either leave the children with her husband's kin or bring them back as non-kin into her own group. In cognatic systems on the other hand, the children belong as much to the mother as to the father, and are as much kin to her kin as to his. Thus although personal conflicts over children may arise, such conflicts are not built into the system as *structural* constraints against divorce. And finally, the differential patterns of female property accession in the two systems also support the differential divorce patterns. We have seen that female land inheritance (versus dowries of moveable goods) is facilitated by the cognatic-endogamous social organization. Such inheritance, unlike a dowry, can in turn provide women with means of self-support in case of divorce, and thus contributes to the greater ease and feasibility of divorce in these systems.

The upshot of all this is seen not only in the differential actual patterns of divorce, and in the differential cultural attitudes toward it; it is seen in the gender ideology as well. Whereas Polynesian women are not characterized as innately weak, dependent, and needy of protection and support from men, such notions are prevalent in the gender ideologies of the patrilineal systems. The Indian woman, for example, is culturally described as a "naturally" weak and dependent creature, requiring lifetime protection – first from her father, later from her husband, and finally from her sons.

The general hegemony of kinship over affinity in defining personal status in Polynesia, Southeast Asia, and similar societies, and the specific point that women are defined more in terms of kinship than of marital roles in such systems, has even more general implications. In exogamous/dowry systems women are seen more in terms of the marriages they will contract, and the affinal connections they will engender for their groups, than in terms of their ongoing value as members of the group itself. I have argued for Polynesia, on the other hand, that there is a priority of kinship over marital role definitions of women, and that this priority tends to accord women more social respect or, if you will, higher status. Correspondingly, it appears that in the dowry systems, in which marital status, present or future, takes precedence over kinship status in defining the overall role identity of women, women's social respect is generally lower. Assessments of low, as of high, status are difficult to pin down, but certainly the women of India or China hardly appear to be "appreciated" in the same way in their societies as the women of Polynesia or Southeast Asia.

We might pause here to consider for a moment why an emphasis on a marital as against a kinship definition of women would tend to have a "downgrading" effect. It seems to me that here again the answers lie beyond the structural logic of particular systems, and lie rather in dimensions intrinsic to marital relations and kinship relations as such. It would seem that in marriage a woman's distinctively *feminine* (as against generically human) attributes – mainly centering on biological reproduction – are highlighted, whereas in kinship roles they are not. Thus in marriage a woman is more open to being seen as a radically different type of human being, whereas in the context of kinship she is more easily seen as simply occupying different social roles. In all societies, of course, women (like men) are both kinspersons and spouses; what is at issue is the relative dominance of one or the other dimension.

There is one pattern that might have been expected to be differentiated by the dowry/female inheritance divide, but is not, namely the guarding of daughters' virginity. This is a pattern that appears throughout virtually all hierarchical societies, whether patrilineal or cognatic. Most of the analyses of the phenomenon have centered on its relationship to marriage implications – keeping up the girl's "value," thus assuring her of a good marriage and/or assuring her family of good marital connections (Goody 1973; Ortner 1976); expressing her natal family's high status by giving the virgin as a precious "gift" in marriage, the same point being made by sending her off with a valuable dowry (Tambiah 1973); or protecting her status group (e.g., her caste) from improper status infusions through wrong marriages (Yalman 1963). One would thus expect that guarding daughters' chastity would be more associated with the dowry systems, where young women are seen primarily in terms of their marital futures. In fact however, we have seen that premarital female chastity is also emphasized in Polynesia, where women are seen more as kinspersons, and less as marriage export items.

It would appear, then, that an emphasis on virginity may have to do with more general features of hierarchical systems (it is virtually nonexistent in "simpler" societies) and less with the specific variations of kinship and marriage organization within them. Both Goody (1973) and I (1976) have separately made this claim, although neither of us, I now think, did so for the right reasons. Based on the discussions of the present essay, I would now suggest that the concern for the virginity of daughters in hierarchical societies, across the dowry/female inheritance divide, relates more to the argument made earlier concerning the general elevation in status of women in such systems. That is, "stratification" by nongender-based principles places women in each "stratum" on a more equal footing with men, raising them toward equivalence with men at any given level. In this sense, I argued, women's status tends to be higher in such societies than in simpler societies in which gender itself is often a dominant principle of social ranking. It must further be noted that the cultivation of virginity, whatever we may think of it coming from our own cultural backgrounds, is in fact associated in *all* hierarchical systems with high cultural value. In Polynesia we have seen that this is the case, but in patrilineal India too the virgin is seen as a "gift," a precious and valuable object (see Tambiah 1973). And of course virginity has very exalted significance in Christian ideology too. Virginity thus appears in its *cultural* contexts to be an expression and cultivation of the overall higher "value" of women in such systems. I would suggest then that the meaning that gives virginity high value in all hierarchical societies is the same as that which gives women relatively higher status in such societies – that women are, first of all, co-members of their own status groups, and only secondarily females. For clearly virginity downplays the uniquely feminine capacity to be penetrated and to give birth to children.[41] A virgin is still a generic kins-person; a non-virgin is downgraded to mere womanhood.

The question then of whether virginity is "really" oriented toward a girl's marital prospects, as the arguments noted earlier would claim, or rather expresses her ongoing importance within her kin group as the Polynesian analysis would have it (see also J. Schneider 1971), is actually a question of secondary interpretations placed by specific cultures on the more generally available symbol. In the dowry systems, with their marital emphasis, the marriage-oriented interpretations correspond with cultural views and are probably appropriate for their cases, whereas in the female inheritance systems the interpretation stressing the symbolic retention of the girl for her kin group is probably more appropriate.

The whole emphasis on dowry and/or female inheritance has tended to focus discussion on women, and I must now also say a few words about the men. Although the Polynesian female patterns are consistent with many of the female patterns common to hierarchical societies in general, and with virtually all of the patterns seen in the Sri Lanka-Southeast Asian area, Polynesian male patterns may appear divergent from all the rest. Nowhere else do we see the extreme emphasis on male sexual activity so characteristic of Polynesia, and here it might be thought that we are in the presence of something culturally idiosyncratic, having little to do with general structural characteristics of hierarchical social organization.

In fact, however, I would argue quite the contrary. The problem of junior male siblings discussed in this essay for Polynesia is in fact endemic to all hierarchical systems. Only one sibling can succeed to the headship, whether that be the position of head of household, or the kingship of the whole realm. The differences of privilege and opportunity between senior and junior siblings in hierarchical societies are thus everywhere potential sources of social cleavage. And everywhere junior siblings must somehow be "taken care of," whether by methods that ensure their dependency and loyalty to the "house," or by methods that effectively remove them from direct interest in kinship and status affairs, or by some combination of the two approaches. The Tibetan system of impartible male inheritance and fraternal polyandry, for example, responds to the first impulse, while Tibetan Buddhist monasteries that took in one-fifth of the male population, ideally always junior siblings, responded to the second (see e.g., Stein 1972).

Focusing purely on "diversionary" or "removal" tactics for dealing with the problem of junior siblings, however, the enouragement of hyperactive (but nonreproductive) sexuality for junior Polynesian males is clearly simply one among several functional equivalents that would serve these purposes. Other possible solutions would include frequent warfare (for which of course there are other motives as well), and/or perpetual warfare training, to which some Polynesian societies were devoted (see also, for example, the Nayar). And as the Tibetan example suggests, another major possibility would be religious monasticism. Monasticism in fact was the great solution of Eurasia, in both Christianity in the West and Buddhism in the East.[42] Polynesia historically escaped the (early) influences of either of these "high" religions, while at the same time not developing an ascetic tradition of its own. It is not too farfetched to suggest, however, that the asceticism of the European and Asian religions and the (nonreproductive) eroticism of Polynesia are simply inverse transformational solutions to the same general problem, the problem of what to do with junior male siblings in hierarchical societies.

In sum, Polynesia is hardly an idiosyncratic case. Polynesian patterns of female "treatment" are well within the range seen in other "hierarchical" societies, and the male patterns appear as functional equivalents of, and simple symbolic transformations upon, male patterns over the same range. It is clearly possible to say that what we have seen in Polynesia is at least as much a set of structural correlates of "hierarchy" in general, as of peculiar Polynesian cultural traits. On the other hand, I have also argued that idiosyncratic, historically evolved, cultural differences play a major role in affecting variations within the general pattern. The marriage-cum-dowry orientation of the patrilineal systems of Europe and Asia, and the kinship-cum-female inheritance emphasis of the cognatic systems of Southeast Asia and Polynesia, are both congruent with hierarchical macro-organization, but are not directly derivable from it. Each in turn has different consequences for the views and treatment of women in their respective areas.

If the prestige system and the kinship system are thus somewhat independent of one another, at least analytically, it may be suggested that we could also look for different kinds of relationships between the two "levels." If, for example, in Polynesia, hierarchy in general raises the status of women, and so (independently) does the fact that kinship encompasses and subordinates the significance of marriage, we can say that the status system and the kinship system are consistent with one another. In India, on the other hand, stratification raises the status of women but the marital orientation of the kinship system has a depressing effect on female status; thus the status system and the kinship system could be said to be in a contradictory relationship with respect to women. It would be interesting to pursue, for example, the high degree of elaboration of notions of female pollution in India, compared to the relatively low degree of elaboration of such notions in Polynesia (or Southeast Asia) in light of this contrast. But that is another paper.

Notes

1 On the basis of an earlier draft of this essay, I solicited and benefited enormously from the generous criticism of Polynesianists: Irving Goldman, Bradd Shore, and Vern Carroll, to all of whom I am extremely grateful. I hope that the most egregious errors have been weeded out. Although it is conventional to assume responsibility for all errors that remain, I do so more than conventionally. I have never done fieldwork in the area, and I remain acutely aware of my own novice-hood in relation to this fascinating body of data.

I also wish to thank the following friends for their very detailed suggestions and criticisms: Jane Collier, Salvatore Cucchiari, Raymond Kelly, John Kirkpatrick, Michelle Rosaldo, David Schneider and Harriet Whitehead. Finally, I am also most appreciative of the comments and reactions of Aletta Biersack, Nancy Chodorow, Keith Hart, Leslee Nadelson, Niara Sudarkasa, and Susan Contratto. Marshall Sahlins kindly sent me the manuscript of his forthcoming work, *Historical metaphors*.

This paper is dedicated to the memory of Margaret Mead, whose writings on Samoa remain in my opinion among the best ethnographic works on Polynesia; they also contain some of the most perceptive observations on gender and sexuality for any society.

2 The rank system throughout Polynesia is by now virtually defunct. I will however use the "ethnographic present" tense in the essay as if it were still operating.

3 The terms are from Goldman's (1970) classification of Polynesian societies, according to an evolutionary scheme that will not be central to the present essay, and that I will thus not discuss here. It need only be understood that the "traditional" societies are the least complex in terms of organization of the rank system, the "stratified" are the most complex, and the "open" societies form a middle category.

Sahlins (1958) also works with an evolutionary scheme, although he does not label the levels (Chapter I, passim). Although his theoretical presuppositions and interests are radically different from Goldman's, the outcome of his classification is similar. I present here the two schemes for the reader's reference.

Goldman (1970: 21): *"Traditional"* – Pukapuka, Ontong Java, Tokelau, Tikopia, Futuna, Tongareva, Uvea, Maori, Manihiki-Rakahanga. *"Open"* – Mangaia, Easter Island, Marquesas, Samoa, Niue; *"Stratified"* – Hawaii, Tonga, Society Islands (Tahiti), Mangareva.

Sahlins (1958: 11–12): *Group III* – Pukapuka, Ontong Java, Tokelau; *Group IIb* – Tikopia, Futuna, Marquesas; *Group IIa* – Mangaia, Easter Island, Uvea, Mangareva; *Group I* – Hawaii, Tonga, Tahiti, Samoa.

4 The discussion in this section is drawn primarily from Goldman (1970) and Sahlins (1958), further informed by the general ethnographic literature on Polynesia as listed in the References. The description of the social organization, as well as of the sex/gender system that follows, is a composite, an "ideal type," to which probably no single Polynesian society perfectly conforms. I am aware of the wide range of variations throughout the area, but I have chosen to ignore them in the interest of establishing a general set of relations between rank and gender over the area as a whole. The merit of this approach must be judged not only by the persuasiveness of

the present essay, but by the degree to which it proves valuable for future analysts in constructing hypotheses to account for the variations.

5 The patterns are clearer if one keeps in mind that the kin group ultimately owns the land, rather than individuals. Individual ownership thus depends on the kinship affiliation of the individual.

6 In some cases (see note 10) the head of the unit has exclusive or predominant control over the disposition of the unit's property. Hence one could run the analysis of sibling rivalry in terms of economic competition or conflict, rather than in terms of prestige and succession. The results would be similar, but in cultural terms less accurate, because property "ownership" (or control), like political power, is a by-product of status position. It is not in any meaningful sense a source of status (apart from the fact that more land can support more kin/followers) and it is certainly not a culturally valued end in itself.

7 Variations between Western and Eastern Polynesia with respect to kinship, marriage, and gender patterns are extremely interesting. In this essay, however, I have limited discussion to patterns that appear over the area as a whole, with only minor exceptions. For the reader's reference on this point, here is Goldman's classification of Eastern and Western societies (1970: xxvii; see also Burrows 1940): *Eastern*: Maori, Manihiki-Rakahanga, Tongareva, Mangaia, Easter, the Marquesas, Mangareva, the Society Islands (Tahiti), the Hawaiian Islands; *Western*: the Samoan Islands, Tonga, Uvea, Futuna, the Tokelaus, Tikopia, Pukapuka, Niue, Ontong Java.

8 Brother–sister marriage is also noted for Rarotonga (Suggs 1966: 177).

9 Parallel cousin marriage, between children of same-sex siblings, is reported for the aristocracy in Mangareva (Buck 1938: 132). Several other accounts report marriage with "cousins," without distinguishing between cross and parallel: Suggs 1966: 110; Oliver 1974: 764; Handy and Pukui 1958: 109.

10 In the Marquesas only the senior child inherits (Linton 1939: 154); in Mangareva (Buck 1938: 163) and in Tonga (Kaeppler 1971: 178) only the senior son inherits. Note however that in none of these cases are women categorically disinherited as against men; the category of noninheritors includes junior males as well as females.

11 There are two additional means of intentionally and controllably enlarging the group: adoption and polygyny. Both are widely practiced, the latter mainly by the aristocracy. Space limitations prohibit discussing the differential advantages and disadvantages of each here.

12 Sisters' daughters would be especially powerful symbols in the process under discussion. They represent the "hold" on kinswomen across two generations. Most sacred maids, as well as the *tamaha* (the "favored" and highest ranking kinswoman of the Tongan chief) are supposed to be sisters' daughters, although as in Samoa they are often daughters, and sometimes even sisters.

13 Except for the very highest wife of the Tui Manua, the highest chief (Mead 1930: 184).

14 A Samoan man who is caught and branded as a sleep crawler, however, appears as shameful, and "no girls will ever take [him] seriously" (Mead 1930: 62).

15 It appears that in Tahiti women may have also occasionally done it to men (Oliver 1974: 365).

16 Because virginity is more strongly enforced for chiefly daughters – Goldman calls it a "privilege of rank" (1970: 564) – it has special aristocratic associations as well. This probably gives added spice to deflowering virgins, in that a man would be symbolically asserting chiefly status in getting to any virgin.

17 The argument has clear Freudian overtones. They seem to me wholly appropriate to the case at hand, which is quite "patriarchal" in the classical sense. Gough's Freudian interpretation of Nayar girls' puberty rites (1955) seems to me similarly appropriate to the Nayar case, Yalman's pointed comments on it notwithstanding.

18 I omit from the discussion chiefly rape of lower-status women, which is also not uncommon, especially in the "stratified" societies (e.g., Gifford 1929: 72, 184; Mariner I 1827: 231; Malo 1903: 255). Essentially it is parallel to (though not exactly legitimately part of) chiefly rights of appropriation and/or disposition of goods and services in his domain.

19 The exception is rape of high-status women by low-status men. This is everywhere severely penalized.

20 Bradd Shore (in this collection) suggests that much of Samoan rape may be explained by the fact that all woman are seen primarily as "sisters," and there is difficulty in transforming a nonsexual into a sexual relationship. I agree that Polynesian women are seen primarily as "sisters," and Shore's suggestion would not be incompatible with many of the interpretations of the present essay.

Vern Carroll (1976) has suggested that rape is "no big deal" to women of Nukuoro, a Polynesian outlier in Micronesia where Carroll did research. Given the discussion just presented in the text, it would make sense that even Polynesian women might find rape less psychologically traumatic, though not necessarily more morally acceptable, than in our own culture.

21 It does occasionally happen that a lower man marries a higher woman, probably when a chief intentionally marries a daughter downward in order to forge a clientship. This is not allowed to interfere with the normative superiority and authority of the husband within the household (see e.g., Gifford 1929: 16).

22 Institutionalized "bond friendships," found in many Polynesian societies, perform many of the same functions (Firth 1967: 108–15 passim; Suggs 1966: 131; Handy 1923: 89; Mead 1949: 48; Oliver 1974: 825, 844).

23 In Samoa this "tabu" on public interaction between people in a sexual relationship applies to married couples, but not to adolescents. The tabu against public interaction between husbands and wives is said to be almost as strong as that against brother–sister interaction (Mead 1949: 83).

24 Much of the following account is drawn from Handy's *Polynesian Religion*. Handy presents an account of an ideal-type Polynesian religion for which he draws heavily on the Maori case, and it appears that he makes many unfounded generalizations for the area as a whole. But Polynesian religion is by and large not well documented. A careful survey of the available fragments, as well as a specification of variations, is beyond the scope of the present essay.

25 The Hawaiians had an Earth Mother goddess; they were apparently the only people in the area who did (Handy and Pukui 1958: 22).

26 But a Tongan wife of a high chief does bring in many of her kin as dependents and helpers in her husband's household (Gifford 1929: 17, 36). She may also bring her younger sisters as secondary wives or concubines for her husband.

27 Among the Maori only wives could cut their husbands' hair (Best II 1924: 533). It is not clear what an unmarried man would do for a haircut.

28 Firth reports little adultery for Tikopia (1963: 118). Adultery in modern Mangaia is said to be "relatively rare" but also "heavily folklorized" (Marshall 1971: 146). Adultery in Tonga is also reported as "rare" (Goldman 1970: 565), but here and there throughout Mariner's marvelous first-hand account of 18th century Tongan

society, largely of high-ranking people, both men and women allude to and joke about their extramarital love affairs (see I: 116, II: 49).

29 Oliver (1974: 804) reports "uxoriousness" for Tahiti, which is stronger than "amiability." Marshall says that Mangaian husbands and wives are not very social or conversational with one another, and that the husband–wife relationship is mostly sexual and economic (1971: 140). He later says however that "over the long term husbands and wives develop emotional attachment" (1971: 159).

30 Throughout the area there are no formal "divorce" mechanisms. Divorce is effected simply by separation.

31 Mead reports jealousy to be rare in both sexes in Samoa (1949: 68, 97).

32 Married women get general "deference" in Tikopia (Firth 1963: 122) and are "respected" as a category in Tonga (Mariner 1827: passim). This does not negate their subordination to their husbands in the domestic context.

33 Firth says that Tikopian girls want to marry more than boys, to get out from under the heavy control of their fathers (1957: 434). This motive would clearly be possible for girls throughout the area, although it is not reported elsewhere.

   At any rate, given the relatively low presumed motivation of girls to marry, it is clear that a girl's best bet when she does marry would be to reside uxorilocally, where she would retain on a day-to-day basis her status and prerogatives as a kinswoman. Thus her interests would coincide with her kinsmen's interest in keeping her (and her children) with the group.

34 In the context of these suggestions, intense wifely jealousy is less explicable than the jealousy of husbands. It is reported rare in Tahiti (Oliver 1974: 826) and also in Samoa (where, however, jealousy in general is rare (see note 31). But in some places it is reported to be intense (e.g., Firth 1963: 120), sometimes leading to suicide (Best I 1924: 475; Buck 1938: 472) or to fatal neglect of children (Marshall 1971: 148). The solution to this puzzle would lie in assuming that women have quite as much pride as men in Polynesian societies, partly because they are raised as valuable persons, and partly because pride is a very generally cultivated emotion in these status-conscious systems. Women's jealousy may thus be parallel to men's at the level of person feeling, even if it is not culturally supported and encouraged as men's is.

35 In Samoa, too, only high-rank women had birth feasts, but these were described as being for the mother (Mead 1949: 113).

36 Despite the high rates of abortion and infanticide, and of giving children up to others in fosterage and adoption, Polynesians are generally reported to be fond of children (see Loeb 1926: 85; Henry 1928: 274; Handy and Pukui 1958: 46, 71, 164–6). It may be suggested that, because children's independence of parents is culturally encouraged, their loyalty and love must be courted and wooed. This perhaps accounts for the great indulgence and affection they are evidently shown.

37 Goldman considers that the status of women in Polynesia was higher in the more complex societies than in the "traditional" ones (1970: 554).

38 Pollution beliefs and practices surrounding women vary significantly between Western and Eastern Polynesia. Comparative analysis on this point would be extremely important.

39 This means among other things that some women, like some men, are in all hierarchies of *very* high status, and occasionally (though far less often than men) succeed to highest offices. The "queens" and other female paramounts that surface here and there in the ethnographic literature are not products of "matriarchies," but of systems organized along the lines discussed in this essay.

40 There are presumed historical links between Polynesia and Southeast Asia. Their languages belong to the same macro-family (Goldman 1970: xxv).

41 Virginity also expresses continuing male dominance *within* the (nongender-defined) "strata," because it is largely maintained by male control of kinswomen.

42 I am hardly suggesting that Christian and Buddhist monasticism evolved *in order to fulfill* this function. Normally I give religion rather more serious treatment in its own terms. See, e.g., my monograph on Sherpa ritual and religion (1978).

References

Beaglehole, Ernest, and Beaglehole, Pearl. 1938. *Ethnology of Pukapuka*. Bernice P. Bishop Museum Bulletin 150. Honolulu: Bishop Museum.

1941. *Pangai, a village in Tonga*. Wellington, New Zealand: Polynesian Society.

Best, Elsdon. 1924. *The Maori*. 2 vol. Wellington, New Zealand: Board of Maori Ethnological Research.

Biersack, Aletta. 1974. "Matrilaterality in patrilineal systems: the Tongan case," Curl Bequest Prize Essay 1974, unpublished.

Buck, Peter. 1932. *Ethnology of Tongareva*. Bernice P. Bishop Museum Bulletin 92. Honolulu: Bishop Museum.

1938. *Ethnology of Mangareva*. Bernice P. Bishop Museum Bulletin 157. Honolulu: Bishop Museum.

1939. *Anthropology and religion*. New Haven: Yale University Press.

Burrows, Edwin G. 1940. "Culture areas in Polynesia." *Journal of the Polynesian Society* 49: 349–63.

Carroll, Vern. 1970. (ed.) *Adoption in Eastern Oceania*. Honolulu: University of Hawaii Press.

1976. "Rape on Nukuoro: a cultural analysis." *Michigan Discussions in Anthropology* I (Winter): 134–47.

Danielsson, Bengt. 1956. *Love in the South Seas*. New York: Reynal.

Dumont, Louis. 1970. *Homo hierarchicus*. Translated by Mark Sainsbury. Chicago: University of Chicago Press.

Firth, Raymond. 1940. "The analysis of *mana*: an empirical approach." *Journal of the Polynesian Society* 49: 483–510.

1957. *We, the Tikopia*. 2d ed. London: George Allen and Unwin.

1963. *We, the Tikopia*. Abridged. Boston: Beacon Press.

1967. *Tikopia ritual and belief*. Boston: Beacon Press.

1970. "Sibling terms in Polynesia." *Journal of the Polynesian Society* 79: 272–87.

1975. *Primitive Polynesian economy*. New York: Norton.

Forster, John. 1960. "The Hawaiian family system of Hana, Maui, 1957." *Journal of the Polynesian Society* 69: 92–103.

Gifford, Edward W. 1929. *Tongan society*. Bernice P. Bishop Museum Bulletin 61. Honolulu: Bishop Museum.

Goldman, Irving. 1955. "Status rivalry and cultural evolution in Polynesia." *American Anthropologist* 57: 680–97.

1970. *Ancient Polynesian society*. Chicago: University of Chicago Press.

Goody, Jack. 1973. "Bridewealth and dowry in Africa and Eurasia." In *Bridewealth and Dowry*, ed. J. Goody and S. J. Tambiah, pp. 1–58. Cambridge: Cambridge University Press.

Gough, Kathleen. 1955. "Female initiation rites on the Malabar coast." *Journal of the Royal Anthropological Institute* 85: 45–80.

1961. "Nayar: Central Kerala," and "Nayar: North Kerala." In *Matrilineal kinship*, ed. D. Schneider and K. Gough, pp. 298–404. Berkeley and Los Angeles: University of California Press.

Handy, E. S. C. 1923. *The native culture in the Marquesas*. Bernice P. Bishop Museum Bulletin 9. Honolulu: Bishop Museum.

1927. *Polynesian religion*. Bernice P. Bishop Museum Bulletin 34. Honolulu: Bishop Museum.

Handy, E. S. C. and Pukui, Mary K. 1958. *The Polynesian family system in Ka-'u Hawai'i*. Wellington, New Zealand: The Polynesian Society.

Hecht, Julia. 1977. "The culture of gender in Pukapuka: male, female, and the *Mayakitanga* 'Sacred Maid.' " *Journal of the Polynesian Society* 86: 183–206.

Henry, Teuira. 1928. *Ancient Tahiti*. Bernice P. Bishop Museum Bulletin 48. Honolulu: Bishop Museum.

Hocart, A. M. 1915. "Chieftainship and the sister's son in the Pacific." *American Anthropologist* 17: 631–46.

Hogbin, H. I. 1931. "The sexual life of the natives of Ontong Java." *Journal of the Polynesian Society* 40: 23–34.

Hooper, Antony. 1976. " 'Eating blood': Tahitian concepts of incest." *Journal of the Polynesian Society* 85: 227–41.

Huntsman, Judith, and Hooper, Antony. 1975. "Male and female in Tokelau culture." *Journal of the Polynesian Society* 84: 415–30.

1976. "The 'desecration' of Tokelau kinship." *Journal of the Polynesian Society* 85: 257–73.

Kaeppler, Adrienne. 1971. "Rank in Tonga." *Ethnology* 10: 174–93.

Kirkpatrick, John T. 1979. "The Marquesan notion of the person." Unpublished doctoral dissertation. University of Chicago.

Leach, Edmund. 1970. "A critique of Yalman's interpretation of Sinhalese girl's puberty ceremony." In *Echanges et Communications*, ed. J. Pouillon and P. Maranda, pp. 819–28. The Hague: Mouton.

Levin, Stephanie Seto. 1968. "The overthrow of the *Kapu* system in Hawaii." *Journal of the Polynesian Society* 77: 402–30.

Levy, Robert I. 1973. *Tahitians: mind and experience in the Society Islands*. Chicago: University of Chicago Press.

Linton, Ralph. 1939. "Marquesan culture." In *The Individual and his society*, ed. A. Kardiner, pp. 137–96. New York: Columbia University Press.

Loeb, E. M. 1926. *History and traditions of Niue*. Bernice P. Bishop Museum Bulletin 32. Honolulu: Bishop Museum.

Malo, David. 1903. *Hawaiian antiquities*. Translated by N. B. Emerson. Honolulu: Hawaiian Gazette.

Mariner, William. 1827. *An account of the natives of the Tonga Islands*. 2 vol. Compiled by John Martin. Edinburgh: Constable.

Marshall, Donald S. 1971. "Sexual behavior on Mangaia." In *Human sexual behavior*, ed. D. S. Marshall and R. C. Suggs, pp. 103–62. New York and London: Basic Books.

Mead, Margaret. 1930. *The social organization of Manu'a*. Bernice P. Bishop Museum Bulletin 76. Honolulu: Bishop Museum.

1949. *Coming of age in Samoa*. New York: New American Library.

Mishkin, Bernard. 1961. "The Maori of New Zealand." In *Cooperation and competition among primitive peoples*, ed. M. Mead, pp. 428–58. Boston: Beacon Press.

Oliver, Douglas. 1974. *Ancient Tahitian society*, 3 vol. Honolulu: University Press of Hawaii.

Ortner, Sherry B. 1973. "On key symbols." *American Anthropologist* 75: 1338–46,
    1976. "The virgin and the state." *Michigan Discussions in Anthropology* 2: 1–16;
    reprinted 1978 in *Feminist Studies* 4: 19–37.
    1978. *Sherpas through their rituals*. Cambridge: Cambridge University Press.
Pitt-Rivers, Julian. 1966. "Honour and social status." In *Honour and shame*, ed. J. G.
    Peristiany, pp. 19–78. Chicago: University of Chicago Press.
    1977. *The fate of Schechem or the politics of sex*. Cambridge: Cambridge
    University Press.
Rogers, Garth. 1977. "The father's sister is black: a consideration of female rank and
    power in Tonga." *Journal of the Polynesian Society* 86: 157–82.
Rubin, .Gayle. 1975. "The traffic in women: notes toward a political economy of
    sex." In *Toward an anthropology of women*, ed. R. Reiter, pp. 157–210. New
    York: Monthly Review Press.
Sahlins, Marshall. 1958. *Social stratification in Polynesia*. Seattle: University of
    Washington Press.
    1963. "Poor man, rich man, big-man, chief: political types in Melanesia and
    Polynesia." *Comparative Studies in Society and History* 5: 285–303.
    forthcoming. *Historical metaphors and mythical realities: structure in the early
    history of the Sandwich Islands Kingdom*. Ann Arbor: University of Michigan
    Press.
Schneider, David. 1968. *American kinship: a cultural account*. Englewood Cliffs,
    New Jersey: Prentice-Hall.
    1976. "The meaning of incest." *Journal of the Polynesian Society* 85: 149–69.
Schneider, Jane. 1971. "Of vigilance and virgins: honor, shame, and access to
    resources in Mediterranean society." *Ethnology* 10: 1–24.
Shore, Bradd. 1976. "Incest prohibitions and the logic of power in Samoa." *Journal
    of the Polynesian Society* 85: 275–96.
Stein, R. A. 1972. *Tibetan civilization*. Translated by J. E. S. Driver. Stanford:
    Stanford University Press.
Suggs, Robert C. 1966. *Marquesan sexual behavior*. New York: Harcourt, Brace and
    World.
    1971. "Sex and personality in the Marquesas: a discussion of the Linton-Kardiner
    report." *Human sexual behavior*, ed. D. S. Marshall and R. C. Suggs, pp.
    163–86. New York and London: Basic Books.
Tambiah, Stanley J. 1973. "Dowry and bridewealth and the property rights of women
    in South Asia." In *Bridewealth and dowry*, ed. J. Goody and S. J. Tambiah, pp.
    59–169. Cambridge: Cambridge University Press.
Turner, Victor, 1967. *The forest of symbols*. Ithaca: Cornell University Press.
van Gennep, Arnold. 1960. *Rites of passage*. Translated by M. B. Vizedom and G. L.
    Caffee. Chicago: University of Chicago Press.
Vayda, A. P. 1961. "Love in the Polynesian atolls." *Man* 61: 204–5.
Yalman, Nur. 1963. "On the purity of women in the castes of Ceylon and Malabar."
    Journal of the Royal Anthropological Institute 93: 25–58.

Index